W9-BSV-011

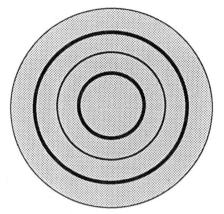

The Changing
FAMILY LIFE CYCLE

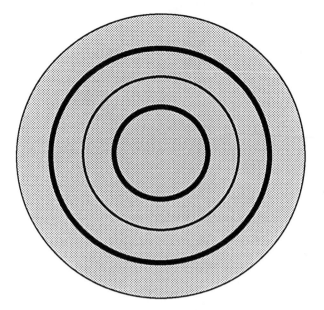

The Changing
FAMILY LIFE CYCLE

A Framework for Family Therapy

SECOND EDITION

Edited by

Betty Carter, M.S.W.

Director, Family Institute of Westchester

Monica McGoldrick, M.S.W.

Associate Professor and Director of Family Training, Psychiatry Department,
UMDNJ-Robert Wood Johnson Medical School and the CMHC at Piscataway

Allyn and Bacon
Boston   London   Sydney   Toronto

Copyright © 1989 by Allyn and Bacon
A Division of Simon & Schuster
160 Gould Street
Needham Heights, MA 02194

All rights reserved. No part of the material protected by this copyright notice may be reproduced or utilized in any form or by any means, electronic or mechanical, including photocopying, recording, or by any information storage and retrieval system, without written permission from the copyright owner.

ISBN 0-205-12063-6

Printed in the United States of America

10   94

The genograms for this book were produced with the MacGenogram program developed by Randy Gerson for the Macintosh Computer. The genograms and other illustrations were done by Neale McGoldrick. Information on the MacGenogram Program can be received from: Humanware, 2908 Nancy Creek Road, N.W., Atlanta, Georgia, 30327

Book Design by Publishers Creative Services

CONTRIBUTORS

ROBERT C. AYLMER, Ed.D.
Newton, Mass.

CLAUDIA BEPKO, M.S.W.
Fair Haven, N.J.

JACK O. BRADT, M.D.
Clinical Assistant Professor
Psychiatry Department
Georgetown University
Washington, D.C.

EVAN IMBER-BLACK, Ph.D.
Director of Family & Group
Studies
Department of Psychiatry
Albert Einstein College of
Medicine
Bronx, N.Y.

BETTY CARTER, M.S.W.
Director, Family Institute of
Westchester
Mount Vernon, N.Y.

EDWIN H. FRIEDMAN, M.A.
Consultant and Family Therapist
Washington, D.C

RICHARD FULMER, Ph.D.
New York, N.Y.
Director, Family Therapy Training
Program, Fordham-Tremont
Community Mental Health
Center
Bronx, N.Y.

NYDIA GARCIA PRETO, A.C.S.W.
Clinical Coordinator
Adolescent Day Hospital
UMDNJ-Community Mental
Health Center
Piscataway, N.J.

RANDY GERSON, Ph.D.
Atlanta Institute for Family
Studies
Adjunct Professor
Georgia State University
Atlanta, Ga.

FREDDA HERZ BROWN, R.N.,
Ph.D.
Director of Training
Family Institute of Westchester
Mount Vernon, N.Y.

PAULETTE MOORE HINES, Ph.D.
Director of Consultation and
Education
New Brunswick Community
Focus Team
UMDNJ R.W. Johnson Medical
School CMHC
Piscataway, N.J.

LYNN HOFFMAN, M.S.W.
Family Therapist and Consultant
North Amherst, Mass.

JO-ANN KRESTAN, M.A., C.A.C.
Fair Haven, N.J.

JENNIFER MANOCHERIAN, M.S.
Family Institute of Westchester
Mount Vernon, N.Y.

PAULINA McCULLOUGH, A.C.S.W.
Assistant Clinical Professor of
Psychiatry (Social Work)
University of Pittsburgh
Pittsburgh, Pa.

MONICA McGOLDRICK, M.A.,
M.S.W.
Director of Family Training
UMDNJ R.W. Johnson Medical

School CMHC and Psychiatry
Department
Piscataway, N.J.
Faculty, Family Institute of
Westchester
Mount Vernon, N.Y.

JOHN ROLLAND, M.D.
Assistant Professor
Department of Psychiatry
Yale University, School of
Medicine
New Haven, Conn.
Medical Director, Center for
Illness in Families
New Haven, Conn.

SANDRA RUTENBERG, Ph.D.
Assistant Professor
School of Nursing
Queens University
Kingston, Ont., Canada

ROBERT M. SIMON, M.D.
Associate Psychiatrist
Ackerman Institute for Family
Therapy
New York, N.Y.
Private Practice, Norwich, Vt.

JUDITH STERN PECK, M.S.
Director of Clinical Services
Family Institute of Westchester
Mount Vernon, N.Y.

FROMA WALSH, M.S.W., Ph.D.
Social Services Administration
University of Chicago
Faculty, Family Institute of
Chicago
Chicago, Ill.

Contents

Acknowledgments   xiii

Part 1. CONCEPTUAL OVERVIEW

1. **Overview: The Changing Family Life Cycle—A Framework for Family Therapy**   3

   Betty Carter, M.S.W., and Monica McGoldrick, M.S.W.

   The Family as a System Moving Through Time   4

   The Changing Family Life Cycle   10

   The Stages of the Intact Middle-Class American Family Life Cycle   13

   Major Variations in the Family Life Cycle   20

   Conclusions   25

2. **Women and the Family Life Cycle**   29

   Monica McGoldrick, M.S.W.

   Male and Female Development   31

   Work   34

   Households   36

   Between Families: Young Adulthood   37

   The Joining of Families in Marriage: The Young Couple   41

   Families with Young Children   43

   Families with Adolescents   49

   Launching Children and Moving On   52

   Older Families   55

   Divorce and Remarriage   58

   Women and Their Friendship Networks   60

   Lesbians   60

   Health and Illness Patterns of Health-Care Behavior   61

   Family Therapy   62

   Conclusions   64

3. **Ethnicity and the Family Life Cycle**   69

   Monica McGoldrick, M.S.W.

   The Concept of Family   70

   Life Cycle Stages   71

The Unattached Young Adult 71

The Young Couple 72

Intermarriage 73

The Transition to Parenthood and the Family with Young
   Children 74

Families of Adolescents 76

Launching 77

Families in Later Life 78

Ethnicity and Death 80

Problems and Their Solutions 82

Ceremonies and Rituals 83

Immigration and the Life Cycle 83

Therapy 86

Conclusions 89

4. The Family Life Cycle and Discontinuous Change 91

Lynn Hoffman, M.S.W.

Evolutionary Feedback 91

Hierarchical Growth 92

Expectable Life-Stage Crises 94

The Concept of Step Mechanisms 96

Paradoxical Injunctions and the "Sweat Box" 98

5. Family Life Cycle Issues in the Therapy System 107

Robert M. Simon, M.D.

Therapist Not Yet at the Family Stage of the Life Cycle 108

Therapist Is in the Same Stage of the Life Cycle as the Family 109

Therapist Is Past the Family's Stage in the Life Cycle 110

Other Life Cycle Issues 112

When the Life Cycles Do Not Fit Well 114

Study of the Therapist's Family of Origin 116

6. Systems and Ceremonies: A Family View of Rites of Passage 119

Edwin H. Friedman, M.A.

Three Myths That Inhibit Forming a Family Process View 121

Three Natural Rites of Passage 128

Three Nodal Life Cycle Events 143

Conclusions 146

7. Idiosyncratic Life Cycle Transitions and Therapeutic Rituals 149

Evan Imber-Black, Ph.D.

Idiosyncratic Life Cycle Transitions 150

The Emergence of Symptoms 151

Therapeutic Rituals 153

Transition Rituals 154

Healing Rituals 157
Identity-Redefinition Rituals 159
Designing and Implementing Therapeutic Rituals for
    Idiosyncratic Life Cycle Transitions 161
Conclusions 162

8. Genograms and the Family Life Cycle 164
Monica McGoldrick, M.S.W., and Randy Gerson, Ph.D.
Marriage and Remarriage 164
The Transition to Parenthood and Families with Young Children 169
Families with Adolescents 174
Families at Midlife: Launching Children and Moving On 176
Marriage, the Next Generation 178
Parenthood, the Next Generation 180
Families in Later Life 183
Conclusions 186

Part 2. THE TRADITIONAL MIDDLE-CLASS FAMILY LIFE CYCLE

9. The Launching of the Single Young Adult 191
Robert C. Aylmer, Ed.D.
Adult Development and Life Cycle Theory 191
Individual Factors 193
Family System Factors 194
Career Issues 197
Intimacy Issues 198
Clinical Considerations 203

10. The Joining of Families Through Marriage: The New Couple 209
Monica McGoldrick, M.S.W.
Fusion and Intimacy 212
Homosexual Couples 218
The Wedding 221
Patterns with Extended Family 224
In-Laws 228
The Importance of Sibling Issues 228
Cultural Differences 230
Issues in Marital Adjustment 231

11. Becoming Parents: Families with Young Children 235
Jack O. Bradt, M.D.
Paradigms in Collision 237
Space for Children 240
Sex 242

Intimacy 243
The Extended Family 243
Rebalancing Work and Home Life: Back to Work 245
Sibling Rivalry 246
The Child-Focused Family 248
Guidelines for Intervention 249
Conclusions 253

12. Transformation of the Family System in Adolescence 255
Nydia Garcia Preto, A.C.S.W.
Three-Generational View of Transformation 256
Tasks of Adolescence 257
Clinical Intervention During Adolescence 270
Conclusions 281

13. Launching Children and Moving On 285
Paulina McCullough, A.C.S.W., and *Sandra Rutenberg, Ph.D.*
Demographic Changes 287
The Changing Function of Marriage 289
Maturity at Midlife 291
Development of Adult Relationships with Grown Children 293
Realignment of Relationships to Include In-Laws and
Grandchildren 296
Resolving Issues with the Older Generation 297
Clinical Considerations 299
Summary 307

14. The Family in Later Life 311
Froma Walsh, M.S.W., Ph.D.
Later-Life Transitions and Tasks 312
Role Flexibility and Successful Aging 326
Clinical Assessment and Treatment Issues 327

Part 3. THE DIVORCE CYCLE

15. Divorce in the Changing Family Life Cycle 335
Judith Stern Peck, M.S.W., and *Jennifer Manocherian, M.S.*
Demographics 336
Review of the Literature 337
The Impact of Divorce at Different Stages of the Family Life
Cycle 346
Clinical Implications 364

16. The Postdivorce Family 371
Fredda Herz Brown, R.N., Ph.D.
The Process of Becoming a One-Parent Family 372

Phase I—The Aftermath 374
Phase II—The Realignment 381
Phase III—Stabilization 386
The Noncustodial Single Parent 389
General Guidelines for Treatment 393
Conclusions 395

17. Forming a Remarried Family 399
Monica McGoldrick, M.S.W., and Betty Carter, M.S.W.
Studies of Remarriage: Clinically Useful Findings 402
Predictable Emotional Issues in Remarriage 405
The Process of Remarriage 408
The Impact of Remarriage at Various Phases of the Family Life
Cycle 410
Family Therapy with Remarried Families: Clinical Procedures
and Illustrations 414
Conclusions 426

Part 4. VARIABLES THAT FURTHER CHANGE THE FAMILY LIFE CYCLE

18. Chronic Illness and the Family Life Cycle 433
John Rolland, M.D.
Psychosocial Typology of Illness 434
Time Phases of Illness 438
Transgenerational History of Illness, Loss, and Crisis 442
Conclusions 454

19. The Impact of Death and Serious Illness on the Family Life Cycle 457
Fredda Herz Brown, R.N., Ph.D.
Factors Affecting the Impact of Death and Serious Illness on
the Family System 458
Social and Ethnic Context of Death 458
The Ethnic Influence 460
Timing of Death in the Life Cycle 462
The Nature of Death 469
The Openness of the Family System 472
The Family Position of the Dying or Dead Family Member 473
Family Treatment Intervention 474

20. Alcohol Problems and the Family Life Cycle 483
Jo-Ann Krestan, M.A., C.A.C., and Claudia Bepko, M.S.W.
Alcoholism and the Life Cycle: General Treatment Issues 484
Staging 486
Characteristic Issues at Specific Life Cycle Stages 489

The Unattached Young Adult   489
The New Couple   493
The Family with Young Children   495
The Family with Adolescents   497
Launching Children and Moving On   500
Alcoholism and Divorce   502
The Family in Later Life   502
General Guidelines for Treatment   505

21. The Family Life Cycle of Poor Black Families   513
Paulette Moore Hines, Ph.D.
The Cycle of Poverty   515
Characteristics of the Family Life Cycle   516
  Truncated Life Cycle   517
  Female-Headed Households   518
  Unpredictable Stress   518
  Reliance on Institutional Supports   518
Stages of the Family Life Cycle   519
  Stage 1—Adolescence/Unattached Young Adulthood   519
  Stage 2—The Family with Children   523
  Stage 3—The Family in Later Life   528
Assessment and Intervention   531
  Multiple-Impact Family Therapy   534
General Guidelines   539
Avoiding Therapist Burnout   541
Conclusions   542

22. Lower-Income and Professional Families: A Comparison of
Structure and Life Cycle Process   545
Richard Fulmer, Ph.D.
Sources of Data   545
Birth and Marriage Patterns   546
Additions to a Theory of the Family Life Cycle   548
Life Cycle Stages for "Professional" Families   550
Life Cycle Stages for Lower-Income Families   557
Strengthens and Vulnerabilities   573

Author Index   579
Subject Index   585

Acknowledgments

We would like to thank a number of people for their support and help in bringing this new edition to fruition. Firstly, our colleagues at the Family Institute of Westchester and the Community Mental Health Center of Robert Wood Johnson Medical School, UMDNJ, especially the Director, Gary Lamson for his unfailing support to my projects. We owe a great debt also to Myra Wayton, Lisa Fine and Jeannine Stone for their administrative support which have made our concentration on this project possible. We thank Mary Scanlon, librarian of the Medical School for so generously responding to our endless calls for references and information. And we thank Andrea Lauritzen, Angela McInearney, and Karen Welch, nannies of John Orranidis, for the support which made this work easier. Our personal networks of friends and colleagues have also been crucial in enhancing our work life. We want to mention in particular, Carol Anderson, Froma Walsh, Michael Rohrbaugh, Evan Imber Black, Ron Taffel, Meyer Rothberg, Sandy Leiblum, Joyce Richardson, Rich Simon, and the other members of the Women's Project in Family Therapy: Peggy Papp, Olga Silverstein, and Marianne Walters for their personal friendship and support. We thank Suzi Tucker and our publisher Gardner Spungin for their help in bringing out this new edition.

We are grateful to Neale McGoldrick for working with her usual incredible vigor, speed and ability to bring the complex artwork into shape.

We dedicate this book to our parents,
to our husbands
and to our children

PART 1

Conceptual Overview

Overview
The Changing Family Life
Cycle: A Framework for Family
Therapy

Betty Carter, M.S.W.
and Monica McGoldrick, M.S.W.

> Time present and time past
> Are both perhaps present in time future
> And time future contained in time past.—T.S. Eliot

In the short span of years since the first edition of this book appeared there have been a great many changes in the family therapy field with regard to this topic, and in life cycle patterns themselves. First of all there is a burgeoning literature discussing families in relation to their developmental phase, and referring to divorce, remarriage, and chronic illness in developmental terms. Second there has been a small revolution in awareness of differences in male and female development (Gilligan, 1982; Miller, 1976; etc). and in their implications for the family life cycle. The conservative, or even reactionary, stance that the family therapy field has taken regarding the role of women has come under strong criticism (Goldner, 1986; Taggert, 1986; Libow, 1984; Hare-Mustin, 1978, 1980 & 1987; The Womens Project in Family Therapy, in press; McGoldrick, Anderson & Walsh, in press, etc) and requires a careful rethinking of our assumptions about "normality," the notion of "family" and who is responsible for its maintenance, and the role of the therapist in responding to changing norms and sociopolitical realities. Awareness has also increased about the importance of ethnic patterns and cultural variability in life cycle definitions of normality (McGoldrick, 1982). In this second edition, we have tried to reassess and reformulate our first edition in light of these changing perspectives.

We want to emphasize two cautions about a life cycle perspective. A rigid application of psychological ideas to the "normal" life cycle can have a detrimental effect if it promotes anxious self-scrutiny that raises fears that

deviating from the norms is pathological. The opposite pitfall, overemphasizing the uniqueness of the "brave new world" faced by each new generation, can create a sense of historical discontinuity by devaluing the role of parenthood and rendering meaningless the relationship between generations. Our aim is to provide a view of the life cycle in terms of the intergenerational connectedness in the family. We believe this to be one of our greatest human resources. We do not mean to oversimplify the complexity of life's transitions or to encourage stereotyping by promoting classifications of "normality" that constrict our view of human life. On the contrary, our hope is that by superimposing the family life cycle framework on the natural phenomenon of lives through time, we can add to the depth with which clinicians view family problems and strengths.

The family life cycle perspective views symptoms and dysfunctions in relation to normal functioning over time and views therapy as helping to reestablish the family's developmental momentum. It frames problems within the course the family has moved along in its past, the tasks it is trying to master, and the future toward which it is moving. It is our view that the family is more than the sum of its parts. The individual life cycle takes place within the family life cycle, which is the primary context of human development. We think this perspective is crucial to understanding the emotional problems that people develop as they move together through life.

It is surprising how little explicit attention therapists have paid to a life cycle framework until recently. Perhaps it is the dramatically changing life cycle patterns in our time that are drawing our attention to this perspective. In any case it is becoming increasingly difficult to determine what family life cycle patterns are "normal," and this in itself is often a cause of great stress for family members, who have few models for the passages they are going through.

In this book we look at the family life cycle in relation to three apsects: (1) the predictable stages of "normal" family development in traditional middle-class America as we near the end of the 20th century, and typical clinical fallout when families have trouble negotiating these transitions; (2) the changing patterns of the family life cycle in our time and the shifts in what is considered "normal"; and (3) a clinical perspective that views therapy as helping families that have become derailed in the family life cycle to get back on their developmental track, and which invites you, the therapist, to include yourself and your own life cycle stage in the equation (Chapter 5).

THE FAMILY AS A SYSTEM MOVING
THROUGH TIME

In our view family stress is often greatest at transition points from one stage to another of the family developmental process, and symptoms are most

likely to appear when there is an interruption or dislocation in the unfolding family life cycle. Therapeutic efforts often need to be directed toward helping family members reorganize so that they can proceed developmentally. Michael Solomon (1973), one of the first therapists to discuss a family life cycle perspective, outlined tasks for a five-stage family life cycle and suggested using this framework as a diagnostic base upon which to plan treatment. Others have divided the family life cycle into different numbers of stages. The most widely accepted is the breakdown of the sociologist Duvall (1977), who has been working for many years to define normal family development. Duvall broke the family life cycle into eight stages, all of them addressing the nodal events related to the comings and goings of family members: marriage, the birth and raising of children, the departure of children from the household, retirement, and death. The most complex breakdown of the life cycle was that proposed by Rodgers (1960), who expanded his schema to 24 separate stages to account for the progress of several children through the nodal events of the life cycle. Hill (1970) emphasized three generational aspects of the life cycle, describing parents of married children as forming a "lineage bridge" between the older and younger generations of the family. His view is that at each stage of the life cycle there is a distinctive role complex for family members with each other. Combrinck-Graham (1985) has suggested an emphasis on oscillations between centripetal and centrifugal periods in family development, emphasizing life experiences, such as birth or infirmity, that require a pulling together and primacy of relationships, and other experiences, such as starting school or a new job, that demand focus on individuality. Obviously the many ways family members rely on one another within the "generation spiral" (Duvall, 1977, p. 153) in a mutual interdependence are part of the richness of the family context as generations move through life.

The development of a life cycle perspective for the individual has been greatly facilitated by the creative work of Erikson (1950), Levinson (1978), Miller (1976), Gilligan (1982), and others in defining the transitions of adult life. Recent studies of the couple over the life cycle have helped us gain a time perspective on the two-person system (Campbell, 1975; Gould, 1972; Harry, 1976; Schram, 1979; Nadelson, et al., 1984). The three-person or family model has been elaborated most carefully by Duvall, who focuses on child rearing as the organizing element of family life.

We should like to consider the motion of the entire three- or four-generational system as it moves through time. Relationships with parents, siblings (Cicirelli, 1985), and other family members go through stages as one moves along the life cycle, just as parent-child and spouse relationships do. It is extremely difficult, however, to think of the family as a whole because of the complexity involved. As a system moving through time, the family has basically different properties from all other systems. Unlike all other organizations, families incorporate new members only by birth, adoption, or marriage, and members can leave only by death, if then. No other system is subject to these constraints. A business organization can fire members it views as dys-

functional, or, conversely, members can resign if the structure and values of the organization are not to their liking. If no way can be found to function within the system, the pressures of family membership with no exit available can, in the extreme, lead to psychosis. In nonfamily systems, the roles and functions of the system are carried out in a more or less stable way, by replacement of those who leave for any reason, or else the system dissolves and people move on into other organizations. Although families also have roles and functions, the main value in families is in the relatinships, which are irreplaceable. If a parent leaves or dies, another person can be brought in to fill a parenting function, but this person can never replace the parent in his or her personal emotional aspects.

Our view is that "family" comprises the entire emotional system of at least three, and now frequently four, generations. This is the operative emotional field at any given moment. We do not consider the influence of the family to be restricted to the members of a particular household or to a given nuclear family branch of the system. Thus although we recognize the dominant American pattern of separately domiciled nuclear families, they are, in our view, emotional subsystems, reacting to past, present, and anticipated future relationships within the larger three-generational family system. We urge you to include at least this much of the system in your thinking and chapter 8 explains how to use the genogram effectively for this clinical mapping and tracking.

Our three-generational perspective should not be confused with what Goode (1963) has referred to as the "classical family of Western nostalgia," a mythological time when the extended family reigned supreme, with mutual respect and satisfaction between the generations (Hess & Waring, 1984). The sexism, classism, and racism of such patriarchal arrangements should not be underestimated. However, we pay a price for the fact that modern families are characterized by choice in interpersonal relationships: whom to marry, where to live, how many children to bear, how to conduct relationships within the nuclear and extended family, and how to allocate family tasks. As Hess and Waring have observed, "As we move from the family of obligatory ties to one of voluntary bonds, relationships outside the nuclear unit similarly lose whatever normative certainty or consistency governed them at earlier times. For example, sibling relationships today are almost completely voluntary, subject to disruption through occupational and geographic mobility, as indeed it might be said of marriage itself" (p. 303). In the past, respect for parents and obligation to care for elders was based on their control of resources, reinforced by religious tradition and normative sanction. Now, with the increasing ability of younger family members to determine their own fates in marriage and work, the power of elders to demand filial piety is reduced. In the past, maintenance of family relationships was understood to be the responsibility of women: they cared for children, they cared for the men, and they cared for the elderly and the sick. This is changing. But our culture is still dedicated to the "individualism" of the frontier and has made no adequate arrangements for society to take up these responsibilities, and many, particularly the poor and the

powerless, usually women and children, are falling through the cracks. We are not, however, trying to encourage a return to a rigid inequitable three-generational, patriarchal family, but rather we want to foster a recognition of our connectedness in life—within any type of family structure—with those who went before us and those who follow after. At the same time it is important to recognize that many problems are caused when changes at the social level of the system lag behind changes at the family level, and, therefore, fail to validate and support the changes.

One of the most complex aspects of the status of family members is the confusion that occurs over whether one can choose membership and responsibility in a family. In our times people often act as though they can choose in this matter, when in fact there is very little choice. Children, for example, have no choice about being born into a system, nor do parents have a choice, once children are born, as to the existence of the responsibilities of parenthood, even if they neglect these responsibilities. In fact no family relationships except marriage are entered into by choice. Even in the case of marriage, the freedom to marry whomever one wishes is a rather recent option, and the decision to marry is probably much less freely made than people usually recognize at the time (see Chapter 10). While partners can choose not to continue a marriage relationship, they remain co-parents of their children and the fact of having been married continues to be acknowledged with the designation "ex-spouse." People cannot alter whom they are related to in the complex web of family ties over all the generations. Obviously family members frequently act as if this were not so—they cut each other off because of conflicts or because they claim to have "nothing in common"—but when family members act as though family relationships were optional, they do so to the detriment of their own sense of identity and the richness of their emotional and social context.

Although family process is by no means linear, it exists in the linear dimension of time. From this we can never escape. Earlier work on the life cycle has rarely taken this complex process adequately into account. Perhaps this is so because, from a multigenerational perspective, there is no unifying task such as can be described if the life cycle stages are limited to descriptions of individual development or parenting tasks. But the tremendous life-shaping impact of one generation on those following is hard to overestimate. For one thing the three or four different generations must accommodate to life cycle transitions simultaneously. While one generation is moving toward older age, the next is contending with the empty nest, the third with young adulthood, forming careers and intimate peer adult relationships and having children, and the fourth with being inducted into the system. Naturally there is an intermingling of the generations, and events at one level have a powerful effect on relationships at each other level. The important impact of events in the grandparental generation is routinely overlooked by therapists focused on the nuclear family. Painful experiences such as illness and death are particularly difficult for families to integrate, and are thus most likely to have a long-range

impact on relationships in the next generations, as has been shown in the impressive work of Norman Paul (Paul & Grosser, 1965; Paul & Paul 1974; see also Chapter 19).

There is ample evidence by now that family stresses, which are likely to occur around life cycle transition points, frequently create disruptions of the life cycle and produce symptoms and dysfunction. Hadley and his colleagues (1974) found that symptom onset correlated significantly with family developmental crises of addition and loss of family members. Walsh (1978) and Orfanidis (1977) both found that a significant life cycle event (death of a grandparent), when closely related in time to another life cycle event (birth of a child), correlated with patterns of symptom development at a much later transition in the family life cycle (the launching of the next generation). There is growing evidence that life cycle events have a continuing impact on family development over a long period of time. It is probably the clinicians' own limited perspective that inhibits our noticing these patterns. Research is rarely carried out over periods of more than a few years, and thus longitudinal connections can easily get lost. One research group, headed by Thomas, studied the family patterns of medical students at Johns Hopkins and then followed them over many years. They found numerous life cycle connections between early family patterns and later symptom development (Thomas & Duszynski, 1974). Such research supports the clinical method of Bowen, who tracks family patterns through their life cycle over several generations, focusing especially on nodal events and transition points in family development in seeking to understand family dysfunction at the present moment (Bowen, 1978).

As illustrated in Figure 1-1, we view the flow of anxiety in a family as being both "vertical" and "horizontal" (Carter, 1978). The vertical flow in a system includes patterns of relating and functioning that are transmitted down the generations of a family primarily through the mechanism of emotional triangling (Bowen, 1978). It includes all the family attitudes, taboos, expectations, labels, and loaded issues with which we grow up. One could say that these aspects of our lives are like the hand we are dealt: they are the given. What we do with them is the issue for us.

The horizontal flow in the system includes the anxiety produced by the stresses on the family as it moves forward through time, coping with the changes and transitions of the family life cycle. This includes both the predictable developmental stresses and those unpredictable events, "the slings and arrows of outrageous fortune," that may disrupt the life cycle process (untimely death, birth of a handicapped child, chronic illness, war, etc.). Given enough stress on the horizontal axis, any family will appear extremely dysfunctional. Even a small horizontal stress on a family in which the vertical axis is full of intense stress will create great disruption in the system.

In our view the degree of anxiety engendered by the stress on the vertical and horizontal axes at the points where they converge is the key determinant of how well the family will manage its transitions through life. It becomes imperative, therefore, to assess not only the dimensions of the current life

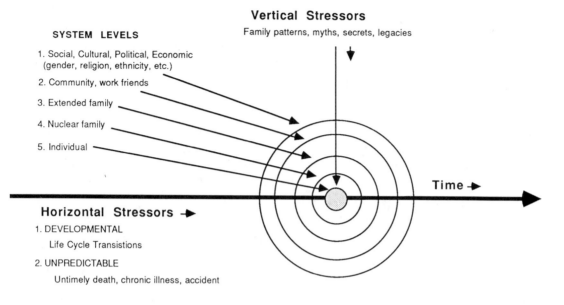

Figure 1-1 Horizontal and vertical stressors

cycle stress, but also their connections to family themes, triangles, and labels coming down in the family over historical time (Carter, 1978). Although all normative change is to some degree stressful, we have observed that when the horizontal (developmental) stress intersects with a vertical (transgenerational) stress, there is a quantum leap in anxiety in the system. If, to give a global example, one's parents were basically pleased to be parents and handled the job without too much anxiety, the birth of the first child will produce just the normal stresses of a system expanding its boundaries in our era. If, on the other hand, parenting was a cause célebrè of some kind in the family of origin of one or both spouses, and has not been dealt with, the transition to parenthood may produce heightened anxiety for the couple. The greater the anxiety generated in the family at any transition point, the more difficult or dysfunctional the transition will be.

In addition to the stress "inherited" from past generations and that experienced while moving through the family life cycle, there is, of course, the stress of living in this place at this time. One cannot ignore the social, economic, and political context and its impact on families moving through different phases of the life cycle at each point in history. We must realize that there are huge discrepancies in social and economic circumstances between families in our culture, and this inequality has been escalating. At present the top 10% of the population have 57% of the net wealth of the country while the bottom 50% of the population share 4.5% of the total net worth (Thurow, 1987). Among working men only 22% will earn as much as $31,000 and among working women only 3% will earn this much. (Society's treatment of working women is

still grossly unequal, with working women earning no more than 65% of what their male counterparts in the work force earn, and with women and children accounting for 17% of those in poverty.) We are rapidly moving to the point where only a family with two full-time working parents will be able to support a middle-class existence (Thurow, 1987).

Cultural factors also play a major role in how families go through the life cycle. Not only do cultural groups vary greatly in their breakdown of life cycle stages and definitions of the tasks at each stage (Chapter 3), but it is clear that even several generations after immigration the family life cycle patterns of groups differ markedly (Woehrer, 1982, Gelfand & Kutzik, 1979; Lieberman, 1974). One must also recognize the strain that the vastly accelerated rate of change puts on families today, whether the changes themselves are for better or for worse.

Even the stages of the life cycle are rather arbitrary breakdowns. The notion of childhood has been described as the invention of 18th-century Western society and adolescence as the invention of the 19th century (Afies, 1962), related to cultural, economic, and political contexts of those eras. The notion of young adulthood as an independent phase could easily be argued to be the invention of the 20th century, and for women as independent persons of the late 20th century, if that is accepted even now. The phases of the empty nest and older age are also developments primarily of this century, brought about by the smaller number of children and the longer life span in our era. Given the present rates of divorce and remarriage, the 21st century may become known for developing the norm of serial marriage as part of the life cycle process. Developmental psychology has tended to take an a historical approach to the life cycle. In virtually all other contemporary cultures and during virtually all other historical eras, the breakdown of life cycle stages has been different from our current definitions. To add to this complexity, cohorts born and living through different periods differ in fertility, mortality, acceptable gender roles, migration patterns, education, needs and resources, and attitudes toward family and aging.

Families characteristically lack time perspective when they are having problems. They tend generally to magnify the present moment, overwhelmed and immobilized by their immediate feelings; or they become fixed on a moment in the future that they dread or long for. They lose the awareness that life means continual motion from the past and into the future with a continual transformation of familial relationships. As the sense of motion becomes lost or distorted, therapy involves restoring a sense of life as process and movement from and toward.

THE CHANGING FAMILY LIFE CYCLE

Within the past generation, the changes in family life cycle patterns have escalated dramatically, due especially to the lower birth rate, the longer life

expectancy, the changing role of women, and the increasing divorce and remarriage rate. While it used to be that child rearing occupied adults for their entire active life span, it now occupies less than half the time span of adult life prior to old age. The meaning of the family is changing drastically, since it is no longer organized primarily around this activity.

The changing role of women in families is central in these shifting family life cycle patterns. Women have always been central to the functioning of the family. Their identities were determined primarily by their family functions as mother and wife. Their life cycle phases were linked almost exclusively to their stages in child-rearing activities. For men, on the other hand, chronological age has been seen as a key variable in life cycle determinations. But this description no longer fits. Today women are moving through the parenting cycle more rapidly than their grandmothers; they may put off developing personal goals beyond the realm of the family, but they can no longer ignore such goals. Even women who choose a primary role of mother and home-maker must now face an "empty nest" phase that equals in length the years devoted primarily to child care. Perhaps the modern feminist movement was inevitable, as women have come to need a personal identity. Having always had primary responsibility for home, family, and child care, women necessarily began to struggle under their burdens as they came to have more options for their own lives. Given their pivotal role in the family and their difficulty in establishing concurrent functions outside the family, it is perhaps not surprising that women have been the most prone to symptom development at life cycle transitions. For men the goals of career and family are parallel. For women these goals conflict and present a severe dilemma. While women are more positive than men about the prospect of marriage, they are less content than men generally with the reality of it (Bernard, 1972). Women, not men, are likely to become depressed at the time of childbirth; this appears to have a great deal to do with the dilemma that this shift creates in their lives. Women, more than men, seek help during the child-rearing years, and as their children reach adolescence and leave home and as their spouses retire or die. And women, not men, have had primary responsibility for older relatives. Surely women's seeking help for problems has much to do with the different ways in which they are socialized, but it also reflects the special life cycle stresses on women, whose role has been to bear emotional responsibility for all family relationships (Chapter 2).

Actually, at an ever-accelerating pace over the decades of this century, women have radically changed—and are still changing—the face of the traditional family life cycle that had existed for centuries. In fact the present generation of young women is the first in history to insist on their right to the first phase of the family life cycle—the phase in which the young adult leaves the parents' home, establishes personal life goals, and starts a career. Historically women were denied this most crucial step in adult development and were handed, instead, from their fathers to their husbands. In the next phase, that of the newly married couple, women are establishing two-career marriages, having children later, having fewer children, or choosing not to have children at all.

In the "pressure cooker" phase of the family life cycle—that of families with young children—the majority of divorces take place, many of them initiated by women; in the next phase, that of families with adolescents, couples have the fastest growth in divorce rates at present. It is during this phase that the "midlife crisis" has sent unprecedented numbers of women back to school and work. Finally, when the children are gone, a married couple—if they are still married—can expect an average of 20 years alone together, the newest and longest phase of the family life cycle. In former times one spouse, usually the husband, died within two years of the marriage of the youngest child. Old age, the final phase of the family life cycle, has almost become a phase for women only, both because they outlive men and because they live longer than they used to. At ages 75–79, only 24% of women have husbands whereas 61% of men have wives. At ages 80–84, 14% of women have husbands and 49% of men have wives. At age 85, 6% of women have husbands and 34% of men have wives (Bianchi & Spain, 1986; Glick, 1984b; U.S. Senate Special Committee Report, 1985).

The recent changes in these patterns make our task of defining the "normal" family life cycle even more difficult. An ever increasing percent of the population are living together without marrying (3% of couples at any one point in time), and a rapidly increasing number are having children without marrying. At present 6% or more of the population is homosexual. Present estimates are that 12% of young women will never marry, three times the percent for their parents' generation; 25% will never have children; 50% will end their marriages in divorce and 20% will have two divorces. Thus families often are not going through the "normal" phases at the "normal" times. If one adds to this the number of families that experience the death of a member before old age and those that have a chronically ill or handicapped or alcoholic family member, which alters their life cycle pattern, the number of "normal" families is even smaller. Another major factor affecting all families at one time or another is migration (Sluzki, 1979; McGoldrick, 1982). The break in cultural and family continuity created by migration affects family life cycle patterns for several generations. Given the enormous number of Americans who have immigrated within the past two generations, the percentage of "normal" families is diminished still further.

Thus our paradigm for middle-class American families is currently more or less mythological, though statistically accurate, relating in part to existing patterns and in part to the ideal standards of the past against which most families compare themselves.

It is imperative that therapists at least recognize the extent of change and variations in the norm that are now widespread and that they help families to stop comparing their structure and life cycle course with that of the family of the 1950s. While relationship patterns and family themes may continue to sound familiar, the structure, ages, stages, and form of the American family have changed radically.

It is time for professionals to give up attachments to the old ideals and to

put a more positive conceptual frame around what *is:* two paycheck marriages; permanent "single-parent" households; unmarried couples and remarried couples; single-parent adoptions; and women of all ages alone. It is past time to stop thinking of transitional crises as permanent traumas, and to drop from our vocabulary words and phrases that link us to the norms and prejudices of the past: children of divorce, out-of-wedlock child, fatherless home, working mother, and the like.

THE STAGES OF THE INTACT MIDDLE-CLASS AMERICAN FAMILY LIFE CYCLE

Our classification of family life cycle stages of American middle-class families in the last quarter of the 20th century highlights our view that the central underlying process to be negotiated is the expansion, contraction, and realignment of the relationship system to support the entry, exit, and development of family members in a functional way. We offer suggestions about the process of change required of families at each transition, as well as hypotheses about the clinical fallout at each phase.

The Launching of the Single Young Adult

In outlining the stages of the family life cycle, we have departed from the traditional sociological depiction of the family life cycle as commencing at courtship or marriage and ending with the death of one spouse. Rather, considering the family to be the operative emotional unit from the cradle to the grave, we see a new family life cycle beginning at the stage of "young adults," whose completion of the primary task of coming to terms with their family of origin most profoundly influences who, when, how, and whether they will marry and how they will carry out all succeeding stages of the family life cycle. Adequate completion of this requires that the young adult separate from the family of origin without cutting off or fleeing reactively to a substitute emotional refuge (Chapter 9). Seen in this way, the "young adult" phase is a cornerstone. It is a time to formulate personal life goals and to become a "self" before joining with another to form a new family subsystem. The more adequately young adults can differentiate themselves from the emotional program of the family of origin at this phase, the fewer vertical stressors will follow them through their new family's life cycle. This is the chance for them to sort out emotionally what they will take along from the family of origin what they will leave behind and what they will create for themselves. As mentioned above, of greatest significance is the fact that until the present generation this crucial phase was never considered necessary for women, who had no individual

status in families. Obviously the tradition of caretaking has had profound impact on the functioning of women in families, as the current attempt to change the tradition is now also having.

We have found it useful to conceptualize life cycle transitions as requiring second-order change, or change of the system itself. Problems within each phase can often be resolved by first-order change, or a rearranging of the system, involving an incremental change. We have summarized the shifts in status required for successful accomplishment of life cycle transitions in column 2 of Table 1-1, which outlines the stages and tasks of the life cycle. In our view it is important for a therapist not to become bogged down with a family in first-order details when they have not made the required second-order shifts in relationship status to accomplish the tasks of the phase.

In the young adult phase, problems usually center on either young adults' or their parents' not recognizing the need for a shift to a less hierarchical form of relating, based on their now all being adults. Problems in shifting status may take the form of parents' encouraging the dependence of their young adult children, or of young adults' either remaining dependent or rebelling and breaking away in a pseudo-independent cutoff of their parents and families.

For women, problems at this stage more often focus on short-circuiting their definition of themselves in favor of finding a mate. Men more often have difficulty committing themselves in relationships, forming instead a pseudo-independent identity focused around work.

It is our view, following Bowen (1978), that cutoffs never resolve emotional relationships and that young adults who cut off their parents do so reactively and are in fact still emotionally bound to rather than independent of the family "program." The shift toward adult-to-adult status requires a mutually respectful and personal form of relating, in which young adults can appreciate parents as they are, needing neither to make them into what they are not nor to blame them for what they could not be. Neither do young adults need to comply with parental expectations and wishes at their own expense. Therapy at this phase most often involves coaching young adults to reengage with their parents in a new way that accomplishes the shifting of their status in the system. When the parents are the ones seeking help, therapy usually involves helping them to recognize the new status of their adult children and to relate to them as such. Family members often get stuck in a "more of the same" struggle, where the harder they try, the worse it gets. Therapy focuses on helping them make the necessary second-order change. Only when the generations can shift their status relations and reconnect in a new way can the family move on developmentally.

The Joining of Families Through Marriage:
The Couple

The changing role of women, the frequent marriage of partners from widely different cultural backgrounds, and the increasing physical distances between

Table 1-1. The Stages of the Family Life Cycle

Family Life Cycle Stage	Emotional Process of Transition: Key Principles	Second-Order Changes in Family Status Required to Proceed Developmentally
1. Leaving home: Single young adults	Accepting emotional and financial responsibility for self	a. Differentiation of self in relation to family of origin b. Development of intimate peer relationships c. Establishment of self re work and financial independence
2. The joining of families through marriage: The new couple	Commitment to new system	a. Formation of marital system b. Realignment of relationships with extended families and friends to include spouse
3. Families with young children	Accepting new members into the system	a. Adjusting marital system to make space for child(ren) b. Joining in childrearing, financial, and household tasks c. Realignment of relationships with extended family to include parenting and grandparenting roles
4. Families with adolescents	Increasing flexibility of family boundaries to include children's independence and grandparents' frailties	a. Shifting of parent child relationships to permit adolescent to move in and out of system b. Refocus on midlife marital and career issues c. Beginning shift toward joint caring for older generation
5. Launching children and moving on	Accepting a multitude of exits from and entries into the family system	a. Renegotiation of marital system as a dyad b. Development of adult to adult relationships between grown children and their parents. c. Realignment of relationships to include in-laws and grandchildren d. Dealing with disabilities and death of parents (grandparents)
6. Families in later life	Accepting the shifting of generational roles	a. Maintaining own and/or couple functioning and interests in face of physiological decline; exploration of new familial and social role options b. Support for a more central role of middle generation. c. Making room in the system for the wisdom and experience of the elderly, supporting the older generation without overfunctioning for them d. Dealing with loss of spouse, siblings, and other peers and preparation for own death. Life review and integration

family members are placing a much greater burden on couples to define their relationship for themselves than was true in traditional and precedent-bound family structures (Chapter 10). While any two family systems are always different and have conflicting patterns and expectations, in our present culture couples are less bound by family traditions and freer than ever before to develop male-female relationships unlike those they experienced in their families of origin. Marriage tends to be misunderstood as a joining of two individuals. What it really represents is the changing of two entire systems and an overlapping to develop a third subsystem. As Jessie Bernard pointed out long

ago, marriage represents such a different phenomenon for men and for women that one must really speak of "his" and "her" marriage. Women tend to anticipate marriage with enthusiasm, although statistically it has not been a healthy state for them. Men, on the other hand, approach marriage typically with much ambivalence and fear of being "ensnared," but, in fact, do better psychologically and physically in the married state than women. Marriage has traditionally meant the wife taking care of the husband and children, providing for them a haven from the outside world. The traditional role of "wife" provides low status, no personal income and a great deal of work for women and typically has not met women's needs for emotional comfort. This is part of the reason for the recent lowering rate of marriage and later age of marriage, as well as the trend for women to delay child bearing, or even to choose not to have children at all. A rise in women's status is positively correlated with marital instability (Pearson & Hendrix, 1979) and with the marital dissatisfaction of their husbands (Burke & Weir, 1976). When women used to fall automatically into the adaptive role in marriage, the likelihood of divorce was much lower. In fact it appears very difficult for two spouses to be equally successful and achieving. There is evidence that either spouse's accomplishments may correlate negatively with the same degree of achievement in the other (Ferber & Huber, 1979). Thus achieving a successful transition to couplehood in our time, when we are trying to move toward the equality of the sexes (educationally and occupationally), may be extraordinarily difficult (Chapter 10).

Although we hypothesize that failure to renegotiate family status is the main reason for marital failure, it appears that couples are very unlikely to present with extended family problems as the stated issue. Problems reflecting the inability to shift family status are usually indicated by defective boundaries around the new subsystem. In-laws may be too intrusive and the new couple afraid to set limits, or the couple may have difficulty forming adequate connections with the extended systems, cutting themselves off in a tight twosome. At times the inability to formalize a living together couple relationship in marriage indicates that the partners are still to enmeshed in their own families to define a new system and accept the implications of this realignment.

It is useful in such situations to help the system to move to a new definition of itself (second-order change) rather than to get lost in the details of incremental shifts they may be struggling over (sex, money, time, etc.).

Becoming Parents: Families with Young Children

The shift to this stage of the family life cycle requires that adults now move up a generation and become caretakers to the younger generation. Typical problems that occur when parents cannot make this shift are struggles with each other about taking responsibility, or refusal or inability to behave as

parents to their children. Often parents find themselves unable to set limits and exert the required authority, or they lack the patience to allow their children to express themselves as they develop. Often, parents with children who present clinically at this phase are somehow not accepting the generation boundary between themselves and their children. They may complain that their four-year-old is "impossible to control." Or, on the other hand, they may expect their children to behave more like adults, reflecting too strong a generational boundary or barrier. In any case, child centered problems are typically addressed by helping parents gain a view of themselves as part of a new generational level with specific responsibilities and tasks in relation to the next level of the family.

The central struggle of this phase, however, in the modern two-paycheck (and sometimes two-career) marriage is the disposition of child-care responsibilities and household chores when both parents work full-time. The pressure of trying to find adequate child care when there is no satisfactory social provision for this family need produces serious consequences: the two full-time jobs may fall on the woman; the family may live in conflict and chaos; children may be neglected or sexually abused in inadequate child-care facilities; recreation and vacations may be sharply curtailed to pay for child care; or the woman may give up her career to stay home or work part-time. This problem is at the center of most marital conflict presented at this stage, and often leads to complaints of sexual dysfunction and depression. It is not possible to work successfully with couples at this phase without dealing with the issues of gender and the impact of sex-role functioning that is still regarded as the norm for most men and women. It is not really surprising that this is the family life cycle phase that has the highest rate of divorce.

Chapter 11 focuses largely on the impact of this transition on the working couple because of its relevance to today's family. However, therapists need also to inform themselves about child behavior and development, learning disabilities, serious disorders of childhood, etc., so that they do not overlook these in their focus on parent-child or marital conflict.

The shift at this transition for grandparents is to move to a back seat from which they can allow their children to be the central parental authorities and yet form a new type of caring relationship with their grandchildren. For many adults this is a particularly gratifying transition, which allows them to have intimacy without the responsibility that parenting requires.

The Transformation of the Family System in Adolescence

While many have broken down the stages of families with young children into different phases, in our view the shifts are incremental until adolescence, which ushers in a new era because it marks a new definition of the children within the family and of the parents' roles in relation to their children. Families

with adolescents must establish qualitatively different boundaries than families with younger children, a job made more difficult in our times by the lack
of built-in rituals to facilitate this transition (Quinn et al., 1985). The boundaries must now be permeable. Parents can no longer maintain complete authority. Adolescents can and do open the family to a whole array of new values
as they bring friends and new ideals into the family arena. Families that
become derailed at this stage may be rather closed to new values and threatened by them and they are frequently stuck in an earlier view of their children.
They may try to control every aspect of their lives at a time when, developmentally, this is impossible to do successfully. Either the adolescent withdraws
from the appropriate involvements for this developmental stage, or the parents
become increasingly frustrated with what they perceive as their own impotence. For this phase the old Alcoholics Anonymous adage is particularly apt
for parents: "May I have the ability to accept the things I cannot change, the
strength to change the things I can, and the wisdom to know the difference."
Flexible boundaries that allow adolescents to move in and be dependent at
times when they cannot handle things alone, and to move out and experiment
with increasing degrees of independence when they are ready, put special
strains on all family members in their new status with one another. This is also
a time when adolescents begin to establish their own independent relationships with the extended family, and it requires special adjustments between parents and grandparents to allow and foster these new patterns.

   Therapy in such situations needs to help families make the appropriate
transformation of their view of themselves to allow for the increasing independence of the new generation, while maintaining appropriate boundaries and
structure to foster continued family development.

   The central event in the marital relationship at this phase is usually the
"midlife crisis" of one or both spouses, with an exploration of personal, career,
and marital satisfactions and dissatisfactions. There is usually an intense
renegotiation of the marriage, and sometimes a decision to divorce. A focus on
parent-adolescent complaints by either the family or the therapist may mask
an affair or a secretly pondered divorce, or may prevent the marital problems
from coming to the surface. This is not to say that common adolescent
symptoms, such as drug and alcohol abuse, teenage pregnancy, or delinquency
or psychotic behavior, should not be carefully assessed and dealt with.

Families at Midlife:
Launching Children and Moving On

   This phase of the family life cycle is the newest and the longest, and for
these reasons, it is in many ways the most problematic of all phases (Chapter
13). Until about a generation ago, most families were occupied with raising
their children for their entire active adult lives until old age. Now, because of
the low birth rate and the long life span of most adults, parents launch their
children almost 20 years before retirement and must then find other life

activities. The difficulties of this transition can lead families to hold on to their children or can lead to parental feelings of emptiness and depression, particularly for women who have focused their main energies on their children and who now feel unprepared to face a new career in the work world. The most significant aspect of this phase is that it is marked by the greatest number of exits and entries of family members. It begins with the launching of grown children and proceeds with the entry of their spouses and children. It is a time when older parents are often becoming ill or dying. This, in conjunction with the difficulties of finding meaningful new life activities during this phase itself, may make it a particularly difficult period. Parents not only must deal with the change in their own status as they make room for the next generation and prepare to move up to grandparental positions, but also with a different type of relationship with their own parents, who may become dependent, giving them (particularly women) considerable caretaking responsibilities. This can also be a liberating time, in that finances may be easier than during the primary years of family responsibilities and there is the potential for moving into new and unexplored areas—travel, hobbies, new careers. For some families this stage is seen as a time of fruition and completion and as a second opportunity to consolidate or expand by exploring new avenues and new roles. For others it leads to disruption, a sense of emptiness and overwhelming loss, depression, and general disintegration. The phase necessitates a restructing of the marital relationship now that parenting responsibilities are no longer required. As Solomon (1973) has noted, if the solidification of the marriage has not taken place and reinvestment is not possible, the family often mobilizes itself to hold onto the last child. Where this does not happen, the couple may move toward divorce.

The Family in Later Life

As Walsh (Chapter 14) has pointed out, few of the visions of old age we are offered in our culture provide us with positive perspectives for healthy later-life adjustment within a family or social context. Pessimistic views of later life prevail. The current myths are that most elderly people have no families; that those who do have families have little relationship with them and are usually set aside in institutions; or that all family interactions with older family members are minimal. On the contrary, the vast majority of adults over 65 do not live alone but with other family members. Over 80% live within an hour of at least one child (Chapter 14).

Another myth about the elderly is that they are sick, senile, and feeble and can be best handled in nursing homes or hospitals. Only 4% of the elderly live in institutions (Streib, 1972), and the average age at admission is 80. There are indications that if others did not foster their dependence or ignore them as functional family members, even this degree of dependence would be less.

Among the tasks of families in later life are adjustments to retirement, which not only may create the obvious vacuum for the retiring person, but may

put a special strain on a marriage that until then has been balanced in different spheres. Financial insecurity and dependence are also special difficulties, especially for family members who value managing for themselves. And, while loss of friends and relatives is a particular difficulty at this phase, the loss of a spouse is the most difficult adjustment, with its problems of reorganizing one's entire life alone after many years as a couple and of having fewer relationships to help replace the loss. Grandparenthood can, however, offer a new lease on life, and opportunities for special close relationships without the responsibilities of parenthood.

Difficulty in making the status changes required for this phase of life are reflected in older family members' refusal to relinquish some of their power, as when a grandfather refuses to turn over the company or make plans for his succession. The inability to shift status is reflected also when older adults give up and become totally dependent on the next generation, or when the next generation does not accept their lessening powers or treats them as totally incompetent or irrelevant. The evidence suggests that men and women respond very differently to their roles in aging and this too must be carefully assessed (Hesse-Biber & Williamson, 1984).

Even when members of the older generation are quite enfeebled, there is not really a reversal of roles between one generation and the next, because parents always have a great many years of extra experience and remain models to the next generations for the phases of life ahead. Nevertheless, because older age is totally devalued in our culture, family members of the middle generation often do not know how to make the appropriate shift in relational status with their parents.

Clinically it is rarely the older family members themselves who seek help, although they do suffer from many clinical problems, primary among which is depression. More often it is members of the next generation who seek help, and even they often do not present with their problem defined as relating to an elderly parent. It is often only through careful history taking that one learns that an aging grandparent is just about to move in or to be taken to a nursing home, and that the relationship issues around this shift have been left totally submerged in the family.

Helping family members recognize the status changes and the need for resolving their relationships in a new balance can help families move on developmentally.

MAJOR VARIATIONS IN THE FAMILY LIFE CYCLE

Divorce and Remarriage

While the statistical majority of the American middle and upper classes still go through the traditional family life cycle stages as outlined above, the largest

variation from that norm consists of families in which divorce has occurred. With the divorce rate currently at 50% and the rate of redivorce at 61% (Glick, 1984a), divorce in the American family is close to the point at which it will occur in the majority of families and will thus be thought of more and more as a normative event. In our experience as clinicians and teachers, we have found it useful to conceptualize divorce as an interruption or dislocation of the traditional family life cycle, which produces the kind of profound disequilibrium that is associated throughout the entire family life cycle with shifts, gains, and losses in family membership (Chapter 15; Ahrons & Rodgers, 1987). As in other life cycle phases, there are crucial shifts in relationship status and important emotional tasks that must be completed by the members of divorcing families in order for them to proceed developmentally. As in other phases, emotional issues not resolved at this phase will be carried along as hindrances in future relationships (Chapter 15).

Therefore, we conceptualize the need for families in which divorce occurs to go through one or two additional phases of the family life cycle in order to restabilize and go forward developmentally again at a more complex level. Of women who divorce, at least 35% do not remarry. These families go through one additional phase and can restabilize permanently as post-divorce families (Chapter 16). The other 65% of women who divorce remarry, and these families can be said to require negotiation of two additional phases of the family life cycle before permanent restabilization (Chapter 17).

Our concept of the divorce and postdivorce family emotional process can be visualized as a roller-coaster graph, with peaks of emotional tension at all transition points:

1. At the time of the decision to separate or divorce
2. When this decision is announced to family and friends
3. When money and custody/visitation arrangements are discussed
4. When the physical separation takes place
5. When the actual legal divorce takes place
6. When separated spouses or ex-spouses have contact about money or children
7. As each child graduates, marries, has children or becomes ill
8. As Each spouse is remarried, moves, becomes ill, or dies.

These emotional pressure peaks are found in all divorcing families—not necessarily in the above order—and many of them take place over and over again, for months or years. A more detailed depiction of the process appears in Table 1-2.

The emotions released during the process of divorce relate primarily to the work of emotional divorce—that is, the retrieval of self from the marriage. Each partner must retrieve the hopes, dreams, plans, and expectations that were invested in this spouse and in this marriage. This requires mourning what is lost and dealing with hurt, anger, blame, guilt, shame, and loss in oneself, in the spouse, in the children, and in the extended family.

Table 1-2. Dislocations of the Family Life Cycle Requiring Additional Steps to Restabilize and Proceed Developmentally

	Phase	Emotional Process of Transition Prerequisite Attitude	Developmental Issues
Divorce			
1.	The decision to divorce	Acceptance of inability to resolve marital tensions sufficiently to continue relationship	Acceptance of one's own part in the failure of the marriage
2.	Planning the breakup of the system	Supporting viable arrangements for all parts of the system	a. Working cooperatively on problems of custody, visitation, and finances b. Dealing with extended family about the divorce
3.	Separation	a. Willingness to continue cooperative coparental relationship and joint financial support of children b. Work on resolution of attachment to spouse	a. Mourning loss of intact family. b. Restructuring marital and parent-child relationships and finances; adaptation to living apart c. Realignment of relationships with extended family; staying connected with spouse's extended family
4.	The divorce	More work on emotional divorce: Overcoming hurt, anger, guilt, etc.	a. Mourning loss of intact family: giving up fantasies of reunion b. Retrieval of hopes, dreams, expectations from the marriage c. Staying connected with extended families
Post divorce family 1.	Single-parent (custodial household or primary residence)	Willingness to maintain financial responsibilities, continue parental contact with ex-spouse, and support contact of children with ex-spouse and his or her family	a. Making flexible visitation arrangements with ex-spouse and his family b. Rebuilding own financial resources c. Rebuilding own social network
2.	Single-parent (noncustodial)	Willingness to maintain parental contact with ex-spouse and support custodial parent's relationship with children	a. Finding ways to continue effective parenting relationship with children b. Maintaining financial responsibilities to ex-spouse and children. c. Rebuilding own social network

In our clinical work with divorcing families, we subscribe to the basic systems view that cutoffs are emotionally harmful, and we work to help divorcing spouses continue to relate as cooperative parents and to permit maximum feasible contact between children and natural parents and grandparents. Our experience supports that of others (Hetherington et al., 1977; Ahrons, 1980), who have found that it takes a minimum of two years and a

great deal of effort after divorce for a family to readjust to its new structure and proceed to the next life cycle stage, which may or may not include remarriage.

Families in which the emotional issues of divorce are not adequately resolved can remain stuck emotionally for years, if not for generations. The predictable peaks of emotional tension in the transition to remarriage occur at the time of serious commitment to a new relationship; at the time a plan to remarry is announced to families and friends; at the time of the actual marriage and formation of a stepfamily, which takes place simultaneously and as the logistics of stepfamily life are put into practice.

The family emotional process at the transition to remarriage consists of struggling with fears about investment in a new marriage and a new family: one's own fears, the new spouse's fears, and the children's fears (of either or both spouses); dealing with hostile or upset reactions of the children, the extended families, and the ex-spouse; struggling with the ambiguity of the new family structure, roles, and relationships; rearousal of intense parental guilt and concerns about the welfare of children; and rearousal of the old attachment to ex-spouse (negative or positive). Table 1-3 depicts the process in somewhat greater detail.

Our society offers stepfamilies a choice of two conceptual models, neither of which work: families that act like the intact family next door; glorified in the situation comedies of TV; and the wicked stepparents of the fairy tales. Our first clinical step, then, is to validate for stepfamilies the lack of social support and clarity in the paradigm of family they are offered. Clinicians can offer them the challenge of helping to invent a new form of family structure, with the following guidelines making good systems sense: giving up the old model of family and accepting the complexity of a new form; maintaining permeable boundaries to permit shifting of household memberships; and working for open lines of communication between all sets of parents and between all natural parents and grandparents and their children or grandchildren. (Chapter 17).

In our experience the residue of an angry and vengeful divorce can block stepfamily integration for years or forever. The rearousal of the old emotional attachment to an ex-spouse, which characteristically surfaces at the time of remarriage and at subsequent life cycle transitions of children, is usually not understood as a predictable process and therefore leads to denial, misinterpretation, cutoff, and assorted difficulties. As in the case of adjustment to a new family structure after divorce, stepfamily integration seems also to require a minimum of two or three years before a workable new structure permits family members to move on emotionally.

The Family Life Cycle of the Poor

The adaptation of multiproblem poor families to a stark political, social, and economic context has produced a family life cycle pattern that varies significantly from the middle-class paradigm so often and so erroneously used

Table 1-3. Remarried Family Formation: A Developmental Outline*

	Steps	Prerequisite Attitude	Developmental Issues
1.	Entering the new Relationship	Recovery from loss of first marriage (adequate "emotional divorce")	Recommitment to marriage and to forming a family with readiness to deal with the complexity and ambiguity
2.	Conceptualizing and planning new marriage and family	Accepting one's own fears and those of new spouse and children about remarriage and forming a stepfamily Accepting need for time and patience for adjustment to complexity and ambiguity of: 1. Multiple new roles 2. Boundaries: space, time, membership, and authority. 3. Affective Issues: guilt, loyalty conflicts, desire for mutuality, unresolvable past hurts	a. Work on openness in the new relationships to avoid pseudomutality. b. Plan for maintenance of cooperative financial and coparental relationships with ex-spouses. c. Plan to help children deal with fears, loyalty conflicts, and membership in two systems. d. Realignment of relationships with extended family to include new spouse and children. e. Plan maintenance of connections for children with extended family of ex-spouses(s).
3.	Remarriage and reconstitution of family	Final resolution of attachment to previous spouse and ideal of "intact" family; Acceptance of a different model of family with permeable boundaries	a. Restructuring family boundaries to allow for inclusion of new spouse–stepparent. b. Realignment of relationships and financial arrangements throughout subsystems to permit interweaving of several systems. c. Making room for relationships of all children with biological (noncustodial) parents, grandparents, and other extended family. d. Sharing memories and histories to enhance stepfamily integration.

*Variation on a developmental scheme presented by Ransom et al. (1979)

to conceptualize their situation. Hines (Chapter 21) offers a thought-provoking breakdown of the family life cycle of the poor into three phases: the "unattached young adult" (who may actually be 11 or 12 years old), who is virtually on his or her own, unaccountable to adults; families with children—a phase that occupies most of the life span and commonly includes three- and four-generation households; and the phase of the non-evolved grandmother, still involved in a central childrearing role in old age—still actively in charge of the generations below.

In addition to the chapter referred to above, readers are referred to Aponte (1974, 1976) and Minuchin and colleagues (1967) for clinical approaches to

poor families, and to Fulmer's provocative contrast of the family life cycle in two different socio-economic classes (Chapter 22). Such polarities have become a characteristic feature of American life in the 1980s, particularly in urban areas where the middle class is often outnumbered by a combination of "yuppies," poor and homeless.

Cultural Variation

Most descriptions of the typical family life cycle (including ours) fail to convey the considerable effects of ethnicity and religion on all aspects of how, when, and in what way a family makes its transitions from phase to phase. Although we may ignore these variables for the theoretical clarity of focus on our commonalities, a clinician working with real families in the real world cannot afford to ignore this. The definition of "family," as well as the timing of life cycle phases and the importance of different transitions, varies depending on a family's cultural background. It is essential for clinicians to consider how ethnicity intersects with the life cycle and to encourage families to take active responsibility for carrying out the rituals of their ethnic or religious group(s) to mark each phase (Chapter 20). It is also extremely important for us as clinicians to help families develop rituals that correspond to the actual transitions of their lives, including those transitions that the culture has not validated (Chapter 8).

CONCLUSIONS

In conclusion, we direct the reader's thoughts toward the powerful (and preventive) implications of family life cycle celebration: those rituals, religious or secular, that have been designed by families in every culture to ease the passage of its members from one status to the next. As Friedman (Chapter 7) points out, all family relationships in the system seem to unlock during the time just before and after such events, and it is often possible to shift things with less effort during these intensive periods than could ordinarily be expended in years of struggle.

REFERENCES

Ahrons, C. H. (1980). Joint custody arrangements in the postdivorce family. *Journal of Divorce*, 3:187–205.

Ahrons, C. R. (1980). Redefining the divorced family: A conceptual framework. *Social Work*, Nov: 437–441.

Ahrons, C. R. (1983). Divorce: A crisis of family transition and change. In D. H. Olsen & B. X. Miller (Eds.), *Family studies: Review yearbook*, Vol. 1. Beverly Hills, Calif.: Sage Publications.

Ahrons, C. R. H. & Rodgers, R. (1987). *The divorced family*. New York: Norton.

Aponte, H. (1974). Psychotherapy for the poor: An eco-structural approach to treatment. *Delaware Medical Journal* 46:15–23.

Aries, P. (1962). *Centuries of childhood: A social history of family life*. New York: Vintage.

Bacon, L. (1974). Early motherhood, accelerated role transition and social pathologies, *Social Forces* 52: 333–341.

Belsky, J., Spanier, G.B., & Robine, M. (1983). Stability and change in marriage across the transition to parenthood. *Journal of Marriage and the Family* 45(3):567–578.

Bernard, J. (1972). *The future of marriage*. New York: Bantam.

Bianchi, S. M. & Spain, D. (1986). *American women in transition*. New York: Russel Sage.

Bowen, M., (1978). *Family therapy in clinical practice*. New York: Aronson.

Butler, R.N., & Lewis, M.I. (1983). *Aging and mental health*. New York: New American Library.

Campbell, A. (1975, May). The American way of mating: Marriage si, children only maybe. *Psychology Today* 37–43.

Carter, E.A. (1978). The transgenerational scripts and nuclear family stress: Theory and clinical implications. In R.R. Sager (Ed.), *Georgetown family symposium* (Vol. 3, 1975–76). Washington, D.C.: Georgetown University.

Cicirelli, V.G. (1985). Sibling relationships throughout the life cycle. In L. L'Abate (Ed.), *The handbook of family psychology and therapy*. Homewood, Ill.: Dorsey Press.

Combrinck-Graham, L. (1985). A developmental model for family systems. *Family Process*, 24(2): 139–150.

Duvall, E.M. (1977). *Marriage and family development* (5th ed.). Philadelphia: Lippincott.

Erikson, E. (1950). *Childhood and society*. New York: Norton.

Erikson, E.H. (1976). *Adulthood*. New York: Norton.

Fishbein, H.D. (1987). The identified patient and stage of family development. *Journal of Marital and Family Therapy* 8(1): 57–62.

Gelfand, D.E. (1982). *Aging: The ethnic factor*. Boston: Little Brown.

Gelfand, D.E., & Kutzik, A.J. (Eds.) (1979). *Ethnicity and aging*. New York: Springer.

Gilligan, C. (1982). *In a different voice*. Cambridge, Mass: Harvard University Press.

Glick, P. (1984a). How American families are changing. *American Demographics*, Jan 21–25.

Glick, P. (1984b). Marriage, divorce, and living arrangements. *Journal of Family Issues* 5(1): 7–26.

Glick, P. (1984c). American household structure in transition. *Family Planning Perspectives* 16(5): 205–211.

Goldner, V. (1985). Feminism and family therapy. *Family Process* 24(1): 31–48.

Goode, W.J. (1963). *World revolution and family patterns*. New York: Free Press.

Goodrich, D.W., Ryder, R.G., & Raush, H.L. (1968). Patterns of newlywed marriage. *Journal of Marriage and the Family* 30: 383–390.

Gould, R. (1972). The phases of adult life: A study in developmental psychology. *American Journal of Psychiatry* 129: 33–43.

Hadley, T., Jacob, T., Milliones, J., Caplan, J., & Spitz, D. (1974). The relationship between family developmental crises and the appearance of symptoms in a family member. *Family Process* 13:207–214.

Hare-Mustin, R.T. (1978). A feminist approach to family therapy. *Family Process* 17: 181–193.

Hare-Mustin, R.T. (1987). The problem of gender in family therapy. *Family Process* 26: 15–27.

Harry, J. (1976). Evolving sources of happiness for men over the life cycle: A structural analysis. *Journal of Marriage and the Family* 2: 289–296.

Hess, B.B., & Waring, J.M. (1984). Changing patterns of aging and family bonds in later life. *The Family Coordinator* 27(4): 303–314.

Hesse-Biber, S., & Williamson, J. (1984). Resource theory and power in families: Life Cycle Considerations. *Family Process* 23(2) 261–278.

Hetherington, M.E., Cox, M., & Cox, R., (1977). The aftermath of divorce. In E.M. Hetherington & R.D. Parke, *Contemporary readings in child psychology,* 3nd ed. New York: McGraw-Hill.

Hill, R. (1970). *Family development in three generations.* Cambridge, Mass.: Schenkman.

James, K. & McIntyre, D. (1983). The reproduction of families: The social role of family therapy. *Journal of Marital and Family Therapy* 9(2): 119–130.

Kitson, G.C., & Raschke, H.J. (1983). Divorce research: What we know, what we need to know. In D.H. Olson & B.C. Miller (Eds.), *Family studies: review yearbook,* Vol. 1. Beverly Hills, Calif.: Sage Publications.

Lieberman, M. (Oct. 1974). Adaptational patterns in middle aged and elderly: The role of ethnicity. Paper presented at the Gerontological Society Conference, Portland, Ore.

Levinson, D. (1978). *The seasons of a man's life.* New York: Knopf.

Libow, J.A., Rashkin, P.A., & Caust, B.L. (1982). Feminist and family systems therapy: Are they incompatible? *The American Journal of Family Therapy* 10(3): 3–12.

McGoldrick, M. (1982). Overview. In M. McGoldrick, J.K. Pearce, & J. Giordano, (Eds.), *Ethnicity and family therapy.* New York: Guilford Press.

McGoldrick, M., Anderson, C., & Walsh, F. (in press). *Women in families: A framework for family therapy.* New York: Norton.

McGoldrick Orfanidis, M. (1977). Some data on death and cancer in schizophrenic families. Presentation at Georgetown Presymposium. Washington, D.C.

Miller, J.B. (1976). *Toward a new psychology of women. Boston: Beacon.*

Minuchin, S., Montalvo, B., Guerney, B., Rosman, B., & Schumer, F. (1967). Families of the slums. New York: Basic Books.

Nadelson, C., et al., (1984). Marriage as a developmental process. In C.C.Nadelson & D.C. Polonsky (Eds.), *Marriage and divorce: A contemporary perspective.* New York: Guilford.

Nock, S.L. (1981). Family life cycle transitions: Longitudinal effects on family members. *Journal of Marriage and the Family,* 43: 703–714.

Norton, A.J. (1980). The influence of divorce on traditional life cycle measures. *Journal of Marriage and the Family,* 42: 63–69.

Norton, A.J. (1983). The family life cycle: 1980. *Journal of Marriage and the Family,* 45(2): 267–275.

Quinn, W.H. (1983). Older generations of the family: Relational dimensions and quality. *American Journal of Family Therapy,* 11(3): 23–34.

Quinn, W.H., Newfield, N.A., & Protinsky, H.O. (1985), Rites of passage in families with adolescents. *Family Process,* 24(1): 101–112.

Paul, N. & Grosser, G. (1965). Operational mourning and its role in conjoint family therapy. *Community Mental Health Journal,* 1: 339–345.

Paul, N. & Paul, B.B. (1974). *A marital puzzle.* New York: Norton.

Rodgers, R. (1960). Proposed modifications of Duvall's family life cycle stages. Paper presented at the American Sociological Association Meeting, New York.

Schram, R.W. (1979). Marital satisfaction over the family life cycle: A critique and proposal. *Journal of Marriage and the Family* 41(1): Feb.

Sluzki, C. (1979). Migration and family conflict. *Family Process* 18(4):379–390.

Solomon, M. (1973). A developmental conceptual premise for family therapy. *Family Process* 12: 179–188.

Spanier, G.B. (1983). Married and unmarried cohabitation in the United States: 1980. *Journal of Marriage and the Family* 45(2): 277–288.

Spanier, G.B., & Glick, P.C. (1980). The life cycle of American families: An expanded analysis. *Journal of Family History* 5: 97–111.

Taggert, M. (1985). The feminist critique in epistemological perspective: Questions of context in family therapy. *Journal of Marital and Family Therapy* 11(2): 113–126.

Thomas, C.G. & Duszynski, D.R. (1974). Closeness to parents and the family constellation in a prospective study of five disease states: Suicide, mental illness, malignant tumor, hypertension and coronary heart disease. *The Johns Hopkins Medical Journal* 134: 251–270.

Thurow, L. (1987). The surge in inequality. *Scientific American* 256(5): 30–37.

U.S. Senate Special Committee on Aging and American Association of Retired Persons. (1985) *Aging America.* Washington, D.C.: U.S. Government Printing Office.

Walsh, F. (1978). Concurrent grandparent death and the birth of a schizophrenic offspring: An intriguing finding. *Family Process* 17: 457–463.

Woehrer, C.E. (Nov. 1982). The influence of ethnic families on intergenerational relationships and later life transitions. *Annals of the American Academy of PSS* 464: 65–78.

Women's Project in Family Therapy (in press). *Feminism and family therapy.* New York: Guilford Press.

2

Women and the Family Life Cycle

Monica McGoldrick, M.S.W.

Women have always played a central role in families, but the idea that they have a life cycle apart from their roles as wife and mother is a relatively recent one, and still is not widely accepted in our culture. The expectation for women has been that they would take care of the needs of others, first men, then children, then the elderly. Until very recently "human development" referred to male development and women's development was defined by the men in their lives. They went from being daughter, to wife, to mother, with their status defined by the male in the relationship and their role by their position in the family's life cycle. Rarely has it been accepted that they had a right to a life for themselves.

In this chapter we focus on the interaction of women's roles throughout the life cycle both in their families and at work. These roles have changed dramatically in recent years. Since 1980 the birth rate has fallen below replacement levels as many more women concentrate on jobs and education. For the first time, more women than men are enrolled in college (Bianchi & Spain, 1985). Although the family therapy field has tended to ignore the overall context of which family patterns are a part, it is becoming increasingly obvious that family relationships cannot be separated from that context, which defines the types of relationships that are possible in families, and delineates who is available to participate in those relationships. The differences in the roles of men and women are illustrated by the fact that in the American workplace women still make on average 64 cents for every dollar a man makes for the same job. Family therapists have ignored the context in which families exist, focusing only on the interactional level of family members, as if they were interchangeable parts with equal control over the outcome of family interactions (Taggert, 1985; Hare-Mustin, 1987). As Goldner (1985) has stated, despite documentation from sociologists and demographers concerning the differences between men and women in family participation, "the category of gender remains essentially invisible in the conceptualizations of family therapists. This blind spot seems extraordinary when one considers the embat-

tled condition of the contemporary family and the extent to which the battle lines have been drawn around conflicting ideologies about how gender relations should be structured" (p. 33). Goldner goes on to point out that, "like the sexual revolution, the breakdown of the traditional family has too often meant a new kind of freedom for men and a new kind of trap for women" (p. 41).

As difficult as adhering to traditional patterns may be for many women, changing the status quo is also extremely painful for them. Even as women are rebelling against having to assume total responsibility for maintaining family relationships, and for upholding traditions and rituals such as holidays and other celebrations, they typically feel guilty when they do not continue to do what they have grown up to expect they will do. When no one else moves in to fill the gap, they feel that family solidarity is breaking down, and that it is their fault.

Being part of a family and then the breaking up of that family have profoundly different implications for men and for women. As Jessie Bernard (1982) has described it, "his" marriage is very different, and a great deal more satisfying, than "her" marriage. Although men remain ambivalent about getting married, fearing "ensnarement," it is women who become more symptomatic and prone to stress in the married state on virtually every indicator. The research reviewed in several places strongly suggests that married women have more symptoms than married men or unmarried women (Brodsky & Hare-Mustin, 1980; Baruch, et al., 1983; Bernard, 1982; Avis, 1985). They experience more depression and more marital dissatisfaction. Women in traditional marital relationships also have poorer physical health, lower self-esteem, less autonomy, and poorer marital adjustment than women in more equal relationships (Avis, 1985).

Women are exposed to higher rates of change and instability in their lives than men (Dohrenwend, 1973) and are more vulnerable to life cycle stresses, because of their greater emotional involvement in the lives of those around them. They are more responsive to a wider network of people for whom they feel responsible. Their role overload leaves them further overburdened when unpredictable stresses, such as illness, divorce, or unemployment, occur. This means they are doubly stressed—they are exposed to more network stresses and are more emotionally responsive to them (Gove, 1972). Kessler and McLeod (1984) found that women are much more affected than men by the death of a loved one and by other network events. Men respond less to events at the edge of their caring networks, and actually hear less about stress in their networks. The help-seeking literature indicates that people in need of emotional support more often seek out women as confidants, and thus women are subjected to even more demands for nurturance. At times their networks are so demanding that some cutting off may be necessary for their mental health (Cohler & Lieberman, 1980; Belle, 1982). As Avis (1985) summarizes the research, "Many writers have concluded that adherence to traditional family roles not only oppresses women, but can have a pernicious effect on all family members, on marriage relationships, and on family functioning" (p. 131).

In recent years women have been marrying later and less often, having fewer children and divorcing more (50%). Those with the most education and income are the most likely to divorce and least likely to remarry, in contrast to men, among whom the wealthiest and best educated are the most likely to stay married or to remarry quickly. It is the woman who is likely to move down to the poverty level if the couple divorces, as she suffers an average income drop of 40%, whereas the man's income rises on an average of 17%. At present 75% of the poor are women or children, mostly living in one-parent households. After divorce men have an ever larger pool of marriageable spouses from which to choose. In first marriage, the average wife is three years younger than her husband; for second marriages the wife is, on the average, six years younger than her husband (Bianchi & Spain, 1985).

Traditionally women have been held responsible for the maintenance of family relationships and for all caretaking: for their husbands, their children, their parents, their husband's parents, and any other sick or dependent family members. Even now almost one-fifth of women aged 55–59 are providing in-home care to an elderly relative. Usually one daughter or a daughter-in-law has the primary care of an elderly mother. Clearly, caregiving for the very old (who are mostly women) is primarily a woman's issue. Increasingly, though, younger women have joined the labor force, and thus are unavailable for caretaking without extreme difficulty. At present more than half of all women aged 45–64 are working outside the home, and most of them full time. With more and more four-generation families on the scene, the caregivers are apt to be elderly themselves, and struggling with declining functioning. Thus today's middle-aged women are caught in a "dependency squeeze" between their parents and their children. (Lang & Brody, 1983; Baruch & Barnett, 1983).

The laws that regulate social services to support families are determined primarily by men and do not support the women who run families. Contrary to the claim that government services sap the strength of family supports, the failure to provide public services to families will most likely exaccerbate intergenerational conflicts, turning family members against each other (Hess, 1985). The overwhelming majority of lawmakers in our society are males and their record on legislation in support of family caretaking is very poor. This is a primary issue for divorced women, mothers of small children, minority women, the elderly (who are mostly women), and other groups that do not have the power to make the laws and so are doubly burdened—with the responsibility but without the resources to take care of their families.

MALE AND FEMALE DEVELOPMENT

There has always been a "his" and "her" version of human development, although until recently only the former was ever described in the literature

(Bernard, 1975). Female development was seen only from an androcentric perspective and involved learning to become an adaptive helpmate to foster male development. Most male theoreticians, such as Freud, Kohlberg, and Piaget, tended to ignore female development. Only very recently has the description of female development appeared in the literature at all (Miller, 1976; Gilligan, 1982; Dinnerstein, 1976; Belenky et al., 1986). Whereas separation, differentiation, and autonomy have been considered primary factors in male development, the values of caring and attachment, interdependence, relationship, and attention to context have been primary in female development. At the same time, these latter values have been devalued by male theoreticians (such as Erikson, Piaget, Levinson, and Valliant).

Women have tended to define themselves in the context of human relationships and to judge themselves in terms of their ability to care. Gilligan has described the woman's place in a man's life cycle as that of "nurturer, caretaker, and helpmate, the weaver of those networks of relationships on which she in turn relies. But while women have thus taken care of men, men have, in their theories of psychological development, as in their economic arrangements, tended to assume or devalue that care" (Gilligan, 1982, p. 17). The major theories of human development have generally equated maturity with autonomy. Concern about relationships has been seen as a weakness of women rather than a human strength. The studies of Broverman and her colleagues on sex-role stereotypes (1970, 1972) have made eminently clear the biases in our cultural attitudes that equate "healthy adulthood" with "maleness." As these studies have shown, we have equated maturity with the capacity for autonomous thinking, rationality, clear decision making, and responsible action, and have devalued the qualities our culture has defined as necessary for feminine identity, such as warmth, expressiveness, and caring for others.

Theories propounded by males have failed to describe the progression of relationships toward a maturity of interdependence. Though most developmental texts recognize the importance of individuation, the reality of continuing connection is lost or relegated to the background. Perhaps this is why there is almost no discussion in the developmental literature of the importance of children in redefining one's adult identity (Daniels & Weingarten, 1982).

Erikson's (1963) eight stages of development suggest that human connectedness is part of the first stage, trust versus mistrust, which covers the first year of life, but this aspect does not appear again until the sixth stage, intimacy versus isolation. All the other stages described by Erikson prior to adulthood involve individual rather than relational issues: autonomy versus shame and doubt; initiative versus guilt; industry versus inferiority; identity versus role confusion. Identity is defined as having a sense of self *apart from* one's family. In addition, from age one to 20, those characteristics that refer to interpersonal issues—doubt, shame, guilt, inferiority, and role confusion, (all of which are associated with female characteristics)—signify failure. It is unfortunate that doubt, guilt, a sense of inferiority and awareness of role confusion are thus defined out of a healthy identity. Do we not need these qualities to deal with

others realistically, just as we need other qualities? Given this idealization of healthy development, it is not surprising that men develop with an impaired capacity for intimacy and experience difficulty in relating to their vulnerability, doubt, and imperfection.

The remarkable development of the ability to talk or communicate, which occurs between the ages of one and three, and is the primary differential characteristic between us and other animals, is not even referred to in this schema. In fact girls demonstrate greater and earlier verbal ability than do boys (Romer, 1981). And remarkably, Erikson's phase of generativity, comes *after* the time of greatest human generativity—producing children—which does not even enter into his schema. The last stage of adulthood, ego integrity versus despair, again appears to relate to individual rather than interpersonal aspects of development. Thus for Erikson the ideal characteristics of a healthy adult (autonomy, initiative, industry, and a clear identity apart from one's family) create a seriously imbalanced human being. In our view all stages of the life cycle have both individual and interpersonal aspects, and the failure to appreciate this has led to seriously skewed human development.

In Levinson's (1978) account, the most significant relationships for men in early adult life are the mentor and the special woman, or helpmate, who encourages the hero to shape and live out his dream. Thus the significant relationships of early adulthood have been construed as "transitional figures" that are the means to an end of individual achievement (Gilligan, 1982, p. 152). George Valliant's (1977) study of male development among high-achieving Harvard graduates, interestingly called "Adaptation to Life" rather than male adaptation, also focuses on work and minimizes the importance of attachment to others.

Even the language that has evolved to describe human development uses peculiarly impersonal terms such as "object relations" to refer to human relationships. The sexist bias of our language appears also in the use of the terms "maternal deprivation," on the one hand, but "father absence," a much less derogatory term, on the other—although what is usually meant is a father who was completely unavailable and a mother who was present but did not give all that was needed.

Developmentally women have been expected from the point of early adulthood to "stand behind their men," to support and nurture their children, and, paradoxically, to be able to live without affirmation and support themselves. Adaptability has probably been the major skill required of women. They were expected to accept being uprooted every time their husbands said it was necessary to move for a better job, to accept their husbands' lack of communication and unavailability, and to handle all human relationships themselves. It is ironic that women, who are seen as "dependent" and less competent than men, have had to function without support in their marriages, to be, indeed, almost totally self-sufficient emotionally. Women have typically had to bolster their husbands' sense of self-esteem, but have been seen as "nags" when they sought emotional support for themselves. [In clinical practice, men's marital

complaints typically center on their wives' nagging and emotional demands (Weiss, 1985) whereas wives' complaints center on their husbands' lack of emotional responsiveness and their own sense of abandonment].

Miller (1976) has called for a new psychology that recognizes the different pattern of women's development, based on a context of attachment and affiliation with others. As she describes it, women's sense of self has been organized around being able to develop and maintain relationships. The threat of disruption of a relationship is often perceived not just as "object loss," but as something closer to a loss of one's identity, and thus as requiring a transformation of self and of the system. Basic to this systemic perspective is the sense that human identity is inextricably bound up in one's relationships with others and that complete autonomy is a fiction. Gilligan's studies suggest that women's moral development has centered on the elaboration of the knowledge of human attachment. In Gilligan's (1982) view, "Attachment and separation anchor the cycle of human life, describing the biology of human reproduction and the psychology of human development. The conceptions of attachment and separation that depict the nature and sequence of infant development appear in adolescence as identity and intimacy and then in adulthood as love and work" (p. 151).

Because of the way women have been socialized, and because awareness of gender issues strikes at the interior of the family, at every woman's closest relationships, these issues have been even more threatening and difficult to accept than ideas about differences in class or ethnicity. As James (1985) points out:

> Patriarchal structures are transmitted through the acquisition of culture, language and gender identity and the family is the site of this transmission . . . To the extent that there is a disjunction between the ideology and a woman's experience, she will tend to blame herself, lose herself and shape herself to fit the picture. This ideology creates women's silence—to speak out against it risks incurring labels and sanctions that mark her as deviant. . . . Women's worth is very much dependent on their roles as wives and mothers. Their value is tied to and derived from their relationships with men (pp. 244–247)

WORK

For men the relationship of family and work is seen as mutually supportive and complementary, but for women work and family have involved conflicting demands. Women have been in a double bind in this regard. (Fox & Hesse-Biber, 1984; Apter, 1985; McGoldrick, 1987; Berg, 1986). Although participation in the labor force is the most important determinant of women's psychological well-being (Kessler & McRae, 1984), the dominant cultural value has been that women belong in the home. We know that women who work show fewer symptoms of psychological distress (Bernard, 1982).

Furthermore, despite the widespread belief that maternal employment is harmful for children, there is evidence that this is not so (Hoffman, 1974). In fact, at least one study has demonstrated that having a working mother with a high-status job has an even more positive effect on the achievement of both her sons and her daughters than does having a father with a high-status profession (Padan, 1965; Lozoff, 1974). And yet there are many pressures against women feeling good about working (Piotrkowski & Repetti, 1984). The family is seen as supporting and nurturing the male worker for his performance on the job whereas women are seen as depriving their families by working, and there is no sense of the family being a "refuge" for women as it has been for men. In fact, the high level of psychological demands in their jobs at home and often in the workplace (nursing, teaching, secretarial work) with little actual control or power over their situation puts them in a particularly stressful situation much of the time (Baruch et al., 1987).

Friedan (1985) has warned that "if the women's movement didn't move into a second stage and take on the problems of restructuring work and home, a new generation would be vulnerable to backlash. But the movement has not moved into that needed second stage, so the women struggling with these new problems view them as purely personal not political, and no longer look to the movement for solutions" (p. 84). Friedan is now urging us again to bring the issue to the forefront, "to free a new generation of women from its new double burden of guilt and isolation. The guilt of less-than-perfect motherhood and less-than-perfect professional career performance are real because it's not possible to 'have it all' when jobs are still structured for men whose wives take care of the details of life, and homes are still structured for women whose only responsibility is running their families" (p. 84). Friedan is urging us to tackle the hard political tasks of restructuring home and work so that women who are married and have children can also earn and have their own voice in the decision-making mainstream of society.

Economic independence for women, which has profound implications for traditional family structures, appears crucial for women's self esteem (Blumstein & Schwartz, 1983), and protection in the face of abuse (Aguirre, 1985), divorce (Weitzman, 1986), and old age (Hess, 1985). The increasing feminization of poverty means that virtually all the poor by the year 2000 will be women and children. To counteract this trend, massive power changes are required in our culture.

As Goldner (1985) has stated:

"By ignoring the complex interpenetration between the structure of family relations and the world of work, family therapists tacitly endorse the nineteenth-century fiction that the family is a domestic retreat from the market place economy . . . The dichotomization of these social domains is a mystification and a distortion that masks a fundamental organizing principle of contemporary family life. The division of labor (both affective and instrumental) and the distribution of power in families are structured not only according to generational hierarchies but also around gendered spheres of influence that derive their legitimacy precisely because of the creation of a public/private dichotomy. To rely on a theory that

neither confronts, nor even acknowledges, this reality is to operate in the realm of illusion." (pp. 43–44)

The indications are that the male-female earnings differential has increased over time from the 1950s to the 1970s (Bianchi & Spain, 1985). As the research has demonstrated, wives' economic dependence on their husbands largely determines their return to abusing husbands (Aguirre, 1985; Strube & Barbour, 1984) and basically creates a seriously problematic power imbalance (Blumstein & Schwartz, 1983).

Fifty-one percent of married women (and 55% of all women over 16, as compared with 36 percent 30 years ago) work outside the home, a large portion in sex-segregated, low-paying jobs. One-quarter of all employed women are crowded into just 22 of 500 occupations distinguished by the Bureau of the Census Thirty-three million people work in low-paying service jobs in which 90% of their co-workers are of the same sex (Fox & Hesse-Biber, 1984; Bianchi & Spain, 1986).

Unfortunately the well-being of both children and the elderly, who are mostly women, may be gained at the expense of the quality of life of the middle generation of women, who are most burdened. Squeezed by overwhelming demands of caretaking for both other generations; they are forced to accept work that limits their options for the rest of their lives (Hess & Soldo, 1984).

Even though the majority of women work, the sharing of family responsibilities to balance the work load is not occurring. While husbands and children participate slightly in housework, the vast majority of household labor is done by wives—between 74% and 92% of major tasks in one study (Berheide, 1984). Employed women continue to do 4.8 hours a day of housework, compared with 1.6 hours for their husbands (Ferree, 1984). As one woman in Berheide's sample put it, "If I don't do it, it doesn't get done" (p. 44). Husbands performed between 12% and 26% of tasks, with the exception of outside errands, where they did 54% and their wives 74% (the overlap reflects work done together or alternated). Children did between 7% and 13% of the tasks. Respondents made it clear that the household remained the wife's responsibility, although other family members sometimes "helped her."

A recent study indicates that in the past decade women have become more aware of the external constraints on their ability to meet their goals in the labor force. They see themselves as having less control over events than they did in the past (Doherty & Baldwin, 1985). This fits reports that women are experiencing high rates of sex discrimination in the workplace (Doherty & Baldwin, 1985).

HOUSEHOLDS

The traditional household is fast becoming a relic of the past. Fewer than 10% of families fit into the traditional ideal of working father, stay-at-home

mother, and children (Friedan, 1985). Very few families can afford to have children unless both husband and wife have jobs (Thurow, 1987). Only 29% of households consist of couples with children under 18, compared with 44% in 1960, and since at least half of those mothers work, many suggest the figure is closer to 6% (Hewlett, 1985). The number of married-couple and couple-with-children households has decreased steadily since 1970, and the number of single-parent households (mostly headed by women) has more than doubled (Rawlings, 1983). For the increasing number of teenaged unmarried mothers, their mothers, aunts, and sisters seem to have full responsibility for the children. The teen fathers are rarely included as part of the picture and other male family members frequently have no primary role in the family's development.

Finally, the majority of people who live alone are women (11 million versus 6.8 million men) and they tend to be widowed and/or divorced elderly (*Current Population Reports,* Oct. 1981; Bianchi & Spain, 1985).

BETWEEN FAMILIES: YOUNG ADULTHOOD

Young adulthood has been, until very recently, a phase for men only. Women passed from their families of origin to their families of procreation, with no space in between to be independent. For men this phase has tended to emphasize their development of a career whereas for women careers almost always have taken second place to the search for husbands. Women are frequently confronted with a clash between the two roles, with family and social pressure conflicting with career demands. The more a woman focuses on career, the less viable are her marital options. In contrast to the situation for men, where education increases the likelihood of marriage, for women with a college education the chances of marrying after age 30 diminish rapidly. In our experience daughters who make full use of young adulthood for personal development tend to do so at a greater distance from their families of origin than do sons, probably because there is less family acceptance of women's individual development. It is perhaps for this reason that the next phase, the young couple, represents different patterns for men and women in relation to their families of origin. For women it brings a turning back to their parents for more connection whereas for men there is an increasing separation from their families of origin, with the marital relationship replacing the family of origin (White, 1986). As Ben Franklin said: "My son is my son til' he takes a wife, but my daughter's my daughter all the days of my life." In fact a daughter is also a daughter-in-law for the rest of her life, since through marriage she typically gains responsibility for the connectedness with her husband's family as well.

The pressure on women not to take full advantage of independent living may be intense. They may lower their sights because of educational, social, internalized, or family attitudes. Women worry that their families may disap-

prove of their high aspirations, fearing it will mean the loss of marital possibilities. Although they are tending to pursue educational and career possibilities longer than in the past, they still tend to drop out of college and employment at higher rates than do men. (It is also true that men have *fewer* options to drop out of the career or work ladder.)

Horner's studies (1972) showed that women feel anxiety about competitive achievement. Such fear "exists because for most women the anticipation of success in competitive achievement activity, especially against men, produces anticipation of certain negative consequences, for example, threat of social rejection and loss of femininity" (p. 125). Sassen (1980) pointed out that Horner found success anxiety present only in women whose success was at the expense of another's failure. Thus, once again, women's behavior is shown to be sensitive to its interpersonal context.

Working with families at this phase of the life cycle is particularly rewarding because of the new options that are available when young adults are able to move toward new life patterns. Interventions directed at connecting young women with the strengths of women in past generations of their families may be especially significant in assisting them at this crucial formative phase. It is important to outline all the unrecognized work that their mothers and grandmothers did to raise their families and to keep a household going in order to emphasize their courage, abilities, hard work, and strengths as role models for positive identification, since women are typically hidden from history (herstory!). An excellent discussion of coaching women on working out family relationships is offered in Lerner's *The Dance of Anger* (1985).

Case Example: Young Adulthood

Mary Smith, age 25, applied for therapy because of conflicts with her Puerto Rican boyfriend and problems with both of her parents. As can be seen on the Smith family genogram (Figure 2.1), Mary is the oldest of four children, and the only one still at home. Her mother was the middle of 3 children with an alcoholic father. After a few sessions, Mary brought in her mother, Barbara Smith, whose anguish about her life with an abusive husband she had been confiding to Mary for some time. Mary felt helpless with her mother. Barbara was offered marital therapy and several months later she decided to return for herself. She had never told anyone that her husband Joe had abused both her and the children for many years. She said her model for her silence was her mother, who had put up with an active alcoholic husband for almost 50 years, and had always said, "You make your bed and you lie in it." Recently Barbara had begun to work in insurance sales. She loved the taste she had of the working world in a position where she could really use her interpersonal and management skills. But the manager was very negative toward women, and she was soon dismissed. She was having great difficulty in finding another job.

Work was done with Mary, Barbara, and Joe individually and together. A life cycle framework was used to redefine their present situation in order to help the family see their lives in the context of time and motion. To assist Barbara in reducing her guilt about having tolerated her abusive husband, I suggested that raising children takes a lot of energy, and only now as her children are becoming young adults is she free to reevaluate her life. In addition, having grown up in a

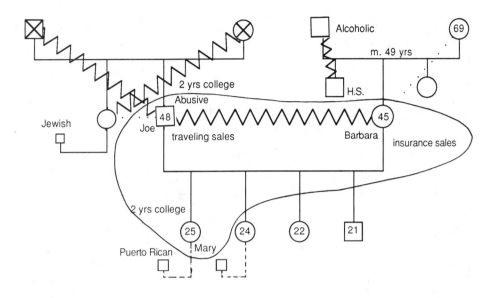

Figure 2-1. Smith Family

family with an alcoholic father, she had learned early not to express her own needs and feelings. As the oldest sister, she had been given the responsibility of caring for her younger sisters from earliest childhood. Nowhere had there been encouragement for her to develop a sense of herself and of her own aspirations and abilities, except as a caretaker.

Once we had taken steps to assure that the abuse would never occur again without police involvement, a similar interpretation was made with Joe, who gradually came to realize the serious damage he had done to his family by his abuse. He had grown up in a family where he himself was abused, had married while young and immature, and the children had come along quickly. Over the years, with a very limited emotional repertoire, he had struggled to make a living for his family and had been caught in the stress of being a travelling salesman, which contributed to his failure to cope effectively with family demands. Sessions were held with him and his young adult children to discuss the past and to help them deal with their current young-adult issues. For example, he discussed the fact that in his own family there had been intense conflicts or cutoffs with regard to the marriages of both his sister and himself, and now that his second daughter was getting married, he did not want to repeat this pattern. He helped Mary work out ways to solve her financial problems in order to get an apartment of her own. And he helped his two youngest children plan for their last years of college and for becoming independent. Planning for these sessions required reassessment of his own relationships with both parents, as well as his own frustrated dreams of becoming an artist and his entering straight into the world of business, where he felt he had lost his identity.

Work with Barbara focused on reinterpreting her mothering to find the strengths in her ability to raise her children, as well as her courage in seeking employment in a clearly sexist occupation. She was encouraged to view each job interview as giving her the skill to handle a new and difficult situation. We also discussed the important ways in which she was providing a new role model for her children by her behavior. A session was held with Barbara and all of her daughters to strengthen their joint resolve never to tolerate abuse in the future. Sessions were also held with Barbara's mother and her sister. Her mother was exceptionally

articulate about her resolve to take responsibility for her own life, even though she had decided to stay with her alcoholic husband. She was clear that she had decided on an independent life-style, in which she travels alone and strictly limits what she will tolerate from her husband. We also discussed their shared dilemma in their earlier years of raising small children, when there was not much leeway for independent action. In the session with Barbara's sister, we talked over their common difficulties in combining career and family, and in learning to speak up about their own needs, even to each other. They discussed their experiences growing up and resolved to support each other in their efforts to express their own feelings.

Mary's sense of loyalty to her mother and fear of leaving the family was only one factor contributing to her difficulty in moving on with her life. She was aware that her relationship with her boyfriend was unhealthy and that he was abusive and possessive, as her father had been. She felt she did not have the ability to handle him effectively, but she feared his reaction if she left him and believed she would not find anyone else to love her. She thought that if she moved into her own apartment, she would not be able to keep him away. She knew she "should" stop seeing him and continue her schooling (she had finished two years of college), but she felt that she was not smart enough to continue her job and take college courses, and that her job was the only security she had; it provided financial independence. Gradually, by changing her relationships with her parents and siblings, she began to feel more confident. When her boyfriend got drunk at a party she ended the relationship. She also decided she could handle one college course, and she worked out a plan to move to her own apartment.

This change happened concomitantly with the parents assuming responsibility for handling their own marital problems, a difficult task for Barbara, since she knew she could not support herself financially if she separated from Joe. Joe's motivation to work on issues was increased by the realization that beyond his family he had no relationships, and his job, was highly stressful, provided little security or gratification. He began the difficult task of developing his emotional side, which had been thwarted so early as well as reconnecting with his sister from whom he had become cut off.

This case illustrates not just the dilemma of a young adult woman about following her mother's choice of a life path (a relationship with an abusive boyfriend) or choosing a more independent path of a career, which might threaten her chances of finding a mate. Mary did indeed have in her mind the myth of being taken care of by a man who would save her from the difficulties of pursuing a college degree and learning how to handle money and an independent life-style. She was able during therapy to recognize strengths in her mother that she had not realized were there, in particular her courage in striving to enter a very difficult job world after many years at home. In this way she could emulate her mother's strengths and still find her own way in life. To do this, however, she, like her mother, had to learn to put her own needs first, rather than always attending to the needs of others. The father's therapy illustrates the important role men can have, not only in overcoming the limitations that gender stereotypes place on their lives, but in serving as role models for their daughters by attempting to change dysfunctional patterns and pass on their strengths.

THE JOINING OF FAMILIES IN MARRIAGE:
THE YOUNG COUPLE

In recent years women have been marrying later, or choosing not to marry at all (12% compared with 3% of their parents' generation). They are having fewer children and having them later, and many (about 25%) are opting not to have children at all. Marriage represents a very different proposition for women than for men. Several recent researchers have found a continuing difference in the values of men and women about their marriages (Sternberg, 1986; White, 1986). Women tend to view this transition as a time to move somewhat closer to their families of origin, while men tend to take another more definitive step away from their families of origin. Although during courtship men are willing to spend time with women in ways that enhance the women's sense of intimacy, after marriage they tend to spend less and less time talking to their wives, often considering that doing chores around the house should be an adequate demonstration of caring and intimacy, and feeling mystified about what women want when they seek more contact and intimacy in the marital relationship (Sternberg, 1986). Generally women are more willing than men to admit to problems, and they are much more likely than their husbands to evaluate their relationships as problematic. Men value their wives' attractiveness whereas women consider their husbands' earning potential a major attraction in marriage. Men say that what is important in marriage is their wives' sexual responsiveness and shared interests; wives say that their husbands' ability to get along with the wife's family and friends is more important. Men generally rate their marital communication, relationships with parents, and sexual relationships as good; women rate all of these as problematic. Furthermore, it seems that the double standard continues to operate, with women considering their husband's fidelity more important than men do, and men more likely to expect fidelity from their wives than from themselves (Coleman, 1986; Sternberg, 1984; Huston, 1983; White, 1986).

Between 1970 and 1982, the proportion of women in their late 20s who had never married rose from 10.5% to 23.4% (Saluter, 1983). For those in their early 30s, the proportion rose from 6.2% to 11.6%. It appears that about 25% of women are still marrying before age 20, but the other 75% are delaying marriage for ever longer periods of time. For every ten women between 40 and 50 with a college education, there are only three single men who are older and better educated (Richardson, 1986). This demographic tendency, as one writer has put it, "makes marital equality a joke. A husband may be fairness itself— wash his share of the dishes, encourage his wife in her work, value her opinions, respect her individuality and all the rest of it. But every eye wanders from time to time and the moment comes when he is comparing his wife with other women, while she is comparing him to solitude" (Pollit, 1986).

For every age bracket, the higher the income of the woman, the lower the rate of marriage—a situation that is just the reverse for men (Bernard, 1982,

p. 35). Although this probably reflects the greater freedom that financial security gives a woman about whether to marry, it also reflects the limitations in her options. Since women have always been expected to marry men who were taller, older, smarter, and wealthier than they were, they have been at a serious disadvantage in finding a mate. Women whose choices did not reflect these differentials have always been stigmatized, as have men who chose women who were older, smarter, taller, or wealthier. Such men might these days be labeled "wimps," unable to find a more desirable woman. The only category where women were allowed to be "more and better" was in physical attractiveness.

It is striking that women are so positive about marrying and men so ambivalent about it, since marriage appears to be so much more advantageous for men than for women.

One clinical intervention that can be used to help couples at this phase to change the traditional pattern of their sex roles is the suggestion to change traditional rituals around marriage to symbolize the move toward nonsexist relationships. For example, both spouses can be encouraged to develop a ritual that allows them to represent the movement from their parents (not just the woman from her father) to the marital bond. Since marriage requires the partners to redefine themselves in relation to their extended family in any case, such a ritual offers them the opportunity to redefine traditional family relationships in a way that may make their future marital accommodation more equitable.

Case Example: The Couple

Joan Woods, 32, and Peter Stern, 28, applied for therapy after four years of marriage because of continuing conflicts. Both were the oldest children in their original families. Peter, who was severely dyslexic, came from a Jewish family. His father had been a lawyer, but had functioned only marginally for many years because of serious depressions. During Joan's childhood her mother had been hospitalized for psychotic episodes, so that Joan had functioned as the parental child to her 2 younger siblings. Joan complained that Peter was never affectionate, did not seem to care about her, and did not seem ambitious, although he was always working. He was employed as a child care worker. Peter's complaints centered on Joan's continuous nagging, criticism, and insistance on doing whatever she wanted, often going away on work-related trips. Joan was an up-and-coming manager for a large corporation, and her salary was about twice that of her husband's.

The couple's struggle was reinterpreted as a reflection of their being in the forefront of our culture's changes, since both of them were doing work that broke them out of the conventional sex role stereotypes for their gender and out of the traditional couple relationships of marital partners. I suggested that the conflicts they were having resulted from their not having yet fully moved toward a new type of marriage. By shifting their emotional patterns as they had their patterns of work, and not locking themselves into certain stereotypes just because others do, they could free up their relationship to each other. We even talked about the fact that their same-sex parents' dysfunction, as difficult as it must have been for them growing up, perhaps played a usefol role by *not* providing them with the typical stereotypic role models that might have limited their own life options.

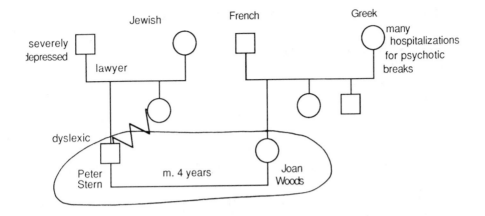

Figure 2-2. Woods/Stern Family

The phase of the transition to marriage is an important time for helping young women (and men) look beyond the stereotypes that have been so problematic for family development. Patterns that get set at this point in the life cycle may have great importance later on. Many young women at this time in their lives resist looking at the problems of their romantic myths about marriage, and they often do not appear for therapy until after marriage, when the problems surface. Even then, in the early years of marriage, it is a lot easier to change patterns than later when they have become entrenched.

FAMILIES WITH YOUNG CHILDREN

With the transition to parenthood, the family becomes a threesome, which makes it a permanent system for the first time. If a childless spouse leaves, there is no system left, but if one person leaves the new triad of couple and child, the system itself survives. Thus symbolically, and in reality, this transition is a key one in the family life cycle.

Even for "modern" dual-career couples this transition tends to mark a reversion to a more traditional division of roles, with women doing the lion's share of household maintenance and childcare planning. The traditional family often has not only encouraged, but even required, dysfunctional patterns, such as the overresponsibility of mothers for their children and the complementary underresponsibility or disengagement of fathers (Avis, 1985). We want to suggest a very different way of thinking about parenthood. As Daniels and Weingarten (1983) have described, "Parenthood is a powerful generator of development. It gives us an opportunity to refine and express who we are, to learn what we can be, to become someone different." One of the mothers in their study put it as follows: "Children battle you into being more than you

thought you were, into giving more than you thought you had it in you to give. Those middle of the nights, you learn something about yourself" (p. 1). The developmental literature, strongly influenced by the male-dominated psychoanalytic tradition, focused almost exclusively on mothers, placing extraordinary emphasis to the mother-child relationship in the earliest years of life, to the exclusion of other relationships in the family and of later developmental phases (Lewis et al., 1984). Kagan (1984) has drawn our attention to the mythology involved in our assumptions about the importance of infancy and early childhood in determining the rest of human life. The psychoanalytic model also stressed the view of human development as a primarily painful process in which mother and child were viewed as adversaries. The assumptions about development in the early years led to a psychological determinism that held mothering responsible for whatever happened. The fantasy that mothers were all powerful has led to a tendency to blame mothers for whatever goes wrong and to expect they should be perfect, all giving and all knowing (Chodorow & Contratto, 1982). Much of the feminist literature has continued to focus on mothering, while locating the mother-child dyad within a patriarchal system (Dinnerstein, 1976; Chodorow & Contratto, 1982). We urge quite a different perspective of human development, one that views child development in the richness of its entire context of multigenerational family relationships as well as within its social and cultural context. Literature and the media continue to focus on the mother as the crucial component of healthy child development. Fathers are still depicted as peripheral adjuncts (usually to provide a bit of extra support for the mother), particularly until the child is verbal and out of diapers. And aunts, uncles, grandparents, and other relatives are almost never even mentioned in the child-development literature (Lewis et al., 1984).

It is also curious how nonsystemic the developmental literature has been in ignoring the powerful impact of children on adult development. Thus the potential for change and growth in parents, as they respond to the unfolding of their children's lives, is lost. As Daniels and Weingarten (1983) put it: "Because men have not traditionally occupied themselves with caring for children, parenthood—the core experience of generativity—is oddly missing from their sense of their own development" (p. 5), as is evident in Erikson's ignoring the subject completely.

The transition to parenthood is typically accompanied by a general decrease in marital satisfaction, a reversion to more traditional sex roles even by dual-career couples, and a lowering of self-esteem for women (Cowen & Cowen, 1985). This tends to be true even for couples with a more equal distribution of roles in the early phases of their relationship and marriage. The transition to parenthood tends to push them back toward more traditional sex roles. Very few couples share household and child-care responsibilities equally.

Recently there has been much talk about husbands and wives sharing in childbirth classes and in the delivery. However, there is still virtually no

preparation of men for the much more complicated and longer-lasting tasks of child rearing. In our view this is an important area for intervention when working with families at this life cycle stage. Fathers rarely have any experience with small children so they need to learn the skills of intimacy with children. This basically requires time alone with the child; when their wives are present, it can be extremely difficult for them to take primary responsibility for a child or to develop close affectional bonds.

Our culture still leaves women with the main responsibility for child rearing, and blames them when it goes wrong. Seventy-three percent of mothers with children in the home work, and 60% of these mothers have no guaranteed maternity leave (a basic right in 117 other countries)—and we have been spending 25% less public money on day care since 1980. Thus it is clear that mothers are not receiving social support for the tasks that are expected of them in parenting. Even when fathers begin to participate more actively in relating to children, it is the mothers, including dual-career mothers, who bear the lion's share of responsibility for seeing that the children's needs are met. This includes keeping doctors' appointments, solving school problems, providing lunch money, and participating in after-school activities.

It is difficult to ascertain what the biological differences between males and females really are, since socialization impacts so powerfully and so early. We do know that female babies are more likely to survive the birth experience and are less likely to have birth defects, and that females are less vulnerable to disease throughout life. Beyond that we wonder how much richer the patterns of both sexes would be if both men and women participated actively in child rearing. For example, studies of newborns show the tendency to encourage more physical activity in boys and more dependency in girls (Romer, 1981; Lewis & Weintraub, 1974; Maccoby & Jacklin, 1974). Given the present socialization, it appears that girls already tend, in their childhood play, to be more sensitive to relationships and to avoid competition. By age three boys already are more oriented to other males, to peers, and to nonfamily members, whereas girls are more oriented toward females, family members, and adults (Lewis et al., 1984). Thus boys may be directed away from the home as early as preschool whereas girls are being socialized toward family relationships. Although boys rarely stop their games because of disputes, girls do so (Lever, 1976). But the major difference in early childhood is that girls develop language skills earlier and boys tend to be more active. Studies of infants show that parents talk and look more at girls and engage in more rough play with boys.

Given the extent of influence of our patriarchal system, it is indeed amazing that more differences between the sexes have not been found. For example, in a study of the ten top children's television programs, four had no females at all and the other six were predominantly male, with any females often portrayed as deferential or as witches or magical creatures. One study of children's stories showed that very few main characters were female, and that those who were female were primarily observers, not central to the action, and they were almost always shown as wearing aprons (even female animals), as if to rein-

force their roles as housekeepers (Romer, 1981). Even on the very popular educational show Sesame Street not a single major character is female.

Kagan and Moss (1962), in a longitudinal study of children, traced achievement-oriented adults back to their relationships with their mothers. (They did not look at their relationships with the fathers, interestingly enough!) They found that the males had very close loving relationships with their mothers in infancy whereas the females had had less intense closeness with their mothers than the average. Hoffman (1972) has suggested that this is so because for a daughter to become achievement oriented, she may do better if she does not experience the training in dependence that has been described as more typical for girls.

The data on children raised with only one parent are not clear. It does appear that a girl raised without a father may have more difficulty in establishing relationships with men, and a boy may display extremely masculinized behavior (possibly because his mother's sensitivity to the lack of a father may encourage her to place an exaggerated emphasis on this behavior (Romer, 1981). On the other hand, children raised with their mothers in a single-parent household may well experience more collaborative, democratic relationships throughout childhood, which may be a particular strength in our competitive, hierarchical society (Hartman, 1987).

In treatment with families at this phase of the life cycle, it is important to inquire in detail about household responsibilities as well as the handling of finances and the specifics of child rearing and child care. Clearly, men who do not develop intimate relationships with their children as they grow up will find it difficult to change the pattern later. It is also important to convey an awareness of the importance of what women have been doing in the family, since their role is most often treated as less important than that of their husbands. Typical questions might be:

• Do both parents always go to your children's school plays and sports events?
• How are your children changing your perspective on the meaning of your life?
• Does the father get to spend time alone with each child? (It is almost impossible to develop intimacy if he does not.) And is the time spent fairly equally divided among the daughters and sons?
• How are domestic responsibilities divided?
• How is money handled and by whom?
• What are each parent's hopes and expectations for each child in adulthood?

Case Example: Family with Young Children

George and Eleanor Durks applied for therapy after four years of marriage (see figure 3). They had a three-year-old daughter together, and George has three grown sons from his first marriage. As is often the case, Eleanor was the one with the complaints: George, she said, gave her no feedback and did not even know the names of her daughter's friends, although in his high level of corporate law he had

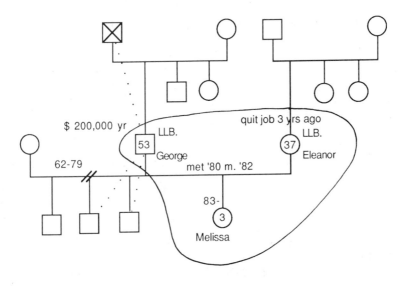

Figure 2-3. Durks Family

a reputation for being an extremely good negotiator. In Eleanor's view her husband spent no time at all with their daughter, Melissa, was negative toward Eleanor's family, toward holidays, and even toward spending time together on weekends, and, in sum, had no interests beyond work. She also felt that he had a great deal of money that he refused to let her even know about, much less share in spending. George was much less verbal in the initial session, saying, when pressed, that he could not understand what his wife was talking about, since he tried to give her everything and did nothing but work to provide a good life for them. He said that Eleanor often acted irrationally, blowing up in front of friends, but basically he seemed to want nothing except for her to stop complaining so that they could get on with their lives. The couple had met while they were both working for the same law firm, where George was a senior partner and Eleanor was a law clerk. The meeting took place shortly after George had been through a stormy divorce from his first wife, whom he described as "frankly crazy." Initially, George said, he had found Eleanor very understanding and helpful. Now, he said, she no longer paid any attention to his concerns, and did nothing but complain. Eleanor had left her job when Melissa was born and had not returned. She was quite defensive about George's having told her that she wasn't as interesting as she used to be.

This couple appeared to have fallen into a common pattern once their daughter was born, in which the way of relating that they had worked out previously, based on George's expression of concern about his previous marriage, and common interests in law and politics now shifted to the traditional marital pattern. However, Eleanor was unhappy with this, though she did not want to return to work and give up her closeness with her daughter just to win George back. She spoke frankly of her anxiety that if she pushed George to the point of separation, her life style would change dramatically for the worse, since his income was almost $200,000, and even if she returned to work, hers would be no more than $40,000. On the surface George appeared unconcerned about the possibility of having a second failed marriage. Being considerably older, and having raised three sons in a very traditional marriage in which he had almost nothing to do with his children until they were old enough to play little-league baseball, he also had not expected to develop a very close relationship with Melissa during her infancy or early childhood.

To highlight the sex-role changes that appeared crucial to this couple's dilemma, therapy began by exploring the early childhood experiences of both spouses, and discussing with them in detail what kind of relationships they had had with each parent, and what they expected for themselves. George came from a family of three sons, with a successful, distant, businessman father and a mother who played the role of hypochrondriacal martyr—in part, he thought, to get his father's attention. George had initially been attracted by Eleanor's competence and her understanding attitude, so unlike his mother. In Eleanor's family her mother had been unassertive and accepting of her father, who was an abusive and irresponsible alcoholic. Eleanor was first attracted to George's success and warmth toward her, so unlike her own father. Several sessions were spent alone with George, discussing his limited relationships with his three grown sons, and the therapist's concern that if he did not change the pattern, he would lose a chance for closeness to his last child as well. He was urged not to compete with his wife for time with Melissa, but to spend time alone with her, since otherwise it would probably be impossible for the two of them to get to know each other. Exploring his feelings about his relationship to Melissa seemed easier than moving directly toward the marriage, since he felt so hurt there and he had so little sense of what was wrong or what he could change. It was suggested instead that he work on getting to know his sons and his daughter, and then his mother, in preparation for finding a different way of relating to his wife.

Meanwhile, the therapist confirmed Eleanor's sense of frustration, and at the same time tried to help her strategize about more effective ways of accomplishing her ends than complaining. She was encouraged to enjoy her daughter and to obtain as much gratification from her friendship network as possible. (Eleanor had many friends, but she felt guilty that she was somehow not able to make a social life that worked for George as well.) She was also encouraged to spend time with her family of origin, which she enjoyed doing, but felt guilty about, since George was uncomfortable with them. The main aspect of these interventions was to help Eleanor define her interests and desires for herself, and not just on the basis of George's feelings.

Gradually George began to enjoy the gratification of being with his daughter and to enjoy spending weekend time as a threesome. Eleanor stopped pressing for a closeness she could not get and to press only where it really mattered to her. She began by clarifying the finances, requesting shared responsibility for Melissa, and having some time together as a couple. Eleanor had been feeling guilty and disqualified whenever she raised her concern about their relationship. Therapy confirmed Eleanor's experience of nonintimacy with George. His limitations were framed for both spouses as arising out of the patriarchal structure of society, which impairs men in human relationships and women in other areas of functioning.

As happens so often for women, Eleanor's voice needed confirmation. Belenky and her colleagues report on an interview study of women in which they spoke repeatedly of "gaining a voice," by which they meant gaining a sense of having something worthwhile to say and feeling the inner security to say it. In their struggle to gain a voice, women often need validation of their experience of not being heard.

Eleanor had felt disqualified whenever she tried to clarify her position to her husband. And he had been raised not to hear or appreciate her complaint. It took repeated efforts on her part to speak up and to make certain that her position had been articulated and heard, and it took a great deal on George's part to realize that he had never really listened to her.

FAMILIES WITH ADOLESCENTS

Erikson (1968) describes the development of adolescent girls as different from that of boys in that they hold their identity in abeyance as they prepare to attract the men by whose name they will be known, and by whose status they will be defined—the men who, as Gilligan (1982) says, will rescue them from emptiness and loneliness by filling the "inner space" (p. 12). Our concern is that such attitudes toward girls, which define their development in terms of their ability to attract a male, are detrimental to their mental health, leaving them lacking in self-esteem they may fear that if they appear smart, tall, assertive, or too competent, they will risk losing their chances of finding an intimate relationship with a male. It is in keeping with social norms that during the adolescent years girls often confuse identity with intimacy by defining themselves through relationships with others. It thus is important to raise questions about such norms, since they put the girl into an impossible bind, in which you are only healthy if you define your identity, not by your self, but by your mate.

For some reason there appear to be certain phases in development, including preschool and adolescence, when children seem to hold more rigidly to sex-role stereotypes—even more than their parents or teachers. It is important not to encourage this stereotyping, but to encourage girls especially to develop their own opinions, values, aspirations, and interests. Clinically it is important when working with adolescents and their families to ask questions about the roles each one is expected to play in the family. What are the chores and responsibilities of boys and of girls? Are sons encouraged to develop social skills or are parents focused primarily on their achievement and sports performance? Are daughters encouraged to have high academic aspirations? Are both sexes given equal responsibility and encouragement in dealing with education, athletics, aspirations for the future, extended family relationships, buying gifts, writing, calling, or caring for relatives? Do both sexes buy and clean their own clothes? Are daughters encouraged to learn about money, science, and other traditionally "masculine" subjects?

Although conventional gender values are particularly high during adolescence, it is also during this phase that crucial life-shaping decisions are made. It is extremely important for the therapist to convey facts about adult life in a compelling manner. As Alexander and his colleagues (1985) say about interventions with delinquent adolescent girls, "Information about the different salaries of a secretary and heavy-machine operator, statistics about women in the work force, and data on the increase of impoverished, single-parent households, increases the probability that the female delinquent will make thoughtful decisions about her future" (p. 141).

During adolescence daughters are particularly torn between identification with their mothers and with their fathers. A daughter who is close to her mother in a traditional family may feel a sense of betrayal if she moves in her

career aspirations toward a life different from that of her mother's and toward role identification with her father (Hare-Mustin, 1978).

A common problem at this phase is the father-daughter relationship. Fathers often become awkward about relating to their daughters as the daughters approach adolescence, fearing their budding sexuality. Given the frequently limited masculine repertoire for handling closeness, at times they may sexualize the relationship, or they may withdraw, and even become irritated or angry as a way of maintaining the distance they feel is necessary. They may need encouragement to engage actively with their daughters rather than avoid them. They may engage more easily with sons, where shared activities such as sports allow companionship without too many pressures for intimate relating. The unavailability of fathers for their daughters may lead daughters to develop an image of the male as a romantic stranger, an unrealistic conception that cannot be met when they reach adult life (Hare-Mustin, 1978).

On the other hand, especially for men who only have daughters, this phase may mark their first conversion to a feminist position, as they want to support their daughters' having the same rights and privileges that men do. This awareness is important to capitalize on therapeutically. Having only daughters increases the likelihood of fathers becoming aware of gender inequities. Particularly as his daughters become adolescents and move into young adulthood, a father may for the first time become cognizant of the limitations imposed by current gender stereotypes on his daughter's future career and life options. This increase in sensitivity is, of course, most likely to occur if the father has already developed a close relationship with his daughter in childhood. Mothers may be feeling a strain as their children pull away, particularly as they realize the limitations of their options, if they have devoted themselves primarily to child rearing.

Case Example: Late Adolescent

Mrs. Reid called for services for her 19-year-old daughter, Joyce, whose eating habits had narrowed to the point that she ate only turkey and lettuce, and Mr. Reid had noticed that in a bathing suit she had begun to look like a skeleton. The genogram (Figure 2-4) shows that Mr. Reid was a consultant whose work took him away from home for about 6 months each year. During his trips Mrs. Reid was required always to be at home in case he should call, but he refused to permit her to accompany him on his business trips, or even to call him while he was away. Joyce was the younger of two daughters, her sister Sara having preceded her at a local college by one year. Mrs. Reid was also the younger of two daughters. Her father was always treated as if he were on a pedestal. His wife and daughters served him—even to ironing his socks—despite the fact that he was carrying on a rather open affair with a neighbor in the same apartment building. Mr. Reid's mother had died in a car accident when he was three, at the same time that he had been sent to a hospital for tuberculosis. Soon after he returned home, his father remarried and had another son. The father had also been away a lot and had had many affairs during Mr. Reid's childhood.

It became apparent that Joyce felt in conflict between a loyalty to her father, which required that she go into business and do well at school, and loyalty to her mother, for whom she served as confidante concerning the father's insensitivity

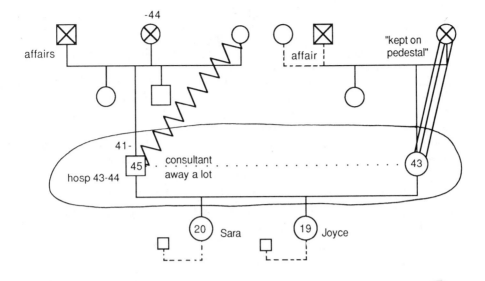

Figure 2-4. Reid Family

and lack of caring. She feared leaving her mother, whose needs she felt intensely, and becoming stuck, if she chose an unsatisfactory relationship like that between her parents.

Since Joyce's eating problem appeared to reflect her life cycle dilemma in relation to gender issues, much time was spent exploring both parents' hopes for their daughters, as well as the daughters' own aspirations and sense of their parents' messages. At one point, to make explicit Joyce's covert central role in the family, she was placed in charge of deciding who should attend the next several sessions. To the first session she brought only her father. It became clear that she wanted to see whether he was ready to take over the relationship with her mother that she felt he had relegated to her. To the next session she brought only her mother, and the theme was the sisterhood of women over the generations. There was discussion of the boyfriends of both Sara and Joyce, and whether the male/female balance in the family would shift in this generation away from the primacy of "the sisterhood" over all other relationships. Mrs. Reid felt sure it would not, saying that Sara's recent distancing with her boyfriend was just temporary, as she herself had distanced while courting Mr. Reid; after marriage she had returned to her primary bond with her mother and sister, and she stated unequivocally that her relationship with her mother had been the most important in her life. As she put it, "Having a mother is everything"—this in spite of the fact that she felt her own mother had died of a "broken heart" after her own husband had died it was almost as if men's idealized images were adored in the abstract but women were where the intimacy really lay. When the question was raised as to whether Joyce's boyfriend might break the pattern and demand more intimacy than the other men in the family had, both mother and daughter felt this was an unnecessary worry, so much had they accepted the patterns with which they were familiar.

During the latter part of therapy, the changing role of women in this generation was a primary focus of attention. Joyce sought her mother's permission, and even encouragement, to lead a different kind of life; Mr. Reid sought to develop more intimacy with his daughters, an entirely new experience for him, not only with his daughters, but with anyone. One important turning point in his relating came during a session in which his older sister participated to discuss their early shared

life experiences and their present relationship. Not surprisingly, Mr. Reid's sister felt the same distance in dealing with him that his wife and daughters felt, but her impressions broadened the context of the therapeutic discussions.

The family members were encouraged in all these ways to increase their flexibility, particularly in their definitions of male and female roles, and to experiment with new possibilities so that the father could be more emotional and the mother and daughters more openly assertive and demanding on their own behalf.

Often a man's relationships with another man—a father, brother, son, an army buddy, or childhood friend—provides the best avenue to his feelings. For those who have served in the military, their war experiences may be the only experiences of sufficient emotional intensity to put them in touch with any strong feelings. Sometimes it may be possible to get into a man's emotional system through a discussion of his work system, particularly of issues with a long-time boss. But often the denial of emotional issues is so powerful a value in the work environment that it is impossible to make any inroad here. In Mr. Reid's case, there were no close males available.

LAUNCHING CHILDREN AND MOVING ON

This is the longest phase in the family life cycle, lasting often 20 years or more. There is a tendency for men and women to be going in opposite directions psychologically at the point where their children move out into their own lives. Men, perhaps realizing that they have missed most of the intimacy of their children's development, may begin to seek closeness whereas women, after years of focusing on caring for others, begin to feel energized about developing their own lives—careers, friendships outside the family, and other activities. The discovery celebrated by men in midlife of the importance of intimacy and relationships is something that women have known from the beginning. The self-esteem and confidence that come from work have always been known to men, at least those of the middle classes. But for women this may be a time of special stress, since they often feel very much behind in the skills to deal with the outside world. Just at the point where their children no longer need them and where they are beginning to be defined by the male world as too old to be desirable, they must venture outward. The initial steps are usually the hardest. Once they have begun to move in this arena, many women experience a new confidence and pleasure in their independence—no longer having to put everyone else's needs first. Because of the social and management skills that they have generally developed in previous life cycle phases, women are remarkably resourceful in building a social network. Their lifelong skills in adapting to new situations also serve them in good stead. But the world of work still does not recognize their efforts in a way commensurate with their contributions. And women have typically not been socialized to expect or demand the recognition they deserve.

Obviously the divergence of interests for men and women, as well as the shift in focus of energies required at this phase, often creates serious marital tensions (Hesse-Biber & Williamson, 1984). These stresses may precipitate estrangement or even divorce. Men who divorce typically miss the caretaking functions provided by a wife and they remarry rather quickly, usually a younger woman. For women, whose options in remarriage are much more limited, the likelihood of remarriage after a divorce at this phase are quite slim. In part this is attributable to the skew in availability of partners and in part to older women's having less need to be married and so, perhaps, being less willing to "settle," particularly for a traditional marriage that will mean a return to extensive caretaking.

Women who have developed an identity primarily through intimacy and adaptation to men will be particularly vulnerable in divorce during the launching phase, when they may feel that their very self is disintegrating. Gilligan's observation that women's embeddedness in relationships, their orientation to interdependence, their subordination of achievement to care, and their conflicts over competitive success leave them at risk in midlife seems more a commentary on our society than a problem in women's development. At present 42% of women aged 55–64 are in the labor force, compared with 27% in 1950, but their benefits are equal to men's and the types of low-paying, sex-segregated jobs generally available to them have not changed much in the past 40 years.

It is at this time also that women typically experience menopause. This transition has generally been viewed negatively as a time of physical and psychological distress as women move toward old age. On the contrary, for many women it is a turning point that frees them sexually from worries about pregnancy and marks a new stabilization in their energies to pursue work and social activities.

This life cycle phase, often referred to as the "empty nest," is often depicted it as a time of depression for women, especially for those whose entire lives have been devoted to home and family. However, the recent literature on this phase suggests that such a phenomenon is much more presumed than real. Often women are grateful for the opportunity to recapture free time and explore new options. They are not nearly as sorry to see the child-rearing era end as has been assumed.

Case Example: Launching Children and Moving On

Nell Byrne, aged 54, applied for therapy because of a total cutoff from her 30-year-old daughter, Elizabeth, who lived in the same two-family house but had not spoken to her mother in a year (see Figure 2-5). Nell had returned to her parents' home after an early separation from her alcoholic husband, although the details of the separation were never discussed. She had been the third of eight children. Her own mother had been chronically ill, and her father had been a quiet alcoholic for many years. From the time she returned home, she became primary caretaker of both parents, even though she worked and her mother cared for Elizabeth during the day. As the years went by; Nell had become increasingly alienated from her

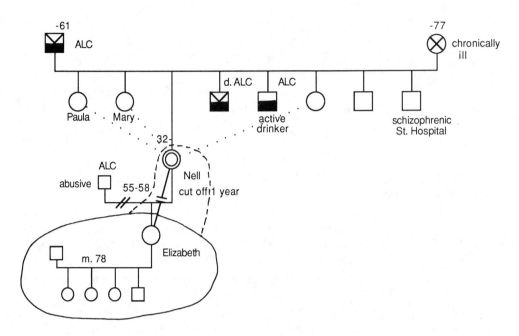

Figure 2-5. Byrne Family

three sisters as a result of hurt and angry feelings, never discussed openly, about the caretaking of the parents. Mr. Byrne died when Elizabeth was five and Mrs. Byrne when Elizabeth was 21. Elizabeth married the following year, and had four children in close succession. Nell inherited the house and Elizabeth and her family lived downstairs, paying rent to her. Two years before she sought therapy, Nell had lost her job as a legal secretary in a firm reorganization and had been unable to seek a new one, fearing that the job loss resulted from her personal inadequacies. She had withdrawn from her friends, since, as she said, "No one likes to be around a depressed complainer." And the tension in her relationship with her daughter had built up to the point where Elizabeth had ceased to talk to her. After this, Nell had also become cut off from her sisters, apparently because they felt that it would be too awkward at holidays to decide whether to invite both Nell and Elizabeth to family functions, since they were not on speaking terms. An additional stress was the fact that two of Nell's surviving brothers were severely dysfunctional—one a chronic schizophrenic and a patient at the state hospital, with Nell as primary responsible relative, and the other a flagrant alcoholic, who also used Nell as his primary resource whenever he was arrested or hospitalized.

Our assessment of the situation in this family was that Nell was experiencing the burnout of a lifelong caretaker, who, for a variety of reasons, felt she no longer was needed by those she cared for, and no longer was able to do for others. We reassessed her work history, which showed she had excellent skills, and had thrived on running an office. As a result of discussions of previous work connections, she recontacted a number of associates, and one of them made her a job offer. As part of the assessment of her family relationships, we decided to invite her next older sister, Mary, for a session, which proved extremely useful. This was done because it appeared that Nell needed a redefinition of the caretaking relationship in order to get some relief from her burdens, and she also needed more personal support. Mary had been the closest to Nell during their childhood, and we hoped now to build on the importance of this early relationship.

The relationships of sisters are generally the longest relationships in life. Because women have always had the primary responsibility for the family, caretaking is generally shared among sisters. Often, because of the responsibilities they must share and without the resources or authority to help, they may turn against each other. Brothers may contribute money, which requires less emotionally, and yet tend to be appreciated much more by aging parents for their contribution. On the other hand, sisters may become powerful resources for each other as life moves on and they are without partners as a result of death or divorce. Unfortunately, the triangulation that develops in families, particularly as a result of the burdens of caretaking for parents can cause feelings of hostility between, or among, sisters and thus preclude the special sharing they might have enjoyed throughout life.

It became evident in the discussion between Nell and Mary that no one in the family had ever known why Nell had separated from her husband. She had felt too ashamed to talk about his alcoholism and abuse, and the other family members had never asked, but had assumed that Nell had taken advantage of her parents by moving back into their home. Mary also had been unaware of most of the details of the father's alcoholism and the mother's disabilities. She had never realized the burden Nell felt in caring for the parents. Nell had been hurt that no one else ever offered to help, whereas Mary, and apparently the others, had felt that Nell had added to the parents' problems in their old age. In discussing the events that had taken place in each of their lives over the past many years, the two sisters were able to begin a rapprochment, which became very significant for them afterward, particularly as they began to share the responsibility for their dysfunctional brothers, together with their other brother and sisters. Nell then contacted her sister Paula on her own, and began the same process of reconnection. Finally, she invited her daughter to come for a session. The daughter's complaint was that Nell had been full of unspoken disapproval and disappointment and had hurt her feelings many times. This was a repeat of Nell's own strongest memories from her own childhood. She talked about her own experiences in growing up, her struggles about admitting that the marriage to Elizabeth's father had failed, and her return to her parents' home. The problems with launching in the previous generation were repeating in this generation. Nell admitted that she had been very fearful that Elizabeth would end up in the same frustrating position as she had been in herself. Undoubtedly her anxieties had been transferred to Elizabeth as disapproval. Elizabeth began to see her mother in a new light, as a very strong woman who managed to keep a career going in spite of many difficult burdens over the years.

Like so many women, Nell had to contend with the guilt she felt in pulling back from being the primary caretaker of the ill and dying members of her family, a situation that is often intensified because there is no one else to take over the job. This is a particular difficulty for women of her generation, who were socialized at a time when such responsibilities were assumed automatically. It is important to help such women enlist the support of others in their families to share the decisions, responsibilities, and emotional squeeze of such relationships.

OLDER FAMILIES

The final phase of life might be considered for women only, since they live longer and, unlike men, are rarely paired with younger partners, thus making

the statistics for this life cycle phase extremely imbalanced (Congressional Caucus for Women's Issues, New York Times, 9/23/84):

• Six out of ten Americans over 65, and seven out of ten over 85, are women.
• Seventeen percent of American women over 65 have incomes below the poverty line, as opposed to 10% of men.
• Almost half the older women have median incomes of less than $5000, as opposed to one in five men.
• More than 80% of elderly female householders live alone and one-fourth of them live in poverty.

The increasing proportion of very old women over the next 20 years presages a number of problems. As Hess and Soldo (1984) put it: "The incomes of women, lower throughout worklife than those of men, remain so in old age. In addition, since the great majority of very old women are widows, and widows typically live alone, their poverty rates increase with advancing age. It becomes ever more difficult to obtain and maintain suitable housing, particularly that which is supportive of declining functional capacity" (p. 2). Since women are the primary caretakers of other women, these problems will affect at least two generations of women, who will be increasingly stressed as time goes along.

Those women who need the care, and those who give it, are statistically the poorest and have the least legislative power in our society. The laws are made mostly by men, and there is little consideration given to services to support the caregivers' ability to provide service to their family members. Several studies indicate that the immediate reason for nursing-home admission is more likely to be the depletion of family resources than a deterioration in the health of the older relative (Hess & Soldo, 1984).

While the increase in remarried families might mean a wider kinship network available for caregiving, the increasing divorce rate and family fragmentation will probably mean that fewer family members will be willing to provide care for elderly parents. Since both those who give care to the elderly and most of those who receive it are women, the subject tends to escape our view. As therapists we can counter this imbalance by redefining both the dilemmas of the elderly and those of their caretakers as highly serious, significant issues.

Case Example: Aging Family.

Lillian and Sam Beal requested therapy initially (see Figure 2-6) because of their oldest daughter, Laura. However, it became apparent in the very first session that the major problem was the place in the family of Sam's 83-year-old mother, Emily. She had been living with Lillian and Sam since their marriage, and there had always been stress between Lillian and her mother-in-law. Sam had refused to consider having his mother live elsewhere, but at the same time rarely spoke to her himself; in Lillian's words, he was "unbelievably cold and unfeeling" toward his

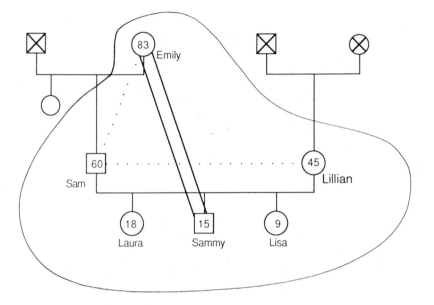

Figure 2-6. Beal family

mother, although he was generally pleasant with other people. Laura, who had been behaving in a moody and negative manner, would soon be graduating from high school and leaving for college; she was the one most sensitive to the pressure her mother was under. Emily had been very attached to the children, often giving in to them when Lillian had set limits. The children felt very attached to their grandmother, but recently the son, Sammy, on several occasions had become annoyed at his grandmother's nagging. Sam refused to discuss or intervene in any of these conflicts, maintaining a quiet pose in the family, trying to get along with everyone when the family was together, and tending to ignore both his mother and wife. Lillian, at 45, had just gone back to work, because Sam, at 60, had been laid off by his company and could only find work at a much lower salary. Lillian had been ambivalent about working. She was glad for time away from her mother-in-law but nervous about handling a job after 18 years out of the paid workforce, and she also feared she would not be able to keep up "her" responsibilities toward the children and family. Now, having worked for six months, she was enjoying the friends she was making, even though her work as secretary was often tedious. She was increasingly resentful of having to be responsible for all household work and meals, even though her husband returned home earlier than she did. And she particularly resented the fact that she had to perform all the caretaking her mother-in-law required.

Therapy involved questioning many of the premises on which this family operated. The first change was based on a simple principle: that each spouse take responsibility for the needs of his or her own parents—sending cards, buying presents, keeping in contact, and caretaking—but such a stance is difficult to implement because women tend to be more sensitive to others' needs and have always had the role of maintainer of relationships in families. Lillian was much more attuned to her mother-in-law's loneliness and lack of status in their house-hold, as well as her physical needs, her desire for privacy, her shopping require-ments, and the necessity to make and keep doctors' appointments. Emily, in turn, turned more readily to **Lillian**, "not wanting to trouble" her "busy" son. Sam was now given primary responsibility for his mother's needs. We had to add a

specific structure to the new arrangements; Sam began to take his mother out to Saturday breakfast every week to have some time alone with her and for a chance to talk to her about her needs for the week. He had to learn to be responsive to her. This change necessitated a fair amount of family-of-origin work, going back to his childhood and his relationship with both parents in order to understand how his emotional cutoff from his mother had developed. Helpful here were several encounters between Sam and his older sister during which they discussed their childhood and their past and present relationships with each other and with their parents. Lillian was coached not to rescue Sam and to give him the emotional space to deal with his mother. Because it was so difficult for her not to respond to others' needs, it was suggested that she leave home at various times, become "forgetful" about dinner and other housekeeping tasks, and sign up for several work-related seminars. Laura's growing responsibility for her mother was discussed, along with her own ambitions for her life. Sam was encouraged to spend time with her to help her with college arrangements, since her mother previously had been the only one who had evinced interest in this area. In one session the grandmother talked about her own life, about how she had had to work from a very early age and how she and her husband had run a grocery store together, until he died and she had to take it over alone. Part of Sam's resentment of his mother had to do with her not being available like the mothers of his friends and his feeling that she did not care about him. This was discussed in relation to the myths about mothers and how anything less than perfect, all-encompassing all-giving care is considered neglect.

Emily's nagging at Sammy was also explored. He was primarily interested in art, which she thought was "frivolous," and she felt that he required surveillance in order to achieve academically. This was discussed with the family in relation to our culture's rigid expectations for girls and for boys; their changing of their patterns was framed as an indication of their flexibility and strength as a family. An important general aim of therapy now becomes the rebalancing of skewed caretaking patterns between spouses, not only in relation to children, but, as in this case, in dealing with the third generation.

DIVORCE AND REMARRIAGE

Divorce and remarriage are two points in the lives of family where the dilemmas of women in our culture are most evident (see also Chapters 15, 16, 17). Given the unequal and unsatisfactory situation for many women in marriage, it is not surprising that they so often divorce; but our society's arrangements regarding divorce are rapidly pushing more and more women and their children below the poverty level. With the recent trend toward joint custody following divorce, many complex issues are raised for women. Until very recently in human history, women never received custody after a divorce. They had no legal rights at all; they belonged to their husbands, as did their children. Gradually we developed a system in which custody went to mothers, unless there was a strong countervailing reason. Now many people are moving toward some form of joint custody, but a number of feminist groups are opposing this as not in the best interests of women. The argument is that the women

continue to have ultimate responsibility for their children anyway, while relinquishing some of the little control they had when they had sole custody through their right to receive financial support.

In our view joint custody is an extremely important concept for both men *and* women, but even more so for children. The difficulty is that for men, who have had little practice in child care during the marriage, it is hard to learn to share real responsibility for the children after the divorce. Men, and their employers, tend to view their work responsibilities as primary and child care as secondary. Thus if a child is sick or either parent will be away, it is usually the mother who will have to make extra arrangements. And yet, because they are working, mothers now lose the opportunity to be with their children full time. In the shifting of roles required by joint physical custody following divorce, however, there is a positive value. It allows the mother some time to herself, and, particularly where the husband has overnight contacts with his children, it involves him in basic child-care responsibilities, such as choosing clothing, overseeing the brushing of teeth, and delivering the children to school—which, in turn, increases the likelihood of a genuine, ongoing intimacy with them, rather than remaining in a Sunday-father role. Current research clearly documents the importance for children of ongoing contact with both parents, and the insufficiency, especially for young children, of seeing their fathers only every other weekend.

It is extremely important clinically not to ignore fathers, even if they are not active in the household or in the family picture. At the same time, it is important not to invalidate the mother by assuming that the father must be involved in the current situation. As Herz Brown (Chapter 16) recommends, it is important to enter a family system of a single-parent household through the mother, and to move only with respect for her responsibility and power toward engagement of her ex-husband.

Remarried families offer a number of particularly trying situations for women. Most difficult of all family positions is probably the role of stepmother. Given our culture's high expectations of motherhood, the woman who is brought in to replace a "lost" mother enters a situation fraught with high expectations that even God could not achieve. One of the major interventions is to remove the burden of guilt from the stepmother for not being able to accomplish the impossible: taking over the parenting for children who are not her own. Our general guidelines involve putting the natural parent in charge of the children, however difficult that may be with a father who works full time and who feels he has no experience with "mothering." The problem for the stepmother is especially poignant, since she is usually the one most sensitive to the needs of others, and it will be extremely difficult for her to take a back seat while her husband struggles awkwardly with an uncomfortable situation. The fact is, she has no alternative. The tendencies of women to take responsibility for family relationships, and to believe that what goes wrong is their fault and that if they tried hard enough, things would have worked out, are the major problems for them in remarried families, since the situation carries with

it so many built-in complexities, structural ambiguities, loyalty conflicts, and membership problems.

WOMEN AND THEIR FRIENDSHIP NETWORKS

Friendship is an extremely important resource for women throughout life (Rubin, 1985; Pogrebin, 1987). Women tend to have more close friends, but the relationships they have are often not validated by the larger society (Bernard, 1981). Men may have acquaintances with whom they spend time, but no close friends at all in whom they confide. Schydlowsky (1983) shows that the importance of women's close female friendships diminishes from adolescence to early adulthood, as they focus on finding a mate and establishing a marriage, and then increases throughout the rest of the life cycle. Close female friendships were reported as more important than close male friendships throughout the life cycle and second only to good health in importance for life satisfaction.

Perhaps socialization enables women to develop deep and boundary-dissolving friendships whereas men are more inhibited in such intimate contact. Perhaps because a male's identity is partly formed by repudiating his identification with his mother, his boundaries are thicker and more impenetrable. In addition, there appears to be a strong American male homophobia that inhibits intimacy between men. Levinson (1978), Valliant (1977), and Weiss (1985) all found that for men friendship was largely noticeable in its absence.

We urge family members to respect the need for both sexes to nurture friendship systems outside the family and to move away from the traditional pattern of women organizing the social schedule of couple activities around business associates of the husband. In such situations women are expected to make friends not on the basis of personal interests, but because their husbands want to cultivate certain contacts. In such traditional arrangements, women are expected to replace friends whenever their husbands' job require them to move. Such arrangements do not respect the importance of friendship as a basic support throughout the life cycle and mistake career networking for friendship.

LESBIANS

Lesbians tend to be perceived as unlaunched adolescents, regardless of their age (Krestan & Bepko, 1980). An important clinical issue in working with them is to help them deal with their families of origin in relation to their lesbian

life-style so that the family will respect their subsystem boundaries and they will not feel the need to distance reactively from the family. Negotiating a way to maintain a sense of connectedness along with a sense of individuality is probably the most serious problem for lesbian couples (Roth, 1985). In the face of family or society's lack of acknowledgment of a lesbian couple's attempt to define boundaries, the couple boundaries may rigidify, pushing them into a fusion and creating an increasingly closed system (Krestan & Bepko, 1980). Several specific problems create difficulty for lesbian couples, in particular their not having "marker events," such as weddings or the birth of children to define their change in status, as other couples do in marriage (Roth, 1985). Other life cycle transitions also tend to be problematic, such as retirement, serious illness, or death, in which the disqualification of the couple by the larger society may lead to ceremonies at which they have to disguise their feelings and relationship, thus intensifying their problems rather than promoting a sense of continuity and connectedness.

In addition, their relationship to their community is most likely to be influenced by the extent to which they have "come out." They may be very isolated from their work and social community if they are not open, and they may be pressured in various ways within a lesbian community if they are (Roth, 1985). Dealing with the issue of "coming out" is an important individual and interpersonal aspect of development for lesbian couples (Roth, 1985). They must deal with the added loss of status as a result of their sexual orientation, if they are open, and with a sense of alienation if they maintain secrecy about their most important relationship. Because of the negative cultural attitude toward homosexuality, the life-style of such couples becomes much more than a matter of choice of love or sexual partner. Necessary secrecy with employers about their relationships, for example, can force them into a much more closed, rigid operating context.

On the other hand, a recent study showed that lesbian couples are the only group for whom money did not determine the power balance (Blumstein & Schwartz, 1983) and this strength may be highlighted in therapeutic interventions.

HEALTH AND ILLNESS: PATTERNS OF HEALTH-CARE BEHAVIOR

Women are much more likely than men to define themselves as patients and to seek help. Pragmatically, the pattern has been for women to seek help from male physicians for both physical and emotional problems. Men tend to avoid seeking help and are thus more likely to become patients only when their problems have become serious and require hospitalization whereas women are more likely to receive help on an outpatient basis. The informal health care of

families has always been done by women. They cared for children, spouses, and parents; they nursed and visited the sick and the dying. Now that the majority of women are in the workforce, this no longer can be an automatic assumption. In addition, the lowest paid and lowest status levels of the formal health-case system—nursing and social work—have been staffed primarily by women. With more women seeking high-status careers in medicine or other fields, many of the most capable women are not available for the provision of lower-level health-care service.

It is hard to predict what will happen to the health-care system as women refuse to continue to play the role of server and unpaid provider and as clients refuse or are unable to pay the high cost of a health-care system that does not meet their needs. We can hope that the value of service industries will increase, along with the values women have been expected to develop, but which have been devalued in the larger culture: caring, relating, and sensitivity to others.

It is also interesting to speculate on what will happen if women cease to define their problems in ways that make them the recipients of the male caretaking establishment: as depressed, anxious, phobic or anorexic women. Much has been said about the cultural determinants of these problems, and changes are occurring gradually. Women, it is hoped, will begin to redefine their lives. Instead of feeling anxious and depressed when they are not happy in a life of selflessness and attention to others, they may come to appreciate the social inconsistencies and irrational demands made upon them. They may learn to change their lives rather than try to adapt to their circumstances. Men also, it is hoped, will refuse to keep paying the dreadful cost physically and emotionally for the values of a culture that requires them to ignore their feelings and relationship needs.

FAMILY THERAPY

As discussed earlier, the family therapy field has tended to accept gender-biased developmental and systems theories, with the result that the field has been working predominantly with male-derived, male-focused ideas about behavior and relationships (Wiener & Boss, 1985). Often the women we see value themselves solely on the approval from external, primarily male sources, and have little sense of their own self worth. As Weiner and Boss put it, "Because severe dependency needs and lack of self-development in women reflect traditional gender role socialization, the superficial, circular explanations for these phenomena reflect the absence of appropriate, female-focused models of development and mental health" (p. 15).

Weiner and Boss recommend four specific ways to strengthen the development of new women-based conceptual frameworks and theories:

1. Clarify the sociocultural and historical components of education in the mental health fields.

2. Establish criteria for sensitivity to gender roles in supervision, training, and consultation.

3. Update and correct negative and unsubstantiated information about female development.

4. Acquire empirical evidence about women's psychosocial development.

To this we want to add some specifics about treatment, to suggest to therapists ways to shift toward gender sensitive therapy, since, as Rampage and her colleagues (1986) have discussed, one is either doing feminist family therapy or sexist family therapy (by failing to respond to the inequalities in families based on gender). There is no middle ground. Needless to say, proselytizing and haranguing are the least effective ways to make therapeutic progress, and the therapist must introduce alternative perspectives without political speeches.

• Pay attention to the income and work opportunities of the husband and wife in a family and the implications for the balance of power in their relationship.

• Pay attention to the relative physical strength of men and women in a family and to the impact of any physical intimidation or incident of physical abuse, however long ago, as a regulator of the balance of power between spouses.

• Have family members examine what they like and do not like about being male and female.

• Help the family clarify the rules by which male and female roles in the family, in education, and in work are chosen and rewarded.

• Help the family clarify rules as to who makes which decisions, who handles finances, who handles legal matters, who handles emotional matters, who handles caretaking, and who cleans the toilet.

• Place the family's attitudes toward male and female roles in context, clarifying the broader political, social, and economic issues of divorce, aging, and child rearing, and encouraging families to educate themselves about these matters.

• Urging women to accept and move toward "male" values is not the solution to problems of female powerlessness. It is important to validate women's focus on relationships at the same time that you empower them in the areas of work and money.

• Be sensitive to the high price men may have to pay if they change their male orientation toward success and give higher priority to relationships, caretaking, and emotional expressiveness.

We also hope that more research will be done on gender differences for male and female therapists of different life cycle stages in working with

different family members. The little evidence we have so far suggests that there are significant differences in how women therapists, especially young women therapists, are related to in therapy by men and women in families (Warburton and Alexander, in press) and in the way they perceive themselves and their work (Woodward et al., 1981).

CONCLUSIONS

We believe that the patriarchal system that has characterized our culture has impoverished both women and men, and we look forward to a changing life cycle in which both men and women will be free to develop themselves equally inside and outside of the family. We hope that family therapy can become a force that fosters adaptive changes in human development to allow more latitude for both men and women in their ways of relating to their mates and peers, in their intergenerational connectedness, and in their stance toward work and community. We do not believe that the relational and emotionally expressive aspect of development is intrinsic to women. We see the romanticization of "feminine" values as inaccurate and unhelpful to families (Hare-Mustin, 1983). It is also not enough for women to adopt the "male" values of the dominant culture and to devalue what have been traditionally "female" values.

We aim toward a theory of family and individual development where both instrumental and relational aspects of each individual will be fostered. The "feminine" perspective has been so devalued that it needs to be highlighted, as Miller (1976), Gilligan (1982), Friedan (1981), Belenky et al., (1986) and others have been doing.

It is clear that traditional marriage and family patterns are no longer working for women, and the statistics reveal their dissatisfaction. In our view it will only be when we have worked out a new equilibrium not based on the patriarchal family hierarchy that these patterns will change.

The dichotomy between the "emotional expressiveness" and "instrumental" spheres, and the devaluation and relegation of the former to women, has been very costly to all family members, men and women alike. We believe that it is the socialization of women that makes them "intuitive" and that men could be raised to be equally sensitive if our patterns of education were changed to include this as a desired value. We believe that our world needs to appreciate both perspectives and to move toward a society in which men *and* women have both abilities: to function autonomously and to be intimate. Basic to this change is the notion that nurturing would not be the province only of women and that work and money would not be primarily a male-controlled sphere.

REFERENCES

Aguirre, B.E. (1985). Why do they return? Abused wives in shelters. *Social Work* 30(3):350–354.

Alexander, J., Warburton, J., Waldron, H., & Mas, C.H. (1985). The misuse of functional family therapy: A non-sexist rejoinder. *Journal of Marital and Family Therapy,* 11(2):139–144.

Apter, T. (1985). *Why women don't have wives: Professional success and motherhood.* New York: Schocken Books.

Avis, J. (1985). The politics of functional family therapy: A feminist critique. *Journal of Marital and Family Therapy* 11(2):127–138.

Baruch, G., Barnett, R., & Rivers, C. (1983). *Lifeprints: New patterns of love and work for today's women.* New York: New American Library.

Baruch, G., & Barnett, R.C. (1983). Adult daughters' relationships with their mothers. *Journal of Marriage and the Family* Aug.: 601–606.

Baruch, G.K., Biener, L., & Barnett, R.C. (1987). Women and gender in research on work and family stress. *American Psychologist* 42(2):130–136.

Belenky, M.F., Clinchy, B.M., Goldberger, N.R., & Tarule, J.M. (1986). *Women's ways of knowing.* New York: Basic Books.

Belle, D. (1982). The stress of caring: women as providers of social support. In L. Goldberger & Shlomo Breznitz (Eds.), *Handbook of stress.* New York: Free Press, pp. 496–505.

Berheide, C.W. (1984). Women's work in the home: Seems like old times. *Marriage and Family Review* 7(3):37–50.

Bernard, J. (1975). *Women, wives and mothers: Values and options.* New York: Aldine.

Bernard, J. (1982). *The future of marriage.* New Haven, Conn: Yale University Press.

Bernard, J. (1981). *The female world.* New York: Free Press.

Bianchi, S.M., & Spain, D. (1985). *American women in transition.* New York: Russell Sage.

Blumstein, P., & Schwartz, P. (1983). *American couples: Money, work, sex.* New York: William Morrow.

Brodsky, A.M., & Hare-Mustin, R.T., Eds. (1980). *Women and psychotherapy.* New York: Guilford Press.

Brody, E.M. (1981). Women in the middle and family help to older people. *The Gerontologist* 21:471–80.

Broverman, I.K., Vogel, S.R., Broverman, D.M., Clarkson, F.E., & Rosenkrantz, P.S. (1972). Sex-role stereotypes: A current appraisal. *Journal of Social Issues* 28(2):59–78.

Broverman, I.K., Broverman, D.M., Clarkson, F.E., Rosenkrantz, P., & Vogel, S.R. (1970). Sex-role stereotypes and clinical judgments of mental health. *Journal of Consulting Psychology* 43:1–7.

Caplan, P.J., & Hall-McCorquondale, I. (1985). Mother-blaming in major clinical journals. *American Journal of Orthopsychiatry* 55(3):345–353.

Chodorow, N., & Contratto, S. (1982). The fantasy of the perfect mother. In B. Throne (Ed.). *Rethinking the family: Some feminist questions.* New York: Longman.

Cohler, B., & Lieberman, M. (1980). Social relations and mental health among three European ethnic groups. *Research on Aging* 2:445–469.

Cowen, C.P., et al. (1985). Transitions to parenthood: His, hers, and theirs. *Journal of Family Issues* 6(4):451–481.

Current Population Reports. Oct. 1981:20, 365.

Daniels, P., & Weingarten, K. (1983). *Sooner or later: The timing of parenthood in adult lives.* New York: Norton.

Devanna, M.A. (1984). *Male/female careers—The first decade: A study of MBAs.* New York: Columbia University Graduate School of Business.

Dinnerstein, D. (1976). *The mermaid and the minotaur.* New York: Harper & Row.

Doherty, W.J., & Baldwin, C. (1985). Shifts and stability in locus of control during the 1970's: Divergence of the sexes. *Journal of Personality and Social Psychology* 48(4): 1048–1053.

Dohrenwend, B.S. (1973). Social status and stressful life events. *Journal of Personal and Social Psychiatry* 28:225–235.

Erikson, E. (1968). *Identity: Youth and crisis.* New York: Norton.

Erikson, E. (1963). *Childhood and society* (2nd ed.). New York: W.W. Norton.

Ferree, M.M. (1984). The view from below: Women's employment and gender equality in working class families. *Marriage and Family Review* 7:3–4.

Foster, S.W., & Gurman, A.S. (1984). Social change and couples therapy: A troubled marriage. In C. Nadelson & D. Palonsky (Eds.), *Contemporary marriage.* New York: Guilford Press.

Fox, M.F., & Hesse-Biber, S. (1984). Women at work. Mayfield Publishing Company.

Friedan, B. (1985). How to get the women's movement moving again. *New York Times Magazine,* Nov. 3.

Gilligan, C. (1982). *In a different voice.* Cambridge, Mass.: Harvard University Press.

Goldner, V. (1985). Feminism and family therapy. *Family Process* 24(1):31–48.

Goleman, D. (1986). Two views of marriage explored: His and hers. *New York Times* 135:19 (Apr. 1).

Gove, W.R. (1972). The relationship between sex roles, marital status and mental illness. *Social Forces* 51:34–44.

Hare-Mustin, R.T. (1978). A feminist approach to family therapy. *Family Process* 17:181–194.

Hare-Mustin, R.T. (1983). Psychology: A feminist perspective on family therapy. In E. Haber (Ed.), *The women's annual: 1982–83.* Boston: G.K. Hall, pp. 177–204.

Hare-Mustin, R.T. (1987). The problem of gender in family therapy. *Family Process* 26(1):15–27.

Hartman, A. (1987). Personal communication.

Hess, B.B. (1985). Aging policies and old women: The hidden agenda. In A.S. Rossi (Ed.), *Gender and the life course.* New York: Aldine.

Hess, B.B., & Soldo, B.J. (1984). The old and the very old: A new frontier of age and family policy. Presentation at annual meeting of the American Sociological Society, San Antonio, Texas.

Hesse-Biber, S., & Williamson, J. (1984). Resource theory and power in families: Life cycle considerations. *Family Process* 23(2):261–278.

Hewlett, S.A. (1985). *A lesser life.* New York: Morrow.

Hoffman, L.W. (1972). Early childhood experiences and women's achievement motives. *Journal of Social Issues* 28(2):129–155.

Hoffman, L.W. (1974). Effects of maternal employment on the child: A review of the research. *Developmental Psychology* 10(2):204–228.

Horner, M.S. (1972). Toward an understanding of achievement-related conflicts in women. *Journal of Social Issues* 28:157–175.

Huston, T. (1983). Developing close relationships: Changing patterns of interaction between pair members and social networks. *Journal of Personality and Social Psychology* 44(5):964–976.

James, K. (1985). Breaking the chains of gender: Family therapy's position, *Australian Journal of Family Therapy* 5(4):241–248.

Kagan, J. (1984). *The nature of the child.* New York: Basic Books.

Kagan, J., & Moss, H.A. (1962). *Birth to maturity.* New York: Wiley.

Kessler, R.C, & McLeod, J.D. (1984). Sex differences in vulnerability to undesirable life events. *American Sociological Review* 49:620–631.

Kessler, R.C., & McRae, J.A. (1984). A note on the relationships of sex and marital status with psychological distress. In J. Greenley (Ed.), *Community and mental health. Vol. III.* Greenwich, Conn.: JAI.

Krestan, J., & Bepko, C. (1980). The problem of fusion in the lesbian relationship. *Family Process* 19:277–290.

Lang, A.M., & Brody, E.M. (1983). Characteristics of middle-aged daughters and help to their elderly mothers. *Journal of Marriage and the Family* 45:193–202.

Lerner, H. (1985). *The dance of anger.* New York: Harper & Row.

Lever, J. (1976). Sex differences in the games children play. *Social Problems* 23:478–487.

Levinson, D. (1978). *The seasons of a man's life.* New York: Knopf.

Lewis, M. Feiring, C., & Kotsonis, M. (1984). The social network of the young child. In M. Lewis (Ed.), *Beyond the dyad: The genesis of behavior series* (Vol. 4). New York: Plenum.

Lewis, M., & Weintraub, M. (1974). Sex of parent x sex of child: Socioemotional development. In R.D. Friedman, R.M. Richart, & R.C. Vandewiele, (Eds.), *Sex differences in behavior.* New York: Wiley.

Maccoby, E.E., & Jacklin, C.H (1974). *The psychology of sex differences.* Stanford, Calif.: Stanford University Press.

McGoldrick, M. (1987). On reaching mid-career without a wife. *The Family Therapy Networker* 11(3):32–39.

McGoldrick, M., Anderson, C., & Walsh, F. (Eds.). (in press) *Women in Families and Family Therapy.* New York: Norton.

Miller, J.B. (1976). *Toward a new psychology of women.* Boston: Beacon.

Padan, D. (1965). Intergenerational mobility of women: A two-step process of status mobility in a context of a value conflict. Tel Aviv, Israel: Publication of Tel Aviv University.

Piotrkowski, C.S., Repetti, R.L. (1984). Dual-earner families. *Marriage and Family Review* 7:3–4.

Pogrebin, L.C. (1987). *Among friends.* New York: McGraw-Hill.

Pollit (1986). *New York Times.*

Rampage, C., Halsted, C., Goodrich, T.G., & Ellman, B. (1986). Panel on Feminism and Family Therapy. Networker Symposium. Washington D.C. March 21.

Rawlings, S.W. (1983). Household and family characteristics: March 1982. *Current Population Reports,* Series P 20 (381). Washington, D.C.: U.S. Bureau of the Census.

Richardson, L. (1986). *The new other woman.* New York: Free Press.

Romer, N. (1981). *The sex-role cycle: Socialization from infancy to old age.* New York: McGraw-Hill.

Rossi, A. (1980). Life-span theories and women's lives. *Signs* 6:4–32.

Roth, S. (1985). Psychotherapy with lesbian couples: Individual issues, female socialization and the social context. *Journal of Marital and Family Therapy* 11(2):273–286.

Rubin, L. (1985). *Just friends.* New York: Harper & Row.

Saluter, A.F. (1983). Marital status and living arrangements: March 1982. *Current Population Reports,* Series P-20 (380). Washington, D.C.: Bureau of the Census.

Sassen, G. (1980). Success anxiety in women: A constructivist interpretation of its sources and its significance. *Harvard Educational Review* 50:13–25.

Schydlowsky, B.M. (1983).

Sternberg, R. (1984). The nature of love. *Journal of Personality and Social Psychology* 47(2):312–329.

Strube, M.J., & Barbour, L.S. (1984). Factors related to the decision to leave an abusive relationship. *Journal of Marriage and the Family* 46(4):837–844.

Taggert, M. (1985). The feminist critique in epistemological perspective: Questions of context in family therapy. *Journal of Marital and Family Therapy* 11(2):113–126.

Thorne, B. (1982). *Rethinking the family: Some feminist questions.* New York: Longman.

Valliant, G.E. (1977). *Adaptation to life.* Boston: Little, Brown.

Warburton, J., & Alexander, J. (In press). Sex of client and sex of therapist: Variables in a family therapy study. In M. McGoldrick, C. Anderson, & F. Walsh (Eds.), *Women in families and family therapy.* New York: Norton.

Weiner, J.P., & Boss, P. (1985). Exploring gender bias against women: Ethics for marriage

and family therapy. *Counseling and Values* 30/1:9–21.

Weiss, R.S. (1985). Men and the family. *Family Process* 24(1):49–58.

Weitzman, L. (1985). *The divorce revolution*. New York: Free Press.

Wheeler, D., Avis, J.M., Miller, L.A., & Chaney, S. (In press). Rethinking family therapy training and supervision: A feminist model. *Journal of Psychotherapy and the Family*.

White, K. (1986). *The Journal of Personality and Social Psychology*.

Woodward, C.A., Santa-Barbara, J., Streiner, D.L., Goodman, J.T., Levin, S., & Epstein, N.B. (1981). Client, treatment, and therapist variables related to outcome in brief, systems-oriented family therapy. *Family Process* 20:189–197.

CHAPTER 3

Ethnicity and the Family Life Cycle

Monica McGoldrick, M.S.W.

Ethnicity interacts with the family life cycle at every stage. Families differ in their definition of "family," in their definition of the timing of life cycle phases and the tasks appropriate at each phase, and in their traditions, rituals, and ceremonies to mark life cycle transitions. When cultural stresses or transitions interact with life cycle transitions, the problems inherent in all change are compounded. In fact *Plath* (1981) has argued that the very definition of human development in Eastern cultures is different from western cultures in beginning with the definition of a person as a social being and defining development as by growth in the human capacity for empathy and connection. By contrast Western cultures begin with the individual as a psychological being and define development as growth in the human capacity for differentiation. This chapter will suggest some of the variability based on ethnicity, outline some of the categories for evaluating ethnic patterns as families move through the life cycle, and provide a clinical case to suggest ways of intervening with families that take into account the ethnic and life cycle interface.

Ethnicity patterns our thinking, feeling, and behavior in both obvious and subtle ways, although generally operating outside of our awareness. It plays a major role in determining what we eat, how we work, how we relate, how we celebrate holidays and rituals, and how we feel about life, death, and illness. We see the world through our own cultural filters and we often persist in our established views in spite of clear evidence to the contrary.

Ethnicity as used here refers to a concept of a group's "peoplehood" based on a combination of race, religion, and cultural history, whether or not members realize their commonalities with each other. It describes a commonality transmitted by the family over generations and reinforced by the surrounding community. But it is more than race, religion, or national and geographic origin, which is not to minimize the significance of race or the special problem of racism. It involves conscious and unconscious processes that fulfill a deep psychological need for identity and historical continuity. It unites those who conceive of themselves as alike by virtue of their common ancestry, real or fictitious, and who are so regarded by others.

The consciousness of ethnic identity varies greatly within groups and from one group to another. Families vary in attitude toward their ethnicity as a result of clannishness, regressive holding on to past traditions, and fear of changing cultural norms, on the one hand, to denial of any ethnic values or patterns, on the other. In groups that have experienced serious prejudice and discrimination, such as Jews and Blacks, family attitudes about allegience to the group may become quite conflicted and members may even turn against each other, reflecting prejudices in the outside world. Some groups have a choice about ethnic identification whereas others, because of their color or other physical characteristics, do not. Ethnicity intersects with class, religion, politics, geography, the length of time a group has been in this country, the historical cohort, and the degree of discrimination the group has experienced. Generally speaking, Americans tend to move closer to the dominant American value system as they move up in class. People in different geographic locations evolve new cultural norms. Religion also modifies or reinforces certain cultural values. Families that remain within an ethnic neighborhood, who work and socialize with members of their group, and whose religion reinforces ethnic values, are likely to maintain their ethnicity longer than those who live in a very heterogeneous setting and have no social reinforcers of their cultural traditions. The degree of ethnic intermarriage in the family also plays a role in cultural patterns (McGoldrick & Preto, 1984). Nevertheless, there is burgeoning evidence that ethnic values and identifications are retained for many generations after immigration and play a significant role in family life throughout the life cycle. Second-, third-, and even fourth-generation Americans differ from the dominant culture in values, behavior, and life cycle patterns.

While we are well aware of the problems of stereotyping and generalizing about groups in ways that may lead to prejudice, and in no way mean to contribute to that tendency in our culture, we have taken the risk of characterizing differences among groups in order to sensitize clinicians to the range of values held by different people. Of course, each family must be dealt with as unique, and the characterizations used here are meant to broaden the therapist's framework, not to constrict it.

THE CONCEPT OF FAMILY

When we talk of families moving through the life cycle together, it is important to note how our clients themselves define "family." For example, the dominant American (primarily WASP) definition has focused on the intact nuclear family, including other generations often only to trace the family geneology to distinguished ancestors who were in this country before 1776, or for southern WASP families, noting family members who took part in the Civil War (McGill & Pearce, 1982). For Italians, by contrast, one might even say

there is no such thing as the "nuclear family." For this group family has tended to refer to the entire extended network of aunts, uncles, cousins, and grand-parents, who are all involved in family decision making, who share holidays and life cycle transition points together, and who tend to live in close prox-imity, if not in the same house (Rotunno & McGoldrick, 1982). Black families tend to focus on a wide informal network of kin and community in their even broader definition of family, which goes beyond blood ties to close long-time friends, who are considered family members (Stack, 1975; Hines & Boyd, 1982). The Chinese go even further, to include all their ancestors and all their descendents in their definition of family. Everything they do is done in the context of this entire family group and reflects on it, bringing shame or pride to the entire set of generations. It should be added, however, that women in Asian families have traditionally been moved into their husband's family at the time of marriage, and their names disappear from the family tree in the next generation, leaving only the males as permanent members of a family (Kim et al., 1981; Kim, 1985). Thus, in a sense, Asian families consist of all one's male ancestors and descendents.

LIFE CYCLE STAGES

Groups differ in the importance given to different life cycle transitions. For example, the Irish have always placed most emphasis on the wake, viewing death as the most important life cycle transition, which frees human beings from the suffering of this world and takes them, it is hoped, to a happier afterlife. Blacks, perhaps as a result of similar life experiences with suffering, have also emphasized funerals; both groups go to considerable expense and delay services until family members can get there. Italian and Polish families instead have placed the greatest emphasis on weddings; they often go to enormous expense and carry on the celebration and feasting for lengthy periods of time, reflecting the importance of the continuation of the family into the next generation for these groups. Jewish families give special emphasis to the Bar Mitzvah, a "transition to manhood," thus reflecting the value placed on intellectual development, a transition most groups hardly mark at all.

THE UNATTACHED YOUNG ADULT

Ethnicity relates family process to the broader context in which it evolves. Just as individuation at this phase requires that we come to terms with our families of origin, it also requires that we come to terms with our ethnicity. For

example, if young people experience their parents as cold, distant, and unfeeling, it may be hard for them, even with the appreciation that their grandparents were the same, to feel sympathy for their parents' life styles. However, if they recognize in that stoicism the determined individualism with which the pioneers forged ahead in this country, they become connected with a fuller, more complex and accurate picture of their heritage, which may be easier to appreciate.

The intervention of choice for this phase of the life cycle—Bowen coaching, to help the young adult differentiate—will vary depending on the family's ethnic background. For a Puerto Rican woman, issues may well arise with her father because she wishes to pursue an independent life and career whereas he believes that she needs, and should accept, his protection. A Puerto Rican male might encounter family problems because he does not wish to conform to the traditional "macho" ideal. In a WASP family, the need will be to reconnect since disengagement has usually already occurred to a great extent and relationships may have already become superficial and ritualized. Bowen's ideas about creating "a tempest in a teapot" (1978) apply well to this group. For Greeks and Italians, the need may be instead to increase emotional distance while remaining connected. Which issues are primary will depend on the ethnic group's basic orientation to the accepted norms of the dominant group in America for this phase. For groups such as WASPs, Germans, and Scandinavians that value the young adult's independence, problems may surface when this cannot be accomplished, either because of a developmental lag, as with a disabled child, or because the necessity for prolonged education makes it impossible for the young adult to become self-sufficient. For other groups that do not value independence from the family (such as Italians and Puerto Ricans), this period may be particularly difficult. For certain groups, such as Greeks and Jews, where success and the family are both highly valued, a young adult may separate from the family in order to accomplish her or his goals for success, but the input of the family remains strong and will be intensified if the young adult's goals are not achieved.

THE YOUNG COUPLE

A number of major differences become evident at this life cycle transition, including the definition of sex roles, the boundary around the couple within the family system, and the relationship of the spouses to friends, activities, and the community. While the couple is viewed as two separate partners in many groups, for others the couple is expected to merge individual identities. In some groups the couple itself only has an identity as part of the family system. In Japan, for example, until 1948, couples had no legally defined status within the family system. Since weddings were not a symmetrical linking of

family groups but a recruitment of a female into the male line, the husband's family, not the individuals, made the decisons regarding the spouse (Morsbach, 1978). In Japanese families the wife traditionally became part of the husband's family and was expected to conform. The obvious triangle involving the husband, wife, and mother-in-law is repeatedly discussed in descriptions of the Japanese family. For other ethnic groups, such as WASPs and the Irish, the boundary around the couple is quite strong and a parent offering advice would be considered "intrusive." For many other groups, such as Blacks and Italians, the extended family is turned to and will offer advice on conflicts and problems that a couple may have with each other or later with their children.

Different cultural attitudes about sex roles may also create difficulties for intermarried couples at this phase. In some groups, such as the Irish, women are expected to be strong and to take care of things. In others, such as Greek and Italian families, males are expected to handle all matters outside the family itself. In WASP and Jewish families, more democratic roles are expected, even though, of course, all these patterns fit within the basically patriarchal system of the larger culture (see Chapter 2). Couples from different backgrounds will vary on the degree of intimacy that is expected between spouses, on attitudes toward sexual relations, and on having independent spheres of activity. For some groups the man handles the outside world and the woman's sphere is the home. For some the couple is expected to socialize primarily with the extended family or as a nuclear family alone. For others friends are an important part of socializing. Here, too, there are differences between "family friends" and individual friends of a spouse. Some go so far as to have separate vacations; for others this would be unheard of.

INTERMARRIAGE

Americans are marrying out of their ethnic groups at an ever-increasing rate. The likelihood of intermarriage generally increases with the length of time an ethnic group has been in this country, as well as with educational and occupational status. Intermarriage is feared because it threatens the survival of the group. Cultural and religious groups have always had prohibitions against intermarriage. Generally the greater the difference in cultural background, the more difficulty spouses will have in adjusting to marriage (McGoldrick & Preto, 1984).

For example, a WASP/Italian couple might run into conflicts because the WASP takes literally the dramatic expressiveness of the Italian whereas the Italian finds the WASP's emotional distancing intolerable. The WASP may label the Italian "hysterical" or "crazy" and in return be labeled "cold" or "catatonic." Knowledge about differences in cultural belief systems can be helpful to spouses who take each other's behavior personally. Couples may

have a sudden and remarkable shift in response when they can come to see the spouse's behavior as fitting into a larger ethnic context rather than as a personal attack.

Couples who choose to marry out of the group are usually seeking a rebalance of the characteristics of their own ethnic background. They are moving away from some values, as well as toward others. As with all systems, the positive feelings can, under stress, become negative. The extended families may stereotype the new spouse negatively—often a self-protective maneuver—reassuring themselves of their superiority when they feel under threat. During courtship a person may be attracted precisely by the fiance's differentness, but when entrenched in a marital relationship, the same qualities often become the rub.

Families may at times use their ethnic customs or religious beliefs selectively to justify an emotional position within the family or against outsiders (Friedman, 1982). But the opposite problem can be equally difficult. That is, couples often react to each other as though the other's behavior were a personal attack rather than a difference rooted in ethnicity. Typically we tolerate differences when we are not under stress—and in fact, find them appealing. However, when stress is added to a system, our tolerance for difference diminishes. We become frustruated if we are not understood in ways that fit with our wishes and expectations. WASPs tend to withdraw when upset, to move toward stoical isolation, in order to mobilize their powers of reason (their major resource in coping with stress). Jews, on the other hand, seek to discuss and analyze their experience together; Italians may seek solace in food, emotional and dramatic expression of their feelings, and a high degree of human contact. Obviously these groups may perceive each other's reactions as offensive or insensitive, although within each group's ethnic context their reactions make excellent sense. In our experience much of therapy with intermarried couples involves helping family members recognize each other's behavior as a reaction from a different frame of reference (McGoldrick & Preto, 1984).

THE TRANSITION TO PARENTHOOD AND THE FAMILY WITH YOUNG CHILDREN

As with other life cycle transitions, whatever the accepted traditions for a particular group, their way is seen as the only right and moral way. The rituals that accompany it are fairly defined practices, and there is often little variation within a given group. Jordon (1980) explored the accepted birth practices in four cultures and the belief systems used to support these practices. The dominant American pattern until quite recently was that birth occurred in a sterilized medical environment, with only medical personnel present, and with

certain drugs almost routinely given. Birth has been conceived of primarily as a "medical event" whereas most other cultures have defined it as a natural process. Now the dominant pattern is changing to include the father at the birth, although other family or friends are rarely included. Caesarean sections are a common practice, representing 25% of births in the United States. In Holland, by contrast, babies are almost always born at home; few or no drugs are given, the husband and a midwife are expected to be present, and caesarean sections are extremely rare. The birth process in both Holland and Sweden is seen as primarily the woman's experience, and one over which she is given primary responsibility. The Swedish use hospitals and drugs at the woman's discretion.

In contrast to these three, Yucatan Indians view birth as a shared, not an individual, responsibility. The husband, the wife's mother, and a midwife are all expected to be present. In fact husbands are criticized if they are not there. In contrast to the dominant U.S. practice, other males are rarely present, the tradition being to exclude people who have not given birth themselves.

In the United States, with birth seen as a medical event, doctors are considered responsible for what happens. Women become "patients" (in wheelchairs, often without their own clothes, without much control over IVs or drugs that are given). Episiotomies are accepted practice "to prevent tears," although reports from other cultures are that tears rarely occur. The dominant American pattern uses "scientific knowledge" (a strong WASP value) to justify the patterns that are used, such as giving birth in a setting that is outside of the family's own familiar territory.

Child-rearing patterns also vary tremendously. The dominant American value is still that mothers should have primary responsibility for child rearing, although this was never true in other cultural groups, and children have traditionally been raised by others: grandmothers, older siblings, or other parental substitutes. The British have used wet nurses and nannys, southern WASPs Black women, and many cultural groups have used grandparents, when mothers work outside the home.

Groups differ also about whether child rearing should be permissive or strict, whether the family should be child focused, as tends to be the case in Jewish families, or whether children should be seen and not heard, as in Irish families. Some groups, such as Greeks and Puerto Ricans, tend to indulge young infants, but then become rather strict with children, especially girls, beyond a certain age. Black families often go by the rule, "Spare the rod and spoil the child," as do the Irish, who disapprove of praising children for fear they will get a "swelled head," whereas other groups are extremely affectionate with children, sleep with them, and encourage them to express themselves, and even to "show off." Jewish families typically pay extremely close attention to the emotional and intellectual development of their children, readily taking them for consultations if their grades fall below "A" or if there is any indication of emotional upset. It is important for clinicians to evaluate families in relation to their ethnic background and to be careful in making judgments

about child-rearing patterns that may be different from the ones with which they were raised.

FAMILIES OF ADOLESCENTS

As families move toward the children's adolescence, issues about separation and openness to new values become more salient. In Jewish families, which tend to be democratic and to move toward new values readily, parents are often receptive to their children's interests. Other groups are more oriented toward tradition (Italians, Greeks, Chinese, etc.) and intergenerational struggles between parents and children are often intense. This is the period when the youth want to bring their friends home and this will alternately be seen as an opportunity or an intrusion on the family system. Certain groups, such as the Irish, tend to welcome outsiders, sometimes to the point of preferring having them present (because it limits the intimacy possible among family members). Others, such as Italians, may take a long time to become intimate with outsiders, but once they do, the outsiders become part of the family.

Adolescence may be a particularly stressful time for daughters in many families because of the rigid rules restricting female independence in most cultures. Daughters in Italian and Puerto Rican families, for example, may undergo intense struggles as they seek more activities outside of the family. The changing role of women may intensify intergenerational struggles of adolescence for daughters from these cultures as they rebel against the traditional role in which women wait on brothers and fathers and later husbands and sons.

Some families, such as the Irish, may move from being very structured and controlling in their child-rearing practices to allowing their teenagers too much freedom, as if the intermediate range of control is difficult for them to negotiate. Other families, such as Greeks and Puerto Ricans, may try to control their adolescents' behavior completely, particularly that of daughters. With the rapidly changing norms in the dominant culture, children are now exposed in school to many risky behaviors and pulls toward freedom from family control at an ever-younger age. This clashes strongly with the values of many cultures.

For certain groups, such as Jewish families, the importance of success may lead to parent-child struggles at this phase. One study comparing Jewish and non-Jewish adolescents and their families has indicated that a high achievement orientation was associated in the Jewish families with a high degree of family conflict (Radetsky et al., 1984). Jewish parents also often provide for their children at the expense of their own happiness (Herz & Rosen, 1982), which may lead to increased levels of guilt and ambivalence in the children, who feel they can never do enough to repay their parents.

LAUNCHING

It is important to check whether families with difficulties at the launching phase had experienced migration during this phase in a previous generation, which may have intensified the meaning of this transition for the family. We must assess carefully what pathway a particular family considers "normal" for young adults in its cultural context (Chapter 21). As mentioned above, WASP families may have the most difficulty if their children are not launched "on time," since dependency tends to be seen as a serious problem in such families. Thus a child who cannot function independently by about age 18 may be perceived as a problem. This may be so even if the youth needs more time, because of developmental lag or because of educational demands for successful functioning in our culture. One might even say that upper-class British families begin launching their children as early as age seven, when they send them to boarding school. There are many upper-class WASP communities in the United States in which it is seen as a mark of dysfunction not to send your child to boarding school at least by age 14.

By contrast, Italian families may not expect to launch their children at all, but rather to absorb newcomers through marriage and birth. The expectation is for everyone to remain working and living together in the same community. They expect adult children to socialize primarily with the family. In such families the children's ambitions for independent achievement may be seen as a threat to the family and may be responded to as a betrayal of family loyalty. In fact Italian families will expect to take care of their children no matter what, and may need help only because the network is not large enough to handle the responsibilities they expect to take for a severely dysfunctional member. Usually there is the utter conviction that family relationships are about interdependence, a sharp contrast to WASP culture, which places such high value on independent functioning and self-discipline.

One might say that for Jewish families a lack of success is considered the primary problem at the launching phase. Separation from the family often seems allowable only to the extent that the young person is successful. The award-winning film "Best Boy," about a middle-aged retarded son in a Jewish family and his first cousin (the film maker), who wished to launch him from his aging parents, is a touching depiction of this problem. The intergenerational ambivalence in Jewish families may be seen at this phase particularly, as children distance guiltily from their parents, or remain ambivalently close. The expectation of active, intimate ongoing relationships, particularly between mother and daughter, is rather different than for other groups, such as WASPs, where the generational boundaries, like all other boundaries, tend to reinforce autonomous functioning. It is not uncommon, for example, for an adult Jewish daughter to confide in her mother about her sexual problems whereas an Irish or WASP daughter may well not reveal even the most ordinary details of her everyday life.

For Irish families the problem at launching may have to do with the family not expecting much "working through" of transitions. The wish to keep up appearances may lead them to be very upset about anything not going "right," although to the outside world they will usually put up a good front and pretend nothing is happening. Cutoffs often occur between parents and children at this point, resulting from their inability to talk to each other about the changes in relationship required for a successful negotiation of this phase. Parents may not go to a child's wedding or hurts may build up over the distance children take, at times a delayed reaction to parental pressures in adolescence to which they could not respond at the time. Now they feel able to react. There may be little or no discussion of the issues. Frequently launching reactivates parents' own feelings of loss or hurt resulting from unresolved issues in their own launching, which may never have been discussed and may now be intensified by their parents' aging or death.

Depending on the sex roles held by the group, the middle generation's difficulties at this phase will vary. For groups in which the woman's role has traditionally been constricted to child and husband care, such as Italians or Puerto Ricans, the launching phase may cause a serious crisis in the marriage and family, since the culture traditionally proscribes the woman's moving beyond the home sphere in her activities. In groups where women have tended to have "significant other" roles all along, this transition may be easier. For example, Irish women have traditionally socialized through the church and participated in a variety of activities beyond child rearing. In addition, marital intimacy was never a high expectation, thus lessening the potential disappointment at the point of launching. Black women have usually worked outside the home. In WASP families women often have had other activities, because they believed in making their children independent from an early age. They either may work or participate in volunteer activities and not expect to spend their entire lives as family caretakers. Black women tend to have a similar outlook.

FAMILIES IN LATER LIFE

Major differences among groups about this life cycle phase concern the responsibility of the middle generation for caretaking of the elderly, attitudes of respect or disregard for older family members, and in particular the role of older women in families, since women typically live longer than men. Older Americans are more likely themselves to be immigrants or the children of immigrants and/or to have grown up in ethnic communities surrounded by others of their own cultural background (Woehrer, 1978).

Certain groups, such as Greeks, Italians, and Chinese families, hold strong beliefs about not "abandoning" family members to nursing homes. Others, such as WASPs, Scandinavians, and Jews, are much more likely to accept the

nursing-home solution. A major factor when families are struggling with issues of health care for elderly family members is the importance of facilities that also provide a culturally adequate environment. It is well known that the meaning of cultural traditions increases as we age (Gelfand, 1982), so that as we lose other faculties, the traditions and rituals of our cultural background take on increasing importance: foods, ways of celebrating holidays, language, and music.

Today it is becoming increasingly difficult for families (that is, for women) to care for older family members even if they wish to. Often they are working, the network of extended family is smaller and more dispersed so that the burdens of caretaking cannot be shared, and our society provides virtually no economic support to families for this activity. In addition, the younger generation may not understand their parents' wish to take on the burden of caring for an aging grandparent, and may be unsupportive, thus adding to the burden. At the very least, clinicians can help families at the point of making decisions about the care of older family members to seek culturally syntonic arrangements, even though these may be hard to find.

Groups differ in their patterns of relating to friends and kin, a factor that becomes increasingly important in later life as family members become more dependant on support networks. Older Blacks tend to draw on a more varied pool of informal helpers while Whites, particularly WASPs, are more likely to limit help seeking to their spouses or a single other family member as they reach old age and then to have difficulties if this support is lost. Older Blacks, who are also more likely to turn to prayer as a resource, appear to have more flexibility in adopting to the use of varied resources, which may help to explain the lower rate of suicide of older Blacks compared with Whites, in spite of their more limited education, resources, and family stability (Gibson, 1982). For groups such as Irish and Black families that tend to prefer peer relationships, there is much emphasis on the friendship network, as well as on sibling relationships (Woehrer, 1978). Whereas Italians tend to evaluate friends according to their ability to act like kin, the Irish tend to evaluate relatives according to their ability to act like friends (Woehrer, 1978). According to Greeley (1972), the Irish tend to experience guilt when they are not friends with their siblings or do not enjoy being with them. Other groups, such as Scandinavians, have a low level of visiting among family members, but they are likely to belong to organizations; others, such as Poles and Italians, tend to socialize most frequently with the family, and are less likely to join organizations. In fact one study some years ago found that 79% of Italian Americans visited their parents weekly, compared with 39% of Scandinavians and WASPs (Greeley, 1971).

Given these differences, as Woehrer (1978) describes it, a Scandinavian senior citizen who lives in a high-rise apartment building and sees her children only occasionally and a Polish grandfather who has no close friends outside the family and belongs to no organizations may both be socially integrated within the context of their own cultural values and expectations. Likewise, a

German grandmother who sits alone sewing clothes for her grandchild and an Irish grandmother employed at the information booth at the state legislature may both find meaning and happiness, but if they had to switch roles, they might become alienated and unhappy (Woehrer, 1978). Scandinavian elderly may be most reluctant to reveal difficulties to their children or to seek their aid. Blacks see friends as kin and as people who help each other. The Irish, who also enjoy friendships, do not like to have to turn to friends for help when in need and are more likely to withdraw (McGoldrick, 1982; Woehrer, 1978). When clients are in need of extra resources, particularly the elderly, who are most tied to their cultural traditions, it is important to check out their preferred mode of connecting.

ETHNICITY AND DEATH

The problem of death is universal. Mourning rituals involve a transition to a new stage of individual and relational identity. But cultures vary in their ways of dealing with their dying members, and in their mourning rituals and their explanations of the meaning of death in human existence. In contrast to the dominant American pattern of denial of death, Alaskan Indians who are dying exhibit a willfulness about their death, participate in its planning and the time of its occurrence, and show a remarkable power of personal choice. In our time we have come to hide death, making the process of adapting to loss all the more difficult. In contrast to traditional cultures, our society lacks cultural supports to assist families in integrating the fact of death with ongoing life (McGoldrick, Hines, Garcia-Preto, & Lee, 1986). Medical practice and technology have increased the problems of adaptation by removing death from the everyday reality of life.

American culture is moving toward the minimization of all rituals for dealing with death. As a result of legislation, public health laws, custom, and work regulations, there is little individual control over the process rituals for dealing with death, and given that has been taken over by the funeral industry. The allowable time for bereavement leave (usually one to three days) makes it very difficult for cultural groups to retain their traditional customs during death and mourning.

Nevertheless attitudes regarding bereavement continue to vary in profound ways and clinicians should be careful about definitions of "normality" in assessing families' responses to a death. For example, in certain Mediteranean cultures, such as Greek and Italian, women have been the primary mourners and bear the outward signs of mourning (black clothing) for the rest of their lives. Some groups have even required a women to kill herself when her husband died. At the opposite extreme, WASPs have tended to value a handling of death that involves "no mess, no fuss," a rational handling of the

experience, with minimal expression of feeling, carried out in the most pragmatic, practical way. As one friend put it when explaining why he had not
attended the funeral of his twin sister, "What would have been the point of
spending the money to go? She was already dead." WASPs tend to prefer
death in hospitals where they are out of the way—not an inconvenience to the
family—and they do not want to incur any unnecessary obligations because of
their dependence. (In hospitals care is provided on the "rational" basis of fee
for service.) For other ethnic groups, to die away from family support or one's
own environment is a double tragedy. Italians, Greeks, Indians, and many
other groups consider human interdependence to be natural to life, and would
consider it an unnatural deprivation not to care for a family member in time of
such need.

As mentioned above, Black and Irish families generally consider death the
most significant life cycle transition and family members will make every effort
to attend a relative's or friend's wake and funeral. Black families in the South
often incurred great expense to have flowers, a band, singing, and other
accompaniments for their funerals. Funerals might be delayed for days to make
sure that all family members could get there. The Irish also spare no expense
for drink and other funeral arrangements, even if they have very little money.
Such customs undoubtedly relate to the belief in these two cultural groups that
life in this world is generally full of suffering, and that death will bring a release
to a better afterlife.

The two groups differ greatly, however, in their handling of the emotional
experience. Black families tend to express their grief directly. The Irish, on the
other hand, are much more likely to get drunk, tell jokes, and relate to the
wake as a kind of party, with little overt expression of their emotions—a
custom that could be perceived by many as unfeeling. In Puerto Rican culture,
by contrast, women "are expected to express their sorrow dramatically
through displays of seizure-like attacks and uncontrollable emotions." (Osterweis et al., 1984). Various Southeast Asians participate in public displays of
emotion but in private retain their composure and are stoic about their feelings
(Osterweis et al., 1984).

Jewish culture has a prescribed pattern of rituals to help family members
deal with death, including burial within 24 hours, and a week of "shiva," or
family mourning, when friends and family visit and bring food. Certain
prayers, "Kaddish," are said for a year, and a memorial service, referred to as
the "unveiling," held eleven months after the death, marked the end of the
official mourning period (Herz & Rosen, 1982). In traditional Eastern European Jewish culture, the belief was that "the worst life is better than the best
death" (Zborowski & Herzog, 1952)—in obvious contrast to beliefs held in
Black and Irish culture.

It is important to appreciate that cultural groups have specific beliefs about
forms of mourning and the clinician must find out from a family what its
members believe about death, the rituals that should surround it, and the
afterlife. Often a failure to carry out such death rituals, for whatever reason, is

an important component of the family's becoming embedded in the mourning process without resolution. In fact, because of the dominance of hospital personnel and funeral directors in the death process, family members may have lost control of their traditions, and thus may come to view participation in ritual as a sign of weakness or of being "unsophisticated" or superstitious. It can be extremely helpful to encourage family members to respect the traditions of their heritage and to be active in determining what cultural forms they will use to deal with their losses.

PROBLEMS AND THEIR SOLUTIONS

Illness behavior is a normative experience governed by cultural rules. We learn approved ways of being ill, and doctors' explanations and activities, as well as those of the patients and their families, are culture specific. Symptoms differ so much among ethnic groups that it brings into question the usefulness of our diagnostic nomenclature. Patients have been shown to have major differences in their attitudes toward complaining (some groups require it; others disapprove of it), in the accuracy of their ability to describe their experience objectively, in their preferred solution to being in pain, and in their attitudes toward doctors. Emotional expressiveness can lead to problems since the dominant (WASP) culture tends to value such expression less than do many minority groups. Certain groups, as a result, are labeled as having psychological problems, although there is no evidence of this apart from their tendency to dramatize their experience.

Every culture has characteristic problems. These problems are often consequences of cultural traits that are conspicuous strengths in other contexts. For example, WASP optimism leads to confidence and flexibility in taking initiative, an obvious strength when there are opportunities to do so. But optimism becomes a vulnerability when people must contend with tragedy. They have few philosophical or expressive ways to deal with situations in which optimism, rationality, and belief in the efficacy of individuality are insufficient. Although independence and individual initiative work well in some situations, WASPs may feel lost when dependence on the group is the only way to ensure survival (McGill & Pearce, 1982).

Naturally the behavior different groups see as problematic will differ as well. WASPs may be concerned about dependency, emotionality, or not being able to function; the Irish about "making a scene"; Italians about disloyalty to the family; Greeks about any insult to their pride or "filotimo" (which means something like carrying out one's responsibility for one's own group); Jews about their children not being "successful"; and Puerto Ricans about their children not showing respect.

CEREMONIES AND RITUALS

Families vary in their patterns of celebration and in the degree and pattern of ritualization of their activities. Sometimes ethnicity is used to promote clannishness in a way that goes beyond reinforcing and reminding members of their group identity. Usually such moves are seen when people feel threatened from without and join against a common enemy. In their positive sense, group holidays (Christmas, Passover, Easter) are opportunities for families to join in celebrations that mark group boundaries and reinforce their common heritage and values. At other times ethnicity may be used for cultural camouflage (Friedman, 1982), as when parents tell a child they cannot attend his or her wedding because the child is marrying someone outside of their group. This is not to say that families do not have feelings about intermarriage or about the need to perform rituals as a reinforcement of their group identity (see section on intermarriage). It is extremely important to reinforce a family's use of rituals so as to reinforce their sense of identity.

IMMIGRATION AND THE LIFE CYCLE

Migration is so disruptive in itself that we could say it adds an entire extra stage to the life cycle for those families who must negotiate it. The readjustment to a new culture is by no means a single event, but is a prolonged developmental process of adjustment that will affect family members differently, depending on the life cycle phase they are in at the time of the transition.

Families' attitudes toward ethnicity depend on many factors, such as how much time has passed since immigration, their life cycle stage at the time of immigration, and the circumstances that led them to migrate: did they come alone as young adults, or as young children with their nuclear family, or in their later years as part of a mass migration because of political or economic oppression? All who migrate must deal with the conflicting cultural norms of the country of origin and of the United States. A person's cultural identity will depend on his or her facility with the new language; economic and political situation; flexibility in making new connections with work, friends, and organizations such as church, schools, government bureaucracies, and the health-care system; and remaining connections to the country of origin. Immigrants may wall off the past, forcing their children to speak English only and never talking about the country they left behind. Or they may wall off the new culture, living and working in an ethnic enclave, never making an effort to learn English or to negotiate the American system. A third approach is to attempt to

assume a pattern of biculturality, passing on to their children stories and traditions and at the same time learning the ways of the new culture.

When families have buried the past under the pressure to accommodate to the new situation and out of the pain of remembering what they have left behind, it may be important to help them break through the cultural cutoff and regain continuity with the culture of origin, which can enrich their sense of identity and broaden their potential for dealing with the present. In this regard it is essential to keep in mind the entire course of the life cycle. In young adulthood people may disregard their culture, but as they get older, their cultural identity may become more important to them and inspire them to reconnecting with their traditions.

The hope of returning to the country of origin may impede the family's efforts to adapt to the new situation. This happened, for example, with the first wave of Cuban migrants, many of whom kept waiting for the revolution to end so that they could return to Cuba. The state of permanent uncertainty or uprootedness is in itself profoundly stressful and will have a long-range impact on family adjustment.

People who migrate in the young-adult phase may have the greatest potential for adapting to the new culture in terms of career and marital choices. However, they are perhaps the most vulnerable to cutting off their heritage, leaving themselves open to emotional isolation at later phases of the life cycle when the need for cultural support and identification tends to increase (Gelfand & Kutzik, 1979). The result is that they may be permanently cut off, unable to maintain continuity between heritage and children.

Therapy involves detailed questioning about a person's background, not only the family but also the country of origin, and helping the person to reconnect with his or her culture.

Families that migrate with young children are perhaps strengthened by having each other, but they are vulnerable to the reversal of generational hierarchies. If the family migrates with small children (even more so with teenagers), there is a likelihood that the parents will acculturate more slowly than their children, creating a problematic power reversal in the family (Lappin & Scott, 1982). If the children must take on the task of interpreting the new culture for the parents, parental leadership may be so threatened that children are left without effective adult authority to support them and without a positive identification with their ethnic background to ease their struggle with life in this new culture Coaching the younger generation to show respect for the values of the older generation is usually the first step in negotiating such conflicts. Families that migrate at this phase may also have problems down the road, particularly at the launching phase where the children feel guilty about leaving parents who are not at home in the culture.

Families migrating when their children are adolescents may have more difficulty because they will have less time together as a unit before the children move out on their own. Thus the family must struggle with multiple transitions and generational conflicts at once. In addition, the distance from the grand-

parental generation in the old country may be particularly distressing as grandparents become ill, dependent, or die. The parents may experience severe stress in not being able to fulfill their obligations to their parents in the country of origin. It is not uncommon for symptoms to develop in adolescents in reaction to their parents' unexpressed distress.

Again, therapy involves helping the family sort through its cultural conflicts. The worry and concern for the extended family in the country of origin must be respected, while the struggle to achieve in this country is also reinforced. Often encouraging such families to build connections to church or other ethnic supports in this country is an important part of therapy.

When families migrate in the launching phase, it is less often because they seek a better way of life and more often because circumstances in the country of origin make remaining there impossible. Migration in this phase causes particular difficulties for families because it is much harder for the middle generation to break into new work and friendship networks at this age. Again, if aging parents are left behind, the stresses will be intensified.

The launching phase may be made more complex when children date or marry spouses from other backgrounds. This is naturally perceived as a threat by parents since it means a loss of the cultural heritage in the next generation. One cannot underestimate the stress it creates for parents, who themselves have had to give up their country of origin, to fear the loss of their traditions when their children intermarry.

Migration in later life is especially difficult because families are leaving so much behind. There is evidence that even those who migrate at a young age have a strong need to reclaim their ethnic roots at this phase, particularly because they are losing other supports around them (Gelfand & Kutzik, 1979). For those who have not mastered English, life can be extremely isolating at this phase. The need to depend on others may be particularly frustrating, as when one is forced to be in a nursing home where one cannot communicate easily.

Sometimes if the first generation is older at the time of immigration and lives in an ethnic neighborhood in the new country, its conflicts of acculturation may be postponed. The next generation, particularly in adolescence, is likely to reject the ethnic values of parents and strive to become "Americanized" (Sluzki, 1979). Intergenerational conflicts often reflect the value struggles of families in adapting to the United States.

Members of the third or fourth generation are usually freer to reclaim aspects of their identities that were sacrificed in the previous generations because of the need to assimilate.

Families from different ethnic groups may have very different kinds of intergenerational struggles. WASP families are likely to feel they have failed if their children do not move away from the family and become independent (McGill & Pearce, 1982) whereas Italian families are likely to feel they have failed if their children do move away. Jewish families will expect a relatively democratic atmosphere to exist in the family, with children free to challenge

parents and to discuss their feelings openly (Rosen, 1982). Greek families, in contrast, do not expect or desire open communication between generations and would not appreciate the therapist's getting everyone together to discuss and "resolve" their conflicts. Children are expected to respect parental authority, which is maintained by the distance parents keep from their children (Welts, 1982). Irish families will be embarrassed to share feelings and conflicts across generations and cannot be expected to do so to any great extent.

Any life cycle transition can trigger ethnic identity conflicts since it puts families more in touch with the roots of their family traditions. How the rituals of transition are celebrated can make an important difference in how well the family will adjust to the changes (Chapter 7). All situational crises—divorce, illness, job loss, death, retirement—can compound ethnic identity conflicts, causing people to lose a sense of who they are. The more a therapist is sensitive to the need to preserve continuities, even in the process of change, the more he or she can help the family to maintain maximum control of its context and build upon it.

THERAPY

Appreciation of cultural variability leads to a radically new conceptual model of clinical intervention. Restoring a stronger sense of identity may require resolving cultural conflicts within the family, between the family and the community, or in the wider context in which the family is embedded. Differentiation involves selecting from our ethnic traditions those values we wish to retain and carry on. Families may need coaching to sort out deeply help convictions from values asserted for emotional reasons.

Defining what response is adaptive in a given situation is not an easy task. It involves appreciation of the total context in which the behavior occurs. For example, Puerto Ricans in this country may see returning to Puerto Rico as a solution to their problems. A child who misbehaves may be sent back to live with family members. This solution may not be functional from the perspective that the child will then be isolated from the immediate family. The living situation in Puerto Rico may also not be adequate to provide for the child's needs. However, it is advisable for the clinician not to counter the parents' plan but to encourage them to strengthen their connectedness with the family members in Puerto Rico with whom their child would be staying in order to make the most of their wish to rely on their own network for support in handling a disruptive child.

The therapist's role in such situations, as in all therapy, will be that of a culture broker, helping family members to recognize their own ethnic values and to resolve the conflicts that evolve out of different perceptions and experiences.

Often it is very difficult to understand the meaning of behavior without knowing something of the value orientation of the group. The same behavior may have very different meaning to families of different backgrounds. The following example of a newly married couple illustrates the importance of therapeutic understanding of the role of ethnicity in relation to life cycle transitions.

Brian Werner, a 28-year-old computer analyst of German/Irish background, and his wife Barbara, a 26-year-old high-school teacher of Eastern European Jewish background, applied for therapy in November 1985, five months after their marriage. Barbara was extremely upset with Brian because he would not confront his mother, whom she thought had treated them very badly. Although Brian was generally mild mannered, their disagreements had escalated to the point where Brian had begun hitting her, which led her to threaten separation. The couple had met in 1983, three weeks after her father had suffered a heart attack. They married on July 28, 1985, without any members of Brian's family present. Apparently his father disapproved of their having a Jewish wedding, and Brian's mother was in conflict up until the last minute about whether to upset her husband by going or her son by staying home. Brian's siblings had become caught up in the conflict as well and had not attended the wedding. Three days later Brian's father died of cerebral hemmorage. During and after the funeral Brian and Barbara were related to by Mrs. Werner and the other family members civilly but with no discussion of what had happened concerning their wedding. Barbara found this extremely upsetting. On two occasions she tried to talk things over with Mrs. Werner, whose response sounded as if there were no problems and she did not know what Barbara was talking about.

During the first therapy session, the therapist took a three-generational genogram (Figure 3-1), which indicated that marriage had been a toxic issue in both families of origin since the previous generation. Barbara's mother had been disapproved of by her mother-in-law from the beginning, and her father, Mr. Fine, had finally cut his family off entirely "because of how they treated his wife." Barbara's mother's father had "demanded" that his son-in-law remain in their neighborhood after marriage or he would cut them off.

As for Brian's parents, they had met in Ireland during the war and came to this country to marry because they could not find an Irish priest who would marry them. Mrs. Werner had never returned to Ireland.

The family stresses related to the conflicts around the transition to marriage, which had a charged meaning in both families. In addition, because their was an ethnic intermarriage, the coping skills Brian and Barbara were using were compounding their difficulties. Barbara kept wanting to "have it out," which only made Brian more anxious. She kept telling him how to confront his mother, demanding it as a necessary test of his loyalty. Brian was sure this would not work, but he could not explain why.

The therapist discussed with Brian and Barbara the ways in which each of their families handled stress and the cultural backgrounds of their families. Barbara had to admit that Mrs. Werner acted very "Irish," but kept reiterating, "She insulted me. She never thanked me for all the things I did for her and she just ignores me." Brian and Barbara were given papers to read on ethnicity (McGoldrick & Presto, 1984) to help them gain perspective on the patterns in their families and Barbara was instructed to back off and let Brian work out his relationship with his mother. Brian then brought his mother in for a therapy session. He had been feeling very rejected by her, but during the session it became clear, as happens so often in Irish families, that his mother was feeling equally rejected by him. He had trouble responding to her.

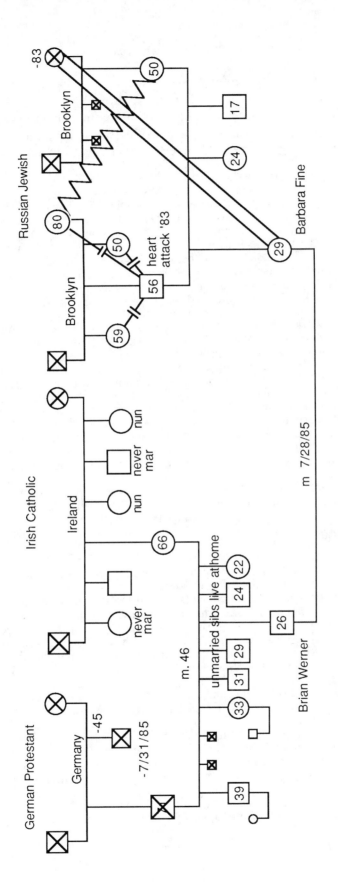

Figure 3-1. Werner family genogram

Because of the level of Brian's anxiety and Barbara's reactivity, it was decided to meet with Brian individually to coach him about developing a relationship with his mother, opening up toxic issues, including his marriage three days before his father died, his parents' marriage and dissolution of ties with Ireland, and his fears about his mother's health. He was also coached about handling Barbara's reactions without withdrawing from her (as he was inclined to do).

Barbara was also coached about responding to her mother-in-law without expressing all her hostilities directly (as she wanted to do).

Their first wedding anniversary (and the anniversary of Mr. Werner's death), as well as the following Thanksgiving and Christmas, provided Brian and Barbara with opportunities to rework the family themes of isolation following intermarriage and to become part of their families in a new way, rather than repeating the pattern of cutoff or submission that was set in their parents' generation, if not before.

CONCLUSIONS

Ethnicity intersects with the life cycle at every phase. Every life cycle transition is an opportunity to repair cutoffs and reinforce continuities of the family. It is important to encourage families to use their life cycle transitions to strengthen individual, family, and cultural identities.

REFERENCES

Bowen, M. (1978). *Family therapy in clinical practice,* New York: Jason Aronson.

Friedman, E.M. (1982). The myth of the Shiksa. In M. McGoldrick, J.K. Pearce, J. Giordano (Eds.), *Ethnicity and family therapy.* New York: Guilford Press.

Gelfand, D.E., & Kutzik, A.J. (Eds.) (1979). *Ethnicity and aging: Theory, research and policy.* New York: Springer.

Gelfand, E.G. (1982). *Aging: The ethnic factor.* Boston: Little, Brown.

Gibson, R.C. (1982). Blacks at middle and late life: Resources and coping. *Annals of the American Academy Annals* (AAPSS 464), Nov.:79–91.

Greeley, A.M. (1971). *Why can't they be like us?* New York: Dutton.

Greeley, A.M. (1972) *That most distressful nation.* Chicago: Quadrangle.

Herz, F., & Rosen, E.M. (1982). Jewish families. In M. McGoldrick, J.K. Pearce, & J. Giordano (Eds.), *Ethnicity and family therapy.* New York: Guilford Press.

Hines, P., & Boyd Franklin, N. (1982). Black families. In M. McGoldrick, J.K. Pearce, & J. Giordano (Eds.), *Ethnicity and family therapy.* New York: Guilford Press.

Jordon, B. (1980). *Birth in four cultures.* Montreal: Eden Press Women's Publications.

Kim, Bok-Lim (1985). Women and ethnicity. Presentation at the American Family Therapy Association, June.

Kim, Bok-Lim, Olcamura, A.I., Ozawa, N., & Forrest, V. (1981). Women in shadows. National Committee Concerned with Asian Wives of U.S. Servicemen, 964 La Jolla Rancho Road, La Jolla, CA 92037

Kubler-Ross, E. (1975). *Death: The final stage of growth.* Englewood Cliffs, N.J.: Prentice-Hall.

Lappin, J., & Scott, S. (1982). Intervention in a Vietnamese refugee family. In

M. McGoldrick, J.K. Pearce, & J. Giordano (Eds.), *Ethnicity and family therapy.* New York: Guilford Press.

McGill, D., & Pearce, J.K. (1982). British American families. In M. McGoldrick, J.K. Pearce, & J. Giordano (Eds.), *Ethnicity and family therapy.* New York: Guilford Press.

McGoldrick, M. (1982). Irish families. In M. McGoldrick, J.K. Pearce, & J. Giordano (Eds.), *Ethnicity and family therapy.* New York: Guilford Press.

McGoldrick, M. (1982). Normal families: An ethnic perspective. In F. Walsh (Ed.), *Normal family process.* New York: Guilford Press.

McGoldrick, M., Hines, P., Garcia-Preto, N., & Lee, E. (1986). Mourning rituals: How culture shapes the experience of loss. The Family Networker, 10/6, 28–36.

McGoldrick, M., & Preto, N.G. (1984). Ethnic intermarriage: Implications for therapy. *Family Process* 23(3):347–362.

Morsbach, H. (1978). Aspects of Japanese marriage. In M. Corbin (Ed.), *The couple.* New York: Penguin.

Osterweis, M., Solomon, F., & Green, M. (eds.), (1984). *Bereavement: Reactions, consequences, and care.* Washington, D.C.: National Academy Press.

Plath, D. ( ) Of time, love and heroes. In (Ed.) *Adult Development Through Relationships.*

Radetsky, D.S., Handelsman, M.M., & Browne, A. (1984). Individual and family environment patterns among Jews and non-Jews. *Psychological Reports* 55:787–793.

Rotunno, M., & McGoldrick, M. (1982). Italian families. In M. McGoldrick, J.K. Pearce, & J. Giordano. (Eds.), Ethnicity and family therapy. New York: Guilford.

Sluzki, C. (1979), Migration and family conflict. *Family Process* 18(4):379–390.

Stack, C. (1975). *All our kin.* New York: Harper & Row.

Welts, E.P. (1982). Greek families. In M. McGoldrick, J.K. Pearce, & J. Giordano (Eds.), *Ethnicity and family therapy.* New York: Guilford Press.

Woehrer, C.E. (1978). Cultural pluralism in American families: The influence of ethnicity on social aspects of aging. *The Family Coordinator* 329–339.

Zborowski, M., & Herzog, E. (1952). *Life is with people.* New York: Shocken Books.

4

The Family Life Cycle and Discontinuous Change

Lynn Hoffman, M. S. W.

EVOLUTIONARY FEEDBACK

A recent paper by Dell and Goolishian (1979) examines the concept of "evolutionary feedback," a term developed by the physicist Prigogine to describe a "basic, non-equilibrium ordering principle that governs the forming and unfolding of systems at all levels." One can turn to Bateson's latest book, *Mind and Nature,* and find a similar description in his comparison of epigenesis and evolution:

> In contrast with epigenesis and tautology, which constitute the worlds of replication, there is the whole realm of creativity, art, learning and evolution, in which the ongoing processes of change feed on the random. The essence of epigenesis is predictable repetition; the essence of learning and evolution is exploration and change.

Prigogine's concept of "order through fluctuation," as described by Dell and Goolishian (1979), emphasizes not stability and homeostasis but the idea of discontinuous change:

> At any point in time, the system functions in a particular way with fluctuations around that point. This particular way of functioning has a range of stability within which fluctuations are damped down and the system remains more or less unchanged. Should a fluctuation become amplified, however, it may exceed the existing range of stability and lead the entire system into a new dynamic range of functioning. An autocatalytic step or surge into positive feedback is needed to obtain such instability. (p. 10)

Dell points out the tendency of systems thinkers in the field of family therapy to deny the epistemological revolution, of which the family movement is part, by using the language of linear causality in place of the very different language of circular causality espoused by Bateson. Dell particularly objects to the vulgar use of the idea of homeostasis. Family theorists have fallen prey to the mistaken notion that a family is like a homeostatic machine with a governor: Thus it is said that a "family needs a symptom," or a "symptom serves a homeostatic function in the family." To use this kind of language is to assume a dualism between one part of the system and another part. It is more correct to say that all parts are engaged in whatever ordering of constancy or change is in question, in an equal and coordinate fashion. To speak otherwise

is to engage in what Bateson calls "chopping the ecology," or what Dell describes as a kind of "fuzzy system animism."

What must be kept in mind is the continuous recursiveness of all circuits in complex systems. It is not valid to say that the parents are "using" the child's problems to keep them together. One could just as well say that the child is using the parents' overprotectiveness to keep him or her safely close to home. Or that without the child's problem, there would be no link between mother and father's mother. Or that a valued older child keeps being drawn back home because of it. Or that the problem child is the primary comforter of mother, and so forth. Dell and Goolishian use analogies to biology and other sciences: "DNA is not a governor of biological systems; biological functions are regulated by the total system of DNA and cytoplasm" (p. 4).

The most important point made by Dell is that one cannot use a cybernetic analogy based on a mechanical model of closed system feedback. Rather one must realize that there is a different cybernetics of living systems that cannot be explained by the negative feedback view. This point is dramatized by the stepwise, sudden leaps to new integrations characteristic of such systems, which are not only unpredictable, but irreversible. The conceptual emphasis is on self-organizing processes that reach toward new evolutionary stages rather than on processes that reach toward equilibrium.

What makes this argument so crucial is that families that come in with distress in one or more members seem to be having difficulty with evolving; they are or seem nonevolved—"stuck" in an outmoded stage. Perhaps it is this "stuckness" that make the early version of the homeostatic model so convincing to therapists working with troubled families. In such families there is too much emphasis on maintaining equilibrium. For this reason the task of therapy should be to make available to a group that is becoming more and more like a homeostatically controlled piece of machinery the power inherent in all living systems—the ability to transcend the stuckness and move to a different stage.

Certainly putting an evolutionary framework around our cybernetic analogy is in itself an evolutionary step forward in family theory and theory of change. For one thing it fits the process we are trying to describe far better than the static model of error-activated feedback mechanisms does. For another it affords a far more satisfying rationale for the success of some of the so-called "paradoxical" approaches to therapy, which produce rapid shifts in families or individuals. These shifts can take place with incredible suddenness, and indeed seem to be self-generated. To go further into this subject, let us turn to the ideas of another physicist who has written about discontinuous change, John Platt.

HIERARCHICAL GROWTH

One property that families share with other complex systems is that they do not change in a smooth, unbroken line but in discontinuous leaps. Platt,

(1976) in an imaginative paper, speaks of a process physics where the emphasis is not on static structure but on what he calls a "flow hierarchy"—forms that maintain a steady state even though matter, energy, and information are continually flowing through them. A bit of thought will convince the reader that families, too, are like waterfalls or cascades, where the many-tiered pattern of the generations persists as an overall structure, even though individuals pass through it as they are born, grow old, and die.

Platt argues that many natural systems are of this type, and that change, in such systems occurs in a startling and sudden way. He cites falling in love, acts of creation, conversions, evolutionary leaps, reformations, or revolutions as examples, and says that when a system is conflicted or dysfunctional, this may not necessarily portend disaster but indicate that pressure toward a new and more complex integration is mounting.

Platt makes a useful distinction between three kinds of change that depend on the way the entity in question is organized. If it is externally designed, like a watch, then a change will have to be made by an outside agent, like the watchmaker who takes the watch apart and reassembles it. If it is internally designed, like a plant that contains a genetic blueprint, then only mutations of the gene pattern can produce a change.

Among living systems that follow a self-maintaining design, a great number present a third model for change. In such entities change takes the form of a transformation, a sudden appearance of more functionally organized patterns that did not exist before. Platt calls this type of change "time emergence." One might think of a kaleidoscope, which keeps the same geometric pattern as the tube being turned until all at once a small particle shifts in response to gravity and the whole pattern changes to an entirely new one. The most interesting feature of a kaleidoscope is that one can never go back.

This is consonant with the way systems, which have what Ashby (1960) calls "bimodal feedback mechanisms" or "homeostats," operate. They will remain stable as long as the environment around them does not change, or as long as internal elements within do not change; but if this happens, the system will either break down or respond by shifting to a new "setting" that will meet the demands of the new field. The change in the setting creates a discontinuity because the range of behaviors, the "grammar" for allowable activities, has changed. Thus a set of completely different patterns, options, and possibilities emerges. It is usually organized more complexly than the previous one. But it, too, is rule governed and will not change again until new pressures from the field enforce a new leap.

The natural history of a leap or transformation is usually as follows: First the patterns that have kept the system in a steady state relative to its environment begin to work badly. New conditions arise for which these patterns were not designed. Ad hoc solutions are tried, and sometimes work, but usually have to be abandoned. Irritation grows over small but persisting difficulties. The accumulation of dissonance eventually forces the entire system over an edge, into a state of crisis, as the homeostatic tendency brings on ever-intensifying corrective sweeps that get out of control. The end point of what

cybernetic engineers call a "runaway" is either that the system breaks down, that it creates a new way to monitor the same homeostasis, or that it spontaneously takes a leap to an integration that will deal better with the changed field.

Families are notable examples of entities that change through leaps. The individuals who make up a family are growing (at least partially) according to an internal biological design, but the larger groupings within the family—the subsystems and the generations—must endure major shifts in relation to each other. The task of the family is to produce and train new sets of humans to be independent, form new families, and repeat the process, as the old sets lose power, decline, and die. Family life is a multigenerational continual changing of the guard. And although this process is at times a smooth one, like the transitions of political parties in a democracy, it is more often fraught with danger and disruption. It is common knowledge now that most psychiatric symptoms (and many medical ones) cluster around these stress periods. One must assume from this evidence that most families do not leap to new integrations with ease, and that the "transformations" referred to by Platt are by no means self-assured. This brings us to an accumulation of research by sociologists and clinicians studying the family life cycle.

EXPECTABLE LIFE-STAGE CRISES

The family life cycle was discovered by a circuitous route. Of major importance was the work of Erik Erickson (1963), whose depiction of individual life stages, and the interplay between these stages and the shaping processes of social institutions, challenged the narrow focus of intrapsychic theories of development. At the same time, clinicians studying the responses of individuals to stress began to question the notion that there were some individuals who had better coping patterns or better "ego strengths" than others. One of the first pioneers in this area, Eric Lindemann, noticed that the difference between a normal and an abnormal grief reaction had to do with the overall makeup of the family network of the bereaved one, not with his or her coping mechanisms as shown by previous attempts to handle stress. Lindemann (1967) notes in his classic study of survivors and relatives of victims of the Coconut Grove fire that:

> Not infrequently the person who died represented a key person in a social system; his death was followed by disintegration of this social system and by a profound alteration of the living and social conditions for the bereaved.

The intensity of a grief reaction did not have to be tied in with a previous neurotic history, but with the type of loss for the person involved.

Not only a loss, it then appeared, but also the acquisition of new family

members can trigger an upset. A now classic study by Holmes and Rahe (1967) who compiled a "Social Readjustment Rating Scale," indicated that there was no correlation between the negative perception of an event and the degree of stress that was attached to it. Out of a list of 43 life-stress events, rated by 394 subjects in terms of intensity and length of time necessary to accommodate to them, ten of the top 14 involved gaining or losing a family member. It is fascinating to realize that events with presumably positive meanings, such as "marital reconciliation," ranked higher on the scale than ones with negative connotations, such as "difficulties with sex."

The stress researchers began to realize that they were dealing with normal, expectable life-stage crises that had to do with bodies entering and leaving the family system. Soon two terms were coined—"crisis of accession" (when somebody joined the family) and "crisis of dismemberment" (when somebody left or died). One could add to this list various shades of departures, or effects attributable to major shifts in roles: a child starting kindergarten might produce a crisis in some families, as would the retirement of the head of the household in others.

At the same time, such pioneering family sociologists as Reuben Hill were studying the relationship between family life stages and their impact on individuals in the family (Hill & Hansen, 1960). It is interesting that no consensus has ever been reached as to the number of stages; some researchers have listed up to 24, and others have limited themselves to seven or eight. Generally courtship, marriage, advent of young children, adolescence, leaving of the children, readjustment of the couple, and growing old and facing death are the major categories. Studies linking these periods to the production of symptoms of all kinds have justified a growing interest. Accompanying this interest has been a gradual realization that a symptom may not be a disturbance pertaining to an individual member, but a sign that a family is having trouble negotiating a transition.

In support of this idea, Haley (1973) has stated that pathological behaviors tend to surface at points in the family life cycle when the process of disengagement of one generation from another is prevented or held up. For instance, members of a family in which a child is mediating a parental conflict may seem to resist this person's departure, or even to block it. A symptom seems to be a compromise between staying and leaving; the child becomes incapacitated to a greater or lesser degree and never really leaves home, or may leave but may find it hard to negotiate the new molecule of marriage and may fall back, or else a child of the new marriage may have to serve as mediator in turn. One can often see the truth of the Biblical statement: "The fathers have eaten sour grapes and the teeth of the children are on edge." One frail, psychotic child can sometimes appear to be holding an entire kin network on his or her shoulders, like the key person in a family high-wire act who displays incredible strength and an impeccable sense of balance.

What we may now justifiably ask is what the mechanism is that somehow prevents people in a family from making the leap to a new integration. The

answer is suggested by the concept of another kind of shift, which occurs when a homeostatically regulated system is about to exceed its parameters or break. For this we shall have to turn to Ashby and his idea of step-mechanisms.

THE CONCEPT OF STEP MECHANISMS

In *Design for a Brain* Ashby (1960, pp. 87–89) describes four types of movement as an entity or a material passes from one state to another. A "full-function" moves in a progressive fashion without a finite interval of constancy between states, like a barometer. A "step-function" has intervals of constancy separated by discontinuous jumps, like a stairway. A "part-function" is like a step-function except that from one state to another the line is progressive, rather than instantaneous. A "null-function" simply indicates an absence of movement or change.

Here we are concerned only with the step-function. Ashby comments on the fact that many step-functions occur in the natural world. He includes as examples the tendency of an elastic band to break when the proportion of pull versus length reaches a certain point, or the tendency of a fuse to blow when the circuit is loaded beyond a certain number of amperes, or the sudden change that takes place when strong acid is added to an alkaline solution.

In looking at more complex entities, such as machines, Ashby notices that some of their variables may exhibit a sudden shift in character whenever they reach a certain value that he calls a "critical state." In fact, he says, it is common for systems to show step-function changes whenever their variables are driven too far from some usual value. He goes on to speculate that it would be useful for a system to have at least one such element. A clear example is the wiring of a house for electricity. If there is no circuit breaker, the whole system will break down and have to be replaced. But the device of the circuit breaker means that only a fuse will blow, and when that is replaced (assuming that the overload has been corrected), the system will still be functioning. Ashby calls this type of arrangement a step-mechanism.

One difficulty with Ashby's ideas is that he is not really concerned with living systems at the group level and above. He is attempting to devise a cybernetic model that would account for the evolution and structure of the brain, and most of his examples are drawn from the world of biology, chemistry, and physics. One has to pull his ideas out of context to make them apply to social systems. However, without some notion similar to that of the step mechanism, the sudden shifts in behavior one often sees in families with symptomatic members could never be explained.

Let us take the psychosomatic child whose symptom deflects parental conflict. In the case of a family, one of many essential variables is the relationship between the members of the executive dyad, who are usually the

parents. There are probably homeostatic arrangements regulating such dimensions as closeness/distance or balance of power that limit the behaviors allowed in this dyad. Let us hypothesize that one of these sets of limits is constantly being overpassed. With a symmetrical couple, a slight advantage accruing to one party may provoke an escalation that, if not blocked, may end in violence or divorce. With a complementary couple, too much inequality may produce depression in the "low" spouse and concomitant anxiety in the "high" one. Whatever the nature of the plateau (and it is usually not a pure example of either model depicted above), there will be a "critical state" that represents some value beyond which the system may not go and still remain intact.

At this point various things can happen. A couple may have techniques for handling the threat, such as a cooling-off period for an angry symmetrical couple or a "good fight" for a distant complementary one. Another way would be for one of the spouses to develop a severe or chronic symptom, which again would prevent a split, though at a cost. However, it often happens that a third party—for example, a child—becomes drawn into the conflict. Once this happens the child's discomfort grows while parental tensions lessen. Perhaps some minimal cue indicating parental conflict will trigger anxiety in the child, who reacts with irritating behavior. At this point one of the parents may start to attack the child while the other moves in to his or her defense. Caught in the tightening spiral, the child may start to respond with a physical symptom— may show signs of an asthmatic attack and start to wheeze. This will cause the parents to stop their covert struggle and unite. A very real issue joins the couple, since the child's physical well-being is at stake. Their getting together, especially if it is accompanied by supportive behavior, allows the child's anxiety to diminish, even though the momentum of the physiological condition carries its own dangers.

In this example one could say that warning signals are at work whenever a feedback chain reaches a critical state in a set of relationships. These signals prevent events from taking place that might endanger the system. For instance, the child's symptom is a warning signal that diverts the parents from having a fight.

But what if the child's discomfort proceeds to a level that is unacceptable, and a positive feedback chain develops that cannot be countered by the usual warning signals? Here we move up to the next level of homeostatic control, where the interface is not between the child and parents, but between the family and the wider society. Ashby calls attention to the fact that:

> A common, though despised, property of every machine is that it may "break." In general, when a machine "breaks" the representative point has met some critical state, and the corresponding step-function has changed the value. . . . As is well known, almost any machine or physical system will break if its variables are driven far enough from their usual value. (p. 92–93)

It is possible that what is known in psychiatry as a "nervous breakdown" is similar in function to what Ashby is talking about. In a family the individual's

"breakdown" operates as a step-mechanism, signalling the failure of the family's homeostatic mechanisms and necessitating the intervention of the larger system, the community. Here is where helpers in various guises come in and an attempt is made to repair the broken element, the person.

However, to return to the image of the electric circuit, as long as it continues to be overloaded, it will not do any good to fix or replace the fuse. Sometimes the problem is temporary; the overload has been due to a sudden plugging in of an extra appliance (a mother-in-law visiting, for instance), and once that is taken away, the system will return to normal. But often the change is permanent. Somebody has died, or there is a shift in family circumstances that is irreversible, or a maturation level has been reached by a family member that is built into the growth of every human being. Then the family must make a shift in its own behavioral responses to meet the new demands. Otherwise the person's symptomatic behavior may continue, or another problematic behavior may replace it. What we are dealing with, in a family with a troubled member, is a situation in which the transformation needed to effect a leap to the next stage might threaten the family by impairing some important member or a subsystem.

Symptomatic displays could thus be thought of negatively as aborted transformations or positively as negotiations around the possibility of change. Antonio Gramsci, in *Prison Notebooks,* says: "The crisis consists precisely in the fact that the old is dying and the new cannot be born; in this interregnum a great variety of morbid symptoms appear." A symptomatic redundancy is an arrangement that usually springs up to handle this interregnum between the old and the new. It represents a compromise between pressures for and against change. The symptom is only the most visible aspect of a connected flow of behaviors and acts as a primary irritant that both monitors the options for change, lest too rapid movement imperil someone in the family, and also keep the necessity for change constantly alive. You then have behaviors that spiral rather than cycle around the possibility of a leap. Sometimes the leap is taken simply because of some accidental shift brought about by the spiral, which is always moving forward in time. Even if a very narrow spiral appears that chronically circles around some central point, it is still always shifting and is never without some potential for change.

The next question to consider is how to help the family make a leap up, rather than continue in this chronic spiral, and achieve a transformation to a new stage that will obviate the presence of symptoms or distress.

PARADOXICAL INJUNCTIONS AND THE "SWEAT BOX"

Platt, as we saw, was stressing the positive—even extraordinary—capacity of living systems to achieve transformations that go beyond what could pre-

viously have been predicted or achieved, thus not only "saving the day," but pointing the way toward a new one. Ashby is looking at a different kind of shift, perhaps equally extraordinary: the ability of one element of a system to "break" if too much pressure for change has been introduced. In a family or other group, the shift to a symptomatic configuration saves the day, but it emphatically does not point the way to a new one. This may be seen as a nonevolution or failed leap, as it not only keeps the family from making a new integration but seems to happen at the expense of one family member, who has often sentimentally been thought of as the "scapegoat" (an appellation that is more apparent than real).

The question for therapy, when cast in this new light, then becomes: How does one interfere with a mechanism that ensures family stability (morphostasis) and instead help the family achieve a transformation that will represent a more complex integration (morphogenesis)? Here a discussion of what Rabkin has called "saltology" (from the Latin *saltus,* "to leap"), and which might more prosaically be called "leap theory," is in order. Also important in this connection is some extremely good thinking Rabkin has done in relating transformations or leaps to the appearance of that communicational oddity, the "paradoxical injunction."

Rabkin (1976) has presented a refreshing examination of the original double-bind concept in a paper called "A Critique of the Clinical Use of the Double Bind." This paper reclassifies most of the examples used by clinician-researchers to illustrate double binds: masked hostility, sarcasm, strategic deceit, or ordinary "damned-if-you-do, damned-if-you-don't" dilemmas.

A case can be made for equating one of these dilemmas, the paradoxical injunction, with the double bind. A paradoxical injunction is described as a statement that intrinsically contradicts itself unless teased apart into a "report" level and a "how this report is meant" level, the second level inclusive of the first. This is also how the researchers in Palo Alto thought of the double bind. The double bind, as we have seen, was associated with manifestations of irrational behavior such as schizophrenia.

The paradoxical injunction is a form of communication, however, that all parents and all children (all superiors and all subordinates, for that matter) have become involved with at some time in their lives—but seldom do they literally go crazy. Of course, they often get upset, which, Rabkin argues, happens because the paradoxical injunction is the best our poor language can do to suggest that a systems change is required.

Rabkin takes an example already used by clinicians to equate a paradoxical injunction with a double bind. The parent says to the child, at a point when the child is about to pass into the grey area of adolescence: "I insist you go to school because you enjoy the beauties of learning." (The Bateson group in Palo Alto used a similar example, a *New Yorker* cartoon in which an employer is telling a baffled-looking employee: "But Jones, I don't want you to agree with me because I say so, but because you see it my way.") Rabkin then quotes Koestler on the process of creation: Before a creative leap can occur, says

Koestler, all previous pathways must be blocked. It is only from the accumulated intensity of the stress that the pressure to take the leap will occur.

Seen in this light, the paradoxical injunction appears the communicational form most likely to create sufficient pressure for change. The paradoxical injunction of parent to adolescent child says, in effect, "I want you to be independent, but I want you to want that independently of my wanting that." What might be called, for want of a better term, a "simple bind" is set up. The receiver is directed to remain simultaneously in a symmetrical and a complementary relationship with the communicant. This being impossible, a leap must be taken to what Rabkin calls an "achievement," his word for the transformation or new integration spoken of by Platt.

The impossible situations set up by the zen master for the student are now understandable in this light. The whole point is for the student to become "equal" to the master, but this cannot be done by an order from the master, or from within the master–student relationship at all. The student must somehow get the idea "on his own or her own" that this is the course that must be taken. In line with this thinking, one should reserve the term "paradoxical injunction" or "simple bind" for the confusing directive that often appears as a harbinger of a leap into a new stage, and the term "double bind" for the very different message sequences that block this leap or imply unthinkable consequences should it occur.

The introduction of this concept of the simple bind solves many issues that have perplexed researchers and clinicians for years. For one thing there is no longer the vexing question: If paradoxical communication is operating in art, fantasy, play, and most creative activity, how do we distinguish between that form of paradoxical communication which is associated with schizophrenic communication and that which is associated with the complex achievements of the artist or the prophet? For another we have a way to explain the idea of the therapeutic double bind or counterparadox, which has been linked to homeopathic medicine: The cure resembles the disease. A therapeutic double bind might be rephrased as a reinstatement of the conditions of a simple bind, although this time within a different context—the relationship between the therapist and the client or family. The bind is reimposed, the period of confusion is gone through, the family or client takes the requisite leap, and the new integration is then rewarded rather than invalidated or dismissed.

An example of this process is described by Bateson (1972) in an essay on "learning to learn." Bateson had become interested in porpoises that had been trained to show "operant conditioning" to the public by exhibiting special behaviors—hearing a whistle and then receiving a fish. The porpoises possessed a considerable repertoire of these behaviors. Bateson realized that these animals, since they did not produce the same behavior every time, must have "learned to learn" how to produce a piece of conspicuous behavior. He asked to watch the process by which a porpoise was taught to do this, and in fact created an experimental situation in which to conduct his observations. First the trainer rewarded the porpoise for a piece of conspicuous behavior,

such as raising its head. The animal repeated this action several times, each time being rewarded with a fish. However, the next time the porpoise came in, there was no fish. The trainer waited for the animal to produce another behavior accidently—perhaps an annoyed tail flap—and then rewarded that. Each behavior was rewarded three times in the session in which it occurred, but not in the next. Rewards were given only when the porpoise again produced a piece of unusual behavior. This process was evidently so disturbing to both the trainer and the porpoise that the trainer kept breaking the rules to reinforce the creature at times that were not appropriate. The porpoise, in turn, began to act more and more agitated as attempts to gain a previously reinforced reward would prove futile, and began to exhibit behaviors that in a human would be called "psychotic."

Before the 15th session, however, a remarkable event took place. The porpoise rushed about the tank, acting intensely excited. When she came on for her performance, she put on an elaborate display of eight behaviors, three of which had never been noticed in this species before. Bateson makes the point that the disruption of habitual patterns of stimulus and response can be intensely upsetting to a creature if this disruption constantly puts the creature in the wrong in the context of an important relationship. He added, however, that if the disruption and pain do not cause the animal to break down, the experience may produce a creative leap, a fact noted also by Wynne (1976) in an essay "On the Anguish and Creative Passions of Not Escaping the Double Bind."

This example reinforces the notion that a prerequisite for creative leaps in complex systems is a period of confusion accompanied by self-contradictory messages, inconsistencies, and, above all, paradoxical injunctions: I command you to be independent; I want you to love me spontaneously; I order you to be the dominant one. These messages, with their threatening implications that the relationship between the communicants may be endangered if the change does not take place, can be called the "sweat box." The "sweat box," in mild or severe form, often seems to be necessary before morphogenetic or rule-setting change can take place in a person, in a family, or in larger systems.

However, if and when a move in an appropriate direction is taken, there must be immediate confirmation and reward. The essence of the double bind is to disconfirm a leap once taken, to indicate that change is not desired, or to disqualify the whole event. In other words, the double bind is a simple bind that is continually imposed, and then continually lifted; pressure to change followed by injunctions not to change; a yes–no kind of thing, that produces the disruption and pain that Bateson argued were untenable for humans and other creatures. Rabkin, carrying this idea further, argues that a paradoxical injunction that brings about a systems change followed by a paradoxical injunction to undo that systems change might well result in intense disorganization in the recipient of such messages.

Consider the example of a mother caught in a struggle with an adolescent son. She wishes him to display more adult ("symmetrical") behavior. But if she

enjoins him to do so, she is defining him as a child (a "complementary" relationship). There is no way out of this difficulty, as every exasperated parent and resentful teenager know, except for some shift whereby both find that they are relating more pleasantly and more as peers than as parent and child, at least in the area the struggle was about. This shift can take place suddenly, or a long back-and-forth battle may be required. But the necessary condition is that the shift in the setting governing their relationship happens "spontaneously," since for the mother to enforce it, or for the child to seize it, would merely reaffirm their previous situation.

If the parent giving the original paradoxical messages responds positively to an integration of the relationship at a more equal level, then this is a successful resolution of the dilemma. There has been no double bind, or at least no harmful one. But if at the moment the child and mother do reach that desired state, one of them, or someone else in the family, signals that this would be bad or would be inadmissible by family rules, then one has the preconditions for a double bind. And then one has the appearance of symptoms embedded in cycles in which the pressure for change builds up, followed by injunctions against change, in endless sequence like a stuck record: the famous "game without end."

The way a simple bind might either become resolved or turn into a symptom can be illustrated by the following hypothetical case.

> Peter, 13, begins to sleep late in the morning and so be late for school. His mother becomes tired of pushing him to get up and finally says, "Why do I always have to kick you out of bed to go to school? Act like a grown-up. You ought to want to go to school for the sake of your own future. Your father used to get up at six and run a paper route before he even got to school, in zero-degree weather," etc., etc.
>
> This is a bind (simple variety) because if the boy "acts like a grown-up," he is demonstrating a symmetrical relationship, but at the same time, if he does go to school, it is in response to his mother's demand, and his relationship to her is thereby defined as complementary. What he does do is to become even more reluctant to go to school. His mother oscillates between washing her hands of him and going after him, a process that only escalates the tension between them. The school calls, saying that the boy is beginning to cut whole days, which means even more pressure. Father, who usually can sleep later than his son and hates to get up early, is constantly awakened by the morning fusses. Although he prefers to stay out of his wife's dealings with his son, he begins to protest. "Lay off the boy," he says to his wife. "You're only making things worse." He compares her to his father, who made his own adolescent years miserable by insisting that he get up and take the paper route. He says that he can sympathize with the boy. This statement brings out the latent split within most parenting dyads, the split between a permissible and a punitive stance. The mother, intensifying her position, says, "It's about time you stopped nagging him." They end up shouting and get into a state of unresolved anger with each other. Peter draws the covers up over his head and succeeds again in not going to school.

This is the normal type of confusion a family faces when children reach adolescence. It is usually resolved if the parents can overcome their differences and establish a united front. Perhaps adolescent rebellion not only serves to establish the beginning of independence for a child but also offers an

issue that the parents, who by a natural process will one day be child-free again, can use to test the nature and strength of the bond between them. It seems not to matter which way the parents go; the situation is solved if the parents can say; "It's your own life, mess it up and take the consequences," or "Get to school, and no more nonsense." Somehow, from this microtest of whether the parents are together enough to survive their son's eventual departure, he gets enough confirmation to begin to leave, and the school issue drops away. The boy may find that an attractive female schoolmate waits at the same bus stop. Suddenly it is no longer "Why don't you get up and go to school?" but "Why aren't you ever at home any more?"

Here is the alternative scenario that might establish a symptom.

The boy does get up and go to school. He finds the female classmate, and he also regains his interest in studying (an unlikely story, but this remains a hypothetical case). However, father begins to feel more and more depressed. His work is not going well and his ulcer's beginning to act up. It seems that this is the last child at home and the one who has been closest to his father, all the more so in that the wife is rather domineering and he chooses to remain distant from her rather than fight openly. He experiences a small feeling of elation when the boy defies his mother over not going to school in a way that was never possible for the father while growing up. The boy is very important to him. The mother, too, is strangely caught up in the fight she has with her son. It is as though he is able to stand up to her in a way that her husband never can, and although she is angry, she gains a kind of satisfaction from his assertiveness. With her husband there is only shadowboxing; with her son someone is really there.

At the same time, perhaps both are unconsciously aware that the boy's growing up means the emergence of many difficult issues between them, and the father's ulcer seems to signal that he will probably turn his feelings about these issues inward rather than hazard an open conflict with his wife. A sense of ominous possibilities fills the air. The father eats little at night and complains about his ulcer. When he does, mother seems annoyed rather than sympathetic and says, "I'm sick of your always going on about your ulcer and never going to the doctor about it. I always have to push you to make an appointment. Why can't you take responsibility for your own problems instead of making the whole family miserable?" The father becomes moody and quiet, and the son feels his own stomach tighten. He says, "I don't want any more supper," and starts to leave the table. Mother says, "You sit right there till we're all finished." The father says, "Let him go, for God's sake. Do you have to run everybody's life like you run mine?" The evening ends with the boy in his room, depressed; the father watching TV in silence; and the mother furiously washing dishes.

The next day the boy complains that he has had an attack of nausea and cannot go to school; in fact, he throws up. The parents fight about whether or not he should be made to go to school. In the end he stays home. This is the beginning of a fine school phobia. Two months later, having tried everything and on the advice of the school, the parents start looking for a psychotherapist.

What the psychotherapist decides falls outside the lines of this story. But a contextual reading of the situation would be to perceive that the boy's appropriate behavior in going to school was not rewarded. Instead there were intimations of catostrophe (parental discord, father's illness). The polarization of views—permissiveness versus punitive action, increased—with the boy's symptom now at the center maintaining these parental behaviors and being

maintained by them in a self-perpetuating loop. This bind evidently cannot be resolved by a creative leap, such as the boy's falling in love (an involuntary act that could be seen as an appropriate response to a simple bind—"he" did not decide to go back to school; "falling in love" is what decided it). In fact the hints of catastrophe redouble when the boy mentions that he has met a wonderful girl. The leap that should be made is invalidated by the context, not by any one villain: it is messages from the people who make up his context that covertly frame his eventual departure as a betrayal, a harmful thing, possibly even a murder. One can even see the school phobia turning into something more serious. The boy hears "voices" telling him that he is the son of God and is destined to save the world, and that his mission requires that he stay in his room and write a long book that describes his new understanding of the meaning of the universe.

To summarize, a theory of discontinuous change suggests that there will be no way to avoid the period of stress and disruption that is the prelude to what we have called a transformation. A common feature of these periods is the type of message known as the paradoxical injunction, or, using different terminology, a simple bind. The double bind only results when this simple bind is negated or denied, so that the necessary pressure for the transformation or leap cannot take place. In such a case, one might expect a symptom to arise that expresses both the family's need for change and the prohibition against it. Since family structures are under most pressure to change at natural transition points, it is no surprise that most symptoms occur at these times. The knowledgeable clinician or student of family life will know that these behaviors are expectable concomitants of family change. He or she will seek to disrupt the homeostatic sequence that forms about a symptom, so that pressure for change will be allowed to build and a transformation will take place that makes the presence of a symptom unnecessary.

REFERENCES

Ashby, W. R. (1960). *Design for a brain*. London: Chapman & Hall, Science Paperbacks.
Bateson, G. (1972). Steps to an ecology of mind. New York: Ballantine Books.
Bateson, G. (1978). *Mind and nature*. New York: Dutton.
Dell, P., & Goolishian H. (1979). Order through fluctuation: An evolutionary epistemology for human systems. Paper presented at the annual scientific meeting of the A. K. Rice Institute, Houston, Texas.
Erickson, E. (1963). *Childhood and society*. New York: Norton.
Gramsci, A. ( )*Prison notebooks*.
Haley, J. (1973). The family life cycle. In *Uncommon therapy: The psychiatric techniques of Milton Erickson, M.D.* New York: Norton.
Hill, R. L., & Hansen, D. A. (1960). The identification of conceptual frameworks utilized in family study. *Marriage and Family Living* 22:299–311.
Holmes, T. H., & Rahe, R. H. (1967). The social readjustment rating scale. *Journal of Psychosomatic Research* 2:213–28.

Lindemann, E. (1969). Symptomatology and management of acute grief. In H.J., Parad & G. Caplan, (Eds.), *Crisis intervention: Selected readings*. New York: Family Service Association of America.

Platt, J. (1970). Hierarchical growth. *Bulletin of Atomic Scientists*.

Rabkin, R. (1976). A critique of the clinical use of the double bind. In E. C. Sluzki & D. C. Ransom (Eds.), *Double bind: The foundation of the communicational approach to the family*. New York: Grune & Stratton.

Bateson, G. (1972). Steps to an ecology of mind. New York: Ballantine Books.

Wynne, L. (1976). On the anguish and creative passions of not escaping the double bind. In C. Sluzki & D. Ransom (Eds.), *Double bind: The communicational approach to the family*. New York: Grune & Stratton.

CHAPTER 5

Family Life Cycle Issues in the Therapy System

Robert M. Simon, M.D.

Family therapists usually talk and write as though they were the outside observers of self-contained family systems, but there are two circumstances that give the lie to this illusion of objectivity: supervision and clinical failure. Both experiences are necessary in professional development, and they force us to ponder a more complex system: *family plus therapist*. From this perspective we must consider not one but two life cycles, our own and the family's. Their combination bodes good or ill for efforts at making a change.

How the two life cycles combine is an important part of what I will call *fit* between therapist and family. Fit, admittedly an inexact term, covers all those elements of personal style, wisdom, charisma, and resourcefulness that give a therapist the edge in introducing change to stuck systems. It is related to the familiar concept of joining (Minuchin, 1974), because both address the essential connection of the therapist with the family. But unlike joining, fit does not have an action or a value connotation. You do not perform fit, it happens. Thus relevant questions in relation to joining (Did you do it? How do you do it?) cannot be applied to fit. One might only ask, "What is the nature of the [inevitable] fit?"

Fit is nonlinear. Unlike technique, which should improve over time, fit keeps changing according to the therapist's life experience and is also different with each client family. For example, suppose a young therapist encounters a midlife couple with a problem adolescent. The therapist's age and life experience are relatively (though not entirely) unimportant in describing the family's dysfunctional interaction. Fit, on the other hand, may play a large role in the therapist's credibility with the family, and also in the scope and power of the intervention strategies. In this instance the fact that the therapist never brought up a teenager is the most obvious issue, but not the only one. The fit will also be influenced by the therapist's adolescent experience with the therapist's own parents, by the experience of siblings, and, in fact, by all of the past family rules and expectations that for the therapist surround the notion of adolescence.

Child rearing is not the only track on which these issues run. Gender, for example, makes a major contribution to normal life experience, so the fit of a male therapist with a family is different from that of a female. Similarly, nonpathological but shaping experiences such as divorce, parent or sibling death, or physical disability may also influence fit in a profound way. All of this may be invisible in the "objective" formulation the therapist makes of the family problem.

Supervision adds yet another level of fit, isomorphic to that between therapist and family; moves within the family-plus-therapist system will be influenced by the family-plus-therapist-plus-supervisor system. Usually this is a positive influence because it rebalances situations where the fit between therapist and family is unproductive. McGoldrick (1982) explored this issue in what she called a "trigger family." She reported the immobilization of a trainee when confronted with a family avoiding the issue of the mother's cancer. This therapist's mother had died of cancer, and in his family of origin the subject had been taboo.

As a rough first approximation, we can assume that the life cycles of therapist and family can combine in three major ways: (1) The therapist has not yet experienced the family's stage: (2) The therapist is currently experiencing the same stage of the life cycle as the family: (3) The therapist has already been through that stage of the life cycle. Each situation has its special flavor.

THERAPIST NOT YET AT THE FAMILY'S STAGE OF THE LIFE CYCLE

I referred before to the young therapist who fits with the older family through memories of his or her own childhood and adolescence. Children like these therapists, but their rapport can have its limitations. In my early days as a family therapist an irate mother yelled at me, "Why don't they have a law against *parent* abuse?" At that moment she was reacting to the warmth I felt and showed toward her difficult son. Our fit was such that I understood his feelings much better than I did hers. My response to this attractive brat would be very different today after having raised my own children, and, also, after having achieved some understanding of my own parents' struggles. (And at the time I treated that family, a woman supervisor of mature years would have been very helpful.)

John, a 28-year-old psychologist, was supervised by a colleague via videotape. The family consisted of a couple in their 40s with two teenage daughters, the older of whom had been threatened with expulsion from school for cutting class repeatedly. The mother berated her daughter and the young therapist intervened several times to defend the daughter. As he finally made

several attempts to get the focus of discussion off the daughter, the other girl made some thinly veiled suggestions that the father was seeing another woman. John completely ignored those comments and returned to the problem of the older daughter's school behavior. He then gave the parents patronizing advice on dealing with their daughter and with the school.

In the supervisory discussion, John realized that he had sided with the daughter against her parents, particularly the mother, and he readily traced this to his reactivity to his own mother. What astounded him, however, was that he had neither heard nor understood the comments of the younger girl until the supervisor pointed them out and replayed the videotape.

Asked whether this blind spot was related in some way to his own family, John reported that his parents had separated briefly when he was about 15. They had given him no specific explanation of that event or of their subsequent reconciliation, but John had suspected that his father was having an affair.

Shaken by the impact of this almost-forgotten incident on his work, John was motivated to spend more time talking with each of his parents, clarifying family history and working on various personal issues in his relationship with them. With periodic coaching in the supervisory group, John identified and worked on many problems that had prevented his understanding his parents and how they came to be who they were. Eventually he discovered that his father had not actually had an affair, but by that time the issue was among the least important on his agenda. His work with older families improved appreciably through the ensuing year.

In another instance a young, unmarried woman trainee interviewed a middle-aged couple on the verge of divorce. The therapist acted curt, scattered, and cold toward the couple. One of the other trainees remarked, "I don't know what's gotten into her; she is usually so much better than this." Another colleague offered the information that the therapist's father was divorcing for the second time. An angry plague-on-both-your-houses child had (temporarily, as it turned out) emerged on encountering a new set of disappointing adults.

THERAPIST IS IN THE SAME STAGE OF THE LIFE CYCLE AS THE FAMILY

Any stage of life transition is apt to be full of pain and upheaval, and therapists can easily empathize with a family going through something that they are experiencing themselves. They are not likely to pathologize the situation unnecessarily since they know it from personal experience. On the other hand, there may simply be too many emotional triggers for the therapist to handle. How these are dealt with, of course, depends on the particular therapist. Some defend themselves with blind spots so that important issues

are overlooked. Some therapists may show reactive contempt for the family, especially notable when the case is discussed with colleagues.

The therapist may react with anxiety or jealousy to the family's attempted solution to a problem. Suppose that in living through the late-adolescent-child phase of the life cycle, a mother and son have moved closer to each other. They connect with a male therapist whose teenage relationship with his own mother was based on avoidance, but whose wife is struggling to stay close to her own children. This therapist may condemn mother–son closeness as unhealthy, "too oedipal", etc. The mother's value as a mentor and as a model for later conjugal relationship is devalued. (Note how gender creeps in at this point. More on this below.) Another example of therapist reactivity might be seen when a midlife couple experiments with a sexually "open marriage". If this arrangement were something the therapist had been attracted to but had failed to achieve, he or she might denounce it as sick or avoid the issue altogether. In any case the therapist's rage, boredom, or helplessness often indicates that a personal wound has been opened, and therapists would be well advised to heal it in their own families rather than react to it in their work.

Special issues in the therapist's life cycle may interfere with his or her work with certain families in therapy. Suppose that a therapist's parents had divorced in their late 40s and the therapist now encounters midlife marital difficulties. He or she may be unduly pessimistic as to whether marital issues can be resolved at this phase and so may remain stuck with some families. Supervisors often observe that major disruption in the family life cycle patterns of the therapist (early deaths, prolonged illnesses, divorce, remarriage, etc.) turn out to be the basis for difficulty in responding to these processes in client families.

This is not to say that having lived through these events is always a negative factor in one's career as a therapist. On the contrary, a successful resolution of the traumatic event (or self-differentiation in Bowen's terms) may lead to understanding and empathy that patients find valuable—a special sort of fit through linked personal tragedies. The development of this resource in trainees can be a unique gift of the supervisory experience.

THERAPIST IS PAST THE FAMILY'S STAGE IN THE LIFE CYCLE

Fit with families gets a little easier as you get older. A therapist who has already lived through some of the trials the family has can be very understanding. Family members feel that older therapists recognize their problem immediately. They are not fazed by it, and have a good fund of anecdotes based on personal experience. The older therapist shows the family that the situation is

basically normal, not pathological. Work with this therapist is, at some unverbalized level, *reassuring.*

John and Terry, a couple in their early 30s, sought help after seven years of marriage. At that time they had two sons age three and one (the children were not included in treatment). I was then 41 and had a teenager and a 10-year-old.

The initial complaint was one of severe marital discord that had only become worse during a period of individual psychotherapy for Terry. The couple was locked into a pattern of mutual blaming, especially over money. His chief weapon was to withhold; hers was to patronize him with psychological expertise, particularly regarding his relationship with the children.

In the first phase of treatment, each presented a "case" as though we were in court. The problem of fit was especially significant at this time because the difficulty of establishing it with the husband was exactly matched by the ease with which it could be established with the wife. Terry was always ready to accept my least opinion as Gospel and to lecture John on the wisdom of my statements. John did not relate easily to another man to begin with, and Terry's unquestioning acceptance of me usually provoked him to a jealous put-down. Therefore, I made a concerted effort to establish a sense of trust between John and me. At the same time, Terry was encouraged to develop her own ideas and to outdo me in understanding herself and her family.

All of this was work for a midlife therapist. My age and professional status were assets in engaging John's interest in an alliance; I think he might have been contemptuous of a younger therapist. I also suspect that, at a younger age, I would have had considerably more difficulty playing dumb. This is not to say that a younger therapist could not have treated the couple, but merely that our particular fit allowed for certain strategies to be brought into play.

Postscript

The couple returned six years later because Terry had decided to divorce John. It became clear during the discussion that the situation was irrevocable, and they were warming up to a bitter custody fight as a metaphorical "antidote" for John's sense of helplessness. Their view of the therapist from the first round of treatment made it possible to intervene with authority, and brief therapy helped them to let go without a pointless and destructive battle. The success of the therapy partly turned on the couple's looking upon me like an elder member of their family.

Finding oneself at a life cycle stage beyond that of the family can have pitfalls as well. Therapists who have had a difficult time in a past stage of the life cycle may find that working with a particular family opens the door on ghosts and ancient curses of their own. In self-defense they may become distant, cynical, or patronizing. They may act as though only their solutions can work for the family, or in other instances convey the feeling that nothing

will work at all. Still another danger is that the therapist will seem too knowledgeable. The family members, or at least the parents, may then abandon their own resources and fall back on trying to imitate the expert. These families want to hang on to therapy forever because life keeps presenting new problems and they always need the therapist's formulas for solving them. Here, too, the therapist has become a family member, but the relationship is one of covert fusion. As with all fusions, reactive cutoff is waiting in the wings. At some point the well of infallibility runs dry and an embittered family now turns against the former guru.

OTHER LIFE CYCLE ISSUES

The first edition of *The Family Life Cycle* made it clear that there are many crucial issues in the natural history of families, not just the central ones of partnering and rearing children. Sickness, death, divorce, and even economics may also powerfully influence the course of family life. There has begun to be some speculation as to whether the nuclear threat poses a subtle warping effect on the normal expectations of the life cycle (Simon, 1984). These are no less meaningful for the therapist than the partnering/parenting issues stressed up to this point.

The relationship between the sexes, however, is of special interest because it touches so directly on all of the other issues, and because of its variation through the family life cycle. Women have generally been the plaintiffs in marital and family work; when the men are the plaintiffs, they are usually griping about how the women express their complaints (sexual unresponsiveness, in particular). Since my career has already spanned a good piece of the adult life cycle (20 years), I was curious to see whether my clinical attitudes had changed over time, and I went back to clinical notes from 12 to 15 years ago. I found that the purely technical level of observation had not changed much, except that I am now more inclined to formulate cases around systemic shifts rather than around assessment of character. What seems most different today is my formulations about women.

Notes on a Depressed Woman and Her Husband in 1969

Much detail about the depressive phenomenology, then a paragraph about husband.

Affable, overly-smiling man who seems to deny anger and resentment. Tends to see her as the irrational patient, himself as reasonable. Has premature ejaculation, yet portrays himself as without any neurotic problems.

At first conjoint session:

He immediately jumps into their sex life, since last night was a typical example of premature ejaculation, guilt, and her getting depressed. He is [compulsively] orgasm-oriented while she is more interested in the closeness of foreplay.

At a later session:

He sent her to the bank three times this week and she is furious: He is supposed to be in charge of that. Is she reenacting her relationship with her father?

Notes on a Family in 1971:

Parents come because of problems with C., their 12-year-old daughter, a gawky and overgrown girl who contrasts with her physically "perfect" and highly prized younger brother. Father is boyish, somewhat infantile. Mother a bit masculine, controlling in a subtle way. Feels anxious because she is two years older than husband.

Second session a few weeks later:

They have changed in an important way. She no longer colludes with him on their 'ideal marriage'. Feels she's always walking on eggshells with him, afraid to speak her mind. She told his mother off many years ago but now feels maybe it was he that she was angry at. He then proceeded to disqualify her, criticizing her choice of words, saying she's not really that upset, why make things worse, etc. There are several hints of a sexual problem.

What strikes me in looking back over these vignettes is not whatever advances I may have made in diagnosis and intervention, but my consistent failure to associate the woman's emotional state, including her sexual responsiveness, with her lack of power in the family. These were women with large responsibilities for their homes and children, for remaining attractive to their husbands, for advancing their husband's careers, and so on. Yet they could experience real power in one area only—raising the children. If this was not enough for them, or if it became not enough, or if the job one day was finally finished, they had no power base. This was ignored in the psychiatric and family therapy literature of the time. When these women became depressed, conventional clinical wisdom either linked the depression to their loss of reproductive capacity or in some way defined their symptoms as being of their own making. Only in the last few years have feminist writers in the family field introduced power realities into our theoretical models (Hare-Mustin, 1978; Hess-Biber & Williamson, 1984).

Although like most men I probably have a long way to go on this issue, I think that my attitude toward women's problems has changed greatly with advancing years. The continued vitality of the woman's movement has of course played an important role in this, and I have had the good fortune to be associated with powerful and articulate women in the workplace. But I have also encountered these issues in a three-woman/one-man household, and when it comes to learning about family matters, it is sometimes small events that count the most.[1]

When she began working parttime as a teacher's aide, my wife suggested that she open her own bank account. Almost by reflex I began to challenge this

---

[1] I include this anecdote not as an exercise in self-congratulation but as an example of how small life experiences shape one's therapeutic posture.

idea—there was so little money involved; we had never had any conflict over spending decisions, I would have to pay all the taxes, and so on. In retrospect I realize that her proposal made me uneasy in some way: Was this a prelude to abandonment?

Later each of us achieved a fuller insight into our motivations at the time: She realized that it was intensely important to her to have money that she alone controlled, no matter what the dollar amount. I realized that some of my resistance had been just because she suggested the idea, and I did not like her having better ideas than I did. We then found the same issue emerging in chance discussions with friends and relatives: In most of these families, the wives work but time and again they remarked that the husband had refused to allow them to have their own bank accounts. These couples usually consider themselves happily married but the financial issues are openly resented by the women. At the same time, they feel powerless to change it. Apparently many still operate under the family rules of an earlier day: a woman's role is to support her bread-winning husband, not to challenge him.

The lack of personal power underlies many of the complaints women have in their home lives, and a lot of men's resistance to change is based upon their lack of understanding the issue, as well as on their reluctance to share power. Men are acculturated to think that (1) power is essential to masculinity and (2) women need taking care of. On both counts they do not see why their wives should be so unhappy, as long as they are being provided for. In my own struggle through the life cycle, I have come to center a lot of marital therapy around that balance of power, but it is clear that therapists of different gender, age, and experience might view the issues in different ways. Suppose that older female therapist meets a young family with some version of this issue. She might be angered by the young husband's chauvinism or by the way his wife falls for it. Or a young male therapist meeting the same couple might fail to connect to the wife's sense of complaint and vague depression. These elements in the fit can be subtle and may not be apparent to the supervisor unless therapy sessions are viewed "live."

WHEN THE LIFE CYCLES DO NOT FIT WELL

There are a few general suggestions that may be helpful to family therapists who find themselves in a poor fit between the family's stage of life and their own. The most overarching recommendation is the rigorous study of one's own family of origin, which has been accorded a separate section. In addition to that major undertaking, the following four issues are worthy of consideration.

Choice of Stance

It does not make sense for a young therapist meeting an older family to adopt a one-up stance ("I'm the expert"). It is equally ludicrous for an older therapist to be too one-down ("You're the experts"). The former therapist will be dismissed as arrogant and the latter as ineffectual. Changing a system can be done from many angles as long as there is a workable fit.

Choice of Model

This is a closely related issue because different models of therapy emphasize different stances. For instance, Bowen and Milan models emphasize a neutral therapist who operates through questions and through a lively research interest in the family system. Structural therapy, on the other hand, requires more charismatic leadership; if a young therapist is dealing with an older family, or a female therapist with a tyrannical father, there may not be enough authority to give the family restructuring tasks. In training, choice of model is usually determined by the philosophy of the institute, but the limitation of choice is compensated for by the support of the supervisor.

Supervisor

Private supervision is a venerable institution in all psychotherapies and is also to be commended for family therapists beyond the training years. For reasons already discussed in this chapter, the supervisor should be chosen not just on the basis of clinical experience but also with an eye toward complementing the life experience of the supervisee. In this regard there is a lot to be said for male therapists seeking female supervisors.

Networking

Even the ideally chosen supervisor is limited to a session every so often and on a necessarily restricted number of cases. Another kind of supervision is experienced when professional life allows therapists to interact with colleagues of varying ages, gender, ethnicity, and sexual orientation. Seeing the clinical world through other people's lenses is like living parts of the life cycle that fate has not decided to award to you personally.

STUDY OF THE THERAPIST'S FAMILY OF ORIGIN

This chapter has emphasized that fit between therapist and family is sometimes a training and self-educational issue. Psychoanalytic institutes have always recognized the need for therapists to undergo their own explorations through the training analysis. The analog in family therapy is the study of one's own family characterized by Murray Bowen (1978) as a complex research enterprise. Its goal is to understand the network of family rules and expectations under which each of us has been socialized, which is not a far cry from the goals of the training analysis. Its method, however, is far different, emphasizing active discussions with family members rather than the development of transference to the therapist.

At this stage in the history of family therapy there is nothing new in recommending that therapists study their own families, but only the Bowen school makes this research integral to training and supervision. Other approaches to family therapy may utilize family-of-origin research when a trainee is stuck with a particular family, but there is no general provision for this work in the training sequence. That, in turn, implies that the supervisors or other instructors may not be trained in how to assist professionals in conducting such research. If one is not in training in a Bowen-based institute, or not in training at all, it can be difficult to find the proper assistance. (The assistance, by the way, is not always a complex matter: I recall being stuck on a painful family issue from the past and was greatly helped when Bowen told me to be patient and not lose heart. Eventually he proved to be right.)

Bowen has emphasized the work of Walter Toman (1969) on sibling position and its organizing influence on the personality. This is also a life cycle issue because the influence of sibling position upon one's expectations of self and other has not, in my experience, been as fixed as Toman seems to imply. Each new epoch in life seems to bring a reassessment and reorganization of these influences. My own "hand of cards," as Toman calls it, is heavily junior. I am a youngest child, and so were both of my parents. Both my parents and I also related most directly to an older sister. My wife, too, is well practiced in juniority as the sister of an older brother. Our typical marital conflict is not a clash of wills but a silent struggle to get the other one to take charge. Until the time I had investigated the ramifications of juniority and its typical combinations in marriage to other juniors, to seniors, and so on, I had no model against which to judge some of the marital conflicts that presented themselves in my office. I did note that I was most uncomfortable with openly battling seniors, and I tended also to be easily intimidated, despite a professional façade, by belligerent men.

For me the investigation of family-of-origin issues involved not only specific bruising events that had transpired in my youth but also an appreciation of how juniority and seniority had been experienced in both families. As a result I

became more able to take charge of certain situations, and was able to depathologize both my patients' actions and my own responses to them. For example, I could now see myself shrinking from conflict with some patients whereas previously I had found a rationalization or else had counterphobically insisted on a confrontation. At the same time, my relationship with women became less a vacillation between accepting everything they had to say versus "cutting them down to size." Since juniority and gender can never change, this is one of those issues that, as Bowen says, will be the work of a lifetime. All in all, research on the family of origin plays the same role for therapists that a Chopin etude does for a pianist: It is a tremendously interesting experience in itself, and it leaves you in a better place for having tackled it.

REFERENCES

Bowen, M. (1978), *Family therapy in clinical practice*. New York: Jason Aronson, Chaps. 21 and 22.

Hare-Mustin, R. (1978), A feminist approach to family therapy. *Family Process* 17:181–194.

Hess-Biber, S., & Williamson, J. (1984) Resource theory and power in families: Life cycle considerations. *Family Process* 23:261–278.

McGoldrick, M. (1982), Through the looking-glass: Supervision of a trainee's 'trigger' family. In *J. Byng-Hall & R. Whiffen, eds, Family Therapy Supervision*. London: Academic Press.

Minuchin, S. (1974). *Families and family therapy*. Cambridge, Mass.: Harvard University Press, Chap. 7.

Simon, R. (1984). The nuclear family. *Family Networker* 8:22–27.

Toman, W. (1969). *Family constellation*. New York: Springer.

CHAPTER 6

Systems and Ceremonies: A Family View of Rites of Passage

Edwin H. Friedman, M.A.

Rites of passage are usually associated with emotionally critical moments of life. Yet most studies of these ceremonies have tended to ignore the crucial role of the family at such events. The convention in the social sciences has been to place primary focus on the culture that provides the rites or on the individuals who are being passed through to a new stage in their life cycle. The role of the family on such occasions has tended to be seen as secondary, as occupying more of an intermediary position between the individual members to be passed and society. From this perspective the family participates in the customs provided by a culture as a way of helping its members take their new position in that culture.

Twenty years of experience as a clergyman and family therapist have given me an almost totally different perception of the role of families in rites of passage. I have found that the family, far from being an intermediary, is the primary force operating at such moments—primary not only in that it, and not the culture, determines the emotional quality of such occasions (and therefore the success of the passage), but also in that it is the family more than the culture that ultimately determines which rites are to be used. Families are far less determined by their culture's customs and ways of doing things than they are selective, according to their own characteristics and pathology, of their culture's ceremonial repertoire. Though, of course, the family will always say, "That's just the way we (Jews, Catholics, Fijis, Aborigines) have always done things (at our weddings, funerals, baptisms, bar mitzvas)." (See also Friedman 1982).

Indeed, so central is the role of family process in rites of passage that it is probably correct to say it is really the family that is making the transition to a new stage of life at such a time rather than any "identified member" focused upon during the occasion.

What may be most significant, however, in switching one's primary focus to the family is that it enables one to see the enormous therapeutic potential inherent in natural family crises. The one phenomenon that has stood out in

my experience with families of all cultures is that the periods surrounding rites of passage function as "hinges of time."

All family relationship systems seem to unlock during the months before and after such events, and it is often possible to open doors (or close them) between various family members with less effort during these intensive periods than could ordinarily be achieved with years of agonizing efforts.

I believe this is true because, with respect to timing, life cycle events are not as random as they appear. Rather they are usually the coming to fruition or culmination of family processes that have been moving toward those ends for some time. Life cycle events are always part of "other things going on." They always indicate movement, and it is simply easier to steer a ship when it is afloat, even if it is drifting in the wrong direction, than when it is still aground.

It will be the purpose of this chapter to strip away the cultural camouflage of rites of passage and to show how family process operates at emotionally significant moments of life cycle change. I will try to show how the time periods surrounding such moments are particularly useful for observing family process in the raw. I will give examples from my own experience to show how members of the helping professions may use a family understanding of rites of passage to turn the crisis always inherent in those events into an opportunity for beneficial change.

The ideas and examples that will be illustrated come out of 20 years of continuous experience in one community (the Washington metropolitan area) as both rabbi and family therapist. Over these two decades, my dual role enabled me to pass perceptions back and forth between positions as in each role I was able to gain a vantage point not usually available to individuals functioning in only one role. For example, my continuous experience in one community often gave me the opportunity to observe the same family throughout an entire generation. As their clergyman I often gained intimate knowledge of that family, not only at important nodal points and rites of passage themselves, but also as I observed the changes that took place between those events. And, of course, all of these observations were informed by what I was learning about family process from my general family therapy experience. Similarly, since my therapy experience has always been ecumenical, and since Washington is a "Mecca" nationally and internationally, I was given an opportunity to observe families of many different cultures and backgrounds intimately. That experience enabled me to realize that what I had been observing among Jewish families had universal application. Eventually I found I could quite successfully extrapolate the insights I had obtained from the rabbinic experience with the life cycle to families I was counseling about other problems, no matter what their cultural background.

The framework of this chapter will be to explore three natural life cycle events (death, marriage, pubescence), and then to comment on three nodal events that are less a natural part of the life cycle and more a creation of the times in which we live (divorce, retirement, geographical uprooting).

Before beginning that process, however, I would like to note briefly three

myths that inhibit forming a family process view of rites of passage and four principles about the relationship of family process to rites of passage that are basic to my conceptualization.

THREE MYTHS THAT INHIBIT FORMING A
FAMILY PROCESS VIEW

Three myths about life that inhibit the development of a family process view of rites of passage are that (1) the family is breaking down; (2) culture determines family process in fundamental ways; and (3) the rite of passage is the same as the ceremony that celebrates it.

The Breakdown of the Family

The notion that the family is "breaking" down is supported by the higher divorce rates and by the greater physical distance between relatives in our highly mobile society. However, nodal events in family life have an absolutely transporting quality, and are able to transcend great distances of gulfs, as can be seen by the presence of family members who come from a distance to attend funerals, weddings, or bar mitzvas. Sometimes only one or two individuals come from another area of the country, but they are there to represent that part of the clan. On the other hand, sometimes it works the other way, of course, and relatives who were expected to come do not, citing the physical distance or the climate as their defense. But whichever the case, it seems important to point out that no correlation necessarily exists between the degree of physical distance or frequency of previous communication between family members and whether they appear at a given family ritual. One member will have trouble getting a car out of the garage to drive 20 miles, and another will, on finding the local airport snowed in, drive 150 miles through a blizzard to another airport. Nor can one always predict, based on previous relationships, who will do what. There is also no correlation between the distance family members have to travel and their punctuality at the ceremony and, in fact, this may be in an inverse ratio.

It is possible, of course, to say that all this is proof of the breakdown of the family and the underlying need for family relationships. It may not be accidental, however, as to who appears at which event. In any case the therapeutic potential inherent in bringing family members together at life cycle events should not be discounted because of distance. A better metaphor for the present state of family life might be to say that the family has gone "underground," and nothing will coax various parts of it to surface at a rite of passage. The umbilical cord is infinitely elastic.

I have involved clients in overseas travel and overnight communication that involved three continents, and found that even after decades, the buried system is very much alive.

There is another reason for not confusing physical distance with emotional potential. One cannot assue that the members of a family who are most distant from home base are those who are necessarily most independent, or least reactive, emotionally. On the contrary, often they are the members of the family who most needed physical distance in order to relate with any independence at all to the family members back home.

For example, a woman has been maintaining an adaptive mode of relating to her critical husband in order to keep peace. She is visited by a sister whose presence makes her feel less alone, or, the opposite, by a mother whose dependency requires a lot of thought and emotional energy. In either case the homeostasis of her marriage will be upset and the husband, feeling the withdrawal of emotional energy, now perceives his wife to be less cooperative or less attentive and becomes more critical than ever. Actually I have found it a general rule of thumb that when one marriage partner is visited by relatives, the other often becomes more reactive during the stay. It is particularly those relationships held together by distance, so to speak, that will surface with all their original intensity at family get-togethers. In addition, what often had been enabling such relationships to maintain great distance was that each family member correspondingly compensated by investing more emotion into nearby relationships, as with a spouse, while cutting off the extended family. When the originally intense relationship comes alive, the energy now drawn away from the spouse is sensed immediately, thus creating problems "at home."

Such phenomena can occur at any family get-together, and probably help explain much of the increased anxiety around Christmas. (See the comparison in family process terms between Christmas and bar mitzva around the issues of drinking, gift giving, and suicide rates.) But at family rituals that are associated with nodal events in the life cycle, the whole emotional energy system is higher to begin with, and thus they are prime times for the confluence and redirection of intensity. It may be more correct to say, therefore, that the major breakdown that occurs during rites of passage is not the family but the family's defense of physical distance.

Culture Determines Family Process

In 1970 I delivered a paper at the Georgetown Family Therapy Symposium entitled "Culture and Family Process." It was the thesis of this work that rather than determining family life in any significant way, culture was more the projection of family process on a societal level. I proposed that to try to understand family life through its customs and ceremonies was, therefore, circular reasoning. The new metaphor I suggested was that "culture is the medium through which family process works its art."

I tried to show that although a strict Catholic family, a rigid Methodist family, or an orthodox Jewish family might claim they are only following their religion when they observe all the customs of their background in the proper way, no culture has general agreement among its leaders as to what is right. Obviously one can often find other families from the same culture, if not members of the same family, who do it differently.

What seems to happen in family life is that individuals and families adhere most closely to those values that coincide with their own life style. Every religious tradition and cultural background has its own neurotic usefulness.[1]

There are some crucially important ramifications of this reversal in conceptualizing how family and culture influence one another. The first is that it gets the therapist out of the middle—between the client and the client's background—when issues come up about rituals or ceremonies, and the client says, "I can't do that because it's against my tradition." Such questions as "Do all the members of your faith do it that way?" or "Do all the ministers of your religion agree with yours on that issue?" can open the door. Sometimes one can go the other way and ask, "How does it happen that you are so strict (orthodox or observant) about this particular religious or cultural matter when you do not follow so many other basic tenents of your faith?" For example, to a woman contemplating divorce: "Well, I can understand your decision never to marry again, as a good Catholic, but how did you decide to go against the Church on birth control?" It is not important whether they can make fine theological distinctions, but that they take responsibility for their decisions and thus make themselves the final judge of who is to be judge.

It might be objected: "That won't be true on all issues; no orthodox Jew would ever sanction a mixed marriage, nor would a strict Catholic sanction marriage to a divorced person." First of all, that is not my experience. Again, as with physical distance correlations, so loyalty to tradition correlations do not seem to hold true when dealing with the complexities of family emotional systems at life cycle events. Beyond that, however, what is important is not the position individuals take at such times but how they function with that position. Even if it were true that an orthodox Jew is more likely to object to a mixed marriage, or an observant Catholic to marriage to a divorcee, the intensity with which they react is another matter, and that tells much about the family and their position in it. For example, an objection simply stated as such, or even a refusal to go to an event because it is against one's principles, can be understood as a definition of position. On the other hand, cutting off, disinheriting, constant harassment, or heavy interference have nothing to do with cultural values and traditions, even though the family members acting that way

---

[1] In ethnic families it is almost impossible for a child growing up to distinguish a feeling about his or her family from a feeling about his or her ethnic background. I have tried to show elsewhere that commitment to tradition has nothing to do with marrying outside that tradition. In any ethnic family, the child marrying out is the child most important to the balance of the parents' relationship. See "Ethnic Identity as Extended Family in Jewish-Christian Marriage," delivered at the Fifth Georgetown Family Therapy Symposium. November 196, published in *Systems Therapy,* edited by Bradt and Moynihan, 1971.

may claim they are defending the faith. The roots of that kind of fanaticism will always be found in that family member's unworked-out relationships with the family of origin. (See discussion on weddings.)

It is just not possible to keep this kind of focus on family process clear as long as one assumes that family members' behavior is determined by, rather than selective of, cultural background. Actually, to the extent that one can keep this focus clear, two other benefits accrue. First, it probably means that every time family members give a cultural explanation for why they do or cannot do something, that cultural explanation at precisely that moment, far from being the enlightening comment it appears, is probably a denial of family process. Therefore, rather than dutifully writing it down as one more significant datum, the therapist should recognize such an explanation as a warning light—an indication of where those persons are stuck in their own family.

That second benefit that comes with keeping one's focus on family process is that culture and custom can then be used as a tracer element for getting a better reading on family members' relationships with one another. Take, for example, five grown siblings in their 50s or older, only one of whom keeps kosher, or only one of whom is still a pillar of the local parish. You may safely hypothesize that he or she was the child stuck with responsibility for Momma's memory.

Noting such clues can often be helpful in understanding why certain family members are functioning the way they are during any rite of passage.

Ceremony Is the Rite of Passage

The third myth that inhibits a family view of rites of passage is the assumption that the ceremony is the rite of passage. After all, some individuals are married long before the ceremony, and some never do leave home. Some family members are buried long before they expire and some remain around to haunt for years, if not generations. This myth has a corollary, which is that the members of the family who are the focus of the ceremony are the only ones who are going through the passage. The whole family goes through the passage at nodal events in the life cycle, and the passage often begins months before and ends months after the ceremony.

Ceremonies celebrate. From an emotional systems point of view, they are not in themselves efficacious. Rather, their effect is determined by what has already been developing within the emotional system of the family. Ceremonies do focus the events, however, in that they bring family members into conscious contact with one another and in that they bring processes to a head.

On the one hand, therefore, the celebration event itself can be a very useful occasion for meeting people, for putting people together, for reestablishing relationships, for learning about the family (both by observation and by the hearing of tales), for creating transitions, as in leadership, or for the opportu-

nity to function outside or against one's normal role—getting "looped," for example, when one has always been expected to be the sober one.

On the other hand, my experience with rites of passage suggests that the more important time for becoming involved with one's family is in the months before and after the celebration, using the event more as an excuse for reentry. Though, naturally, the more one prepares the soil before the celebration, the richer the harvest will be at the event itself.

For example, it would be nice to use the state of flux in a family system usually present at a funeral to bring a brother and sister into verbal communication again. But this is more likely to happen at the funeral if one initiates communication with each of them while the family member to be buried is dying.

Perhaps the most important point to be made about distinguishing the ceremony from the passage is that the potential for change that I have found near nodal family events could not be that great if the event were just the event.

The notion feeds back into itself. If you can get things going right before any given ceremony, then all the natural healing processes that ageold traditions have captured in their rites of passage will take over, and at the celebration, do much of your work for you. Elsewhere I have been developing this theme for clergy of all faiths, suggesting that an awareness of family process can enable a minister to draw on the natural strengths in families to enrich religious experience. The idea is not to psychologize religion. Rather the thesis is that when clergymen facilitate the meaningful involvement of family members at life cycle ceremonies, they are in fact allowing natural healing processes to flow, and doing what religion had always intuited but what modern times has come to be called therapy.[2]

As I often put it to couples worried about relatives' opinions: if the family relationship is not operating pathologically, and this marriage is no more than a routine upset of the balance of your family system, then you could even include a ritual murder as part of the wedding and everyone would still probably walk out commenting, "Wasn't that a lovely wedding?" If, on the other hand, there are severe rifts in the family, or if the marriage is particularly disturbing to the balance of the parents' marriage, then it is a different matter. Then no amount of precaution about following customs and ceremonies properly will shield the couple from the infinite capacity that intensity harbors for the manufacture of criticism.

The logical conclusion to be drawn from this is that if you are worried about the length of your gown or the shape of the baptismal fount, go to work on the triangles with your parents. In fact, you may never have a better opportunity.

---

[2]I have expanded on the notion that mature traditions already are in touch with family process in "Enriching the Lifecycle Through Creative Family Participation," Draft 40 pp., 1977. Paper written for the Committee on Family Life of the Central Conference of American Rabbis. Presented to the full Conference, Toronto, June, 1978. See also section on pubescence—bar mitzva.

Giving up these myths leads to some very useful principles, which in turn lead to the observation of confirming patterns. For the other side of the notion that the rite of passage is more than the ceremony, and the individuals going through the passage are more than those identified with the ceremony, is the idea that rites of passage always indicate significant movement in a family system. Therefore, not only can a family approach to rites of passage make them smoother journeys, but the crises these events precipitate become golden opportunities for inducing change in otherwise stable dysfunctional relationship patterns. As mentioned earlier, family systems seem to unlock during these periods.

On the basis of my experience with families of many cultures, I would assert the following principles regarding rites of passage for families regardless of cultural background.

1. Rites of passage are family events that arise at the time they do because of emotional processes that have been at work in the nuclear and extended family of the member(s) who is (are) the focus of the ceremony.

2. The ceremony or the event itself reflects the fact that processes in the family have been undergoing change and are in a state of flux.

3. The ceremony and the time before and after it are therefore opportune periods for inducing change in the family system.

4. There seem to be certain "normal" time periods for the change and working through of emotional processes at times of life cycle transition, and attempts to hasten or shorten those periods unduly are always indications that there are important unresolved issues in the family relationship system.

This last principle leads to the observation of certain patterns. The incredible similarity in the way the first three principles appeared, no matter what the culture, made me realize I was observing something natural and organic to the human phenomenon. Then it became clear that a key to understanding families not only in the midst of a rite of passage, but at any time, was to note in the family history how the family had functioned at past rites of passage as per indication of the major issues in the family. While it is not possible to pinpoint the exact range of "normality," and here culture will affect the norms, enough of a range may be established to create a benchmark for judging the extremes.

In Table 6–1 are seven continua describing time periods around the rites of passage of marriage, birth, and divorce. The center column represents a range that, I have found most people fall within when they are objectively considering the decision to make a change. This is the benchmark period. It is not meant to be all-inclusive, and perhaps could be seen as a sliderule that might expand or contract between the extremes, depending on the culture. What is important is not how exact this column is but what it points to in each direction. On the basis of my experience, I would say that to the extent that members of a family come near those extremes, they are making decisions

Table 6–1

EXTREME	BENCHMARK PERIOD	EXTREME
1. Age when married		
teenage elopement	21–27	no marriage or mid-forties
2. Length of courtship		
		five years of going steady
love at first sight—10 days	6 months to 1 year	or living together
3. Length of engagement		
eloping right after decision	3–6 months	many years of putting it off
4. Time to birth of first child		
		childless for whatever
pregnancy before marriage	2–3 years	reason
5. Time between separation and divorce		
	1–2 years after legal	
attempt to hasten legal limits	limits	till death do us part
6. Time between separation from one mate and going steady with future mate		
affair with future mate	2–4 years	withdrawal, promiscuity
7. Time between divorce and remarriage		
same as examples 5 and 6	2–5 years	same as examples 5 and 6

from *The Curvature of Emotional Space*

more with their guts than with their heads and there are important unworked-out issues still to be resolved with the family of origin.

The table also suggests that the opposite extremes say something similar. I emphasize this because these opposite extremes may show up in different generations or different siblings, but reflect similar patterns.[3]

I am in no way saying, however, that families with members who fall on the extremes in one scale will necessarily fall on the extremes in the other scales. It is important to realize also that these continua should not be taken too literally. They are designed primarily to create a tool for gaining perspective and will be less specifically accurate at any given point along the line, though more generally accurate as one moves toward the extremes. (*Warning:* Anyone caught trying to rate himself or herself by means of these "scales" will be considered to have fallen off the ends completely.) While the scales still need refinement, I think the model may hold, even if it makes it appear that some families have members going through life holding one end of their umbilical cord in their hand, looking for someone else to plug it into, or the reverse, as when family members are unable to commit themselves to anyone.

What can be said about individuals who tend to operate near the extremes is that they come from families that have trouble elasticizing their rela-

---

[3]In emotional life any situation can produce exactly opposite effects and any effect can come from totally opposite situations. An awareness of this is important in observing patterns that may superficially appear different. I tried to develop this theme more fully in "The Curvature of Emotional Space," delivered at the 14th Georgetown University Family Therapy Symposium, 1977, unpublished.

tionships, by which I mean they have difficulty maintaining different distances with a person over time. They tend to control their feelings with an on/off switch—it is all or nothing. Other clues have tended to show this also. For example, when either no one or everyone is invited to an event, it may say something similar. And with regard to funerals, cremation hints the same sort of difficulty in allowing the pain of the emotional processes to operate naturally. Generally speaking, anything that shows a rush to replace loss or an inability to fill the gap indicates a lack of flexibility in the system.

But the most important ramification of these findings for a family approach to rites of passage is, I believe, that in their universality they support the notion that the human species has developed rites of passage out of its own nature. Traditions, no matter what the culture, reflect or capture this, and ultimately that is why in the emotional life of any family, the rites of passage through the life cycle are ideal times for learning about the family, as well as for helping it to heal itself. For the application of these concepts to entire organizations, see *Generation to Generation* (Friedman, 1985).

THREE NATURAL RITES OF PASSAGE

The following discussion covers three natural rites of passage—funerals, weddings, and puberty rites—and includes examples of how a family approach can make the passage less fraught with anxiety, and even turn it into an opportunity for helping the family in broader terms. I also comment briefly on three nodal points in the modern life cycle that are not as natural but are becoming so widespread as to approach traditional rites of passage in emotional significance—divorce, retirement, and geographical uprooting.

Funerals

I begin with an event that is usually considered to mark the end of the life cycle because death is undoubtedly the single most important event in family life. Over the years I have seen more change in families—marriage, divorce, pregnancy, geographical moves, other deaths—occur within a year after the death of a family member than after any other nodal point in the life cycle. Another reason for beginning with the end is that this event, especially if it is associated with a particularly important member of the family, can influence the celebration of other nodal events that follow. For example, at the first wedding, baptism, bar mitzva, and so on, following the death of a person important to the system, there is likely to be a larger turnout than one might have been otherwise led to expect. When that occurs the phenomenon itself may give an indication of who is going to replace the deceased member of the

family. On the other hand, the turnout for a funeral appears less likely to be influenced by the nodal events that preceded it.

Death creates a vacuum, and emotional systems, as physical systems, will rush to fill it. In the process cutoffs between family members will begin and end, and freedom and getting stuck will be the fate of others. Shifts in responsibility are normal, and replacement becomes a goal for many. The fluidity of a system around the time of death is thus also greater, though not necessarily for an indefinite period. In other words, if one is going to take advantage of that period, the funeral, its preparations, and its "celebration" can be a crystalizing experience. And while there may be more anxiety and pain for the family when a death is expected, such cases offer more opportunity for change. Six major kinds of opportunity become available during this rite of passage:

1. The chance to take or shift responsibility;
2. The opportunity to reestablish contact with distant relatives (or close relatives who live at a distance);
3. The opportunity to learn family history;
4. The chance to learn how to deal with the most anxious forces that formed one's emotional being;
5. Though this may subsume the previous, the opportunity to shift energy directions in the family triangles, all of which seem to resurrect themselves at such moments;
6. The opportunity to reduce the debilitating effects of grief.

The last has the character of a time warp, since it involves affecting what usually comes after death by what one does in the family before death. But it may be the most crucial one of all, and better than any other notion it encapsulates the idea that a rite of passage is more than a ceremony. The basic notion is: grief is the residue of the unworked-out part of a relationship.[4]

Several of these are exemplified by the following story, in which I was involved as clergyman, but where I was able to use my knowledge of family process to let flow the natural healing forces released by rites of passage.

A woman who was very involved in community mental health called and asked if I would be willing to do a "nonreligious" funeral for her husband, a renowned scientist, aged 46, who was terminally ill and might die any day. The rub was that she didn't want him to know about it. He was very areligious, but she wanted to do this for her sons, ages 19 and 12. I replied that I couldn't agree to do a funeral for a man while he was still alive unless I could meet him. (There were additional reasons for my taking this position, having to do with my general ideas that secrecy almost always stabilizes dysfunction and increases anxiety in a system. I

---

[4] I am indebted to Dr. Murray Brown for this insight as reported at a Georgetown clinical monthly meeting after the death of his father.

concluded this after observing numerous clients in therapy where the impending death of a loved one was handled in a hush-hush way.)[5]

The woman said that meeting her husband was out of the question, and I just said, "Think it over." She called back later that day to say that she had spoken to her husband and he had agreed to meet with me. I told her that I did not want to see him alone, but with her and her two sons. She agreed, but warned me that she did not want any therapy. I said I would only ask questions.

The husband had just come back from the hospital to die at home. When I arrived he was lying in bed, and while physically weak, was perfectly lucid. He was an only child, and kept a phone next to his bed so that when his aged parents called from the Midwest, they would not realize how bad things really were.

The older son was there, but I was informed that the younger son, who had asthma, had been sent to the home of his mother's mother. I began by telling the dying man (in front of his wife and son) that I had never met anyone who knew he was going to die, and wondered what he thought about it. He responded in a self-denying way, seemingly trying to convey that he was approaching his end with perfect equaniminity. I pushed the point by saying that his wife had said he was a very nonreligious man, and I wondered if he was now hedging his bet before he met his maker. He again responded lucidly and with a great sense of character, "No." He knew this was really going to be final. I then asked him what he wanted said at his funeral. (I already told him that I had found some passages from Albert Einstein that I thought would be appropriate, but I was now speaking in terms of a eulogy.) He then replied with amazing humility that there was nothing particular about himself that he wanted emphasized.

As far as I was concerned, to this point all the questions were just "probing the line." I now turned to the son and asked him in front of his father what he wanted said at his father's funeral. At this point, by the way, a fortuitous ringing of the phone took the mother out of the room; she never came back in. I proceeded to catalyze a conversation of the most personal kind between father and son over the issue of what was to be said at father's funeral. The man died the next day. The son, at my urging, wrote and delivered the eulogy, and the mother, several days later, sent me a long thank-you note and a copy of Kubler-Ross's *On Death and Dying.*[6]

As a clergyman I had an unusual opportunity in this situation, but I think that what happened there could only have occurred in that family during such a rite of passage. Such experience clarified for me that there are ways of encouraging such a process if you are "lucky" enough to be seeing a client around the time of a death in the family.

My own experience with the dying, the dead, and their survivors is that it is not an individual who is dying as much as it is a member of a family—that is, part of an organism is dying. When this focus is maintained, as impersonal and cold as it may seem at first, many new ways of seeing things unfold. For example, using the principle of extremes mentioned before, I believe that where extraordinary efforts are made, either to end the person's life, "to reduce suffering," or to prolong a person's life when he or she is biologically alive but existentially dead, the family either is desirous of rushing through the

[5]The full expansion of this view of the pernicious effects of secrets in families is in "Secrets and Systems," delivered at the 10th Georgetown University Family Symposium, 1973. Published in volume 11, *Selected Papers,* edited by Lorio and McClenathan, 1977.

[6]In another experience I had with the shifting emotional forces that take place at funerals, a woman tried to kidnap her mother after her father's death because the distance from her husband made her feel that she would mourn alone. It is described in "Family Systems Thinking and a New View of Man," *CCAR Journal,* vol. 18, no. 1, Jan. 1971.

passage or fearful of entering it. In either case it will say something about the family and the importance of the dying person to it at that moment. Such an approach also refocuses the so-called ethical issues around the "right to die."

There is another important way in which the focus on the dying person, rather than the family, misguides this rite of passage: it requires that the dying be *compuis mentis*. In many cases such persons are psychotically senile, unconscious, in a coma, obstreperously denying, or hopelessly confused. In those situations, from the point of view of that individual's existence, the person "might as well be dead." But that is in no way true from the point of view of the family. As long as the dying person is above ground, he or she is a live part of the organism. (Compare the extraordinary efforts to keep political leaders alive even though they are no longer capable of ruling.) Systems know the extraordinary significance of burial.

Recently I had the opportunity to put into practice much of what I have been preaching, when my own mother, who had been deteriorating for several years with artereosclerosis, went into her final decline. I present here in outline how I functioned during the period, since I believe the recounting of my own experience will capsulize much of what I have been trying to convey about funerals.

In August 1977, my mother, aged 79, whose mental and physical condition had been deteriorating for several years, and who, throughout this period, had to live with a home attendant, fell and broke a small bone in her leg. Because she had almost no pulse below her waist, the cast almost immediately created a pressure sore that would have become gangrenous without constant attention. She was put in the hospital in an attempt to debride the wound and save her leg.

Since my mother had all but stopped walking anyway, the surgeon wanted to amputate. The decision would have to be mine as I was her only child and my father had died 25 years previously. She seemed no longer capable of really understanding what was happening. Remembering my mother as a person who did not give up easily, I stayed on the side of trying to save the leg, but I was already thinking of her funeral. What complicated my own ability to think clearly during this period was the incredible anxiety of her sister, who lived next door to my mother. My aunt had made it to her 80s by using her anxiety to get others to take responsibility. Throughout those last four months, she would constantly criticize the home attendant to me, and me to everyone else. In an effort to defuse the intensity of the triangle involving my mother, my aunt, and myself, I began to contact other members of the extended family whom I perceived to be in inter-locking triangles with me and my mother or with me and my aunt. I started a process in which I tried to establish or reestablish as many relationships as possible with other members of the family and close friends of my mother all over the United States. I kept informing them of what I was doing and what was happening. I found great support in doing this; the process of involving family members at a distance also seemed to redistribute the guilt and the responsibility, spread the risk, and make me more objective about what was happening nearby.[7]

For six weeks the situation stayed the same, and then, just as we were all about to give up, I made one last attempt to break through to my mother, directly telling

[7]For more background on my family system, and a glimpse of my anxious aunt ten years earlier (she is the one who goes through the glass sliding door), see "The Birthday Party: An Experiment in Obtaining Change in One's Own Extended Family," *Family Process*, vol. 10, no. 3, Sept. 1971.

her I was giving up. To our surprise the leg began to heal and my mother was able to return home. However, shortly afterward the visiting nurse tied the bandage too tight and my mother developed gangrene. At this point positions switched, the surgeon now saying that my mother was so close to death that amputation would be a "heroic" act. Since I had done a lot of thinking about how unresolved attachment makes it difficult to let someone die, I had difficulty with this one. My aunt, who from the beginning had been against amputation, was still against it. I, however, made the decision for the amputation on the ground that I could not let my mother's body poison itself when that was preventable; she would have to die "naturally." After the amputation she actually seemed to perk up for a while. Again, throughout this period, I stayed in constant touch with the family and friends, informing them of what was happening, but in each case only after I had made the decision, so that I could keep my decisions clear of family anxiety. Throughout this period my aunt and those closest to my mother kept attacking me for my failure to put my mother in a nursing home much sooner where "she" would have been more comfortable (meaning they would have been more comfortable).

Shortly after my mother came home from the hospital, it became clear to me that her body had gone beyond all thresholds and I began to prepare for her death and funeral. Then the same visiting nurse, severely chastened by the doctors for her previous mistake and feeling anxious about her condition, wanted to put her back in the hospital. Luckily I was called first. For three years I had fought against much family pressure to keep her out of institutions. It was now clear that she had less time left than it would take to reverse the process of her illness. With great difficulty I made the decision not let her go back to the hospital and die in the institution, but to let ill-nature take its course. I stopped interfering. Within five days she was dead.

I had prepared a list of family telephone numbers, and when I received word of her death, I began to follow out a plan I had thought out while my mother was dying. I called each relative to report my mother had died and took advantage of the natural reminiscing we went through to make notes of what each person said about my mother. At the funeral I read a "family eulogy," which included my own remarks and those of the other family members. Then I asked those present to add anything they wished.

My remarks about my mother were as straightforward and honest as I could make them. I talked about how I thought her qualities had influenced (or spoiled) me and made reference to how she had taken care of her mother for the family. As for me, after the funeral I felt a greatly strengthened sense of my ability to deal with acutely anxious crises.

Here are some things that happened during the rite of passage in my personal life and in my work with families.

1. Three years previously I had become cut off for one reason or another from everyone who eventually came to the funeral. Now things had swung so far the other way that one cousin even invited my whole family to stay for a visit. I felt I was a member of the family again.

2. My anxious aunt's grandson, who had recently married, unbeknownst to the family, a woman he had been living with for years, introduced his wife to the family for the first time.

3. Knowing how money channels are emotional channels and having seen so many families split up over inheritance, I tried to use that phenomenon in

reverse by giving the newlyweds my mother's furniture, which they appreciated greatly.

4. I found myself able to go back to work immediately and with enthusiasm, with no depression, and I found, if anything, an increased sense of creativity and competence in my work.

5. There were ramifications for my work systems also. With regard to family therapy clients, several families went into crisis around this time. As I saw it, when I learned to deal with the forming forces of anxiety that had made me "me," I inadvertently pulled out some of the supports with which I had been previously buttressing these clients in my anxiety over their anxiety. They almost all made leaps of growth, however, as it seems that I did not respond anxiously to these "inviting" crises either.

6. There was also an interesting analogous reaction within the small congregation I served and that I had helped to establish 14 years previously. Annually, at contract time, I had come to expect some attack from the "loyal opposition." In the past I usually became quite engaged with these members, often going to great lengths to refute the content of their charges—motivated, I believe, by anxiety over my own security or over continuation of the congregation's philosophy. This time, however, the content of their charges, though not different in nature, seemed almost silly, if not boring, and I did not take the initial complaints very seriously. (Not surprisingly the reactions to my disengagement escalated.[8])

One last point: 25 years previously I had for several months helplessly watched my father slowly die in a hospital. I had not dared to take the opportunity to tell him what he meant to me, to discuss with him his impending death or to function in any way that might have proved helpful to my survivorship or my mother's eventual widowhood. The atmosphere had been overcast with anxiety and denial. His wake left me with a sense of relief that it was all over, but it was a relief wrapped in confusion, guilt, and a pervasive feeling of something left incomplete. He had made one statement to me when it seemed he knew he was going to die, something enigmatic like, "Eddie, do what you want to do." Totally out of the context of a more intimate surrounding experience, it became over the years like some mysterious pearl of advice one carries away from an audience with an oracle, which one is bound to plumb and ponder for a lifetime. On the other hand, after my mother's death, it was an entirely different story. Though she had been anything but concerned about my future—in fact she had often been bitter, complaining, contrary, and sometimes, in the confusion of her senile psychosis, a name-calling witch—I had a sense of completeness, fulfillment, and peace. Finally, I would say that treating a funeral as a family rite of passage and making the most of that

---

[8]I have not discussed here the effects of rites of passage on work systems, simply because of lack of space. I have developed the theme somewhat in "Leadership and Self in a Congregational Family," *CCAR Journal*, Winter 1978.

opportunity for one's own differentiation is the only way I know to get out of that horrible, forever-after haunting dilemma of wishing it would all be over soon.

Weddings

If death is the most portentous event in family life, marriage may be the most symptomatic in two senses. First, my experience with over 2000 couples before marriage has led me to the conclusion that the timing of weddings is far from random. I have found, for example, that many couples either meet their spouse or decide to marry within six months of a major change in the family of origin of one of the partners. It is not that romance does not count, but simply that it is not enough to move a relationship to marriage. Weddings can also be symptomatic of family process in that stresses surrounding the engagement and wedding preparation period seem really to make the seams show. This can be true with funerals also, but there are some major differences. More likely than not, death will have an implosive effect on a family, in which all the members pull together, even if after the funeral they fight over the inheritance. With weddings one must decide whether to invite those one does not want to be with and the burden of choice can become almost overbearing, depending on how many sides one is trying to please. Whereas with a funeral the need for comfort makes the closest relatives willing to be with one another, with a wedding the desire to be joyous makes some of those same relatives anathema. Another major difference between weddings and funerals is that in death one is dealing with the loss of an insider whereas with marriage the problem is the inclusion of an outsider—despite the old saw, "I am not losing a daughter but gaining a son."

There can be, of course, a light side to weddings: the obsessive concern with etiquette, the inappropriateness of some gifts, even the jealousy of who gets seated with whom. Once again, however, when viewed in family process terms, these little things may be more significant than we might think. Sometimes it is blatant, like the mother who during the wedding whispered to the bride as she partook of the ceremonial wine, "Not too much now, dear." Similarly, a humorous but often significant warning signal comes when the mother or father makes the first contact with the clergyman, either because their son "works," or because their daughter lives in Alaska and "it would be a long-distance call."

On the other hand, some families handle such situations with amazing perceptiveness. One man who was marrying a woman with a five-year-old daughter turned to the little girl immediately after the pronouncement and also gave the child a ring. He knew what he was doing; under those conditions he really did marry both, and not only his bride.

One of the aspects of family ceremonies that has always appalled me, and yet has also proved to me that the unseen family process has more power than

the ceremony, is the loss of critical taste at family events. I have performed very sloppy weddings in the most uncomfortable settings (bees literally in my bonnet) and had everyone come up afterward to congratulate me on the warmest wedding they have ever attended. But I have also been part of such anxious systems that even in the most elaborately arranged settings, the most eloquent homilies were ignored and I had all I could do to keep from inadvertantly stepping on the bridal gown and tripping the bride.

As an opportunity for inducing change, I have found that the rite of passage surrounding a wedding is the most propitious for redirecting focus. The opportunities for learning about the family and reworking triangles described with regard to funerals are there also, but the time around weddings stands out primarily as the time to redirect a parent's focus, and once again crisis is opportunity.

Though this is clearly the case, most couples who experience difficulties with their parents over a wedding see this period as just something to be gotten through until they can get married and get away. This avoidance of the experience might be similar to cremation after death. Of course, the real getting away only occurs if the young people use that period to develop more differentiation of self in the relationships with their parents. And again, couples who are experiencing pain at such moments (as with terminal deaths) may be more fortunate. Where problems arise in the family of origin during wedding preparations, the opportunities for redirection of focus are plentiful.[9]

To begin with, I can say categorically that I have never seen a religious, social, or other issue worked out regarding a marital choice where the efforts have been made directly on the content of the issue. For example, if parents are critical of the marital choice on the ground of different religious or social backgrounds, efforts to change the parents' minds by saying such things as, "But Mom, you were always so liberal yourself," of "Dad, you always taught me to treat everyone equally," are doomed to failure. I have seen many a bride or groom spend an entire weekend with critical parents trying to show them how illogical their views were and, leave in the belief that they had changed their parents' minds, only to receive a letter later in the week showing that they were back at ground zero. These efforts to deal with the content of the parents' complaint are ineffective because one is dealing with symptom, not cause. The cause of almost all severe parental reactions to marital choice is the failure of the reacting parent to have worked out something important in other relationships. The focus has been misplaced. On the other hand, I have found almost 100% success in reducing the significance of such issues, if not eliminating them altogether, when the bride or groom is able to refocus the reacting parent on his or her own parents.

---

[9] I have developed the general notion of the interrelationship between marriage and family of origin in two papers: "The Nature of the Marital Bond," delivered at the 11th Georgetown University Family Therapy Symposium, 1974, published in volume 11, *Collection of Selected Papers*, edited Lorio and McClenathan, 1977; and "Engagement and Disengagement—Family Therapy with Couples During Courtship," delivered at the eighth Georgetown University Family Therapy Symposium, 1971, published in *Collection of Symposium Papers*, vol. 1, edited by Andres and Lorio, 1977.

Three major factors are always present in the reacting relative's position in the family: (1) he or she is having great difficulty differentiating from the child getting married; (2) not necessarily distinct from this, the child getting married is very important to the balance of the parents' marriage; and (3) that parent or relative is caught up in some emotionally responsible position in his or her own family of origin.

There is little question that the third is most important, but it is also often the most difficult to get to. Some starting moves for refocus that I have found helpful in factors one and two are: "Well, Dad, it's all your fault, you should have sent me to Hebrew school (church on Sundays) more often." If the response is "We tried, but you wouldn't go," the point is carried further. "Well you were the parent, why didn't you try harder?" "It's a good thing your mother isn't here to see this." Or, for an interfering mother telling her daughter what to do at the wedding: "Mom, here is a list of 100 aspects of the wedding; I know how important it is to you to please your sister (mother, mother-in-law, friends); would you look it over at your leisure and give me as full answers as possible? I am particularly interested in knowing whether you want the traditional approach to putting the knives next to the spoons, or the newer idea that the knife should be in front of the plate." These will not bring complete change, but they are sure to afford breathing room. One refocusing effort, however, has worked without fail. While to some readers it may seem merely an effort to lighten a toxic issue and to others a sarcastic or nasty remark, I have yet to find a better way for a bride to refocus her mother's attention. It goes something like this.

"Mother, I know you are opposed to John, and you have the right to your position, but you are still my mother and I believe you owe me one more thing before John and I marry. We have never had a frank talk about sex. What has been the secret of your marital success? How many times a week would you say a man likes it? And when you don't want it, how do you keep a man away?" I have yet to find a better way to refocus a parent on her own marriage (parents satisfied in their own marriage just do not put that much energy into their children). But not every daughter can make that little speech. So, from the other side, maybe the 100% success I have seen with this one is that any daughter who can say that to her mother is well on her way to disengagement anyway.[10]

Sometimes a wedding gives one the opportunity to go to work in the primary triangle with mother and father. The key to any triangle is not to get caught in the middle as the focus of an unresolved issue between the other two. If one family member is caught, not only does he or she have less maneuverability, but the other two wind up with a pseudostabilization of their relationship. One of the best ways to get "detriangled" is to put the other two members of the triangle together. This is true whether the triangle is classic, as

---

[10]For a description of the kind of family emotional system that I believe most objects to "outsiders," see "Conversion, Love and Togetherness," *Reconstructionist*, vol. 39, May 1973.

with an extramarital affair, or where the third member is a symptom (physical or emotional) of one's partner, parent, or child. By seeming to encourage a togetherness that really has more appearance than substance, it is often possible to make the hidden issue surface where it belongs. (Anyone who doubts this should try the opposite, namely, separating the other two persons, or the other person and his or her symptom and watch them respond by absolutely falling in love with each other.) When a person getting married can avoid the content of the objecting parent's remark and concentrate instead on the emotional processes of the triangle, that bride or groom will become defocused as a natural part of any new process, which now focuses the parents on one another.

For example, usually it is the mother who tends to be more reactive about a marital choice or over wedding preparations. If this turns out to be the case and Dad starts to react also, then one has a wonderful opportunity to tell Dad how terrific it is to see the way he stands up for the mother even when it goes against his principles. If it is the father who is the primary reactor and the mother will not stand up to him, similar statements can be made about how true she is to the old-world standards of the adaptive wife. The key is to keep pushing them together and praising their togetherness as one goes along.

There is also an obverse side to this. This occurs when the parents agree to come to the wedding, but very reluctantly, conveying that they are only coming out of a sense of duty. This is a trap. Here they have again put the bride or groom in the middle by making their child responsible for their behavior. Under such circumstances they will come with a vow not to enjoy themselves (which can be infectious.) They will stay by themselves in a corner, perhaps with a sibling, standing like gaunt, Midwestern farmers from a Grant Wood painting, adamantly unsmiling. The detriangling here involves making them come for themselves by giving them permission not to come: "Dear folks, I know you are only coming to please me, and I don't want to see you give up your principles just because I am your favorite; I would like you to be there, but I'll understand if you can't make it."

A typical pattern that often needs addressing is the parents' reference to their own extended families. In my experience when the parent says, "My parents are upset," that has always been a projection; likewise, when the parent says, "This will kill them." I have never seen the grandparent react more than the parent, even when their old-worldliness would lead one to expect more reaction. This is more evidence that the issues have to do with the closeness of the relationship, not the subject of the issue. In all events the following type of letter has met with excellent success in my experience:

Dear Grandma or Aunt, or Uncle:
    As you may have heard [they probably haven't], I am going to marry a Jew [a Catholic, a Black, a Martin]. I would like to invite you to the wedding even though I know this probably goes so much against your principles that you may feel you cannot attend. I did want you to know, however. Also, I wondered if you could give me some advice. Your daughter, or "kid sister" [not "my mother"], is absolutely off the wall about this. She keeps telling me this will be the end of our relationship,

calls me every night, says if you found out you would drop dead, etc. I wondered if you could give me any information that would explain why she is behaving this way, or any advice on how to deal with her.

My own experience has been that whenever that type of letter has been sent, although no reply is received, within weeks the issue has calmed down.[11] Sometimes the unresolved issue behind parents' reactivity near the rite of passage of a wedding has to do with a relationship the parents and a relative who is dead—perhaps, their own parent, a spouse, or another child. When this is true, a visit to the graveside with that parent can offer an opportunity for unlocking fixed attitudes and enabling refocus. The key, however, no matter which way of refocusing one chooses, is that an impending wedding is a sign of a relationship system in flux. Some members are going to feel the pull of the forces of change more than others. Who is going to react most depends on who stabilized his or her own life through some kind of emotional dependence on the person getting married. For example, some parents use a child as an anchor to keep from getting drawn back into the vortex of the parents' parents' pull. Or they invest in a child to compensate for the absence of affection in a marriage. The road to no change at such moments is to elope, cut off, or try to placate the parents as much as possible until one gets married and can start one's own family. Those approaches guarantee a transference of emotional intensity into the new family being formed. But where individuals can be taught to seize the opportunity at the rite of passage of a wedding, they leave a lot of unnecessary baggage at home.

Here is a clinical experience and a short case history that illustrate the extent to which a wedding as a rite of passage is a family event.

A divorced man came in to get married, mentioning in the premarital interview that he was not going to keep up with his young child from his previous marriage, since it would "complicate things for the child." I gingerly pointed out that by doing this, he might create ghosts. He didn't buy it and I didn't pursue it. I did, by the way, have the impression that it all somehow had to do with his mother, who was not coming to the wedding. After the wedding he refused to give me my fee, saying that he had only come in to get married, not for counseling. It was the only time that had ever happened, and I made a mental note that I had touched something deep.

Several years later a prospective groom came in who was in an identical situation. Remembering the first experience, and being a fool rather than an angel, I told this man what had happened the previous time I had raised such an issue, and added, "I know this must be a touchy subject, but have you thought about the possibility that for all your good will, your child might grow up wondering why her natural father rejected her by cutting off in such an

---

[11] It can work in the opposite direction also. I have seen parents who were never really motivated to work on their relationships with a child, induced to begin when they originally came in concerned over the child's marital choice, and stay, literally for years after the ceremony, as they continue to bring change to the entire family.

absolute manner?" And I mentioned how often I had done family histories with adults who reported similar stories of how their fathers or grandfathers became ghosts in the system and how the residue of guilt those cutoffs had left continued to haunt the family. He laughed about the first groom, but said he simply didn't see it my way. Two days laters he called to say he had decided to get married by someone else. Again I had the impression that it had something to do with his mother.

Several years after that, a man came in to get married who happened to mention that after several years of cutoff he had just reestablished relationships with his children. I said, "Oh, then you must have made some major changes with your mother." This time the groom looked at me as if he had seen a ghost and responded, "How the hell did you know that?" I am still not sure how I knew, other than to say that whenever a relationship changes suddenly near the rite of passage of a wedding, whether it is a cutoff or the reestablishment of a dormant relationship, my experience has taught me that there is usually a third member of the family involved. The wedding as a rite of passage is like the movement of an iceberg, with most of what is in motion unseen by the human eye.

The second case example is about a family of five children in which the eldest came in at age 40 for her second marriage. While well educated, she was the black sheep of the family. Her father, a very successful tyrant, had died several years previously. The family—that is, the mother (and one unmarried brother, in particular—was in a fury about her marital choice, and) threatened to disinherit her. In a session with the mother and daughter, the father's beatings of this daughter came out.

Though she had had a lot of therapy throughout her childhood, she found the subject very painful. I asked her at this point if she had ever seen the father's beatings as symptomatic of the mother's closeness with her. Her chains disintegrated before my eyes. She became motivated to lead the family instead of fighting it. And for two months before and six months after the wedding, she went to work on the triangles with her siblings, her mother, and every relative she could find. The mother, who was being shown great attention by a man for the first time since her husband's death, was told not to marry this man, that he was not good enough, etc. And what would *her* mother (now in her 80s) say? The brother, who had inherited the father's superresponsible position (and who had not come to the wedding), was repeatedly complimented for being willing to give up his own personal happiness in order to keep the family together.

Both relationships almost immediately began to shift. It was as though they were now seeing this woman for the first time. It turned out that the other brother, a wandering Ph.D. in his late 20s, was between jobs or hobbies, and the youngest sister was an absolute slave to her rigid husband, with physical symptoms beginning to show up in her child.

Every one of these dysfunctional symptoms, which had been helped to operate covertly through the perpetual focus of the family on "poor sister," became approachable again, as if for the first time, around her wedding. Putting to service all the energy and intelligence characteristic of the family, which had been allowed previously to intensify pathology or to become sopped up by rebellion, the black sheep used the opportunity made possible by the family scapegoat position, and the family in every respect began to change.

Pubescence

The third most universal rite of passage is that of puberty, the onset of adulthood. Of the three this one has lost much of its family significance in modern culture, becoming associated often with cultural phenomena, graduations, dating, and so on. My own religious tradition, of course, has maintained it with the celebration of the bar (boy) or bat (girl) mitzva. I would like to shift gears in this section and talk within my own tradition's metaphor about this rite of passage.[12]

The major reason I wish to stay within my own tradition here is that I have experienced with changes in the tradition based on what I have learned about family process, and the results have been both astounding and enlightening. What I wish to show is, first, how something as obviously individual, no less child focused, is really very much a family rite; and second, how making everyone aware of that fact actually increases the effectiveness of the passage. There are other lessons that come forth also—that the message of the emotional system is a more powerful medium than the culture tradition, establishing it or perverting it; and that, old traditions, even without articulation of family process, have recognized it all the time.

The Jewish tradition of bar mitzva (literally, son of, or worthy of, the commandments) is at least 1500 years old. On a day close to a boy's 13th birthday, he is called up to bless the scripture reading or to read a portion. From the point of view of traditional Jewish law, he is now an adult able to give witness in court, be responsible for his own wrongdoing, and be counted as one of the ten men needed for a public service (minyon). In the 1920s (around the time of the 19th amendment, which gave women the right to vote), progressive branches of Judaism introduced bat mitzva for a girl, though the ceremony has only become widespead only recently, since the renaissance of the women's movement.

Today, from the religious point of view, depending on the branch of Judaism, the ceremony can be just the scripture blessing, a reading of the portion in Hebrew, which the child may have just memorized, or a rite with more emphasis on the meaning of the portion, with the child giving more than a sterotyped thank-you speech and, adding a talk that interprets his portion.

In terms of contemporary sociology, the bar mitzva, especially for the Jews of middle-class suburbia, often appears to be an event of great social importance. In some places it has been joked, "The bar has become more important than the mitzva." And it might be added, "The caterer more important than the rabbi."

But in either case, from the family process point of view, the ceremony always appears to be child focused.

---

[12]An improvisional approach to the whole life cycle that tries to show how tradition can actually be preserved through the insights of family process can be found in "Enriching The Life Cycle Through Creative Family Participation," *op. cit.*

The first time I began to think of bar mitzva in family terms was actually before I had trained to do family therapy. I was doing some work as a community relations specialist for the White House. For the first time in my life, I began to sense the pressures non-Jews feel around Christmas time. Colleagues I had worked with all year began to become extremely anxious. They began to shop compulsively for gifts beyond their means, and drinking became more frequent. Then one Friday evening, as I was leaving a staff Christmas party on my way to a weekend that was to include a bar mitzva, things seemed strangely familiar. The anxiety, the gift giving, the drinking— there was something the two had in common. Years later when I had the conceptual framework I began to understand.

It was the force of family togetherness: All the family intensity, the prob- lems with relatives, the unspoken feelings, the pressure to relate that many individuals spend much of a year trying to avoid, become unavoidable for a Christian near Christmas; for Jewish families something similar occurs around a bar mitzva. As I began to explore this notion, other events and findings propelled me further in that direction of observing family force fields. First, a father of a bar mitzva boy (unbeknownst to me, in line for a transplant) went into heart failure during his son's service, and died. He was an only child, sitting next to his widowed, terribly dependent mother at the time. This experience led me to an extraordinary amount of additional information. As I related what had happened to others, I began to hear an incredible number of reports about parents going into dysfunction near the time of a sons's bar mitzva, including suicides, breakdowns, and other forms of physical illness. (It is, of course, well known that the suicide rate goes up nationally in late December.)

I began to put things together. No wonder I had never been really suc- cessful in calming a bar mitzva child's anxiety no matter how well prepared he was. It was not his anxiety I was dealing with. No wonder mothers whom I had previously perceived to be models of efficiency and astute reasonableness approached me almost on the verge of hysteria in seeking bar mitzva dates. No wonder fathers running top government agencies and used to living with daily crises seemed to go limp at this period. I was dealing with phenomena with far- ranging effects.

Since I knew that a most effective means of dealing with panic was to offer an alternative mode of behavior, I immediately hit upon involving the family members more in the ceremony and the preparation. I soon found to my surprise and delight that these efforts had more reward than I expected.

The first change I made was in the method of choosing the portion. Traditionally there is no choice; one goes by the calendar cycle. I began to meet with the child, learn a little about him and his family, add what I already knew, and then make several suggestions based on interest and style, leaving it to the child and parents to make final selections. Then I had a study session with the entire family—parents, siblings, grandparents, if they were in town— in which discussion (even argument) was promoted about interpretation. At

the end of the discussion, the child was given the charge that he would be the teacher for the day. He was told to divide his talk into three parts—a synopsis in his own words of the portion, his interpretation of what the Biblical author was trying to say, and any interpretation he wished to make for the day.

After the family meetings, I continued to meet with the bar mitzva child several times to help with the writing of his talk, but I began to assume less responsibility. Whereas in former days I used to become terribly concerned about the articulation, coherence, and overall conceptualization of the talk, I was now primarily concerned to ask questions (which I wanted taken back to the family) that helped with the development of the ideas.

Soon I realized that my role had changed significantly. Instead of bearing the burden of helping this child through his rite of passage, I had a team, a team on which I was more a coach than the star player. With that in mind, I also began to make changes in the ceremony. First I stopped giving any sermon myself other than an introduction, which described the development of bar mitzva in Jewish tradition and its further shaping by our congregation. The child was called "our teacher for today," and the father (or, in some cases, both parents) was asked to bless the child, publicly or privately. Since the congregation had a tradition of creative services from the beginning, families started creating their own services. Continuing with my role as coach, I would make available source books, ask for about six to ten passages, and then take responsibility for fitting them into the prayer order. Families, of course, differed in the extent to which I could select, some becoming so involved that they printed, at their own expense, a supplement that even contained the scripture portion itself in Hebrew and English, and artistic members of the family (sometimes the child himself) began to create designs for the cover. Sometimes a sibling wrote a poem for a frontpiece. One family had a coat of arms that went back for generations and decorated the cover with that.

All families were given the option of having the bar mitzva at home if they chose. Sometimes musical members of the family played an overture or background music during the silent prayer. A musical child might play on a guitar or trumpet a tune he or she had created for the service. The parents also gave out portions of the service to incoming relatives, who read them to the congregation. Blessings over the meal were distributed also, each family being encouraged to allot these responsibilities as seemed natural.

The results have been beyond what I could have foreseen. Family anxiety seems greatly reduced, there is much less focus on materialistic expression, and, despite less direct involvement by me, the child generally does a better overall performance. In other words, though I have been trying less to "teach" the child myself, whatever process has been released by the transfer of my functioning to the family is also producing more thoughtful, deeper intellectual efforts on the part of the child. Finally, though I am less "out front," I seem to get more thanks than before from visiting relatives. The systems seem to know.

THREE NODAL LIFE CYCLE EVENTS

Funerals, weddings, and the onset of puberty have been universal rites of passage as long as the human species has had culture. Our modern culture seems to be producing three other nodal points of great consequence for the life cycle: divorce, retirement, and geographical uprooting. I should like to discuss these changes as family events also. However, I wish to make clear that I think there is an important difference between these three and the former three. The former are all connected to the life cycle biologically. They are part of being human. It is not as clear to me that in themselves the latter have the same power for change, unless perhaps they are, as is often the case, residuals of the former events—for example, where the divorce, or at least the separation, came within a year after an important death; or the geographical move soon after a marriage. And, of course, both could be symptomatic of even larger forces flowing through the family arteries. These latter also differ in that they are not complete passages, but more like the openings to a passage. With marriage, death, and pubescense, an individual is not simply leaving one state, but going to another that is well defined. Somehow the beginning and the end are all subsumed as part of the complete passage of six months to a year; and the new state toward which the family is headed is in some ways teleologically pulling the family through the crisis. Similarly, while the biological rites of passage all deal with loss and healing, these latter rites tend only to deal with loss. They are thus more open ended. All of this is not to say that they are not ripe times for bringing change to a family, or in some cases are not symptomatic of changes already going on in the family, but they may not be in themselves natural family phenomena with all the power for healing that those experiences contain.

Divorce

The rate of divorce today is becoming so high as to suggest it is reaching the level of a biological imperative. And of these latter nonbiological nodal points in life, divorce would seem to portend more family change. Several religious groups have experimented with the creation of a divorce ceremony. (Jewish tradition has had one for 1500 years in which the man hands the bill of divorce to his wife personally, if possible, and says, "I divorce you.") Since the thrust of this chapter has been that rites of passage are family events, it may be that in many cases only the second marriage or a funeral really completes that passage. I do know of one person who sent out divorce announcements with an invitation to a party: "Mrs. _____ announces the divorce of her daughter from Mr. _____ on the steps of the Court House of _____." She said that many of her female cousins took one look at it and destroyed the card before their husbands could see it.

To bring the full power of a family rite of passage to divorce, perhaps the following perspective would be helpful: To the extent that a divorce comes about because the rite of passage of marriage did not do its work (that is, successfully bring about disengagement in the family of origin), the divorce is not likely to bring real change if the original triangles are still stuck. To the extent, on the other hand, that the divorce is a result of changes in that originally stuck situation with the family of origin, which in turn unbalanced the marriage, then the divorce is more likely to offer opportunity.

In either case, if clients who come in to work on their fears of loneliness, instability, adjustment of their children, loss of moorings, and so forth (the focus of most of the self-help books on divorce) can be focused on relationships with the family of origin instead—and they often are more motivated to do so during this period—one will have made divorce a rite of passage in the fullest sense of the term.

Retirement

Retirement may have more ramifications for family life than has been realized, though therapists near military bases do not have to be told this fact. The number of divorces that occur after early military retirement is quite high. The general rule would seem to be this: Where the marriage was balanced by the mother being intensely involved with the children and the father with the service (which becomes a sort of extended family), his retirement often unbalances the relationship, particularly if he now tries to reenter the family and finds himself excluded, or seeks a replacement in the form of an extramarital relationship. This phenomenon is not limited to the military and can occur with any profession that involves the husband who is deeply in his work relationship system (lawyers, clergy, etc.). That it has far-reaching ramifications may be seen from the following tale.

> A couple, both of whom were only children, and both 27 years old, came in to get married after going steady for five years. They had must made the decision and wanted the wedding in a month. Naturally I asked them what they thought moved the relationship on to marriage. Though well educated, introspective, and in no way threatened by the question, they had no idea. In poking into the family history, I could find none of the usual family changes, such as deaths, marriages, or births. Then innocently she remarked, "Well, the only thing I can say that changed is that both our fathers retired last year." Five years of going steady and they suddenly realized that they were right for one another.

One possible explanation of this is that when the fathers retired, they got closer to their wives, who inadvertently let go of their children. Or perhaps this was more true of the one who was the real holdout. In any event, theoretically this is the exact opposite of the military situation where divorce results when the wife refuses to be drawn closer to the now more available spouse and still clings to the child.

It is thus clear that retirement can have significant family ramifications, and can also be induced by family events as when a parent, after a loss (through death, divorce, or marriage), begins to wonder, "What's the point of working so hard?" and begins to change his or her sights. The so-called "leaving the nest" syndrome may be similar. Another major family ramification of retirement is the onset of senile processes. If the experience with my mother and aunt has more universal application, the following rule may be true: If, around the time any older person begins to reduce significantly his or her functioning (through retirement or an illness) there is available an overfunctioning, anxious family member who, at that moment, has no receptacle for his or her energy, the likely outcome is senility for the former.

Geographical Uprooting

Geographical uprooting can also have severe consequences, particularly to the extent that it means leaving an emotionally important house or community. What is also crucial is the extent to which it changes the balance of a marriage. For example, if it takes a wife further away from her mother, it can either free her or lead her to become more dependent. In general, it might be said that such uprooting, to the extent it takes a couple further from one spouse's extended family and closer to the other's, will shift the balance, though not necessarily always in the same direction. I have seen situations where couples move toward an area in which both extended systems reside and almost blow apart in months, despite a previously content relationship.

From the other side, I have seen more than one family in therapy stuck for months on a marital problem or a problem with a child become suddenly motivated to "resolve things" as a deadline nears so that they can get on with their new life.

Here the principle given earlier is borne out again: families in flux during a rite of passage sometimes can be more easily changed at such periods. It also suggests that the changes that accompany, and often precede, geographical uprooting or retirement may be much more powerful forces than we realize. And once again the visible change, that is, the actual retirement or the move, may be symptomatic of emotional changes in the family that had been growing toward a climax for some time.

Our culture, of course, has done little to prepare families for the emotional shock waves of moves or retirement. Interestingly, the U.S. government, sensing the life cycle importance of retirement in recent years, has instituted a program of trial retirement, where the person can change his or her mind during the first year. But even that program may be little more helpful than are trial marriages. It is the homeostatic forces of emotional balance that count, and it is very hard to get a true reading on changes in that balance until commitment is made.

What then about new ceremonies that might help such transitions? It might

be possible to create these, but they would have to be centered in the family rather than the work system or the larger community, though members of those systems could be included.

Here we come face to face with what ceremonies are all about. From an individual point of view, a ceremony can help mark a feeling of change or renewal, and perhaps make one conscious of a benchmark period in one's life cycle. But it is much more than that. Ceremonies, even today, get at processes the most ancient tribes were trying to deal with in their most primitive rites. After all, it is only when we think of a person as a member of the family that the term "life cycle" makes any sense. Otherwise we should be talking in terms of life lines.

CONCLUSIONS

I have tried to show that the notion that families are primarily passive vehicles during rites of life passage, with little influence on either the outcome of the passage or the selection of the particular rites and ceremonies, does not hold up. The traditional social science focus on different cultures' customs, aided by concentration on the individual to be passed, completely ignores the possibility that the very obvious cultural differences are really rather unimportant in themselves. They may be fun to compare, but are not nearly as crucial as the unseen family process forces wearing those very cultural disguises. Indeed, all cultures as they become more sophisticated may be participating in a great illusion—namely, that the medicine men for all their hocus-pocus have only succeeded in driving the spooks and spirits further from view, and making them harder to exorcise or control. It is the demons that now wear the masks. There is a great irony here for the function of ceremonies at rites of passage. Now the culture disguises they have been enabled to assume allow them to go slipping through, right into the next generation.

An example is the parent who is having difficulty separating from a child. Instead of focusing on her difficulties in separating from her own parents, she attacks a culturally different child-in-law. For that matter, a child having difficulty separating from a parent who, instead of focusing on the emotional processes in the family that reared him or her, chooses a mate from a culture that does not operate as intensely, is participating in the same process.

But the shiktza (non-Jewish or generally nonethnic woman) to whose bosom the ethnic man runs always turns out to relate at least as intensely as the ethnic mother from whose bosom the man has fled. Indeed, further research will probably show that in-law problems existed in the previous generation even when everyone was of the "same faith."

On the other hand, there is a different ending where members of a family can see through the cultural camouflage and the diversion of the focused

individual. When they can maintain their gaze on the family process that contributed to a rite of passage occurring at that particular time, as well as observe how these processes are at work during the rite of passage itself, that family is in a position to influence both the effectiveness of the passage and its own emotional system.

REFERENCES

Friedman, E. H. (1982). The myth of the shiksa. In M. McGoldrick, J. K. Pearce, & J. Giordano (Eds.), *Ethnicity and family therapy*. New York: Guilford Press.

Friedman, E. H. (1985). *Generation to generation: Family process in church and synagogue*. New York: Guilford Press.

CHAPTER 7

Idiosyncratic Life Cycle Transitions and Therapeutic Rituals

Evan Imber-Black, Ph.D.

Normative life cycle events and transistions, such as weddings, births, and deaths, are most frequently marked with rituals. Many religious and ethnic groups also have rituals to mark young adult development (e.g., bar mitzvah, confirmations), or such development may be marked by secular rituals such as graduation. These rituals, while often seen as discrete events—such as a wedding, the christening or naming of a baby, and so on—are actually processes occurring over time and involving advance preparation and reflection afterward. Choices regarding who participates in the planning and execution of a life cycle ritual may be regarded as metaphors for family rules. Negotiations that occur during the preparation for life cycle rituals may be opportunities for second-order change Thus such rituals may be seen as the visible and condensed drama of the life cycle transitions they mark.

Relying on symbols, metaphors, and actions, which are capable of multiple meanings, life cycle rituals function to reduce anxiety about change. According to Schwartzman (1982), rituals make change manageable, as members experience change as part of their system rather than as a threat to it. Similarly, Wolin and Bennett (1984) suggest that rituals contribute to a family's "identity," its sense of itself over time, facilitating the elaboration of roles, boundaries, and rules. A sense of self and a sense of family and group membership are enabled through rituals. Emotional and physical well-being may be promoted during times of intense relationship change. Rituals have the capacity to assist in the resolution of conflict. Contradictions may be resolved as rituals incorporate contradictory elements. Thus a wedding, at once, marks the loss of members in particular roles from the families of origin, while at the same time it marks the beginnings of the new couple and in-law relationships. Since the ritual event is time and space bounded, a safe and manageable context for the expression of strong emotions is created. Rituals marking normative life cycle transitions function at many levels, enabling individual change (e.g., from adolescent to young adult; from single adult to married

adult), relationship change (e.g., from parent–child to two adults; from dating couple to married couple), family system change (e.g., expansion through the addition of members or contraction through members leaving), and family–community change (e.g., graduation marks not only a child leaving school, but a change in the family's relationship to larger systems; a retirement party marks not only a person ending work, but a change in the family's relationship to the outside world). Rituals may function to connect a family with previous generations, providing a sense of history and rootedness while simultaneously implying future relationships. The performance of and participation in such rituals link a family to the wider community through the repetition of familiar rites. Rituals may function to prevent dysfunctional isolation, especially crucial in times of grief and loss. Thus the final formal step of many funeral rituals involves the reincorporation of survivors into the community through required meals or visiting (Van Gennep, 1960).

IDIOSYNCRATIC LIFE CYCLE TRANSITIONS

While all individuals and families experience some normative life cycle transitions and participate in rituals that facilitate these transitions, many individuals and families are faced with idosyncratic life cycle transitions that, by virtue of their seemingly different or unusual nature, may not be marked by rituals. Such idiosyncratic transitions may include the birth of a handicapped child; pregnancy loss; forced separation through hospitalization, imprisonment, or terror; reunion after such forced separations; migration; living-together relationships; the end of nonmarried relationships; homosexual marriages; foster placement and the reunion after foster placement; sudden unexpected or violent death, including suicide; families formed by adoption when there is overt or covert nonsupport from family members; the leaving home of a mentally or physically handicapped young adult, especially when this leaving has not been anticipated; and chronic and incapacitating illness.

This list, which is intended to be suggestive rather than exhaustive, is shaped by broad social processes that may change over time and may differ with various cultural and socioeconomic groups. Thus pregnancy outside of a legal marriage may or may not be an idiosyncratic life cycle event with all of the aspects described above attendant to it, depending on the norms of the family, the family's reference group, and the response of the wider community. While the list may seem an unusual combination, all of the transitions named have several elements in common.

1. Familiar, repetitive, and widely accepted rituals do not exist to facilitate required changes, and to link individual, family, and community.
2. All require complex reworking of relationships, similar to normative life

cycle transitions, but lack the available maps that attend to more expected transitions.

3. Contextual support from the family of origin, the community, and the wider culture is often lacking. Individual and family events and processes are not confirmed by the family of origin, larger systems, and the community.

4. A balance of being both like others (e.g., a family with a severely handicapped member shares many features of other families) and being unlike others (e.g., a family with a severely handicapped member has certain aspects of their functioning that are different from other families) is often difficult to achieve, resulting in a skewed sense of either denying the differences or maximizing them to the exclusion of a sense of connectedness with others.

5. A sense of stigma is often experienced as a result of prejudice from the wider community. This, in turn, may lead to the emergence of secrets and conspiracies of silence that constrain relationship possibilities.

6. Involvement with larger systems is often problematic. Families with handicapped members, hospitalized members, imprisoned members, or fostered members are required to deal with larger systems in ways that alter family boundaries and relationships, often over many years. Families experiencing forced migration or migration for economic reasons are often involved with intimidating larger systems. Families whose organization and membership are not affirmed by the wider culture, such as gay couples and their children, are often stigmatized by larger systems. Since family identity and sense of competency include reflections from larger systems with whom they interact, families with any of the various idiosyncratic life cycle events and transitions listed may be at greater risk of incorporating negative images.

7. The family may abandon or interrupt familiar rituals that contribute to its sense of itself, especially if these elicit painful memories.For instance, after the loss of a member through sudden death, hospitalization, or imprisonment, members may avoid family rituals. Families who are unable to accept gay relationships of their offspring, or nonmarried heterosexual relationships, may interrupt participation in rituals. Paradoxically, such ritual abandonment or interruption functions to prevent healing and relationship development.

THE EMERGENCE OF SYMPTOMS

Family life cycle theorists (Carter & McGoldrick, 1980; Haley, 1973; Terkelson, 1980) have described the connection between normative life cycle-event derailment and the emergence of symptoms in individuals and families. Building on Haley's interpretation of Erickson's use of family life cycle theory, Carter and McGoldrick alerted the clinician to assess for both horizontal and vertical stressors in family development, while Terkelson added the category "paranormative" to include such transitions as marital separation, illness, and

severe extrinsic and unexpected events with which a family must cope, and under the stress of which may become symptomatic. Families experiencing idiosyncratic life cycle events and processes may be at particular risk for the development of symptoms in members. The convergence of lack of social support, relational cutoffs and isolation, stigma, secrecy, sense of shame in one or more members, and frequently stressful relationships with larger systems with whom the family must interact, may be mirrored by a paucity of rituals to mark developmental change. Rigid and repetitive symptoms and interactions of family members in response to symptoms metaphorically express the family's stuck position. The clinician searching for normative life cycle issues in order to hypothesize regarding the emergence of symptoms may find that idiosyncratic and often hidden life cycle processes are salient.

Case Example

An elderly woman was referred for therapy because of a "phobia." Her symptoms included compulsive handwashing, refusal to touch anyone except her children, and an inability to go to public places such as stores and restaurants. She was married and had two grown daughters and several grandchildren. The family insisted that her problems had started when she and her husband retired five years earlier, following the husband's development of ill health. A hypothesis linking her symptoms to the life cycle developmental stage of retirement and old age seemed tempting, but proved ineffective. As therapy proceeded and rapport developed through a number of interventions (see Imber-Black, 1986a, for a complete description of this case), an idiosyncratic life cycle event became available for discussion. During the 1940s the woman had become pregnant before marrying her husband. Her family had insisted that the couple move far away. The pregnancy was kept secret from the husband's family, as he had been frightened of their response. The secret was subsequently discovered, and great criticism was heaped on the woman by her new mother-in-law. The couple married with no celebration and with a great sense of shame. The birth of their first child was not marked by any celebration by the couple or by the extended family. In describing these events, the woman cried as if they had occurred yesterday, rather than nearly 50 years earlier, as they were just as alive and unresolved in the present as in the past.

The couple decided to lie to their children regarding their wedding date, and lived in constant fear that the children would find out. They avoided the celebration of their anniversary. The couple constricted their relationships with others, both among extended family and with the outside world, and became more and more turned inward. The woman's so-called "phobia" seemed now to be a metaphor for a family that lived in fear and secrecy. Her "compulsive" handwashing and family members' responses to it were highly ritualized, in a family that shared no other rituals. Many of her fears had been with her since the inception of her marriage, but like the circumstances of the marriage itself, had been kept secret until she couple's retirement and the husband's ill health. It was as if she sensed that sharing her seemingly irrational fears with other family members would finally lead to resolution of family relationships, and open the family to the outside world, which, in fact, occurred through the process of a therapy during which the couple told their secret to their children. The children responded that they had known the secret for years, but felt compelled to keep their knowledge of the secret a secret! Thus four decades of relationships had been marked by fear and

distance, as more and more topics became off-limits lest they touch on the family's origins. By the time therapy ensued, only "mother's phobia" was a safe topic for discussion. Therapy ended with a celebration of the couple's anniversary for the first time in 48 years!

In this example normative life cycle transitions had been derailed by an idiosyncratic one. The family, met by disapprobation and condemnation by the family of origin and stigma by the wider community, responded by erecting a wall of secrecy. Normative life cycle rituals to guide their development were avoided, paradoxically adding to their sense of shame. Symptoms and the interactions in response to symptoms replaced rituals as context markers for relationships. The family's resurrection of rituals (e.g., the anniversary celebration) may serve as a guide to the therapist working with families marked by idiosyncratic life cycle events and processes.

THERAPEUTIC RITUALS

The efficacy of therapeutic rituals to facilitate systemic change has been described by many clinicians (Imber-Black, 1986a, 1986b; Imber Coppersmith, 1983, 1985; O'Connor, 1984; O'Connor & Hoorwitz, 1984; Palazzoli et al., 1977; Papp, 1984; Seltzer & Seltzer, 1983; van der Hart, 1983). Differing from simple tasks whose intent is to target the behavioral level, and which the therapist expects to be performed as prescribed, rituals are intended to effect the behavioral, cognitive, and affective levels, and the family or individual is expected to improvise, in order to tailor the ritual to particular and personal circumstances. Rather than relying only on concrete instructions, rituals utilize symbols and symbolic actions that may be capable of multiple meanings. In designing therapeutic rituals, the clinician must discover which symbols are appropriate, which represent the possibility of new relationship options, and which carry enough familiarity to not be totally foreign. Thus, in designing therapeutic rituals, the therapist takes a clue from cultural rituals, which, according to Grainger (1974), "starts out from ideas which 'fit' and carries us to new,the strange, the 'unfit,' which has the power to radically transform our previous notions of fitness" (p. 11).

Therapeutic rituals as interventions for idiosyncratic life cycle events and processes often draw on elements attendant to normative life cycle rituals, in order to highlight similarities to others while at the same time including unusual elements capable of affirming differences rather than hiding them.

Although there are several categories of rituals that may be useful in therapy, three categories are particularly beneficial for idiosyncratic life cycle events and processes. These include transition rituals, healing rituals, and identity-redefinition rituals.

TRANSITION RITUALS

Transition rituals have been described extensively by van der Hart (1983), primarily in reference to normative life cycle transitions. Such rituals mark and facilitate transitions of specific members and of membership in the family, altering boundaries and making new relationship options available. The transitions needed in idiosyncratic life cycle events and processes often have no rituals. Indeed, the very transition, and all of the relationship changes attendant to it, may be unanticipated by the family.

Case Example: The Giving of Gifts

A family was rerferred for therapy by a physician for what was identified as "depression" in the mother. The family consisted of two parents, Mr. and Mrs. Berry, and two young adult children, Karen, 22, and Andrew, 20. Karen was diagnosed as "severely mentally retarded" shortly after her birth. Mrs. Berry was advised by Karen's pediatrician to quit her job, and to remain at home to care for Karen. Extended family supported this advice, and visited often while Karen and Andrew were small. The parents were told Karen would never function on her own, and would always remain "like a child." Eventually Karen went to a special school, but the parents were never counseled in ways to prepare for Karen's adolescence or adulthood. Karen developed language and self-care skills.

The family functioned well during Karen and Andrew's childhood. However, as both children became teenagers, severe difficulties ensued. No one in the nuclear or extended family knew how to cope with Karen as an emerging young woman. The family felt fearful that Karen might be exploited sexually and became increasingly protective of her. Andrew was required to spend most of his free time taking Karen to any outside events that were scheduled by her special school, and he grew increasingly resentful and withdrawn. His own plans to go away to college seemed impossible to him. Karen became rebellious and difficult for the family to be with, and the parents felt they had failed her and needed to try harder. At the same time, Karen's school began to push the family to put Karen in a group home. This option had not existed at the time of Karen's birth, and had never been anticipated by the family. For a period of two years, the parents and the school struggled regarding Karen's future. The parents were unable to articulate their fears to the school personnel, who saw them as "overinvolved" with Karen. Consequently adequate explanations of what the group home could offer Karen and her family were not forthcoming. During this time everyone in the family deteriorated emotionally and functionally, culminating in the referral for family therapy by the mother's physician.

Through the course of a therapy that affirmed the family's unanticipated life cycle change of Karen eventually leaving home, and that richly credited the family for their contributions to Karen, the family became able to ask and receive adequate information from the group home regarding Karen's future there. As the leaving home was normalized, the parents were able to articulate expectations regarding the visiting and holiday time together that mark the relationship of most young adults with their families. Andrew became freer to live his own life, and made plans for going away to college in four months, after Karen was to go to the group home. The family was preparing itself for many changes. However, as Karen began to visit the group home, first for dinners, and then for brief overnights, fights began to break out between Karen and her parents. Mr. and Mrs. Berry became

alarmed that Karen was not as ready to move out as they had thought, and in a session alone with the therapist they cried and said they feared for her future.

Since the family had made so many changes in the direction of Karen's leaving home and were just on the verge of completing the actual leaving when the fighting emerged, the therapist decided that a ritual to mark Karen's leaving home was needed. The parents had stated frequently that they "didn't think they had given Karen enough in order to equip her for life in the outside community. This sense of not having "given her enough" was intensified by the school's criticism of the family. Their phrase "given her enough" was utilized to construct a leaving-home ritual that would confirm Karen's young adulthood, would promote the family's confidence in her and themselves, and would highlight ongoing connectedness among the members.

The parents and Andrew were asked to each select a gift for Karen for her to take to her new home—one that would remind Karen of them, and would also ease her way in her new setting. Karen, in turn, was asked to select a gift for each member that would remain with them when she left. The family members were told not to buy these gifts, but to choose something of their own, or to make something. They were asked to bring these gifts to the next session, and not to tell anyone else in the family about their gift before the session.

When the family arrived, they seemed very excited and happy in a way that had not been seen before during therapy. They had not shared their gifts before the session, but had decided during the two weeks to wrap then and put them in a large bag, which Karen carried to the meeting. Mrs. Berry began by saying that during that week they had decided on a definite date for Karen to move out, which they had not been able to do previously. Karen had gone for several visits to the group home. She also said there had been a lot of secretive laughter during the two weeks, as people prepared their gifts, and no fighting!

The therapist suggested a format for the exchange of gifts that was simple and largely nonverbal, which involved each member giving his or her gift, with a brief explanation if needed, and the recipient simply saying "thank you," with other discussion reserved for after the gift exchange. This was done to highlight the family as a group together and to facilitate equal participation, since Karen often fell silent when verbal discussions became rapid.

Mr. Berry began the ceremony. He reached into the bag and gave Karen an unusually shaped package, which turned out to be his favorite frying pan. Mr Berry traditionally made Sunday breakfast. As Karen was learning some simple cooking skills in school, she had always wanted to use this frying pan, but her father had been afraid that she would ruin it and so would not let her do so. Karen beamed and said, "Thank you."

Mrs. Berry's package was small and she shyly handed it to Karen. It contained an almost full bottle of perfume and a pair of earrings. Mrs. Berry related briefly that she had often scolded Karen for using her perfume and had never allowed her to wear earrings. She looked at Karen and said, "I think you're grown up enough for these—they belonged to my mother and she gave them to me and now I'm giving them to you." With tears in her eyes, Karen said, "Thank you."

The mood changed profoundly when it was Andrew's turn. He remarked that he could not bring his whole gift to the session, but that Karen would understand. She opened his package to find a partially used box of birdseed. Leaving for school meant that Andrew could not take his parakeet. He had been allowed various pets and had been responsible for them, whereas Karen had not. He explained that he called Karen's group home and they would permit her to bring the bird. He said he would teach her to care for it before she moved out. Karen thanked him, and Mrs. Berry expressed relief that the parakeet was leaving home too!

Karen then gave her gifts. To her mother Karen gave her favorite stuffed

animal, which she had had since early childhood, and with which she still slept. She said to her mother, "I can't sleep with this in my new home—please keep it." To her father she gave a photograph of her that had been taken on one of her visits at the group home. The photograph showed her sitting with several young men and women, and she said to her father, "These are my new friends." To Andrew she gave her clock radio. This was a prized possession that had been a Christmas gift. As she presented it to Andrew, she said, "Don't be late for school!"

Two weeks after this session, Karen moved into the group home, and a month later Andrew left for college. The family ended therapy. At the one-year follow-up, the family reported that both children had adjusted well to their new settings and were to visit home for holidays. Mrs. Berry had also returned to school in order to train for paid employment.

DISCUSSION OF THE RITUAL

This leaving-home ritual seemed to function in a number of ways. Through the course of the family therapy, the family had been preparing for Karen's leaving home, but seemed to get stuck just at the verge of her actual leaving. Like many normative life cycle rituals, the therapeutic ritual worked to confirm a process that was already in motion, and was not simply a discrete event. The ritual symbolically affirmed and made simultaneous the contradictions of separation and ongoing connectedness involved when any child leaves home. The family members, in their giving of gifts, were able both to give permission for separation and to affirm their ongoing, but changing, relationships.

The ritual was designed to introduce symmetry into a system primarily marked by complementary relationships. Thus all members participated in the giving and receiving of gifts, and in the planning and thoughtfulness that went into gift selection, thus altering the previous pattern in the family whereby the parents and Andrew were seen to be the "givers," the "providers," the "protectors," and Karen the recipient of care, advice, and protection.

The ritual was also designed to confirm individual boundaries as each member was individually responsible for his or her own planning and selection of gifts. Individuation was promoted through the instruction of "secret planning" by each member. Dyadic relationships between Karen and every member were also confirmed, in a family that previously operated with triads involving Karen as their primary mode of relationship. Finally, each member's contribution to the ritual was highlighted as important to the entire process, thus symbolically celebrating the whole family unit. Thus various aspects of the ritual functioned to introduce differences in pattern to the family system.

By asking the family to bring their gifts to the therapy session, the therapist was able to serve as witness to the process. Witnesses are frequently a part of nomative life cycle rituals. The therapist also may be seen symbolically to represent an outside helping system in a celebratory stance with a family who had been used to criticism and disparagement from outside systems.

This ritual, "the giving of gifts," has also been used successfully with other families that are struggling with either difficult or precipitous leaving-home processes (e.g., children leaving one parent to live with another or children leaving temporarily for an outide placement).

HEALING RITUALS

Healing rituals are a part of human tradition. Every culture has rituals to mark profound losses, deal with the grief of survivors, and facilitate ongoing life after such loss. Healing may be necessary, however, not only in the case of the loss of a member through death, but also for losses sustained through the breakup of relationships, for the reconciliation of relationships after painful revelations (e.g., affairs), for unresolved grief when normative healing rituals have not occurred or have not succeeded, for losses of bodily parts and functions due to illness, and for the often attendant loss of roles, life expectations, and dreams (see Imber Coppersmith, 1985, and Palazolli, et al., 1974, for case examples of healing rituals). Therapeutic healing rituals are particularly useful when normative healing rituals do not exist (e.g., pregnancy loss; the end of important relationships, especially those unconfirmed by the wider community; recovery from political terror) or are not sustaining for the magnitude of the loss (e.g., suicide or other sudden, violent, or unexpected death).

Case Example: Setting Fire to the Past

Alice Jeffers, 35, requested therapy, saying that she was depressed and unable to live her life normally. Alice was single and lived alone. She was a trained and practicing veterinarian. At the first session, she said that she had been in an eight-year-long relationship with a man. The relationship, which had included periods of living together, had been very stormy, and had finally ended two years previously at his insistence. When the relationship was ongoing, Alice's family had not approved. They were relieved when it ended, but seemed unable to extend any support to Alice for the pain she felt. Friends told her she was well rid of him. Over the two years, Alice grew increasingly isolated, and by the time she came to therapy, she did not go out with any friends, spent all her free time thinking about her former lover and dreamed about him nightly, had gained a lot of weight, and felt that her work was being affected. Her own family and friends' inability to confirm her pain and loss seemed to contribute to her own need to do nothing else but think about him and feel sad. She said she felt that if she had been married and divorced, people would have been more supportive, as they had been of her sister in such circumstances.

The therapist began with a simple confirmation of Alice's loss and grief, and highlighted the fact that there are no agreed-upon processes for the end of a nonmarried relationship. Alice was asked to do a task that would allow her both to grieve and to begin to get on with other aspect of life. For one hour a day, Alice was told, she should do nothing but review memories of the relationship, since this was something that obviously still needed to be completed. The therapist sug-

gested that she write these memoirs on separate index cards and bring them to the next session. Except for that hour a day, Alice was urged to do other things. If she found memories intruding into this outside time, then it meant that an hour a day was not enough, and she should increase the time to an hour and a half.

Alice returned with a stack of index cards, which she had creatively color coded, using purple for "mellow' memories, green for 'jealous" memories, and blue for "sad" memories. Then, with laughter, she stated, "And, of course, my anger ones are *red!*" As the therapy session focused on the cards and their meanings, Alice stated that she had felt much better during the three weeks, that she had begun to find that an hour a day was too much time, and that she had stopped dreaming about her former lover. The therapist asked her if there were cards she felt ready to let go of, and she said that there were. She was asked to take all the cards home and sort them out, differentiating between those she still wanted to hang on to and those she felt ready to release.

Alice arrived two weeks later, dressed more brightly than previously and eager to talk. She had started to go out with friends, and had considered an aerobics class. After reporting this, she took out two stacks of cards. She said she had decided she wanted to keep the purple "mellow" memories, as these were a part of her that she wanted to maintain. She felt the good parts of the relationship had changed her in positive ways, and she said she wanted to carry this into any new relationship she might have. This was the first mention of a sense of the future. She also wanted to keep most of the red "anger" memories, as these helped her to remember how shabbily she had been treated many times and so kept her from romanticizing the past. She was, however, very ready to let go of the green "jealousy" memories, which often made her feel bad about herself, and the blue "sad" memories, as she felt she had been sad long enough! At that point the therapist left the room and returned with a ceremic bowl and a book of matches and silently offered these to Alice, who smiled and said "Oh, we should burn them!" It is important to note that she saw the burning as a joint endeavor of herself and the therapist. The therapist handed the cards back to Alice, who put them in a pile in the bowl and lit them. She used several matches in order to get a good fire going and then sat silently for several moments watching the flames. At one point she said, "It's so final, but it's good." A few minutes later, she joked, "We should toast marshmellows—that would be the final irony," referring to the fact that her boyfriend had often criticized her body and her weight and yet brought her treats. Toward the end she said, "This is good—my final memory is of warmth."

In sessions subsequent to the burning ritual, Alice dealt with many family-of-origin issues that were previously unavailable due to her stuck position vis-à-vis her boyfriend. She was able to renegotiate several relationships, began going out more with friends, and started a scuba class. When therapy ended she was beginning flying lessons, an apt metaphor for her new beginnings.

DISCUSSION OF THE RITUAL

Several elements that are common to therapeutic healing rituals were utilized in this case, including affirmation of pain and loss, alternation of holding on and letting go, and action to symbolize finality. When appropriate healing has not occurred in a relationship or situation, well-meaning friends and family often discourage the expression of pain or otherwise attempt to

minimize turmoil. As in Alice's case, this frequently has the opposite effect, and the person may become doubly troubled, both by sadnes and by the subsequent sense of isolation. Therapeutic healing rituals should begin with an affirmation of this sadness, and then lead to a gradual process of letting go that respects the client's pace. Symbolic action in therapeutic healing rituals often mirrors that which occurs in normative healing rituals, such as burning and burying. In this case the therapist served as a witnes to and coparticipant in the healing process. This coparticipation was spontaneously invited by Alice, and was an important element due to her sense of isolation. Healing rituals may be followed by celebration rituals. In the case under discussion, Alice designed her own celebration ritual, the buying of several new outfits to define what she called her "new style."

IDENTITY-REDEFINITION RITUALS

Identity-redefinition rituals function to remove labels and stigma from individuals, couples, and families, and often realign relationships between the family and larger systems, especially necessary when the larger systems have held negative points of view toward a family. A reworking of an earlier idiosyncratic life cycle transition that went awry may be accomplished. New relationship options, previously unavailable due to the constraints of labels, become available (Imber Coppersmith, 1983). A balance of being both similar to others and different from others becomes achievable.

Case Example: An Adoption Celebration

A family was referred for therapy by social services. The family consisted of the father and mother, Mr. and Mrs. Oscar, and their son Wayne, 10 years old. At the time of referral, Wayne, who had been adopted as an infant, was living in a foster home, and the parents were considering interrupting the adoption, because, as they both stated, they were "bad parents." Their proof that they were "bad parents" included Wayne's behavior and learning problems at school and at home. They believed that if they were "good parents," Wayne would be "good."

The therapist investigated the origins of and contributions to the parents' idea that they were "bad parents' and discovered that this idea began when they could not have biological children. Mrs. Oscar said she knew she must somehow be a "bad" person or God would have given her children. Both sets of grandparents disapproved of the adoption of Wayne, and there were no celebrations or gifts to mark his entry into the Oscar family. When Wayne was quite small, and began to do the normal mischievious things that little boys do, Mrs. Oscar had nobody to talk it over with, and began to feel more certain that she was a "bad mother." This process escalated when Wayne began school. He had learning difficulties and was quickly labeled a problem. Mrs. Oscar frequently attended school meetings. These meetings reinforced her sense that they were "bad parents."

The therapist asked the parents to tell her in what ways their family was like other families and what ways it was unlike other families. They were unable to

define any ways in which they were like other families, except for such things as living in a house and eating meals together. They saw themselves as completely unlike other families because their family had been formed by adoption. For this same reason, Wayne was defined as totally unlike other boys. His similarities to other boys his age went unseen, and only his differences were highlighted. The family's interactions with larger helping systems over several years had reified this view, culminating in Wayne's placement in foster care. As the session continued, it became apparent that the parents sincerely wanted to have Wayne return to them and that the idea of interrupting the adoption had come from social services. Therapy began with the theme of highlighting both the family's similarities to and differences from other families.

Over the course of therapy, Wayne's behavior in the foster home, at school, and on visits home began to improve. Plans were made for his return home. The therapist decided to use the occasion of Wayne's return for an identity-redefinition ritual that would alter all members' perceptions of themselves and their family. The therapist explained to the parents that one problem for Wayne and for their family began when Wayne was adopted and no celebration was held because of the attitudes of their families of origin. This set the family on a course of feeling different from other families, because families generally celebrate the arrival of babies. Wayne's leaving to go to foster care was reframed as an opportunity to redo his entry into the family. The parents were asked to plan an adoption party that would celebrate Wayne as their son. Wayne knew about the party, and in a separate brief meeting with the therapist, he was asked to do something to celebrate his mother and father as his parents. The Oscars chose to invite friends and family. They also invited the therapist, Wayne's prior foster mother, and the social service worker. Not all members of their families were willing to come, but several did, and brought gifts for Wayne. Regarding the members who chose not to come, Mrs. Oscar said later, "It says more about them than it does about us!" Pictures of Wayne as a baby were displayed, which they had not been previously. The parents served ice cream and cake, and Wayne, who had listened attentively during the sessions when his parents talked about being "bad parents," put up a sign that said, "I'm glad I have good parents!"[1]

After the adoption celebration, Wayne's behavior at home and school continued to improve. On follow-up the therapist inquired about Wayne, and Mr. and Mrs. Oscar were able to relate any misbehavior of Wayne's to "normal preteen activities" rather than to his adoption or to their being "bad parents."

DISCUSSION OF THE RITUAL

This identity-redefinition ritual functioned to redefine Wayne, his parents, the family as a whole, and the family's relationship to the extended family and the outside world, as exemplified by larger systems. Placed in a therapy that had successfully challenged the parents' negative views of themselves and their son, the adoption celebration ritual recontextualized Wayne's place in the family as a cause for celebration rather than as a cause for shame. Stigma was lifted, and the family refused to accept further stigma from the families of

[1]A variation of this adoption celebration was first created and utilized by the Family Therapy Training Team at the University of Massachusetts, including Richard Whiting, Linda Giardino, Janine Roberts, John Anderson, and David Armstrong, with Evan Imber-Black, supervisor.

origin or larger systems. The family's similarities to other families (e.g., families have parties to celebrate the entry of children) and their uniqueness as an adoptive family were highlighted and confirmed.

DESIGNING AND IMPLEMENTING THERAPEUTIC RITUALS FOR IDIOSYNCRATIC LIFE CYCLE TRANSITIONS

Watzlawick (1978) has referred to therapeutic rituals as "the most comprehensive and the most elegant of all the interventions" (p. 154). Palazzolli (1974) has suggested that rituals require great creativity on the part of the therapist. Designing and implementing the rituals under discussion in this chapter, however, are a learnable skill. Several guidelines will enhance this process.

1. Just as normative rituals are processes, rather than discrete events, so therapeutic rituals are part of a larger therapeutic process. Their efficacy relies on planning, careful assessment, especially regarding life cycle phases and idiosyncratic life cycle events, and respect and rapport between family and therapist. The rituals intended here are not "games" or "tricks" but rise out of a relational context that appreciates the ritualizing tendency of human beings and the need for meaning in human relationships.

2. The therapist searches to discover the appropriate symbols and symbolic acts of the individual, family, and ethnic and cultural group, which represent the possibility of relationship development. Such symbols and metaphorical action should connect the family with the familiar, while also being capable of leading to the unfamiliar. The therapist must remain open to the development of multiple new meanings the family elicits from the symbols used, and not predetermine these outcomes.

3. The therapist designs the ritual, utilizing family input for the dimensions of time and space. Thus rituals may occur at a particular time or over time. Time may be used to draw particular distinctions or to highlight simultaneity. A sense of connection to past, present, and future is made. The ritual may occur in the therapy session or at home or some other agreed-upon place, such as near a body of water, in a woods, or in a cemetery. If the therapist determines that having a witness is important, then the therapy session is often the preferred time and space.

4. The therapist attends to alternations in order to incorporate contradictions. Thus holding on may be alternated with letting go in a single ritual, or a ritual of termination or separation may be followed by a ritual of renewal or celebration.

5. The therapist is careful to leave aspects of the ritual for the family to

design and improvise in order to facilitate imagination that may lead to problem solving and enhanced functioning. A sense of humor and playfulness are utilized when appropriate.

6. Therapeutic rituals for idiosyncratic life cycle events borrow heavily from normative rituals.

7. The therapist remains open to the family's development of the ritual, including the choice not to do the ritual. Therapeutic rituals, just like normative rituals, should not be hollow events, practiced simply because someone said to do it. They are opportunities for the confirmation of existing relationships and for the beginnings of relationship change. Family readiness must be carefully gauged and respected. In successful therapeutic rituals, the ritual and its outcome ultimately belong to the family.

CONCLUSIONS

Idiosyncratic life cycle events and transitions pose particular difficulties for individuals and families. Lacking both available maps that attend to more expected transitions and wider contextual support and confirmation, complex feedback processes may be set in motion, resulting in symptoms and a high level of distress and isolation. Therapeutic rituals, creatively designed to enhance family or individual client participation in the shape of their ultimate form, and borrowing richly from normative life cycle rituals, facilitate necessary transitions, healing, and the expansion of relationship possibilities.

REFERENCES

Carter, E. A., & McGoldrick, M. (1980). The family life cycle and family therapy. In E. A. Carter & M. Goldrick (eds.). *The family life cycle: A framework for family therapy,* New York: Gardner Press.

Grainger, R. (1974). *The language of the rite.* London: Dacton, Longmann & Todd.

Haley, J. (1973). *Uncommon therapy: The psychiatric techniques of Milton H. Erickson,* New York: Norton.

Imber-Black, E. (1986a). Odysseys of a learner. In D. Efron (Ed.), *Journeys: Expansion of the strategic-systemic therapies.* New York: Brunner/Mazel.

Inber-Black, E. (1986b). Toward a resource model in systemic family therapy. In M. Karpel (Ed.), *Family resources.* New York: Guilford Press.

Imber Coppersmith, E. (1983). From hyperactive to normal but naughty: A multisystem partnership in delabeling. *International Journal of Family Psychiatry* 3/2: 131–44.

Imber Coppersmith, E. (1985). We've got a secret: A non-marital marital therapy. *In A. Gurman (d.), Casebook of marital therapy.* New York: Guilford Press.

O'Connor, J. (1984). The resurrection of a magical reality: Treatment of functional migraine in a child. *Family Process* 23/44: 501–509.

O'Connor, J., & Hoorwitz, A. N. (1984). The bogeyman cometh: A strategic approach for difficult adolescents. *Family Process* 23/24: 237–249.

Palazzoli, M. (1974). *Self-starvation: From the intrapsychic to the transpersonal approach to anorexia nervosa.* London: Caucer Publishing Co.

Palazzoli, M., Boscolo, L., Cecchin, G., & Prata, G. (1974). The treatment of children through the brief therapy of their parents. *Family Process* 13: 429–42.

Palazzoli, M., Boscolo, L., Cecchin, G., & Prata, G. (1977). Family rituals. A powerful tool in family therapy. *Family Process* 16/4: 445–453.

Papp, P. (1984). The links between clinical and artistic creativity. *The Family Therapy Networker* 8/5: 20›9.

Schwartzman, J. (1982). Symptoms and rituals: paradoxical modes and social organization. *Ethos* 10/1: 3–23.

Seltzer, W., & Seltzer, M. (1983). Magic, material, and myth, *Family Process* 22/1: 3–14.

Terkleson, K. G. (1980). Toward a theory of the family life cycle. In E. A. Carter & M. McGoldrick (Eds.), *The family life cycle: A framework for family therapy.* New York: Gardner Press.

Van der Hart, O. (1983). Rituals in psychotherapy: Transition and continuity. New York: Ivington Publishers.

Van Gennep, A. (1960). *The rites of passage.* Chicago: University of Chicago Press.

Watzlawick, P. (1978). *The language of change: Elements of therapeutic communication.* New York: Basic Books.

Wolin, S. J., & Bennett, S. A. (1984). Family rituals. *Family Process* 23/3: 401»20.

8

Genograms
and the Family Life Cycle

Monica McGoldrick, M.S.W., and Randy Gerson, Ph.D.

When evaluating a family's place in the life cycle, we have found genograms and family chronologies to be useful tools. They provide at a glance a three-generational picture of a family and its motion through the life cycle. This chapter explores how genograms can elucidate the family life cycle framework and how an understanding of the life cycle can aid in the interpretation of the genogram. We consider both the patterns that typically occur at various phases of the life cycle and the issues to be predicted when life cycle events are "off schedule." The family of Sigmund Freud is used to illustrate life cycle issues on a genogram.

The family life cycle is a complex phenomenon. It is a spiral of family evolution as generations move through time in their development from birth to death. One might compare this family process to music, in which the meaning of individual notes depends on their rhythms in conjunction with each other and with the memories of past melodies and the anticipation of those yet to come. Genograms are graphic pictures of the family history and pattern, showing the basic structure, family demographics, functioning, and relationships. They are a shorthand used to depict the family patterns at a glance. Table 8-1 shows the basic format for constructing a genogram according to the standardization described by McGoldrick and Gerson in 1985.

MARRIAGE AND REMARRIAGE

Since the life cycle is circular and repetitive, one can start at any point to tell the story of a family. With the Freud family we begin a few years before the birth of its most famous member, Sigmund, at the time of his parents' marriage. It should be remembered that much of what we suggest about the Freud family is speculative, since a great deal of information is missing from the historical

Table 8-1 Genogram Format

A. Symbols to describe basic family membership and structure (include on genogram significant others who lived with or cared for family members—place them on the right side of the genogram with a notation about who they are).

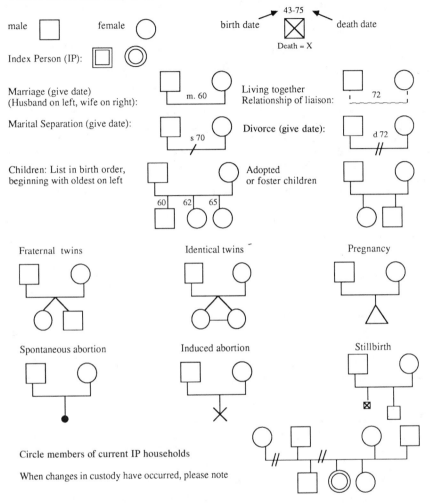

[continued on page 166]

[*continued from page 165*]

B. Family interaction patterns. The following symbols are optional. The clinician may prefer to note them on a separate sheet. They are among the least precise information on the genogram, but may be key indicators of relationship patterns the clincian wants to remember:

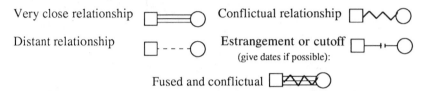

Very close relationship   Conflictual relationship

Distant relationship   Estrangement or cutoff
(give dates if possible):

Fused and conflictual

C. Medical history. Since the genogram is meant to be an orienting map of the family, there is room to indicate only the most important factors. Thus, list only major or chronic illnesses and problems. Include dates in parentheses where feasible or applicable. Use DSM-III categories or recognized abbreviations where available (e.g., cancer CA; stroke CVA).

D. Other family information of special importance may also be noted on the genogram:

    1. Ethnic background and migration date
    2. Religion or religious change
    3. Education
    4. Occupation or unemployment
    5. Military service
    6. Retirement
    7. Trouble with law
    8. Physical abuse or incest
    9. Obesity
    10. Alcohol or drug abuse (symbol = ◧ ○)
    11. Smoking
    12. Dates family members left home: LH '74
    13. Current location of family members

It is useful to have a space at the bottom of the genogram for notes on other key information: This would include critical events, changed in the family structure since the genogram was made, hypotheses, and other notations of major family issues or changes. These notations should always be dated, and should be kept to a minimum, since every extra piece of information on a genogram complicates it and therefore diminishes its readability.

record. The following is meant only to illustrate the use of the family life cycle in evaluating family patterns with genograms.

At the marriage or remarriage phase, the genogram shows the coming together of two separate families, indicating where each spouse is in his or her own family life cycle. In order to start a new family, both partners must come to terms with their families of origin. The genogram gives clues to the connectedness of the spouses to their own families, and their respective roles in these families. When one spouse competes with the other's family or when parents do not approve of their child's choice, in-law triangles may begin at this phase. The genogram also shows the previous relationships that may interfere with current marital bonding.

As can be seen on the genogram of the Freud family in 1855 (Figure 8-1), the marriage of Jacob Freud and Amelia Nathansohn had a number of atypical aspects. Jacob, who was 40, was marrying for the third time. Amelia was just 20. In fact, the new wife was even younger than one of Jacob's sons from his first marriage. These differences between spouses would tend to complicate their transition into a new family.

We know that Jacob Freud and his first wife, Sally Kanner, had two sons, and two other children who did not survive, but little is known about Sally, and less about Jacob's second wife, Rebecca (Clark, 1980; Glicklhorn, 1969). We do not know what happened to either wife—whether the couple divorced or the wife died. The missing information evokes curiosity about Jacob's first marriages and their implications for his third marriage, to Amelia. Jacob's first marriage took place when he was only 16, suggesting the possibility of an unexpected pregnancy (Anzieu, 1986). The second marriage is even more mysterious. This wife, Rebecca, was never mentioned by any family member and we only know of her existence from the public records. It appears that she married Jacob in about 1852, so Jacob's sons Emanuel and Philip would have been grown, and they would obviously have known her. Surely Amalia would at least have known of her existence, as they all lived in the same town; and yet, if anyone ever did mention her to Freud, he never told anyone. One wonders why. Was there something about her of which the family was ashamed? In any case Jacob and Amelia obviously began their new family in the shadow of Jacob's earlier marriages.

When examining the genogram, it is particularly important to note the ages of family members as they move through the life cycle. There is a normative timing for the transition to each of its phases. These norms are ever-changing, and have varied across cultures and throughout history, but they can serve as a starting point for understanding more about life cycle transitions in a family. For example, if children marry late or never leave home, this may speak to the difficulty of differentiating from their family. With any newly married couple, it is important to note the spouses' positions within the life cycles of their respective families. Jacob was already a grandfather whereas Amelia, 20 years younger and a peer of his sons, was at the young adult phase. How did these two happen to marry? We know that Jacob had no particular business pros-

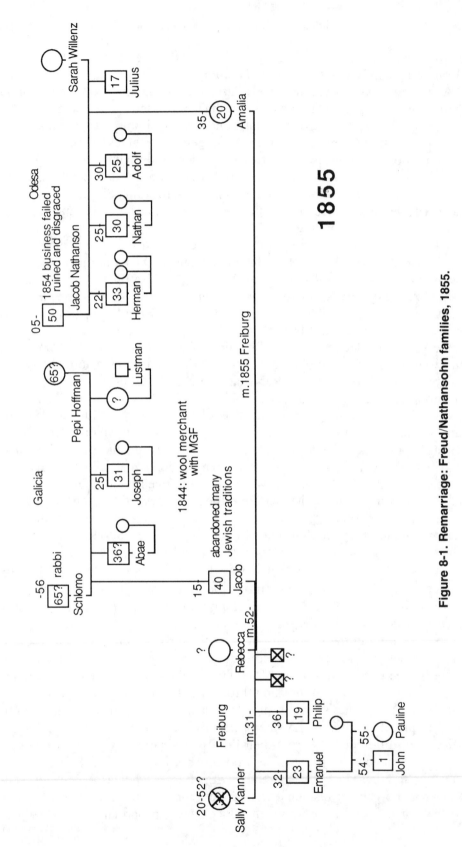

Figure 8-1. Remarriage: Freud/Nathansohn families, 1855.

pects at that time (Swales, 1986), so we may wonder what led Amalia to agree to marry a man so much older, with grown sons and two previous marriages. It seems that Amalia's father had recently lost his fortune, which may explain the situation (Swales, 1986). In any case, Amalia was a vivacious young woman, one of the youngest in her family. Jacob, for his part, had experienced many ups and downs. Having done fairly well in his 30s as a traveling salesman with his maternal grandfather, he seemingly came to a standstill in midlife. One would predict, upon seeing these indications on a genogram, that differences in experience and expectation could lead to a problematic life cycle transition.

Our life cycle framework suggests that unresolved issues in earlier phases of the life cycle lead to more difficult transitions and complexities in later life cycle stages. Thus it is likely that with Jacob's previous marriages and mysterious past and the discrepancies in age and expectations, as well as their financial precariousness, Jacob and Amalia entered their marriage with many complex issues unresolved.

It is also useful to examine the genogram for predictable triangles and patterns at different life cycle stages. As discussed by McGoldrick and Carter in Chapter 17, remarried families are formed on an entirely different basis than first families, as they are built on the losses of the first family. They require an additional phase of the life cycle. There are at least two predictable triangles to search for in the genogram of a remarried family: (1) that involving the two new spouses and the previous spouse (or the memory of the previous spouse), and (2) that involving the two new spouses and the children of the previous marriage. We know nothing of Amalia's relationship with Jacob's previous wives, nor do we know details of her relationship with Emanuel and Philip. We do know that in Freud's fantasy, his mother and Philip were lovers, and that within three years of the marriage Jacob helped arrange for his sons to emigrate to England. Might he have done this partly to have his sons at a safe distance from his wife?

THE TRANSITION TO PARENTHOOD AND FAMILIES WITH YOUNG CHILDREN

During the transition to parenthood and to becoming a family with young children, the parents must bear the heavy responsibility of child rearing while trying to maintain their own relationship. The genogram often reveals stressors that make this phase particularly difficult for the parents. By providing a quick map of the sibling constellation, the genogram may also reveal the particular circumstances surrounding the birth of a child and how those circumstances may contribute to the child's having a special position in that family. Finally, the genogram will show the typical mother–father–child triangles of this period.

As can be seen on the genogram of the Freud family for 1866 (Figure 8-2),

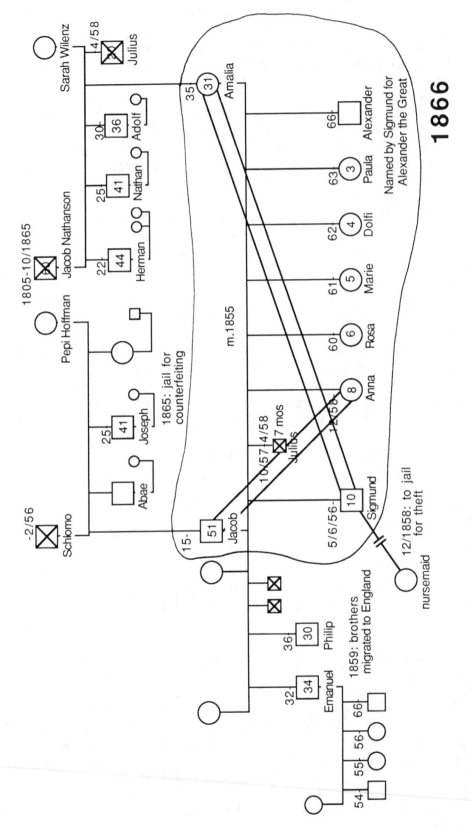

1866

Figure 8-2. Family with young children: Freud family, 1866.

Sigmund was born in 1856 in Freiburg, Moravia. He was the first of eight children so his birth marked the beginning of the life cycle transition of a second family with young children. Being born into a remarried family, he had two grown stepbrothers from his father's previous marriage. All of these particulars, seen on the genogram, suggest an important role for Sigmund as the first member of a new nuclear family.

It is the birth of the first child, more than the marriage itself, that most profoundly marks the transition to a new family. The previously married spouse begins to shift toward the new spouse and child. For the new spouse, the child tends to signify greater legitimization and power in relation to the partner's previous family. Sigmund definitely seemed to have a special place in his mother's heart. He had an extremely intense relationship with her (Nelken, in press) and she always referred to him as her "golden Sigi." By all accounts he was the center of the household. There is the proverbial family story that when his sister Anna wanted to play the piano, their mother bought one, but got rid of it immediately when Sigmund complained that the noise bothered him. His sisters did not have any further piano lessons. Sigmund's special position is further indicated by the fact that the family gave him the privilege of naming his younger brother, Alexander, born when Sigmund was ten. (Interestingly, in his own marriage he himself named every one of his six children, all for his male heroes or one of their family members!) The Freuds' cultural preference for sons further exalted Sigmund's position in his family.

It is also important in evaluating a life cycle transition to examine the stressors impinging on the family at the time. When one sees coincidental losses and traumatic events on the genogram, one should begin to explore their possible effect on the process of the life cycle.

From a systemic perspective, loss is viewed as a major transition that disrupts life cycle patterns of interaction, and so requires family reorganization and poses shared adaptational challenges. A family's sense of motion through the life cycle may become stuck or distorted after a loss, and genograms allow one to track the effect of losses over time.

As can be seen on the genogram for 1859 (Figure 8-3), there was much going on in the Freud family around the time of Sigmund's birth. Sigmund's specialness for his father may have been intensified by the fact that Jacob's own father died less than three months before Sigmund was born and Sigmund was named for him. This grandfather, Schlomo, was a rabbi, and perhaps Sigmund was raised to follow in his footsteps by becoming a teacher and intellectual leader. Sigmund's family role was obviously also influenced by his brilliance. Another factor accounting for his special role was probably that he was born at the high point in the family's hopes. Shortly afterward they had to migrate twice and Jacob suffered from various business failures. Sigmund's younger siblings, particularly Anna and Dolfi, may have borne the brunt of the negative effects of these changes on the family.

Equally important, it can be seen on the genogram that Sigmund's brother Julius, born when Sigmund was 17 months old, lived for only seven months.

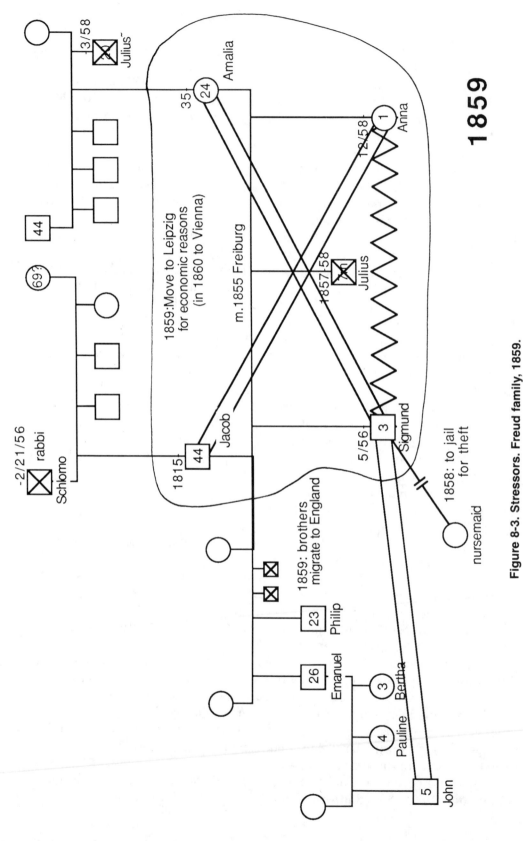

Figure 8-3. Stressors. Freud family, 1859.

172

The death of a sibling tends to intensify parental feelings about the surviving children. The child nearest in age, especially a child of the same sex, often becomes a replacement for the lost child. Thus Sigmund's closeness to his mother may have become even more important to her after the death of her second son. The loss of this infant would itself have been intensified by the fact that exactly one month before his death, Amelia's youngest brother, also named Julius, died at the age of 20 from pulmonary tuberculosis (Krull, 1986). Probably she knew that her brother was dying when she named her son for him seven months earlier. In later life Sigmund said that he had welcomed this brother with "ill wishes and real infantile jealousy, and his death left the germ of guilt in me" (cited in Krull, 1986).

The oldest sometimes resents the later born, feeling threatened or displaced by the new arrival. From a very early age, Sigmund may have seen Anna as an intrusion, and she may have resented his special position and privileges in the family. She was conceived the month before the death of the second child, Julius. Sigmund's sibling rivalry might have been compounded by family ambivalence about the first child born after a lost son. These feelings of rivalry can linger into adulthood. Sigmund's relationship with his sister Anna seems never to have been very close, and they were alienated as adults.

Another complicating factor in terms of the sibling constellation can be seen on the genogram. For the first three years of his life, Sigmund was raised almost as a younger brother to his nephew John, who was a year or so older than he. Sigmund has commented on the importance of this relationship: "Until the end of my third year we had been inseparable; we had loved each other and fought each other and . . . this childish relationship has determined all my later feelings in intercourse with persons my own age. My nephew, John, has since then had many incarnations, which have revived first one and then another aspect of character and is ineradicably fixed in my conscious memory. At times he must have treated me very badly and I must have opposed my tyrant courageously" (Jones, 1953, p. 8).

This beginning phase of a new family, of which Sigmund was the first, finally concluded with a splitting and emigration of the old family. We do not know the details of why the Freud family left Freiburg. It seems that Jacob and Amelia shared a nursemaid with Emanuel and his wife and the cousins played well together. The nursemaid was eventually dismissed from the household for stealing, and this was another loss for Sigmund. Perhaps there were tensions between Amelia and her stepsons Emanuel and Phillip, who reminded her of Jacob's earlier loyalties. As already mentioned, there is even a hint of a possible affair. In any case, when Sigmund was three, his stepbrothers and their families went to England to find their fortunes, and Jacob moved his family first to Leipzig, and then to Vienna, possibly because of economic reversals. Thus, within a period of a few years, Sigmund experienced a multitude of losses: his priority as the earliest born, the death of his brother, the dismissal of the nursemaid, the emigration of his stepbrothers and their children, and, finally, the uprooting of his own family.

FAMILIES WITH ADOLESCENTS

Once the children reach adolescence, the task is to prepare the family for a qualitative change in the relationships between the generations, as the children are no longer so dependent on their parents. During this period triangles are likely to develop involving the adolescents, their peers, and their parents, or the adolescents, their parents, and their grandparents. The genogram often reveals the family boundaries and multigenerational patterns that are predictive of how easily the family will adjust to this phase.

Figure 8-4 shows the Freud family in 1873, the year Sigmund turned 17 and entered medical school. We have little specific information on family events at that time, but the genogram suggests a family with many burdens of child rearing, with seven children all still in the home. We may also wonder if the discrepancy in age between Jacob and Amelia would not be felt even more at this stage in the life cycle. Jacob, at 58, may have been feeling his age. Sigmund later described his father as rather grouchy and disappointed in the last part of his life. Jacob was particularly disappointed in his sons Emanuel and Philip. Sigmund later reported that he felt as through he had to make up for their absence. We also know that Jacob's brother was jailed for counterfeiting, an experience that Sigmund later said turned his father's hair gray. [It appears that Jacob was implicated in the scheme—or at least his sons were, which could account for their earlier move to England (Krull, 1986; Swales, 1986).] In contrast, Amelia, at 38, was still energetic, attractive, and youthful. We do not know whether these differences in age, energy level, and outlook led to tension or conflict between Jacob and Amelia, but, given her devotion to Sigmund and the demands of a large household, it is likely that her energies were more focused on her children than on her spouse.

It is during adolescence that children begin to have interests outside the family, both in school and with friends. Sigmund did very well in school, and was at the top of his gymnasium class for six of his eight years there (Prause, 1978). His success with his peers was less spectacular. The genogram will sometimes indicate important peers in a child's life and whether family boundaries easily include outsiders. We know of Sigmund having only one close friend at school, Eduard Silberstein, with whom he corresponded and formed a secret society. At 16 he had a crush on a friend's sister, Gisela Fluss, but never expressed his feelings to her. By all accounts he was a shy, intense, serious young man who focused more on his studies than on socializing. Perhaps he was responding to a mandate from his family: to excel in school and to succeed in life, and so justify his special position in his family.

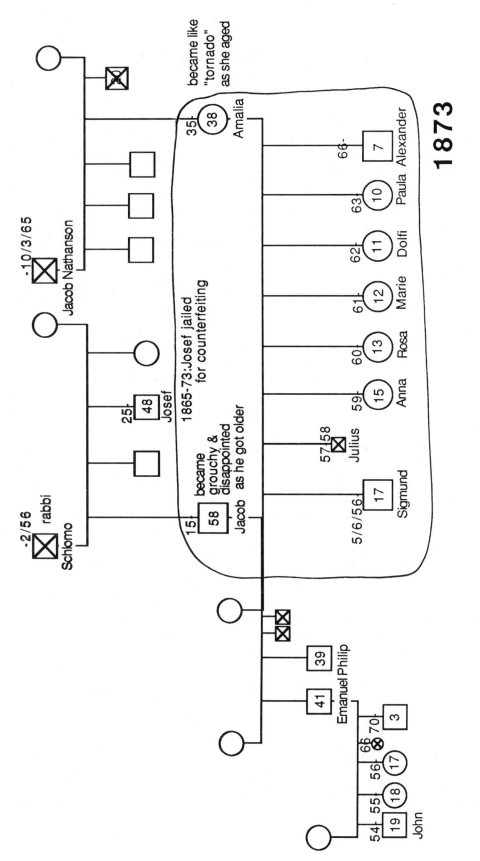

Figure 8-4. Family with adolescents. Freud family, 1873.

175

FAMILIES AT MIDLIFE: LAUNCHING
CHILDREN AND MOVING ON

The genogram also allows us to anticipate the developments of the next generation. If we look at the genogram of the Bernays family (Figure 8-5), we see that the early years, and particularly the adolescence and young adulthood of Martha, Sigmund's future wife, were turbulent and displayed certain parallels with the Freud family. Her older brother Isaac had had medical problems in childhood that required a great deal of medical attention and left him lame. As he was growing up, Isaac was reportedly a difficult child with destructive tendencies (Swales, 1986), and kept the household in an uproar. In addition, the three children following Isaac all died in early childhood. Finally came Eli, Martha, and Minna. Like the Freud family, the Bernays had to deal with the death of young children. When Martha was eight, her father was briefly jailed for fraud, undoubtedly bringing a sense of disgrace to the family. Like Sigmund (whose uncle and perhaps father and brothers were involved in counterfeiting), Martha grew up in an atmosphere of secrets and forebodings of potential ruin and disgrace. When Martha was 11, her older brother Isaac, then 17, died. And when she was 18, Martha's father died of a heart attack. The family was left in very poor financial circumstances. Like the Freud family, with Jacob's apparent continued unemployment in his later years, it is not clear how the Bernays survived. Eli, who took over the running of the family, eventually fled Vienna to avoid bankruptcy and the payment of debts owed to friends. One could speculate that the similarities in background and experience of Sigmund and Martha may have been part of their attraction for one another.

The phase of launching is the period when children leave home to be on their own. In the past this phase usually quickly blended into marriage, since children often did not leave home until they married. Now many go through a period of being a single adult. In our view this phase is the cornerstone of the modern family life cycle, and crucial for all the other phases that are to follow. The short-circuiting of this phase, or its prolongation, may affect all future life cycle transitions. The genogram often reveals the duration of the launching phase, as well as factors that may contribute to a delay of launching.

The information we have on the Freud family during the launching phase is quite scanty. As already mentioned, Sigmund held a favored, almost exalted, position in his family. Sometimes this can lead to difficulties in the launching phase, where a young adult is hesitant to leave such a favored position and the parents may be unwilling to let their special child go. In Sigmund's day children usually did not leave home as single young adults, but lived in their parents' household until they married and established a household of their own. This was also true of Sigmund, who lived with his parents until he was 30, when he married Martha Bernays.

One interesting fact from the perspective of the life cycle is how long it took Sigmund to complete his medical studies. He took seven years to get his

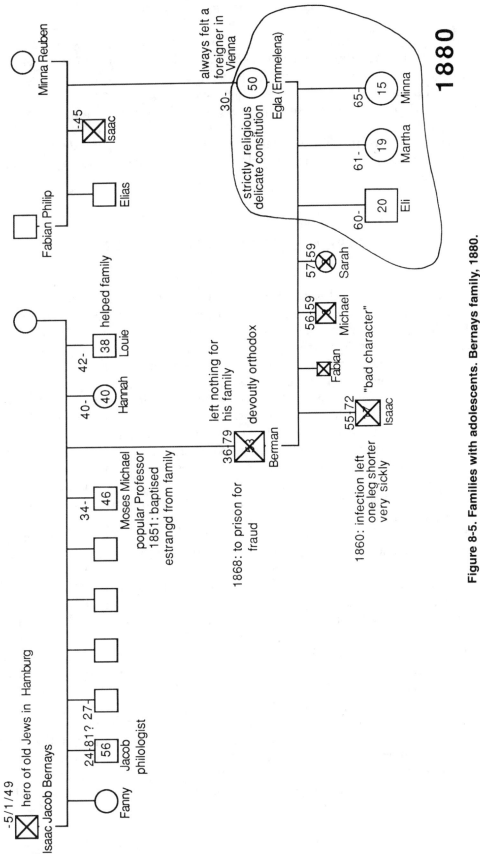

Figure 8-5. Families with adolescents. Bernays family, 1880.

177

degree, and did not practice for many years after that. This was unusual for students in those days, particularly those who were not independently wealthy. Perhaps he was hesitant to finish and move on to the next phase—supporting himself. Or perhaps he felt he was needed at home. In any case he did not seriously think about supporting himself until he wanted to marry Martha. When a delay in moving on to the next phase is indicated by the genogram, as in Freud's case with his prolonged time as a student and his lengthy engagement, one should explore the impediments to moving on in the life cycle.

MARRIAGE, THE NEXT GENERATION

Having gone through several transitions of the Freud family life cycle, we come to the next phase: the marriage of Sigmund Freud and Martha Bernays. The marriage genogram will often provide valuable clues to the difficulties and issues involved in the joining together of two family traditions in a new family.

What is immediately apparent from the genogram (Figure 8-6) is the unusual double connection between the Freuds and Bernays in Sigmund's generation. Such unusual configurations often suggest complicated relationships between the two families, and the possible existence of triangles. The oldest son in each family married the oldest daughter of the other family. As mentioned earlier, Sigmund and his sister Anna never got along very well. Perhaps Sigmund felt the usual sibling rivalry of an oldest child with a younger sister. Whatever the reason, Sigmund seemed to resent the marriage of Anna to Eli Bernays, who had previously been a friend of his, and to whose sister he was himself engaged. Sigmund and Martha's engagement lasted for more than four years, from 1882 to 1886, during which time Sigmund was very anxious to marry, but could not do so because he lacked the money. Eli and Anna were married in 1883, and Sigmund apparently did not attend the wedding. In fact, he did not even mention the event in his letters to Martha, although he wrote to her almost daily, and shortly after that discussed the possibility of attending the wedding of one of her cousins, certainly a much less important family event. Perhaps Sigmund resented Anna's marriage because his own marriage seemed so far off. Sigmund's negative feelings toward his sister and brother-in-law seemed to intensify when the couple moved to New York and the less educated Eli became very wealthy while the highly educated Sigmund had to struggle for the money to support his family.

We know that before their marriage there were difficulties between Sigmund and Martha regarding their families. Both came from families with financial problems, and financial concerns stood in the way of their marrying for more than five years. In addition, Freud felt threatened by Martha's relationship to her family of origin and was demanding and possessive about her

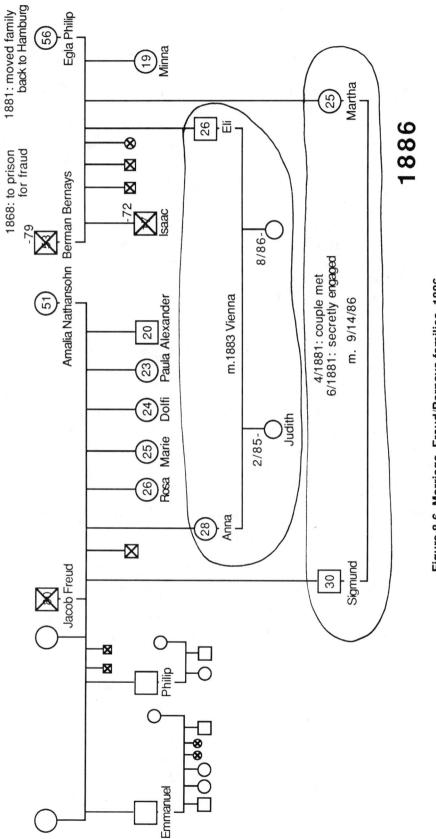

Figure 8-6. Marriage. Freud/Bernays families, 1886.

179

loyalty to him. During their long courtship, Sigmund wrote to Martha: "Are you already thinking of the day you are to leave, it is no more than a fortnight now, must not be more or else, yes, or else my egotism will rise up against Mama and Eli-Fritz and I will make such a din that everyone will hear and you understand, no matter how your filial feelings may rebel against it. From now on you are but a guest in your family . . . For has it not been laid down since time immemorial that the woman shall leave father and mother and follow the man she had chosen?" (letter in E. L. Freud, 1960, p. 23) Sigmund particularly resented his mother-in-law, who had moved her family, including Martha, from Vienna to Hamburg at the beginning of their engagement. Sigmund was overtly jealous of Martha's relationship with Eli, and even threatened to break off their engagement if she did not give up her loyalty to her brother. Nevertheless, throughout their marriage Martha did maintain contact with other members of her family and remained true to their faith, Orthodox Judaism, despite her husband's intellectual rejection of religion.

PARENTHOOD, THE NEXT GENERATION

As can be seen on the Freud genogram for 1896 (Figure 8-7), Sigmund and Martha married and had six children within eight years. The early years of a family with young children are always an eventful time. Martha was busy raising their ever-increasing brood while Sigmund struggled to enlarge his medical practice and begin some of his most creative intellectual work. It can often be a difficult time for marriages, with the spouses' energies so focused on their children and work. When this phase is seen on the genogram, one should be alert to child-rearing issues and normative strains in the marriage.

It was during this life cycle phase that Sigmund experienced a major life crisis that led to his greatest intellectual discoveries, and his major formulation, and then recanting, of the seduction theory. It was also during these years that Sigmund showed symptoms of depression and "pseudo"-cardiac problems. He complained of lethargy, migraines, and various other somatic and emotional concerns. He was clearly in a great deal of distress. During this period he began his famous self-analysis, and constructed the edifice of a new theory, which led to the publication of possibly his most famous book, *The Interpretation of Dreams.*

A look at the genogram may elucidate why this was such a turbulent, but productive, time in Sigmund's life. In December 1895, Anna, their last child, was born. Martha was worn out by five pregnancies in nine years, had been surprised and unhappy to learn that she was pregnant again, and it seems that Sigmund and Martha decided not to have another child. Sex between the couple apparently began to diminish considerably at this point (Anzieu, 1986).

Often the last child has a special position in the family. This was true of

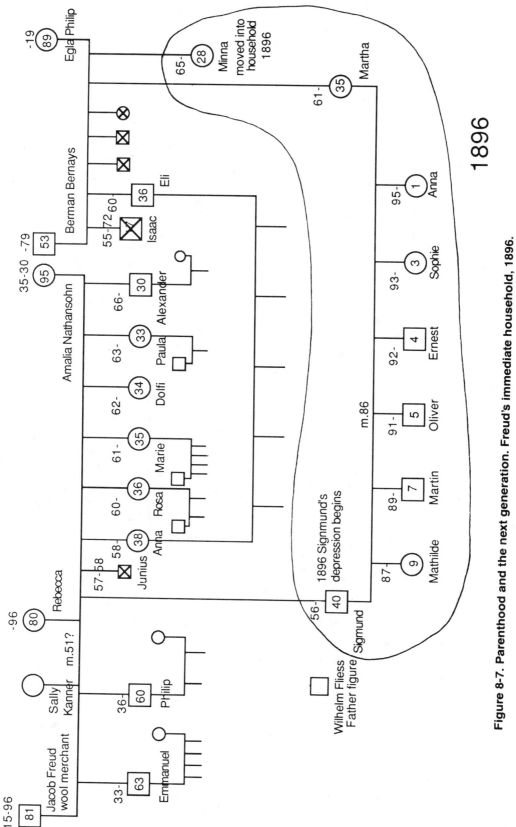

Figure 8-7. Parenthood and the next generation. Freud's immediate household, 1896.

181

Anna, who was not named for Freud's sister, but for the daughter of his friend and beloved teacher, Samuel Hammerschlag. This young woman, Anna Hammerschlag Lichtheim, also was a friend of the Freuds (Krull, 196). Throughout his life Sigmund and his daughter Anna were very close (she, rather than his wife, took care of him when he was ill), and she alone among the children never married, devoted herself to her father, who even became her analyst for several years, and she alone chose to carry on his life work. The birth of the last child may be an important turning point in family life. It seems that Martha became very preoccupied with raising her six children and Sigmund who was not very much involved with the children, moved closer intellectually and emotionally to his sister-in-law, Minna, whom he had described in May 1894, in a letter to Fleiss, as "otherwise my closest confidante" (Masson, 1985, p. 73).

Minna moved into the Freud household in early 1896. Fourteen years earlier she had been engaged to Sigmund's best friend, Ignaz Schonberg, who had broken off the relationship shortly before his death from tuberculosis. According to Jones (1955), Sigmund's view in that early period was that he and Minna were alike because they both were wild, passionate people who wanted their own way, whereas Ignaz and Martha were good-natured and adaptable.

Minna was never to marry. When other relatives appear as household members on a genogram, one should speculate about the possibility of triangles involving the spouses and the children. By all accounts Sigmund and Minna had an extremely close relationship. Minna's bedroom in the Freud household could be entered only through the master bedroom (Eissler, 1978). They took at least 12 vacations together (Swales, 1987), apparently because they both enjoyed traveling whereas Martha did not, at least not at Sigmund's pace (Freeman & Strean, 1981). Minna was much more interested in discussing Sigmund's ideas than was Martha. Recent research supports the suggestion that Sigmund may have had an affair with Minna that led to an abortion in 1901 (Swales, 1985). We know nothing about Martha's attitude toward her husband's relationship with her sister. [Interestingly, as can be seen on the Freud genogram for 1939 Figure 8.9, Sigmund's oldest son, Martin, repeated this pattern and had an affair with his wife's sister (Freud Lowenstein, 1984).]

Also in 1896, Sigmund's father died, a loss Sigmund said was the most significant and upsetting event in a man's life. He wrote, shortly after his father's death: "By one of those obscure paths behind official consciousness the death of the old man has affected me profoundly . . . His life had been over a long time before he died, but his death seems to have aroused in me memories of all the early days. I now feel quite uprooted." The death of a parent marks a critical point in the life cycle. In addition to the loss, it is a painful reminder of one's mortality and that the mantle of tradition and responsibility has been passed to the next generation. Now, Sigmund had his mother to support as well. It was around this time that Sigmund adopted Fliess as a father figure in his self-analysis.

One can view Sigmund's self-analysis as the culmination of a number of events in the family's and his own life cycle. He had just turned 40. He had had

his last child. He was struggling to support a large family. His wife's sister had moved in for good. His father had died. Apparently the passion of his marriage had cooled. In modern-day terms, Sigmund was suffering a "midlife crisis." The crisis seemed to be resolved with the consolidation of his career: the publication of his book, his appointment as a professor, and his growing recognition as the father of a new theory.

FAMILIES IN LATER LIFE

During the phase of aging, the family must come to terms with the mortality of the older generation, while relationships must be shifted as each generation moves up a level in the developmental hierarchy and all relationships must be reordered. There are special problems for women who are more often the caretakers (Dolfi and Anna) and who tend to outlive their spouses (Amalia and Martha). Often the genogram will reveal which child was delegated to become the caretaker of the aging parents, as well as the likely struggles and triangles in which siblings become involved in managing these responsibilities. When the last parent dies, the relationships between siblings become independent for the first time. Sibling conflicts and cutoffs at this point usually reflect triangles with parents that have come down from much earlier life cycle phases, especially with regard to who was the favored sibling in childhood.

We can see on the genogram (Figure 8-7) that Sigmund's father died in 1896 at the age of 81, leaving Amalia to be cared for by her children for the next 35 years. Sigmund and his youngest brother, Alexander, took financial responsibility for their parents and sisters in later life, although it was the middle daughter, Dolfi, who remained at home, unmarried with their mother, who lived to be 95. Sigmund also lived a long time, to the age of 83 (Figure 8-8) and was cared for by his daughter Anna. Anna became her father's main follower and the inheritor of his mantle. Anna apparently was his primary caretaker through his 17 operations for jaw cancer, although Martha Freud was still alive (she lived until 1951). Her assuming this role meant, as it had previously for Sigmund's sister Dolfi in relation to their mother, that Anna never had her own family, since she was 44 at the time of her father's death, and he had been unwilling to function without her for so many years. Even after his death, Anna did not marry.

The genogram may be helpful in predicting or understanding the reactions of family members at different points in the life cycle. For example, Sigmund had a very strong reaction to the death of his three-year-old grandson in 1923, shortly after he himself was diagnosed with cancer (Figure 8-9): "He was indeed an enchanting little fellow, and I myself was aware of never having loved a human being, certainly never a child, so much . . . I find this loss very hard to bear. I don't think I have ever experienced such grief, perhaps my own

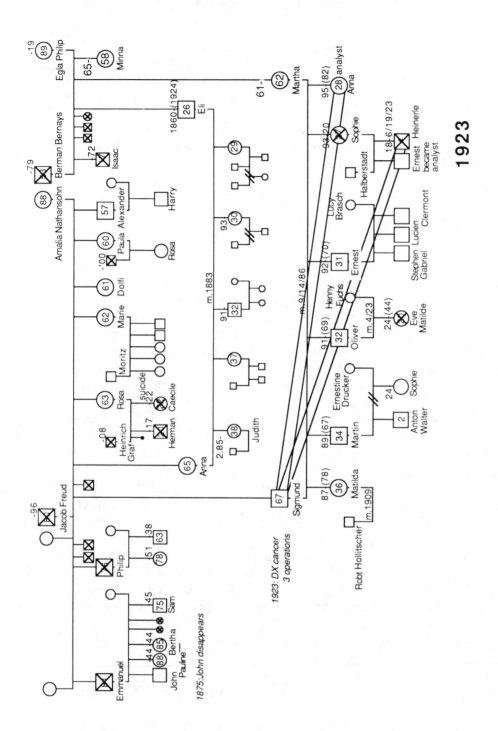

Figure 8-8. Aging. Freud family in 1923.

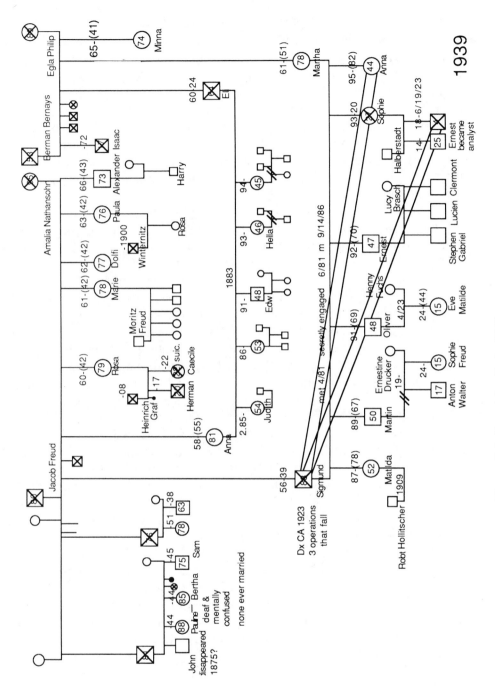

Figure 8-9. Freud family in 1939.

sickness contributes to the shock. I worked out of sheer necessity; fundamentally everything has lost its meaning for me" (6/11/23). A month later he wrote that he was suffering from the first depression in his life (Jones, 1955, p. 92). And three years later he wrote, to his son-in-law, that since this child's death he had not been able to enjoy life: "I have spent some of the blackest days of my life in sorrowing about the child. At last have taken hold of myself and can think of him quietly and talk of him without tears. But the comforts of reason have done nothing to help; the only consolation for me is that at my age I would not have seen much of him."

Sigmund's words suggest he was having to come to terms with his own mortality. This would be particularly difficult since his daughter Sophie (the child's mother) had died three years earlier at the age of 27, and also because that his grandson's death was so untimely in the life cycle.

Contrast this grandson's death with Sigmund's reaction to the death of his own mother seven years later in 1930: "I will not disguise the fact that my reaction to this event has because of special circumstances been a curious one. Assuredly, there is no saying what effects such an experience may produce in deeper layers, but on the surface I can detect only two things: an increase in personal freedom, since it was always a terrifying thought that she might come to hear of my death; and secondly the satisfaction that at least she has achieved the deliverance for which she had earned a right after such a long life. No grief otherwise, such as my ten years younger brother is painfully experiencing. I was not at the funeral; again Anna represented me as at Frankfurt. Her value to me can hardly be heightened. This event has affected me in a curious manner . . . No pain, no grief, which is probably to be explained by the circumstances, the great age and the end of the pity we had felt at her helplessness. With that a feeling of liberation, of release, which I think I can understand. I was not allowed to die as long as she was alive, and now I may. Somehow the values of life have notably changed in the deeper layers." (Quoted in Jones, 1955, p. 152)

In this case Sigmund at 74, more reconciled with his own eventual death, is relieved that the sequential order of the life cycle will be honored: first the parents die, and then the children. The untimely or traumatic loss of a family member typically is extremely difficult for families to mourn, and therapists are urged to be alert to dysfunctional patterns that develop in response to such losses (Chapter 19; McGoldrick & Walsh, 1983; Walsh & McGoldrick, 1988).

CONCLUSIONS

The genogram can be used to map the family at each phase of the family life cycle. Different configurations on the genogram suggest possible triangles and issues that can be explored for each phase. The genogram is only a schematic

map of a family. Gathering the necessary information must be part of an extensive clinical interview and the genogram is a summary graphic of the data collected. Much information, of course, must be omitted to make a genogram comprehensible. Despite these limitations we believe that the genogram with an accompanying family chronology (McGoldrick & Gerson, 1985; Gerson & McGoldrick, 1986) is the best tool yet devised for tracking the family life cycle. Table 8-2 presents a sample chronology of the Freud family that covers various events in the family history, some of which could be clearly shown on the genogram, and some of which, as can be seen, would get lost there.

REFERENCES

Anzieu, D. (1986). *Freud's self-analysis.* Madison, Conn.: International Universities Press.

Clark, R. W. (1980). *Freud: The man and the cause.* New York: Random House.

Eissler, K. R. (1978). *Sigmund Freud: His life in pictures and words.* New York: Helen & Kurt Wolff Books, Harcourt, Brace, Jovanovich.

Freeman, L., & Strean, H. S. (1981). *Freud and women.* New York: Frederick Ungar Publishing Co.

Freud Lowenstein, S. (1984). My three mothers. *Radcliffe Quarterly* Dec.: pp. 14–17.

Freud, E. (Ed.) (1960). *The letters of Sigmund Freud.* New York: Basic Books.

Freud, M. (1958). *Glory reflected: Sigmund Freud—Man and father.* New York: Vanguard.

Gerson, R., & McGoldrick, M. (1986). Constructing and interpreting genograms: The example of Sigmund Freud's family. In *Innovations in clinical practice: A source book (vol. 5).*

Glicklhorn, R. (1969). The Freiberg period of the Freud family. *Journal of the History of Medicine* 24:37–43.

Jones, E. (1954, 1955). *The life and work of Sigmund Freud.* 3 volumes. New York: Basic Books.

Krull, M. (1986). Freud and his father. New York: Norton.

Mannoni, O. (1974). Freud. New York: Vintage.

Masson, J. (Ed.) (1985). *The complete letters of Sigmund Freud to Wilhelm Fleiss: 1887–1904.* Cambridge, Mass.: Belnap Press.

McGoldrick, M., & Gerson, R. (1985). *Genograms in family assessment.* New York: Norton.

McGoldrick, M., & Walsh, F. (1983). A systemic view of family history and loss. In M. Aronson (Ed.), *Group and family therapy.* New York: Brunner/Mazel.

Nelken, M. (In press). Freud's heroic struggle with his mother. Manuscript in preparation.

Prause, G. (1978). *School days of the famous.* New York: Springer.

Swales, P. (1987). "What Freud Didn't Say." UMDNJ-RWJ Medical School. May 15.

Swales, P. (1985). Freud, Minna Bernays, and the conquest of Rome: New light on the origins of psychoanalysis. *The New American Review* 1, 2/3:1–23.

Swales P. (1986). Freud, his origins and family history. UMDNJ-RWJ Medical School. November 15.

Walsh, F., & McGoldrick, M. (In press). Loss and the family cycle. In C. Galicor (Ed.), *Family transitions: Continuity and change over the life cycle.* New York: Guilford Press.

Table 8.2.
Chronology for the Freud Family

1854 Sigmund's nephew John is born.
1855 (July 29) Jacob and Amalia are married.
1856 (February 21) Schlomo Freud, Jacob's father, dies (Jacob is 40).
1856 (May 5) Sigmund is born in Freiberg, Moravia (now Pribor, Czechoslovakia).
1857 (October) Sigmund's brother Julius is born.
1858 (March) Julius Nathansohn, Amalie's 20-year-old brother, dies of tuberculosis.
1858 (April 15) Julius dies.
1858 Fleiss is born. [Schur (1972) says Freud identified him with Julius.]
1858 (December) Sigmund's sister Anna is born.
1859? Sigmund's nursemaid leaves—arrested for theft, reported by Sigmund's half-brother Philip
       (during Amalia's confinement with Anna)
1859 Emmanuel and Philip emigrate with their families, including Sigmund's nephew, to whom he is
       very attached.
1859 Freud family moves from Freiberg to Leipzig (?) because of economic reversals.
1860 Family settles in Vienna.
1860 (March) Sigmund's sister Rosa is born.
1861 (March) Sigmund's sister Marie (Mitzi) is born.
1862 (July) Sigmund's sister Dolfi is born.
1863 (May) Sigmund's sister Paula is born.
1866 (April) Sigmund's brother Alexander, named by Sigmund, is born.
1868? Sigmund enters the gymnasium.
1873 Sigmund enters medical school.
       *   *

1882 (June 17) Sigmund and Martha become engaged.
1883 Minna becomes engaged to Ignaz Schonberg, close friend of Sigmund.
1883 (June 14) Martha's mother moves with her daughters to Wandsbek.
1883 (September) Sigmund's friend Nathan Weiss commits suicide.
1883 (October) Eli Bernays and Sigmund's sister Anna are married. Sigmund does not attend, or
       even mention the wedding in letters to Martha (at least not in published correspondence—
       although apparently only a small part has been published).
1884 (July 18) Sigmund publishes cocaine paper.
1884 Jacob Freud has business problems.
1885 (April) Sigmund destroys all of his papers.
1885 (June) Schonberg breaks his engagement to Minna.
1886 (February) Schonberg dies of tuberculosis, diagnosed in 1883.
1886 Paper on male hysteria.
1886 (September 14) Sigmund and Martha are married, enabled by a gift of money from Martha's
       aunt.
1887 (October) Mathilda, Sigmund and Martha's first child, is born (named for colleague Breuer's
       wife).
1889 (December) Martin, the second child, is born (named for French hypnotist Jean Martin Charcot).
1891 (February) Oliver, the third child, is born (named for Freud's hero, Oliver Cromwell).
1892 (April) Ernst, the fourth child, is born (named for Freud's teacher, Ernst Brucke).
1892 Eli Bernays goes to America.
1893 Eli returns to take his family to the United States with him. (? Two daughters, Lucy and Hella,
       stay with Freud's family for a year.) Sigmund gives Eli some money for the trip.
1893 (April) Sophie, the fifth child, is born (named for the niece of Freud's teacher Samuel
       Hammerschlag).
1883 (Fall) Cardiac symptoms—Sigmund is told to give up smoking. Breuer is his doctor but he
       seeks advice also from Fleiss. (Fleiss' wife later becomes jealous of his relationship with Freud.)
1894 Sigmund writes of having heart problems, trying to give up smoking, depression and fatigue,
       and financial problems
1895 (January) Fleiss operates on Sigmund's nose. [Fleiss is apparently treating Freud for a
       pseudocardiac condition (Mannoni, 1974).] Freud is still using cocaine.
1895 (February) Emma Eckstein episode begins.
1895 (March) Anna is conceived. Sigmund and Martha decide this will be their last child.
1895 (May–June) Sigmund begins self-analysis.
1895 (July 24) Sigmund has Irma dream.
1895 (August) Sigmund goes to Italy with brother Alexander.

1895 (November) Minna comes to stay with the Freud family.

1895 (December) Anna, the sixth and last child, is born [named for Freud's teacher Samuel Hammerschlag's daughter, a young widow and patient of Freud's, who may have been "Irma" in the Irma dream (Anzieu, 1986)].

1896 (April) Sigmund writes of migraines, nasal secretions, fears of dying.

1896 (May) Sigmund writes of the medical community isolating him.

1896 (October 23) Jacob Freud dies. (Sigmund is 40 at the time. His wife apparently is away for a few days and does not return for the funeral. The father had been very ill for a month or so.)

1896 (November) Freud family moves to new apartment in same building.

1897 (January) Sigmund is passed over for university promotion.

1897 (March) Mathilda has very bad case of diphtheria.

1897 (May) Sigmund again is passed over for promotion—becomes anxious.

1897 (May) Sigmund has incestuous dream about daughter Mathilda.

1897 (July) Sigmund arranges for father's gravestone.

1897 (August) He writes of self-analysis.

1897 (October 15) Freud develops idea of Oedipus complex.

1899 *Interpretation of Dreams*
******

1900 End of Sigmund's self-analysis.

1902 (March 5) He becomes professor extraordinary.
******

1919 Martha has bad case of pneumonia, goes to sanitorium.

1919 Sigmund and Minna go to a spa for a "cure."

1920 Daughter Sophie contracts pneumonia and dies.

1923 (May) Sigmund goes to friend Felix Deutsch for diagnosis of his cancer and first operation.

1923 (June 19) Favorite grandson dies of tuberculosis. Sigmund weeps for first time. He never gets over this loss, which follows so shortly on his own illness.

1923 (October 4) He has a second operation.

1923?(October 11) Sigmund undergoes a third operation. (Over next 16 years, he will have 30 more operations.)

1923 Eli dies in New York. Sigmund writes bitterly about his money and suggests that maybe now his sister Anna will do something for her four indigent sisters.

PART

2

The Traditional Middle-Class Family Life Cycle

CHAPTER 9

The Launching of the Single Young Adult

Robert C. Aylmer, Ed.D.

The life cycle stage of the unattached young adult comprises that period of time when the individual has physically, if not emotionally, left his or her family of origin, but has not yet established a family of procreation. Being thus viewed as "in between," this stage has traditionally not been explored in much detail by family theorists, and its largely ignored by family therapists as well.

Although this stage might appear to be the most individual of the family life cycle stages, its satisfactory resolution is perhaps more centrally rooted in ongoing family-of-origin issues than any other. In moving out of the family and beginning to establish an identity in the worlds of work and of intimate relationships, success is probably determined more by the degree, quality, tone, and completeness with which original family relationships (with parents, siblings, and extended kin) are renegotiated than any other factor.

For the purpose of this chapter, the family life cycle stage of the single young adult includes those individuals in their 20s who are (1) physically separate (although possible short-term returns to the nest may occur); (2) postcollege and/or military or (if under 21) working and living apart from the parental home; and (3) largely financially independent (although this may be an evolving issue). It includes individuals who married young and were divorced after a year or two as well as those who are living together without permanent commitment. It does not however, include children of any age who have never left home.

ADULT DEVELOPMENT AND LIFE CYCLE THEORY

The problem with most life cycle frameworks and theories of adult development of recent decades is that they use research on the lives of men to describe

all "adults." As a consequence they focus on chronological age and career development, emphasize the importance of individuation and separation, and fail to acknowledge the equal importance of attachment. In the past this focus on male development fitted the norms of society, which did not permit young women to experience a period of personal development before marriage. Until this generation young women were handed from their fathers to their husbands without expectation that they would develop personal life goals or the skills that lead to economic independence.

For example, in tracking the main process of development, Levinson (1978) charts the success or failure of the man's engagement in his career, with his marriage and family relationships taking an adjunctive role to the main task of getting on with his "dream." Similarly, in the work of George Vaillant (1977), the variables that correlate with adult adjustment, as well as the interviews that generate those data, are related chiefly to occupation, with a minimum concern for relationships. In fact, Vaillant said to his subjects before his interview with each that the hardest questions he could ask would be to "describe your wife."

Even Erik Erikson, the patron saint of the life cycle, failed to articulate a process of development in which adult women can be considered as mature as men. Erikson (1968) wrote that a young woman's identity was already defined through "her kind of attractiveness" and the selective nature of her search for a man, and that female identity is a primary biological, psychological, and ethical commitment to child care. Thus Erikson appears to describe, and thus prescribe, dependency as the norm for women, leading sociologist Jessie Bernard (1975) to complain that a female's normative development in our society consists first of learning to achieve dependency and then (for some) learning to overcome it.

Carol Gilligan's landmark work *In A Different Voice* (1982) describes the different orientations of males and females throughout development, with men pursuing identity in self-expression and women in self-sacrifice. This creates reciprocal problems in later adult development, when men may perceive that their focus on individual achievement has left them emotionally distant and isolated from their wives and children, and women may discover that having formed an identity so based on relationships that they have not developed the skills needed to support themselves financially in the face of divorce or the death of a spouse.

Thus both autonomy and attachment are functional adult goals, in love and work, for both men and women. However, in our society, each sex has been taught to pursue one and neglect or eschew the other. Gilligan emphasizes, contrary to the main body of adult-development literature, that there is no single mold of social experience and interpretation for young adults to follow, but rather a more complex truth of ongoing separation and attachment in the lives of women and men. Jean Baker Miller (1976) adds her voice to this view, saying that an understanding that human affiliation is just as important as self-

enhancement contains the possibility for an entirely different, more advanced, and nonviolent approach to living and functioning for both women and men.

INDIVIDUAL FACTORS

Following the bias toward separateness as the key to maturity, virtually every author writing on the topic of adult development highlights independence from family as the essential developmental task of the entry phase to adulthood. Having provisionally left home for college and/or military service, job "apprenticeship," or travel, the young adult is faced with the task of being in the adult world "for real." While there is still plenty of time for trying on multiple possibilities of identity, work, and relationships, the individual at this stage is faced with the harsh realities of "taking care of business" in terms of having an independent residence, self-care and maintenance, financial responsibility, and general life management. Levinson (1978) writes that the individual (male)

> . . . must now shift the center of gravity of his life from the position of child in the family of origin to the position of novice adult with a new home base that is more truly his own. It is time for full entry into the adult world. This requires multiple efforts: to explore the available possibilities, to arrive at a crystallized (though by no means final) definition of his self as an adult, and to make and live with his initial choices regarding occupation, love relationships, lifestyles and values.
>
> The distinctive character of this developmental period lies in the co-existance of its two tasks: to explore, to expand one's horizons and put off making firmer commitments until the options are clearer; and to create an initial adult life structure, to have roots, stability and continuity. Work on one task may dominate but the other is never totally absent. The balance of emphasis on the two tasks varies tremendously. (pp. 79–80)

Clearly this is no simple task and requires enormous reserves of courage, energy, tolerance for ambiguity, and willingness to risk. It is no wonder that many young adults fail to enter this stage by staying at home as delayed adolescents; do not progress in the issues of independence and identity development, and, while physically separate, simply flounder vocationally and interpersonally; or short-circuit the developmental process of independence by premature marriage and assumption of new family responsibilities.

Satisfactory initiation of and progression through this phase necessarily depend on the resolution of the tasks of the adolescent stage that immediately precedes it and establishes a context for autonomous development and functioning. Adolescence in turn owes much of its success or failure to the quality of the interpersonal and family framework which accompanies earlier developmental stages. The personal and psychological factors of trust, autonomy, competence, self-esteem, and hope which emanate from a proper "holding

environment" (Kegan, 1982) are essential at any stage of development and particularly this venturesome one. It is important to keep in mind, however, that these aspects of self always exist in an ongoing context of a viable nuclear and extended family network. The importance of this context of relationships, emotional forces, and events continues to exert a direct influence on the evolution of self long after the impact of traditional child-rearing effects have ended.

FAMILY SYSTEM FACTORS

Due to primacy of the disengaging *nuclear* family system, most of the issues described here will involve relationships between the young adult and his or her parents. However, it is important to recognize that transactions and decisions in this primary parental triangle are inherently determined by and constantly subject to stresses in the extended family kin networks (including the parents' relationships with their *own* parents) as well. Some of these more general system factors will be dealt with as appropriate here.

Having surrendered ongoing day-to-day supervision of adult children's living arrangements by permitting them to establish independent living arrangements, the primary task for the nuclear family unit is to continue the letting-go process regarding control and power in the formerly dependent relationship. Aspects of this complicated transition from adolescence to adulthood include the handling of financial support (gifts versus loans, with or without an agreed-upon interest rate and repayment schedule, by both parents explicitly or by one covertly or secretly without the knowledge of the other, etc.); respecting residential boundaries, for example, including choice of residence, which may or may not be consistent with the parents' values, or by visiting children's dwelling only by prearrangement or invitation (rather than unannounced "drop-ins"); and allowing for the offspring's premises to be furnished and cared for independently in a manner preferred and supervised by the young person (rather than a struggle over furniture, dishes, food, housecleaning services, and the like, foisted upon the all-too-willing although protesting "child").

The young adult's career development presents the family system with a challenge reguarding the degree to which it can tolerate the blend of tentativeness and commitment required for successful resolution of the phase. Middle-class "deviations," such as a decision not to go to college, or taking a year off between high school and college or between college and graduate school, can be respected as transitional identity experiments and resolution of incomplete childhood or adolescent dreams, or they can be seen as disloyal, destructive, or hurtful attacks on the family's purpose and meaning.

Naturally such provisional identities may also be undertaken by the young adult in a playful, adventuresome spirit or as a hostile, reactive, nose-thumbing gesture of defiance against parents and their values. As steps are taken along more serious career lines, tolerance for ambiguity, confusion, and sudden change, becomes important. The parents' anxiety level and reactivity may otherwise inappropriately limit the natural "bouncing around" of this stage.

Young adult intimate relationships also require a high degree of tolerance for range and change of choices. While parents have had to contend with rivals for affection throughout adolescence, the freedom to make choices about relationships, sex, and cohabitation totally free from parental scrutiny or supervision is often a more serious threat to parents' sense of closeness with their child than the intense but not quite "for real" earlier attachments. Similarly, young adults, in learning how to set goals and boundaries in a totally unsupervised environment, may experience increased anxiety. They may withdraw from relationships (to the concern of would-be grandparents), or engage in experimental relationships and life styles that trigger reactivity in the parental or extended system.

Parent–child reactivity to choice of companions or to nature of living arrangements is often a considerable problem as the generations vie for a balance between attachments outside the family system and a redefinition of parent–child intimacy. As in the issues of independence and career development, parents whose issues of separation, intimacy, and autonomy regarding their own families of origin, family, and personal identity are more resolved will have an easier time responding to the vagaries of this phase.

From this viewpoint of the family system, successful resolution of this transition requires (1) an ability to tolerate separation and independence while remaining connected; (2) a tolerance for differentness and ambiguity in career identity of adult children; and (3) the acceptance of a range of intense emotional attachments and life styles outside the immediate family. Of course, the degree of tolerance possible for parents is determined in part by the degree of reactivity sent their way by their children. However, since some degree of upset and crisis is inherent in the young adult's progression through this phase, a more important factor in the parents' response will be the degree of satisfaction and success in their resolution of the other family life cycle transitions in which they themselves are embedded. The degree to which parents have mastered the struggle for independence from their own parents, as they may be reactivated by issues of aging, retirement, disability, or death in that generation, will have a major effect on the degree to which they can permit more entrenched autonomy and independence in their own children. The degree to which parents have confronted and resolved the issues of limitation and constraints on career goals in their own midlife crisis will have a profound impact on the degree to which they can tolerate the apparent "waste of time" that their offspring may engage in while trying on different career identities. Finally, the more successfully parents as husband and wife are renegotiating

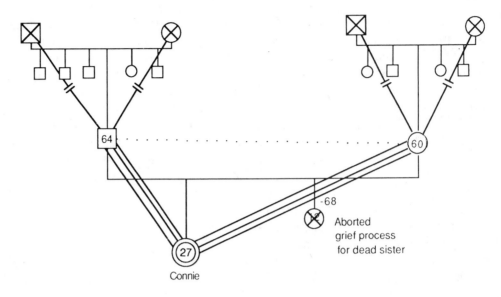

Figure 9-1. Connie

issues of intimacy in their "empty nest," the better able they will be to tolerate variations, excesses, and crises in their young adult children's further exploration of sexuality and intimacy.

Case Example

Connie is a single school teacher, age 27, who is very dissatisfied with her career. She is the sole surviving child of a Jewish family whose younger daughter died in adolescence of cancer, an event from which the family has never recovered and has never discussed. Connie has never visited her sister's grave, never mentions her name in the family, and does not know whether her parents ever talk about her sister or visit her grave. Both parents are estranged from their own parental and sibling systems, and their marriage is distant, except for concern about Connie.

Connie lives in a condominium purchased by her parents "as an investment" but which is clearly their way of continuing to support her. There is no lease or formal agreement about Connie's contributing to the upkeep of the condominium. She is always months behind in her "rent," has allowed the premises to deteriorate, and spends her substantial salary in a spendthrift way so that she is always needing to borrow additional funds from her parents.

She is constantly besieged separately by each of her parents to visit and to take care of the other parent's emotional needs. Father will invite her to a secret dinner at which he implores her to call mother because "you're her whole life." Mother will call Connie and caution her not to bring up sensitive issues because "your father would have a heart attack and die." Connie describes her romantic entanglements with people her parents wouldn't approve of as "my secret life" and believes that knowledge of these relationships would destroy her parents if they knew of them.

Therapy with Connie was initially aimed at clarifying her goals, helping her to make informed choices about sexuality and intimacy, and to become less reactive to her parents' intrusions in her life and more responsible for her own finances.

Later, it moved toward confronting her own unaddressed grief reaction about her sister, and the possibility of gradually reopening this issue in the family system by her talking about it with her parents and with extended family members.

CAREER ISSUES

In career development the anxiety can be high if the young adult is not yet at the level of entry to the career of choice or at least involved in serious committed apprenticeship such as graduate school by the mid- to late 20s. By this time the "trying on" of various provisional identities to test or perfect career-development skills and interests is rapidly becoming dangerously obsolete. The individual who is still uncommitted to a career path or occupational choice is vulnerable to self-doubt, substantial loss of self-esteem, and depression. This vulnerability, and the defensiveness likely to accompany it at the individual level, often interacts counterproductively with increased anxiety inthe parental generation about whether the offspring will "make it." In extreme cases, individuals with difficulty in making or maintaining committed efforts toward career goals, such as staying with a job or remaining in graduate school, may periodically return home as these efforts fail. While sometimes useful in allowing more complete resolution of parent–child relationships in adulthood, repeated reentry into the preadult family structure, especially if triggered by disfunction, can have a debilitating effect on the progression of the entire family system toward its later more differentiated life cycle stages.

Considerable stress and anxiety may exist even in those cases in which progress is not aborted. Issues of competitiveness, expectations, and differentness regarding career achievements between the older generation and goals in the younger one frequently distort and inhibit the further differentiation of self from family that career commitment entails. For the young adult, reactive competitiveness to outdo the parents or, at the other extreme, reactive opposition by showing them just how wrong they have been in their life choices, frequently binds up energy needed for the outside world into unproductive family enmeshments. These struggles can then cause inappropriate deviations in career paths from what would be more appropriate for the individual's actual capacities and needs.

Even if this struggle for more complete vocational identity is not so conflictual, young adults are often highly ambivalent about turning to parents and other family members for advice and counsel in this period of high stress. Reactive sense of pride, the need to maintain "independence," or invalidation of parental wisdom, can all deprive the young adult of a much needed support system during this stormy transition period.

At the family system level, the capacity to provide this support is primarily related to the ability of the other family members to detach their own expectations and conflicts about achievement from those of their offspring. This

capacity, of course, is intrinsically rooted in the degree of satisfaction or at least resolution of midlife career issues affecting parents themselves. Parents' reactivity to their children's achievement may also be rooted in the birth order of the child (Toman, 1969), the relative achievements or difficulties encountered by their other children, or the clarity of their own vocational adjustments relative to their own siblings and parents. Particular struggles for young men on this issue often have to do with wanting a more balanced allocation of energy toward family rather than investing all their resources in their careers. This can often give rise to real or perceived disapproval by their fathers for not being "serious" enough about job advancement. For women, particularly those with traditional at-home mothers, there is often extreme ambivalence and overexpectation of themselves to be able to "do it all" in areas of career, relationship, and family.

It is in the area of intimacy and relationships, however, that most stress seems to arise in this phase, particularly when career development is proceeding smoothly. With a separate base of operations established from the family of origin, along with financial independence and a growing sense of personal security and self-esteem in vocational development, questions of isolation, sharing, and personal completeness come to the fore.

INTIMACY ISSUES

Despite the obvious importance of intimacy and commitment in this phase, writers on adult development have not provided much useful information. For example, the index to Levinson's (1978) seminal book contains no entries under "intimacy" or "commitment" as factors in adult (male) development. Sheehy (1974), who used Levinson's work as her model, does address these issues but only in the context of redefinition or divorce in existing marriages. She does not address the problems of commitment and intimacy for individuals or couples who have not yet reched marriage or serious commitment.

Gilligan (1982) maintains that such studies have overemphasized career achievements and ignored intimacy. She states that Levinson, in particular, relegates women and relationships to a position subbordinate to the career advancement of men, particularly in the role of the "special woman" who is "the helpmate who encourages the hero to shape and live out his vision" (Levinson, 1978). She therefore sees Levinson's description of early adult relationships as "the means to an individual's achievement. . . . These 'transitional figures' must be cast off or reconstructed following the realization of success" (Levinson, 1978).

This exploitational use of others in the service of one's own narrow self-interest is hardly intimacy. Kegan (1982) makes the useful distinction between fusion (relationships that are seen and used as the *source of self*) versus

intimacy (in which relationships are a step toward *sharing self*). Kegan's description of the shift in balance from what he terms the institutional or *autonomous* self to the interpersonal or interconnected *mutual* self comes closest to bridging the "autonomy–attachment" gap in adult development research, which Gilligan (1982) points out. Prior to the stage of interpersonal balance, "There is no self to share with another; instead, the other is required to bring self into being. Fusion is not intimacy and the pre-existence or maintenance of self that is involved has powerful reverberations between the individual and the family of origin system" (p. 97).

The composite picture of development that evolves from all of these authors is that this phase is one of unavoidable stress and upset as the individual passes from an *individual orientation* to an *interdependent orientation* of self. However, as Kegan demonstrates, the nature and degree of this stress, and of successful resolution, are primarily determined by the degree of self the individual brings to an intimate encounter rather than what he or she expects to elicit from the encounter. It is in this notion of differentiation of self, which is at the core of Bowen's (1978) family theory, that the interrelationship between the developing young adult and the family system is primarily apparent, through the mechanisms of the family projection process, family-of-origin triangles, and nodal events.

Family-of-origin programming describes how people learn functional or dysfunctional expectations, attitudes, orientation, and concepts (about self, others, and relationships) in the family that then exert powerful effects on an individual's behavior in intimate relationships and other areas of adult life. This learning occurs through two primary channels, the family projection process (Bowen, 1978) in the extended-family system and parental triangles in the nuclear-family system.

In the family projection process, individuals are imbued with the characteristics ("serious," "irritable," "overresponsible," "unreliable," etc.) and emotional obligations ("take care of mother," "make up for wastrel uncle," "replace dead sibling") of predecessors with whom . . . relationship issues in the family are unresolved because of incomplete mourning (Paul & Paul, 1975); family loyalties (Boszormenyi-Nagy & Sparks, 1973); divorce (Aylmer, 1977); or cutoffs (Carter & Orfanidis, 1976). Thus individuals come out of the family of origin into the world and marriage, "programmed" to enact roles and characters belonging to people, relationships, and events long buried (Aylmer, 1986, p. 110).

It is not difficult to see how these extended-family dramas can inhibit self-development or to connect the resulting incompleteness with the process of fusion (i.e., completing self through another) described by Bowen (1978) and Kegan (1982). Bowen also uses the term *pseudo-self* to describe the aspects of personality that are evoked by, and therefore highly dependent on, relationships. Clinically the more such extended-family fusion issues can be resolved prior to the development of new relationships, the more likely an individual will be to move into the interdependent, mutual phase of true

intimacy freer of family-of-origin projection. The individual and new relationships (or marriage) can exist in the context of sharing of self, rather than in a futile and vulnerable attempt to derive a self from the relationship.

In addition to coping with these multigenerational dramatic scriptings of the whole extended-family system, individuals mature in the immediate circumstances of a nuclear family and in highly charged emotional relationships with each parent. The triangle connecting an individual with each of his or her parents can also set up potentials and limitation for intimacy.

For example, a man growing up in a typical parental triangle of negative distance from father and enmeshment with his mother (who has given up on reaching her husband) may come to adult intimate relationships with an emotional allergy to closeness that he will experience as invasion and loss of independence, and a compensatory, distant, critical stance which was modeled after his father (see Figure 9-2).

Correspondingly (Figure 9-3), a woman growing up in another typical parental triangle of an aloof, idealized father and an enmeshing conflictual relationship with her mother might come to adulthood with an emotional addiction to distant men whom she pursues, but never succeeds in catching, and an inability to relate to women (Aylmer, 1986).

The final extended-family factor affecting individual development involves rections throughout the system to nodel events and stressors. Nodal events can be recent (conflict over choice of friends) or remote (dispute over grandfather's will ten years ago); instantaneous (heart attack in father) or longstanding (Alzheimer's disease in mother); positive (new job) or negative (death

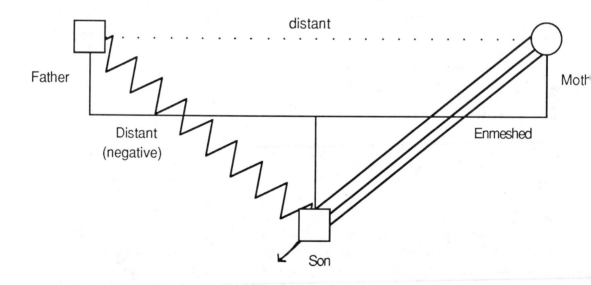

Figure 9-2. Nuclear-family triangle: enmeshment–sensitive.

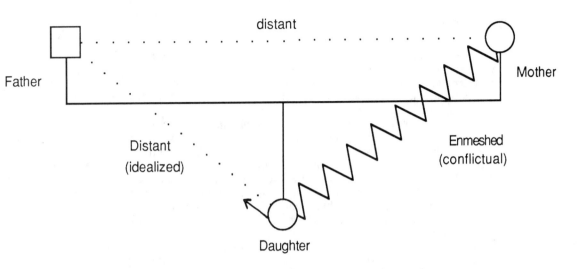

Figure 9-3. Nuclear-family triangle: distance–sensitive

of a sibling); serious (threat of nuclear war) or mild (friend moves slight distance away). Nodal events may also occur at the level of an individual (job loss), a relationship (sister's divorce) a social group (women's issues), or society as a whole (the energy crisis).

Nodal events, therefore, are either family phenomena per se (marriage, divorce, birth, death, etc.) occurring within the system or nonfamily phenomena (employment, social changes, etc.) that intrude on family members from outside. In either case, nodal events can influence distress by raising the anxiety level in the extended-family systems(s), thereby intensifying the operation of dysfunctional family patterns (triangles, cutoffs, enmeshment) that increase stress on individual family members while simultaneously decreasing their range of relationship options and appropriate connectedness in the kin network.

In summary, the higher the frequency and severity of nodal events in the extended-family system, and the lower the emotional maturity (differentiation) and connectedness of that system, the higher the level of anxiety and the greater the likelihood of individual or relationship symptoms (Aylmer, 1986).

Stressful events and unfinished business in the nuclear- and extended-family system are unavoidable and universal in human development. However, the more intense and unresolved these issues remain, and the more they are dealt with simply by distance and even total cutoff from the relationships and people from which they were derived, the more they place extra stress and limits on the individual's capacity to develop a self and therefore to share this self in intimate relationships. A high level of anxiety related to poorly handled nodal events in the family can greatly complicate the path for emerging young adults.

Case Example.

Charlie is an energetic, successful, athletic, WASP stockbroker trainee of 28, who was referred for therapy by his internist who was treating him for an array of gastrointestinal and other psychosomatic complaints. Charlie is a very tense and competitive individual who is currently zooming ahead in his firm's training program.

Discussion of his life uncovers the fact that Charlie and Nancy, his girlfriend of several years, are living together, and indeed have bought a house jointly. However, they have no definite plans to marry and Nancy complains that they have sex too infrequently. Closeness is primarily in a "buddy" sense, and Charlie is very dependent on Nancy's encouragement and support and has asked his firm not to send him on out-of-town assignments to avoid being away from her overnight. Further exploration reveals that Charlie gets very anxious about sexual or emotional intimacy issues in the relationship, feeling that he will "lose himself" or "dissolve in a puddle."

Charlie is the only son of a famous scientist father, whose own father was a bankrupt failure at business. Charlie has never been sure of the degree to which he has measured up to father's expectations, and while progressing well in his career, has a great deal of anxiety about both the level of his success and the choice of his occupational field.

While Charlie's career ambivalence seems clearly tied to the ambiguity of whether he is to take after his father or grandfather, and is not without its problems for him, it is primarily in the area of intimate relationships that his development is hindered. When questioned, Charlie says he can't imagine his father having the same anxieties about sex and closeness that he has, and wouldn't dream of revealing this "weakness" to his father.

When Charlie was coached by the therapist to share his difficulties with his

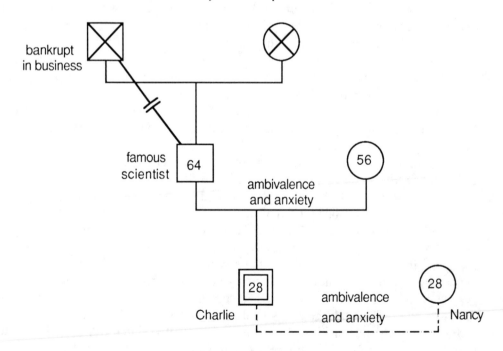

Figure 9-4. Charlie

father, he was astonished to learn that the father had been engaged three times to three different women, only to back out in terror each time as the marriage date approached. Indeed, it was only after two years of intensive therapy (which Charlie would never have dreamed his father was capable of) that Charlie's dad was able to meet, commit to, and marry Charlie's mother.

Armed with this information, and a stronger sense of validation of himself, Charlie and Nancy were able to confront more directly their sexual problems, which were closely tied to Charlie's overdependence on Nancy's support. As Charlie was able to feel more confident, taking risks in the area of sex and intimacy, he also became less dependent on Nancy and began to travel more for his firm, and actually to enjoy the freedom and power he experienced. Soon they made plans to marry. Learning to discuss with his father his fears about work, along with the issue of the grandfather's failure and its effects on the father, dispelled much of Charlie's driven anxiety in the area of career as well.

CLINICAL CONSIDERATIONS

Since many problems of young adulthood are directly traceable to ongoing difficulties in nuclear- or extended-family relationships and events, therapy is often most effective when it focuses actively and directly on these issues. Bowen (1978) and his colleagues use the term "coaching" to describe the ongoing consultation process in family or origin therapy. [For a fuller discussion of the rationale and logistics of the coaching process, see Carter and Orfanidis (1976).]

Coaching consists of working (usually individually) with a family member, initially to tease out the multigenerational dynamics and issues that are inhibiting individual and family functioning. Strategies are then formulated to guide the individual in relating deliberately and consciously to selected nuclear- and extended-family members in order to normalize relationship patterns and deal appropriately with toxic issues.

A method that emphasizes reengaging the family during a life cycle stage of emancipation may, seem paradoxical (and is frequently seen so by clients!). However, direct renegotiations of preexisting emotional ties is essential to the critical stage task of initiating a lifelong balance of autonomy and attachment.

Coaching is intended to reverse the tendency of family systems to build up tension over generations and create intergenerational patterns of *enmeshment, cutoff,* and *triangles.*

Enmeshment is a pattern of emotional overinvolvement among family members, which can range from too frequent telephone contact to total symbiotic fusion. At its worst enmeshment stunts individuals' emotional and psychological development, promotes pathological interdependences, and isolates a family from the community.

Cutoff is a family pattern characterized by extreme disengagement and distance, to the point of no involvement at all. It can occur angrily and suddenly, with extreme bitterness and projection, or gradually and innocuously over years or generatons, without apparent cause. Cutoff robs

families of their essence and vitality, and contributes a sense of hollowness and vulnerability to the individual members it launches but does not support.

Both of these patterns are highly charged emotionally, deeply embedded in the family structures, and therefore very difficult to change. While seemingly opposite in nature, enmeshment and cutoff serve similar functions in families, by allowing relationship issues and needs for distance and closeness to be acted out or avoided but never resolved.

Distance and closeness can characterize the relationship patterns of whole families and even cultures, or be found reciprocally in the same nuclear- or extended-family system. Within a system, distance–closeness dynamics usually take the form of a *triangle,* in which two members are (overly) close and one is (overly) distant. Families can be seen as a network of interlocking triangles in which each member is close to some and distant from others in a complicated web of alliances and tensions.

While problematic at all stages of the family life cycle, these processes of enmeshment, cutoff, and triangles have special impact on the young adult. Enmeshment keeps individuals overinvolved with family-of-origin forces at a time when entry into the outside world and new committed, intimate relationships are essential. Cutoff separates individuals prmaturely and arbitrarily from the nuclear and extended family resources that fuel identity and support new endeavors and attachments. Triangles prevent seeing others in the family as real people rather than as characters in a multigenerational drama and create unrealistic and inappropriate expectations for partners in developing relationships.

Coaching aims at replacing these dysfunctional patterns in the nuclear and extended system with open adult relationships characterized by ongoing sharing of self without reactivity to others. Steps or stages in achieving this result can include the following.

Detriangling—deliberately shifting allegiance from an overclose or affectionate parent (or other family member) to a distant or difficult one, to move toward a more balanced relationship with each parent as individuals. Examples are taking father's side in an argument or refusing to listen to mother's criticism of father.

Person-to-person contact—creating opportunities for individual sharing and exchange with family members, especially parents, to move from extremes of distance or closeness to more genuine intimacy. Examples are writing letters describing one's personal concerns or worries or acknowledging a parent's contribution to one's life.

Reversals—deliberately behaving in an opposite fashion from family expectations, to free up opportunities for new behavior. Examples are asking advice of younger or scapegoated family members; changing pattern of attendance at family rituals; or responding humorously to criticism instead of reacting defensively.

Reconnecting—establishing or enhancing nuclear- or extended-family relationships in order to broaden relationships options, find out historical informa-

tion, or diffuse overinvolved nuclear-family relationships. Examples are writing extended-family members for genogram information or visiting relatives never before seen.

The following case illustrates in more detail how multigenerational problems can emerge in young adulthood and how family-of-origin coaching can facilitate successful resolution of these crises and progression through this crucial developmental stage.

Case Example

Joan is a 32-year-old researcher, who enters therapy with feelings of depression, low self-esteem, lack of assertiveness, ambivalence about her career, and a pattern of brief unsatisfactory involvements with men. Although she has been in both individual and group psychodynamic therapy for the past two years, her situation is not improving.

The genogram (Figure 9-5) indicates that Joan is the younger of two daughters of a working-class Jewish family. Mother and father are Eastern European, having married late after emigrating following World War II. Joan's mother had lost many relatives in the concentration camps and most of her father's family was destroyed during World War I, after which he wandered around Europe as an orphan. Joan's older sister is married, with two children, and seems quite successful, although she and Joan are fairly distant. This could be partly due to the six-year age difference, but also reflects the triangular structure of the family. Joan reports that she always recalls her parents' marriage as being conflictual, with her sister generally siding with her father while she was aligned with her mother and angry at her father.

In 1967, when the older sister married, the father experienced a financial reversal and abruptly left the family. Seven years later, Joan's older sister decided to find the father, tracked him down through union records, and prevailed upon him to return to the family. Within one month of the father's return, Joan took a job in a distant city and remained virtually cut off for several years, before recently returning home (ostensibly for career reasons). When asked about the timing of her father's return and her departure, Joan replied, "I had been left saddled with my mother once, and I was not going to let that happen again. I got out while the getting was good."

The timing of these events and her lack of contact after moving suggest that Joan's actions were based more on reactivity to family-of-origin issues and events than to genuine development of her career. In this context the emergence and exacerbation of symptoms since she moved back can be seen as the return in more direct form of the unfinished developmental business that Joan had aborted in her sudden move. Multigenerational therapy was initiated to unravel the triangle connecting Joan with her mother and her father that was preventing her from moving on in her individual development.

Initially Joan was coached to try to move more directly toward her father in order to improve the relationship and to resolve some of her hurt and anger about his abandoning her. At the same time, Joan attempted to bridge her enmeshed reactivity with her mother by finding out more about her mother's family of origin, including the experience of the concentration camps. This was a straightforward application of Bowen theory in renegotiating family-of-origin relationships, wherein distant relationships are approached directly in order to enhance closeness, while close relationships are approached indirectly in order to provide perspective and detachment.

These approaches were not met with much initial success due to Joan's own reactivity and anger at her father and her anxiety about opening up painful issues

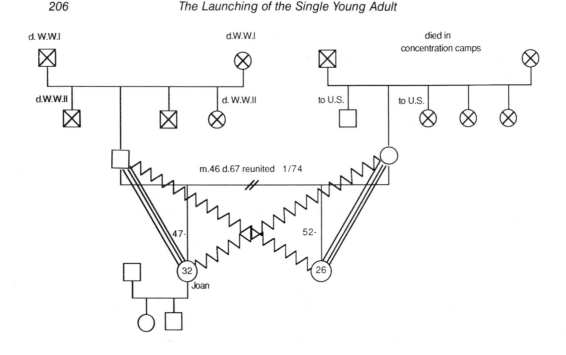

Figure 9-5. Joan

with her mother. For example, Joan had taken the heroic step of traveling to Israel with her father to visit the grave of his brother. She reported that while she felt considerable empathy with his grief as he stood tearfully at his brother's grave, she was unable to comfort him either with words or with gestures. With her mother she became tongue-tied and frozen whenever she attempted to ask questions about the past. For this reason, an in-office consultation meeting was held with Joan and her two parents. The purpose of this meeting was to facilitate Joan's detriangling from her parents by attempting to "break the ice." (Joan's older sister was not at the meeting but later viewed a videotape of the session.)

The consultation interview was therefore structured to assist Joan in moving directly to her father, exploring mother's reactivity to this idea, and to get permission from both parents to begin looking at the painful past. This was to be presented to them in terms of their daughter's needing to get to know them better, and to have a better relationship with them in order to move on in her life. Finally, the interview was intended to conclude with the establishment of an ongoing plan for Joan's efforts to resolve her relationships with her parents in the context of the extended families.

In the course of this interview, which Joan had prepared for by rehearsal, including tape recording and replaying statements to her father about her feelings about their relationship, Joan was able to tell her father that she loved him, and although she had been angry with him for leaving, she was no longer angry with him and now wanted a closer relationship. She asked her mother if she would consider sharing with Joan some of her past. Mother agreed to these requests once she realized how important they were to her daughter, and in the course of the session rolled up her sleeve to display her concentration camp tatoo while describ-

ing in some detail what the experience had been like, including which members of her family had died and how she had managed to survive. Father, for his part, tearfully explained to his daughter some of the circumstances of his leaving, and agreed to sit down with her and review some of his earlier life so she could come to know him better.

While powerful and moving as an experience, this session was viewed in the context of the therapy as only the beginning of Joan's efforts at detriangling with her parents, not the culmination. Following the meeting, Joan obtained a map of Poland and spent many hours with her father following his wanderings as an adolescent after his parents were killed in World War I. This understanding allowed her to be less reactive to her father's harsh, abrasive way of communicating, and also allowed her to pace her involvement with him so that she did not expose herself to more of his toxic behavior of her reactive feelings than she could handle at one time. Gradually, as she elicited more information from him about his life, she began to see him as a tragic figure, deserving more empathy than anger. Moreover, as this was the first time in her memory that she had spent time individually with her father, she began to experience more of a sense of closeness and connection to him. For the first time they began to have a relationship.

To facilitate her moving toward her mother and exploring the holocaust history, Joan enrolled in One Generation After, an organization formed to facilitate the collection of oral histories of holocaust survivors. Joan, like many other children of the holocaust, found this structure and support enormously useful in learning how to address such painful issues with her mother. While this area remains tender and tentative for both Joan and her mother, they are continuing gradually to explore this part of her mother's life in more detail.

Within a year after undertaking these efforts to free her adult development by detriangling from her family of origin, Joan had applied to and been accepted in a Ph.D. program at a major university and had met and developed a committed relationship with a man with whom she is currently considering marriage. She is no longer depressed or ambivalent about relationships with men and is progressing well toward her professional career goals. She remained somewhat anxious about her competence and has had periodic anxiety attacks associated with examinations in graduate school. These concerns about catastrophic consequences of not measuring up cleared up as she completed her exploration of her reactivity to her mother's terrifying concentration camp experiences.

The case of Joan illustrates how career and intimacy issues in adult development resonate with individual tasks and family-of-origin issues. The issues in Joan's family stand out in bold relief due to their tragic nature, and certainly not all individuals will pursue change with Joan's absolute determination. However, this work illustrates how careful attention and systematic effort to explore and resolve in the context of present family relationships the family-of-origin determinants of developmental difficulties can free individuals from restrictive scripts that have inhibited growth for years, or even generations.

REFERENCES

Aylmer, R. C. (1977). Emotional issues in divorce. *The family*.
Aylmer, R. C. (1986). Bowen family systems marital therapy. In N. S. Jacobson & A. S.

Gurman (Eds.) *Clinical handbook of marital therapy*. New York: Guilford Press, pp. 107–148.

Bernard, J. S. (1975). *Women, wills, emotions: Values and options*. Chicago: Aldine Publishing.

Boszormenyi-Nagy, I. (1973). Invisible loyalties. New York. Harper.

Bowen, M. (1978). *Family therapy in clinical practice*. New York: Jason Aronson.

Carter, E. & Orfanidis, M. (1976). Family therapy with one person and the therapist's own family. In P. J. Guerin (Ed.) *Family therapy: Theory and practice*. New York: Gardner Press, pp. 193–219.

Erikson, E. H. (1968). *Identity, youth and crisis*. New York: W. W. Norton & Co.

Gilligan, C. (1982). *In a different voice*. Cambridge, Mass.: Harvard University Press.

Kegan, R. (1982) *The evolving self*. Cambridge, Mass.: Harvard University Press.

Levinson, D. J. (1978). *The seasons of a man's life*. New York: Ballantine Books.

Miller, J. B. (1976). *Toward a new psychology of women*. Boston: Beacon Press.

Sheehy, G. (1977). *Passages*. New York: Bantam.

Toman, W. T. (1969). *Family constellation* (2nd ed.). New York: Springer.

Vaillant, G. E. (1977). *Adaptation to life*. Boston: Little, Brown.

10

The Joining of Families Through Marriage: The New Couple

Monica McGoldrick, M.S.W.

> Older man to younger one who is on the verge of divorce: "I guess in our time we didn't expect so much of marriage and perhaps we got a lot more." Older woman to younger woman on the verge of divorce: "I guess in our time we didn't expect so much of marriage and we settled for what we got."

Becoming a couple is one of the most complex and difficult transitions of the family life cycle. However, along with the transition to parenthood, which it has long symbolized, it is seen as the easiest and most joyous. The romanticized view of this transition may add to its difficulty, since everyone—from the couple to the family and friends—wants to see only the happiness of the shift. The problems entailed may thus be pushed underground, only to intensify and surface later on.

Weddings, more than any other rite of passage, are viewed as the solution to problems such as loneliness or extended-family difficulties. The event is seen as terminating a process, though it does not; "And they lived happily ever after" is the myth. Families will often say, "At last they're settled," as though the wedding resolved something rather than coming in the middle of a complex process of changing family status.

This chapter will outline the issues in becoming a new family and discuss clinical interventions for those who have trouble negotiating this phase. The meaning of marriage in our time is profoundly different from its meaning throughout previous history, when it was tightly embedded in the economic and social fabric of society. The changing role of women and the increasing mobility of our culture, along with the dramatic effects of widely available contraceptives, are forcing us to redefine marriage.

Marriage requires that two people renegotiate together a myriad of issues they have previously defined individually, or that were defined by their families of origin, such as when and how to eat, sleep, talk, have sex, fight, work, and relax. The couple must decide about vacations, and how to use space, time,

and money. There are also the decisions about which family traditions and rituals to retain and which ones the partners will develop for themselves. These decisions can no longer be determined solely on an individual basis. The couple will also have to renegotiate relationships with parents, siblings, friends, extended family, and co-workers in view of the new marriage. It places no small stress on a family to open itself to an outsider who is now an official member of its inner circle. Frequently no new member has been added to the system for many years. The challenge of this change can affect a family's style profoundly; the tendency of members to polarize and see villains and victims under the stress of these changes can be very strong.

The joke that there are six in the marital bed is really an understatement. It has been said that what distinguishes human beings from all other animals is the fact of having in-laws. In the animal kingdom, mating involves only the two partners, who usually mature, separate from their families, and mate on their own. For humans it is the joining of two enormously complex systems. It is possible that if couples could fully appreciate the emotional complexity of negotiating marriage right at the start, they might not dare to undertake the proposition.

The place of marriage in the life cycle has been changing dramatically. Men and women are having sex earlier but marrying later than ever before. An ever-increasing proportion are living together before marriage, or even living with several partners before deciding to marry. Marriage used to be the major marker of transition to the adult world, because it symbolized the transition to parenthood; now it often reflects a greater continuity with the phase of young adulthood or even adolescence, since childbearing is increasingly postponed for a number of years after marriage.

In fact, the status changes of marriage may not be fully appreciated by the family until the next phase. It is this transition to parenthood that confronts couples more sharply with the problems of traditional sex roles and of multi-generational patterns. Women are wanting their own careers and are increasingly resistant to having the primary household and childcare responsibilities and to having husbands who are absent from family life. But change comes very slowly.

In most societies to talk of the choice to marry or not would be almost as relevant as to talk of the choice to grow old or not: it has been considered the only route to full adult status. To marry has been simply part of the "natural" progression through life, part of the inevitable, unless catastrophe intervened. Only recently has our society been modifying its norms on this, as more of the population do not fit into the traditional patterns, and even raise questions about their viability.

The cultural ideal is still that in marriage men should be in the one-up position. The husband "should be" taller, older, smarter, more educated, and have more income-generating power. For more than a generation, Jessie Bernard has been discussing the fact that marriage produces such profound discontinuities into lives of women as to constitute a genuine health hazard

(Bernard, 1982). In spite of the widespread cultural stereotypes that marriage is something men should dread and fear, all the research supports the opposite—that in every way marriage improves men's mental health, while in almost every way, mentally, physically, and even in crime statistics, single women are healthier than married women (Apter, 1985).

Contrary to the popular stereotypes of the frustrated old maid and the free unencumbered bachelor life, spinsters do very well and bachelors do very poorly (Gurin et al., 1980 p. 42). And statistically, the more education a woman has and the better her job, the less likely she is to marry. Just the reverse is true for men.

Paradoxical as it seems, having been raised to see themselves as dependent, women after marriage often devote a great part of their efforts to keeping their husband's self-image intact. Often, because the wife has put so many eggs in the one basket of marriage and given up so much for it, she has a great deal at stake in making a go of it.

A surprising 10% of women are choosing not to marry at all and the estimates are that as many as 20–30% of women in the present generation will choose to remain childless. To this must be added the couples waiting until much later in the marriage cycle to begin having children. According to a 1985 census report, 75% of American men are still single at age 25. This is an increase from 55% in 1970. For women the rates are now 57% compared with 36% in 1970, reflecting a remarkable shift (Glick, 1984).

We have no real evidence about the impact on later marriage of the tremendous recent increase in the number of unmarried couples living together; but we know that more and more couples are passing through a stage of living with one or several partners before marriage, making the transition to marriage much less of a turning point in the family life cycle than in the past. There is an increase to 4% in the number of unmarried couples living together at any given time, although a much higher overall percent live together for some period before marriage. Obviously the meaning of a wedding changes when a couple has been living together for several years and participating jointly in extended-family experiences. Nevertheless, as the movie "Best Friends" depicted, even after a couple has been living together for several years, the transition to marriage can still create great turmoil, the more so if the partners have not dealt with their extended family as a couple during the period of living together.

In any case there seems to be a timing and a pattern to this phase. With those who marry early, it often means having more difficulty adjusting to its tasks. Women who marry before age 20 (about 25% of women) are twice as likely to divorce as those who marry in their 20s. On the other hand, those who marry after 30 (about 20% of women) are less likely to divorce, but if they do, they do so sooner than those who marry earlier (Glick 1984). Thus it appears that in our culture there is a timing for coupling and while it seems to be better to marry later than sooner, those who fall too far out of the normative range on either end may have trouble making the transition. Such people are often

responding to family stresses that make the process of coupling more difficult to achieve. Those who marry early may be running away from their families of origin or seeking a family they never had. They may leave home by fusing with a mate in an attempt to gain strength from each other. Later on they may have more difficulties as a result of their failure to take the step toward independent development first. Women who marry late are frequently responding to a conflict between marriage and career and their ambivalence about losing their independence and identity in marriage. An increasing number of men also seem to be avoiding commitment and prefer living alone to becoming involved in the interdependence that marriage entails. Some who marry late may also have seen a negative image of marriage at home, or they have been enmeshed in their families and have trouble forming outside relationships, developing a secure work situation, and leaving home.

In spite of the trend toward delaying both marriage and pregnancy, the majority of couples do marry and have children before age 30. Naturally those who have children shortly after marriage have relatively little time to adjust to the status changes of marriage and its accompanying stresses before moving on.

What is amazing, considering the long-range implications of the decision to marry, is that so many couples seem to spend so little time thinking out the decision. Aylmer (1977) has commented that many Americans seem to spend more time deciding which car to buy than selecting the spouse they expect to keep for life. It seems that the timing of marriage decisions is often influenced by events in the extended family, although most couples are unaware of the correlation of these events and the process which underlies their decision to marry (Ryder, et al., 1971; Friedman, 1977; McGoldrick & Walsh, 1983). People often seem to meet their spouses or make the decision to marry shortly after the retirement, illness, or even untimely death of a parent, or after other traumatic family loss. The sense of loss or aloneness can be a strong contributing factor in the desire to build a close relationship. This may blind a person to the aspects of a prospective spouse that do not fit the idealized picture that the other will complete him or her and make life worthwhile. This desire for completion is likely to lead to difficulty accepting the spouse's differentness, which will necessarily show itself in the course of the relationship. As one woman put it, "My husband and I have always been afraid of the stranger in each other. We kept wanting to believe that the other thought the same as we thought they were thinking, which could never be. We just couldn't appreciate that here was a new and different person, with his or her own thoughts and feelings, who would make life more interesting."

FUSION AND INTIMACY

A basic dilemma in coupling is the confusion of intimacy with fusion. Fogarty has clarified the problem in the following way: "The forces of together-

ness spring from the natural human desire for closeness. Carried to extremes they lead to a search for completeness. Carried beyond the possible, such forces lead to fusion, a uniting of two people and resultant distance. Spouses try to defy the natural incompleteness of people and systems, as if one can become complete by fusing into a united twosome (Fogarty, 1976, p. 39).

There is a vast difference between forming an intimate relationship with another separate person and using a couple relationship to complete one's self and improve one's self-esteem. The natural human desire to share one's experience often leads to this confusion between seeking intimacy and seeking fusion in coupling. Poets have long talked about the difference. Rilke (1954) writes: "Love is at first not anything that means merging, giving over, and uniting with another (for what would a union be of something unclarified and unfinished, still subordinate?); it is a high inducement to the individual to ripen . . . it is a great exacting claim" (p. 54).

There are, of course, sex differences in the way fusion is experienced, since women have traditionally been raised to consider "losing themselves" in a relationship as normal, and men have been raised to see intimacy as frightening. Thus men more often express their fusion by maintaining a pseudo-differentiated distant position in relationships and women by maintaining a pseudo-intimacy, which is really a giving up of themselves.

Frequently others expect a couple to fuse and view the wife as somehow joined to the identity of her husband, thus increasing the difficulties for women in differentiating and maintaining their separate identities. For men the fear of intimacy and the social expectations of his "independence" and of his wife's adaptiveness work together to inhibit his establishment of intimate relationships that permit differences to exist.

Bowen systems theory (1978) elucidates the universal tendency to seek fusion as related to a person's incomplete differentiation from her or his family of origin. In other words, couples seek to complete themselves in each other to the degree that they have failed to resolve their relationships with their parents, which would free them to build new relationships based on each person's freedom to be him or herself and to appreciate the other as he or she is. The process whereby people seek to enhance their self-esteem in marriage is based on denying their "differentness" from their spouse, and can result in severe distortions in communication to maintain the myth of agreement (Satir, 1967).

During courtship couples are usually most aware of the romantic aspects of their relationship. Marriage shifts the relationship from a private coupling to a formal joining of two families. Issues that the partners have not resolved with their own families will tend to be factors in marital choice and are very likely to interfere with establishing a workable marital balance.

It may be that much of the intensity of romantic love is determined by one's family values. From this perspective Romeo and Juliet might have felt intensely attracted to each other precisely because their family situation prohibited their relationship. Such obstacles may lead to an idealization of the forbidden person. They, and many other romantic heroes, from Tristan and Isolde on

down, were conveniently spared a more complete view of their relationship by their untimely deaths, thus preserving the romance, and perhaps obscuring the more pedestrian underlying family dramas that probably fostered their attraction in the first place.

In everyday life the outcome of such love affairs is often not so romantic, as the following case illustrates (see Figure 10-1).

Nancy met her husband, Tom, during her last year of high school. Her parents had been very unhappily married and had invested all their energies in their children's success. Nancy planned to go to college and her younger brother was expected to go even further academically. A month after her high-school graduation, Nancy's lawyer father had a severe stroke and became an invalid. Her mother, who had never responded well to stress, became even more critical of her husband now that he was so dependent. Nancy began college, but the same week met Tom, with whom she fell "madly in love." Within three months she had decided to drop out and marry Tom, who had begun working for an insurance company after finishing high school the previous year. He was an only child from a lower-middle-class family. For him not only was Nancy very attractive, but her family represented a step up socially. She was an intense, dynamic, and attractive woman. Her intensity appealed to him, perhaps because his own family life had been marred by his father's inability to work because of a war disability and his mother's added disappointment in being able to have only one child. Tom hoped to escape the lonely and rather depressed atmosphere of his home by marrying Nancy. He had always felt responsible for his parents' well-being, but powerless to make them happy. He was delighted when Nancy left college and began pushing to marry him. He had been threatened by her college pursuits anyway. For Nancy he represented the only way she knew to get away from her family's expectations. She had been conflicted about school since her mother had had to give up college in favor of her own younger brother. She feared that surpassing her mother in education would be a sign of disloyalty. She had also been receiving mixed messages from her family about continuing her education after her father's stroke. And since she had grown up not believing she was really smart, she felt under great pressure about schoolwork. Tom would free her from these pressures. He would not push her to achieve. He accepted her as she was. He had a steady income, and this would mean she

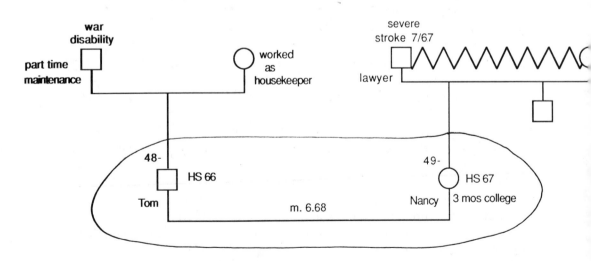

Figure 10-1. The young couple.

would not have to worry about her inability to concentrate on her studies, for fear of failure, or being disloyal to her mother by achieving success. She would become Tom's wife; they would raise a family and her worries would be over.

Both Tom and Nancy found the other attractive and saw their relationship as making them feel better than they ever remembered feeling before. Tom's parents were not generally disapproving, but suggested strongly that they wait, since they were both so young. Nancy's father disapproved of her marrying someone without a college education and thought she should finish school herself. In private moments Nancy wondered if she might find someone more intelligent and with more promise, but her parents' disapproval pushed her to defend her choice and to reject their "snobbism." Prior to marriage Nancy and Tom had little chance to be alone together. What time they did have was filled with wedding arrangments and discussion of the families' pressures on them. Almost immediately after the wedding, Nancy felt restless. Things with her family had quieted down after the marriage—they had no more reason to protest. Nancy quickly became bored and began to pressure Tom to get a better job. Tom felt guilty about having "abandoned" his parents, something he hadn't let surface during courtship. To improve things financially, and to deal with his feelings about his parents, he suggested buying a two-family house that his parents had been considering. They could share expenses and it would make a good investment. Nancy agreed because it meant they would have much nicer living quarters. Almost immediately she began to feel pressure from Tom's parents to socialize with them and to have children for them. Having married to escape her own parents, she now felt saddled wilth two others, with the added burden of not knowing them well. Suddenly Tom's personality irritated her. Where initially she had liked him for his easy-going style and his acceptance of her, she now saw him as lacking ambition. She was embarrassed to have him spend time with her friends because of his manners and lack of education, so she began avoiding her friends, which left her even more isolated. She tried pressuring him to fulfill her dreams and satisfy all her relationship needs. He felt increasingly inadequate and unable to respond to her pressure. Sexually she felt he was clumsy and insensitive and began to turn him away. His sense of inadequacy led him to retreat further and he took to going out in the evening with his friends, with whom he felt accepted and not on trial.

Nancy's resistance to parental expectations had now been transferred into the marriage. Tom's hopes for moving beyond his parents' disappointing lives had now been transformed into pressure from Nancy for him to succeed, and he resented it. Neither Nancy nor Tom had worked out for themselves individually what they wanted in life. Each had turned to the other to fulfill unmet needs and now each was disappointed.

What began to happen between Nancy and Tom is what happens to many couples when the hope that the partner will solve all problems proves to be in vain. There is a tendency to personalize stress and to blame someone for what goes wrong. At times one blames oneself; at times, one's spouse. Given enough stress couples tend to define their problems solely within the relationship. They may blame the spouse ("He let me down; he doesn't love me.") or themselves ("I'm no good; I'd be able to satisfy her if I were.") Once this personalizing process begins, it is very difficult to keep the relationship open. Nancy began to lay the blame for her disappointments in life on Tom and he saw himself as responsible for her unhappiness.

A major factor that tightens couple relationships over time is their increasing interdependency and their tendency to interpret more and more facets of their lives within the marriage, which is often supported by others who also

promote the couple's narrow focus. For example, during courtship, if one partner becomes depressed, the other is not likely to take it too personally, assuming. "There are many reasons to get depressed in life; this may well have nothing to do with me." Such an assumption of not being responsible for the other's feelings permits a supportive and empathic response. After several years of marriage, however, this partner has a much greater tendency to view the other's emotional reactions as a reflection of his or her input and to feel responsible for the partner's depression. After five years of marriage, the partner may think, "It must mean I'm not a good wife, or I would have made him happy by now." Once each starts taking responsibility for the other's feelings, there is a tendency for more and more areas in the relationship to become tension-filled. Over time they will avoid dealing with more and more areas. For example, she may feel inadequate, guilty, and resentful. She may then decide to avoid dealing with him because she does not want to be blamed, or she may become very protective of him and not say anything upsetting for fear of making him feel worse. In either case the more her reactions are a response to his, the less flexibility there will be in the relationship and the more the couple's communication will become constricted in the areas that are emotionally charged.

The period when couples are courting is probably the least likely time, of all the phases of the cycle, to seek therapy. This is not because coupling is so easy, but rather because of the romanticization of the attraction between the partners. They will have a strong tendency to idealize each other and to avoid looking at the enormous and long-range difficulties of establishing an intimate relationship. While the first years of marriage are the time of greatest overall marital satisfaction for many, they are also the time of the highest rate of divorce. The degree of disillusionment and mutual disappointment will usually match the degree of idealization of the relationship during courtship, as in the case of Nancy and Tom. During courtship the pull toward the relationship is likely to prevent realization of potential difficulties (Friedman 1977), so they do not show up until further down the road. On the one hand, there is the tendency toward pseudomutuality during courtship, and on the other, as Bowen has observed, this can be the time of greatest openness in the relationship because years of interdependence have not yet constricted the relationship. Most spouses have the closest and most open relationships in their adult lives during courtship. It is common for living-together relationships to be harmonious, and for fusion symptoms to develop when those involved finally get married. It is as if the fusion does not become problematic as long as there still is an option to terminate the relationship (Bowen, 1978, p. 377). While marriage frequently tightens a relationship, the fusion often starts developing during courtship, when couples say they like everything about each other, share all their free time together, and so on.

The failure to appreciate or allow for the differentness in the other person comes from never really having become emotionally independent of one's parents. This leaves a person in the position of trying to build self-esteen in the

marriage. Neither partner dares to communicate his or her fears to the other. He may be thinking: "I must never let her know that I am really nothing or I will lose her, and I will never tell her that at times she is boring and talks too much." Meanwhile she may be thinking: "I mustn't let him know that I am really worthless or he will leave me. And I mustn't let on that he is boring, only wants to watch sports and TV, and has nothing interesting to say." Each puts the other in charge of his or her self-esteem: "I am worthwhile because you love me." This leaves both vulnerable to the converse possibility: "If you do not love me, I am worthless." Thus couples can become bound in a web of evasiveness and ambiguity, because neither can dare to be straight with the other, for fear of things turning out unhappily, as they did in their families of origin. Messages between them may become more and more covert as more and more they define their own worth by the relationship. It can lead to the content of communication becoming totally obscured by the need of both partners to validate themselves through the spouse. It may end with the absurdity of couples spending their time doing things neither wants to do because each thinks the other wants it that way.

While many couples seem to make it to couplehood with the help of romance, pseudomutuality, or the resistance of their parents to the idea, some couples, perhaps an increasing number, get stuck in the process of becoming a pair.

> Mary and David applied for counseling over the question of whether to marry after living together for eight years. Mary saw David's refusal to marry as a rejection. David saw Mary's push to marry as a reflection of other insecurities, since they were happy in their life together. He saw marriage as tying them into unpleasant obligations such as his parents had shared. He also feared becoming the caretaker for her, should she inherit the disabling genetic disease from which her mother suffered. Mary was preoccupied with David's refusal to marry her, saying she would leave him unless he changed his mind, though she admitted they were compatible in most things and she was very happy with their life together. She was obsessed with the possibility of his leaving her.

In such situations family patterns contribute to the inability of each successfully to negotiate the transition to couplehood. In such instances the concept of "marriage" has taken on a meaning far beyond the fact of two people sharing their lives with each other. Very often couples fall into the stereotypic roles Mary and David were playing here. She can think of nothing but marriage, and that is the one thing he cannot think about. These patterns reflect opposite sides of the same lack of differentiation from their families of origin. Men who are not comfortable with their level of differentiation typically fear commitment whereas such women typically fear being alone.

It is not uncommon for two people who have been living happily together to find that things change when they do get married because they have now added to the situation the burdensome definitions of "husband" and "wife." These words often bring with them the conceptions of heavy responsibility *for* rather than *to* each other, which living together did not impose. There may also

be the burden of having definitely passed beyond youth into "serious" adulthood.

> Another unmarried couple who had lived together for four years, Ann and Peter, both in their early 30s, applied for therapy because of an unsatisfying sex life. The couple had always avoided discussing marriage. Peter said he was just too unprepared and Ann that she feared learning that he did not want to marry her. She heard his silence as a statement of his basic indifference to her. For Peter marriage signified a loss of spontaneity, such as he saw in his parents. Both his parents had left college to marry when his mother became pregnant, and they saw this as a serious mistake. With the burden of a family to support, they felt stifled in their ambitions, and had never moved past this frustration. Peter felt that he had to resolve all his insecurities and become completely self-sufficient before marrying. Ann feared that if Peter did not marry her she would have to start a new relationship soon or she would be too old to have children. This had affected their sexual relationship, which had become increasingly tension-filled.

This couple viewed marriage as such an enormous task that they could never be sufficiently prepared for it. Many couples have the opposite misperception, that marriage will fulfill them regardless of all other aspects of their lives. Family attitudes and myths about marriage filter down from generation to generation, making such transitions proportionately smoother or more difficult.

HOMOSEXUAL COUPLES

The patterns described here for heterosexual couples are similar, but frequently more difficult for homosexuals for several reasons (Krestan & Bepko, 1980: Roth, 1985; Nichols & Leiblum, 1986). The horrendous implications for gay men as well as for heterosexual couples brought on by the AIDS crisis in the formation of couple relationships is hard to anticipate. One large study carried out prior to the AIDS crisis suggests that in many respects the impact of gender on the couple has outweighed the effect of their gayness in terms of the patterns that couples developed regarding sex, power, and work (Blumstein & Schwartz, 1983). We can only predict that the forced changes in sexual behavior brought about by the AIDS epidemic will radically influence gay men and heterosexuals (lesbians have a very low likelihood of developing the disease), both in their sexual patterns and in their relationships with their family members. At the same time that the similarity or identification of homosexuals being of the same sex may increase the understanding between partners, it is also likely to make them more vulnerable to fusion. A second and related area of difficulty comes from the lack of acceptance that most gay couples experience from their families and from the culture at large throughout the life cycle. This increases the risk that they will develop boundary problems with each other in response to their family or society's negative reactions to

their couplehood; the stigma of being homosexual may lead either to having a secret identity or to having a fusion with others in the gay community and cutting off the straight world.

Related to this familial and societal negativity is the lack of normative rituals for homosexuals as they move through the life cycle. They do not have the benefit of formal marriage, or even divorce, to mark their relationship transitions. Often the family of origin tends to view them as perpetual adolescents. It requires special efforts on their part to receive adequate recognition for their relationship transitions.

Case Example

Kathy Bailey, aged 28, and Ellen Carr, 35, who had been living together for a year and a half, sought therapy in January 1986. Kathy was not sleeping and Ellen was concerned that she was depressed, anxious, and drinking too much. Kathy had struggled since her mid-teens with her homosexuality. In college she dated occasionally, and upon graduation she had married very briefly, hoping that this would release her from her homosexual feelings and the disruption she felt a homosexual life-style would create for her and her family of origin. After her divorce she kept a great distance from her parents, with whom she had always had a stormy relationship. She had been known in her family as the problem child since elementary school. Her conservative WASP family operated on the basis of preserving appearances. Her older sister always played the "good girl," and never went beyond the limits accepted by the family. Kathy was always the outspoken one in the family, seen as the rebel. She always argued politics with her father, and when she became involved in women's rights, he became particularly incensed. Kathy felt that her mother was sympathetic to her at times, but the mother never dared to disagree openly with her husband.

After her divorce Kathy had become more involved with lesbians in the various political activist jobs she had. She had several attachments, but Ellen was her first live-in relationship. After beginning the relationship with Ellen, she had decided to go to law school, but had recently dropped out.

Ellen, who came from a Jewish family, had known clearly since she was in high school that she was a lesbian and had socialized within a gay social group from the time she began college. She had never told her parents that she was a lesbian, but she occasionally brought home female friends and sensed that her parents, who had a very conflicted relationship, were not unhappy that she never dated men. She suspected that her mother might be lesbian without knowing it, and a paternal aunt who had never married as well.

What precipitated Kathy's turmoil was her announcement to her parents during a visit (which she always made without Ellen) that she was a lesbian. Kathy said she had decided to tell her parents about this because she was tired of keeping her life a secret. Her mother initially looked fairly supportive. Her father, however, became extremely angry and told her that this was just the last in a series of her "bad judgments" for many years. In several phone calls to her parents over the next weeks she was greeted with stony silence by both. Kathy's symptoms had begun just after this. Ellen tried to be supportive but had disapproved of Kathy's telling her parents about her homosexuality, believing that "parents never understand and there's no point getting into all that." Since then Kathy had spoken to a number of her lesbian friends about the situation, and the general advice they gave her was that she should forget about her parents: her father sounded like an insensitive redneck" and why bother—just write him off. Her conflict was that at

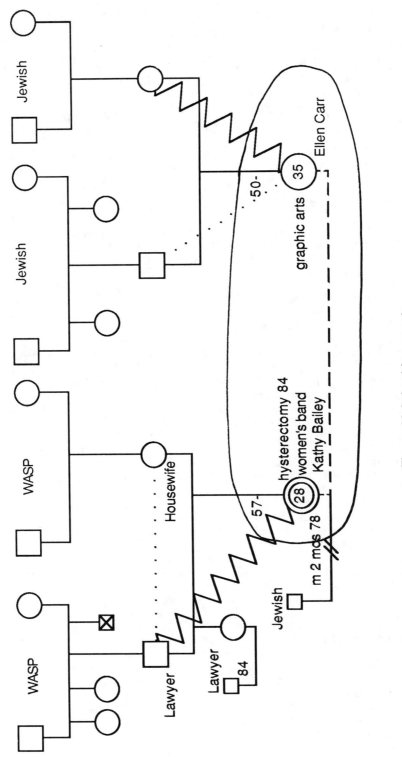

Figure 10-2. Lesbian couple.

some level she was still seeking, not only greater closeness with her parents, but their approval.

The initial therapy sessions focused on helping Kathy sort out for herself the different aspects of her feelings and behavior. She tried, for example, to differentiate her wish for parental approval of her career path from her lesbian life-style. She worked on allowing her parents to disapprove of her homosexuality, if that was their need, without rejecting them. She also had to think through how she wanted to deal with her parents and not make decisions based on the feelings of her friends. She was encouraged to put herself in her parents' place regarding her announcement of her homosexuality. Having worked on this she was coached to write a response to her father in which she acknowledged his disappointment that she had left law (his profession) and told him how frustrating she knew her career vacillation must have been for him over the years. She then talked about her earlier fears that he would cut her off completely if he knew of her homosexuality and her relief that he had not; she said she appreciated how hard this must be for him and her mother, since it meant they would never have grandchildren (a particularly painful issue for them since her sister had had to have a hysterectomy two years earlier). She acknowledged that it would probably be very difficult for them to deal with the issue with their friends. She said she wished her life had not taken this turn, for their sake, and told him now much she loved him and wanted to have a close relationship.

The letter helped her to clarify for herself that her lesbianism was not a matter for her parents' approval, and that discussing it with them came at the deepest level from a need to end the secrecy and solidify her identity as an adult. Luckily, through her motivation to understand herself and her respect for her parents' limitations, she was able to achieve a relationship with them over the next several years in which the issue of her sexual identity became a fact of life that was accepted by them in a matter-of-fact way. She and Ellen became accepted in the family as a couple, included for holidays together, and with a boundary of respect around their relationship.

As can be seen from this example, the systemic problems around couple formation are generally similar, regardless of the content of the problems. However, certain patterns are quite predictable for homosexual couples, as for religious, class, ethnic, or racial intermarriages. Where the extended family is extremely negative toward the couple for whatever reason, we encourage couples to take a long view, not trying to turn the acceptance of their relationship into a yes-or-no event, but working gradually over time to build bridges for family closeness. Other life cycle transitions, particularly births and deaths, often create a shift in the family equilibrium, which allows for redefinitions of family status for the couple.

THE WEDDING

One of the best indicators of the family process at the time of couple formation, and one of the best places for preventive intervention, is the wedding itself. As family events, weddings are the only major ceremonies organized by the family itself, and they are the family ceremonials that involve

the most planning (Barker, 1978). The organization of the wedding, who makes which arrangements, who gets invited, who comes, who pays, how much emotional energy goes into the preparations, who gets upset and over which issues, are all highly reflective of family process. It seems generally that those who marry in unconventional ways, in civil ceremonies, or without family or friends present, have their reasons. Most often the issues in such situations are family disapproval, premarital pregnancy, an impulsive decision to marry, a previous divorce, or the inability or unwillingness of the parents to meet the costs of the wedding (Barker, 1978). From a clinical point of view, the emotional charge of such situations, when it leads to downplaying the marriage as a family event, may well indicate that the family members are unable to make the status changes required to adapt to this new life cycle stage and will have difficulty with future stages. Weddings are meant to be transition rituals that facilitate family process. As such they are extremely important for marking the change in status of family members and the shifting in family organization.

The opposite problem ensues when the family overfocuses on the wedding itself, perhaps spending more than they can afford, putting all their energy into the event and losing sight of the marriage as a process of joining two families. Families and couples often assume that once the wedding has occurred, everyone should feel close and connected. Today, with the changing mores, this focus on the wedding may be less intense, but there is still a large overlap of myth associated with marital bliss, which gets displaced onto wedding celebrations in a way that may be counterproductive.

Surprisingly, few couples ever seek premarital counseling, in spite of the obvious difficulties in negotiating this transition (Friedman, 1977), and in spite of the fact that preventive intervention in relation to the extended families might be a great deal easier at this time than later in the life cycle. The most that can be said is that it is extremely useful when working with any member of a family around the time of a wedding to encourage him or her to facilitate the resolution of family relationships through this nodal event. One can only encourage all participants to make maximum use of the event to deal with the underlying family process. For example, it is often fruitful to convey to the couple that in-law struggles are predictable and need not be taken too personally. It is important for couples to recognize that the heightened parental tension probably relates to their sense of loss regarding the marriage. When families argue about wedding arrangements, the issues under dispute only cover up underlying and much more important system issues, as in the following example:

> A couple about to marry was very upset because of the woman's mother's preoccupation with invitations and seating arrangements. The prospective wife's previous marriage had been annulled, and this had never been announced or dealt with openly by the family. Initially the daughter got caught up in anger at her mother for not accepting her new marriage. The mother was embarrassed to invite her family, since they had come to the first wedding and would now know for

certain that it had not worked out. The mother hoped that with a small wedding "no one would notice," and over time the issue of the annulled marriage would be totally forgotten. She hoped her relatives would think that the new husband was the same one the daughter had married at the first wedding. The daughter was incensed at what she perceived as her mother's rejection of her and her new husband. Once she was able to begin talking to her mother about this, emphasizing how hard this second marriage must be for her mother, the tension diminished considerably. The daughter was able to give up her indignation and move toward her mother with some compassion for her mother's fear of her family's reaction. The daughter's move released the tension binding the system.

Since family members so often view others as capable of "ruining" the event, a useful rule of thumb is for each person to take his or her own responsibility for having a good time at the wedding. It is also useful for the couple to recognize that marriage is a family event and not just for the two of them. Looked at from this perspective, parents' feelings about the service need to be taken into consideration in whatever meaningful ways are possible. An interesting example is the young woman mentioned above, who was having conflict with her mother about the undiscussed annulment. She had always been allied with her father. For the wedding she asked both parents to escort her down the aisle, since, she said, they had both helped to bring her to the point of marriage. The mother was extremely touched by the invitation, and this small gesture allowed the young woman to make a significant family statement to her parents about their meaning in her life. Probably the more responsibility the couple can take for arranging a wedding that reflects their shifting position in their families and the joining of the two systems, the more auspicious this is for their future relationship.

An ideal to work toward in planning a wedding would be that achieved by Joan and Jim Marcus. They were one of the unusual couples who sought coaching to help them through the premarital period. They were aware of budding conflicts between them and wanted to resolve them before they got worse. Jim's parents had divorced when he was five. His father remarried briefly when Jim was eight and again when he was 16. He had grown up in his father's custody, with several housekeepers involved between his father's marriages. Jim had distanced from his alcoholic mother and from both stepmothers for many years, but was able to reverse the process of cutoff in his planning for the wedding. He called each of them to invite them specially to his wedding, discussing with each her importance in his life and how much it would mean to him to have her present at his wedding celebration.

The next problem was Joan's parents, who were planning an elaborate celebration and wanted everything to go according to the book. This would have made Jim's less affluent family very uncomfortable. Initially Joan became quite reactive to her mother's fancy plans and to her making decisions without discussion. At the suggestion of her therapist, she spent a whole day with her mother, discussing her own feelings about marriage and approaching her mother as a resource on how to handle things. She discovered for the first time that her mother had been married in a small civil wedding because her parents had had little money and disapproved of her wedding. They had married during the Koren war, just before her father went overseas. Joan learned how much her mother had yearned for a "proper wedding." She realized that her mother's wishes to do everything in a fancy way had grown out of her own unrealized dreams and were an attempt to give Joan

something she had missed. With this realization Joan could share her own wish for a simple celebration and especially her anxiety about Jim's family's discomfort, which she had not mentioned before. She asked her mother for advice on how to handle the situation. She told her how uncomfortable she was about the divorces in Jim's family and her fears that her own relatives would disapprove of him, especially if all his mothering figures attended the wedding. Suddenly her mother's attitude changed from dictating how things had to be done to a helpful and much more casual attitude. A week later Joan's mother told Jim that if there was any way she could facilitate things with his mother, stepmothers, or other guests she would be glad to do it.

Another couple, Ted and Andrea, perhaps the only couple I have seen who sought premarital counseling specifically to work on extended-family issues, were able to field stormy emotional reactions in the family so well that they probably prevented years of simmering conflicts that had hampered both extended families over several generations. When they sought help, they said they planned to marry with only a few friends present, unless they could bring their families around to accepting them as they were. Andrea's parents had eloped after their parents refused to agree to the marriage because of "religious differences." Ted's paternal grandfather had had a heart attack and died three days after Ted's father married. Weddings thus became dreaded events for both extended families. The couple began the work by contacting extended-family members personally to invite them to their marriage, and raise any concerns during the conversations. For example, the husband called his father's mother, who was 85 and whom his parents had assured him would never be able to come. He told her his parents were sure she couldn't make it, but that it meant a great deal to him to have her there, since he feared his father might have a heart attack and he needed her support. The parents had been acting to protect the grandmother "for her own good." She not only made her own arrangements to have a cousin fly with her, but she arranged to stay with her son, the groom's father, during the week after the wedding. At the wedding both the bride and groom made toasts in verse to their families, in which they ticked off the charged issues with humor and sensitivity, and made a special point of spending time with family members.

It frequently happens that friendship systems and extended-family relationships change after the wedding. Many couples have difficulty maintaining individual friendships and move, at least in the first years, toward having only "couple friends." We encourage the spouses to keep their individual friendship networks, since "couple friends" typically reinforce fusion, and do not allow the spouses their individual interests and preferences.

PATTERNS WITH EXTENDED FAMILY

Marriage symbolizes a change in status among all family members and generations and requires that the couple negotiate new relationships as a twosome with many other subsystems: parents, siblings, grandparents, and nieces and nephews, as well as with friends. Most often women move closer to their families of origin after marriage, and men become more distant, shifting their primary tie to the new nuclear family. In any case spouses deal with their

families in many different ways. Many find marriage the only way to separate from their families of origin. They tend to be enmeshed with their families, and this pattern continues even after marriage. Patterns of guilt, intrusiveness, and unclear boundaries are typical of such systems. Other couples cut off their families emotionally even before marriage. In these situations the partners may not even invite their parents to the wedding. Parents are seen as withholding and rejecting and the couple decides to do without them. Another pattern involves continued contact with parents, but with ongoing conflicts. In such families there is usually involvement of the extended family in the marriage plans, but often with fights, hurt feelings, and "scenes" around the time of the wedding. This pattern is perhaps the most helpful for future resolution of the issues. The conflicts indicate that at least the family is struggling with separating and is not forcing it underground as in enmeshed or cutoff families. The ideal situation, and the one very rarely found, is where the partners have become independent of their families before marriage and at the same time maintain close, caring ties. In such instances the wedding would serve for all the family as a sharing and a celebration of the new couple's shift in status.

Arlene and Howard are a clear example of the difficulties of enmeshment. They married when both were 19. They had met and dated perfunctorily in high school. Arlene's father worked 18 hours a day and her mother devoted herself exclusively to her son and daughter. Arlene feared her mother's loneliness if she left her, so she remained at home while her younger brother left for a college far away. After high school Arlene got a job selling in a department store. She considered moving away for work or study but felt her parents, especially her mother, would feel rejected if she got an apartment of her own in the same city and she feared a move further away on her own. Following the pregnancy "scare" during which she and Howard decided they would have to marry, she concluded this was the best thing to do anyway, and a few months later they were married. Her family paid for the wedding and exerted primary control over the guest list, which bothered Howard. However, he felt he was not financially in a position to complain. His family was rather poor and could not contribute to the costs, and he had no extra money himself. After the wedding the couple moved to their own apartment, but Arlene and her mother were in daily phone contact and couple visited her parents most weekends. Howard began using the excuse of work to avoid these family gatherings. Arlene's mother was centrally involved in decorating their apartment, offering to pay for items the couple could not afford on their own. Howard resisted these presents, since they left him feeling indebted and guilty, but Arlene said that rejecting her parents' gifts would only hurt them. It was not until many years later, when their own children began to break away, that Arlene and Howard recognized the need to find new ways to cope with this enmeshment. Intervention at the time of the marriage might have helped this couple establish the necessary boundaries and balance in their relationship to avoid these later complications.

The second pattern of dealing with parents involves cutting off the relationships in an attempt to gain independence.

Jack and Mary were married in a civil ceremony with two friends as witnesses. They were "not into marriage" and only got married for convenience. Jack had won a scholarship to college at 18 and worked nights to pay his extra expenses. He had decided to do it all on his own because he hated his alcoholic father's abuse.

At first he kept up contact with his mother, but when she refused his urgings to leave her husband, Jack decided she deserved what she got and he kept up only perfunctory and sporadic contact. He met Mary in college and afterward they began living together. She had had a stormy adolescence, during which her parents disapproved of her boyfriends, her politics, and her use of pot. She disapproved of what she called her parents' hypocrisy, since they drank rather heavily. After many stormy fights, she began to avoid going home. Jack also discouraged her family contact. He said it only upset her and that her parents were never going to change. After she told her parents she and Jack were going to live together, the relationship became even more strained. They disapproved and she disapproved of their disapproval. Jack was just as happy to have her cut off her relationship with her parents, since in his view parents just meant trouble and they could make it better on their own. The couple drew in on each other in a "two against the world" stance that remained balanced until their own children reached adolescence. At this point the children began acting out, and when Jack and Mary tried to set limits, the children challenged their pseudomutual stance, saying, "Why should we listen to you. You never listened to your parents or kept up any relationship with them." The couple could no longer maintain their fusion in the face of their children's challenges. They needed at this point to reassess their pattern of closing out the outside world under stress. Now they had to open up to other connections to help them respond to their children's distress.

Many couples develop restrictive couple patterns like Jack and Mary that work until later developmental stages destabilize them.

The third common pattern of relationships with extended family involves some contact, some closeness, some conflict, and the avoidance of certain issues. In such families the time of coupling is an excellent opportunity to reopen closed relationships, for example, inviting to the wedding relatives with whom parents are out of touch. It is a good chance to detoxify emotional issues, reviewing marital and family ties over several generations as part of redefining the system. However, the underlying tensions often surface reactively at the time of transition in emotional scenes or arguments around wedding plans, only to go underground again as family members try to act happy and friendly so as not to "create unpleasantness." The attempt to smooth things over in itself often increases the likelihood of outbursts. The fact that all change creates disruption and uncertainty in the system needs to be dealt with in the family if the developmental processes are to move along. For example, it may be easier for the family to move on if they are in touch with their sense of loss at the time of the wedding, and if they are a bit confused and uneasy about how to manage the new relationships. Whatever the patterns of difficulty with extended family—conflict, enmeshment, distance, or cutoff—the lack of resolution of these relationships is the major problem in negotiating this phase of the family life cycle. The more the triangles in the extended family are dealt with by an emotional cutoff of the relationship, the more the spouse comes to represent not just who he or she is, but also mother, father, brother, and sister. This input of intensity will surely overload the circuits in time. If the husband's relationship with his wife is his only meaningful relationship, he will be so sensitive to her every reaction, and especially to any hint of rejection, that he will overreact to signs of differentness by pulling her to agree with him or blaming her for not accepting him. The intensity will

probably make the relationship untenable eventually. Our culture's social mobility and overfocus on the nuclear family to the neglect of all other relationships contributes to this tendency to place more emotional demand on a marriage than it can bear. Once a spouse becomes overly involved in the other's response, both become bound up in a web of fusion and unable to function for themselves.

> Paul and Lucy, two graduate students, applied for marital therapy after a marriage of two years, because they were both concerned about the tensions between them. They thought they were not enjoying their relationship as much as other couples, in spite of their best efforts. Among other things, Paul said he tried to take Lucy out to dinner as often as possible, a struggle, he said, because they had so little money. Lucy said she never enjoyed it and she could sense his discomfort and did not like spending money that way herself, but went along, since it seemed to mean a lot to Paul. Paul got annoyed and said she always seemed to want to go and he was doing it to please her. She said she only acted happy because it seemed to mean so much to him. It turned out that Paul's mother, who had died of cancer the year Paul and Lucy married, had always seen his father as stingy. She frequently complained about her husband for not taking her out. Paul did not want to appear like his father. Lucy was trying to be accommodating to Paul because she did not want to end up with a divorce as her parents had done. The couple was well on its way to a life pattern that neither of them wanted, out of fear of disappointing each other.

Therapy for this couple involved reducing their focus on the marriage and placing their relationship in the broader context of their extended families. This therapeutic approach, the hallmark of Bowen systems therapy, appears to have great merit for couples who become myopic and see their partners as the source of all pain and joy in their lives.

Some couples transfer parental struggles to the spouse directly. One such young couple's marriage foundered when the husband's possessiveness led to his striking his wife for starting an affair. The wife, Roberta, had played the role of the "bad girl" and rebel in her family of origin. Her incestuous affair with a first cousin at the age of 17 had led to a thunderous response by her parents. She met John while still involved with her cousin and married him the following spring. Within a few months, the cycle of John's possessive intrusiveness and Roberta's rebellious acting out had developed full swing.

A related coupling problem occurs when people choose partners to handle their families for them. A man may choose a wife totally unacceptable to his parents and then let her fight his battles with his parents, while he becomes the "innocent bystander." The price everyone pays in such situations is the failure to achieve any real intimacy, since issues can never be resolved when other members are brought in to handle one's relationships.

When family members have served a central function in their parents' lives or in the preservation of their parents' marital balance, they may not feel the parents have granted "permission" for them to marry successfully. We would suggest that most marital problems derive from unresolved extended-family problems, and not from the specific marital conflicts on which spouses may focus.

While it is less common in our time that a parent dies before the children marry, when this does occur, the power of death-bed instructions regarding the marriage, and of other unresolved parental directives about marriage, are crucial in evaluating a couple's functioning expectations of themselves and each other in marriage.

IN-LAWS

Among the problematic triangles for the couple, the one involving husband, wife, and mother-in-law is probably the most renowned. In-laws are easy scapegoats for family tensions (Ryder et al., 1971). It is always much easier to hate your daughter-in-law for keeping your son from showing his love than to admit that your son doesn't respond as much as you wish we would. It may be easier for a daughter-in-law to hate her mother-in-law for "intrusiveness" than to confront her husband directly for not committing himself fully to the marriage and defining a boundary in relation to outsiders. In-law relationships are a natural arena for displacing tensions in the couple or in the family of origin of each spouse. The converse of this is the pattern of a spouse who has cut off his or her own family and seeks to adopt the spouse's family, forming a warm, enmeshed fusion with the in-laws, based on defining his or her own family as cold, rejecting, uninteresting, and so on.

It is important to mention also the sexism of our culture that so often focuses blame on the mother-in-law rather than on the father-in-law, who is usually seen as playing a more benign role. Just as mothers get blamed for what goes wrong in families because of their being given primary responsibility for family relationships, so do mother-in-laws get primary blame by extension. Many factors contribute to this process. Just as wives are given responsibility for handling a husband's emotional problems, so are they often put in the position of expressing issues for all other family members, and then being blamed when things go wrong.

THE IMPORTANCE OF SIBLING ISSUES

Siblings may also displace their problems in dealing with each other on the intrusion of a new spouse. Predictable triangles are especially likely between a husband and his wife's brothers or between the wife and her husband's sisters. The sisters may see their brother's wife as having "no taste," as infusing the brother with superficial values, and so forth. What is missed by the system in such instances is that the brother probably chose his wife intentionally as a

protection from his sisters, perhaps to set the limits he never dared set alone, or to allow him to distance without the guilt of doing it directly. Often the brother will get his wife to take over dealing with his family altogether, which usually succeeds only in escalating the tension. Of course, a person may also use the extended family to distance from his spouse without taking responsibility for it, under the guise of family duty: "I'd love to spend all day with you honey, but I have to visit my parents."

Good clues about a new couple can be found in the marital relationships of the parents, the couple's primary models for what marriage is about. The other basic model for spouses is their relationship with their siblings, their earliest and closest peers. Research indicates that couples who marry mates from complementary sibling positions enjoy the greatest marital stability (Toman, 1976). In other words, the older brother of a younger sister will tend to get along best with a younger sister of an older brother. They will tend not to have power conflicts, since he will be comfortable as the leader and she as the follower. In addition, they will tend to be comfortable with the opposite sex, since they have grown up with close contact with their opposite sexed siblings as well. Those who marry spouses not from complementary sibling positions will have more adjustments to make in marriage in this regard. An extreme case would be the oldest of many brothers who marries the oldest of many sisters. Both would expect to be the leader and would probably have difficulty understanding why the other does not take orders well, since they are used to having their orders taken at home. In addition, they will be less comfortable with the opposite sex, since they grew up in strongly single-sexed environments (Toman, 1976).

The most difficult thing about sibling-position differences is that we are not generally aware of how many of our assumptions about life are based on them. In fact, a great number of our basic life expectations come from implicit assumptions we formed in our families. We rarely realize how much we have to learn about differentness when we join with someone else, as in the following example.

A couple married for two years applied for therapy for vague complaints that the relationship was not working out. Both spouses were the youngest in rather large sibling systems. Their complaints focused on the vague feeling that their needs were not being met in the relationship and the other one never seemed to be doing his or her share. In was pointed out that since each had been considered the "baby" in the family of origin, they were probably both waiting for the other to be responsible, as youngests grow up assuming that a good, appreciative parent or older sibling can always be relied on to take care of things. They laughed and said that it was true that they had been the prince and princess of their families. They now had to do considerable work negotiating the taking of responsibility in the marriage, since this was a new task for both of them and one they had not known they needed to learn.

The dilemma presented by this couple is typical of many marital problems that are not really marital problems. They are problems that get focused in the marriage, but really derive from the couple's finding in the marriage a different

situation than they were used to in their families of origin. Again the biggest problem is that these differences in experience are so difficult to recognize. So often, if one's expectations are not met, the assumption is that the spouse is at fault for not responding "correctly." One often hears complaints, "If you loved me, you would know how I feel," or "If you loved me, you wouldn't always challenge my plans," as if "love" included mind reading.

CULTURAL DIFFERENCES

Another arena that becomes problematic in a marriage under stress is the cultural or family style differences. This may be more of a problem in the United States where people from so many diverse cultural backgrounds marry and find themselves in conflict because each starts out with such different basic assumptions (McGoldrick & Preto, 1984).

A young couple applied for therapy after a year of marriage because the wife said she was convinced her husband did not love her and that he had changed after they got married. The wife was the fifth of seven children from a Brooklyn family of Italian extraction. She had met her husband in college and was extremely attracted to his quiet, stable strength and strong life ambitions. He was from a midwestern Protestant family, where, as an only child, he was strongly encouraged by his parents to work hard and have a morally upright life. He had found her vivacious and charming, and had also been attracted to her family, because of their open affection and because, in contrast to his own "uptight" parents, they always seemed to have a good time.

Under stress the couple found that the very qualities that had attracted them to each other became the problem. The husband became for the wife "an unfeeling stone." She complained: "He doesn't care about my feelings at all and ignores me completely." For the husband the wife's vivaciousness now became "hysteria" and he found her "nagging, emotional outbursts, and screaming" unbearable.

As we discussed in therapy their very different family styles of coping with stress, their opposing assumptions became obvious. In the husband's family the rule was that you should keep your problems to yourself and think them out; with enough effort and thought, most problems could be worked out. The wife's family dealt with stress by getting together and ventilating. The family related intensely at all times, but especially when family members were upset. These styles had been turned inward in the marriage and were tightening things even more. The more the wife felt isolated and needed contact, the louder she sought attention and the more the husband withdrew to get some space and to maintain his balance. The more he withdrew, the more frustrated and alone the wife felt. Both partners had turned their differences, initially labeled as the source of attraction, into the problem, and had begun to see the other's behavior as a sure sign of not caring. Neither had been able to see that their family styles were just different. They were compounding the difficulty by moving further into their own pattern, with each blaming the other for the other's response. Once the family patterns could be clarified in the context of the extended-family and ethnic backgrounds, the spouses were able to temper their responses and to see their differences as neutral, rather than as signs of psychopathology or rejection.

ISSUES IN MARITAL ADJUSTMENT

Generally speaking, it is possible to predict that marital adjustment will be more problematic if any of the following are true:

1. The couple meets or marries shortly after a significant loss (Ryder, 1970, Ryder et al., 1971).

2. The wish to distance from one's family of origin is a factor in the marriage.

3. The family backgrounds of each spouse are significantly different (religion, education, social class, ethnicity, the ages of the partners, and the like).

4. The spouses come from incompatible sibling constellations.

5. The couple resides either extremely close to or at a great distance from either family of origin.

6. The couple is dependent on either extended family financially, physically, or emotionally.

7. The couple marries before age 20 (Booth & Edwards, 1985).

8. The couple marries after an acquaintanceship of less than six months or more than three years of engagement.

9. The wedding occurs without family or friends present.

10. The wife becomes pregnant before or within the first year of marriage (Christensen, 1963; Bacon, 1974).

11. Either spouse has a poor relationship with his or her siblings or parents.

12. Either spouse considers his or her childhood or adolescence an unhappy time.

13. Marital patterns in either extended family were unstable (Kobrin & Waite, 1984).

Most of these factors have already been given support by sociological data on divorce (Burchinal, 1965; Goodrich, et al. 1968; Ryder, 1970; Bumpass, 1972; Becker et al., 1977; Mott & Moore, 1979).

A number of other factors probably add to the difficulty of adjusting to marriage in our time. Changing family patterns as a result of the changing role of women, the frequent marriage of partners from widely different cultural backgrounds, and the increasing physical distance from families of origin are placing a much greater burden on couples to define their relationship for themselves than was true in traditional and precedent-bound family structures (Rausch, 1963). While any two family systems are different and have conflicting patterns and expectations, in our present culture couples are less bound by family traditions and are freer than ever before to develop male–female relationships unlike those they experienced in their families of origin. Couples are required to think out for themselves many things that in the past could have been taken for granted. This applies also to the enormous gap that often exists

in our culture between parents and children in education and social status. While it is much better for marital stability for children to be more successful than their parents (Glick, 1977), any large gap is obviously a strain, since parents, siblings, and child will have to adjust to large differences in experience.

The economics of our culture have meant that a fair percentage of children are able to leave their families and support themselves financially much earlier than was previously possible. Economic independence may increase the tendency to distance from the extended family. At the other extreme, the requirements of our lengthy educational process for many professionals may also complicate the adjustment to this phase of the life cycle by setting up the problem of prolonged dependence on parents (see Fulmer, Chapter 22). For example, couples who are trying to define themselves as separate from their families but are still being supported by them are in a difficult and ambiguous position. It is impossible to become emotionally independent while still relying on one's parents financially, so many couples struggle to develop couple boundaries in relation to their parents, but are basically unable to maintain them.

The changing role of women also influences marital relationships. It appears that the rise in women's status is positively correlated with marital instability (Pearson, 1979), and with the marital dissatisfaction of their husbands (Burke, 1976). When women used to fall automatically into the adaptive role in marriage, the likelihood of divorce was much lower. The adaptive spouse was not prepared to function independently either economically or emotionally. In fact, it appears very problematic for marriage when both spouses are equally successful and achieving. There is evidence that either spouse's accomplishments may correlate with the same degree of underachievement in the other (Ferber, 1979). Thus achieving marital adjustment in our time, when we are attempting to move toward equality of the sexes (educationally and occupationally), may be extraordinarily difficult.

REFERENCES

Apter, T. (1985). *Why women don't have wives*. New York: Schocken.

Aylmer, R. C. (1977). Emotional issues in divorce. *The Family* 4/2.

Bacon, L. (1974). Early motherhood, accelerated role transition and social pathologies. *Social Forces* 52: 333–341.

Barker, D. L. (1978). A proper wedding. In M. Corbin, Ed., *The couple*. New York: Penguin.

Becker, G., et al. (1977). Economics of marital instability. *Journal of Political Economy* 85: 1141–1187.

Bernard, J. (1982). *The future of marriage*. New Haven, Conn.: Yale University Press.

Blumstein, P. & Schwartz, P. (1983). *American couples*. New York: Morrow.

Booth, A., & Edwards, J. N. (1985) Age at marriage and marital instability. *Journal of Marital and Family Therapy* 47/1:67–75.

Bowen, M. (1978). *Family therapy in clinical practice*. New York: Jason Aronson.

Bumpass, L. & Sweet, J. (1972). Differentials in marital instability, 1970. *American Sociological Review* 37: 754–766.

Burchinal, L. G. (1965). Trends and prospects for young marriages in the United States. *Journal of Marriage and the Family* 27/2.

Burke, R. J., & Weir, T. (1976) The relationship of wives' employment status to husband, wife and pair satisfaction. *Journal of Marriage and the Family* 38/2.

Christensen, H. T. (1963). The timing of first pregnancy as a factor in divorce: A cross-cultural analysis. *Eugenics Quarterly* 10: 119–130.

Fogarty, T. (1976). On emptiness and closeness, Part II. *The Family* 3/2.

Friedman, E. (1977). Engagement and disengagement: family therapy with couples during courtship. In F. Andres & P. Lorio, Eds., *Georgetown Family Symposia*, Vol 1.

Glick, P. C. (1977). Updating the life cycle of the family. *Journal of Marriage and the Family* 39/1.

Glick, P. C. (1984). Marriage, divorce, and living arrangements. *Journal of Social Issues* 5/1: 7–26.

Goodrich, W. et al. (1968) Patterns of newlywed marriage. *Journal of Marriage and The Family* 30/3.

Gurin, G. Veroff, J., & Feld, S. (1980). *Americans view their mental health*. New York: Basic Books.

Kobrin, F. E., & Waite, L. J. (1984). Effects of childhood family structure on the transition to marriage. *Journal of Marriage and the Family* 4:807–816.

Krestan, J., & Bepko. C. (1980). The problem of fusion in the lesbian relationship. *Family Process* 19:277–290.

McGoldrick, M., & Preto, N. G. (1984). Ethnic intermarriage: Implications for therapy. *Family Process* 23/3:347–364.

McGoldrick, M. & Walsh, F. (1983) A systemic view of family history and loss. In L. R. Wolberg & M. L. Aronson (Eds.), *Group and family therapy* New York: Brunner/Mazel.

Mott, F. J. & Moore, S. F. (1979). The causes of marital disruption among young American women: An interdisciplinary perspective. *Journal of Marriage and the Family* 41/2.

Nichols, M., & Leiblum, S. R. (1986). Lesbianism as a personal identity and social role: A model. *Affilia* 48–59.

Pearson, W. & Hendrix, L. (1979) Divorce and the status of women. *Journal of Marriage and the Family* 41/2.

Rausch, H. L., et al. (1963). Adaptation to the first years of marriage. *Psychiatry* 26/4:368–380.

Rilke, R. M. (1954). *Letters to a young poet,* translated by M. D. Hester. New York: Norton.

Roth S., (1985). Psychotherapy with lesbian couples: Individual issues, female socialization and the social context. *Journal of Marital and Family Therapy* 11/3:273–286.

Ryder, R. (1970). Dimensions of early marriage. *Family Process* 9/1.

Ryder, R. G., Kafka, J. S., and Olson, D. H. (1971) Separating and joining influences in courtship and early marriage. *American Journal of Orthopsychiatry* 2: 450–464.

Satir, V. (1967). *Conjoint family therapy* Palo Alto, Calif.: Science & Behavior Books.

Toman, W. (1976). *Family constellation* (3rd ed.). New York: Springer.

CHAPTER 11

Becoming Parents:
Families with Young Children

Jack O. Bradt, M.D.

> Being a parent, whether father or mother, is the most difficult task humans have to perform. For people, unlike other animals, are not born knowing how to be parents. Most of us struggle through.—Karl Menninger

Like all developmental stages of the family life cycle, becoming a parent shares the common characteristic of a change of membership and a change of function of its members. After 25 years as a family practitioner, the author is clear that there is no stage that brings about more profound change or challenge to the nuclear and extended family than the addition of a new child to the family system. Over the past two generations in a world that has become massively disposed to destruction, our nation has become self-conscious about overpopulation and destruction through new life. Layered over this global emotional backdrop are the dramatic changes in the number of women working outside the home, the divorce rate and the stability of marriage, the common use of contraception and abortion, and inflation and the lifetime dollar cost of having a child.

In this context of massive social change, the challenge of new membership—a new child in the family—is reviewed. The household considered is an increasingly uncommon one: a couple married only once, who become parents of a child or children with whom they live in one household. The focus is on new parents and young children at a time of extreme change and challenge to relationships.

Biologically, becoming a parent is the event that identifies this stage. But being a parent is the psychological and social outcome and is more than a bonding between two generations. It changes the balance among work, friends, siblings, and parents. Moreover, there is a profoundly different meaning for this stage for a male or for a female. Contemporary young parents in the United States struggle to integrate their place of gainful employment, usually

away from home and their family life at home. Once physically two separate worlds, distinctively populated by men or by women and children, the work world—the place of status and power—has become a man's and a woman's world with clearly felt psychological as well as fiscal value. The domestic world has been left to the children and the elderly, with neither women nor men clear about who should or who will raise the children, or how to raise them in a world with fewer community supports than generations before knew.

Driven by psychological need, while perhaps acknowledging the interdependence of the need for a balance of investment between one's work life and home life, young parents struggle with the seemingly mutually exclusive pulls of work and home responsibilities and satisfactions, and relate to this pressure as if the best answers were different for men than they are for women. For grandparents this may have been so, but today it seems less often the case as the nature of our country's work shifts increasingly in the direction of information exchange rather than smokestack industry, from a work world of brawn to a work world of artificial intelligence. While the nature of household work has been significantly altered by the products of an industrialized nation, the nature of helping children grow into responsible adults has remained stable, still basically requiring flexible interaction with loving adults who feel rewarded by raising children.

It has always been possible for men and women to overlook their own relationship, their lack of intimate experience in their marriage, by emphasizing "the children" or "the job." The successful outcome of this developmental stage (for men and women) is further differentiation of themselves and further capacity to nurture, which the author believes is interdependent with intimacy. The child-focus process, which will be discussed, avoids intimacy, differentiation, and the marriage.

The chapter can best be read with the following concepts in mind.

1. The adult self is experienced through multiple relationships in two spheres: the domestic sphere, made up of friends and multigenerational family, and the nondomestic sphere, which consists of paid employment and public life, usually away from home.

2. The domestic sphere is represented by the image of the children's toy, the jack. Like the jack, domestic relations are organized on a vertical axis and two horizontal axes. Specifically, the metaphor represents the grandparent–parent–child axis as vertical, moving up and down through time, intersected by two horizontal axes, to some extent time phasic, one's siblings and friends before marriage, and one's spouse and friends after marriage. Vertical-axis relationships tend to be unequal. Horizontal-axis relationships are more egalitarian.

3. Positive resolution of the tension between spheres enhances and differentiates self. Negative resolution and fusion result from disconnection of spheres, unipolar fixation, or disconnection of axes.

4. Nodal events are the usual and unusual happenings of family and work

life that create instability in membership and function, events that bring up the possibility of loss or gain of membership and challenge the integrity and growth of the system. Nodal events affect the balance of the system and have the potential of catalyzing fusion and/or differentiation.

5. Reactive closeness and distance are manifestations of fusion. The author sees closeness and distance as interdependent variables of the triangular process in which one member is out and the others are in.

6. True intimacy is distinguished from "closeness" and is independent of third parties and fusion. It is dialogue emerging with differentiation between equals. Intimacy encourages greater self-awareness and change in the conceptualization or integration of human relationships.

PARADIGMS IN COLLISION

Marriage with children creates a collision of paradigms, a concept presented by Armstrong (1971), between the espoused beliefs or attitudes of men and women and the attitudes or policies of the older generations and the work world. Among these are (1) the belief in sexual equality, (2) the egalitarian marriage; (3) cultural norms and attitudes; (4) national and corporate policies regarding working families with dependent children; and (5) the balance of work life and home life.

Men and women may aspire to sexual equality—and privately doubt that the sexes are equal in psychic endowment and individual capacity. As a nation we generally aspire to provide equality of opportunity, but our experience tells us it is not established. When the couple becomes a threesome, the collision is manifest between the sexes, as well as between the family and societal institutions. When it comes to caring for a child, we encounter both the major challenge to sexual equality and perhaps the pivotal issue for the resolution of inequality.

The facts of sexual differences are few. "Despite the . . . importance of intrinsic biological differences and the considerable belief in them . . . it is easier to demonstrate *belief* in these differences than the differences themselves" (Seiden, 1976). Macoby and Jacklin (1974) summarize three fairly well-establlished differences: (1) Girls on the average have greater verbal ability than boys after about age 11. (2) Boys on the average have greater visual, spatial, and mathematical ability beginning about age 12–13 and increasing through the high-school years. (3) Males are more "aggressive" with differences appearing as early as social play does (ages two to 2 1/2 years). Even these differences may be the outcome of social factors.

Gilligan (1982) and others attribute the generational constancy and nearly universal differences in masculine and feminine personality and roles not to anatomy, but to "the fact that women, universally, are largely responsible for

early child care." Despite the limit of immutable differences, our heritage of roles and tradition has made it seem that the differences are the basis for how men and women organize their relationships and the distribution of responsibility for the raising of children and the making of money.

While egalitarianism—equality—is a relatively old political attitude, it is only in very recent times that men and women have tried to live it in their personal and work life. World War II marked the beginning of the trend for married women to work outside the home. That the contemporary couple aspires to equality maritally as well as in the workplace is no proof of its durability or stability once stressed by the test of the birth of a child and the difficulty fitting this new person into the two spheres of life.

Equality is a vulnerable belief, wish, ideal. When young married couples with a new child confront the real world: How can they make it financially? Who can they trust with their child if they both go off to work every day? Who has a job that integrates being a parent with the job description? Who makes the better salary? Who expects to be cared for at home? But most stressed of all with the advent of a child are the male and female psyches.

Deep down, when all is said and done, the image of a real man and of a real woman is not one of equality, equal competence, or equal responsibility in the home life and work life. Despite the social and legal effort to change, the personally held view of the young and educated is still that men more than women belong in the world of work outside the home, and that women more than men belong in the home with the task of nuturing the young.

In Gilligan's (1982) view, "These differences arise in a social context where facets of social status and power combine with reproductive biology to shape the experience of males and females and the relations between the sexes" (p. 2). "Given for both sexes the primary caretaker in the first three years of life is typically female, the interpersonal dynamics of gender identity formation are different for boys and for girls" (p. 7). "Because infant girls most often end up cared for by their own gender, and males do not, feminine personality more than masculine personality comes to define itself in relation and connection to other people" (p. 7). Males, on the other hand, are encouraged to be separate, to be autonomous, to compete with more than to cooperate with men.

Why does equality give way if different roles give different satisfaction to men and women? The answer: because our culture does not give special status and power to women and certainly not to men who carry on domestic life. Rather social status and power are in the work world. Some women find it there, but mainly women care for children, and the imbalance leads to burden and ultimately to sexual inequality.

As pointed out by McGoldrick (Chapter 10), today's marriages are less often contracts for life bringing two persons together in complementary fashion. Marriage without children often seems like little change for either husband or wife who maintain their unmarried relationships and interests and use their time pursuing their own lives.

For today's men, and their fathers before them, work comes first, before

caring for others. The difference today is that the work world, the economy, is not the economy of the 1940–1960 period. There are a few men who choose to nuture children rather than being forced to stay at home because of economic circumstances (see below), but in general men more often talk about equality than live it with their mates.

The United States is the only industrialized nation that does not provide paid maternity leave as a matter of national policy. It has been estimated that one quarter of women working 20 hours per week are employed by companies where policies do not guarantee their return to the same or comparable job after time off for children Lewin (1984). Today's young parents see a different world than their grandparents and parents saw. And yet, more often than not, they aspire to the same end—worldly success. For some young adults, success for their parents, pleasing their parents, would be an acknowledged goal. But living either the traditional life of a man's world or a woman's world as one's parents did has as many hazards as the pioneering life of dual-worker couples with children. In either circumstance, national and corporate policies support neither marriage nor parents with children. Corporate policy places the corporation first, the family second. Work is not meant to support the family, but the family is expected to support the requirements of the job and the worker.

"The competent young women who have joyfully begun to climb the ladders opened to them within the last 10 years are now, many in their 30's becoming mothers and are running into what might be called the 'second wave' of male resistance. They have been accepted as work equals. Their skill and expertise are recognized. But nobody wants to deal with the fact that they are mothers. It's O.K. for a man to talk abut his kids at work. But if a woman wants to get ahead she better just keep mum" (Barko, 1984).

In 1977 the census data first recorded a majority of married mothers with children under 18 in the workplace. In 1983 59% of mothers were in the workplace, and for the first time, a majority of mothers of children under six were in the workforce—58% of all mothers of children three to five. Today half of all women with children under three years old, and 70% of women whose youngest child is six to 13 years old, are in the labor force.

Factors that contribute to this shift of women from an exclusive role in the domestic sphere are economic (often necessity), opportunity (Title XI legislation passed in the 1970s), desire and peer support (the women's movement has encouraged women to enter the domain of men), and the statistically high probability that one's marriage can end. Current projections of divorce for persons first married in the late 1970s—early 1980s is between 10 and 50%.

The birth of a child disturbs the uneasy heterosociality of the workplace and sends women in the domestic direction. The flow of men toward the domestic sphere does not match the departure of pregnant women from work to home, encouraging the primative belief that the workplace is the domain of the male.

Assume the partners are fully employed, enjoying their separate relationships from singlehood as well as their marital relationship, and are feeling

like sexual equals, living in balance in both spheres of life. What happens about work and home life when she becomes pregnant? They may assume there will be minimum disruption. "I should be back to work in three to six weeks." "If all goes well, I should be able to work practically until I deliver." Even is this proves to be the case (which it can, but with considerable stress), the wife's transient absence from work and the addition of a baby forever imbalances the feelings and assumptions of equality of choice about work and the home life.

SPACE FOR CHILDREN

The environment into which children are born can be one in which there is no space for them, there is space for them, or there is a vacuum they are brought in to fill. Many factors determine which context will be present in a family at the time of birth. All available family space may already be taken up with other activities or relationships. Or there may be little space because there are few available family members.

Space for parenting (space for children) is difficult for contemporary parents to make. As the workforce becomes more evenly populated by men and women, there has been no comparable shift of men to the domestic sphere, no revaluing of domestic life, and a devaluing of child rearing. Urie Bronfenbrenner (1977) asks, "Who cares for America's children? Who cares?" We are a nation of single-parent families—those who actually have only one and those who functionally lack a parent, usually a father.

This disproportionate shift in the direction of the nondomestic sphere leaves children often in a relatively adultless relationship context, particularly since the increased mobility of career-oriented parents occurs during the childbearing years. Moving away usually encourages "permanent" psychological distance from the extended family as well. An added effect on this situation is that children are tending to give greater allegiance to their peer group than to parents, teachers, the church, or the state. In fact, today the question becomes pertinent: Are children raising each other? Is the society becoming age stratified? In effect, the outcome is that adults have less space in their lives for children.

At the other extreme are adults overinvested in the domestic sphere. Overcloseness in the parent–child relationships is often the outcome of filling the vacuum created by a relationship loss with another generation. It tends to involve generational blurring, and overloading of the parent–child relationship. Interpersonal intensity derives from two factors: (1) urgency; the emotional conditioning prevalent within our culture; and (2) exclusivity; the degree to which drives are focused upon one or very few persons (Gorney, 1968, p. 146).

Conditioning to intensity, born of discontinuity, is often followed by discontinuity or cutoff (loss).

Children may be used to fill an emptiness in the lives of the adults, often resulting from the loss of their own parents (Bradt & Moynihan, 1971; Fields, 1985), from a lack of marital intimacy or nonparticipation in the nondomestic sphere of life by choice or by failure. Clinically this may emerge as the child-focused family (see below) in which a child becomes a replacement for the unrealized achievement or place in the world or the loss of relationship with a family member who is dead or out of contact (cutoff). Although strength of character is a possible adult outcome of adversity or an unfavorable environment in childhood, in general the yield of a generation of children is greater when the social soil that surrounds the family is more nourishing.

Increasingly, young adults seem to be asking, "Why choose to become a parent?" We may wonder why this attitude is developing and what it has to do with the family experiences these young adults had themselves. Are they uncomfortable about the burdens in their parent's lives, and avoiding a family situation that cultural anthropologists describe as possibly the most unsupported family structure to emerge in social evolution? In 1965 it was considered selfish not to have children, as many children as a couple could afford (Rainwater, 1965). Through the 1970s and into the 1980s, the quest for self (self-actualization, self-potential, self-fulfillment) has been a counterforce, along with the great worldwide economic uncertainty, against having children.

Changes in educational and job opportunities for women, the increased necessity of women being in the workforce, and the use of birth control and legalized abortion are contemporary factors influencing the decision as to whether to have a child. The divorce statistics, affirming the uncertainty of a lasting marriage, and our nation's low priority on working parents and on children, add to the conflict about having children. In any case the time between marrying and the birth of the first child has been dramatically increased with each new statistical survey. Men, who do not usually look upon fatherhood as a dramatic and testing change in their lives, so often have more enthusiasm for a pregnancy than their wives.

This burdened, imbalanced place of parenting may explain why contemporary childlessness seems to be more determined by wives than husbands. Now, more than ever in history, a woman is aware of her role as burdened by motherhood, a heavy and largely unacknowledged (socially unrewarded) role with the added vulnerability of an increasingly high risk of divorce.

It is the author's belief that the usual automatic decision regarding who leaves work to parent and who continues to be the primary financial provider sets the stage for a regressive evolvement of men and women, again alienating them from one another, aligning them in separate worlds of work and home in which many ultimately become alienated from themselves.

Past the benchmark event—the birth of the baby—the next three months are often overlooked as part of the pregnancy. They are more accurately

identified as the fourth trimester. During this period there are endocrine shifts that are more abrupt than the hormonal shifts of puberty, the menses, or the pregnancy. As always with hormonal shifts there are affectual changes and instability that make the new mother more vulnerable to the response of her husband, the extended family, and her baby. Often the arrival of the baby begins an experience of feeling overlooked, isolated, and, especially for mother, overwhelmed with the greater complexity of tasks and relationships. Postpartum depression is a risk during this time and can be assessed on the basis of the complex interweaving of biopsychosocial factors.

SEX

The presence of a child in the home, especially an older child, deprives parents of privacy, even in their bedroom. There is a threat of too little time and too many levels of concern occupying the minds of both husband and wife for sexual intimacy to be achieved. Wives may place sex without intimacy in the category of wifely duties to be kept to a minimum. Husbands, self-righteously occupied with being good, hard-working husbands and fathers, interpret their wives' seeming lack of interest as a rebuff, or failure to appreciate all their hard work.

Both parents may feel themselves taken for granted by the other. Marriage seems tedious and less fulfilling.

The American myth of parenthood, if current literature is reflective of continuing trends of society, is still that parenthood equals motherhood. Happily there are some fathers who are discovering the pleasure and challenge of becoming a participant father-parent, actively involved in the domestic sphere, a peer with their wives and full parents to their children. Unfortunately there may be fewer males who find fatherhood in marriage rather than through divorce. The typical notion of the good father has been, "He's a responsible father: he's always worked hard and provided for his wife and children."

For couples whose bond was more fusion than intimacy, the arrival of a child brings the nuclear-family triangle into play (Bowen, 1966), challenging the stability of the parents' relationship with the close position threatened by the baby. The baby's presence and behavior may draw one parent close to the child leaving the other distant. Commonly the triangle shifts so that the father is in the distant position and mother and child become close. For some distant couples, the baby represents a desired closeness of each to the other through the baby. The involvement of the infant in the closeness–distance process of the parental triangle may be good enough to sustain the infant's growth and development, but developmental achievements of the child can become "nodal events" that threaten the stable triangular family patterns.

INTIMACY

Intimacy is a caring relationship without pretense, revelation without risk of loss or gain by one or the other. It is giving and receiving, an exchange that enhances because it facilitates the awareness of selves, of their differences and sameness. It is discriminant, encouraging elaboration of facets of each person. It creates and sustains belonging, while appreciating each individual's uniqueness. Intimacy encourages continuity. It is the sustaining energy of the human tide moving through time. It allows us to belong not only in the present, but with those who came before and those who come after.

Belsky et al. (1985), in summarizing a number of studies, including their own, state that "marital quality declines modestly, though reliably, from the time passed before to after the birth of the first child. This decline is more pronounced for women than it is for men. Those families experiencing the most marital satisfaction prenatally experience the most marital satisfaction postnatally." With the change of household membership from two (the wage-earning couple) to three (and baby makes three), tasks and demands, many real, some self-imposed, reduce the chances for private dialogue, for intimacy.

The failure of either spouse *both* to change to a parent and to continue to grow as a spouse contributes to an inequality of relationships and is a threat to intimacy. A marriage that has developed intimacy is a marriage better able to respond to the challenge of parenthood, to integrate the lifelong change that parenthood brings, not only to the new parents but to the entire family.

THE EXTENDED FAMILY

The extended family is a resource to the nuclear family in calm and troubled times. There are some families in which the majority of members consider the children of the family as their collective responsibility. This means initiatives for contact and relationships are mutual. Older, middle, and younger generations participate in sustaining the sense of membership and belonging. Geographic mobility of nuclear families make it more difficult to draw from the extended family the support and help a new baby and the new young parents need. Which extended family is more involved and directly influential (non-relating is influential too) to the nuclear family is indicated by whom they turn to for help with the new baby.

The decision to have a baby is the beginning of a shift away from the horizontal axis of marriage toward a realignment with the vertical thrust of the generations of the future and of the past.

With the arrival of a child, all existing family members advance a notch in

the relationship system, from niece or nephew to cousin, from brother or sister to uncle and aunt, from parent to grandparent, from husband and wife to mother and father—a dialectic between peer and nonpeer relationships. The questions become: If there is a vertical realignment of the new family with the extended family, is it more the husband's or the wife's? Is this alignment supportive or detrimental to the marital relationship? How is the balance between the autonomous and interdependent directions of the family adjusted?

For some family members, the change is a nominal rather than a developmental or functional change. The most essential change of the extended family for the well-being of all is to be active resources for the new family. For some who were not close before, the addition of a child to the family may promote a conversion to nurturant resources.

Sometimes one set of grandparents has difficulty accepting the other set as peers. Sharing interest in the new grandchildren can facilitate this, as well as reconciling a grandparent to this later stage of the life cycle. Becoming a grandparent brings to mind the finite reality of one's own life, as well as the possibility of having to take a secondary place in relationship to both child and grandchild. Some parents want to overlook their child's marriage, and expect their child's loyalty to be greater to themselves than to their daughter-in-law or son-in-law. As one mother reminded her son "I come first, then your children, then your wife." Other prospective grandparents, anxious about the style of their children's marriage, welcome the announcement of a grandchild, an answer to their wish that they "should have a child and settle down." So the child is seen as a stabilizer to the marriage rather than a person whose life course is to emerge with time. Some of these children end up in domestic and worldly careers as "peacemakers." Other children, far from peaceful, stabilize a marriage by their disturbing ways.

Some parents use being parents to justify reduced contact with the extended family, as when they offer the excuse "Our children need us at home." How often do adults with children have contact with their own parents without the presence of (or subject of) their children? The focus of attention and activity around the grandchildren keeps parents away from the depression or anxiety they experience when in contact with the older generation. Through their parents children are vulnerable to the multigenerational process. Children add their own reflexive behavior with their parents, short-circuiting the multigenerational process and containing it in the nuclear family until the birth of the next generation. The unipolar vertical process—an involvement with children, noninvolvement with one's parents—is circular. Avoidance of one's own parents creates a void or vacuum that can be filled by children, leaving less space for grandparents. When families are locked in fusion relationship, they cannot be intimate. Misguided attempts are often made to find it, but cutoffs from the extended family and overintensity with children prohibit intimacy.

The extended family has a stabilizing influence on the unstable nuclear

family, particularly if there has been avoidance or aloofness between the older and middle generations. A troublesome child may settle down considerably if cutoffs with the extended family are bridged. And, on occasion, a less intense family member may be able to deal with a child more dispassionately, with more appropriate expectations of responsibility and accountability. Older members of the extended family may be called upon to provide the missing authority or leadership in a dysfunctional family; an unmarried or childless aunt or uncle may assume leadership and parental functions in the place of a dysfunctional or absent parent. Children who relate to older family members will probably have more data, more identity, than those who are expected to be "like" someone with whom they have little or no personal relationship.

To summarize the theory: To overemphasize relationships with spouse and friends and neglect parent–child relationships is to risk becoming neglectful of children and the elderly and to sacrifice the lessons and nourishment of continuity. To overemphasize parent–child relationships is to risk the decay of marriage and may lead to overly intense emotional bonding of parents with their children. Rebalancing the distribution of time, energy, and psychosocial connections can activate powerful resources of a system to heal itself.

REBALANCING WORK AND HOME LIFE:
BACK TO WORK

For the dual-worker household, a return to full-time work for both spouses is an impossibility without providing for their child's needs while they are working away from home. Whether work is a financial necessity or a choice, each parent has to adjust emotionally to a plan that leaves the children with someone other than themselves. If they are living close to extended family, the wish for self-sufficiency and exclusivity of their marriage and lives is compromised by the involvement of a relative as a surrogate parent. If no substitute from the extended family is available, appropriate, or willing, the alternative is to employ someone whose livelihood is raising other people's children. This is expensive, and ususally it is difficult to find both competent and convenient child care. And the younger the child, the more is the feeling of risk and the more difficult it is to find the help needed. Recent exposure of professional day-care abuse of children highlight the plight of young parents.

Sometimes couples work it out on their own by having different work schedules. Pleck (1985) has found that if shifts are different, the child may benefit by being cared for only by parents but the marriage suffers because the contact between husband and wife is diminished.

Usually the mother is the parent whose vistas have been obscured by child care. Her intention to get back into the nondomestic work world becomes a critical point in the family process. She may be motivated by a desire to

restitute her sense of self and rebalance her adult relationships and achieve social validation. Of course, greater role stresses are experienced by parents who attempt to coordinate two jobs with the responsibility for children. This is especially true if they cling to the concept that only mothers are parents.

Most pivotal to working it out is the rebalancing of responsibilities between husband and wife. Some men and women feel that once they are parents, the wife should not work. Conflict arises between husbands and wives: Whose needs come first? Whose job comes first? Is it fair to assume that only one parent is needed? Usually the question as to who is best qualified to parent never comes up. A youngest daughter married to a firstborn and oldest brother who "raised" his younger siblings may be less qualified to parent than her husband. But the assumption is almost always that the wife is the parent who should stay home. If the couple dares to design parent functions as well as work out of the home in an equitable way, the usual inflexibility of employers makes this an arduous effort. Negotiating for flexibility or a work schedule that places equal value on family life usually results in punitive or derogatory action as well as lowering the career potential of the employee. Success in the work world is usually awarded those who work as if their family only needs their salary and/or their worldly reputation. The negotiations between new fathers and mothers are seldom conducted with a conviction that they can both be psychologically fulfilled by letting go of some of the career satisfaction and ambition and they both can be rewarded by caring for their child.

Even when a plan is developed, it is vulnerable to disruption. Suppose the hired child-care person becomes ill, what then? Will it be the husband or the wife who adapts to this and sets aside work schedules to be at home with the child? And what about the unexpected at the job—to go out of town, to work late, to start early? Or suppose the child is in a day-care program and becomes ill. Will the persons in charge remember that this is the father's day to cover for the unexpected or will mother automatically be called? The ingrained traditional behavior of those who live traditional roles discourages the effort to respond differently to the difference in family life today.

SIBLING RIVALRY

Optimum space between children is truly a matter of perspective. From the parents' standpoint, one child at a time is challenge enough, and multiple births or births too close in time a potential disaster. From the child's standpoint the perfect companion would be an identical twin, the optimum peer, a perfect mirror of oneself, an alter ego extraordinary. For parents the birth of twins is far more stressful than single births, in large part because of the additional tasks involved. With the nuclear family generally isolated from the ongoing assistance of the extended family and in a culture where child care is often mainly mother's responsibility, with little support or assistance from

others, twins are a major challenge to her physical and emotional stamina, as well as to the marriage relationship.

That siblings inevitably create "a trauma" for one another seems more a function of availability of caring adults than of the inherent rivalry of children. The long-standing family pattern of parenting by the mother alone seems as much an explanation for sibling rivalry as siblings being close in age. Cooperation can be as likely an outcome as competition, depending perhaps more on the parents' availability and cooperation than on their children.

Competition is determined not only by the availability of parents, but by how parents relate to children. A parent who habitually tries to judge sibling squabbles encourages "sibling rivalry." A common error of parents is to hold one of their children accountable (to blame) rather than holding all children involved in the action accountable for working things out. Children are usually more cooperative with one another in the face of collective adversity, such as parents who expect all their children to cooperate. Paradoxically, one of the more poignant examples of cooperative interaction between siblings is among children who have been deprived of parents through death or other disruptions of the parent–child relationship, such as placement in an orphanage.

An egalitarian philosophy of family life encourages sibling rivalry. Egalitarianism—equal rights, privileges, and authority for parent or child— seems to some like the optimum state for family life. Just as it is important to learn to live cooperatively with peers (e.g., siblings), it is important to experience living with someone other than oneself in authority and to have responsibility for someone less able. In fact, childhood is a misnomer if a child has no parent in charge—see Boszormeny-Nagy & Spark (1973) on parentification. A child who already has adult privileges does not welcome another child as peer and potential companion. Almost inevitably, an only child is included in more adult activities than when there is more than one child. After the birth of a second child, the firstborn is often given the message to remember to set an example: "You're older." This may help the firstborn to fit descriptions of firstborn children, but it may also undermine the potential of siblings to become cooperative peers. Some children who should be peers escape the close association, the opportunity of learning cooperation and of competing, because their parents urge them to develop distinctly different and unrelated interests, friends, behaviors, and attitudes.

Toman (1978) provides insight into the compatibility of parents with their children—for example, that a parent may identify with the same ranked child, as firstborn fathers may be more identified with their firstborn child than their youngest. Other factors influence this; for example, children who symbolize certain overvalued or undervalued family members, not simply themselves. Alliances with or against particular children are often based on such intrafamilial transferences and encourage sibling rivalry.

Although circumstances, such as the physical presence and potential availability or absence of a parent, is an important factor, the sympathetic alignment of children with one parent more than the other is the outcome of a

repetitive triangulation process that produces a sense of closeness with one parent and distance with the other. Sometimes the conflict (overt or covert) between parents is manifest in the interaction of siblings who fight over their parents' issues as if their own.

The birth rate has declined in recent years, indicating a popular swing toward one- or two-child, or even no-child, families. Current statistics indicate that couples are averaging slightly less than two children

THE CHILD-FOCUSED FAMILY

At one extreme of unbalance, the nuclear family's overinvestment in the parent—child relationships preclude the involvement in relationships outside the family and erodes all spouse relationships. The child-focused family is representative of this extreme.

In 1971, Carolyn Moynihan and the author wrote a study describing their experiences in working with 50 child-focused families (Bradt & Moynihan, 1971). Experience with several hundred more such families since then has further clarified this family process. The presence of a child with unusual problems does not constitute a child-focused family. The child focus is a process that seems to compartmentalize family tension by channeling it through a particular child. Thus it can be seen as a coping mechanism, which, like all mechanisms, has its limitations, its failure point. In this instance, the manifestation of breakdown is represented as a particular child. The child plays an active part in the process.

What the author calls the authentic child-focused family process is operative even before the child's birth, and is only amplified by his or her presence and life course. The child's failure to advance successfully through the usual psychological developmental milestones intensifies the family process and encourages the label "problem" early in life. A history usually reveals multiple consultations with child health experts beginning early in life. Family therapists are not usually among the consultants who have been involved. The parents are highly invested in the child and express no other concerns, "It's a child problem, not a family problem."

There are payoffs for children caught in this process, although they and other family members are arrested in the development of a variety of relationships both in and outside of the family. The child-focused process helps all to cope, and also to fail in achieving a richness and diversity of human relationships.

GUIDELINES FOR INTERVENTION

Parents with young children who seek family counseling are in the main concerned about a deterioration of the marriage, the threat of disruption, contemplation of separation or divorce, or the disturbed function of a spouse. Children are part of the consideration of quality of family life, but are not usually the presenting problem. In clinical practice the authentic child-focused family is on the decline. Because this book includes a chapter on divorce, this discussion on intervention is more about the family with a significant child focus. The intensity of parents' preoccupation with a child has two origins (1) the historic or current relationship of each parent with his or her mother and father; or (2) the relative weakness of spousal, sibling, or peer relationships currently and/or historically.

But family therapists do not rank high on the list of experts who might be consulted when the parents are concerned about one of their children. More often a child specialist—child psychiatrist, pediatrician, or teacher—is consulted about a child, especially a younger child. Assuming that the child specialist is systemically oriented, the task will be to place the specific concerns in the context of the multigenerational family relationships and friendships, and to rebalance the nondomestic and domestic spheres of the family.

To find solutions, one must ask the right questions. One must define the dysfunctions and resources of a system rather than of an individual. Equally important is the definition of power and motivation: Who can and who will effect change? The process of shifting away from individual toward systemic considerations is begun in a concrete way through the construction of a family chart (genogram) in the initial sessions (Bradt & Moynihan, 1971). Questions that have to do with the information recorded on the family chart refocus attention, energy, and the investment about a multigenerational system, including the living and the dead, rather than only discussion of various individuals and symptoms.

All reliably effective clinical techniques should be based on conceptual understanding of the family. For the family who presents a child as their concern, it is important to:

1. Assess the parents' child concern as a coping process. What is the family trying to cope with?
   a. Historically the childhood loss experience of the parents or the loss experience of grandparents, with whom the parent(s) are (were) fused (the authentic child-focused family).
   b. Contemporary stresses.
   c. Covert or overt marital dysfunction—issues too threatening to address or patterns of long-standing avoidance that make open consideration of the marriage taboo.
2. Consider how much the child's symptoms are intensified by a stage in

the psychological development of the child as well as the state of balance between the horizontal and vertical process of the family.

One must judge whether the inclusion of the child in ongoing work is essential to engage the parents. If the child is seen separately, which is sometimes useful directly or indirectly (as a support to the family shift of focus), there are risks of reinforcing the child-focused process rather than bringing into awareness (1) problem redefinition and (2) rebalancing tasks. The best outcomes when a child is seen are those in which the family receives relief of the total "child problem." As they become productive and hopeful about other concerns, the child is more free to move out of the "fixed position."

Shifting the Process Away from Child Concerns

Questions that use the child as a reference point allow entry into the extended family, for example: "How would your mother deal with that kind of behavior from Rick?" "How much contact had you and Nelle had the week before Rick kicked over the lamp?" "How often do you notice that pattern?"

Shifting the Process Toward the Child

Parents who are anxious about a particular subject may shift away from the subject by making reference to the child, or the therapist may elect to refer back to the child if either parent is becoming too threatened or seems overly impatient with discussions about extended family. And the child may represent the only existent bridge between parents who have otherwise effected total distance in the marital relationship.

Case Example: Alex and Marion

A year and a half after their marriage, which had taken place when both turned 30, Alex and Marion began discussing when to have a child. During the first year of their marriage, they had made some major educational and professional decisions. Alex had successfully completed the comprehensive examinations for his doctoral degree and had his dissertation research well under way. He had also started a full-time job that would provide economic support while he wrote his dissertation. Marion had begun a master's program in a field that united several of her interests and was carrying out community work of concern to her.

They felt ready to consider having a child, although they could not predict with certainty at what stages academically or professionally they would be when the child was born. Becoming parents was important to both of them, although Alex was more vocal about his desire to become a parent sooner rather than later. Nine months before their wedding, six months before their decision to get married, Marion had become pregnant. At that time Marion had decided to have an abortion, and Alex reluctantly supported her in that decision. As with the first

pregnancy, they concieved quickly. After the pregnancy was confirmed, they happily informed their close friends and Marion's family but not Alex's, as he had been cut off from his family for several years.

After the nausea and tiredness she experienced during the first trimester, Marion felt healthy and strong for the remainder of the pregnancy. She and Alex explored the chances of the baby having birth defects, since two of Marion's first cousins had been born with defects. A genetic counselor assured them that the risks in their case were minimal.

Marion celebrated the successful completion of her graduate courses and the community program she had directed by traveling to California to visit close friends. After two years of marriage, this was her first trip by herself, and she enjoyed it greatly.

But that trip set a note of separation between Alex and Marion that was to characterize the rest of the pregnancy and the first months of the baby's life. Alex was focused on combining full-time work with writing his dissertation, as well as looking ahead to locating a job once he had finished his doctoral program. Marion began a professional internship and was concerned to arrange employment for herself after the birth of the baby.

Alex and Marion attended birthing classes, but they rarely practiced together. They timed the sessions to end a month before the baby's due date, and Alex planned his first job-hunting trip to Washington, D.C., to take place six weeks before the due date. Marion's mother came to visit and help prepare the baby's room and clothes while Alex was gone.

To everyone's surprise (including the doctor's), the baby came six weeks early, the day after Alex had left town. Marion's mother took her to the hospital, where the baby was born after two hours of labor. Alex returned the next day to greet his small but healthy son, Christopher.

Alex took two weeks off work, and Marion's mother stayed another three weeks to help the new family get established. When Alex returned to work and her mother left, Marion was at home with the baby. Her work plans had been thrown awry by Christopher's early birth; the project she would have worked on had to be postponed. At home she felt very much alone and lonely, although she knew a few other mothers in similar situations. Both she and Alex were exhausted from caring for a baby who had to be fed every two or three hours. They had no other relatives in the area who could help. When the baby was two months old, Marion began using a part-time babysitter, the daughter of Alex's secretary, so that she could complete work unfinished because of Christopher's early birth.

Alex and Marion focused on their work and on their child. Although Marion did most of the child care, Alex was closely attached to the baby and would do anything for him when he was home. Their sharing of household tasks was not so easily accomplished. Work was proceeding well for both of them. Marion had returned to half-time work when Christopher was five months old and to full-time work a year later. They were fortunate in finding a succession of caring and competent sitters for Christopher. Alex completed his dissertation a year after Christopher's birth and concentrated thereafter on locating a job in his field.

At this point in their marriage, they had very little time for themselves. They did not enjoy a night away from Christopher until he was a year and a half old. They had never had a very active sexual relationship, but after the baby's birth it languished due to their exhaustion and to a series of severe infections Marion experienced after the insertion of an IUD. Not until Christopher was nine months old were the infections cured. Marion resumed using a diaphragm, although she and Alex wanted to use a form of contraception that would allow more spontaneity. The following year, when Marion went to the doctor to get a prescription for the birth control pill, her Pap smear was abnormal. Although the situation cured itself in several months, it occasioned some concern and forced them to wait longer to change their form of contraception.

They began seeing a family therapist when Alex's job pressures became serious. The therapist helped them through a period of limbo when they did not know when or where or what kind of job Alex would find, and then, once he accepted a job, through the transition. Alex moved to Washington, D.C., two months before Marion and Christopher. He would find a house to rent; she would finish her job and prepare their belongings for moving; her mother would take care of Christopher when they made the actual move.

Marion's mother was an active participant in her daughter's family, the father had died several years before her marriage. Marion and Alex had developed close relationships with several of Marion's relatives who lived in the Midwest, and they saw her brothers regularly at family celebrations.

However, they were not in contact with Alex's family. Alex's parents divorced when he was nine years old; subsequently each parent had remarried, and his father had two more children—a boy and a girl—born exactly ten years after Alex and his sister. Alex's relations with his family had become strained when he entered graduate school and when his relationship with a long-term girlfriend ended. He had cut off contact voluntarily with his mother and his sister, but he struggled to maintain contact with his father, despite the active disapproval of his stepmother.

Neither parent attended Alex and Marion's wedding, although Alex had invited his father. Alex informed his father of Christopher's birth, and shortly before Alex moved to Washington, he took Christopher to visit his father on a weekend when the stepmother was out of town.

In Washington Alex and Marion began seeing a family therapist—the author— to whom they had been referred by their first therapist. Soon after the initial sessions, their work came to focus on how to reconnect with Alex's family. The therapist helped them develop a strategy to bridge the gap after years of separation and to anticipate responses from different family members. The therapist stressed opening channels of communication to all family members, not just selected ones.

Alex sent a letter to his mother and one to his father and stepmother. In the letters he described their reasons for moving, their new home, and their job situations, and included pictures of Christopher. He immediately received a warm response from his mother and began making plans to have her visit. No response came from his father. Through an aunt Alex discovered that his father had just had two strokes. Alex telephoned his father and made plans with his stepmother to visit right away. Within two months of sending letters, Alex had visited his father and stepmother at their home and Alex's mother had come to Washington to visit her son, daughter-in-law, and grandson for the first time.

Throughout the next year, Alex and Marion worked on strengthening their relationship with Alex's family. Twice they traveled to the Midwest to visit Alex's relatives and participate in family rituals—first his father's funeral (he had died a few weeks after Alex's first visit) and next a family Thanksgiving. With the therapist's active encouragement and support, Alex (who is an experienced film-maker) made a videotape of his family. Alex and Marion maintain an active relationship with his family through telephone calls and letters. Christopher recognizes the pictures of all of his relatives and tells stories of visiting them.

Fundamental to the process of family therapy for Alex and Marion was the exploration of Alex's family and it's history of connections and cut offs. Gaining a new dimension in their family meant rebalancing in terms of their relationship with Marion's mother, who had been the only parent and grandmother to them for several years. The therapist worked with them to include Marion's mother in the new family system.

The other issue of key importance to Alex and Marion in the family therapy was the balance of work and home responsibilities they hoped to achieve and the roles they wished to play in each sphere. Alex had moved to Washington for professional reasons. Marion had moved there for family reasons as well as

professional reasons. Marion planned to undertake her own job search once the family was settled and she had located day care for Christopher.

Marion's experience in their new community was focused on the needs of her child and on the resources for families with young children. She met mothers and children but felt increasingly cut off from the professional world, even though she tried to make contacts and arrange interviews one or two days a week. After a few months, she was offered a job and accepted it. In order to survive financially in the expensive Washington area, the family needed Marion's income. The job was exhausting, and Marion felt that she had no energy for family or home considerations. When the job ended due to a loss in funding, she was not unhappy, but she was unemployed. Again her world reverted to the mother–child culture she had gotten to know earlier. Alex was changing job assignments at this point and had no additional experience in job hunting to share with her.

In their second year in Washington, Alex and Marion are beginning to evolve a new balance of work and home life, one more to their liking. Ever since moving, Alex resolutely refused to work overtime at his job; now he has made the decision to cut his hours from 40 to 30 per week. In the meantime Marion has started doing free-lance work, which gives her a schedule of intense work punctuated by periods of no work. Christopher attends a local day-care center every day when Marion is working, and three days a week when she is at home between assignments.

As Alex moves toward wanting more flexibility for himself in order to explore other professional options and to devote more time and attention to his family, Marion is beginning to look for a stable full-time job that will provide the income and benefits they also need.

CONCLUSIONS

In January, 1986 the Family Policy Panel, an offshoot of the United Nations Association of the United States, concluded that the American workplace has failed to adapt to dramatic changes in the American family. They urged that both government and corporations adopt policies to make it easier for employees to work and rear children.

In April 1985 Rep. Patricia Schroeder introduced the Parental and Disability Leave Act in Congress, which could lead to more support for the couple with young children. And a predicted labor shortage developing in the 1990s may encourage government and corporate management to be more responsive to contempory family needs.

Currently marriage with young children is incompatible with our nation's attitude toward the primacy of work. Even with reform—a change in policy of government and industry along the lines of that of European countries—the failure of men and women to share more equally in the nurturance of the young and of one another will undermine the success of marriage and the emergence of a more androgenous new generation.

When children are commonly raised by men and women, then girls and boys will see women working side by side with men away from home not as deprivation but as an extension of caring and cooperation between the sexes. The heterosexual tension of the workplace, born in large part of old traditions

of sexual inequality and dominance, will be replaced by nonsexualized hetero-sexual friendships, peer relationships encouraging intimacy that are supportive rather than threatening to family life. Psychologically and philosophically today's young parents are stressed and are receptive to changing how life is lived. The family therapist has an opportunity to help them identify that roles assigned by gender are part of the stress between them, that choices to be different can succeed, that standing up for their family at work will ultimately make a difference in corporate and government policies.

The optimum outcome of this stage of the family cycle is not simply to bond adults as parents to children. It is to enhance the intimate relationship of marriage—to help men and women realize men's nurturant potential in young and middle adulthood, and to take their life-fulfilling, possibly life-extending, place in the family. It is to join the sexes and the generations together in the present and the future, and to place love in an equal position with work.

REFERENCES

Armstrong, R. (1971). Two concepts: Systems and psychodynamics. Paradigms in collision. In J. O. Bradt and C. D. Moynihan (Eds.), *Systems therapy*. Washington, D.C.: Groome Child Guidance Center.

Barko, N. (1984). Corporate etiquette, *Working mother,* vol. 7, 5.0. Los Angeles: McCall Publishing Co.

Belsky, J., Perry-Jenkins, M., & Crouter, A. (1985) The work–family interface and marital change across the transition to parenthood. *Journal of Family Issues* 6/2.

Boszormenyi-Nagy, I., & Spark, G. (1973). *Invisible loyalties*. New York: Harper & Row.

Bowen, M. (1966) The use of family therapy in clinical practice. *Comprehensive Psychiatry* 7:3: 45–74.

Bradt, J. O., & Moynihan, C. (197). Opening the safe—the child-focused family. In J. O. Bradt and C. J. Moynihan (Eds.), *Systems therapy*. Washington, D.C.: Groome Child Guidance Center.

Bronfenbrenner, U. (1977). *Who needs parent education. Working conference on parent education*. Flint, Mich.: 29–30.

Fields, E., Fisher J. (1985) A Generation Apart (video), City Lights Production Inc., New York, N.Y.

Gilligan, C. (1982). *In a different voice*. Cambridge, Mass.: Harvard University Press,

Gorney, R., *The human agenda*. New York; Simon and Schuster, 1968.

Lewin, T. (1984). Maternity leave: Is it included? *New York Times* July 22.

Macoby, M., & Jacklin, J. (1974). *The psychology of sex differences*. Palo Alto, Calif.: Stanford University Press.

Rainwater, L. (1965). *Family design, marital sexuality, family size, contraception*. Chicago: Aldine

Seiden, A. (1976). Overview: Research on the psychology of women 1. Gender differences and sexual and reproductive life. *American Journal of Psychiatry,* 133/9.

Toman, W. (1976) Family Constellation, Third Edition, New York, Springer.

CHAPTER 12

Transformation of the Family System in Adolescence

Nydia Garcia Preto, A.C.S.W.

The adaptations in family structure and organization required to handle the tasks of adolescence are so basic that the family itself is transformed from a unit that protects and nurtures young children to one that is a preparation center for the adolescent's entrance into the world of adult responsibilities and commitments. This family metamorphosis involves profound shifts in relationship patterns across the generations, and while it may be signaled initially by the adolescent's physical maturity, it often parallels and coincides with changes in parents as they enter midlife and with major transformations faced by grandparents in old age.

These changes take place within a larger social context, which has become increasingly complex. In highly technological societies, such as the United States, the family no longer functions as a comprehensive economic unit and has become dependent on external systems for teaching children, setting limits on them, and finding them employment. Whereas in the past the family was able to offer practical training to children in the form of jobs, it must now provide them with the psychological skills that will help them differentiate and survive in an evermore rapidly changing world. As a result the family's major function has been transformed from that of an economic unit to that of an emotional support system.

This chapter focuses on the overall transformation that families experience as they try to master the tasks of adolescence. Most families, after a certain degree of confusion and disruption, are able to change the rules and limits and reorganize themselves to allow adolescents more autonomy and independence. However, there are certain universal problems associated with this transition that can result in family dysfunction and the development of symptoms in the adolescent or in other family members. Clinical cases will illustrate some of the blocks that families experience during this phase, as well as factors that may contribute to family disorganization or symptomatic behavior, and therapeutic interventions that may be effective with these families.

THREE-GENERATIONAL VIEW OF
TRANSFORMATION

Adolescence demands structural shifts and renegotiation of roles in families involving at least three generations of relatives. Adolescent demands for more autonomy and independence tend to precipitate shifts in relationships across generations. For instance, it is not uncommon for parents and grandparents to redefine their relationships during this period, as well as for spouses to renegotiate their marriage, and for siblings to question their position in the family.

Because adolescent demands are so strong, they often serve as catalysts for reactivating emotional issues and they set triangles in motion. The struggle to meet these demands often brings to the surface unresolved conflicts between parents and grandparents, or between the parents themselves. Requests for greater autonomy and independence, for example, often stir fears of loss and rejection in parents, especially if, during adolescence, they felt rejected or abandoned by their own parents. In families with adolescents, triangles generally involve the following players: the adolescent, the father, and the mother; the adolescent, a parent, and a grandparent; the adolescent, a parent, and a sibling; or the adolescent, a parent, and the adolescent's friends.

As the adolescent enters into conflict with a parent, efforts to ameliorate the tension often repeat earlier patterns of relating in the parents' family of origin. Parents who have made a conscious effort to raise their children differently by avoiding the same "mistakes" their parents made often have a particularly rude wakening. When their children reach adolescence, they are often surprised to observe similarities in personality between their children and their parents. The following caption from a cartoon by Jules Feiffer illustrates this well (Heller, 1982):

> I hated the way I turned out . . . So everything my mother did with me I tried to do different with my Jennifer. Mother was possessive. I encouraged independence. Mother was manipulative. I have been direct. Mother was secretive. I have been open. Mother was evasive. I have been decisive. Now my work is done. Jennifer is grown. The exact image of my mother.

Parents in this situation may react with extreme confusion, anger, or resentment, or in many other ways. In fact, there appears to be a reciprocal chain reaction of meeting and making demands across the generations that is precipitated by the adolescents of the younger generation. Parents, while responding to the adolescent's demands for greater support and autonomy, may themselves get in touch with similar needs, and, in turn, make the same requests of their own parents or each other.

Families during this period are also responding and adjusting to the new demands of other family members, who themselves are entering new stages of the life cycle. In most families with adolescents, the parents are approaching

middle age. Their focus is on such major midlife issues as reevaluating the marriage and careers. The marriage emerging from the heavy caretaking responsibilities of young children may be threatened as parents review personal satisfaction in the light of the militant idealism of their adolescent children. For many women this may actually be the first opportunity to work without the restrictions they faced when the children were young. Many women may be starting a career at this point whereas men are involved with maximizing their professional careers (Prosen, et al., 1981). The normal stress and tension posed to the family by an adolescent are exacerbated when the parents experience acute dissatisfaction and feel compelled to make changes in themselves. At the same time, the grandparents face retirement and possible moves, illness, and death. These stressful events call for a renegotiation of relationships, and parents may be called upon to be caretakers of their own parents or to assist them in integrating the losses of old age.

What often forms is a field of conflicting demands, where the stress seems to be transmitted both up and down the generations. So, for example, the conflict between parents and grandparents may have a negative effect on the marital relationship that filters down into the relationship between the parents and the adolescent. Or the conflict may travel in the opposite direction. A conflict between the parents and the adolescent may affect the marital relationship, which ultimately affects the relationship between the parents and grandparents.

TASKS OF ADOLESCENCE

The origins of this family transformation are the adolescent's developmental tasks that begin with the rapid physical growth and sexual maturation during puberty. As a result of sexual maturation, moves toward solidifying an identity and establishing autonomy from the family (which are really lifelong developmental processes) are accelerated during adolescence. Changing and often conflicting social expectations about sexual roles and norms of behavior are imposed on adolescents by the family, school, peers, and the media. Their ability to differentiate from others depends on how well they handle the expected social behaviors for expressing the intense emotions that are precipitated by puberty. To establish autonomy they need to become gradually more responsible for their own decision making and yet feel the security of parental guidance.

Flexibility is the key to success for families at this stage. For instance, increasing the flexibility of family boundaries and modulating parental authority permit greater independence and developmental growth for adolescents. However, in an attempt to lessen the conflicts generated during this period, many families continue to reach for solutions that used to work in

earlier stages. Parents often try to tighten the reins or to withdraw emotionally to avoid further conflict. Or they either blindly accept or reject the adolescent. Adolescents, on the other hand, in an effort to win their way, resort to temper tantrums, withdraw emotionally behind closed doors, turn to grandparents for support, or present endless examples of friends who have more freedom.

This section focuses on the normal challenges and typical fears or blocks that parents and adolescents experience during this transition.

Sexuality: Transformation of the Physical Self

Puberty brings about a great number of changes that not only transform the physical self, but signal the beginning of the psychological transition from childhood to adulthood (Hopkins, 1983). There are variations in the age at which it begins, but it generally starts earlier for girls than for boys. Also, there has been a trend toward earlier maturation for both girls and boys, referred to as the "secular trend." Menarche, for instance, has shown a regular trend toward earlier occurrence since the 1800s. The average age for onset of menstruation is now 13, whereas in the 1800s it it was over 16 (Hopkins, 1983).

The physical and sexual changes that take place have a dramatic effect on how adolescents describe and evaluate themselves, and radically alter how they are perceived by others. Coping with this upsurge in sexual thoughts, feelings, and behaviors is a major task for all family members. It is not uncommon for family members to experience confusion and fear when adolescents begin to express their new sexual interests. The Lornes illustrate a familiar pattern observed in families coping with these changes.

> Mr. and Mrs. Lornes had always been proud of their 14-year-old daughter, Sandra, who was an excellent student, active in the school band, a gymnast, and a dancer. When they discovered that she was interested in older boys who drank, drove, and had the reputation of being "jocks" at school and in the community, they reacted with fear and confusion. Their initial response was to monitor all her calls and outings, and to drive her to all activities. She, confused by their reaction and frightened by her own feeling, began to lie and "sneak around."

The Lornes' initial reaction was similar to the way many parents respond when they first become aware of a daughter's increased sexuality. Parents want to protect their daughters from the dangers of the world, fearing the possibility of sexual exploitation, rape, or an unwanted pregnancy. Although a daughter may be physically mature, parents fear that she is unable to protect herself from the reality of her environment. These fears are not unfounded, since sexual abuse, rape, and teenage pregnancy are problems that seem to be on the rise in this country (Dickman, 1983). Worries about male children are somewhat different. A boy's parents may worry more about sexual interests distracting him from his studies and jeopardizing his future than about sexual exploitation.

Usually parents who are comfortable with their own sexuality are more

able to accept the heightened sexuality of adolescents and to convey their acceptance. Also, when the home has been a place where information is openly shared, the possibility is greater for setting realistic, sensitive limits and for tolerating minor transgressions. This provides adolescents with an accepting framework within which to express and experiment with this new and important aspect of their lives. On the other hand, if the adolescent's growing sexuality is denied, ignored, or rejected by the parents, the possibilities for the development of a positive sexual self-concept are diminished. The probability of increased feelings of alienation between adolescents and their parents is greater and risks of premature, excessive, or self-endangering sexual activity are increased.

Personal experiences with sexuality influence the way in which parents set limits and expectations and affect the extent to which they include the adolescent in the process of establishing rules. In general, parents who had positive experiences at home and with peers during their own sexual transformation are more likely to provide a similar experience for their children than parents who were neglected, rejected, or sexually abused. This does not imply that all parents who had these negative experiences will repeat the pattern, but it is not uncommon to observe in families the repetition of abuse, neglect, or rejection, as well as the recurrence of teenage pregnancy and children born out of wedlock.

In fact, incestuous impulses between the adolescent and the opposite-sex parent are likely to increase with the adolescent's emerging sexuality. The energy and unacceptability of these urges easily develop into heightened conflict. Perhaps adolescents act so obnoxiously to make it easier for parents to let them go, and perhaps parents become difficult to make it easier for adolescents to want to go. A previously special and loving relationship between father and daughter may rapidly evolve into a mutually hostile one, with the father being possessive and punitive and daughter being provocative. Mothers who are especially close to their sons may experience confusion and conflict when sons begin to demand more privacy and distance from them. The mother's request for closeness may be met with aggression and rejection, and the mother, feeling hurt, may react in a similar manner.

Parents and children of the same sex, on the other hand, tend to become involved in struggles that are more competitive. One assumption that has been extensively discussed, especially in psychoanalytic theory, is that they compete for the attention and love of the opposite-sex parent (Freud, 1962; Blos, 1962). Another assumption, however, is that they compete over their conflicting perceptions of appropriate gender roles. Since adolescents appear to be more stereotyped in their view of sex-type behaviors for men and women than any other age group (Hopkins, 1983), it seems natural that they would confront and challenge parental behavior that does not conform to their perceptions. It follows that the overall struggle during adolescence may be more intense with the parent of the same sex, who usually serves as the primary role model during childhood. To be certain, much of the conflict between parents and

adolescents reflects differences in the way each generation interprets the stereotypes and double standard about sexual roles that exist in this society.

Although the general trend is toward a breakdown in the double standard, adolescent girls continue to exhibit more emotional commitment in their sexual experiences than do boys (Peplau, 1976; Schulz, et al., 1977). However, among adolescents of both genders the trend seems to be toward earlier sexual experiences than do boys (Peplau, 1976; Schulz et al., 1977). This implies that most parents of adolescents will need to review their standards and attitudes about sexual roles, and possibly make changes that will better fit increasing liberalized sexual norms. For many parents this may be a very difficult task, especially if their values fit the more traditional double standard.

Identity: Transformation of the Self

Identity refers to a person's private view of those traits and characteristics that best describe him or her. This self-structure undergoes its greatest transformation during adolescence (Marcia, 1980), when it seems to become more abstract and psychologically oriented.

Attempts to understand this process have been primarily based on Freud and Erickson's theories. Freud focused on sexual drives and on the process of individuation (Blos, 1962), while Erickson (1968) identified adolescence as a period when individuals experience an identity crisis, which, when resolved, leads to commitments to sociopolitical conceptualizations and occupation.

One critical issue that these theories neglect is that, apart from the obvious physical characteristics that distinguish males from females, there are basic differences in the way that both sexes structure their identities. Few studies address this issue, but those that do seem to support the general assumption that females rely more on the relationships and connections they make and maintain whereas males place the emphasis on separation and individuation (Chodorow, 1974; Gilligan, 1982). Based on studies of men, most developmental theories assume that male patterns are the norm. This has created a double bind for women in this society, since traits that characterize the concept of "ideal women" are different from those that describe the "ideal adult" (Broverman et al., 1970). The "ideal adult is seen as having more of the traits that characterize the "ideal man." This inconsistency in role expectations makes gender consolidation especially difficult for females during adolescence when this process seems to be accentuated. Male adolescents who do not have strong sex-typed identities may also experience more difficulty than their more "masculine" counterparts.

Regardless of differences in theoretical frameworks and in gender, the sudden and dramatic acceleration of identity formation that takes place during adolescence can become a source of excitement and energy, but also of conflict, for adolescents and their families. A new-found ability to formulate

intellectual hypotheses expands adolescent creativity and feelings of mastery (Inhelder & Piaget, 1958). They become amateur philosophers and moral judges of social values and mores, often acting as ambassadors between home and community, bringing new ideas and attitudes that serve as catalysts for other family members to make changes. Their propensity for questioning and challenging rules and standards tends to precipitate transformations at home, at school, and in the community.

The struggle to gain a separate, clear, and positive self-image can also cause confusion and immobilization for adolescents and their families. New experiences in the world may subject them to anxiety, disappointment, rebuff, and failure. As with clothes and hair styles, roles may be tried on, prized briefly, and then discarded or clung to in an attempt to anchor a sense of self. While some of these roles are consistent with family values, they frequently challenge, if not assault, the mores of the family.

While attempting to establish self-identity, adolescents often disagree with parents about ideas, beliefs, and values. Comments such as, "My parents are so old-fashioned, they can't understand me," or "I never want to be like my parents, they are so boring" are familiar to those who work with adolescents. Also easily recognizable are parental comments such as, "I was so different at that age," "I didn't dare question my parents," or "I can't believe how girls call boys and initiate going out with them." These differences tend to create conflict among the generations, and sometimes lead to struggles over rules, roles, and relationships. Fears of conflict may inhibit the adolescent's asking questions or sharing ideas, and this creates distance and lack of trust.

Parents with a strong sense of self can be expected to be less reactive to adolescent challenges. This is not to say that they will not experience confusion or fear, but they may personalize their reactions less. Rather than feel attacked or threatened by criticisms, they will be more likely to ask questions, listen to explanations, and share feelings—methods that help parents and adolescents negotiate differences and conflicts (Offer et al., 1981)

Since gender has always been an integral aspect of self-identity, during adolescence same-sex, child–parent relationships have a powerful effect on the process of gender identification. Adolescent views about who they are will be greatly connected to their feelings about being male or female. Relationships with opposite-sex parents are just as influential in validating the adolescent's sense of gender identity, and to a certain extent serve as a program for shaping future relationships with the opposite sex.

Although there are always exceptions, as a rule daughters learn how to be female from mothers, and sons learn from fathers how to be male. Unfortunately, in their attempt to provide positive role models, parents often teach ideals about sexual roles rather than communicate to their children the value of their own experience. Betty Carter (1980) clearly describes this pattern: "Mothers in an effort to fulfill their responsibility, namely raising perfect children, routinely tell their daughters what they think would be helpful, instead of how they really feel, especially if the latter would convey the

mother's doubts, fears, struggles and uncertainties. So, trying desperately to be 'good mothers' and to guide their daughters, mothers withhold their *deepest personal experience* and try to convey to their daughters *how it should have been* and *how they want it to be for their daughters*—instead of how it *really is or was for them"* (p. 16).

Striving for ideals themselves, adolescents often experience their parents as hypocritical, and angrily reject advice. A similar pattern takes place between fathers and sons. In other words, what parents say is often not what they do. Inconsistencies in this process are as unavoidable as the conflict that emerges when adolescents confront and challenge the differences.

Autonomy: Transformation of Decision Making

Adolescents need to venture out of the home to become more self-reliant and independent. Alliances outside the home increase and the influence of peers becomes stronger. While needing nurturance and acceptance to develop strong separate identities, they also need permission and encouragement to become more responsible for themselves. Autonomy does not mean disconnecting emotionally from parents, but it does mean that an individual is no longer as psychologically dependent on parents and has more control of making decisions about his or her life.

Certainly, from an adult perspective, the adolescent's decisions in a rapidly expanding era of behavioral choices can leave much to be desired. The distinctions between choices that are merely unwise and self-defeating, and those that are self-destructive, even life-threatening, are often hard to determine. Uncertainty concerning when and how to act is common for parents of adolescents. The following example describes how decisions about discipline and/or protection become more difficult when the stakes for all concerned escalate.

The Prousts are becoming increasingly anxious and indecisive about how to parent Wendy, who, at 15, is their oldest child. Should she have a curfew? If so, what time? Should they continue monitoring her school work? Insist she attend "family events"? And what about parties? Didn't several of her friends get quite drunk at one two weeks ago? And what about birth control? The rumor of her friend Olivia's recent abortion increases the Prousts' fears. And there is the example of Joe, down the block, a seemingly healthy, friendly child. Now, at 17, he is always stoned, and increasingly involved in serious delinquency.

Wendy's mother can resentfully recall the restrictions of her own teenage years. Shouldn't Wendy have an opportunity for the fun that she was deprived of? True, she sometimes makes some unwise decisions, but isn't that what growing up is about? Perhaps she would do best if she knew her parents trusted her, but do they dare? Her father has agonized over the possibility of his daughter being sexually assaulted or otherwise mistreated. But what should he do?

Wendy wants to be popular and to have friends. She wants a boyfriend, and is curious about sex. But what about her parents? How will they react? And what

about her friends? Anne and Judy are both going with boyfriends and not having sex, but Mary and Sue talk about it all the time. But, if she gets pregnant, who could she tell? Would her parents make her have an abortion, like her friend Olivia? Of course, there is birth control, but she is too embarrassed to ask. She is also afraid of drugs, but they are hard to resist when parties are full of them, and most kids at school have tried at least pot and alcohol.

It has been found that adolescents are more likely to move toward autonomy in families where they are encouraged to participate in decision making, but where parents ultimately decide what is appropriate. In this type of family, adolescents are also likely to model their parents and to seek parent-approved peers. In contrast, adolescents raised in families where participation in decision making and self-regulation is limited tend to become more dependent and less self-assured (Newman & Newman, 1979). As the researchers note, these findings pose an intriguing paradox: "The same conditions that foster a sense of independence also build a bond of closeness and affection between parents and children" (p. 230).

Retaining control while being objective, supportive, and democratic is not an easy task for most parents to accomplish, especially when they feel judged and criticized by their own children. Parental tolerance will tend to be low if they have not been able to achieve emotional autonomy from their own parents. Also, if parents have unresolved conflicts with each other, their ability to accept the adolescent's desire for autonomy becomes impaired. The adolescent may then be triangled into power struggles between spouses or between parents and grandparents, which will complicate the process by increasing tension, dissatisfaction, misunderstanding, and conflict for all.

Although adolescence is a time when both boys and girls move steadily toward autonomy from parents, differences have been found in the way each accomplishes the task. Douvan and Adelson (1966), in a dated but still relevant study, found that boys appeared to be behaviorally dependent for a longer period than girls. However, boys seemed to achieve emotional autonomy at a much faster rate than girls. Their findings also imply that independence is a more important concern for boys than for girls, and that parental expectations seem to reinforce that pattern. More recent studies seem to indicate that differences may still be valid (Gilligan, 1982).

Gender role expectations certainly influence adolescents as they become involved in making decisions about life goals. Traditionally families have given males greater encouragement than they have females for educational and occupational advancement, independent living, and financial self-sufficiency. Recently females have been demanding the same opportunities as families with female adolescents find themselves making choices that challenge the values held by previous generations. When there are no prototypes to provide role models, the conflict and confusion that are normally experienced during this phase may increase dramatically for families with female adolescents.

For adolescents to master the developmental tasks that have been discussed, the family must be strong, flexible, and able to support growth. This is

often easier with each successive child, and particularly difficult if the marital dyad is severely threatened. For example, the case of 17-year-old Tom Murphy illustrates some of the shifts that may occur during adolescence when the child is in a triangle with parents who are in a struggle.

> Adolescence had heightened Tom's fears, as he felt an urgency to differentiate and grow more autonomous. He no longer wanted to be an engineer, as his parents were planning for him, but had become interested in lighting and theater, and was enjoying working with a semiprofessional group. His parents, however, disapproved of his interest, and were constantly urging him to go to college. The thought of going away to college frightened him. He was anxious about living in a dorm, and about leaving his parents alone with all their unresolved conflicts. Unable to talk freely at home about his insecurities, and without close friends outside, Tom had become depressed.
>
> Afraid to cause arguments, he avoided conversations with his parents, and refused to go places with them, especially with his mother, to whom he had been a constant companion. At school he gave up, failing to do assignments that were required for graduation, and dropping courses he did not want. His behavior alarmed the teachers enough to ask the psychologist to see him. When his parents were told, they reacted with fear and anger, confused by his behavior, which they experienced as a rejection of their values and efforts to give him a good future.
>
> Tom had been caught in a classic triangle, trying to please his parents and feeling responsible for their arguments. But pleasing one parent meant disappointing the other. Marital problems and arguments in this family had gone on for years. Mrs. Murphy was very dissatisfied with the marital relationship and claimed that Tom, their only child, was the only reason she stayed in it. Mr. Murphy was resentful and tried to minimize the problems, claiming she and Tom were against him. Overwhelmed by conflicts in their marriage, Mr. and Mrs. Murphy had been unable to be objective and supportive of Tom's moves toward autonomy. Behavior that otherwise could have been interpreted as representing movement toward autonomy was experienced by them as Tom's collusive alliance with one parent against the other. His growth represented a threat to the system, especially to the parents' relationship. In a situation such as this, family therapy can be quite helpful.

Attachment, Separation, and Loss During Adolescence

All transformations threaten previous attachments. The task of adolescence precipitates feelings of loss and fears of abandonment in most families. As adolescents strengthen their alliances outside, their decreasing participation at home is often experienced by other family members as a loss. Indeed, the transition from childhood to adolescence marks a loss for the family—the loss of the child. Parents often feel a void as adolescents move toward greater independence because they are no longer needed in the same way and the nature of their caretaking needs to change.

The difficulties inherent in the task of separation are greater when the parental support system is not working or is unavailable and there are no adults who can provide assistance. Under such conditions parents are likely to

become overwhelmed and to respond either by attempting to control their adolescents arbitrarily or by giving up control completely.

Attempting to control adolescents may arbitrarily lead to serious symptomatic behavior. This type of control is often seen in families where, as Stierlin (1979) suggests, centripetal forces operate to keep members from leaving the system. For instance, families that have experienced early losses and rejections tend to become overprotective, and parents may try to exert control by reinforcing excessive childlike behavior. The message given is that separation is dangerous, and strenuous efforts are made to protect members, especially children, from outside threats. Through mystification, or by demanding such strong loyalty ties that extreme guilt is induced when separation is considered, the family stays close and isolated from others. Members of families that are so tightly bound attempt to meet each other's needs, but fail to promote growth. As a result adolescents may become stuck when they feel the urgency to grow, but stay home to meet their parents' needs. Parents experience a similar dilemma when fears of loss interfere with their attempts to help the children grow. The dilemma is often solved by adopting symptomatic behavior.

Often families find themselves caught in ongoing struggles that only seem to reach resolution with a premature separation. Parents who are overwhelmed by the tasks of adolescence may give up all responsibility and call outside authorities to take control. Frustrated and feeling hopeless about changing the behavior of delinquent or emotionally disturbed adolescents, they may ask courts, social agencies, or hospitals to take them out of the home. Adolescents may also marry precipitously, go to live with friends or lovers, and at times run away in an attempt to escape the conflicts at home. At the extreme, there are those adolescents who are essentially expelled from their families. In those families, as Stierlin (1979) suggests, there seem to be centrifugal forces that impel the adolescent from the system. For example, parents who themselves were abused or neglected tend to abuse and reject when they lose control and feel helpless. Especially when parents are emotionally disturbed or substance abusers, adolescents may be forced into premature autonomy.

The expulsion of adolescents (Sager et al., 1983) may lead to a permanent family rift. This type of separation, while less intense than that following death, has significant and traumatic ramifications. For the adolescent who is cast out or runs away, the casualty rate due to other-inflicted or self-inflicted violence (including drug overdose) is high. Vulnerability to exploitation is also high. Unemployment, underemployment, prostitution, and involvement with an abusive partner are more likely outcomes for the adolescent without family supports. The remaining members of the evicting or deserted family are likely to confront heightened guilt, mutual blame, self-reproach, bitterness, continued anger, depression, and unresolved feelings of loss. The family's capacity to move ahead along its own life cycle course may be severely compromised. Both parents and other adolescents, or soon-to-be adolescents, in the family

are significantly affected by the experience as they attempt to negotiate their own transitions.

All change implies the acceptance of loss. Sometimes parents, unable to cope with the loss of the dependent child, experience serious depression. Likewise, the adolescent must deal with the loss of the childhood self and the family as the primary source of love and affection. The loss of an early romantic attachment can also trigger depression in adolescents.

Early loss in a parent's history can make this stage difficult. A number of studies have found life cycle connections between early loss or life cycle disruption and later development of symptoms (Orfanidis, 1977; Walsh, 1978). They also found a correlation between the death of a grandparent at the same time of the birth of a grandchild and that child's patterns of symptom development during adolescence.

In the following example, both Mr. and Mrs. Olson had experienced unpredictable and tragic losses at early stages in their lives. Divorce, suicide, emotional cutoffs, and physical illness had been used in previous generations as solutions to emotional conflicts.

> Mr. Olson, an only child, remembered always feeling worried about his mother's health and fearful of losing her. During infancy he had lost his father, who died unexpectedly from pneumonia. His mother had never remarried. Mrs. Olson was also an only child, whose parents had been divorced when she was 13. She had felt rejected and abandoned, feelings that increased when both parents remarried, and after her mother had committed suicide, following the stepfather's death. At that time she learned from a cousin that her maternal grandmother had also committed suicide, as had the cousin's sister. Mrs. Olson's father had died of a heart attack ten years after she married. Mrs. Olson also felt rejected by her mother-in-law, who had resented the marriage and taken no interest in her or the children. Now she felt rejected by her husband as well, and by the girls whenever they disagreed with her. She would express her anger and hurt while Mr. Olson withdrew emotionally, made sarcastic remarks, and sometimes burst out angrily.
>
> When their daughter Christina entered adolescence, she had begun to express her ideas more loudly. Around that same time, Mrs. Olson had also grown more expressive of her disapproval and anger toward Mr. Olson. She had wanted to divorce him, but didn't when he promised to change. They tried to keep this from the children, but Christina had been aware of it. Since then her father had been trying very hard to change, especially by talking during dinner.
>
> Two years later, Christina had given up any sign of rebellion. She had become very close to her mother, sharing the same interests and openly talking about her school concerns and problems with friends. She had begun to withdraw from friends and to limit any social contact. It had become very important for her to differentiate from her friends and not be part of their childish behavior. She idolized her mother, was afraid of her father's disapproval, and was worried about her sister, Sylvia's withdrawal from the family. Sylvia, who had also entered adolescence, had begun to spend more time with friends and to take an interest in rock music.
>
> Recently Christina had also started to worry about her weight. Her weight loss and fears about food had become a focus of concern for the whole family. Both parents were actively involved in trying to feed her, and Sylvia had begun to talk more with her. Everyone had become alarmed when Christina's pediatrician diagnosed her as having anorexia nervosa, and referred them to therapy.
>
> In response to extreme fears about parental divorce at such a vulnerable time

in her life, Christina began to change in a way that served to protect her family. The parents themselves were afraid of the feelings of loss and rejection. They were attempting to avoid repeating patterns that in their own families of origin had led to divorce, suicide, and conflicting emotional relationships.

Sociocultural Factors Influencing the Family

Social class, education, race, ethnicity, sex, and place of residence strongly influence the life cycle of families. For example, the experience of poor families with adolescents is significantly different from that of middle-class and upper-class families. Adolescents from poor families usually leave school earlier to look for jobs in an attempt to become financially independent. Unfortunately their lack of skills makes it difficult to succeed. Resultant frustration, combined with the pressure of living in a home with limited resources, may lead them to leave precipitously, or the family to throw them out. Parents in these families often have difficulty with their own role definitions and are not able to provide the guidance and control that would assist their children in mastering adolescence. The possibility of becoming involved in crime, prostitution, drug addition, and alcoholism is very high for this group.

In recent years more attention has been given to the significant role that ethnicity and culture play in the lives of families. Relationship patterns are deeply influenced by ethnic values and attitudes that are passed down through the generations. Ethnic groups differ remarkably in the rituals used to facilitate life cycle stages (Chapter 3). For instance, British-Americans tend to promote the early separation of adolescents and their transition into adulthood (McGill & Pearce, 1982). Unlike most Italian, Hispanic, and Jewish families, they do not struggle to keep their adolescents close to home. McGill and Pearce (1982) observe that British-Americans are good at promoting separation, but may provide insufficient guidance and support for adolescents. The result could be a premature separation that leads to a pseudoadult identity and the establishment of immature relationships in an attempt to replace the family.

In contrast, Portuguese families, while also expecting adolescents to make an early transition into adulthood, handle separation very differently. Adolescents are encouraged to find employment and to make financial contributions to the home, just like adults. However, socially and emotionally they are expected to remain loyal and under the supervision of their parents (Moitoza, 1982). They are expected to live at home until they marry. Leaving home before marriage involves the risk of being ostracized by the family. When these expectations are challenged, serious conflicts between parents and adolescents can occur. Parent–adolescent interaction and contact may substantially diminish or cease. Such cutoffs obviously interfere with healthy transitions to adulthood.

Another factor influencing adolescents and their families is the kind of community in which they reside. For example, the pressure and expectations experienced by families living in rural areas are different from those experi-

enced by families in urban areas. Adolescents who grow up in cities tend to be less dependent on their families for recreation. With public transportation and a greater concentration of recreational options, their potential for independent activity increases. Generally they are exposed to a greater diversity of life-styles and role models, both positive and negative. This may increase the distance between parents and adolescents and escalate the normal conflicts of that stage. Parents may be less able to keep track of their children's friends and their whereabouts, or be less concerned about doing so, than their suburban or rural counterparts.

By contrast, adolescents in suburban and rural areas, due to geographic distance, may find themselves isolated from their peer group and dependent on the family for transportation and social stimulation. Greater dependence on the family may intensify the normal adolescent struggle for independence or slow down the growth process. The acquisition of a driver's license and availability of a car represent a transitional event that permits a major increase in independent actions by the adolescent.

Divorce is another social factor that has a tremendous effect on families with adolescents. Peck and Manocherian (Chapter 15) describe some of the patterns that emerge in families where adolescents are unable to maintain appropriate emotional distance from parental conflicts after divorce or separation. The change in family structure may cause a blurring of boundaries and an intensification of bonds between parents and adolescents. Adolescents may assume adult roles in an effort to replace the missing spouse and support the remaining parent. Single parents who do not have a network of peers sometimes lean inappropriately on their children for emotional support. The case of Mrs. Callahan illustrates some of the issues and patterns that can become salient in single-parent families during adolescence.

Mrs. Callahan, a 39-year-old Puerto Rican woman, had come to the United States after graduating from college. She had left to avoid conflicts with her parents, especially with her mother, whom she experienced as rejecting. She and her parents had always lived with her father's extended family. Growing up, Mrs. Callahan had felt closer to her father's extended family than to her mother, who, she felt, ignored and criticized her. According to Mrs. Callahan, her mother always felt rejected by the paternal family, and resented Mrs. Callahan's closeness to them.

Mrs. Callahan married Mr. Callahan, an Irishman, shortly after coming to this country. Two years later, after Clara's birth, and while pregnant with Sonia, Mrs. Callahan learned that Mr. Callahan was having an affair. She was angry and hurt, feeling betrayed, abandoned, and rejected. She tried to forget and make the marriage work, but after eight years she decided to divorce him. She could not forgive and trust, and he had begun to use alcohol to deal with his feelings. He had felt guilty about the affair, and hurt and angry about the divorce, which he didn't want. She had worried about his drinking, feeling that, on some level, her rejection had caused his problems. Unable to resolve their conflicts, divorce became the solution.

The divorce had been traumatic for them all, especially for Clara, who was ten at the time, and Sonia, who was almost eight. Mr. Callahan had remained a responsible parent, and with Mrs. Callahan's agreement, had frequent contact with the girls. The visits took place in Mrs. Callahan's home, since she was afraid to

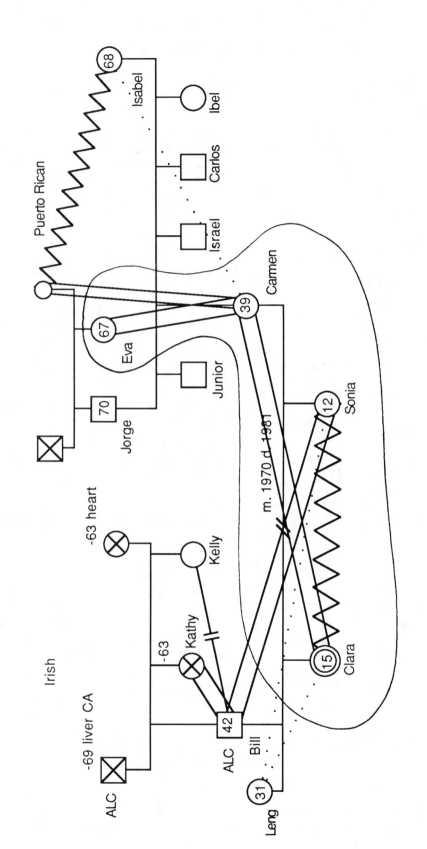

Figure 12-1. Callahan family.

trust him while he drank. She was afraid that he would lose control while driving, or make sexual advances toward the girls. She had no proof of that; she had asked the girls about it and she knew that he loved them, but she couldn't trust an alcoholic.

Five years later, Mrs. Callahan remained unmarried. She had returned to graduate school and was working as a professional; however, fearful of rejection, she had isolated herself from her peers by placing her energy into being a good mother. Before her daughters were born, she had decided to be a very different type of mother from her own. Mr. Callahan, in contrast, married an Oriental woman whom the girls didn't like. This new wife was not very involved with them, and Mrs. Callahan was afraid that Mr. Callahan would also lose his interest. She sometimes regretted the divorce, feeling that she should have been more understanding.

At school Clara, who was now 15, had been doing poorly academically, and recently had written a letter to her mother in which she threatened to run away and kill herself. Her mother became frightened and angry, unwilling to listen to her daughter's criticisms and complaints. Her daughter's expression of dissatisfaction had been extremely painful. She was feeling rejected again, this time by her daughter. She felt that she had sacrificed so much for her daughters, and could not forgive Clara's ungratefulness. Clara, who had always been very close to Mrs. Callahan, wanted to please her, but feeling a need to become autonomous, was confused and frightened by her mother's reactions of pain and anger when she attempted to differentiate. She was able to speak about this to a teacher at school, who called Mrs. Callahan and suggested therapy.

The therapeutic interventions that helped this family will be discussed in more detail later. However, helping Mrs. Callahan and her daughters talk about the divorce, the father's alcoholism, and the emotional distance that she maintained from her family allowed for movement and change in this family. Discussing differences that related to cultural values and feelings about Clara's confusion regarding her ethnic identity was also helpful.

Another factor that this case elucidates is the considerable impact that the lack of extended family or other support group may have on how families manage adolescence. Some ethnic groups, such as Puerto Ricans, rely heavily on extended family members to help with the discipline of adolescents and the clarification of boundaries. It is common for Puerto Rican parents to send a rebellious adolescent to live with an uncle or godparent who can be more objective about setting limits. This move also serves to provide time for parents and adolescents to obtain enough emotional distance from each other to regain control and reestablish a more balanced relationship. Relying solely on the nuclear family, especially when it is a single-parent family, to provide control, support, and guidance for adolescents can overload the circuits and escalate conflicts.

CLINICAL INTERVENTION DURING ADOLESCENCE

If there is a time in the life cycle of families when referrals to family therapy are at a peak, adolescence is likely to be it. Although most families are able to

cope with the demands of this transition and move on, many reach impasses that call for help. They may seek therapy voluntarily, but usually external systems, such as schools, courts, or physicians, refer them or become involved at some point in the process. However, regardless of how they are referred, or whether they welcome or resist the referral, families tend to arrive feeling confused, angry, and out of control, and present problems that reflect the family's inability to deal with the tasks of adolescence.

Often families continue trying solutions that are ineffective in helping them meet the demands of adolescence. Unable to make the necessary shifts that facilitate growth, they become stuck, repeating dysfunctional patterns that eventually lead to symptomatic behavior in adolescents. Helping those families find solutions that may break those cycles by precipitating a second-order change is a primary goal of therapy.

The problems presented by families with adolescents vary in severity and duration, and may range from school phobia in early adolescence to schizophrenia in late adolescence. Psychosomatic illness, eating disorders, depression, suicidal behavior, delinquency, substance abuse, running away, and impulsive behavior of the adolescent are among the most frequently presented.

The following clinical interventions are aimed at taking a life cycle approach to adolescents and their families. Their application will be demonstrated by using some of the cases discussed in previous sections as examples.

Reframing the Family's Conceptions of Time

In therapy the initial presentation made by families with adolescents typically reflects the stopping of time. Stuck and frightened, they experience the present as endless and the future as dangerous. The symptoms they bring often represent the family's attempt to solve conflicts created when they are unable to negotiate relationship shifts that must take place during adolescence. Meant to solve the relationship dilemma, the symptoms also stop the family system's evolution (McGoldrick & Garcia-Preto, 1982). In these families adolescents usually stop growing emotionally, as well as physically sometimes, and parents often appear unable to help their children grow. In most cases the way is blocked by unresolved conflicts that have created emotional distance between parents and grandparents and among other family members across the generations. Present patterns make sense only in relation to the total evolutionary patterns of the system (McGoldrick & Garcia-Preto, 1982).

The goal of reframing the family's conceptions of time is to free the system from the situation in which time has stopped. Tracking the system in relation to different time spheres helps identify the points in the life cycle at which the family appears stuck. Questions about differences between family relationships at the time of symptom onset and at earlier periods in family history underline the continuing process of change in a family whose sense of time has stopped. While respecting the positive value of the family's present symp-

tomatic adaptation, the notion of future change can be introduced into the system by offering new connections between present and past, and by pushing toward new options (McGoldrick & Garcia-Preto, 1982).

In the case of Tom and his family, reframing the family's conceptions of time helped free the system from viewing the present as infinite and the future as dangerous. Asking the family whether they agreed or disagreed with each other's impressions and reactions to Tom's behavior elicited differences in their relationships that helped them to understand some of the patterns that seemed to maintain the present symptoms. It became clear, for example, that Mr. and Mrs. Murphy disagreed about everything under the sun, except on their plans for Tom's future. Tom, on the other hand, disagreed with their plans for his future, but was afraid to express differences at home.

To obtain a clearer picture of the present, the parents were asked about differences in relationships during their own adolescence. It surfaced that Tom's father had felt deeply hurt and resentful at age nine when his mother died after a short physical illness. During adolescence he had left home, and had never been able to establish a close relationship with his father, whom he described as never home because he was always working to support his family. He was trying desperately to change that pattern with his son, but felt blocked by his wife, whom he experienced as critical and distant—the same way he had felt about his stepmother. He accused her of taking Tom away from him, and making him into a "mama's boy." On the other hand, Mrs. Murphy, an only child like Tom, had experienced her father as critical and distant, a pattern she was now experiencing again in the relationship with her husband. Her father had been an alcoholic, and her parents had always been in conflict. She, however, had been nurtured, supported, and accepted by her mother, something that she was trying to repeat with her son. After her mother's death, two years prior to the present situation, she had felt very sad about the loss, and angry that her husband was unable to give the emotional support she needed. She had raised Tom to be different from the men she knew, but now he was also rejecting her. She accused her husband of pushing Tom away by not accepting him.

The patterns observed offered new connections for understanding the problems presented. Relationships between Tom's parents and grandparents had clearly influenced the present situation. Mrs. Murphy's mother's death had set the family off balance. After the death Mrs. Murphy had become more dependent on her son and husband for emotional support, but since she and Mr. Murphy were in conflict, the pressure was on Tom to fill the void. Needing guidance and support himself to meet the challenges of adolescence, Tom felt as helpless as they did. Depleted from her loss, Mrs. Murphy could not give, and Mr. Murphy did not know how to give. To help the family move, it was suggested that Tom's behavior was an attempt to stop time because he saw the future as dangerous. It was conveyed that on some level Tom was probably afraid to leave them alone, because he felt he was the glue keeping the family together. Questions about future time explored the family's perceptions of how Tom's leaving would affect relationship patterns. Asking Mr. and Mrs. Murphy

to visualize Tom as an adult, and to talk about the kind of relationships they would want to have with him in the future, helped clarify some of their present expectations. Questions about their plans for retirement and old age brought to the surface some of the family's fears about survival. Asking Tom hypothetical questions about his own adulthood and his parent's old age crystallized some of his fears and anxieties about growing up.

The family was told to take a break from making any further plans for Tom's future. They were asked to concentrate on the present, to find ways that would help Tom become less fearful and more confident. He needed to learn how to make decisions about his future. The present situation at the high school was given as an example of the type of decisions he needed to make. Mr. and Mrs. Murphy were advised to back off and let him take responsibility for negotiating at school. It was suggested that they make a plan clarifying their expectations of Tom, if he did not go to college. It was also predicted that Tom would probably continue to act depressed until the family was able to think about the future in a less disastrous manner.

The initial focus on the present helped the family gain some control by making plans for handling the immediate problem. By suggesting that now was the time for them to work on tasks that would help Tom differentiate and grow into a responsible adult, the present was reframed as a transition in the family's life cycle. Questions about the parents' adolescence helped them become more objective about each other, as they made connections between the past and present. Pushing the family to think about the future introduced the notion of evolutionary time, and freed the family to consider different possibilities.

Working with Subsystems

Working with family subsystems is a powerful intervention for restructuring and redefining relationships when families with adolescents become developmentally stuck. After meeting with the whole family initially to assess patterns, meeting with parents and adolescents separately increases the therapist's maneuverability to support both generations at once, while clarifying boundaries. It also helps the therapist avoid getting caught in power struggles, such as when adolescents become belligerent or refuse to say anything in sessions (Nicholson, 1986). Meeting with the adolescent and siblings, or asking other significant family relatives to join sessions, adds information and opens the system to new possibilities. This intervention allows the therapist to promote support across the generations, while encouraging a more autonomous exploration of issues by family members (Minuchin, 1974).

Meeting the Parents

Most parents welcome the opportunity to speak in private with the therapist about fears and suspicions they may have regarding their adolescent's

behavior. The therapeutic goal for these sessions, however, is to create a safer atmosphere in which they can feel freer to be more objective about their role as parents, and to explore struggles they may have in other areas of their lives, such as marriage, work, being single or divorced, or problems with their families of origin. In most cases, in order to engage parents in this way, the therapist must first address the concerns they bring.

Mr. and Mrs. Olson, for example, were extremely anxious to meet alone with the therapist to discuss Christina's anorexia. They had a thousand questions concerning weight, hospitalization, the pediatrician, and the therapist's opinions and plans for treatment. Asking for individual impressions and reactions to the symptom resulted in heated discussions and friction between them. Questions about how the symptom was affecting their marriage led to a lengthy description of marital problems by Mrs. Olson, with brief and minimizing statements from Mr. Olson, who otherwise was in general agreement with his wife. Inquiring about their support systems clarified that they did not trust each other and had no friends or relatives who could help.

The immediate goal in that session was to unite them as parents, struggling together as a team to help Christina grow. Mr. and Mrs. Olson were advised to stop struggling with her over food, even if it meant putting blinders over their eyes. A suggestion was given for them to take turns reading the newspaper to each other at the dinner table, to have discussions about the stories, and respond to their daughter only when she made comments about the news.

Of course, they did not follow through on these suggestions, but they were able to stop forcing Christina to eat, and to focus on other areas of concern— such as the family's isolation from friends, their fears about Sylvia's withdrawal from them, and their own difficult marriage. Meeting with them alone at different intervals in therapy made it easier to explore dysfunctional patterns in their relationship as parents and spouses. Encouraging them to be clear about expectations of each other, and to negotiate differences about rules and limits at home, increased the emotional support between them.

Parenting became easier after they had spent some time looking at relationship patterns in their families of origin and connecting present fears to past experiences. Mrs. Olson was able to connect her fears about Christina's starvation and Sylvia's isolation to her reactions to the suicides in her family. She had felt helpless, angry, and empty after her mother's suicide, and as her mother had done in the previous generation, she had tried to keep the suicide secret. Sharing these feelings with the whole family opened up communication with her daughters. Mr. Olson was able to connect his fears of inadequacy as a father to the lack of fathering he experienced from such an early age. He also feared losing his family in the same way he had feared losing his mother when he was a child, when she had been seriously ill and hospitalized for two years with tuberculosis. Concerned about his mother's health, he had always tried to avoid conflicts with her, and now was afraid to tell her that he was hurt when she didn't accept his family. He accepted a suggestion to write letters to his mother in Europe, telling stories about his daughters and wife. Later, on a visit

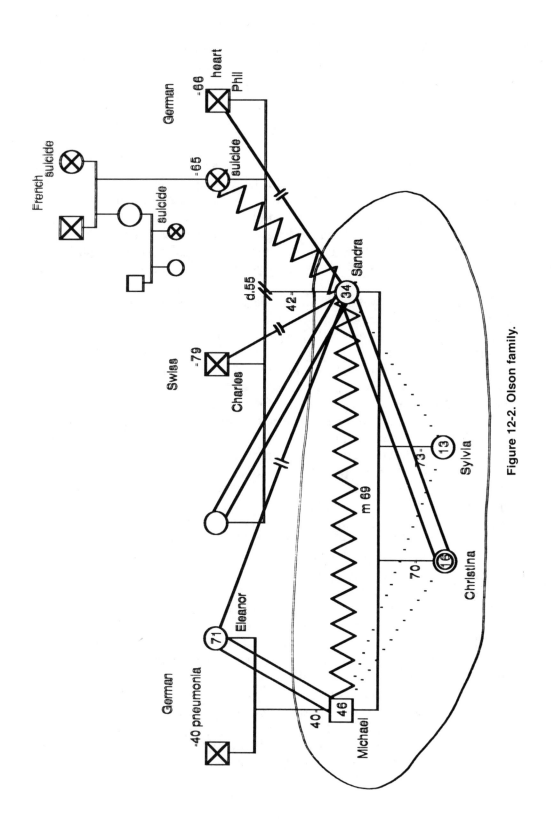

Figure 12-2. Olson family.

to his mother, he was able to follow through by asking her impressions of the stories he had told. Sharing her impressions with his family helped him feel more connected to them.

Meeting with Adolescents

Individual sessions with adolescents provide an opportunity to assess their functioning outside their family system. Often they present a very different picture when seen alone, feeling freer to explore and express their views of the world. Questions that address values and beliefs about life, love, sex, responsibility, education, drugs, friends, family, and the future help clarify their concept of self, or identity. Focusing on how these ideas are similar or different from parental views identifies conflict areas that may be blocking the process of differentiation.

Tom, for instance, was silent and appeared rigid and angry when seen with his parents. He answered questions about the suicidal threats he had made in monosyllables, contributing little information. Alone he continued to present the same picture, but once the conversation was geared toward his interests in radio, electronics, theater, and restaurants, he began to relax and show more feeling. Tom was not sure that he wanted to go into electronic engineering now that he had developed such a passion for the theater and for stage lighting. However, he was afraid to raise the issue with his parents, which would surely start a fight about the one thing they seemed to agree upon—his future. They both wanted him to go to college to become an electronics engineer.

When Mr. and Mrs. Murphy fought. Tom's way out was to be quiet and to retreat to his room. If he agreed with his mother, Mr. Murphy would feel rejected and angry, claiming that they were both against him. If he agreed with his father, which happened infrequently, Mrs. Murphy would feel hurt and stop talking to him. If he spoke about problems, his father would blame Mrs. Murphy. His solution to the dilemma was to stop everything, and in the process he became depressed and suicidal.

Sessions with Tom served to validate his feelings of fear, hurt, anger, and confusion, and to encourage his wish for autonomy by coaching him to confront his parents. In a session with his parents, and with much support from the therapist who had met with Mr. and Mrs. Murphy alone to foster their understanding, Tom was able to tell them about his dilemma. The sessions also gave Tom an opportunity to establish a relationship with an adult outside the system who supported and confronted his wishes to be different from his peers and his parents, and acknowledged his need for greater autonomy.

Meetings with adolescents also offer a safer context in which they can reveal secrets and ghosts that may be plaguing them. Incest, rape, abortions, drugs, alcohol, sex, and physical abuse are issues that sometimes lie beneath the surface or are deeply buried.

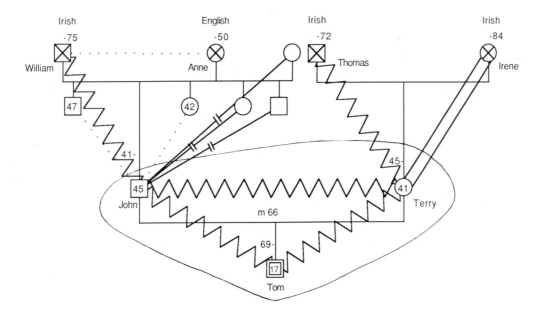

Figure 12-3. Murphy family.

Meetings with Siblings

Changes the family makes to accommodate adolescents affect the position of other siblings in the system. Rules and limits that reflect increased autonomy and responsibility for the adolescent often stir resentment in younger children, or in older siblings who did not enjoy the same privileges. As adolescents become more active with peers in the community, functions they held at home may need to be filled by other children.

In families where the adolescent is symptomatic and parents seek therapy, younger siblings are usually anxious about their own adolescence. Parents, as well, may be afraid of having to go through similar problems with the others. Anxious about the impending conflicts awaiting siblings, the adolescent may have difficulty moving away. Sessions that include adolescents and their siblings can help to allay fears and build support in that subsystem.

Since Christina's anorexia began, Mr. and Mrs. Olson had become increasingly concerned about their younger daughter, Sylvia, who was quiet and kept herself distant from the family. Sylvia rarely shared anything about herself with the family unless coaxed by Mrs. Olson, who felt extremely hurt and angry about her daughter's behavior. Sylvia was the opposite of Christina, who had become Mrs. Olson's confidante and friend, and told the family everything about herself. Christina felt that her parents were being too hard on Sylvia, not giving her a chance to be herself. Although she was accepting of

Sylvia, she also wanted to feel closer to her, to talk more about how to make friends, and to share impressions about their parents.

Therapy sessions with Christina and Sylvia focused primarily on their relationship, and on trying to build support between them. Questions that elicited their impressions about the way each other functioned at home and outside with friends helped to clarify images they held of each other, their family, and the world. Alone they were able to discuss more openly beliefs and values about friends, and to explore how the family's isolation and limited social contacts had contributed to Christina's difficulty. Sylvia, although withdrawn at home, had a number of friends with whom she socialized. In contrast, Christina, who at home was loquacious and the center of attention, felt painfully inadequate among her peers and avoided them. Christina's function in the family system had allowed room for Sylvia to move out, but now the positions in which they appeared stuck were dysfunctional.

A suggestion in the therapy was for Sylvia to give hints to Christina on how to make friends, and Christina to coach Sylvia on how to approach their parents. They were also asked to consider defending each other when they thought their parents were being unfair. The idea of a party was offered as a situation in which they could work together to change some of the patterns that seemed problematic. Sylvia was to present the idea of the party to their parents with coaching from Christina. Christina was to handle making invitations and answering phone calls with Sylvia's help. They were both to negotiate rules and limits for the party with their parents.

The therapeutic goal was to foster support between them and to encourage their developmental growth by asking them to take risks with their parents and friends.

Meeting with Other Relatives

In the case of Clara and her family, inviting Mrs. Callahan's aunt, who was living with them, to some of the sessions made it easier to identify patterns that had operated in the previous generation and were repeating themselves in the present.

Interestingly, Clara's adolescence had activated a triangle similar to one that had operated in the previous generation. The triangle, triggered by discipline issues, involved Clara, Mrs. Callahan, and a maternal grandaunt who had lived with the family since the divorce. Clara felt that her grandaunt, who still adhered to Puerto Rican values, was too old-fashioned and resented her attempts to discipline. Both would complain to Mrs. Callahan, who would try to mediate by explaining cultural differences, but was confused herself about which values to keep and would end up feeling powerless. The aunt would react by moving in to support Mrs. Callahan, and Clara would distance feeling rejected by both. During her adolescence Mrs. Callahan had been involved in a triangle with her mother and this aunt, who was her father's youngest sister.

The aunt would try to mediate between Mrs. Callahan and her mother when they had arguments, but would usually end up defending her niece. The mother would then get angry and distance from Mrs. Callahan, who in turn would feel rejected. The aunt would then move in to explain the mother's behavior and support Mrs. Callahan.

Inviting the aunt to some of the sessions with Mrs. Callahan made shifting this triangle easier. They were told that Clara needed support from them both, but primarily from her mother, with whom she had identified and from whom she needed to differentiate now. It was suggested that Clara was as confused as they were by the different ways in which both cultures dealt with adolescence. Asking them to identify which Puerto Rican values were creating the greatest conflict at home led to thinking about a compromise. They agreed that dating was the greatest source of conflict, since in Puerto Rico this practice has very different rules and connotations. Dating does not start until much later and it is usually in the company of family or friends. Dating different boys is frowned upon, and girls gain bad reputations. It was pointed out that for Clara to live in this culture and feel comfortable with her peers, her relatives needed to adapt to some of the values of this culture. As a compromise they agreed on letting Clara go on double dates, but only with people whom they knew. A curfew was to be negotiated with input from Clara.

Inviting the aunt to the sessions helped to shift the present triangle, but to make additonal changes in the relationship between Clara and her mother, work had to be done with Mrs. Callahan and her mother, who lived in Puerto Rico. Coaching Mrs. Callahan to share with her mother through letters, and on a visit to Puerto Rico, some of her conflicts, and to ask her advice about disciplining Clara was a way to lessen the emotional distance between them. Mrs. Callahan became more accepting of her mother's limitations, and began to appreciate the attention she gave. This helped her listen more attentively to her daughters.

Rituals

Therapeutic rituals have been defined by Watzlawick (1978) as the most elegant synthesis of intervention and technique. Prescribing them to families that are having difficulty negotiating the tasks of adolescence can reduce anxiety about change by offering stability, while at the same time promoting traditions or imagination for making the transition from adolescence to adulthood. Perhaps, in some cases, the development of symptomatic cycles may be a replacement for the lack of rituals.

In general, this society lacks rites to demark movement toward adulthood (Quinn, Newfield, & Protinsky, 1985). Except for some cultural or religious rituals such as barmitzvahs and confirmations, there is a paucity of rituals to mark the transitions of adolescent development. However, proposing to families that are stuck in that transition to plan celebrations around such events as

16th birthdays, obtaining a driver's license, and graduations provides them the opportunity to mark growth toward maturity.

In the Callahan family, for example, prescribing the planning of an event to celebrate Clara's 16th birthday not only shifted relationship patterns, but also introduced an old cultural tradition into the system that symbolizes growth and maturity.

In Puerto Rico, as in many other Hispanic countries, a girl's 15th birthday symbolizes a change in status. Friends and relatives are invited to celebrate the "Quinceañera," the 15-year-old girl, at the family's home, or at a special place, where they usually eat and dance. From that time on, she can attend dances and parties with friends, but usually no single dating is allowed until she is 17 or 18.

During a discussion about Mrs. Callahan's adolescence in Puerto Rico, a description of this custom was given. Mrs. Callahan was able to remember the sadness and loss she felt when her 15th birthday was not celebrated. She had felt different from her friends and resentful toward her parents, but especially her mother, who, she felt, did not love her. Actually, in her mother's family this custom had not been practiced either. Mrs. Callahan's aunt, however, remembered having had a celebration when she turned 15. Both Mrs. Callahan and her aunt excitedly reported memories of parties they had attended for "Quinceañeras." Clara, who had not attended such a party, shared with them descriptions of how her friends were planning to celebrate their "sweet 16" birthdays, which is the custom in this culture.

Clara's 15th birthday had not been celebrated, and they were not planning a sweet 16 party. The suggestion was made that they plan such a party that would reflect the two cultures.

The goal of prescribing this ritual was to encourage cooperation among the generations while at the same time promoting the acceptance of differences into the system. The event enabled Clara, Mrs. Callahan, and her aunt to connect with each other in a more autonomous way and to share with peers and family a happy occasion.

Uses of Self

To engage families with adolescents in therapy, therapists must feel free to join, support, or confront either generation when necessary. This is a difficult task, especially for therapists who are themselves struggling with their own adolescent children, or whose own adolescence was marked by conflictual relationships with parents. The natural pull in these situations is for the therapist to side with parents or adolescent, to view one as the victim and the other as the villain, and to intervene by protecting or defending one from the other.

Asking the following questions can help therapists maintain a more neutral and circular view of the problem.

1. How did parents experience their own adolescence?

2. What was the nature of the parents' relationships with other family members during adolescence?

3. Were there changes in expectations and behaviors among family members during the parents' adolescence? For instance, did they become more distant from or closer to father or mother?

4. If there were siblings, did those relationships change?

5. How close or distant were they with grandparents and other extended family?

6. How were limits set and conflicts resolved?

7. How connected was the family to its sociocultural context?

8. Did they have fun, and were they receptive to new friends, ideas, and values?

Asking these questions about their own adolescence can also help therapists become more aware of personal issues that may influence their reactions and render them powerless with some families. Seeking consultation from a supervisor or colleague who can observe a live session or videotape of cases where therapists feel stuck can further elucidate these issues. Therapists can also make significant shifts in their use of themselves as change agents with families previously experienced as difficult and resistant after changing personal patterns of behavior in their families of origin (McGoldrick, 1982).

In general, working with this population, although challenging and exciting, can also be frustrating and exhausting. For therapists a way to avoid burnout is to establish support networks with other professionals. This is crucial when adolescents are severely depressed and suicidal. Just as the family needs to be connected with extended systems, so does the therapist.

CONCLUSIONS

Adolescents grow up to become adults, have children of their own, and tend to adopt values and attitudes that reflect their parents' beliefs, unless while growing up they were seriously injured psychologically. Families handling the tasks of adolescence experience transformations in structure and organization, which are initially disruptive and create confusion. Most families, however, adjust to the changes without major difficulty and move on in the life cycle, but some, unable to make the transition, become symptomatic. In therapy unlocking the system to allow movement becomes the goal.

Assessing how families are coping with adolescent tasks is crucial to understanding the problems they bring to therapy. To diagnose what they present, therapists must broaden their perspective to consider not only the multiple ways in which families function, but also external factors that have an

impact on them. Usually, without a relatively stable social framework, families have more difficulty providing the flexibility and protection that adolescents need to grow.

Interventions that take a life cycle approach to adolescents and their families, and that are three generational in scope, tend to precipitate transformation in the system. Reframing the family's conceptions of time, working with subsystems, and proposing rituals that promote traditions or imagination are interventions that promote change in the system's organization. Tracking relationship patterns across the generations and connecting present conflicts to past unresolved conflicts allows families to be more objective about their interactions with each other. By offering new connections, the therapist can help families negotiate relationship shifts that must take place during adolescence, and to view the future in a less dangerous way.

REFERENCES

Ackerman, N. J. (1980). The family with adolescents. In E. A. Carter and M. McGoldrick (Eds.), *The family life cycle: A framework for family therapy.* New York: Gardner Press.

Blos, P. (1962). *The adolescent passage: Developmental issues.* New York: International Universities Press.

Broverman, J. K., Broverman, D. M., & Clarkson, F. E. (1970). Sex roles stereotypes and clinical judgements of mental health. *Journal of Consulting and Clinical Psychology* 34:1–7.

Chodorow, N. (1974). Family structure and feminine personality. In M. Z. Rosaldo & L. Lamphere (Eds.), *Woman, culture and society.* Stanford, Calif.: Stanford University Press.

Carter, E. A. (1980). Legacies, intergenerational themes. In E. Carter, P. Papp, O. Siverstein, & M. Walters (Eds.), *Mothers and daughters.* Washington.

Dickman, J. R. (1983). Teenage pregnancy: What can be done? Public Pamphlet No. 594.

Douvan, E., & Adelson, J. (1966). *The adolescent experience.* New York: Wiley.

Erickson, E. H. (1968). Identity: Youth and crisis. New York: Norton.

Freud, S. (1962, originally published 1905). *Three contributions to the theory of sex.* (A. Brill, trans.). New York: Dutton.

Garcia-Preto, N. (1982). Puerto Rican families. In M. McGoldrick, J. K. Pearce, & J. Giordano (Eds.), *Ethnicity and family therapy.* New York: Guilford Press.

Gilligan, C. (1982). *In a different voice: Psychological theory and women's development.* Cambridge, Mass.: Harvard University Press.

Heller, S. (1982). *Jules Feiffer's America: From Eisenhower to Reagan.* New York: Knopf.

Hopkins, J. R. (1983). *Adolescence: The transitional years.* New York: Academic Press.

Imber-Black, E. (1986). Rituals: In session and end of session creative interventions. Paper presented at Family Training Unit, UMDNJ, CMHC.

Inhelder, B., Piaget, J. (1958). *The growth of logical thinking.* New York: Basic Books.

Jessor, S., & Jessor, R. (1975). Transition from virginity to nonvirginity among youth: A psychological study over time. *Developmental Psychology* 11:473–484.

Marcia, J. E. (1980). Identity of adolescence. In J. Adelson (Ed.), *Handbook of adolescent psychological.* New York: Wiley.

McGill, D., & Pearce, J. K. (1982). British families. In M. McGoldrick, J. G. Pearce, & J. Giordano (Eds.), *Ethnicity and family therapy.* New York: Guilford Press.

McGoldrick, M. (1982). Through the looking glass: Supervision of a trainee's "trigger" family. In J. Burg Hall & R. Whiffen (Eds.), *Family therapy supervision*. London: Academic Press.

McGoldrick, M., & Garcia-Preto, N. (1982). Edited tape on: Milan use of time. UMDNJ, CMHC, Piscataway, N.J.

McGoldrick, M., Pearce, J. V. & Giordano, J. (1982). *Ethnicity and family therapy*. New York: Guilford Press.

Moitoza, E. (1982). Portuguese families. In M. McGoldrick, J. K. Pearce, & J. Giordano (Eds.), *Ethnicity and family therapy*. New York: Guilford Press.

Minuchin, S. (1974). *Families in family therapy*. Cambridge, Mass.: Harvard University Press.

Newman, B. M., & Newman, P.R. (1979). *An introduction to the psychology of adolescence*. Homewood, Ill.: Dorsey Press.

Nicholson, S. (1986). Family therapy with adolescents: Giving up the struggle. A.N.Z.J. *Family Therapy* 7:1–6.

Offer, D., Ostrov, E., & Howard, K. I. (1981). *The adolescent: A psychological self portrait*. New York: Basic Books.

Orfanidis, M. (1977). Some data on death and cancer in schizophrenic families. Paper presented at the Symposium Meeting of the Georgetown Symposium, Washington, D.C..

Peplau, L. A. (1976). Impact of fear of success and sex role attitudes on women's competitive achievement. *Journal of Personality and Social Psychology* 34:561–568.

Peck, J., & Manocherian, J. (1987). Divorce. In E. A. Carter & M. McGoldrick (Eds.), *The family life cycle*. New York: Gardner Press.

Prosen, H., Toews, J., & Martin, M. (1981). The life cycle of the family: Parental midlife crises and adolescent rebellion. In S. C. Feinstein, J. C. Looney, A. Z. Schwartzberg, and A. D. Sorosky (Eds.), *Adolescent psychiatry: Developmental and clinical studies*, vol 9. Chicago: University of Chicago Press.

Quinn, W. H., Newfield, & Protinsky, H. O. (1985). Rites of passage in families with adolescents. *Family Process* 24:101–111.

Sager, C. J., Brown, H. S., Crohn, H., Engel, T., Bodstein, E., & Walker, L. (1983). *Treating the remarried family*. New York: Brunner/Mazel.

Schulz, B., Bohrstedt, G. W., Borgatta, E. F., & Evans, R. R. (1977). Explaining pre-marital sexual intercourse among college students. A casual model. *Social Forces* 56:148–165.

Stierlin, H. (1979). *Separating parents and adolescents: A perspective on running away, schizophrenia and waywardness*. New York: Quadrangle.

Walsh, F. (1978). Concurrent grandparent death and the birth of a schizophrenic offspring: An intriguing finding. *Family Process* 12:179–188.

Watzlawick, P., Weakland, J., & Fisch, R. (1974). *Change: Principles of problem formulation and problem resolution*. New York: Norton.

Watzlawick, P. (1978). *The language of change*. New York: Basic Books.

13

Launching Children
and Moving On

Paulina G. McCullough, A.C.S.W.
and Sandra K. Rutenberg, Ph.D.

For families in the stage of life that begins with the launching of the children and continues until retirement, there are particular developmental issues, transitions, tasks, and clinical problems. In terms of the age of the parents, this stage usually extends from the mid-40s to the mid-60s.

The chapter's title reflects what is generally thought to be the main purpose of family life—that is, the care, protection, and socialization of children until such time as they become independent adults. Thus this phase used to be termed the "empty nest," and was thought to be a largely negative transition, particularly for women, the primary caretakers. However, while this transition may begin with the first child's exit from the home, it involves a myriad of familial transitions and tasks of personal growth beyond the parenting function (Carter and McGoldrick, Chapter 1). Broadly, these transitions and tasks relate to:

1. The changing function of marriage.
2. The development of adult-to-adult relationships between grown children and their parents.
3. The expansion of family relationships to include in-laws and grand-children.
4. The opportunity to resolve relationships with aging parents.

These tasks provide an inherent opportunity to reexamine the meaning of family at every level. If the middle-aged couple previously functioned as though they existed merely for the procreation of children, this phase can loom as empty and meaningless. Such couples may be unable to adapt to a life that no longer counts on the parenting function to organize their relationship. Similarly, if adult children no longer need their parents, or chose divergent or opposing life-styles, then the parents may see few reasons for staying con-nected to these adult children. Given that the older generation is now entering

a phase of physical decline and may require more care and attention, the middle-aged adult must come to terms with his or her responsibility to meet these needs, along with looking to institutions or social agencies for assistance. The previous meaning of family is further enlarged by the marriages of adult children, which create linkages to other family systems. The marriages of one's children also signal the beginning of a new family life cycle, and portend the birth of grandchildren who share in the heritages of two extended families.

The duration of this stage, between the leaving home of the last child and the death of one spouse, has increased since the first decade of the century from a median of less than two to almost 20 years. This reflects both the younger age of the mother when the last child leaves home and greater life expectancy. The smaller family, the greater employment of women, and the changing role definitions of women and men both before the launching period and continuing into the middle years have importance in shaping the activities and interests of the couple at midlife. These changes, which will be discussed in detail below, suggest that this stage of life deserves to be thought of more in terms of its own strengths and resources and less in terms of the "empty nest."

Schram (1979) states that research efforts in the area of families with grown children have been partial, inconclusive, and at times contradictory in their premises and subsequent findings. After reviewing literature on marital satisfaction for this stage, she concludes there are three competing descriptions of what happens for the couple in the post-child-rearing stage: (1) the "empty-next syndrome," which posits that there are problems for one or both of the parents; (2) the "curvilinear model," which claims increased freedom and independence for the couple; and (3) variations in marital satisfaction that are minor in nature. These competing explanations need further exploration. Certainly, for some families, reaching this stage may be seen as a time of fruition, completion, and a second opportunity to consolidate or expand by exploring new avenues and new roles. For others, taking a second look may lead to disruption (divorce and other problems) a sense of overwhelming loss (empty-nest syndrome), and general disintegration (illness and death). A broad theoretical model would postulate that families fall on a continuum of functioning. For the more functional families, rites of passage are dealt with as part of family life: the more dysfunctional families may find many of the nodal events to be either more disruptive or possibly conflictual. Many of these families have dealt with events during previous stages as "crises" of one kind or another. For still other families, previous stages have been completed with difficulty and unresolved problems have been brought along to the present stage. To some degree, within each stage there is a "recapitulation" of previous issues. In more functional families, issues get dealt with and resolved as they occur. The families seen in therapy may be those that are more likely to see the transition in negative terms, and to experience significant difficulty in accomplishing any or all of the above tasks.

While this chapter will take an intergenerational approach, it will focus

primarily on the middle generation, as their tasks relate to each other, their adult children, and their aging parents. Particular attention will be paid to the marriage itself, as well as coming to terms with aging parents, for it is the quality of those primary connections to the spouse and the family of origin that will determine how successfully the children will be "launched." The focus will be on those families in which both parents were present through the child-rearing stage and who are continuing together into the launching period. There is a fairly large population where divorce has occurred previously. Moreover, many of the divorced parents remarry rather quickly, creating "reconstituted families." In these and in one-parent families, there are extra tasks for this stage that are dealt with elsewhere in this book (McGoldrick & Carter, (U.S. Bureau of the Census, 1981).

The first section of the chapter will discuss demographic changes relating to this stage of the life cycle as they illuminate its various tasks. The second section will examine the four major tasks of the phase, and suggest some typical problems arising for families at this time. The third section will focus on clinical approaches to launching families. It is the thesis of the authors that thinking about this phase in terms of its unique challenges and possibilities can contribute greatly to effective treatment, and provide an opening for the resolution of what may well be long-standing difficulties in the family system.

DEMOGRAPHIC CHANGES

The most salient changes that can be statistically observed about this stage of the family life cycle are (1) the increased life expectancy in the general population, (2) the reduction in size of the nuclear family, (3) the increase in the number of women involved in the workforce, and (4) the increase in the divorce rate. Each of these changes reflects shifts in the general population that are manifested in changing attitudes, demands, and possibilities for this stage, and are felt with varying degrees of intensity by the individual families making this transition. The increased life expectancy is of primary importance, as the longevity of adults actually created this stage in the first place.

The Census Bureau 1981 special report on Americans during midlife includes in middle age all those between the ages of 45 and 64. In 1979 the middle-aged included 44 million persons, about 20% of the U.S. population. By the year 2010, the number will almost double, to 75 million, approximately 25% of the population. Not only is this group great in numbers, but it is also significant to our discussion that "nine out of every ten middle-aged persons currently live in families and the vast majority of them live with their spouses" (US Bureau of the Census, 1981).

The reduction in size of the nuclear family means that parents are finished with the primary task of launching children at an earlier age. An analysis of the

age of mothers at the time of various life events (Glick, 1977) highlights the increased duration of the post-child-rearing stage and permits some speculation about its significance. The median age of first marriage has remained fairly constant over the last 80 years (although increasing in recent years), as has the age of the mother at the birth of the first child. However, the age of the mother at the birth of the last child has dropped appreciably. The age of the mother when her last child marries has also dropped. Lastly, the age of the mother at the time of the death of her spouse has increased greatly. The last three points mean that at present people are facing much longer periods of marriage in the post-child-rearing stage.

In fact, this midlife stage might be considered as encompassing a two-part process. As described by Duvall (1971), these two stages are: (1) families as launching centers (the time from the first child's exit from the family until the last child leaves home) and (2) middle-aged parents (from the empty nest to retirement). Solomon (1973) addressed the processes involved, stating that the task for the parents involves "relinquishing the primary nature of the gratification involved in the role of parents. . . . This necessitates the existence of a stabilized marital relationship."

At present the time period between the departure of the last child and retirement is astonishingly long, making marital adjustment pivotal to this stage. The average couple today can anticipate 13 years together between the time their last child leaves home and retirement. Concurrent with this is a changing social emphasis on middle age as a time of new opportunities and life expansion. Marriage at this stage is beginning to reflect these changes. Couples run the gamut from those who seem contentedly to embrace middle age and live vicariously through married children and grandchildren to those in which one suddenly realizes that "life out there is beckoning." This realization can lead to overt conflict and a need for a different marital relationship.

The increase in divorce affects the family at nearly every stage of the life cycle. For the family entering this phase, when the couple's "mission" as parents appears complete, divorce offers one option for renegotiating an unsatisfactory relationship. Although most divorces occur in the first ten years of marriage, a recent survey showed that 11% of divorces and annulments during 1982 were for individuals who had been married 20 or more years (PHSVital Statistics of the United States, 1986). The present middle-aged generation was married at a time when divorce rates were much lower. These couples are therefore more likely to see divorce as a personal failure (Hagestad & Smyer, 1982). Hagestad and Smyer state that because most divorces occur in the 20s and 30s, those people divorcing after age 40 will experience less peer support. Moreover, "the prospects of new marital roles and relationships are drastically different for men and women, due to the combined effects of sex differences in the death rates and the double standard of aging. Men have a much larger pool of possible partners to choose from" (p. 167).

Middle-aged households are, in general, well off economically. The age group 45–54 had the highest mean household income ($31,516 in 1986) of any

age group (U.S. Bureau of the Census, 1986). Increased labor-force participation by women generally, and specifically in the 45–64 age range, represents another factor that is changing the economic situation of couples in the post-child-rearing period. In fact, 62.9% of all women 45–54 and 41.7% of all women 55–64 were in the labor force in 1984 (U.S. Bureau of the Census, 1986).

The kinds of work women are doing is relevant. In 1970 women represented 33.9% of all workers in managerial and professional occupations. In 1980 that had risen to 40.6%. In 1970 they represented 59% of the "technical sales and administrative support" positions in the workforce. In 1980 that figure was 64.4%. In the service occupations, women represent 58.9% of the total labor force. With children leaving home at this stage, many women may experience this transition as a release from the dual demands of family and career. But family needs do not cease as the children leave; the growing old-old population is presenting unprecedented dilemmas to the generation in the middle regarding caregiving responsibility and the nature of autonomy.

The questions these social changes raise are important. How will these changes affect the relationships between the adult generations? Are families in the midlife stage evolving a new role in overall family development? Will new family rituals as well as new roles be needed? The fact that technology and demographic changes have made this stage almost as lengthy as the child-rearing stage lends further impetus to the need for research on this period to help families negotiate their many transitions productively.

THE CHANGING FUNCTION OF MARRIAGE

The marital bond regains prominence at this time of transition. Many forces within the family system seem to accentuate the need to refocus, review, and often establish a different arrangement in the marriage. Letting go of child-rearing leaves more time available for couples to devote to self-reflection. With those couples for whom the rearing of children has been the central force organizing and maintaining their relationship, the task will involve a more drastic shift, requiring them to rethink the meaning of family, and in particular the meaning of marriage. In addition, the marriage of the children often propels the parents (and grandparents) to think about their own marriages. The death of an elderly parent, or a growing awareness of their frailties, further highlights the need to ensure a good quality to one's own life. For many individuals the shift has been gradual, or there does not seem to be a great urgency to change; for others, there seems to be a sudden awakening to some forgotten aspect of life, or an impulse to undertake some very different direction.

By this time the marriage has endured many shifts; from the more romantic, idealistic, and/or sexual emphasis, through the more prosaic, child-rearing, team-mate era. These previous sequences might have culminated in a rela-

tionship that is seasoned, stable, and more satisfactory than at any other time. It might also be more conflictual, more tenuous, and more alienated. In the absence of children, the conjugal bond, whatever its nature, will gain prominence. By the same token, more reliance on it will make existing strains more obvious.

Schram (1979), in reviewing research focused on this stage, suggests that the lessening of traditional sex role constraints in the post parental stage may be an important variable related to marital satisfaction. The couple may adopt either more constricted or more expanded roles. Greater freedom from parental responsibilities may prompt the husband toward expansion and the wife toward "holding on" to the marriage and her husband. On the other hand, the wife might start a move in the direction of expansion by pursuing a separate venture or career. If the marriage was based on her being adaptive, essentially a caretaker, and responsible for fulfilling most of the husband's wants, the shift will create an imbalance that will be keenly felt by the husband, and will contribute to temporary or extended disruption. Swensen, Eskew, and Kohlepp (1981) distinguish the more mature (postconformist) from the less mature (conformist) couples. They note that for the postconformists, relationships have more depth and there is more expression of love than at any other time in the life cycle. Conformists couples, however, reach this stage after having curtailed their individual development. For the conformist couples, the marital trajectory shows that "both the amount of love expressed between a husband and wife and the number of problems they have declines. That is, there appears to be less happening between them, for either good or ill" (p. 849). They add that in long-term conformist marriage, there seems to be less interaction, areas of conflict seem to be sealed off, and there is significantly less self-disclosure. Altman and Taylor (1973) and Bowen (1978) advance the notion that a combination of anxiety and immaturity will lead the members of a couple to veer away from potentially conflict-laden subjects to more emotionally safe areas, so as to limit exchanges that cause arguments. This veering away from each other may lead to emotional distance, physical distance, and the development of physical symptoms or continued "child" focus (Bradt & Moynihan, 1971). One obvious question is to what degree the marriage has accommodated the needs for intimacy and separateness. In other words, how well has the interdependency worked? Too much dependence may stress the bond in at least one partner (the more adaptive, usually the wife). Too much distance may make one partner feel "out of touch," "uncared for," leading to stress and dissatisfaction, which at this age may show up as physical symptoms.

At this age a relationship appears to exist between marital status and certain health indices. The psychophysiologist Lynch (1977) notes that "the single, the widowed, and the divorced were two to four times more likely than married people to die prematurely from hypertension, stroke and coronary heart disease." However, he states that "both the presence and the absence of human contact can be critical factors leading to disease and premature death." He adds that "the mere presence of another . . . is not an unmitigated blessing

. . . for unpleasant human interactions may even be physically destructive" (p. 121). Working with a family coping with a chronic illness at this stage is complex. Although the family may be struggling with ongoing difficulties antedating the onset of the illness, families will often use fear of stirring up illness-related repercussions as a reason for avoiding the underlying issues. Those who are able to take a productive and thoughtful role in relation to the disabilities or impending death of an elderly parent will often be more adaptive when it comes to dealing with these issues in themselves or in the spouse.

Marriage for certain families is synonymous with conflict; conflict represents a chief mechanism by which the family deals with anxiety and "undifferentiation" (Bowen, 1966). Chronic marital conflict may at this stage take the form of either overt warfare or silent distance. In such families individuals cannot live with, but cannot live without, their family relationships. However, even marital difficulties of long standing may be spurred toward change "in the course of events" when individuals come face to face with unavoidable transitions such as launching.

More often than not, the state of the marriage is a good measure of individual functioning and autonomy (Vaillant, 1977). However, demands at this stage pose different issues for the wife and for the husband and deserve separate consideration.

MATURITY AT MIDLIFE

Erickson (1964) first described the maturation pattern for individuals as it developed from identity formation in the adolescent to intimacy in early adulthood, and to generativity, or its obverse, stagnation, in midlife. Since then a number of authors have studied individuals at midlife and delineated and expanded our understanding of this stage. Male profiles have been studied by Levinson (1978) and Vaillant (1977), and female profiles by Gilligan (1982) and others. Common to authors describing middle age is the attempt to differentiate successful from unsuccessful outcomes, mature from immature profiles. Bowen (1978)—in a general description that cuts across gender and age lines—bases his definition of maturity or differentiation on how individuals have managed the individual/togetherness balance. Any individual stands at the apex of multiple family forces. Viewed in this manner, experiences with which individuals have to deal at any stage, and their outcome, will depend as much on what that individual's position has been in the family as on the events themselves. A common clinical finding is that individuals in one family seem able to sail through the different stages, where as for individuals in other families, their behavior seems more problem-prone in all the life-cycle transitions. For instance, in some families men in successive generations experience rather tumultuous changes at 40, whereas in other families men make the transition more gradually.

Gilligan (1982) conceptualizes that biological and psychological dicta direct women along a different developmental path than men. Relationships and attachments have primacy for women, and maturity is eventually reached by integrating this focus on intimacy with a capacity for autonomy and separateness. Neugarten (1976) states that to the extent that a woman has been able to build on her own individuality, major life transitions will be accomplished more smoothly. This suggests that the constricted cohort of women at this stage is composed of those who have built their lives by concentrating on the needs of family at the expense of their own needs. Unless they are able to continue to do so by caring for adult children and for grandchildren, the absence of offspring will in this case be experienced as attrition.

There have been too few comprehensive studies of this period of life. In one study Harkins (1978), reviewing a sample of 318 "normal" women, determined that effects of "empty nest" are slight and disappear within two years. She found no effect of the transition on the physical well-being and, in fact, a positive effect on psychological well-being. This same study suggests one clue as to what might be classified as the "intermediate" group—those having some difficulties with the transition. The only variable showing a relationship to adjustment was what she termed "being off schedule." She concluded, "The only threat to well-being may be in having a child who does not become successfully independent when expected" (p. 555). Glenn (1975) reported that "postparental" mothers experience greater happiness, enjoyment of life, and marital happiness than women of similar age who have a child at home. What we do not know is how many of these happier women considered by Glenn were in the workforce.

In the past two decades, the women's movement has provided added momentum in making women and men more aware of the possibilities for expansion within the marriage and in the wider world. More women have embraced possibilities for expansion into paid work. At present women make up approximately half of the labor force. Furthermore, women are increasingly defining careers as an important component in reaching optimal maturity. The most recent cohorts of middle-aged couples have shown a capacity to negotiate dual careers, and even commuter marriages, both of which require flexibility, creativity, and a capacity to be both independent and connected. In previous stages of the life cycle, dual careers might be a source of some anxiety in that work had to be balanced against the need for nurturing younger children. At this stage, however, both spouses are more able to pursue careers unhindered by the concerns associated with caring for youngsters. On the other hand, there is evidence that many women are continuing to take on responsibility for the growing elderly population. Moreover, women, who have heretofore expressed autonomy through voluntarism or part-time employment, discover a new kind of self-fulfillment by embracing work or career. For still another group of women who have considered work mostly in financial terms, this becomes the stage to pursue a better-defined career choice.

Male profiles have been studied by Levinson (1978) and Vaillant (1977). Vaillant (1977) reported that of 95 men, 26 reported stable marriages after an

average of 20 years. The author adds that "no single longitudinal variable predicted mental health as clearly as a man's capacity to remain happily married over time" (p. 320). Career goals, although not pursued with the same intensity of previous stages, are still very important in middle age. For many individuals careers continue along the same ascending line, as evidenced by job promotions, appointment to executive functions, wider recognition, and financial success. It was previously stated that individuals reach their peak, as measured by per capita income, at this period. However, it is also a crossroads for many who will feel that they have gone as far as they can go in their job (Levinson, 1977). As corporations and industry reorganize, some men become unemployed. If the wife is also working, the consequences may not be as deleterious as if the man is the main support. Also, the growing public consideration in the 1980s of early retirement may be experienced by some men as constricting, and by others as liberating. The more resourceful individuals will use these socially induced changes to reach new competence by developing heretofore unknown talents, or by setting out on a path to a new career. However, if the couple is continuing to provide financial assistance to grown children in graduate school, or to elderly parents for medical expenses, then these pressures may counter any inclination to make career changes at this stage.

Men who have single-mindedly pursued a career now face changes in self, family, and/or environment, and may realize the limited and limiting nature of their pursuits. Change seems essential. They may accomplish it by expanding or adding new activities to the existing one, or they may change careers altogether. In many instances the impetus to change is provided in the marriage. The wife may insist on and demand a different, deeper, more expansive relationship; formerly the husband would have resisted, but now he may be able to envisage change. At other times a momentum to change comes from some kind of temporary limitation, such as illness, mental fatigue, or unremitting job pressure (Vaillant, 1977). It should be noted that some men may experience the leaving of the children as a personal loss. Though more at a distance, they, too, may have perceived the raising of the children as a central purpose for their lives. Furthermore, children engaging in fully adult lives are a reminder to the parents that they are in the latter part of their own lives. The impact of losses and shifts that are occurring at this time are sometimes demonstrated indirectly through affairs, or emphasis on material possessions such as the purchase of sports cars or boats, or in some kind of acting out.

DEVELOPMENT OF ADULT RELATIONSHIPS
WITH GROWN CHILDREN

The existence of positive relationships with grown children represents the culmination of a long process of gradually "letting go," starting in childhood,

gaining momentum in adolescence, and leading to some kind of physical separation of the young adult through college or work. The completion of this process is what has been called "launching." Some indicators of successful separation in the young adult are acquisition of skills to embark on a job or career, independent living arrangements (or plans in this direction) and development of stable peer associations and of intimate relationships. Two subsequent developments—marriage and reproduction—balance out individual pursuits by building the "self–other" dimension that rounds out the development of the young adult.

If previous stages proceeded uneventfully, then at this point parents will be able to respond with support and interest to the new tasks undertaken by their children. They may acknowledge a "remembrance of things past," which usually does not interfere with launching. Positive attitudes of parents will vary, based on family norms. In some families choosing a college, a career, or a spouse is left largely up to the young adult. In other families the younger generation, or one of its members, is supposed to achieve many of the goals and aspirations for prior generations. When this dictum centers on one person, this particular individual, even though successful by all outward standards, may be "locked in" in much the same manner as a seemingly impaired child; however, these individuals and families have not been within the purview of mental health services.

There have been a variety of studies focused on the issues involved in launching children. Anderson et al. (1977) studied 100 asymptomatic families through self-reports. One of the questions asked parents how they expected they would feel when their children, now in adolescence, finally left home. The researchers found that "although 33 percent expected a loss of sense of family, 51 percent anticipated new opportunities and 21 percent even expected a sense of relief" at having completed this stage. For the last two groups, "the often cited empty nest syndrome did not appear to be a major problem."

The separation involved in launching the young adult seems, at first glance, to be an interaction primarily involving the young adult and his or her parents. In reality established multigenerational family patterns regarding the degree of autonomy allowed, and the ways in which it may be gained, are equally decisive. In some families there seem to be "loaded" and "freer" positions following definite patterns over the generations—for instance, oldest or youngest. In most families expectations seem to be quite different for men and for women. Extremes of closeness and distance between the older two generations will have a negative impact on launching. A middle-aged parent who has emotionally cut off from his or her parents will show heightened sensitivity to the separation of his or her children. Conversely, emotional overinvolvement of parents with their own aged parents can lead to problematic responses in their own children.

Once again the status of the marriage will play a major role in the outcome of this process. Solomon (1973) states that "if the solidification of the marriage has not taken place and reinvestment is not possible, the family usually

mobilizes itself . . . to hold on to the last child . . . prior to that, the family may avoid the conflict around separation by allowing one child to leave and subsequently focusing on the next in line" (p. 186). It is an axiom of family functioning that reciprocal dependence between parents and child will manifest itself as a focus on one of the children (Haley, 1980, p. 30).

Another common mechanism by which families deal with difficulties in "letting go" is by "cutting off" (emotionally and/or physically). Cutoff can look like emancipation but emotional dependence drives the process. Cutoff may involve one individual or a whole segment of the family. It may be triggered by any event, for example, the marriage of a young adult that is opposed by the parents, and it is particularly frequent after a death of an important family member, when underlying toxic issues have not been resolved. Similarly, families may be split into two clumps by matters involving estates, money, who was favored, or any conflictual issue with regard to which people cannot resolve their differences. Both cutoffs and polarization may last from weeks to years, depending on the existing anxiety and the triangles involved. Cutoffs over marriage are often the most pervasive, elusive, and difficult to surmount (Bowen, 1978).

Physical independence without the accompanying emotional autonomy could be defined as pseudolaunching. Running away from home by joining the armed forces, precipitous marriages, out-of-wedlock pregnancies, drug dependence, and alcohol abuse all point to difficulties with separation. The underlying dependence comes to light when the young adult gets into difficulties and needs to be "bailed out" by parents (Haley, 1980). Other variations of pseudolaunching are extended reliance on family for support (particularly financial) and returning home after a first stint at launching (in one family all three sons returned home after college, claiming that there were no jobs open to them). Vicissitudes in the marketplace will sometimes make it difficult to differentiate between family process and societal processes.

The most common pattern when trouble surfaces with the launching process is for parents to identify the problem as residing in the young adult. The history and the intensity of the difficulties will influence the degree of this projection. The parents typically adopt one of the following postures:

1. "It is a bolt out the blue." The family has regarded itself as highly functional and is "shocked" at the realization that something might be wrong. Here there had been an idealized way of dealing with life, an avoidance of conflict, and a premium placed on harmony and closeness and the successes of the young adult. Successful launching of the first child can prolong the myth of the "happy family."

2. At the other extreme is the family that has traditionally dealt with conflict by seeing it in one child. Symptomatic behaviour is treated as one more instance of a problem in that individual. A family approach will provide the opportunity to look at the youngster more broadly and address the systemic issues that keep the problem alive. However, knowledge of systems on

the part of the expert is not always sufficient to gain the family's acceptance of this view. A number of special strategic approaches have been developed to deal with strongly resistant families (Haley, 1973, 1980; Palazzoli et al., 1978; Wright et al., 1982).

3. "There's nothing wrong with it": here family and offspring coalesce to hold onto each other. The family where all three sons returned home, jobless, after college illustrates this. The mother, in a passionate discourse (silently supported by the father), provided all kinds of good reasons for her children to be home. What she did not discuss so clearly was that the marriage was stagnant and the presence of the sons provided a sense of vitality and movement otherwise lacking in the household.

4. "We thought we were finished with this." In these families the couple has been "looking forward to the time when the last child will leave home and become financially independent." Failure to launch may represent a transgenerational struggle. In other cases the young adults are responding to unresolved issues in either the total family or the couple. Motivation of parents to see the grown child go will be a powerful adjunct to successful outcome in these cases.

5. A less common problem involves emotional or physical symptoms in the parent. The most common version is some form of depression when the last child leaves. The profile is that of an individual (usually the mother) who has depended on her children for emotional sustenance and whose spouse is unwilling or unable to invest more in the marriage as the children grow up. In these cases launching is perceived very much as a loss. Sometimes the emotional or physical symptoms will act as a trigger to reinvolve the more distant spouse. When this is not the case, the symptoms may go unchecked. In some cases the perceived loss is dealt with by an affair, a separation, or a divorce.

6. An even more unusual pattern is one where a failure in emancipation alerts parents to problems in themselves. Motivation to explore the issue independently of the troubled young adult is in itself a positive sign and augers good progress.

REALIGNMENT OF RELATIONSHIPS TO INCLUDE IN-LAWS AND GRANDCHILDREN

The marriage plans of the young adult may generate trouble with the middle generation. These difficulties represent manifestations of unsuccessful separation between the middle-aged parents and their offspring. Incorporating in-laws will be more difficult when the offspring chooses a mate in a reactive or challenging stand taken against parents, and where the action appears to be a rejection of values the family holds as important (McGoldrick, Chapter 10). In other instances the young adult chooses the mate to fend off the family, and so the mate is literally a wedge against the family. Very often this mate will

embrace the negative views that the adult child/partner has of the family. It is rare that difficulties with in-laws are not displacements from long-standing unresolved family problems. Conflicts may be expressed in terms of which set of parents is favored, or in a tug of war over which set of parents will be visited for the holidays, and so on.

Marriage represents one of the main transitions for the young adult and creates a common denominator between the generations. The middle generation faces the task of "coming to terms" with new levels or conditions of attachment in the marriages of the other two generations. Problems the middle generation has in adjusting to the married state of the new generation may range from one extreme of too much interference to the other of feeling that their children no longer need them and thus they feel superfluous, unwanted, or displaced. For the middled-aged couple, marriage of a child will set in motion a whole host of reflections, feelings, and strong emotions, depending on the state of their own marriage. By the same token, witnessing how successfully or unsuccessfully the older generation is coping with changes in the conditions of their marriage will provide a glimpse into their own (middle-aged) future.

Birth of the fourth generation leads to a new state of relatedness; children become parents; siblings become aunts and uncles, parents become grandparents. Feikema (1978) has elaborated on the meaning of this transition for the family system. As is true for other markers in this stage, the grandparenting function has wide variations (Hagestad, 1985; Bengston, 1985). For many families this role is steeped in tradition. Grandparents are authority figures who help the parents with the socialization of children by articulating expectations regarding them. For other families, especially in the case of younger grandparents, the role is more of "fun seeking" (Neugarten, 1976), where the adult joins the grandchild for the specific purpose of having fun. Other functions that grandparents seem to serve are "as an indicator of intergenerational continuity or as a buffer against the family's potential mortality" (Bengston, 1985, p. 25). Another is one of "family watchdog," a third is that of "arbitrator . . . in issues of intergenerational continuity," and finally as "figures in the social construction of biography for younger family members, interpreting and giving meaning to the personal past" (Bengston, 1985, p. 25). For some families, when they live in the same physical location, some grandparents serve either a temporary or regular babysitting function. In any case it is increasingly clear that the grandparents have important functions in the life cycle of their grandchildren (Blau, 1984).

RESOLVING ISSUES WITH THE OLDER GENERATION

In the bulk of work with adults in the middle years, there seems to be "unfinished business" of all gradations with their parents. In some cases the

unfinished business may take a new form upon the death of a parent. The underlying dynamic is a failure in successfully separating emotionally from the parents. This is operative in varying degrees with all families. Unfinished business blocks both generations from accomplishing the expected tasks of that particular life stage.

The life issues that the older generation are tackling—for instance, retirement, financial security, increased time together, decreased physical functioning, and an increase of physical symptoms—will all have an impact on the middle generation. Women are almost always the physical and emotional caretakers in the family, while men often take most of the financial responsibility. The problems of aging in the older generation, not only have to be dealt with, but they also portend the problems that their middle age children will soon face themselves. Death of one spouse is one of the major tasks facing older adults. Neugarten (1976) found that the elderly spouses' reactions to death cover a wide range. She concluded that a considerable number of elderly show great acceptance, and in these cases the death causes little disruption. All of the above will require decisions about autonomous living versus moving in with a middle-aged son or daughter, or selecting a nursing home. The state of intergenerational relatedness will affect these decisions. Conflict in the middle or younger generations usually has a negative impact on older adults. Realistic interdependence with the rest of the family will be conducive to less stress and/or better stress management in the older generation.

In some instances the adults minimize the elderly parent's concerns about his or her life situation, and become impatient or in other ways deny the aged person's perceptions. The clinician can gear the adults to concentrate on what triggers their evasive or angry responses to older family members. In most cases it relates to an inability on the part of the son or daughter to accept the parent on the parent's own terms, and feeling enveloped by the parent's negativity. In a study of adult Jewish-American children of aging parents, Simos (1973) found that the middle-aged adults felt guilty and powerless to help if their parents were depressed and unhappy. Aging parents may sense their children's confusion, but misinterpret it as rejection. When the son or daughter can become less critical and feel less responsible for their parents' happiness, the parents will often take a less negative view of their own lives.

Individuals in the middle generation may also have trouble with what they consider the parents' uninvolved, uncaring, or sometimes rejecting attitudes toward their own difficulties. Many times these feelings are prompted by the grandparents' responses to the vagaries of the growing grandchildren. The unspoken or perceived criticism from grandparents that parents have been too lax or incompetent will cause strife in the relationship. Being able to hear the grandparents' criticism as a measure of their interest, and an expression of their anxiety, will usually help the middle-aged parents respond less defensively.

For the middle-aged person, a major transition occurs with the death of elderly parents. This can involve awareness of new responsibilities as the lead

generation and heightened awareness of their own mortality. For the middle-aged child, death of an older parent need not be a crisis. In support of this notion, Neugarten (1976) describes the attitudes of functional families toward these deaths as more of a natural happening. Problems arise when general relationship difficulties in the family have not been resolved. For some families the overriding reaction to the death of the parent is guilt, which signals unresolved issues. Guilt is not necessarily related to having been distant or in conflict with a parent. Often it is seen in those who have been overresponsible for and overinvolved with parents for a greater portion of their lives. Another issue, common for family caregivers, is resentment toward their siblings, who are often minimally involved and apparently lacking in anxiety regarding the parents' care.

Finally, when family members are unable to deal with the issue of loss of the grandparents, the unresolved issues are likely to reappear in some other form. Bowen (1978) has written about pervasive chain reactions after certain deaths, much like "shock wave effects." Orfanidis (1977) and Walsh (1978), in their studies of families of schizophrenics, have independently noted that the death of a grandparent marks as special the child born around that time. In these cases such connections and the impact of the death are denied by the family. Many factors may be associated with the toxicity surrounding a death. As with other life events, general flexibility of the system, its openness, and the level of functioning maturity are the most significant factors (Bowen, 1978; McGoldrick & Walsh, 1984; Paul & Paul, 1982).

CLINICAL CONSIDERATIONS

A three-generational view of this midlife stage orients us to issues that exist between nuclear and extended families. The degree of success that the parents have demonstrated in dealing with issues of autonomy, responsibility, and connectedness with their respective families of origin will have definitive impact on their success in handling these issues with their grown children. This framework does not merely reframe the presenting problem as part of a historical overview, but subtly changes the family members' outlook from the problem and crisis to one of context.

The family life cycle perspective transforms the experience of the family members from a narrow focus on a problem or crisis to a process orientation involving succeeding generations. When one sees himself or herself as part of a larger whole, the sense of being overwhelmed may lessen. Also, the feelings of guilt or fault, common to the early phase of therapy, may be replaced by a gradual recognition of how the family influences and shapes behavior.

By the same token, the larger framework enables the therapist to be less at the mercy of the opposing forces that seem to polarize family members into

different camps or opposing causes and that provide wide oscillations from one generation to the next: the grandfather being a heavy drinker, the father being a teetotaler, and the grandson drinking heavily again in the course of three successive generations (Carter, 1976). A different view of issues and symptoms as part of a larger whole sets the present experience (heretofore defined as pathological, intractable, or hopeless) within the context of a natural (or at least understandable) occurrence.

Underlying unresolved issues may be triggered in any of the three generations. Depending on the degree of anxiety generated, all three subsystems may respond with accompanying shifts or upsets of the family equilibrium. The following case examples by no means convey the full range of possibilities, but are suggestive of the scope and interrelatedness of events in any family. The first (Figure 13-1) highlights how a family that had been outwardly successful in dealing with previous stages—mainly through insistence on togetherness and conformity—experience a "rude awakening" during the launching of the last child. Failure to emancipate turned out to be secondary to unresolved marital familial issues of long standing.

About seven years previously, Mrs. Doane, a woman in her 40s, had consulted a therapist about problems with her younger daughter Lily, aged 21. Her older daughter had graduated from college and was living away, but Lily was floundering, both about career and life away from home. She had moved back home after two unsuccessful stints at college. She was excessively dependent and demanding of Mrs. Doane, who resented her daughter's intrusiveness and constant bids for attention. Mrs. Doane regarded Lily's move back home as impulsive and her unsuccessful college career as immature. She did not see problems in herself, her husband, or her marriage. After three sessions she claimed she knew what to do about Lily, and promised to return if she needed to.

Six months later she returned to therapy announcing that her husband had suddenly left her, calmly stating that he needed a separation "for himself." He provided no further explanation. She was at a loss to understand his behavior and was quite depressed. She subsequently learned that her husband's departure followed a yearlong affair with a woman in her 20s. Mr. Doane's actions were in sharp contrast with his previous behavior; he had been a "good" son, following in his father's footsteps by working in the business the father had created, and had been a "perfect" husband and father. Then, shortly after his father's death, he plunged into an artistic venture that he enjoyed. There he met this new woman. He was experiencing a strong desire to "leave everything behind" and start a new life. It was three years ago, when he first started to pull away from his wife, that Lily had moved back into the family.

Before discussing the therapeutic course, a few reflections on the marriage are in order. In marrying her husband, Mrs. Doane had hoped to attain what she thought his family represented: a happy family and pillars in the community. Her own parents had a conflictual relationship and struggled to make ends meet. She was the most forceful and functional one in her family, and had made it through college on her own resources. She saw the Doanes as a much better fit for her than her own family. She became more of a Doane than the Doanes. Interestingly enough, even though Mrs. Doane had been successful in her career as a school counselor, she had seen herself as first and foremost a wife. Thus by far the greater portion of her thoughts and efforts had been geared toward making both extended and nuclear families "happy." In short, her self-concept and self-esteem were attained mostly by "being for" and "doing for" others.

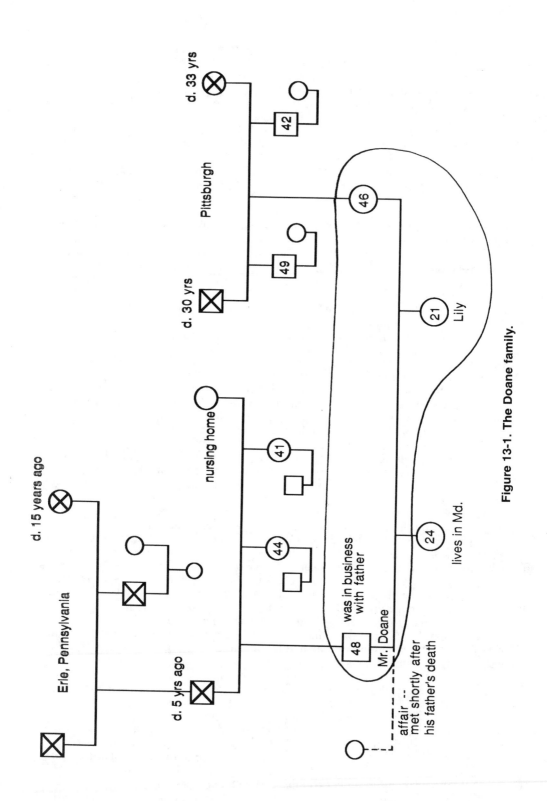

Figure 13-1. The Doane family.

Erie, Pennsylvania

d. 15 years ago

nursing home

Pittsburgh

d. 30 yrs

d. 33 yrs

d. 5 yrs ago

42

49

46

21
Lily

41

44

24
lives in Md.

48
Mr. Doane

was in business
with father

affair --
met shortly after
his father's death

301

Mrs. Doane held strong implicit views regarding marriage. One was the assumption that her husband reciprocated and shared her outlook and priorities. A natural extension was that his priorities would remain stable and unchanged over time. A touchstone for these beliefs was the sanctity of marriage. Therefore, the seemingly sudden turn of events found Mrs. Doane emotionally ill-equipped to deal with the martial difficulties. She was overcome by an powerful sense of betrayal, which she experienced as shock and numbness. These initial responses were followed by equally strong feelings of upheaval and confusion: "Where have I gone wrong?"

This is a common scenario for families facing similar situations. Like the majority of women of her cohort, Mrs. Doane had engaged her capabilities and resourcefulness in the service of the family. Moreover, in the past the hints of any difficulty had led her to try harder. She was pained and felt loaded with the responsibility for trying to figure out the whole upheaval. In his turn Mr. Doane felt he had abrogated his own ideas and wants in an effort to satisfy his wife. It was after the death of his father, the person who had most strongly influenced his responses to others, that Mr. Doane was catapulted into seeking a transformation in his life, culminating with an affair. To his wife Mr. Doane seemed "outward bound" and unconcerned about the result of his actions. He disavowed his own initiative, and failed to express his own views, particularly as they related to his ill-defined discontent with the marriage.

In keeping with the family dynamics and her socialization as a woman, Mrs. Doane was the one to seek and pursue therapy, a common clinical finding for a woman in her position (Lerner, 1985). Therapy had the encompassing goal of allowing her to apprehend the problem by understanding her functioning in the context of the family. Without disavowing her hurt and pain, she was given the opportunity to explore it as it shed light on her relationship with important others. For a woman who had prided herself on her ability to resolve difficulties, her husband's affair made her feel a failure and lowered her confidence. Underlying these hurts had been covert blame and anger. Anger, as in many other cases (Lerner, 1985), was tempered by insight that she had allowed some important dimensions of her sense of self to be submerged, and the ensuing realization that she would have to "let go" of some of her old feelings, thoughts and coping mechanisms.

As expected, when Mrs. Doane was able to let go of the need to "hold on" to the marriage, her husband started making moves to reengage her. She was considering for the first time whether or not she wanted to stay in the marriage. The extent to which individuals can redefine their life course by attending to matters that are important to them will auger well for progress for therapy. Mr. Doane had to deal with the realization that he, too, was in danger of losing his spouse. The separation, besides being a hindrance, became an opportunity to take a second look at the marriage and at the range of aspects, that had not worked. The new arrangement had to include both members' new perceptions. His wife's newly found autonomy required that Mr. Doane deal with her and the relationship in a new way. Mr. Doane found that he had less need to keep himself unavailable. He was coming to grips with his perceived needs, and with what he could realistically expect from himself, from the affair, and from the marriage. The couple agreed that Mr. Doane move back home after six months of conjoint therapy. As soon as he moved back, Lily found her wings, and began a process that led toward a career, and eventually marriage. Since this family was first presented (McCullough, 1980), Mrs. Doane has continued on a course of self-definition. After 15 years as a school counselor, she decided to become an independent entrepreneur, established her own advertising firm, and found increasing satisfaction in this new vocation. Her concerns over the marriage have not completely disappeared, but she feels much more able to deal with both her feelings and with her husband.

The Doanes exemplify some central therapeutic considerations in dealing with

these issues. If the therapist assumes the existence of a strong interdependence among all involved family members, an interdependence that is being taxed from different angles, this approach can be helpful in settling down the crisis. The rejected spouse can be helped to defocus the affair and to view it as part of a larger process. If this spouse becomes less critical and concentrates on improving his or her part in the relationship, then the other spouse may, in turn, realize that the affair is only one of many issues in the system. In such cases the chances to resolve both the separation and the affair are considerably enhanced. The therapist's knowledge that temporary strain often accompanies the movement toward a new level of individual autonomy and higher functioning for the family will serve as an important adjunct in allaying anxiety, mistrust, and anger.

Marital strife tends to be particularly vitriolic at this stage of life. Guerin (1982) conceptualizes four stages of marital conflict, adding that knowledge of the stage of conflict will facilitate prognosis and aid in predicting pitfalls. In those marriages in which an "emotional divorce" has been in operation for a protracted length of time, or in which one of the protagonists perceives divorce as the answer to all existing troubles, the focus may be less on reviving the marriage and more on calming down and easing the separating process.

Another version of family interaction is one that fixes responsibility for parent and offspring with the middle generation. This book has made plain that the separation involved in launching only *seems* to involve primarily the young adults and their parents. In reality established multigenerational family patterns regarding the degree of autonomy allowed, and the ways in which it may be gained, are equally decisive. The following vignette attests to an instance where failure of the parents-in-the-middle to separate successfully from their own parents contributed to impairment in their adult daughter. Furthermore, for the Bartok family, responsibility for both elderly parents and offspring was fixed on the middle generation.

Dr. and Mrs. Bartok were referred to the office by a psychiatrist who was treating their 23-year-old daughter, Laura. Laura had returned home to live after having failed college in the middle of her sophomore year. She was largely nonfunctional and had few friends or outside interests. A review of the various subsystems revealed that the father, a physician, had rather stilted, impersonal relations with both of his parents and his only sister. He maintained a seemingly detached attitude toward his wife and children, but was also dependent on his wife, and he was overly responsive to her criticism. Mrs. Bartok, on her part, had a history of close involvement with her parents and her children. After the death of her father two years earlier, she had become her "mother's keeper." Her mother's intense dependency and demands triggered resentment and guilt in Mrs. Bartok, reactions she also had toward her daughter. Dr. Bartok's aloofness further taxed the intense emotional fusion in the system, and thus perpetuated the dysfunctional circularity.

This example highlights interlocking generational issues. The most striking is a pattern often found in families of impaired offspring: not only does the young one fail to individuate, but there is often a recurrence of that failure in several generations. The death of her father left Mrs. Bartok, the oldest daughter in that generation, responsible for her mother. The fact that Laura was the only daughter in the next generation contributed to making her the focus in the next generation. The failure of Laura to emancipate left Mrs. Bartok apparently "in charge" here, as well. The pattern was a reciprocal one in which Dr. Bartok abrogated his emotional responsibilities for the family.

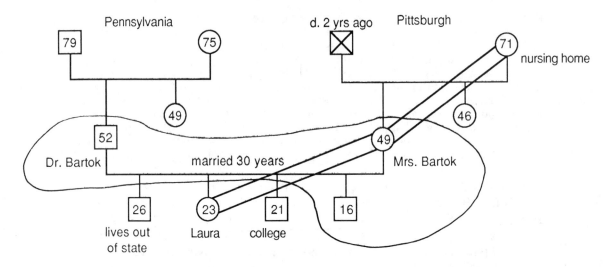

Figure 13-2 The Bartoks.

Despite the presenting problem of an impaired young adult, initial moves in therapy were oriented toward addressing the marital imbalance, which had made Mrs. Bartok the one responsible for all relationships. Dr. Bartok, in spite of a pattern of dealing with emotional issues chiefly through denial and withdrawal, was willing to become more available to the whole family. Therefore, he was actively engaged in plans that needed to be made regarding his mother-in-law and his daughter, Laura. Moreover, issues between the couple were brought to the fore and addressed. Mrs. Bartok remained disappointed in her husband's tendency to become passive and unavailable, but he was somewhat more able to verbalize his care and concern so she did not feel so overburdened and helpless. A fair amount of work was devoted to helping Mrs. Bartok let go of her feelings of not having any choice regarding her mother. Her husband's increased availability and her ability to enlist her younger sister's involvement in locating the best nursing home, finally allowed Mrs. Bartok to tackle this sensitive issue. The therapeutic effort focused on coming to terms with the marriage and overcoming the guilt of separating from her mother. The accompanying emotional readjustment gave the parents new momentum to take a stance with Laura and "push her out of the nest."

Mrs. Bartok decided to join the labor market, becoming employed in a private health center where she had previously served as a volunteer. In spite of not having employed for over 20 years, she found the work challenging and made a good adjustment.

It is worthy of note that unless the therapist is aware of interlocking triangles, problems with the older generation may go untouched and unnoticed for a long time. Particularly where there has been some version of a "cutoff" between the middle-aged person and parent(s), the resulting resentment and or guilt may make the subject unbroachable. This was not the case with the Bartok family. Although they did not present their issues with Mrs. Bartok's mother immediately, neither did they attempt to deny them. Mrs. Bartok's mother, although evidencing some signs of mental impairment, was still able to recognize her loved ones and her surroundings, but impaired enough that she could not accept the serious curtailment of her capacity to care for herself. Given this situation, she and her daughter both responded to the pattern in their family, and the pattern in society—the older

woman expected her daughter to care for her and Mrs. Bartok became the caretaker.

How to include the elderly in plans that affect them is no easy matter. Very often, in the absence of therapy or exposure to what is entailed in the aging process, many caretakers respond to the elderly person's demands as unreasonable. Furthermore, their signs of disorientation or senility can be seen as ploys to keep the upper hand, or worse, as ways to punish and upset their families. If the person traditionally in the caretaking role is motivated to untangle family themes and the proclivities in self that foster and maintain the behavior, then in time anger or fear of hurting the older parent is replaced by a more realistic approach to the situation.

The "stuck together" condition between middle-aged people and their parents, or the failure to reach a more functional emancipation, may take more subtle forms. Numerous indicators signal this pattern—inability or reluctance to disclose important aspects of one's life, or discuss emotionally laden subjects, or incapacity to take a stand or come to some resolution around important points of disagreement. The therapist's orientation will predicate how this process will be addressed. A more encompassing view can often be reached if the client can take a position of standing back, letting go, or reaching some more realistic attachment with parents, and children and spouse. Some family therapists believe that the matter of emancipation merits more specific approaches to deal with the issue (Williamson, 1981; Framo, 1976). In the above histories, both Mr. Doane and Dr. Bartok showed signs of arrested emancipation but an equal denial that the transgenerational issues were part of therapy. Mr. Doane related to his mother in a rather circumspect fashion punctuated by infrequent contact (the mother lived in a retirement village). Otherwise he was in good contact with a sister and closely involved with a cousin, with whom he worked. Except for some efforts to clarify work issues with the latter, Mr. Doane would not modify any fundamental patterns with his mother. As for Dr. Bartok, he was instrumentally more available to his parents, but shared little of his personal life. The more substantial changes were for his nuclear family, but little was changed with his parents.

Of equal importance in dealing with separation from parents, or perhaps a specific demonstration of the process, is dealing with the impending death of one, or both, parents. In the more functional families, matters relating to death, such as wills, executors, and the like, transpire over a long period of time. The onset of critical illness and impending death are sometimes more difficult for the son or daughter to absorb. Clinically the optimal result is achieved if the client is aware of the importance for himself or herself of addressing the situation and his or her feelings with an ailing parent. Fears of making the situation worse, of not knowing the "right way" or the right words, or of taking hope away from the ill member are some of the forms in which individuals couch their anxieties and hesitations. In therapy the unresolved parts of the relationship can be brought out in bold relief. Some are painfully aware that discussing personal matters was not part of the relationship; for

others the realization is one of too much existing emotion, with the accompanying fears of being overwhelmed, of crying, or of totally losing control. The therapeutic focus is to help the individual obtain a better grasp of the situation, and his or her role in it, and to encourage personal contact and communication with the members of the extended family. Furthermore, the individual in middle age can learn a lot for herself or himself while supporting elderly parents through their life review. This entails encouraging older people to ponder out loud what their lives have meant, what their successes and failures have been, and who the significant people involved were. Nevertheless, it is not universal that elderly persons want to reflect on or review their lives openly. The important point is that what elderly people appreciate is a friendly and accepting person, rather than somebody who will attempt to reassure or convince them that things were really better or different than their perceptions.

It is not essential to have the older generation in the room to resolve unfinished business. It suffices to coach the motivated middle-aged adult to engage in different behavior. Also, this middle generation varies considerably in the motivation to modify patterns. Death of the parents seems to compound the difficulties. This finding is consistent with Bowen's (1978) belief that the probability of successfully resolving past problems seems to diminish with the death of both parents.

An interesting clinical finding is that the death of a parent may also resolve an attachment and help the offspring feel more responsible for self, providing him or her with a never known sense of freedom. In some cases (McCullough, 1978), it can propel this middle-aged individual into a veritable metamorphosis.

In relation to the young adult who becomes identified as the problem, the two clinical examples illustrate some of the outstanding dynamics. One overall principle is that the young adult "stuck" in the parental triangle will have the most difficulties around launching, although in some families each youngster may have difficulty with this task. Concentrating efforts on areas other than the offspring will often ameliorate, and sometimes resolve, problems with the impaired young adult. Success in approaching the issue of a "problem" adult child depends to some extent on the capacity to determine the function that the symptomatic behavior serves for the family, as well as the position that the problem-prone adult holds. The triangled child is often the most dysfunctional member of the family. In most instances the "stuck" young adult seems to be satisfied with letting the parents be primary movers in therapy.

Finally, Friedman (Chapter 6) points out that family rituals and rites of passage around engagements, marriage, birth, and death can give people an opportunity to work out previous unfinished business. We have found this to be true, particularly in those cases where the person is motivated for an ongoing venture or engagement with the extended family.

SUMMARY

The post-child-rearing stage is often a time of consolidation, and functioning, as expressed by experience and maturity, and financial solvency (in the middle and upper classes) is generally at its peak. With the child-rearing period behind them, parents can look forward to realizing their full potential. Difficulties at this stage relate to reworking of the marital bonds, as well as the bonds with their parents and their offspring, and adding the new roles of "inlaws" and "grandparents." Most individuals in the middle generation lose one or both parents at this juncture, and they themselves become the older generation.

Thinking about families within a life cycle framework clarifies the predictable tasks to be accomplished at a given stage. The use of the intergenerational dimension offers a means for tracing familial patterns that indicate how the family has traditionally dealt with transitions, especially separations. Experience bears out the principle that whenever there is a serious family problem at this stage—even when there had been no previous evidence of turmoil—there are always preexisting dysfunctional patterns in the family system.

REFERENCES

Altman, I. & Taylor, D. (1973). *Social penetration: The development of interpersonal relationships.* New York: Holt, Rinehart & Winston.

Anderson, C. A., et al. (1977, October). A computer analysis of marital coping styles in families of children of normal and atypical development. Unpublished paper presented at the American Academy of Child Psychiatry Annual Meeting, Houston, Texas.

Bengston, V. L. (1985). Diversity and symbolism in the grandparental roles. In V. L. Bengston (Ed.), *Grandparenthood.* Beverly Hills, Calif.: Sage Publications.

Blau, T. (1984). An evaluation study of the role of the grandparent in the best interests of the child. *American Journal of Family Therapy* 12/4:46–50.

Bowen, M. (1966). The use of family therapy in clinical practice. *Comprehensive Psychiatry* 7:345–374.

Bowen, M. (1978). *Family therapy in clinical practice.* New York: Jason Aronson.

Bradt, J. O., & Moynihan, C. J. (1971). Opening the safe—the child focused family. In J. O. Bradt and C. J. Moynihan (Eds.), *Systems therapy.* Washington, D.C.: Groome Child Guidance Center.

Carter, E. A. (1978). Transgenerational scripts and nuclear family stress: Theory and clinical implications. In R. Riley (Ed.), *Georgetown family symposia:,* Vol. 3 (1975–76), Georgetown University.

Duvall, E. (1971). *Family development.* Philadelphia: J. B. Lippincott.

Erikson, E. (1964). *Childhood and society.* New York: Norton.

Feikema, R. J. (1979). Birth and the addition of a new generation and its impact on a family system. In P. McCullough & J. C. Carolin (Eds.) *Second Pittsburgh Family Systems Symposium: A Collection of Papers.* University of Pittsburgh.

Fogarty, T. (1973–78). On emptiness and closeness, Part 1, Part II. "The best of the family." New Rochelle: Center for Family Learning.

Framo, J. (1976) Family of origin as a therapeutic resource for adults in the marital and family therapy: You can and should go home again. *Family Process* 15(2): 193–210.

Gilligan, C. (1982). *In a different voice*. Cambridge, Mass.: Harvard University Press.

Glenn, N. (1975). Psychological well-being in the postparental stage: Some evidence from national surveys. *Journal of Marriage and the Family* 37 (1): 105–110.

Glick, P. (1977). Updating the life cycle of the family. *Journal of Marriage and the Family* 39(1): 5–13.

Guerin, P. (1982). The stages of marital conflict. *The Family* 10(1): 15–26.

Hagestad, G. O. (1985). Continuity and connectedness. In V. L. Bengston (Ed.), *Grandparenthood*. Beverly Hills, Calif.: Sage Publications.

Hagestad, G. O. & Smyer, M. A. (1982). Dissolving long-term relationships: Patterns of divorcing in the middle age. In S. Duck (Ed.), *Personal relationships 4: Dissolving personal relationships*. New York: Academic Press.

Haley, J. (1973). *Uncommon therapy: The psychiatric techniques of Milton H. Erikson*. New York: Norton.

Haley, J. (1980). *Leaving home: The therapy of disturbed young people*. New York: McGraw-Hill.

Harkins, E. (1978). Effects of the empty nest transition: A self report of psychological well-being. *Journal of Marriage and the Family* 40(3): 549–556.

Lerner, H. (1985). *The dance of anger*. New York: Harper & Row.

Levinson, D. J. (1978). *The seasons of a man's life*. New York: Knopf.

Lynch, J. J. (1977). *The broken heart: The medical consequences of loneliness*. New York: Basic Books.

McCullough, P. (1980). Launching children and moving on. In E. Carter & M. McGoldrick (Eds.), *The family life cycle: A framework for the family therapy*. New York: Gardner Press.

McGoldrick, M., & Walsh, F. F. (1984). A systematic view of family history and loss. In Aronson and Woldberg (Eds.), *Group and family therapy*. New York: Brunner/Mazel.

Neugarten, B. (1976). Adaption and life cycle. *The Counseling Psychologist* 6(1).

Orfanidis, M. M. (1977). Some data on death and cancer in schizophrenic families. Paper presented at the Georgetown Family Symposium, Washington, D. C.

Palazzoli, S. M. , Cecchin, G., Prata, G., & Boscolo, L. (1978). *Paradox and counterparadox*. New York: Jason Aronson.

Paul, N. L. & Paul, B. B. (1982). Death and changes in sexual behavior. In Froma Walsh (Ed.), *Normal family processes*. New York: Guilford Press.

Schram, R. (1979). Marital satisfaction over the family life cycle: A critique and proposal. *Journal of Marriage and the Family* 41(1): 7–12.

Simos, B. G. (1973). Adult children and their aging parents. *Social Work* 18: 78–85.

Solomon, M. (1973). A developmental conceptual premise for family therapy. *Family Process* 12(2): 179–188.

Swensen, C. H., Eskew, R. W., & Kohlepp, K. A. (1981). Stage of family life cycle, ego development, and the marriage relationship. *Journal of Marriage and the Family* 43(4): 841–853.

U.S. Bureau of the Census (1981). Social and economic characteristics of Americans during midlife. June 1981. Current Population Reports, Series P-23, No. 11, Washington, D. C.: U.S. Government Printing Office.

U.S. Bureau of the Census (1986). Statistical abstract of the United States. Washington, D. C.: U.S. Government Printing Office.

U.S. National Center for Health Statistics (1986). Vital statistics of the United States: 1982, Vol. III, Marriage and Divorce. DHHS Pub. No. (PHS) 86–1103. Public Health Service. Washington, D. C.: U.S. Government Printing Office.

Vaillant, G. E. (1977). *Adaptation to Life*. Boston: Little, Brown.

Walsh, F. W. (1978, December). Concurrent grandparent death and the birth of a schizophrenic offspring: An intriguing finding. *Family Process* 17(4): 457–463.

Williamson, D. (1981). Termination of the intergenerational hierarchial boundary between

the first and second generations: A new stage in the family. *Journal of Marital and Family Therapy* 7(4): 441–452.

Wright, L. M., Hall, J. S., O'Connor, M., Perry, R. & Murphy, R. (1982). The power of loyalties: One family's developmental struggle during the launching years. *Journal of Strategic and Systemic Therapies* 1(4): 57–70.

CHAPTER 14

The Family in Later Life

Froma Walsh, M.S.W., Ph.D.

> Old age. We dread becoming old almost as much as
> we dread not living long enough to reach old age.
> The elderly in our society have been stereotyped
> and dismissed as old-fashioned, rigid, senile, boring,
> useless, and burdensome.

In defiance of such negative cultural expectations and constraints new images
of the elderly have emerged in such films as "Trip to Bountiful," "Harold and
Maude," and "Harry and Tonto." Each film reflects and fosters a growing
sensitivity to a person who is attempting, with courage and daring, to adapt to
losses and challenges of later life in ways that fit needs for self-identity,
satisfying companionship, and meaningful experience.

Yet rarely in the media are options seen for healthy later-life adjustment
within family and social context. Instead the elderly person is seen to be
marginal to the social community and each finds solutions only by choosing to
become more deviant, by breaking with society altogether, and even by flaunt-
ing legal, moral, or sexual codes. Notably the elderly are portrayed as widowed, and either as having no family or as taking flight from the family.

Pessimistic views of the family in later life prevail. Myths hold that most
elders either have no families or, at best, have infrequent, obligatory, and
conflictual contact; that adult children don't care about their aged parents and
abandon them or dump them in institutions; and that families in later life are
too set in their ways to change long-standing interaction patterns. Through
such misconceptions the family in later life, like the older individual, has been
stereotyped and dismissed.

In fact, family relationships continue to be important throughout later life
for most adults in our society. Seventy percent live with spouses or other
relatives, including children, siblings, and aged parents. The proximity of
family members and contact by telephone are especially important to those
who live alone, 80% of whom are more elderly women, typically widowed.
Most of those with children report that a child could be there within minutes if
needed and tend to maintain at least weekly contact; only 3% never see a child.

Thus total isolation is rare. Although most older adults prefer to maintain households separate from adult children, nevertheless frequent contact, reciprocal emotional ties, and mutual support bonds are sustained by most families in a pattern that has been aptly termed "intimacy at a distance" (Blenkner, 1965; Butler & Lewis, 1983; Spark & Brody, 1970; Taeuber, 1983; Treas, 1977; Troll, 1971; Streib & Beck, 1981). Moreover, a preponderance of evidence indicates a link between social contact, support, and longevity: the vast majority of elders who visit with friends and family often are likely to live longer than those who seldom have contact.

The family as a system, along with its elder members, confronts major adaptational challenges in later life. Changes with retirement, widowhood, grandparenthood, and illness require family support, adjustment to loss, reorientation, and reorganization. Past and current family relationships play a critical role in the resolution of the major psychosocial task of later life, the achievement of a sense of integrity versus despair regarding the acceptance of one's own life and death (Erikson, 1959). The salient transitions and tasks of later life hold potential for loss and dysfunction, but also for transformation and growth.

The mental health field, unfortunately, has not given sufficient attention to the later phases of individual and family life, despite the fact that adults over 65 are the group most susceptible to mental illness (Butler & Lewis, 1983). The incidence of psychopathology increases with age, particularly organic brain disease and functional disorders such as depression, anxiety, and paranoid states. Suicide also rises with age, with the highest rate among elderly white men. While older adults comprise 11% of our population, they account for 25% of all suicides. Many disturbances are associated with difficulties in family adaptation to the transitions and tasks of later life.

LATER-LIFE TRANSITIONS AND TASKS

Launching: Setting the Stage

Each family's response to later-life challenges evolves from earlier family patterns developed for stability and integration. How the family and its members cope depends largely on the type of system they have created over the years and the ability and modes of the system to adjust to losses and to new demands. Certain established patterns, once functional, may become dysfunctional with the changing life cycle of members.

Launching of the last child from home sets the stage for family relations in the second half of life (Deutscher, 1964). The structural contraction of the family from a two-generational household to the marital dyad presents tasks of parent–child separation and a shift for the parents from investment in their

children to refocusing on their marriage. The loss in maternal role functioning makes this transition especially crucial for women.

While most adjust well to this "empty nest" transition (Neugarten, 1970), the ability to do so may depend, in part, on how empty the nest feels. The transition may be impeded by an unsatisfying marital relationship and overattachment to a child. In some families a young adult child who is locked into such a triangle may become symptomatic at that time. In other cases a failure to negotiate this transition can have a delayed impact, interfering with the family's subsequent ability to deal with later-life transitions. The following clinical case[1] illustrates such a time bomb effect:

> Stanley, age 67, was hospitalized at his wife's insistence for serious alcohol abuse of onset following retirement. Living in the home were Stanley, his wife, and their 42-year-old son, who had never left home. Long-standing overinvolvement between mother and son had served to stabilize a chronically conflictual marriage over the years as long as Stanley had been involved in his work outside the home. Retirement shifted the homeostatic balance as Stanley, now home all day, felt himself to be an unwanted intruder. Lacking his work source of self-esteem, he felt like an unworthy competitor to his son for his wife's affection, at a time in his life when he was longing for more companionship with her. The rivalry between father and son erupted into angry confrontations when Stanley was drunk, with his wife siding with the son and threatening divorce. (See Figure 14-1.)

In this family the tasks of the launching stage were never mastered and a postparental marital relationship was never established. The family's defensive mode of adaptation served to avoid conflict and intimacy in the marriage for many years, but it broke down when retirement demanded new adjustments and reorganization of the system.

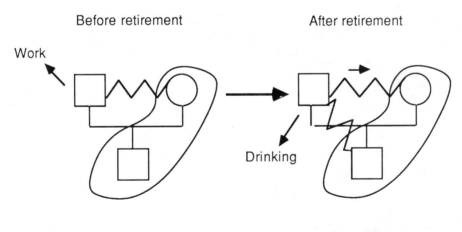

Figure 14-1. Failure to resolve earlier family developmental task complicates later-life transition.

[1]This case and several of the following were adapted from a clinical research sample gathering by the author and colleagues in a joint Northwestern University/University of Chicago Clinical Training Program in Later Life. Acknowledgment is given to David Gutman, Ph.D., Morton Lieberman, Ph.D., Joanna Gutmann, M.S.W., Jerome Grunes, M.D., and Leslie Groves, Ph.D.

Retirement

Following an ebb in marital satisfaction when children are in adolescence, most couples experience increased marital satisfaction after adjustment to the launching of children and throughout their later years together (Lowenthal, et al., 1975). Companionship and mutual caring and caretaking become highly valued in the marital relationship, as well as in sexual intimacy, which continues for many into advanced years (Masters & Johnson, 1968; Lowenthal et al., 1975).

Retirement represents a significant milestone and adjustment for the marital pair (Medley, 1977). For the individual who retires, particularly for men in our society, there is a loss of meaningful job roles, productivity, and relationships that have been central throughout adult life. Whether retirement was desired or forced will affect adjustment. Loss of the role as family provider and a likely income reduction may bring additional stress. Working women may experience less difficulty with their own retirement if they maintain role continuity as homemakers. Wives in traditional marriages often have greater difficulty with their husbands' retirement (Heyman, 1970), which may bring loss of job-related status and social network. Residential change at retirement adds further dislocation and loss of connectedness with family, neighbors, and community. The transition involves reorientation of values and goals and a redirection of energies.

The major task facing traditional couples with the husband's retirement is his incorporation inside the home, with a change in age-role expectations and the quality of interaction. Most couples work out this reintegration well. Some couples, however, experience difficulty, as the following case illustrates.

> Mrs. Barnett sought treatment for depression a year after her husband's retirement from a business management position. Mr. Barnett seemed to adjust well to his retirement. In place of his job investment, he had taken up and excelled at gourmet cooking. In doing so he virtually took over the kitchen, formerly his wife's domain. Also, he found ready application of his business expertise in assuming management of the household budget, another former responsibility of Mrs. Barnett. He expressed satisfaction with his new activities and was proud that he could continue to be a good husband by sharing the household work load and relieving his wife of burdensome chores she had carried alone over the years. Mrs. Barnett, thinking she ought to feel grateful for her husband's consideration, was puzzled as to why she was so depressed in her new leisure. She began phoning her married daughter several times a day, becoming increasingly concerned about her daughter's marriage. The more mother and daughter talked, the worse the daughter's marital discord became. Finally, the daughter, exasperated with her mother's intrusion and feeling helpless to alleviate her mother's depression, arranged psychiatric consultation for her. (See Figure 14-2.)

Couples therapy brought out the main issues straining the family system. Before retirement each partner had maintained separate fields, or spheres of influence and activity, from which they each derived satisfaction, meaning, and self-esteem. Clear boundaries maintained differentiation. With retirement Mr. Barnett invaded his wife's turf, taking over her major activities. The outlets he found for himself were precisely those responsibilities that had given her life

income has become essential to maintain a moderate standard of living in two-parent and, especially, in divorced families, financial and caretaking resources for elderly parents have diminished. Women at midlife are increasingly overburdened by conflicting physical and emotional demands, as job responsibilities are juxtaposed with expectations to maintain traditional roles as homemaker, wife, and mother, as well as care for aging parents, and, increasingly, very aged grandparents (Brody, 1979).

While only 5% of the elderly are maintained in institutions, 86% of all older adults have chronic health problems that, as they age, require increasing hospitalizations, medical expenditure, and family caregiving for daily functioning (Cantor, 1983; Zarit et al., 1982). The lack of useful management guidelines by most medical specialists adds to the confusion, frustration, and helplessness family members experience in the face of chronic and terminal illness. Some aspects of chronic illness are especially disruptive for families, such as sleep disturbance, incontinence, delusional statements, and aggressive behavior. One symptom and consequence of family distress is elder abuse, increasingly reported to occur in overwhelmed families, stretched beyond their means and tolerance (*Elder Abuse*, 1980).

Among the most difficult illnesses for families to cope with are the senile dementias—progressive brain disorders that affect 5–7% of persons over 65. Alzheimers disease, accounting for 60% of dementia cases, produces severe intellectual and behavioral deterioration until death, usually in four or five years but sometimes as long as ten years. Since medical treatment of the illness is limited, a custodial bias prevails in the management of dementia patients. Because of the poor prognosis and a widespread belief that dementia patients cannot be cared for at home, nursing-home placement is usually advised. However, observations suggest that patients kept at home on low-dose or drug-free regimens do not show as severe decrements as those in institutions, where they are typically highly medicated (Zarit & Zarit, 1982). Family intervention is crucial to support caregiving and coping with stress (Ware & Carper, 1982). Adult daycare for patients and their families is another option to partially relieve family burden (Woehrer, 1982).

It is important for clinicians not to assume that the presence of family dysfunction indicates that the family has played a causal role in the deterioration of a chronic illness. Family dysfunction may be, at least in large part, a consequence of the stress associated with the illness. Family intervention priorities should include (1) reduction of the stressful impact of chronic illness on the family; (2) provision of information about the medical condition, functional ability and limitations, and prognosis; (3) concrete guidelines for maintenance and problem solving, and (4) linkage to supplementary services to support family efforts to maintain elderly members in the community (Pinkston & Linsk, 1984; Walsh & Anderson, 1987; Zarit & Zarit, 1982).

A disequilibrium in the marital relationship may ensue with the illness of one spouse. The capacities of the partner can be drained if caretaking has little outside financial and emotional support. In some cases the partner may use the

caretaking role and focus on the spouse's illness in avoidance of his or her own vulnerability, anxiety, or longings to be dependent and taken care of. The need for the spouse to be underfunctioning in relation to the overfunctioning care-taker can impede recovery of maximum potential.

The issue of dependency comes to the fore in intergenerational relations as aging parents experience—or fear—a decline in their capacities, as in illness. In a normal family, handling increased needs for dependency of aging parents does not involve a "role reversal" as some imply (Goldfarb, 1966). Even when instrumental and emotional support is given by adult children to aging parents, the child remains in the relationship of child to parent and does not become a parent to his or her parent. It should be kept in mind that despite childlike appearances, the aged parent has had over 50 years of adult life and experience (Spark & Brody, 1970).

The resolution of dependency issues requires a realistic acceptance of strengths and limitations by the older adult, and the ability to allow oneself to be dependent when need be. It also requires the adult child's ability to accept a *filial* role (Blenker, 1965), taking responsibility for what he or she can appropri-ately do for aging parents, as well as recognition of what he or she cannot or should not do. This capacity may be constrained by the child's own physical, emotional, and social situation. If, for example, adult children are confronting their own aging demands that require major adaptation of functioning, the expectation of meeting their parents' dependency needs may not be realistic (Brody, 1974).

In other cases an aging parent may become overly dependent on adult children. If the children, through their own anxiety, become overly responsible, a vicious cycle may ensue, whereby the more they do for the parent, the more helpless or incompetent the parent becomes, with escalating neediness, bur-den, and resentment. Ambivalent overattachment and dependence are com-mon (Kahana & Levin, 1971). Siblings may go to opposite extremes in regard to filial responsibilities, as in the following case.

Mrs. Z., a 74-year-old widow, was hospitalized with multiple somatic problems exacerbated by symptoms of senility including disorientation, recent memory loss, and confusion. She reported that she had two sons, Tim, age 46, and Roger, age 43, but complained that they didn't care whether she lived or died. The sons reluctantly agreed to come in for a family interview. On the phone Roger stated that, in his opinion, the hospitalization was merely a ploy for sympathy on his mother's part, an attempt to make him feel guilty for not being at her beck and call as Tim was. He said he had learned years ago that the best relationship with her was no relationship at all. In contrast, Tim had become increasingly responsible for his mother, particularly since she had been widowed. Yet the more "helpful" he became, the more dependent and helpless she became in managing her own life. At the point of hospitalization, he felt drained by his mother's growing neediness.

Two stages of therapeutic work were undertaken. First the overresponsible son was coached to be more "helpful" by challenging his mother to function max-imally rather than doing for her. The underinvolved son was asked to join with his brother and to relieve him of some limited, specific burdens. Both sons were encouraged to communicate their feelings and concerns directly with their mother and to be patient in listening to her. They were advised not to be alarmed if their

mother was initially resistant to the changes. With anxiety in the system reduced and the family working together, Mrs. Z.'s thought disorder cleared and her functioning improved markedly.

The second phase of treatment involved a "family life review," in which mother and sons shared reminiscences of their family life history. Members were assisted in exploring developmental periods of particular emotional import, and evoking crucial memories, responses, and understanding. The brothers' long-standing rivalry was explored and put in perspective. Roger's cutoff became better understood in recalling a late adolescent conflict over dependency that he handled by leaving home in anger, severing contact, and vowing to remain self-sufficient. His relationship with his parents had become frozen at that point, but now could be brought up to the present. Finally, mother and sons mourned, for the first time together, the death of the father, and each revealed a secret fear they had overburdened him with their own concerns and had hastened his death. Most important, the therapy accomplished a reconciliation and new understanding and caring among the surviving family members.

The application of life-review therapy (Lewis & Butler, 1974) to whole families has been found by the present author to be of potentially great benefit to many families in later life. It extends the process of reminiscence, which facilitates resolution of the tasks of acceptance of one's life and death, to include the perceptions and direct involvement of significant family members who are central to such resolution. Family albums, scrapbooks, geneologies, reunions, and pilgrimages can assist this work. The resolution of later-life issues rests on the foundation of all earlier life stages. Conflicts or disappointments in earlier stages that may have resulted in cutoffs or frozen images and expectations can be reconsidered from a new vantage point at a later-life stage and from perspectives of other family members. Successive life phases can be reviewed so that relationships can be brought up to date. The transmission of family history to younger generations can be an additional bonus to such work.

The importance of supporting maximal functioning and competence in elderly family members, as seen above, is underscored in the next case, where clinical staff became overly responsible caretakers and underestimated the potential functioning and assets of an elderly patient.

Rita, a 78-year-old widow, was admitted to the psychiatric inpatient unit with a diagnosis of confusional state and acute paranoia, following an incident in which Rita accused her landlord of plotting to get rid of her. When asked what brought her to led the hospital, Rita replied that her only problem was failing vision. When asked if she lived alone, she responded, "I live with my books."

Rita's increasing blindness was making independent living more difficult and hazardous. The landlord reported that her apartment was in disarray and that she seemed unable to manage simple living tasks like grocery shopping. She angrily refused any assistance from neighbors and maintained social isolation. Her only surviving family was a married sister, who lived in another state. Rita's deteriorating eye condition and lack of supportive network the hospital staff to predict that she would be unable to continue to function independently. A nursing-home placement was recommended. Rita vehemently objected, insisting that she wanted only to return to her own apartment. Hospitalization was extended to "deal with her resistance" to the treatment plan worked out *for* her. Fortunately a sensitive

interview with Rita led to a new appreciation of her and to a very different discharge plan arrived at *with* her.

Rita had been happily married, without children, until her husband's sudden death 16 years earlier. In response to that painful and unexpected loss, she withdrew from family and friends, never to become dependent on anyone else again. She centered her life on her work and on her books. A job colleague remembered Rita as a "tough cookie," who was respected for her high functioning and perseverance through difficult assignments, until her forced retirement at 70. Since then Rita had immersed herself in her books, which served many vital functions. They were a source of knowledge, giving her a sense of competence and mastery. The novels, biographies, and atlases offered pleasurable contact with the world, with other people, places, and times. Most important, the books had special meaning because she had inherited them from her father, a scholar, who died shortly after her husband's death. The books linked her to her father, reviving her close childhood relationship with him. Now Rita's failing eyesight was cutting her off from these contacts she valued most.

In Rita's strong identification with her father was an intense pride in his part-Indian heritage, carrying a sense of constitutional superiority that showed itself in a perseverance in adversity, a toughness, and a will to survive and adapt. These strengths are revealed in a visit to Rita's apartment. At first glance all appeared chaotic: piles of books everywhere; clothing and food containers on every counter, table, and chair. However, a closer inspection revealed that Rita had carefully ordered her environment in a system that made sense to her need to adapt to visual impairment. With a magic marker she had color-coded all food: clothes were arranged according to function; books were stacked by their subject and meaning to her. Almost blindly, she could easily locate everything she needed.

Rita's denial of dependency needs could be regarded as pathological, yet self-reliance had served Rita well for many years. It was the breakdown of her mode of adaptation—her vision—that brought confusion and anxiety. Still, realistically, Rita would require some assistance to maintain independent living. Her reluctance to become dependent on any caretaker made her reject any aid with one exception: she herself had contacted a religious organization that sent someone to read to her whenever she called. She could allow help when she maintained control over the circumstances—when she initiated the request, when they came to her, and when she herself determined the limits and boundaries of the dependent relationship.

A new treatment plan was worked out supporting Rita's objective of independent living and incorporating her values. Her natural ability to take responsibility for herself and her determination to function as autonomously as possible were reinforced. To help her feel less out of control and cut off by her sight limitation, a network therapy approach was employed. She was encouraged to select, and initiate contact with, a few neighbors and shopkeepers who could provide occasional backup service. In exchange, she would teach them about American Indian culture and relate Indian lore that had been passed on to her by her father.

The point at which failing health requires consideration of institutionalization or nursing-home placement is a crisis for the family (Kramer & Kramer, 1976; Tobin & Kulys, 1981; Butler & Lewis, 1983). Contrary to myth, adult children generally do not dump their elderly in institutions. Only 4% of all elderly live in institutions, almost half of these may have organic brain disease, and the average age at admission is 80. Institutions tend to be turned to only as the last resort, usually when family resources are strained to the limit. Nevertheless, feelings of guilt and abandonment can make the decision for institutionalization highly stressful for families, and particularly for adult daughters,

on whom the caretaking responsibility is typically concentrated, as the following case illustrates.

> Mrs. Arletti called the psychiatric facility for help, stating that she feared that her teenage son needed to be institutionalized. Mrs. Arletti was seen with her son, who admitted to truancy and behavior problems that the mother felt helpless to control. A full assessment of the family system revealed that the problems had developed over the past eight months, since Mrs. Arletti's aged mother had been taken into their home. The son acknowledged that he frequently cut school and spent all day in his room, which was next to his grandmother's room. Mrs. Arletti burst into tears as she described her mother's Parkinson's condition, and her difficulty in taking care of her mother, who required round-the-clock attention, when she herself, a single parent, had to keep a full-time job. She was alarmed by her mother's occasional loss of balance and falling, feeling helpless and out of control to assist her if it should occur while she was at work. Her concern about institutionalization was primarily with regard to her mother.

This case underscores the importance of a full family assessment and inquiry about elderly members even when presenting problems appear elsewhere in the system and may function in the service of the family in crisis.

When institutionalization is being considered, or when a family is realistically overburdened but fearful of raising the possibility, family sessions that include the elder member can be useful in weighing advantages and costs of the various options, taking into account the strengths and limitations of the elder member and the family, and sharing feelings and concerns before arriving at a decision together. Often through discussion new solutions emerge that can support the elder's remaining in the community without undue burden on any member. Organizations such as the Visiting Nurses Association can be helpful in providing homebound services and informing families of community backup.

Dealing with terminal illness is perhaps the most difficult task for a family, which is complicated by prolonged illness and decisions about life versus facilitating the dying process. Family adaptation to loss (Walsh & McGoldrick, 1988) involves shared grieving and a reorganization of the family relationship system. Denial, silence, and secret keeping tend to be ultimately dysfunctional. When patient and family hide knowledge of a terminal illness, and try to protect their own and each other's feelings, communication barriers create distance and misunderstanding and prevent preparatory grief. The therapist can be helpful in encouraging family members to share feelings of helplessness, anger, loss of control, or guilt that they did not do more (Cohen, 1982). It may be easier for younger family members to accept the loss of elders whose time has come, than for elders to accept the loss—and their own survival—of peers or of their own children who die first. The death of the last member of the older generation is a milestone for a family, signifying that the next generation is now the oldest and the next to face death. It is important, also, not to ignore the impact of an elder's death on grandchildren, for whom the loss of a grandparent may be their first experience with death.

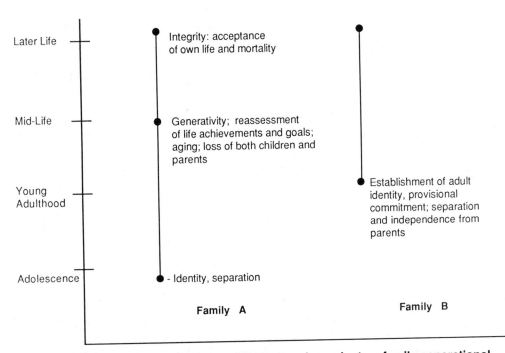

Figure 14.3. Family response to later-life issues dependent on family generational composition and interaction of life-stage concerns of all generations.

Cross-generational Interplay of Life Cycle Issues

Within every family the later-life tasks of the elderly interact with the particular concerns prominent for child and grandchild generations at their own life phases, as has been seen in the cases described. With the increasing diversity in life-styles and family patterns, and the tendency toward later marriage and child rearing (Walsh, 1982), different pressures and conflicts may be generated. As illustrated in Figure 14.3, the issues that come to the fore in one family (Family B) between an older adult and young adult child may be different, and more complicated, than those that arise in another family (Family A) between older adult, middle-aged child, and adolescent grandchild.

A lack of complementarity or fit may occur when diverse developmental strivings are incompatible. In the case of Family B, the needs and concerns of an aging mother, confronting painful deterioration and death, collided with separation, identity, and commitment issues of her young adult daughter.

Julia was in her mid-20s, beginning a social work career, and engaged to be married when her 69-year-old mother, 2000 miles away, developed cardiovascular disease and began a long and painful physical decline. Julia had always been close to her mother and felt torn in response to her mother's strong, but indirect, pleas to return home. She felt an inner pull to go to her mother, but an even stronger resistance to giving up her new job and postponing marriage plans indefinitely.

The situation was complicated by Julia's recently emerging separation and identity issues. She had always been her mother's daughter, a "good girl" who never opposed her mother's wishes or values. Only after leaving home had she begun to differentiate. In attempting to do so, she accentuated differences between

herself and her mother and disagreed openly about issues that mattered most to her mother, especially religion. The geographic distance she established from home helped to bolster efforts to test herself on her own without relying on her mother for direction and support. Now, just at the time Julia was needing to pull away, to function autonomously, and to be self-directed, her mother needed to be close and dependent on Julia. Julia feared losing her sense of self and having her own priorities submerged by her mother's needs.

Weekly phone calls became increasingly strained, erupting into open conflict. Julia's failure to return home was labeled by her mother as uncaring and selfish. She snapped, "What kind of social worker can you be if you can't even care about your own mother?" Julia made a brief visit home, feeling guilty and yet resentful that no matter how long she stayed, it wouldn't be enough for her mother. Anxious just before leaving, Julia defiantly announced that she no longer believed in God and did not intend to bring her children up in any religion. Her mother was devastated, taking this as a total rejection of her and her values, and feeling that she had failed as a mother.

Julia sent her mother gifts. One was picked with special care and affection: a leather-bound book inscribed "For your memoirs." On her next visit home, Julia discovered all her gifts stacked away on a closet shelf, unused. Deeply hurt, she screamed at her mother to explain, particularly, the empty book. Her mother replied, "If I wrote my memoirs, I'd have to write how much you've disappointed me." Julia cut her visit short. Returning to her own home, conflict erupted with her fiance and the wedding plans were soon canceled. Julia, deeply upset by the breakup, phoned her parents for consolation. Her mother replied coldly, "Well now that you aren't going to be married, I have nothing left to live for." A few hours later, she had a stroke. Julia, furious at her mother's self-centeredness and apparent manipulation, did not return home again before the long-anticipated call came one night from her father informing her, "Mom is dead."

Julia scarcely grieved. She married within weeks to someone she had only recently met. It was not until the breakup of that marriage that feelings of loss of her mother surfaced, with guilt and regrets that the final alienation and the fact that it was too late to change things. She determined that she would repair her strained relationship with her father—whom she had not visited since her mother's death—before that was too late. With family therapy coaching, she also initiated new relationships with her mother's family, learning about her mother's life from various perspectives, and coming to appreciate her more fully as a person. She also learned that her mother had lost her own mother shortly after making a life choice that had greatly disappointed the older woman and had not seen her to repair the cutoff before her mother's death. Julia's own process of differentiation was catalyzed by her work. Finally, using gestalt techniques with her therapist, Julia had an important conversation "with her mother," expressing what she wished she had been able to share with her.

This case illustrates that the timing of events can be critical in adjustment (Neugarten, 1970). The mother's developmental needs to come to terms with her life and her impending death occurred "off-time" from the perspective of the daughter's developmental readiness. The aging mother was needing to draw her family close at the end of her life, to reaffirm her life values, and to feel she had successfully fulfilled her role as a mother. The young adult daughter was threatened by the surge of longings for closeness and dependency at a time of impending loss when she was not yet secure in her own individuation. In this case cross-generational anniversary reactions complicated the picture as issues from the mother's relationship with her own mother at life's end were

revived and replicated, with disappointment projected into the daughter and cutoff ending the relationship before death.

Further study of parent loss in young adulthood is needed. As Erikson (1959) has noted, the young adult is emerging from the search for identity into issues of commitment. The fear of ego loss in situations calling for self-abandon may lead to isolation and self-absorption. As Levinson (1978) has observed in young men, this may accentuate the normal preoccupation with making the first choices and commitments, especially marriage, occupation, and residence, that define one's place in the adult world. Responding to the needs and threatened loss of aging parents at this life stage may be fraught with complications.

ROLE FLEXIBILITY AND SUCCESSFUL AGING

Studies of normal adult development and family functioning indicate that a variety of adaptive responses, rather than one single pattern, may be associated with successful later-life adjustment. This diversity reflects differences in family structural patterns (Walsh, 1982), individual personality styles (Maas & Kuyper, 1977), sex roles (Troll, 1971; Gutmann, 1977), and sociocultural context (Gibson, 1982; Woehrer;, 1982 and Gelfand, 1982).

Traditional sex-role distinctions of earlier adulthood tend to shift. Older men show increasing passivity and accommodation in response to environmental challenges, and greater needs for nurturance and affiliation, whereas older women become more assertive and active in the service of meeting their own needs (Gutmann, 1977). The development of more androgynous modes of response, of aspects of the personality that were earlier denied, can enable a greater role flexibility that may be related to longevity and greater life satisfaction in old age (Sinott, 1977).

Likewise, the successful functioning of families in later life requires a flexibility in structure, roles, and responses to new developmental needs and challenges. Patterns that may have been functional in earlier stages may no longer fit and new options must be explored. The loss of functioning and death of significant family members require that others be called upon to assume new roles and responsibilities (Walsh & McGoldrick, 1988). Previous losses and adaptive patterns also affect responses to later life challenges. (Walsh, 1983c; Caspi & Elder, 1986).

The diversity, complexity, and importance of family relations in later life can be expected to become even greater in the future. By 1990 the number of persons 65 and over will jump from the present 20 million to 28 million, with the largest increase in the "old old," over 85. When the baby boom generation reaches old age, they will make up at least 20% of the population. The declining

proportion of younger people and the increasing workforce participation of women will likely exacerbate the strain on families in provision of financial and caretaking support (Taeuber, 1983). As social institutions take over more instrumental aspects of life, such as income maintenance and health care, the family may become even more important in providing lasting emotional ties, a sense of identity, and a sense of self-worth (Neugarten, 1974).

With the lengthening life span, couples may have 30 to 40 years ahead after the children leave home. Four- and five-generation families will become common. More "young old" couples at retirement age with diminishing resources will be involved in caring for their "old old" parents. The growing number of remarriage families will enlarge and complicate the extended-family network. On the other hand, the trend is toward having few or no children. The implications of nonparenthood for later-life adjustment are unknown and warrant study given the significant role of children and grandchildren in the resolution of later-life tasks. Of note is the large proportion of older adult psychiatric inpatients who are childless, in the experience of the author and colleagues.

Because people are living longer than elders did in the past, we lack role models for later-life family relations, just as we lack appropriate labels and role definitions. The term "post-parental" is unfortunate, as parents never cease to be parents. Instead it is the *nature* of parent–child relationships that changes in later life. We are only beginning to explore the possibilities in that transformation. Maggie Kuhn, the vibrant 73-year-old cofounder of the Grey Panthers, sees the responsibility of elders to be innovative and to explore new role options, as society's futurists. She believes that the wisdom and experience of old people, linked with the energy and new knowledge of the young, can be the basis for rich interchange and planning for the future (Kuhn, 1979). Important is a sense of pride in age, in one's history, in life experience, and in the capacity to cope with change.

Clinical services must be flexible to fit the diversity of family constellations and to support optimal functioning and independent living in the community. New treatment options need to be developed to fit new demands and needs.

CLINICAL ASSESSMENT AND TREATMENT ISSUES

The mental health profession has been largely unaware of and unresponsive to the service needs of older adults and their families. Several factors, including the invisibility of the elderly and professional "ageism," have contributed to this neglect.

Invisibility

Functional problems involving family relations with elderly members are often "hidden." First, older adults are much more likely to present somatic problems to medical services than to present emotional problems to psychiatric facilities. In a medical assessment, such functional problems as depression, confusion, and anxiety may not be detected, or may be assumed to be merely an irreversible accompaniment to organic disease. Family stress concomitants may not be addressed.

Even when organic brain disease or other serious physical disorders are present, the family may play an important part in maintaining or exacerbating the condition and can be crucial determinants in the course and outcome. As noted above, the vicious cycle of family overfunctioning/patient underfunctioning can hasten and perpetuate symptoms labeled as "senility." It is important for clinicians to assess the family component—in contribution and reaction—in any medical dysfunction and to involve family members directly in relating to the patient and encouraging maximal functioning. The stressful impact of chronic illness on the family also requires attention to family needs for support information, caregiving guidelines, and linkage to community resources.

A second problem of visibility occurs when clinicians mistakenly assume or accept an older adult's initial claim—that there is no family or that the family is not important in later life. Given the prevalent pattern of "intimacy at a distance," the clinician must look beyond the sharing of a household to identify significant relationships. Emotionally meaningful bonds may transcend geographic distance or apparent biological distance, as with a daughter-in-law, a nephew, or a "distant cousin." With the loss of one's spouse, not only descendants, but also family of origin and spouse's family of origin, may hold more importance. The very statement that one "has no family left" may indicate continuing emotional significance and unresolved mourning issues regarding multiple family members who may have died within a short period of time. Other long-standing cut offs may hold potential for repair. The complexity and diversity of family networks require careful clinical assessment. Drawing a genogram with an elder can be particularly useful in identifying significant others and potential supportive linkages.

A third problem of visibility occurs when younger generations present themselves or their children for treatment. Problems involving elderly family members may be hidden behind complaints or symptoms elsewhere in the system. It is not uncommon in a "complete" diagnostic evaluation of an adult requesting treatment to include a detailed assessment of early family history with little or no mention of current ongoing relationships or recent changes that may have precipitated presenting symptoms. Whatever the age or problem of the symptom bearer, it is important to inquire about elder members in the family system.

Clinicians are trained and accustomed to evaluate families from a model based on early developmental stages when structure, roles, and functioning

are geared to child-rearing imperatives and integration of a two-generational household. We must be careful not to transfer assumptions unquestioningly to family functioning in later life. Clearly the later-life challenges and the diversity in family networks require that we develop new and more flexible conceptualizations for understanding family functioning and dysfunction as they bear on the accomplishment of later-life tasks. Family assessments should determine how a family, given its particular composition, style and modes of adaptation, and needs of its members, has responded to later-life imperatives. Where it has broken down in response to challenges, we need to consider the variety of options possible for reorganization of the family and transformation of relationships to meet changing needs and requirements.

Ageism

Negative stereotyping of older people and their families by mental health systems and professionals has lead to assumptions that they are a poor investment for therapy, too resistant to change, or simply untreatable. Functional problems may be discounted as merely a natural and irreversible part of aging and organic deterioration. The label of senility is indiscriminately applied to elders presenting a range of symptoms of impaired intellectual functioning or responsiveness to others (Nowakowski, 1978). Clinical training programs emphasize early developmental stages and offer limited exposure to elders and their families. Outpatient and inpatient psychiatric settings tend to be organized around the treatment needs of younger patients deemed more interesting and treatable. Elders are too often treated custodially or expected to fit into programs geared to younger patients.

Butler (1975) views professional ageisms as stemming from an attempt to avoid the personal reality of aging and death. It is important for clinicians to develop awareness of our own apprehensions, a perspective on the whole life span, and an appreciation of what it is like to be old.

Clinicians' interface issues with our own families—particularly with our own aging or deceased parents—may contribute to anxiety, avoidance, over-responsibility, or empathic difficulties with elders. As we reach out to become better acquainted with the elders in our own families, as we attempt to resolve our own losses and grievances, and as we explore new relational possibilities for ourselves, therapeutic work with families in later life will take on new meaning and options for growth.

REFERENCES

Blenkner, M. (1965). Social work and family relationships in later life with some thoughts on filial maturity. In E. Shanas & G. Strieb (Eds.), *Social structure and the family: Generational relations.* Englewood Cliffs, N.J.: Prentice-Hall.

Boszormenyi-Nagy, I. & Spark, G. (1973). *Invisible loyalties: Reciprocity in intergenerational family therapy*. Hagerstown, Md.: Harper & Row.

Bowen, M. (1978). *Family therapy in clinical practice*. New York: Jason Aronson.

Brody, E. M. (1974). Aging and family personality: A developmental view. *Family Process* 13:23–37.

Brody, E. (1979). Women's changing roles and care of the aging family. *Aging: Agenda for the eighties*. Washington, D.C.: Government Research Corporation.

Butler, R. & Lewis, M. I. (1983). *Aging and mental health: Positive psychosocial approaches* (3rd ed.). St. Louis: Mosby.

Cantor, M. (1983). Strain among caregivers: A study of experience in the United States. *The Gerontologist* 23:597–604.

Caspi, A., & Elder, G. (1986). Life satisfaction in old age: Linking social psychology and history. *Journal of Psychology and Aging* 1:18–26.

Cicirelli, V. (1983). Adult children's attachment and helping behavior to elderly parents: A path model. *Journal of Marriage and the Family* 815–825.

Cohen, M. (1982). In the presence of your absence: The treatment of older families with a cancer patient. *Psychotherapy* 19:453–460.

Deutscher, I. (1964). The quality of post-parental life. *Journal of Marriage and Family* 26:52–60.

Elder abuse. (1980). Department of Health & Human Services. Pub. No. (OHDS) 81-20152. Washington, D.C.: U.S. Government Printing Office.

Erikson, E. H. (1959). Identity and the life cycle. *Psychol. Issues*, vol. 1, no. 1, Monograph 1. New York: International Universities Press.

Finkle, A. L. (1976). Sexual aspects of aging. In L. Bellak & T. Karasu (Eds.), *Geriatric psychiatry*. New York: Grune & Stratton.

Framo, J. (1976). Family of origin as a therapeutic resource for adults in marital and family therapy: You can and should go home again. *Family Process* 15:193–210.

Gelfand, D. (1982). *Aging: The ethnic factor*. Boston: Little, Brown.

Gibson, R. (1982). Blacks at middle and late life: Resources and coping. *The Annals of the American Academy* 79–90.

Glick, P. (1977). Updating the life cycle of the family. *Journal of Marriage and the Family* 39:5–13.

Goldfarb, A. (1965). Psychodynamics of the three-generation family. In E. Shanas & G. Streib (Eds.), *Social structure and the family: Generational relations*. Englewood Cliffs, N.J.: Prentice-Hall

Gutmann, D. (1977). Notes toward a comparative psychology of aging. In J. Birren & K. Schaie (Eds.), *Handbook of the psychology of aging*. New York: Van Nostrand Reinhold.

Hadley, T. R., et al. (1974). The relationship between family developmental crisis and the appearance of symptoms in a family member. *Family Process* 13:207–214.

Haley, J. (1973). The family life cycle. *Uncommon therapy*. New York: Norton.

Headley, L. (1977). *Adults and their parents in family therapy*. New York: Plenum Press.

Herr, J. & Weakland, J. (1979). *Counseling elders and their families*. New York: Springer.

Heyman, D. (1970). Does a wife retire? *Gerontologist* 10:54–56.

Kahana, R. & Levin, S. (1971). Aging and the conflict of generations. *Journal of Geriatric Psychiatry* 4:115–135.

Kramer, C. and Kramer, J. (1976). *Basic principles of long-term patient care*. Springfield, Ill.: Charles C. Thomas.

Kuhn, M. (1979). Liberating aging, an interview by Ken Dychtwald. *New Age Magazine*.

Levinson, D. (1978). *The seasons of a man's life*. New York: Knopf.

Lewis, M. I. & Butler, R. N. (1974). Life review therapy. *Geriatrics* 29:165–173.

Lopata, H. (1973). *Widowhood in an American city*. Cambridge, Mass.: Schenkman.

Lowenthal, M. Thurner, M., & Chiriboga, D. (1975). *Four stages of life*. San Francisco: Jossey-Bass.

Maas, H., & J. Kuypers (1977). *From thirty to seventy*. San Francisco: Jossey-Bass.

Masters, W. H., & Johnson, V. E. (1968). Human sexual response: The aging female and the

aging male. In B. Neugarten (Ed.), *Middle age and aging.* Chicago: University of Chicago Press.

Mead, M. (1972). *Blackberry winter.* New York: William Morrow & Co.

Medley, M. (1977). Marital adjustment in the post-retirement years. *Family Coordinator* 26:5–11.

Neugarten, B. (1970). Dynamics of transition of middle age to old age: Adaptation and the life cycle. *Journal of Geriatric Psychiatry* 4:71–87.

Neugarten, B. (1974). Successful aging in 1970 and 1990. In E. Pfeiffer (Ed.), *Successful aging: A conference report,* Duke University.

Neugarten, B., & Weinstein, K. (1968). The changing American grandparent. In B. Neugarten (Ed.), *Middle age and aging.* Chicago: University of Chicago Press.

Nowakowski, L. (1978). *Utilization of knowledge of aging in clinical practice.* Paper presented at 15th Annual Georgetown Symposium, Washington, D.C.

Pinkston, E., & Linsk, N. (1984). *Care of the elderly: A family approach.* New York: Pergamon Press.

Saltz, R. (1977). Fostergrandparenting: A unique child-care service. In L. Troll., J. Israel, & K. Israel (Eds.), *Looking ahead: A woman's guide to the problems and joys of growing older.* Englewood Cliffs, N.J.: Prentice-Hall.

Sands, D. & Suzuki, T. (1983). Adult daycare for Alzheimer's patients and their families. *Gerontologist* 23:21–23

Sinott, J. D. (1977). Sex-role inconstancy, biology, and successful aging: A dialectical model. *Gerontologist* 17:459–463.

Sorensen, E. M. (1977). Family interaction with the elderly. In P. Watzlawick & J. Weakland (Eds.), *The interactional view:* New York: Norton.

Spark, G. Grandparents and intergenerational family therapy. *Family Process* 13:225–238.

Spark, G., & Brody, E. M. (1970). The aged are family members. *Family Process* 9:195–210.

Sprey, J., & Matthews, S. (1982). Contemporary grandparenthood: A systemic transition. *Annals of the American Academy* 91–103.

Streib, G., & Beck, R. (1981). Older families: A decade review. *Journal of Marriage and the Family* 42:937–956.

Sussman, M. (1976). The family life of old people. In R. Binstock & E. Shanas (Eds.), *Handbook of aging and the social sciences.* New York: Van Nostrand Reinhold.

Taeuber, M. (1983). *America in transition: An aging society.* U.S. Department of Commerce, Bureau of Census, Current Population Report, Special Series no. 128.

Tobin, S., & Kulys, R. (1981). The family in the institutionalization of the elderly. *Journal of Social Issues* 37:145–157.

Treas, J. (1977). Family support systems for the aged: Some social and demographic considerations. *Gerontologist* 17:186–191.

Troll, L. (1971). The family of later life: A decade review. *Journal of Marriage and the Family* 33:263–290.

Walsh, F. (1982). Conceptualizations of normal family functioning. In F. Walsh (Ed.), *Normal family processes.* New York: Guilford Press.

Walsh, F. (1983a). Family therapy: A systemic orientation to treatment. In A. Rosenblatt & D. Waldfogle (Eds.), *Handbook of clinical social work.* San Francisco: Jossey-Bass.

Walsh, F. 1983b). Normal family ideologies: Myths and realities. In C. Falicov (Ed.), *Cultural dimensions of family therapy.* Rockville, Md.: Aspen Systems.

Walsh, F. (1983c). The timing of symptoms and critical events in the family life cycle. In *Clinical implications of the family life cycle.* Rockville, Md.: Aspen Systems.

Walsh, F., & Anderson, C. (1987). Chronic disorders and families: An overview. In F. Walsh & C. Anderson (Eds.), Chronic disorders and the family, special issue, *Journal of Psychotherapy and the Family*, 3:3.

Walsh, F., & McGoldrick, M. (1988). Loss and the family life cycle. In C. Falicov (Ed.), *Family transitions: Continuity and change.* New York: Guilford Press.

Ware, L., & Carper, M. (1982). Living with Alzheimer disease patients: Family stresses and coping mechanisms. *Psychotherapy* 19:472–481.

Woehrer, C. (1982). The influence of ethnic families on intergenerational relationships and later life transitions. *Annal of American Academy* 65–78.

Zarit, S., Reever, K. E., & Bach-Peterson, J. (1982). Relatives of the impaired elderly: Correlates of feelings of burden. *Gerontologist* 22:373–377.

Zarit, S., & Zarit, J. (1982). Families under stress: Interventions for caregivers of senile dementia patients. *Psychotherapy* 19:461–471.

PART

3

The Divorce Cycle

15

Divorce in the Changing Family Life Cycle

Judith Stern Peck, M.S.W.
and Jennifer R. Manocherian, M.S.

Divorce has become endemic to the American society. Two decades ago it was relatively rare; today almost 50% of couples will choose divorce as the solution to marital dissatisfaction. Despite its prevalence, few spouses are prepared for the emotional and physical impact of divorce. Divorce affects family members at every generational level throughout the nuclear and extended family, thus producing a crisis for the family as a whole as well as for each individual within the family.

Divorce is a major disruption in the family life-cycling process, adding complexity to whatever developmental tasks the family is experiencing in its present phase (Carter & McGoldrick, Chapter 1). The normal life cycle tasks, interrupted and altered by the divorce process, continue with greater complexity due to the concommitant phases of the divorcing process. Each ensuing life cycle phase becomes affected by the divorce and must henceforth be viewed within the dual context of the stage itself as well as the residual effects of the divorce.

With the shape of the family irrevocably altered, the family continues to go on in a new form. Research indicates that family systems require one to three years to engage in the divorce process and restabilize and continue their "normal" developmental process (Hetherington, 1982). If a family can negotiate the crisis and the accompanying transitions that must be experienced in order to restabilize, it will have established a more fluid system that will allow a continuation of the 'normal' family developmental process.

The sociocultural context of the family is another aspect to consider in understanding the impact of divorce, adding a vital and often overlooked dimension to the divorce process (McGoldrick, et al., 1982). Some ethnic and religious groups accept divorce far more readily than others; some religions do not accept divorce at all. While the specific ways in which different cultures view divorce will not be dealt with here, it is important to understand that the

ramifications of a specific culture's perceptions of divorce greatly influence the families adaptational process.

DEMOGRAPHICS

During the past two decades, there has been a dramatic increase in divorce in the United States. The steepest rise occurred during the decade from 1966 to 1976 (U.S. Bureau of the Census, 1983). In 1962 there were 413,000 divorces; by 1983, 1,179,000 (National Center for Health Statstics [NCHS], 1984). Thus the number of divorces has almost tripled in 20 years. Although in 1982–1983 there was a slight downward trend (NCHS, 1984), preliminary data from the NCHS indicated that in 1985 the divorce rate was up again, matching the 1983 level (*The New York Times,* April 14, 1986). All evidence suggests that divorce has become and will remain a variant life-style in almost half of the marriages of today's young adults (Glick, 1984).

In 1981 the length of marriage at the time of divorce peaked at two years, declining gradually every year thereafter, with the median duration time for marriages seven years and the average age of the spouses at the time of divorce between 25 and 34 (NCHS, 1984a). Thus *the time marriages appear to be most at risk is during the first phases of the family life cycle, before and soon after children arrive.* According to divorce data from 31 states, in 45% of the divorces there were no children; in 26%, one child; in 20%, two children; and in 9%, three or more children (NCHS, 1984a). About 1.2 million children were affected in 1981—a ratio of about one child per divorce (NCHS, 1984a). It is estimated that if the current pattern continues, by 1990 a third of all (minor) white children and three-fifths of black children will experience the separation or divorce of their parents; of those children it is far more likely that the white children will live in a remarried household within five years (Bumpass & Rindfuss, 1979).

Of the people who divorce, five-sixths of the men and three-quarters of the women will remarry (Glick, 1984), with the chances of remarriage far greater when the couple is in the early stages of the family life cycle. Of those remarriages, the divorce rate is even higher than for first marriages, with statistics varying according to sex and age groups. For men and women in the 30s who remarried in 1980, the predicted divorce rate is as high as 61% for the men and 54% for the women (Glick, 1984).

There are a number of etiological factors associated with marital instability.

1. *Age and premarital pregnancy:* Brides less than 18, husbands less than 20 (Norton & Glick, 1976), or couples who marry when there is a premarital pregnancy (25% of brides are pregnant [Furstenberg, 1976]) are twice as likely to divorce.

2. *Education:* Less educated men and better educated women are more at

risk than better educated men and less educated women (Levinger, 1976). Compared with those who have not completed college or have postgraduate degrees, women who have completed four years of college are the group least at risk for divorce (Glick, 1984a).

3. *Income:* Women who earn more money are more likely to divorce than women with lower incomes (Ross & Sawhill, 1975). Also the greater the wife's income in relation to the husband's income, the greater the risk of divorce (Cherlin, 1979).

4. *Employment:* When the husband has unstable employment and income, or his income declines from the previous year, the marriage is at higher risk (Ross & Sawhille, 1975).

5. *Socioeconomic level:* Though the gap is narrowing, the relatively disadvantaged tend to be disproportionately at risk (North & Glick, 1976).

6. *Race:* Black couples have a higher divorce rate than whites, and interracial marriages are even more at risk (Norton & Glick, 1976).

7. *Intergenerational transmission link:* Divorce appears to run in families, though studies on the correlation between parental divorce and marital instability in the next generation have yielded mixed results. One possibility is that it is not the pattern of divorce per se but economic factors related to the divorce that often push children into early marriages with poorly selected mates (Mueller & Pope, 1977).

REVIEW OF THE LITERATURE

Divorce: A Crisis of Transition

In the past research focused on the relationship between divorce and psychopathology, with marital status linked to mental disorder. Evidence to support this view stems from the psychological vulnerability of many people at the time of separation/divorce. Divorced people are six times more at risk to be hospitalized for psychological disorders as married people (Bloom et al., 1978; Briscoe, et al., 1973). In addition, divorced people have twice the suicide rate of married people, more car accidents, more physical illnesses culminating in death (cancer and heart disease), and more problems with substance abuse (Bloom et al., 1978).

In our view this pathological perspective on divorce has both major methodological and conceptual shortcomings. More recent work on the impact of divorce, started in the past decade, views divorce as a transitional crisis (Ahrons, 1980a), forcing an interruption of the developmental tasks to be negotiated at the family's particular life cycle phase (Carter & McGoldrick, Chapter 1), creating in their place a series of separation/divorce-related adjustments that throw all family members into a state of chaos and disequilibrium

for a period of one to three years (Hetherington, 1982) until restabilization takes place. Thus the distress is seen as a "normal" short-term response to crisis.

The lack of societal support or guidelines for the family going through this process adds to the difficulties. We need a model for divorce as a normative family transition (Ahrons, 1980a) and believe this framework, based on a crisis theory paradigm, is a useful tool for conceptualizing the divorce experience for the family. Encompassing stages and processes for divorce-related adjustments and accompanying life stresses, it offers a more positive perspective, providing the potential for a growth-inducing experience as family members develop new capacities to adapt.

In the past decade, there has been considerable research on the impact of divorce on the couple and their children. While recent media coverage has called attention to the plight of grandparents with respect to visitation rights, the divorce-adjustment process of the family system as a whole—grandparents, siblings, and other extended-family members—is often overlooked. We believe that each and every member of the nuclear and extended family is affected in ways that influence the process for all, depending in part on the life cycle phase of the family. For example, there is evidence that close grandparent/grandchild contacts is of value to all three generations of family members (Kivnick, 1982). In reviewing the literature, we look first at the impact of divorce on the family as a system and then at special issues for children of divorce.

The Impact of Divorce on the Family

According to the Holmes and Rahe (1967) scale of stressful life events, divorce ranks second only to the death of a spouse. Major individual adjustments must be made at two levels, emotional and practical—adjustment to the separation, with all the emotional upheaval that accompanies it, and adjustment to the new life, with problems in one area affecting adjustment in the other area (Spanier & Casto, 1979). Many interrelated factors influence the response: the circumstances surrounding the dissolution of the marriage, the nature of the postseparation life, age, sex, length of marriage, where the family is in relation to the tasks specific to its life cycle stage, initial psychological stability, the quality of the postseparation life, education, socioeconomic level, ethnic context, other stresses occurring at the time, prior experience with stress, and available support.

The adjustment process takes place in stages over a two- or three-year period, beginning with the predecision period and ending either with some sort of homeostasis established within the new one-parent household or with remarriage (Hetherington, 1977; Ahrons, 1980a). The transition is gradual, beginning long before the actual decision is made, often with only one spouse struggling with the idea of divorce as a solution to his/her dissatisfaction, and

ending when the family has restabilized in a way that is understood by all members of the nuclear and extended family (Ahrons, 1980a). Ahrons (1980a) postulates five overlapping stages of this adjustment process, each one involving specific role transitions and tasks.

In the first stage *(Individual Cognition)*, at least one spouse is considering divorce and beginning the process of emotional disengagement, maintaining distance through separate activities and involvements. This period is often characterized by heightened stress, with considerable fighting, bitterness, blaming, devaluing the partner, depression, anxiety, and, always, ambivalence. There may be an affair, which often serves to expedite the decision.

One of the most important initial factors in adjustment involves the spouse's participation in—or lack of participation in—the decision itself. For the initiator the decision-making period is perhaps the most difficult of all as he/she struggles with tremendous remorse and guilt (Wallerstein & Kelly, 1980).

In the second stage *(Family Metacognition)*, also preseparation, the secret is revealed. A time of great distress, for some families this may be the time of greatest disequilibrium. If the family copes well at this point, the couple may be able to separate with well-thought-out decisions.

In the majority of divorces, one partner wants out more than the other. In studies on couples with children married an average of ten years, the majority of decisions were nonmutual (Wallerstein & Kelly, 1980; Ahrons, 1981). Women tend to take the initiative (Wallerstein & Kelly, 1980; Ahrons, 1981); men to oppose it (Wallerstein & Kelly, 1980).

For the noninitiator spouse, the more sudden and unexpected the decision is perceived to be, the more difficult is the initial emotional adjustment (Spanier & Casto, 1979). Many nonintiator spouses are totally unprepared for the decision (Wallerstein & Kelly, 1980), and experience an overall sense of low self-esteem, powerlessness, and humiliation.

In the third stage *(System Separation)*, the actual separation takes place. This is a very hard time for all the family, the outcome depending largely on how the preceding stages were handled. The more reactive the family, the greater is the crisis. Initially each spouse is in a state of heightened emotional vulnerability that can interfere with normal functioning. Common symptoms include the inability to work effectively, poor health, weight changes, insomnia and other sleep disturbances, sexual dysfunction, and use of alcohol, tobacco, and other substances (Hetherington, 1982).

There is always ambivalence. For the vast majority, lingering attachment persists despite anger and resentment—the more the attachment, the greater the distress (Weiss, 1979). Over time the anger and attachment decrease, with anger remaining longer. There is a sense of helplessness, a lack of control over life events, feelings of incompetence—socially and sexually, loss, loneliness, anger, frustrated dependency needs, and identity problems. Many are not satisfied with the new life-style and wish they had tried harder to make the marriage work. The person who initiated the separation may regret it and want

to reconcile, while the noninitiator spouse may have gone into therapy or started to rebound and be unwilling to risk becoming vulnerable again.

Throughout this stage and all ensuing stages, each spouse is prone to tremendous emotional upheavals, to highs and lows. As soon as the emotional turmoil appears to be abating, something new will occur that sets the individual reeling one more time. This process repeats itself over and over for a period that usually peaks at one year, and may last as long as two years or more. With time the intensity of each swing slowly diminishes—like an upward spiral swinging back and forth, gradually reaching an end point. For those who functioned marginally before the separation, divorce may increase their difficulties; for others divorce stimulates their personal growth in a way that was not possible within the marriage. For many women it may be the first time in their lives they have felt autonomous; consequently they experience a newly found sense of competency and well-being.

There may be a series of separations and reconciliations—half of all married couples separate at least once (Weiss, 1975)—creating boundary ambiguities as the marriage moves back and forth from off to on, with family members uncertain as to whether or not to reorganize to fill absent roles. Premature contact with lawyers often escalates the crisis. When the separation becomes public and legal proceedings are initiated, the crisis may escalate still further.

In general men and women respond differently, with different issues and different coping styles (Berman & Turk, 1981; Chiriboga et al., 1978). At the time of initiating proceedings, women tend to be significantly angrier than men at their spouses, especially if they perceive the spouse as angry at them (Kelly, 1986). They tend to meet the stress of divorce head on; go through a period of emotional turmoil, become angry or depressed, and then recover (Chiriboga et al., 1978). Many men deal with their unhappiness by throwing themselves into work and later experience an overall low sense of well-being (Chiriboga et al., 1978). In the long run, there seems to be a significant difference between how women and men adjust emotionally to divorce. Wallerstein's (1986) ten-year postdivorce follow-up to the Wallerstein and Kelly (1980) study found that 55% of the women versus 32% of the men felt that their lives had improved, and that 64% of the women versus 16% of the men reported a sense of emotional/psychological growth as a result of the divorce.

Many people will play a pivotal role: children, extended-family members, friends, lovers, co-workers, lawyers, and others. Support from family and friends is crucial for both men and women. While initially married friends may be supportive, after the first months there is often a sharp decline, particularly for women. Without such support the overall adjustment is more difficult. It may be self-imposed, as some people respond by withdrawing from family and friends at the time support is most needed. It may be that those around him/her are disapproving or are tired of hearing the same story repeated or are caught in loyalty ties with the other spouse. In any case the social network of separated people often shifts from old, married friends to new, single, more

casual acquaintances. The adjustment tends to be faster when there is more social interaction (Hetherington, 1977).

The fourth stage *(System Reorganization)* involves the difficult process of clarifying new boundaries. All members of the family experience the disruption and confusion that accompanies the divorce process and have difficulty negotiating the transition during this stage. The loss of one parent from the household, the many changes in family functioning, and the stresses on each parent affecting his/her ability to parent all contribute to the impact on the children. The more the nonresident parent is excluded, the greater is the potential for family dysfunction.

The challenge for the family systems becomes one of reorganization rather than dismantling. New rules and patterns must be developed for all the habits and routines of daily life that were taken for granted no longer apply. Membership changes: the households include one spouse each, possibly with new partners, and their families; siblings may be separated; caretakers may assume an important position in the family; children who had left home or other extended-family members may return. Roles, boundaries, membership, and hierarchal structure change, with virtually every subsystem within the family affected: husband/wife, parent/child, sibling/sibling, grandparent/grandchild, spouse/family of origin, spouse/in-laws, spouse/nonfamily relationships (friends, work, community, etc.). Relationships with all systems outside the nuclear family change as well: extended family, friends, work, school, community. All of this takes place in the absence of norms or social supports for divorced families. Consequently the changes are a source of great stress, creating added conflict that interferes with making the transitions.

For the couple the process of terminating the marital relationship while maintaining interdependent ties as parents is difficult, especially since there are few useful role models to use as a guide. In fact many divorced people are clearer about what they do not want to do, based on seeing the experience of others, than what they do want to do. What makes the process even harder is that any ongoing relationship is considered suspect—a form of holding on. A recent five-year study that examined the nature of former spousal relationships (all parents) found that half the couples studied were able to achieve an amiable relationship: 12% were "perfect pals," 38% "cooperative colleagues," 25% "angry associates," and 25% "fiery foes" (Ahrons, 1986).

Other studies looking at the quality of the coparental relationship indicate that the first year is the hardest, with 95% reporting that their feelings changed considerably in the year after the divorce in a way that enabled a better relationship (Goldsmith, 1980). Preliminary findings of a recent study by Kelly (1986) found that child-focused communication was significantly better than discussion of marital issues, an encouraging indicator for cooperative postdivorce parenting. A combination of positive and negative feelings coexist, though neither to an extreme. Most discussions center around issues of parenting, with the major areas of disagreement revolving around finances and child-

rearing practices. Some former spouses get together as a family for such events as children's birthdays, school plays, graduations, and other events related to the children's lives (Ahrons, 1981; Goldsmith, 1980).

Despite a high incidence of conflict (Ahrons, 1981; Goldsmith, 1980), on the whole the relationship is satisfactory to most, though there are significant differences in the way men and women perceive the relationship, with men reporting considerably more parental involvement than their former spouses reported for them (Goldsmith, 1980; Ahrons, 1981). What makes the relationship work is not the interaction itself but clear and agreed-upon boundaries (Ahrons, 1981; Goldsmith, 1980).

For the spouses, the single most powerful factor in defusing the marital bond and restoring self-esteem is the establishment of a new love relationship (Hetherington, 1982; Spanier & Casto, 1979). Just as a new relationship aids the emotional adjustment process, economic stability eases the transition to a new life. For some the adjustment to a new life may be the hardest part (Spanier & Casto, 1979). Frequently a host of practical and financial concerns serves to escalate the crisis, and unless there is a great deal of money, economic necessity will dictate many changes. Separation may herald an entire change in life-style; in any case financial concerns become a major preoccupation for most divorcing people, regardless of income level.

The economic consequences are significantly different for men and women; with the majority of men reporting themselves as financially "well off," women as worse off after divorce (Spanier & Casto, 1979). Sweeping changes in divorce laws across the country, intended to treat both sexes more fairly, have led to some form of no-fault divorce in 48 states, with the financial decisions based on the view of marriage as an economic partnership. Marital assets are evenly or equitably divided and, for the most part, alimony has become outdated. In a ten-year study on the effects of no-fault divorce in California, Weitzman (1985) concluded that women and children have become "the victims of the divorce revolution." With the exception of young women with marriages of brief duration and/or women who have always worked during the marriage and make enough money to be self-supporting, most women are unprepared financially or occupationally for divorce. This is especially difficult for women who have been out of work for a long time or have never worked at all, have no marketable skills, or have young children.

Women with children depend in part on the father for support, which may or may not be forthcoming—47% of support agreements are not adhered to (U.S. Bureau of the Census, 1983). The incidence of defaulting on support during the first year postdivorce is estimated to be as high as 75% (U.S. Bureau of the Census, 1983). In 1984 Congress enacted legislation to enforce child-support collection through mandatory income withholding to cover overdue payments. However, even when support is forthcoming, the average child support payment (averaging 13% of the husband's income) is only $2110 per year (U.S. Bureau of the Census, 1983), a small portion of the actual costs. The average annual income for women with children receiving support is $9000,

and $6500 without support (U.S. Bureau of the Census, 1983). As a result we are faced with a new, divorce-related social problem, called "the feminization of poverty," with over 50% of mother-headed households living in poverty (*The New York Times*, Sept. 7, 1983).

The fifth and final stage *(System Redefinition)* begins when the family has resolved the tasks of the previous stages and has a new self-definition. New roles and boundaries have been clarified, and all members are included if good parenting is to take place. Where there are continued, cooperative ex-spousal relationships, the family restabilizes faster and more effectively. Wallerstein's (1986) ten-year follow-up to the Wallerstein and Kelly (1980) study on divorce found that the mutuality of the decision to divorce often remains an issue, with the initiator spouse reporting significantly greater satisfaction in the quality of life than the noninitiator spouse.

Children and Divorce

While divorce may be perceived as a solution to parents' problems, few children seem to want divorce, no matter how much marital tension preceded the split (Wallerstein & Kelly, 1980). Their reactions varying according to age, temperament, sex, position in the family, past experiences, support systems, and cognitive and social competence. For many children divorce means a change in the nature of the relationship with and access to extended-family members as well—grandparents, aunts, uncles, cousins. Where there is a bitter divorce, loyalty conflicts often become transmitted across the generational lines in ways that serve everyone poorly.

In the past research focused on the impact of father absence on children, and examined the connection between delinquency, underachievement, promiscuity, and confused sexual identity and father absence. A review of 200 studies on father absence found that while father absence is indeed a factor, the cumulative impact of other psychosocial factors (such as poverty) was more central to the behavioral disturbances (Herzog & Sudia, 1973).

More recent studies have examined the impact of divorce on children by comparing the two-parent household with one-parent households. Lowery and Settle (1985), in their comprehensive review of the research literature on children and divorce, found that while some studies showed statistically significant differences between children in intact families and children in divorced families, others showed no differences at all. Further, they found that there were favorable findings in different areas for children in both intact and divorced families. Some children were able to adapt successfully to the stresses associated with divorce, whereas others had more difficulty. It seems that it is not divorce per se that creates long-range disturbances but, the specific circumstances emanating from the separation—namely, the loss of a parent, ongoing conflict between parents (Ahrons, 1980; Wallerstein & Kelly, 1980), the quality of the postseparation life, and the number and degree of

other stress-inducing changes resulting from the separation. Lowery and Settle (1985) concluded that the data are more meaningful when looking at specific variables, such as age, sex, parental conflict, life changes after divorce, and the nature of the parenting arrangement.

Age

The concensus of many studies of all types of arrangements was that the younger children are at the time of divorce, the greater the short-term impact. (While the findings may well apply to infants and toddlers, there has been little systematic investigation on the effects of children less than two years old.) However, in the ten-year follow-up to Wallerstein and Kelly's (1980) study, Wallerstein (1984) found young children who have no memory of the pre-divorce life adjust better over time than older children, who remember the family that was and consider the divorce the central event of their childhood. In addition, recent research indicates that many young adult children whose parents have recently divorced experience a number of difficulties involving loyalty conflicts and anger at their father, no matter who initiated the divorce (Ahrons, 1986; Cooney, et al., 1986).

Sex

Many studies indicate that divorce is harder on boys than girls, though the reasons have not been examined. There may be correlation between distress and the leaving of the same-sex parent, affecting the structure and/or function-ing of the one-parent household. Another possibility is that since boys appear to have a greater constitutional vulnerability to stress (Rutter, 1979), the moving about involved in joint custody is inherently harder on them.

Parental Conflict

Several studies on children's adjustment have found a strong correlation between poor adjustment in children and parental conflict, regardless of mar-ital status (Hess & Camera, 1979; Raschke & Raschke, 1979). The results of many different studies indicate that the postdivorce relationship between the parents is the most critical factor in the functioning of the family. While an important factor in children's postseparation adjustment is the continuing, qualitative contact with both parents, the level of interparental conflict may be more central to the child's postdivorce adjustment than parental absence or the divorce itself (Hetherington, 1977; Emery, 1982). Luepnitz's study (1982) of nonclinical families' coping styles in different kinds of custody arrange-ments found that ongoing conflict was the only predictor of poor adjustment in children.

Life Changes After Divorce

The number and degree of changes to which the children are exposed affect their ability to adapt. As has been noted, father absence is directly related to economic instability, which in turn affects adjustment.

Nature of the New Parenting Arrangements

Many studies have indicated that children want and need a qualitative, ongoing relationship with both parents. In the vast majority of cases, children reside with their mother, by mutual parental agreement. However, in a study on women and custody of children, Chester (1986) reported that where there is a custody battle and both parents are "fit," the father stands a far greater chance of getting the children.

Common divorce terminology refers to the mother-headed household as the single-parent family, conceptually wiping out the role of the father in a way that all too often parallels reality. Furstenburg and colleagues' (1983) sociological study revealed that 50% of the children of divorce have had no direct contact with the noncustodial parent in a year. By six years after the divorce, less than a quarter of the noncustodial fathers see their children more than monthly, with contact less likely if the children are girls and if the father has remarried (Hetherington, 1982). For all children the father remained a significant person, even if there had been no actual contact.

Different studies have found that all family members benefit when there is continued shared parenting. Where there is mutually supportive, cooperative coparental relationship, there is a greater chance that the father will remain involved, both physically and financially (Ahrons, 1981). Fathers, as well as children, do better when there is continued contact (Jacobs, 1982; Greif, 1979). Single mothers, often pushed into the role of emotional and financial caretaker of the family, experience tremendous task overload, which diminishes their capacity to adjust in all areas (Ahrons, 1981; Hetherington et al., 1978).

Most children are dissatisfied with traditional access (every other weekend with their father), feel cut off from the noncustodial parent, and want more contact (Wallerstein & Kelly, 1980; Ahrons, 1981). Joint custody is emerging as a possible replacement for the traditional sole-custody arrangement, based on the assumption that it more closely parallels the structure and functions of the predivorce family, allowing greater and more natural access to both parents. In addition, with the vast majority of single mothers working, the assumption that the mother is at home and available is no longer valid. Both mother and father now have about the same time available for their children.

While most, if not all, studies report a high degree of satisfaction with the arrangement (Greif, 1979; Abarbanel, 1979; Ahrons, 1981), most research has been conducted on the response of early enthusiasts of the concept, and little on the children's experience. One study found that a third of the children experience intense loyalty conflicts and an overconcern for being fair to both

parents (Steinman, 1981). Another small study conducted on same-sex custody found evidence that children like and do well with same-sex custody (Santrock & Warshak, 1979). However, the impact of splitting siblings—a bond that tends to strengthen with divorce—was not measured and cannot be overlooked. Luepnitz (1982) examined all types of arrangements, interviewing all household members, and found that joint custody at its best is superior to sole custody at its best.

From the research findings to date, it would seem that no matter what role the father held in the predivorce family, he is capable of assuming all the responsibility involved in single parenting. A different quality of psychological involvement grows out of the father's participation in a joint-custody arrangement. However, despite the notion that shared parenting might be the ideal solution to divorce, it is by no means a panacea for all. When the mother has assumed primary responsibility for the children prior to separation, tremendous adjustments must be made by both parents. Women are significantly less positive about shared-parenting arrangements and want their children with them for a greater amount of time than men—70% versus 40% of the time (Kelly, 1986). And while it may be hard for the mother to let go of her role as primary parent, it will also be an adjustment for the father to take a more active role, especially if there are young children.

For the former spouses, joint-custody arrangements may tie them together in a way that impedes forward movement of their own lives. For the children coparenting in the presence of continuing, intense conflict appears to be more harmful than no contact. In short, continued access to and qualitative relationships with both parents appear to be more important than the particular form of custodial arrangement.

In any case, despite all the talk about joint custody, there has been little change in type of arrangements in the past ten years. The judicial system may force the issue, however, by defining that what is 'in the best interests of the child' is joint custody. A handful of states already have joint-custody statutes in effect, and the majority of states have joint-custody statutes pending.

THE IMPACT OF DIVORCE AT DIFFERENT
STAGES OF THE FAMILY LIFE CYCLE

As previously noted, divorce is a crisis in the family life cycle, creating a state of disequilibrium for everyone at all generational levels throughout the nuclear- and extended-family system. The disruption is associated with shifts and changes in membership and boundaries, requiring a major reorganization of the family system. The degree to which the family will be affected depends on the phase of the family life cycle during which the divorce occurs, as well as on other factors related to the ethnic, social, and economic context of the

arrangement that would work for them. They were able to agree to an equal-time-sharing plan, with needed adjustments as Alissa got older. They were referred to a mediator to work out the details.

Once the battle ended, both were overwhelmed by the notion of even half-time single parenthood. Finally, each was ready to examine his/her own family-of-origin issues that this evoked, not in the service of saving the marriage but in order for each to carry on alone. Georgia wanted badly to find a face-saving way to reconnect with her family, which the therapist saw as an important goal. Each was seen individually to discuss his or her own issues, and then once a month together to discuss coparenting. Georgia continued in therapy for several months, and Jack even longer, though both remained committed to the idea of using a neutral forum such as therapy to continue to discuss Alissa. Eventually they cut back to three or four such routine visits a year, with as-needed visits always available in between. Perhaps because it was always an option, there has never been the need to schedule an emergency visit.

Families with Elementary-School-Age Children

The impact of divorce on children of this age is more profound. Wallerstein and Kelly (1980) found that children six to eight seem to have the hardest time of any age group, as they are old enough to realize what is happening but do not have adequate skills to deal with the disruption. They often feel a sense of responsibility, experience tremendous grief, and have a pervasive sadness and yearning for the departed parent. At the same time, they experience recurring fantasies of reconciliation and often think that they have the power to make it happen.

When the divorce is bitter, children may be at risk psychologically if involved in loyalty conflicts. Some children assume or are drawn into parent-ified roles, taking on inappropriate adult responsibilities that are damaging emotionally. They may develop school and/or peer problems characterized by poor performance, problematic behavior with peers or authority, and/or somatic symptoms (Wallerstein & Kelly, 1980).

The older the children are at the time of separation, the easier it will be for the father to establish an effective parental role as he knows them as people, with personalities and interests to which he can relate. However, as they get older and more involved with peers and outside involvements, they may draw back from the father both physically and emotionally, unless he is sensitive to their general desire to cut back on their time with parents, and does not take it personally.

Again, parents need to present the fact that they are divorcing to the children together, giving them time to process the idea. Children need a chance to think and talk about their reactions and help in understanding the consequences for them in terms of the impact it will have on their lives and their continuing relationships with parents, relatives, and friends.

The potential for unresolved marital issues to become smoke-screened through the children increases as children get older, with the result that children may carry the loss, anger, and guilt for their parents.

The following case illustrates three goals of clinical work with divorcing

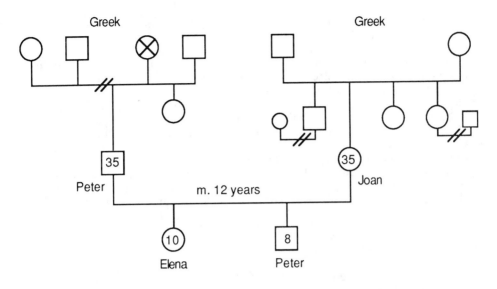

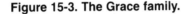

Figure 15-3. The Grace family.

parents. The first goal was to slow down the divorce decision so that if and when the couple decided to separate, it could happen in a less disruptive way. The second goal was to prevent the noninitiator spouse from drawing the children into taking sides against the parent who chose separation. The third goal was to help the couple recognize the benefits for the children of a cooperative coparental relationship.

Case Example: The Grace Family

Joan, 35, made the initial contact, mentioning that she was unhappy in her marriage and wanted out. She said that she had already spoken to her husband, Peter, about divorce. The therapist asked her to come with Peter, suggesting that it would be most helpful if both came to talk about the imminent decision. Joan had been married to Peter, 35, who was of Greek-American extraction, for 12 years. They had two children—Elena, ten, and Peter, eight. With marriage Joan had hoped to be taken care of by her husband emotionally and financially. Peter, on the other hand, the younger son in a family that was chaotic following his father's desertion, was attracted by what he thought was Joan's strength, seeking in a wife a woman on whom he could lean. Tired of the caring for everyone's needs, a few years previously, Joan had gone back to school to pursue a graduate degree. Peter had assumed many of the household and child-care responsibilities to help Joan achieve her goal, thinking he was doing it for the family. In the process he put his life on hold while Joan was flourishing, both socially and intellectually, and he had absolutely no idea that Joan was growing away from him. When Joan told him

she was thinking of leaving him, he was devastated, especially since he himself had as a child experienced the pain of his parents' divorce.

The first move was to slow down the decision-making process to help Peter absorb it and to allow the couple time to put the decision in a context that both could comprehend. To do this the treatment involved a review of the history and development of the marriage as well as work on issues connected to their families of origin. Throughout this phase Peter begged Joan to rethink her decision; he even threatened suicide. A contract was made for the couple to take three more months to continue their family-of-origin work and to finalize their plans. During that time they lived in pseudo-roommate style, dividing the household and child-care responsibilities as if they were separated. This "trial separation" led to discussions of the future relating to financial and child-care arrangements. Before they had made any specific plans, Peter told the children that their mother was breaking up the family. He aligned with them, presenting the notion that they were all victims. The therapist suggested more appropriate ways of handling this sensitive area and saw the couple with their children to help the process along and to attempt to intercept loyalty conflicts.

During the last phase of treatment, coparenting became the key focus of discussion and postseparation plans were made. As a result of focusing on concern for the children's adjustment as well as the emotional process of separating for a couple, they were able to work out a cooperative coparental agreement and to separate in a minimally disruptive way. Peter came to see that his life and his close relationships with his children could continue and that he had the capacity to develop his own potential for future work and relationships. He also recognized the impact of his parents' divorce on his response to the present crisis.

Divorce in Families with Adolescents

Once again, the issues families face relate to the developmental phase of the children. Adolescence is a stage filled with many changes, physical and emotional. It is a time when children are beginning their own process of leaving home, forming an identity separate from their parents. This family life-cycle phase requires a new definition of children within the family and of parents' roles in relation to their children. Families need to establish qualitatively different, more permeable boundaries. Parents are no longer the complete authority; yet the children still need the stability they represent. Adolescents tend to want to be dependent at times and to test their independence at other times.

Because of their own unsettled nature, adolescents' reactions to divorce include anger, a desire for a stable home, and a need for clear boundaries between them and their parents, especially around such issues as sexuality, dating, and household responsibilities. As with toddlers, adolescents depend upon a secure base so they can leave. Divorce threatens this base, and they are angry with the changes. They do not want to have to think about their parents' lives. Many feel they have to hurry and grow up, others that they cannot leave. They worry about sex and marriage and may become preoccupied with their parents' sexuality.

Teenagers can go two ways. For those who are already having difficulties, divorce creates an added burden, increasing the risk of emotional problems;

for others the change in participation in family life is a maturing experience. However, they may get drawn into unwanted loyalty conflicts or assume positions of blame. They want their parents' lives to be in order; they want parenting. They may be pushed into or assume parentified roles with siblings. They want to be left alone but each parent may seek their companionship to fill the loneliness. When children do fill that void, it isolates them from peers and prevents them from moving on. Children at this age may engage in self-destructive behavior: truancy, school failure, substance abuse, sexual acting out. When divorce occurs, the transitional process needs to allow for continued adolescent movement. Divorce is further complicated because of the convergence of many similar issues for adolescents and parents—dating, dealing with one's own sexuality, learning to be independent.

Managing teenagers is difficult, even when the marriage is intact. Handling adolescents without the support of the other spouse compounds the difficulty, especially for mothers with sons (Hetherington, 1982), who accept the social myth that adolescent boys can only be "controlled" by men or the psychoanalytic myth that the mother–son relationship is somehow prone to becoming eroticized if there is no husband around. Continually confronted with new situations, the single parent can feel overwhelmed and not in charge. Coparenting may become nasty. When the teenager's behavior is problematic, neither parent knows what to do, and may compound the difficulty by blaming one another. The ability to coparent is directly related to the capacity to communicate and cooperate.

Each parent will have already established a relationship with the children. To the extent that it is a close tie, it will remain intact—unless the children are drawn into loyalty issues. While they have more contact with the custodial parent, teenagers usually see the other parent as often as they choose and/or is feasible. Depending upon the ages of the children, they often have input into the custodial arrangement. The danger is when they find themselves called upon to fulfill the role of the absent spouse, to become mother or father's confidant and coparent, especially if there are younger siblings.

For women at this stage, the economic ramifications of divorce vary greatly depending upon whether they worked during the marriage. Few can depend upon receiving ongoing alimony, and even if it is forthcoming, it is unlikely that it would allow them the same life style. Most will either have to seek employment based on whatever skills they have or struggle to upgrade their skills, seeking greater economic self-sufficiency for the long haul.

Most men at this stage have invested 15–20 years in developing themselves vocationally and are at their peak, with many productive years ahead. While they may anticipate hefty college tuitions for their children in the near future, it is unlikely that they will have to support their former wives indefinitely, and their concern often centers around preparing for a future in which they may have another family to support.

The following case illustrates the problems involved in single parenting an adolescent when the father effectively cuts off from the family after a bitter

divorce. The presenting problem was the adolescent daughter's running away from home. The first phase of this postdivorce therapy treatment involved the mother and daughter. Once their relationship was restored, the next step involved opening up the system by bringing the father back into an active parenting role. This led to work in restructuring the coparental relationship for the benefit of the child. The third phase focused on the mother working on her own personal issues and their relation to her family of origin. As is often the case, the father was not interested in any further therapy.

Case Example: The Jones Family

Joanne, 43, called to seek help for her fifteen-year-old daughter, Barbara, who had run away from home three times in four months. Joanne and Barbara's father, Bob, had been involved in a bitter court battle at the time of their divorce two years before and, as a result, Barbara had no contact with her father during that period.

During the initial session attended by both mother and daughter, Joanne let the therapist know that she was having problems disciplining Barbara and supporting their household and that she wanted Barbara "fixed". A recently dry alcoholic, she said that she was attending AA meetings regularly and that while she had her own problems, she did not want them addressed in the therapy. By the end of the first session, it was clear that mother and daughter had a strong emotional attachment. Barbara, a pseudo-mature adolescent, was experiencing the need to be close to her mother and at the same time needing to pull away from her. She also wanted to restore contact with her father.

During the first phase of therapy, Joanne and Barbara talked a great deal about what it was like for them to live together in a confined space, with no family or

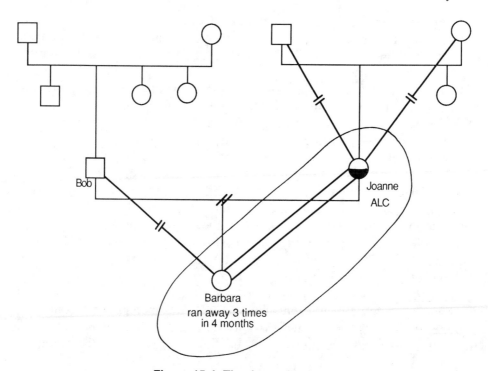

Figure 15-4. The Jones family.

social support network. Joanne was not on speaking terms with her parents or sister, all of whom lived outside the city. She had few friends and had no social contacts with the people at work. There were few people Joanne could turn to for help or support. This bothered Barbara as she felt her mother relied too much on her for companionship.

After seeing the mother and daughter for one month, reframing the runaway behavior as Barbara's caring for her mother, the therapist felt that is was time to help Barbara reconnect with her father. Joanne finally agreed to let the therapist call Bob, though she predicted that he would refuse to come. To her surprise he agreed to come, but only if she agreed not to ask for money.

The next phase of therapy lasted six months, involving Bob and Barbara; Joanne and Barbara; and, finally, all three together on issues of finances and discipline. Work with Bob and Barbara focused on reestablishing their relationship. Bob set up regular visiting days with Barbara. By the end of this phase, he also began making Barbara's final high-school-tuition payments and a long overdue orthodontist bill. Within this time Barbara was attending school regularly, being more cooperative at home, and enjoying ongoing visits with her father.

As her relationship with her daughter improved, Joanne began to realize how lonely, isolated, and angry she felt. Now ready to deal with her own issues, the last phase of therapy focused on Joanne alone—on her work, on her role as a mother, and on her relationships with family and friends. Throughout treatment Bob was unwilling to go into anything other than what was directly related to parenting.

Divorce in Families with Children Being Launched

Because of increased life expectancy, this phase of the family life cycle is the newest and the longest. At this time, after a long-term marriage, divorce can create a great upheaval because the couple has such a long history together. The children, generally, are on their way out of the home. Caretaking functions of the couple often switch to responsibility for elderly parents. Marriages can become vulnerable when children are no longer the major focus of the couple, and the restructuring of the marital relationship necessitated by their leaving home can bring with it the decision to divorce.

Children can have a separate well-defined relationship with each parent. However, despite the fact that they may be out of the parental home, divorce can be very stressful for young adult children, with a sense of increased responsibility to their parents and a vulnerability to loyalty conflicts (Ahrons, 1986; Cooney et al., 1986). Often much of the anger is directed at the father for leaving the mother in their care, even when he did not initiate the divorce (Ahrons, 1986). The father–daughter relationship seems particularly at risk (Cooney et al., 1986). In addition, young adults may experience a sense of loss of family home, abandonment by their parents, and a concern about their own marriage (Ahrons, 1986). There is evidence of an increase in alcohol abuse (Cooney et al., 1986). The biggest risk for children is when the parents hold on to them or they assume the role of substitute spouse to fill the loneliness,

It may be that the divorce occurs when parents who have stayed together 'for the children' now feel free to end a long and unhappy marriage. Under those circumstances each spouse will have spent years disengaging and have developed enough separate friends and interests to make the transition relatively easier. One or both may have a new mate waiting in the wings. Unhampered by parental responsibilities, divorce can be a welcome chance to start a new life.

When a spouse is left unwillingly at this phase, however, divorce is devastating, especially for women, in terms of adjustment both to the separation and to the new life. Wallerstein (1986) found that women over 40 have a harder time rebuilding their lives socially, economically, and psychologically. For those whose primary role has been inside the home, divorce can be extremely difficult with both husband and children leaving at the same time. The social aspects are particularly difficult due to changes in the friendship network and reentry into an alien dating world in which youth and beauty are sought in women. For the wife who has never worked and now must support herself, the challenge may be impossible to meet. The job market is competitive, with age and lack of experience severe handicaps. Combined with all this is the continuing desire to have someone to depend upon. There may be the additional burden of caring for sick or aged parents. Some may develop psychological or physical symptoms that prevent forward movement. Other women may rise to the challenge, tackling the changes well. Much depends on age, career opportunities, interests and network outside the home, and the willingness to give up the idea of marriage as essential to happiness.

For a man divorce at this stage of life is usually inherently easier from a financial standpoint, as he has, most likely, been self-supporting all his adult life. The more difficult adjustments involve loss of home and being taken care of and beginning to date. Statistics show that while women at this and later stages have a remote chance of remarrying (Glick, 1984), men often deal with the difficulties by quickly recoupling, for which they find easy opportunity.

Children can have a separate well-defined relationship with each parent. However, recent research by Constance Ahrons on the impact of divorce of young adults ages 19–24 (AFTA Conference, Washington, D.C., June 1986) indicates that parental divorce can be very difficult. Although they do not feel responsible for the divorce, they experience loyalty conflicts, a sense of loss of family home, abandonment by their parents, anger toward dad at their increased responsibility for having to take care of mom, even when he did not initiate the divorce, and a sense of concern about marriage. There is evidence of an increase in alcohol abuse. The biggest risk for children is when the parents hold on to them or they assume the role of substitute spouse to fill the loneliness. When the parents are unable to make a meaningful new start, the children may have difficulty moving forward with their own lives.

The tasks of this transitional phase fall less on the parenting aspects of family life and more on the individual ability to adapt to life alone. This includes maintaining connections to children, relatives, and friends of the past,

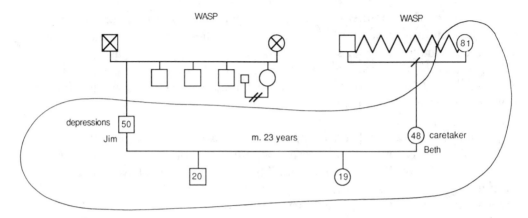

Figure 15-5. The Smith family.

as well as having the ability to make new friends and engage in new activities and life-styles.

The following case illustrates how the decision to divorce evolves when neither spouse is willing to make a commitment to work on marital issues. The technique of "future orientation" was used in an attempt to help the couple test the ramifications of their decision on all generations. They were also able to make cooperative plans for their postseparation lives, based on a discussion of their individual needs.

Case Example: The Smith Family

Jim, 50, and Beth, 48, both WASPs, had been married for 23 years when they came for therapy at the suggestion of their family physician, who was concerned that both spouses were exhibiting stress-related symptoms. Their presenting problems was the deterioration of their marriage. For many years they had been steadily growing apart. The couple spent no time together and had no sexual or emotional relationship. Beth's domain was the home, where she had full responsibility for care of the house, children, and extended-family relationships, including the care of her aging mother who lived with them. Jim spent most of his time preoccupied with his business, struggling to make ends meet financially. Both children, ages 19 and 20, were in college and for the most part out of the house.

Beth said that she had been wanting to leave Jim for years but was afraid of how he would react, especially since he was prone to periods of depression, "black moods" as he described them. Jim said that he, too, had occasional thoughts of divorce but felt that it didn't make sense to start over at their "advanced" ages. Beth felt that Jim's resistance stood in the way of allowing her to move forward with her life—she wanted his okay to go ahead with a separation.

When it was pointed out that she would have to either accept Jim's decision to stay together or make up her own mind about what she wanted, she said that she wanted to at least give the marriage one more try. The therapist reviewed with them the history of their marital relationship and its potential for change. When suggesting ways that each might change to help the relationship, it became clear to both that neither had sufficient motivation to do what was recommended to help the marriage. When Beth finally decided that she wanted a divorce, Jim was ready to accept it as well.

The next phase of therapy was "future oriented," involving an exploration of pragmatic and emotional divorce-adjustment issues for both Jim and Beth. There were financial problems to contend with. Because of Jim's business difficulties, they decided that their home would have to be sold. Jim felt that Beth should remain in their house and that he could live in a boarding house. When the long-range consequences of this plan were explored, both agreed that this was not an equitable arrangement. While they realized that Beth's job prospects were not very promising since she had not worked in 21 years, Beth decided that she wanted to work, both to fill her time and to ease the financial crunch. All this was quite difficult for them, and though they often considered staying in the present state, both felt that to continue to live in a loveless marriage was no longer tenable.

The ramifications of their divorce on this three-generational family system were explored. The dilemma of care for Beth's mother as well as Jim's continued relationship with her was discussed. They agreed that each would have to pursue his/her own relationship with the children and talked about the importance of not calling upon the children to choose sides or to fill the void and loneliness that each anticipated. As each area was discussed, Jim and Beth felt better equipped to act on the decision that had become theirs. The therapist served as a consultant to both during the transitional phase on an as-needed basis.

Divorce in Families in Later Life

When divorce occurs for the couple in later life, it reverberates like a shock wave throughout the entire family, with every aspect of the previous phase that is problematic—financial insecurity and emotional adjustment—exaggerated. In addition, there are now three generations of family members whose lives will be altered by divorce.

There are many ties that bind after a long marriage—children, probably grandchildren, family, and friends. Because the individuals identify themselves in relation to the roles that emerged from the marriage, the process of redefinition is very difficult, especially in light of the fact that they grew up at a time when divorce was less accepted and that the present social climate is so changed.

The children's reactions and perceived responsibilities become key aspects of the divorce-adjustment process during this phase. Each parent may want to become reinvolved with the children in a way that is inappropriate. In a role reversal, children may now feel burdened by their parents.

Much of how people manage depends upon the circumstances of the divorce decision. An unwanted, unexpected divorce at this stage is traumatic, even when the marriage has been unsatisfactory to each for many years. When this is the case, much of the brunt of the hostility and bitterness will be felt by

the younger generations (Ahrons, 1986). Starting over as a single person is very difficult, particularly when there is not a clear sense of identity apart from the roles within the marriage. It is especially hard to find renewed meaning in life at this stage of life. Loneliness is a big problem. Emotional support may have to come from outside the family. The spouse's parents may be dead, their children and siblings involved with their own lives. They may feel very isolated from their usual social network to the degree that it involves couples, finding that social life revolves around couples and that their opportunities are limited. If one spouse has been left by the other, he/she often feels ashamed, humiliated, and as a result may isolate him/herself from former ties and may not have the energy or desire to form new relationships.

There are individual adjustment issues for men and for women. For the housewife who has not worked in many years or never worked at all, divorce may bring with it drastic financial changes. There may be ongoing alimony, but unless there is a great deal of money, it will not be enough to manage the same life-style. If the woman must start work, job opportunities are extremely limited. The husband may be facing retirement, which means he will in all likelihood have less money to live on and more time on his hands. The divorce may be welcomed; however, more likely it will bring with it a void, accompanied by depression. The tasks for each spouse revolve around maintaining their own lives and continuing nonburdensome relationships with people in their support network—family and friends. The children's and grandchildren's reactions and perceived responsibility become key aspects of therapy as well. Pitfalls of this phase include "choosing sides" and reversing of roles.

The following case illustrates short term divorce counseling for an entire family when an elderly couple decides to divorce. Because it had been a well thought out, mutual decision, the focus of the concern was on the impact of the decision on the children and grandchildren of the couple rather than on adjustment issues relating to the couple. As the separate lives of both parents were discussed, their children calmed down and the family was able to productively plan for the changes ahead.

Case Example: The Rubin Family

Ben, age 38, called for an appointment, anxious over the fact that his parents, Rebecca and Sam, both 65, has just informed him, his sister Rachel, 28, and their respective spouses that they were going to divorce. He felt a great deal of concern about what impact their decision would have on the future of the entire family and needed guidance. While he knew nothing specific, he was sure that his father had taken up with a younger woman and was very worried about the emotional and financial impact this would have on his mother. As he presented the situation, the therapist realized that despite the years of tension in the parents' marriage, this was a Jewish family with many close ties and religious traditions that would be affected by a divorce. She suggested that Ben bring the adult members of his family in for a session to discuss the impending separation. Ben felt that his parents were resolved in their decision and would not come. Therefore, the therapist suggested that Ben tell them that he was experiencing the news as a crisis

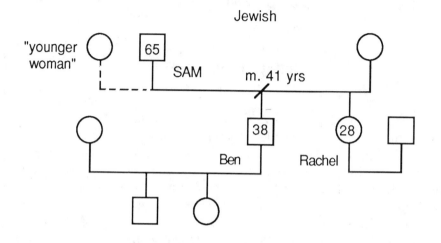

Figure 15-6. The Rubin family.

for the family and that they would be helping him if they came for a consultation session.

During the long and emotional session, Rebecca and Sam affirmed their intention to divorce. Rebecca spoke of their long and difficult 41 years together, reminding their children of their brief separation over a decade ago when she had learned that Sam was having an affair with his secretary. She said that at the time, they resolved to stay together until both children were settled. Now that Rachel was married, it had become increasing difficult to continue a life together. Both wanted different things at this stage of their lives. Sam was about to retire and wanted to move to Arizona, his dream for many years. Rebecca, active in volunteer activities and her children's lives, did not want to leave her children, grandchildren, and community ties. Sam said that he was still involved in the affair, and his lover was planning to move with him.

The therapist saw that this was a well-thought-out decision and that the couple's emotional divorce had actually occurred during the past ten years of separate lives in the same house. She switched the focus onto the concerns of Ben and Rachel, both of whom were upset and angered by the revelation of the affair. Ben confronted Sam with his financial responsibility to Rebecca. Sam assured Ben that he had every intention of making it possible for Rebecca to maintain the same life-style. Both Ben and Rachel expressed their fear at the prospect of having their mother alone in the community. They felt embarrassed by it and concerned about being placed in an obligatory responsible position—both emotionally and financially. Rebecca assured her children that she did not want to become a burden to them, saying that she had many friends and interests to keep her busy. They were also having problems with their father's plans, worried about how he would handle retirement in a community where he knew no one and how his grandchildren would feel not having him nearby. He told them that he expected to return East several times a year and hoped that his children and grandchildren would visit him in Arizona as well. Once Ben and Rachel's fears and concerns were articulated and Sam and Rebecca were able to present their future plans, everyone started to calm down. It was evident that this was not an impulsive decision, and once the children

began to accept the decision and were reassured that their own lives would not be drastically altered by it, the therapist used the remaining time to focus on plans that assured the continuation of relationships with children and grandchildren.

CLINICAL IMPLICATIONS

As we have stated repeatedly throughout this chapter, the divorcing family presents itself with a multitude of complex and far-reaching issues for which there are no simple solutions. All family members are emotionally at risk at the time of separation and divorce, the issues depending, in part, on the particular life cycle phase of the family. Each family has its own idiosyncratic set of associations and behaviors that will unleash strong feelings, depending on its ethnic and family patterns. Certain events inherent in the separation process are potential emotional landmines for every couple: the decision-making period, announcing the decision to family and friends, the actual separation, the initial and ongoing discussions around finances and the children, consulting with lawyers, and, finally, redefinition to a new life.

Individuals within the family, the couple, and the family as a whole may seek therapy at different points along the route. Clinical assessment and interventions vary according to the stage of the separation process and the nature of the presenting problem. Given the charged emotional atmosphere and the complexities inherent in the three-generational relationships of divorcing families, it is easy for therapists to become overwhelmed and narrow the field, accepting the family definition of its membership and excluding, in particular, the noncustodial father or one or more grandparents. In treating these families, therapists must include all family members in their understanding of the problems. If there is a history of abuse of any kind (addictions, spousal or child abuse), the clinical assessment and treatment plan must incorporate this information. Interventions must then be based on dealing with the ongoing problem in the context of the divorce-adjustment process.

Predecision Phase

During the decision-making phase, either one spouse or the couple may seek therapy. If it is one spouse, the first task is to convince the person to bring the other spouse in to discuss the decision together. With the couple the therapist's initial goal is to slow down the process sufficiently so that the couple can contract to explore the divorce decision and related issues. The decision belongs solely to the couple and not the therapist. It is the job of the therapist to help them clarify the process that brought them to view divorce as a solution, and each spouse needs to understand his/her share of responsibility

in the disintegration of the marriage. This will allow them to come to a well-thought-out decision.

Another tactic is to raise future-oriented decisions, helping the couple to see the ensuing ramifications of such a decision, identifying issues specific to their particular life cycle stage. For many women, who may not have thought through the economic consequences of the decision and are totally unaware of the realities facing them, therapy should include a complete discussion of future plans. It might be appropriate to refer the spouse(s) to a psychoeducational group focussing on the process of divorce and encompassing financial and child-related issues.

Another alternative might be to recommend a trial separation with no legal implications, as a cooling-off period. For a trial separation to be effective, the couple needs to structure the following: a time limit, at the end of which the relationship will be evaluated and a decision will be made on whether to extend the separation, reconcile, or divorce; temporary nonbinding living arrangements with provisions for money and children; if, when, and how the couple will have contact, including phone calls, dating, and sex; and the forum for working on the marriage (i.e., therapy). During the specified time period, rather than allow the couple to obsess about whether or not to divorce, the decision itself will be put on hold. The focus shifts to examining the relationship and the participation of each in the problems.

Another intervention aimed at helping the couple face reality is to recommend a consultation with a divorce mediator. A new field, divorce mediation, has emerged in the past decade as a rational and humane alternative to the adversarial divorce process. Basically a systems approach to divorce, mediation requires the couple to meet with a trained third party, the mediator, to discuss and negotiate any or all of the terms of the separation agreement: child and spousal support, property division, and child custody and visitation. Thus the couple participates in the process of reorganizing the family rather than turning the decisions over to lawyers. Lawyers are used instead at the end of mediation in order to formalize it. As a therapeutic strategy, referring a stalemated couple to a mediation consultation challenges their decision. When confronted with the reality of changed access to the children and financial hardship, they may return to therapy to work out the marital issues if their ambivalence, regarding divorce, is high enough.

Separation Phase

Once the decision is made, the focus for therapy becomes the separation itself: how to make the decision public, discussions around children and finances, and the initial adjustment to the separation and the new life. If the couple has been in marital therapy, it is not the time to terminate therapy. Rather the focus of treatment shifts to divorce counseling—work with the couple and family in planning moves for the transitions ahead. It is a time of

important decision making that affects the long-range future of all family members at a time the couple is least emotionally or intellectually prepared to think and act clearly. The therapist can walk the couple through the steps, taking into consideration the needs of everyone involved. Ironically, while in marital therapy the couple is directed toward separate spheres of interest, in divorce counseling the focus is on making sure they maintain appropriate roles together as coparents, with the emphasis on working out cooperative parenting and financial arrangements. In addition, since their relationships with their parents and in-laws will be affected, it is important to help them make the necessary adjustments while staying connected to them.

Children need to be prepared, yet most couples overlook this critical step or think that if they tell the children once that their parents no longer love each other but still love them, that constitutes preparation. The therapist can help the couple figure out what to tell children and extended families about the impending separation. This becomes the beginning of a process that will continue for years. Often the burden of responsibility for the children's well-being falls on—or is assumed by—the woman. When this occurs, the therapist can help both parents share parental responsibility.

The resolution of the emotional attachment, commonly referred to as the emotional divorce, becomes a key therapeutic focus (Bowen, 1978). For each spouse to get on with his/her life, it is necessary to disengage emotionally, to retrieve a sense of self from the marriage that enables him/her to go forward alone. Working through the emotional divorce is a threefold process: mourning the lost marriage and family, examining one's own role in the deterioration of the marriage, and working out a way to go forward without distortion or cutoff from the past.

There are different strategies to use when confronted with a high level of emotional attachment. The initial task is the grief work. The person has to mourn many losses: the hopes, dreams, and expectations of a shared life that have now been shattered as well as the loss of the marital partner and the family unit. Concurrently the individual needs to look at his/her own role in the breakup with perspective rather than blame. Unless and until he/she is able to assume some responsibility for the problems, he/she will never be free to move forward without repeating the same mistakes in the future relationships.

Different members of the family—adults, children, and/or grandparents—may best be directed into psychoeducational or support groups as a follow-up to or instead of divorce counseling or one-on-one therapy. These modalities of treatment provide input and support from others going through the same experience.

Another painful aspect of divorce is the business of the legal dissolution of the marriage. Any and all discussions around the pragmatics of parting are potentially inflammatory, especially when the legal proceedings are initiated. The adversarial nature of the traditional divorce process makes it difficult for even the most amicable of couples to remain on good terms, and yet, as we have seen, it is essential for the well-being of all family members that the

spouses maintain a coparental relationship. Anyone looking to do battle or prolong the marriage can make use of the legal arena. And when the divorce process itself becomes bitter, it is extremely costly, financially and emotionally, hindering the emotional adjustment process for everyone involved. Therapists have a professional responsibility to inform their clients about divorce mediation, a process that has the potential of fostering healing and allowing for closure in a way that is lacking in the adversarial divorce process.

By now it should be apparent that divorce therapy is a difficult business. The therapist must maintain a position of neutrality while joining with each member. In order to explore the issues with an open mind, the therapist needs to be very clear about his/her own personal issues and biases. It is probably not possible for a therapist who "doesn't believe in divorce" to be helpful to couples struggling with the decision or going through the process of divorce. On the other hand, therapists in the process of going through their own divorce, a process that takes at least one to three years, are going to have a hard time being objective and dealing with the pain triggered in themselves. Under all circumstances it is helpful for a therapist dealing with many divorces to have a peer-group or colleague-support system.

REFERENCES

Abarbanel, A. (1979). Shared parenting after separation and divorce. *American Journal of Orthopsychiatry* April.

Ahrons, C. R. (1980). Divorce: A crisis of family transition and change. *Family Relations* 29.

Ahrons, C. R. (1980a). Redefining the divorced family: A conceptual framework. *Social Work* Nov.

Ahrons, C. R. (1981). The continuing co-parental relationship between divorced spouses. *American Journal of Orthopsychiatry* July.

Ahrons, C. R. (1986). Divorce when the children are older. American Family Therapy Association Conference, Washington, D.C., June.

Ahrons, C. R., & Rodgers, R. H. (1987). *Divorced families: A multi-disciplinary developmental view.* New York: Norton.

Berman, W. H. & Turk, D. C. (1981). Adaptation to divorce: Problems and coping strategies. *Journal of Marriage and the Family* 43.

Bloom, B. L., White, S. W., & Asher, S. J. (1978). Marital disruption as a stressor: A review and analysis. *Psychological Bulletin* June.

Bowen, M. (1978). *Family therapy in clinical practice.* New York: Jason Aronson.

Briscoe, C. W., Smith, J. B., Robins, E., Marten, S., & Gaskin, F., (1973). Divorce and psychiatric disease. *Archives of General Psychiatry* 29.

Bumpass, L., & Rindfuss, R. (1979). Children's experience of marital disruption. *American Journal of Sociology* 85.

Cherlin, A., (1979). "Work life and marital dissolution. In G. Levinger & O. Moles (Eds.), *Divorce and separation: Context, causes and consequences.* New York: Basic Books.

Chester, P. (1986). *Mothers on trial.* New York: McGraw-Hill.

Chiriboga, D. A., Roberts, J., & Stein, J. A. (1978). Divorce, stress and social supports: A study in help seeking. *Journal of Divorce* 2.

Cooney, T., Smyer, M., Hagestad, G., & Klock, R. (1986). Parental divorce in young adulthood: Some preliminary findings. *American Journal of Orthopsychiatry* July.

Emery, R. (1982). Interparental conflict and the children of discord and divorce. *Psychological Bulletin* 91.

Furstenberg, F. F. Jr., Nord, C. Winquist, Peterson, J. L., & Zill, N. (1983). The life course of children of divorce: Marital disruption and parental contact. *American Sociological Review* vol. 48.

Furstenberg, F. F., Jr. (1976). Premarital pregnancy and marital instability. *Journal of Social Issues* 32.

Glick, P. C., (1984). How American families are changing. *American Demographics* Jan.

Glick, P. C., (1984a). Marriage, divorce, and living arrangements: Prospective changes. *Journal of Family Issues* March.

Goldsmith, J. (1980). Relationships between former spouses: Descriptive findings. *Journal of Divorce* 4.

Greif, J. B. (1979). Fathers, children and joint custody. *American Journal of Psychiatry* April.

Herzog, E., & Sudia, C. (1973). Children in fatherless families. In B. M. Caldwell & H. N. Ricuiti (Eds.), *Review of child development research: Volume 3: Child development and child policy*. Chicago: University of Chicago Press.

Hess, R., & Camara, K. (1979). Post-divorce family relationships as mediating factors in the consequence of divorce for children. *Journal of Social Issues* 35.

Hetherington, E. M., Cox, M., & Cox, R. (1978). The development of children in mother headed households. In H. Hoffman & D. Reis (Eds.), *The American family: Dying or developing*. New York: Plenum.

Hetherington, E. M. (1982). Modes of adaptation to divorce and single parenthood which enhance healthy family functioning; implications for a preventative program. University of Virginia.

Hetherington, E. M., Cox, M., & Parker, R. D. (1977). Beyond father absence: Conceptualization of the effects of divorce. In *Contemporary Readings in Child Psychology*. New York: McGraw-Hill.

Holmes, T., & Rane, R. (1967). The social readjustment rating scale. *Journal of Psychsomatic Research* 11.

Isaacs, M. (1982). Helping Mom fail: A case of a stalemated divorcing process. *Family Process* 21 (2).

Jacobs, J., (1982) The effects of divorce on fathers: An overview of the literature. *American Journal of Orthopsychiatry* 139.

Kelly, J., Gigy, L., & Hausman, S. (1986). Mediated and adversarial divorce: Initial findings from the divorce and Mediation Project. In J. Folberg & A. Milne (Eds.), *Divorce mediation: Theory and practice*. New York: Guilford Press.

Kivnick, H. Q. (1982). Grandparenthood: An overview of meaning and mental health. *The Gerontologist* 22.

Levinger, A. (1976). A social psychological perspective on marital dissolution. *Journal of Social Issues* 32.

Lowery, C., & Settle, S. (1984). Effects of divorce on children: Differential impact of custody and visitation patterns. *Family Relations* 34.

Luepnitz, D. (1982). *Child custody: A study of families after divorce*, Lexington, Mass.: Lexington Books.

McGoldrick, M., Pearce, J. K., & Giordano, J. (1982). *Ethnicity and family therapy*, New York: Guilford Press.

Messinger, L., & Walker, K. (1981). From marriage breakdown to remarriage: Parental tasks and therapeutic guidelines. *American Journal of Orthopsychiatry* 51(3).

Mueller, C. W., & Pope, H. (1977). Transmission betewen generations. *Journal of Marriage and the Family* 39.

National Center for Health Statistics, (1984). Advance report of final divorce statistics, 1981. *Monthly Vital Statistics Report*, Vol. 32 No. (9) (supp. (2)). DHSS Pub. No. (PHS) 84-1120. Public Health Service, Hyattsville, Md. Jan.

National Center for Health Statistics (1984a). Births, marriages, divorces and deaths, U.S. 1983. *Monthly Vital Statistics Report,* Vol, 32, No. 12, DHHS Pub. No. (PHS) 84-1120. Public Health Service, Hyattsville, Md., March 26.

Norton, S. J., & Glick, P. C. (1976). Marital instability: Past, present and future. *Journal of Social Issues* 32: 5–20.

Raschke, H., & Raschke, V., (1979). Family conflict and children's self concepts: A comparison of intact and single-parent families. *Journal of Marriage and the Family* 41.

Ross, H. L., & Sawhill, I. V. (1975). *Time of transition: The growth of families headed by women.* Washington, D.C.: Urban Institute.

Rutter, M., (1979). Sex differences in children's responses to family stress. In E. J. Anthony & C. Koupernik (Eds.), *The child in his family.* Huntington, N.Y.: Krieger.

Santrock, J., & Warshak, R. (1979). Father custody and social development in boys and girls. *Journal of Social Issues* 35.

Spanier, G. B., & Casto, R. F. (1979). Adjustment to separation and divorce: An analysis of 50 case studies. *Journal of Divorce* 2.

Steimnan, S., (1981). The experience of children in a joint custody arrangement: A report of a study. *American Journal of Orthopsychiatry* 51.

U.S. Bureau of the Census (1983). Current Population Reports, Series P-20, No. 380. *Marital statistics and living arrangements: March 1982.* U.S. Government Printing Office, Washington, D.C.

Wallerstein, J. (1986). Women after divorce: Preliminary report from a 10-year follow up. *American Journal of Orthopsychiatry* Jan.

Wallersein, J., & Kelly, J. B. (1980). *Surviving the breakup: How children and parents cope with divorce.* New York: Basic Books.

Weiss, R. S. (1979). The emotional impact of marital separation. In G. Levinger & O. Moles, (Eds.), *Divorce and separation: Context, causes and consequences.* New York: Basic Books.

Weiss, R. S. (1973). *Marital separation.* New York: Basic Books.

Weitzman, L. (1985). *The divorce revolution.* New York: Free Press.

16

The Postdivorce Family

Fredda Herz Brown, R.N., Ph.D.

In 1980 51% of the households in the United States were headed by women (National Center for Health Statistics, 1984) representing the highest rate of growth of any family form. Indeed the number of children living in one-parent households is considerable. By 1990 the National Center for Health Statistics estimates that approximately *half* of all school-aged children will reside in households with either one parent or a stepparent ("Changing USA Family"; 1984; Glick, 1979.) Since the rate of divorce among remarried couples is projected to reach 60% by 1990 (Glick, 1980), many children living in a stepparent family can expect to live again in a one-parent household before establishing themselves as independent adults.

In light of these figures on divorce and remarriage, the single-parent household has been viewed as a steppingstone to another marriage. Yet with estimates that approximately one-third (35%) of these households will not become remarried households, it is also clear that single-parent households are becoming a new family form (U.S. Bureau of the Census, 1985). Whether the custodial parent marries or not, it is the contention of the author that the family, and the therapist who treats the family, will benefit from a view that defines its members not as a family "in transition" to another two-parent binuclear household, but as a family "in transition" to a different structure or organization, a bona fide family form. The goal of therapy is not to help them endure a period of waiting, perhaps for help to arrive, but to view themselves as active participants in establishing a new way of living. "Waiting" sets the stage for a sense of failure because it perpetuates a perennial women's issue that "help is coming," or that a woman cannot plan a satisfactory life without a partner. Such a notion further intensifies the realistic feelings of being overwhelmed by the task at hand and tends to create a sense of powerlessness, further impeding the family's attempts to deal with the disruption of divorce.

Not the least of the areas in which a sense of powerlessness can develop is the realm of finances. It has been suggested that by the year 1990, families with women and their dependent children will comprise the nation's poor (Weitzman, 1985). Certainly one major reason a woman may remarry is for the economic security marriage may provide for her and her children (Glick, 1986).

Several recent studies have suggested that poverty accounts for the majority of child-related problems in single-parent households. While a therapist cannot change a family's financial status, she/he can contribute to the woman's sense of power in dealing with it. The therapeutic goal is to help the single-parent mother not to seek to replicate what "was" in the two-parent household but to create new ways for meeting the emotional and financial needs of her children as a household with one parent. The reality of her position is that she cannot use the traditional model of family as her guide, and that all expectations, responsibilities, and relationships must be completely reorganized.

In this chapter the author developes a framework for understanding the process of reorganization of structure and relationships in a single-parent household. Understanding the complexities of this process will help clinicians who work with families of divorce approach this stage as more than just a temporary transition to remarriage.

THE PROCESS OF BECOMING
A ONE-PARENT FAMILY

There can be no doubt that divorce is a major disruption in the family system that results in a series of changes in the basic family structure and all its relationships. Single-parent families, most of which are headed by women, exist in a social and economic context that still relates to the traditional two-parent family as the norm. Divorce requires a major shift in how these families function in many areas and a new definition of normal family life. Regardless of the individual dynamics of the family, all single-parent families experience a number of problems in establishing themselves as a viable unit. Three interrelated problem areas dominate their lives: money, parenting, and social relationships. Generally difficulties in these areas appear immediately after separation and persist in some form throughout the entire adjustment phase, lasting some three to five years.

Many of the most pressing problems faced in all stages are related to the financial realities of divorce in the United States where the legal system disadvantages women by acting as if men and women have equal financial opportunity, as if they receive equal pay, as if child care were readily and cheaply available, and as if the woman will probably soon remarry—none of which is true. In fact the average income for these households is $9000 for those who receive support and $6000 for those who do not (Weitzman, 1981; Bouton, 1984; "Changing USA Family", 1984)

Women are generally ill prepared to provide for themselves and their children alone as they have traditionally expected to have husbands to care for them financially while they raised the children and freed their husbands for work. Although the increased cost of living has brought many mothers of

young children into the workforce before the time of divorce, the jobs they hold often barely augment the husband/father's income. Lower-socioeconomic-class women (Goldberg & Dukes 1985) may perceive the financial hardships of divorce as less severe than middle- and upper-class women because their life-style does not change as much. Their more financially affluent counterparts, on the other hand, discover that divorce is nothing less than an economic disaster that spells an end to life as they once knew it.

Parenting problems in new single-parent families relate to the difficulty of disciplining and nurturing children while feeling overwhelmed by a major emotional loss. The father's absence not only leaves a gap in the family hierarchy but also it places an incredible demand on the resources of the remaining parent. Confronted with the need to work full-time (perhaps for the first time since having children) and manage all household tasks alone, many mothers lack consistency. Often there may be little time or energy to attend to the emotional needs of children, who themselves are undergoing a major loss.

Certainly the stage of the family life cycle when divorce occurs has some bearing on the kinds of parenting difficulties a single mother is likely to encounter (see Chapter 15). Very young children present a long list of basic caretaking needs; older children entering adolescence may be more difficult to discipline. Regardless of the stage at which divorce occurs, the custodial mother must establish herself as the sole daily manager of her children, and find the emotional reserves to deal with their normal developmental tasks. To do this effectively, she must feel confident of her own abilities.

Single-parent families also face social isolation (Minuchin, 1974; Hetherington et al., 1977; Cashion, 1982; McLanahan, 1981). Old couple friends frequently are uncomfortable remaining friends with both ex-spouses and feel they must take sides. Or they may extend invitations to child-centered events only, excluding the woman from couple-focused social gatherings. On the other hand, the single parent may refuse invitations to social gatherings with couples, feeling inadequate to go alone, or too exhausted to socialize.

The prospect of dating naturally looms ahead of all new single parents. Some women may fall into an undesirable relationship immediately after separating, only to suffer disappointment soon again. The fear of remaining alone, combined with fears about money, propels many into premature remarriages (Bouton, 1984; Norton, 1983). Others may avoid the entire issue of intimacy for many years, preferring to devote themselves to parenting.

The actual process of resolving these issues, and becoming a one-parent household, consists of three distinct phases: (1) the aftermath; (2) the realignment; and (3) the stabilization. Each phase has its own distinct characteristics, tasks, difficulties, and triangles related to the above issues. During the process of stabilizing as a single-parent household, the usual ebb and flow of the family life cycle are disrupted and additional tasks are added. Unfortunately many such families fail to stabilize in their new form. However, it is a process that, when successfully complete, results in a family that *can function well whether the mother decides to remarry or not.*

PHASE I—THE AFTERMATH

The aftermath is so named because the first year following separation and/
or divorce can be as devastating as any natural disaster. A family may actually
feel as if an earthquake, tornado, or hurricane has attacked their home, and few
are able to articulate their experience during this phase amid their bewilder-
ment and confusion. Families in this phase are responding to an intense
situational crisis and the resultant disruption in the way they live their everyday lives.

Divorcing families frequently think that by getting legally divorced, they
will get emotionally divorced. Couples most often use lawyers to negotiate the
process, failing to realize that having someone else (especially a trained
adversary) does not eliminate the need to resolve the process. It is the author's
experience that a legal divorce may or may not aid in resolving the emotional
divorce. In fact a total emotional divorce is never possible, especially when
children are involved. As long as one must deal with one's ex-spouse, old
emotional connections and reactions are reawakened. However, it is essential
to work on the process of becoming less emotionally reactive to the ex-
spouse's behavior, and eventually to develop an overview of the marriage and
divorce that does not blame the other spouse for everything, nor make oneself
an innocent victim. For an adequate emotional divorce, it is necessary to
retrieve one's self and one's personal life goals from the marriage and reinvest
these expectations in one's self.

In beginning this ongoing emotional process, there is the reality of negotiating a settlement with regard to support, division of marital property, custody,
and visitation. In working through the legal process, the spouses are often
confronted with the obvious—that one does not get rid of one's problems by
divorcing. In fact the divorce process frequently exacerbates old problems
even as it adds new ones.

Women, in particular, in facing the severe economic threat that emerges in
divorce, may feel overwhelmed even if they are the ones initiating the divorce.
"Her" marriage is usually one in which she has been handed from her father to
her husband for economic caretaking (Bernard, 1971). She has been taught to
look to marriage for economic security, intimacy, and companionship. For a
great number of women, the end of marriage marks the first time they have
ever lived alone. Yet they are charged with maintaining the continuity of the
home environment for the children during a major emotional upheaval.

At the same time that there are tremendous nuclear-family changes, there
are also changes in extended-family relationships. The first change that must
be accomplished is the new basis for the connection to the ex-spouse's family.
It is important for families to maintain as open a relationship system as
possible, and yet relationships with ex-spouse's relatives often test a divorcing
spouse's ability to do so. It is not uncommon for each extended family to
protect its members, and to hold the other spouse *totally* responsible for the
divorce. Often divorcing spouses hold their in-laws responsible for the prob-

lems in their marriage, either directly or through their real or imagined negative influence on the ex-spouse during childhood. Much energy needs to be put into keeping the children free to see in-laws, and, if possible, to feel comfortable including them at family celebrations.

Relationships with one's own family also change during this time. The intensity and degree of the shift in these relationships depend partly on the nature of the single parent's previous relationship with her parents, the frequency of divorce in the extended family, and the family's feelings regarding the marriage and the subsequent divorce. Families that are "used to" dealing with divorce often feel more comfortable in negotiating the associated issues; others, less experienced in this area, suffer throughout the transition. If the marriage was viewed negatively, the divorce may change the nature of relationships in a more positive direction.

This transitional phase, however, often leads to negative changes in the single mother's relationships with her parents in one of two directions. Some single-parent mothers, especially very young ones, move in with their parents, allowing them to supplement their own functioning. On the other hand, many cut off from the extended family to protect themselves from criticism, tightening the boundaries on an already stressed system, and ultimately increasing the intensity of their isolation.

Money

Society tends to hold women responsible for the maintainance of family before, during, and after divorce. In spite of this, women frequently experience an abrupt decrease in income in the first year after separation, which continues every year thereafter (*Family Therapy News,* 1984; Bouton, 1984). In fact Weitzman (1985) reports that the income of the average mother-headed, single-parent household decreases by 73% during this period.

In addition to her more immediate financial problems, a woman faces the reality of managing her own and her children's financial future. Sometimes the woman's father will fill in as "wage earner," continuing to support her financially for years after the separation. Such support is rarely free of emotional strings, as seen in the following case.

> Susan's wealthy father offered considerable support to her during her marriage, which had been a source of conflict between her and her ex-husband. Four years after the divorce, her father was still providing the balance between alimony, child support, and Susan's expenses. Susan was still focusing her attention on mothering her children and did not work. Although she lived in a separate household, her father saw his financial help as giving him the "final say" regarding problems with his grandchildren.

A homemaker who has either put off or never had ambitions for her own career may have a hard time conceiving of herself in a particular occupation, and may hesitate to place her children in the care of others. Others may realize

that a once supplementary income is woefully insufficient to maintain their previous standard of living, particularly if the child-care costs must be considered. In fact it may be difficult for a woman to reorganize herself to seek new or better employment during this phase. There are those "superwomen" who find new self-esteem in this period and plunge directly into efforts to take control of their economic situation; however, most will wait until the next phase to tackle this problem.

Parenting

Relationships with the children undergo rapid change during the aftermath phase. Even mothers who are generally able to manage and nurture their children are often overwhelmed at this time (Chiriboga et al., 1979; Goldsmith, 1982; Hetherington et al., 1977, 1979). Children describe infrequent follow-through and/or inconsistency in requirements for daily living (Wallerstein & Kelly 1975, 1976, 1977; Hetherington et al., 1977 & 1979; Minuchin, 1984). Because of the increased responsibilities and demands on her time, it is not uncommon for a mother to look for someone to fill in the gap in functioning that she experiences. The more sudden the change in structure, the more drastic the financial change, the younger the children, and the less functional the mother has been before the divorce, the more difficulty she experiences in the absence of the husband/father.

A mother's sense of powerlessness is proportional to her perception of the vacuum created by the father's absence from the home. To the extent that she feels a gap in her own personal competency, she is likely to pull her children, the father, or the grandparents into the empty space. These moves provide temporary assistance, but may lead to long-term dysfunction.

The 1979 film "Shoot the Moon" depicts a common triangle used to fill in the power gap: the oldest daughter as parental and spousal child. In this type of family triangle, the oldest daughter, who has always been her "father's girl" and her "mother's helper," fills in for the overwhelmed mother by caring for her younger siblings. The positive effect of this for the daughter is that she becomes closer to mother, becoming her confidante and sharing peer activities or interests. However, the long-term difficulties of this triangle create problems frequently seen by family therapists. When mother's boyfriend takes her place as chief confidante, daughter becomes hurt and rebellious. Her alliance with her father is reactivated and she runs to him after an uproar with mother and her boyfriend.

A second triangle is seen when the father functions as the ongoing powerful parental figure in the household. This often happens when he has long held this role, and everyone colludes to keep him involved in the same way. Generally the underlying basis of this triangle is the father's continuing overfunctioning that undermines the mother's ability to function independently. The following case provides an example of such a triangle.

Jane had a highly conflictual relationship with her older daughter, who was now having trouble in school and becoming incorrigible at home. Any differences of opinion between them resulted in her daughter yelling obscenities at her, and subsequently calling her father. John, the father, was more than willing to console "his girls" and handle the daughter's problem. John and Jane had had a long relationship in which he overfunctioned with his wife and daughters. The family continued playing out the same escalating pattern after the separation.

Another common way the shifting balance of power is dealt with in the aftermath phase is by an extremely intense and often bitter set of triangles involving mother, father, and the children. Fathers may use the power of support payments as mothers may use visitation of the children in their struggle with each other. Neither seems to realize that the feelings of emotional powerlessness cannot be resolved by such actions; and, in fact, they only tend to exacerbate whatever negative feelings exist. No one wins, but the battle rages on.

The mother may also pull her own mother into the vacuum created by the father's absence. She may either move in with her parents so that the grandmother can watch the children while the young mother works or goes to school, or she may live nearby to facilitate such caretaking arrangements. This pattern is especially common in ethnic groups where mothers and daughters maintain their respective parent/child roles throughout the life cycle. In such groups there tends to be a different approach to relationships between the generations, and the grandmother, seeing her daughter overwhelmed, will often volunteer to help with the children.

Celeste moved in with her parents immediately following the divorce because she felt she needed her mother to babysit so that she could work. Three years later, the children were calling their grandmother "Mom-Mom," and the older woman was blocking all attempts by Celeste to discipline her own children. By the time she entered therapy, Celeste was spending most of her time at work and away from home, and was labeled "irresponsible" by her mother.

The more overwhelmed the single parent, and the more rigidly her mother and she have adhered to the earlier parent/child roles, the more likely it will be that the grandmother will begin to function as the mother of her grandchildren as well. Thus the daughter, rather than being helped, is further disenfranchised in relationship to her children. Since women generally view their maternal role as a vital part of their identity, particularly after divorce, this can lead to decreased functioning in other areas as well.

Social Relationships

Without the built-in companionship and social networks provided by marriage, many women find social life difficult to arrange. Often a recently separated woman does not seek new friends because of the tremendous stress

she is under on all fronts (Hetherington et al., 1977, 1979: Wallerstein & Kelly, 1980; Rice & Rice, 1986). Frequently potential sources of new social contacts may be limited to local singles' bars or groups for separated and divorced people—alternatives that may be unappealing to many newly single parents. Lack of "single" identity and profound exhaustion may make the simple logistics of planning an evening out an insurmountable task. If the breakup was relatively harmonious, she may relay upon her ex-spouse to take her and the children out for dinner or a day trip occasionally. Money, again, may be an obstacle to taking up new hobbies or activities, which might be more fulfilling than the above choices.

> Barbara reported that she spent most of her free time at home reading, even when the children were spending time with their father. She had dated her ex-husband all through college and had moved six times during the course of their marriage. She had worked full-time since the divorce and was attending graduate school. When her children spent Christmas Day with her father, she refused several invitations to dinner and passed the day in bed with a "good book," a present to herself.

While one of the benefits of divorce can be, and is in many cases, a new sense of self-reliance for women, many effectively isolate themselves from significant relationships with other adults because they are overwhelmed with tasks, or out of the sense of failure that divorce brings with it initially. This tendency to avoid social situations and fail to make use of friendships as a source of support may leave the single mother looking to her children, or even the ex-spouse. Children have a healthy interest in their own activities, and cannot satisfy a parent's need for closeness and cooperation. The father attempting to negotiate his own new life cannot assist the mother in this area without undermining his own and her independence. Ultimately the lack of interaction with peers may exacerbate the mother's tendency to take her children's misbehavior personally, rather than as part of their normal development.

Some single mothers may also isolate themselves from their families. Often these women continue to pull on their ex-spouses for support or experience highly conflictual relationships with their children. Old unresolved issues with parents are likely to surface as problems with a child, as in the following case.

> Mary came for treatment with her 13-year-old daughter, Cara, claiming that she was selfish and demanding. After much exploration, Cara admitted that she had been somewhat more self-absorbed lately. However, the young girl thought that her mother's reaction seemed out of character and rather intense. When asked for the reason for this, Mary suddenly said, "I know. Cara's just like my Mom!"

Interventions

The single parent faces a multitude of personal choices during this phase. Positive choices can be described as those that facilitate her autonomy—e.g.,

taking a job and establishing peer support—rather than relying totally on her children or her family for support. Her ability to negotiate with her ex-spouse mutually satisfactory financial and custody agreements also bodes well for the next phase. Unfortunately the choices made in this phase often create temporary and negative solutions for the basic issues that further complicate and escalate existing triangles in phase II.

Mothers often enter treatment around difficulties with their children. *Interventions during this phase need to be oriented toward decreasing the experience of a power gap in the family.* Women may first need to develop some financial and legal competencies to relieve their personal stress. They need to be told the facts about divorce and finances, so that they can negotiate knowledgeably. Therefore, the clinician must either be well-informed about these facts, or be able to refer clients to a professional (a lawyer or mediator) who is.

If a woman has not been employed, she needs to be assisted in thinking about how she will support herself. Unfortunately lawyers frequently recommend that women not seek work until the divorce settlement is completed. However, it is the author's experience that the sooner a woman begins to consider her options, the better off she will be. While she negotiates a settlement, even a small part-time job may make her feel less overwhelmed and more in control of her own life.

At this time triangles that appear to help the mother, but which eventually may hinder her capacity to protect her children, are likely to have already developed. Although one may be tempted to bring in the father, or the grandparent in some cases, *the first priority is to help the single mother to be competent with the children on her own.* Bringing in the father prematurely will usually feel like a statement about her inadequacy to the mother. Hetherington and her colleagues (1977) have found that a good housekeeper is often the best help to a family at this stage because she/he is "employed by" the mother, works at her request, and aids rather than undermines her success. If her financial resources make this alternative possible, the therapist can encourage the single mother to hire outside help.

In most cases, however, and especially those in which the family includes a grandmother, the single parent needs to be taught to define how she wants others to help her. This increases her sense of power in and control over the situation at home. The therapist may need to coach her to "employ" others rather than let them take over for her. By "employing" others the mother retains the right to direct their assistance, and to do or not do certain things. For example:

Mrs. Brown came to a session with her mother and her three children. It was clear that with her mother present, Mrs. Brown was experiencing herself as disconnected from and unsuccessful with her children. If she told them what to do, they looked to their grandmother, who would then motion for them to listen. The therapist sympathized openly with the grandmother's plight, saying "it must be difficult not to know how to help your daughter." She then suggested that Mrs.

Brown tell her mother what kind of help she needed from her. This was stated explicitly and demonstrated structurally in the next three sessions. The therapist consistently intervened between the grandmother and the children, requesting both adults to consult with each other. Mrs. Brown began to experience success with the children, while her mother developed a sense of her daughter's competence and began to trust her judgment.

Social support is critical to decreasing the isolation and the sense of powerlessness that accompany this phase. As in all crisis situations, multifamily and self-help groups are important in the early treatment stage. Often they calm anxiety and shore up the power of the individual so that an active approach to her situation is possible.

When a newly separated woman calls the author for treatment, an initial appointment is established during which a standard evaluation interview is conducted and the presenting problem is defined and elaborated. If it appears that the woman is defining the presenting problem as her divorce but cannot be specific about any problems that derive from this, she is told that her feelings are normal and that therapy is not a treatment for divorce. In this way the crisis and her attendant feelings are normalized and stage is set for viewing therapy as a place you come to work on problems that have become symptoms. The author frequently defines the "solution" or treatment for her current upset as finding others with whom she can share her experiences and who can offer her guidance and support in negotiating the typical issues that arise. At this time the woman may be referred to the next name on a phone list, developed by the author, of single parents who have more or less successfully mastered the process. When a psychoeducational group focusing on the postdivorce process is available, or about to be formed, she can be referred to that resource. Because all families tend to look dysfunctional during crisis, it is difficult for a therapist to evaluate the need for treatment in a particular case. It has been the author's experience that most single parents at this phase may look or sound dysfunctional just by the nature of their situation. However, to begin "treatment" at this phase often assures a process of dysfunctionality where the therapist is easily incorporated into the family to fill an empty position. Waiting for the dust to settle by providing other supports and resources, such as groups and a resource list, often prevents this treatment casualty.

Clinically there seem to be several situations that, during the evaluation process, should serve as warning lights for treatment. The first is when the family is experiencing dual crises—the separation and the launching of a child or the death of a grandparent and the separation. Dual crises create so much disruption that it is often impossible for a family to deal with them simultaneously without therapeutic help. The second indicator of the need for treatment is when one of the potential first-phase triangles has begun to be solidified. Thus a child or grandparent has moved into the "empty spot" as they see it, and the seeds of potential dysfunction are sown. A third indicator would be any history of cutoffs or problematic relationships in the family of

origin that have worsened, or can be expected to worsen, under the stress of divorce.

PHASE II—THE REALIGNMENT

During this phase the family moves from a state of crisis to one of transition. Some families describe it as if it were a roller-coaster, marked by alternating euphoria and depression as life begins to take some shape. The transition lasts two to three years and is characterized by efforts to "regroup," that is, to make external changes in the family's social, economic, and extrafamilial circumstances, and internal changes in relationships between nuclear and extended-family members. (Ahrons, 1980, 1981, a, b, c; McLanahan, 1981).

Although marriage ends legally when one or the other spouse leaves the marital home, it is to be hoped that by the end of this phase the marriage will end emotionally. No matter how right the decision to end a marriage is, it creates a sadness. Most people run from this sadness, filling their time and emptiness with other people and worry. In fact it is possible to get through the entire three-phase process, and even remarry, without ever letting oneself deal with the pain engendered by losing one's spouse. Couples who fight constantly and who involve their children in their battles are among those who have failed to resolve these emotional issues. Others continue to stay involved in the relationship in the same way, sharing personal problems and staying directly involved in each other's daily concerns. Frequently such couples never institute divorce proceedings, remaining "married but unmarried." When this happens any move into the social arena by either one is experienced as a threat, if not to the ex-partner, then to the children. The normative upset of the children regarding the mother or father's new relationship is often exaggerated in these instances.

Accomplishing the emotional divorce is an arduous and active process that involves accepting one's own mistakes in the marriage and knowing emotionally what one could or could not have done to make the marriage work. The essential question that must be asked and resolved is: "What did the divorce solve or not solve for me?" Resolving this emotional issue has a tremendous bearing on the single parent's ability to face the continuing concerns of the family.

Money

The most pressing problem facing women in this stage continues to be economic. The old family unit must adjust to living as two households instead

of one, with each parent taking responsibility for his or her own financial needs. For women, in particular, this almost always means readjustments in the standard of living as they usually earn much less than their ex-husbands and do not receive enough child support to cover the children's actual expenses. This may bring with it concomitant changes in their status in the community, which has often been defined by their husband's job. Two important changes are likely to be made in response to these issues: (1) selling the marital home and (2) taking a job.

Divorce often means deciding whether it is feasible financially (or socially) to stay in the family home. Women sometimes feel stuck for two reasons. First, they view their home as their one source of equity and hesitate to leave it, even when the maintenance costs far outweigh the long-term value of that equity. In addition, for many (if not most) women, "the home" has a special emotional significance. It has traditionally been their domain, and a great deal of energy has been put into its decoration and upkeep. As one woman said: "Although I can no longer afford to keep this old house 'up to snuff,' and all the neighbors are married, I can't seem to part with it."

While the father's leaving may signal the beginning of the shift to a single-parent household, it is often not until a final decision is made by the mother as to whether she will keep their original home that a full transition is made. Remarried couples frequently purchase a new home as a means of defining their new marriage and family, but divorcing couples rarely view this as a way of redefining their situation. Thus it is generally assumed that the mother should keep the marital home for the children, even though she most likely will be unable to afford it.

Clinicians often fail to take into consideration the impact of this decision on the single parent and her children. Women may feel torn between their emotional desire to feel some security in old surroundings and the desire to be rid of the past. (One client described the marital home as a "museum.") Moving in itself is a monumental task that many women may hesitate to undertake alone.

Mothers also feel conflicted by the feelings of their children. Children typically experience the move from the marital home as *the* major loss, symbolizing the end of the family as they knew it. Such a move means giving up the last vestige of their fantasies of an intact home, as well as all the normal issues involved in changing schools and making new friends.

For most women this phase means rethinking their goals for the future. With the financial settlement and the initial emotional trauma over, a woman is often better able to engage in effective long-term planning. It may mark the first time since her marriage that a woman has had to deal with the realities of the job market and the business world. A woman's success or failure in negotiating this area of her new life may well depend on the extent to which she can overcome the very real economic disadvantages experienced by women. Generally the more objective she can be about the problem, and the more she realizes it is not a personal defect of hers, the more effective she can be in taking the steps necessary to deal with it. Some women faced with the

challenge of these realities become a "supermom" who takes on school and work in addition to parenting. Others go about preparing themselves in step-wise fashion for better work positions. Finally there are women who are not able to master the economic realities themselves, and who continue to rely on their ex-spouses for financial solvency.

Parenting

The child's major need is for continued contact with both parents, and a feeling of support from each that does not threaten his or her loyalties to the other (Hetherington, 1977; Wallerstein & Kelly, 1980; Rice & Rice, 1986; Ahrons, 1986). Many children adjust well in this phase to a variety of parental arrangements that are incomprehensible to two-parent families, while others continue to experience overt or covert hostility between their parents.

Divorce often means a change in the way both parents relate to their children. Because of the increased workload, single-parent mothers tend to make more demands on their children to take care of themselves than do mothers in two-parent families (Hetherington et al., 1977, 1979; Nehls & Morganbesteelf, 1980; Wallerstein & Kelly, 1980). While in the history of the family, children have participated heavily in household tasks, the modern middle-class, two-parent family operates in a context where children have few demands placed on them other than to achieve in school. In the single-parent family, the extent to which new responsibilities interfere in their own activities or their focus on peer relationships determines whether they are viewed positively or negatively by the children.

If a woman has relied on her children, her parents, or her ex-husband for assistance in parenting during the initial family crisis surrounding the divorce, she must now make efforts to reestablish her autonomy in this area. If the mother has not been an effective disciplinarian, she must establish her authority now. Otherwise the family will be stuck in a pattern that defines her as weak and/or powerless, and the *temporary triangles of Phase I become solidified.* For example:

> After her separation and divorce, Mrs. Green had to establish herself in a job, and had struggled successfully for the last two years to get on her own. Initially she had felt quite overwhelmed and her father had helped tremendously by "filling in for my husband." He often interfered with her discipline of the children, and they typically cried when she reprimanded them or attempted to give them instructions, saying: "Grandpa wouldn't do that to us." Her ex-husband complained that the children were too attached to their grandfather, and that they said the same thing to him when he disciplined them.

In this example a temporary adaptation in the aftermath of the divorce had become a problem in the second phase for both parental households. With parenting the critical task for the single parent is to learn how to manage her children by herself.

Social Relationships

The other major external change for the single parent is adjusting to social life as a single person. Since the single parent is not actually alone, this phase often involves balancing life as a "a single person" with life as a parent. While men turn to women, women seem to turn to other women for support. Having female friends becomes a tremendous source of self-esteem, and often allows women to experience a period of personal growth that may have been cut short by marriage during the young-adult phase (Aylmer, Chapter 9.).

When women become divorced, they join the ranks of the large numbers of unattached women in their 30s and 40s who have been divorced or never married. There is a different status afforded to men and women in the single world because sexism and ageism deem older men more desirable than older women.

A greater stigma may also be due to the fact that women usually have custody of children and thus present "a package deal," and its associated problems, to potential male companions, whereas a man's children are usually in the custody of his ex-wife. Also, since men tend to marry younger women, a single-parent mother will be less sought after than younger unmarried women, and, finally, a divorced man brings much more money (and thus power) to the singles scene.

When mothers actually begin dating, children must accommodate to these new circumstances. To the children dating signifies the reality that their parents are no longer interested romantically in each other. It becomes more difficult to hold onto fantasies about parents getting back together when they date other people. As the single parent moves out into other relationships, children often adopt very creative methods of expressing their negative reactions. They may try to split up relationships by becoming pests, bad boys/girls, or chaperones. They may combine any or all of these techniques with comparisons with the father (or mother, in the case of the father's dating), and cast aspersions on the person's appearance, manner, etc. For instance:

> Jeannie came to treatment because she was very upset about the behavior of her daughter, Carole, age 15, who had become "glued" to her since she started dating Rick. Rick was the father of one of Carole's friends and she had initially seemed pleased with their relationship, but now had become their constant chaperone. She had also begun questioning Jeannie in detail about their dating behavior, e.g., kissing, petting, etc.

As in the case above, teenagers struggling with their own sexuality often become prudes regarding their parents' dating and/or sexual relationships. Some mothers make their children confidantes and form a peer relationship, sharing the details of dating. This tends to happen most often with mothers and daughters who are fairly close in age. The mother may even foresee this as a solution to potential issues the daughter may raise about her dating. However,

it begins to lock the child into a spousal role with the mother, inhibiting the teenager's freedom to grow and gain experience with peers.

Intervention

Since the intense anxiety of the crisis has decreased, dysfunctional patterns will tend to show themselves during this phase. The temporary triangles that may have enlisted a child, a grandmother, and/or a father into the perceived vacant position in the hierarchy tend to become solidified, creating symptoms or dysfunction in one or more family members. Interventions during this phase often center on realizing or reinitiating the power relationships in the family. Throughout this phase the mother is also working to establish herself economically. Thus these issues are also directly relevant to the relationships within the family and to the movement to the third phase of the process. The single mother may need to be counseled on job hunting or career strategies, as well as on money management. Therapists need to be aware of the difficulties for women in this area and assist them in seeking appropriate education on these subjects.

Therapy often involves getting whoever has been functioning as mother's partner, as if there were an empty position, to do things more appropriate to his or her role, while helping the mother to take over the executive functioning within the family. The first step is to identify and intervene in whatever relevant triangles may be present. In the following case, the person who had "taken over" the system was actually the mother's therapist, who sought a consultation with the author because she had been unable to bring about movement on the mother's primary complaint.

> Joan was a young welfare mother with two children, Jeanie, 5, and Brian, 18 months. She had begun to see the first therapist for what she called her "poor self-esteem." During the consultation the author observed that the therapist regularly moved to help Joan with the children whenever they became disruptive. As the author began to block the therapist's access to the children, Joan began to react directly to both of them, often struggling with her daughter over the care of her son.

As in the case above, more than one important triangle may exist simultaneously. Generally all function in the same way, as various persons attempt to take over the mother's functioning with her children to the detriment of her personal power in this primary role. In this case not only was Joan involved in a triangle with her therapist and the children, as well as a second triangle with her daughter and her son, but she was also involved in yet a third triangle:

> It became obvious that Joan's sister, Marie, functioned much like a "circus daddy," arriving on the weekends with gifts for the kids. She often took one or both children out, leaving Joan at home, either by herself or with the remaining child. Joan felt terribly inadequate since she was unable to provide gifts or plan "good times" with the children.

Such triangles need to be carefully tracked and often dealt with one at a time. After realigning structural difficulties within the system, interventions need to be directed towards establishing as many open and balanced relationships with the extended system and network as possible. The single parent may also have to deal with her relationship to the ex-spouse and family. This first requires sessions alone with the single parent, and perhaps later some sessions to work out details of coparenting and grandparenting.

As in the aftermath phase, the single parent may need encouragement to seek peer relationships. Issues around dating and intimacy often arise. Encouraging the client to cultivate female friendships is often a first positive step. By contact with other women, the single mother can gain a sense of positive identity in her current role that bolsters her self-esteem and enables her to choose male companions for genuine compatibility and mutual interests, rather than out of sheer loneliness or desperation.

PHASE III—STABILIZATION

Unfortunately some single-parent families think they get to this phase without having negotiated the major problem areas associated with the process of becoming a one-parent family. What frequently passes for stabilization, or a return to "normal," is the remarriage of the mother. In many cases the single mother remarries without having achieved financial management, parental authority over her children, or a viable social network. Thus, at a time when the process should be complete, old issues are still very much alive and unresolved, as in the following case.

> Mr. and Mrs. Jones had married six months previously. It was a first marriage for Mr. Jones and the second for Mrs. Jones, whose three children lived with them. Mr. Jones described his current problem as his conflict with the children. He claimed the children were often unruly, interrupting him and fighting with each other. Mrs. Jones calmly sat by and let her new husband hassle with the eldest boy, John, for authority over the younger children. It became clear that she had not negotiated the major tasks of the realignment phase before marriage, and that the children were as yet unable to attend to her direction.

A second-phase triangle with a spousal child, a custodial parent, and the other children is especially likely to "become a problem" following the parent's remarriage. However, even in cases where the parent does not remarry and the family appears to have stabilized, the normal tasks of the young-adult stage of life cycle may cause underlying difficulties to surface. The pulls of this child to stay involved with the parent as he or she continues to mature may create problems for both parent and child. The following case is one where both the remarriage of the mother and the daughter's entry into the young-adult phase combined to cause a major family unheavel.

The Gordons came for treatment because Mrs. Gordon's 18-year-old daughter by a previous marriage, Vanessa, was continually threatening suicide. Vanessa had returned home from college at the urging of her counselor due to the suicide threats. She had been home for two weeks and did not want to return to school. Mrs. Gordon felt this was unwise, but was scared to send her daughter back to college. She said that her ex-husband, Mr. James, was also concerned and willing to come in. She and Mr. Gordon had been married only four months, just before the start of Vanessa's first college year and five years after the divorce from her father. Both mother and daughter made it clear that Vanessa was very close to her father. Vanessa worried about his well-being and he, in turn, felt both his ex-wife's marriage and his daughter's departure for college to be major losses.

Certainly it is more difficult to deal with Mr. James' ongoing feelings of loss with regard to his ex-wife and daughter when both have ostensibly moved on to the next phase of the life cycle. Going back and accomplishing tasks of previous phases is more problematic because, as time goes on, the process becomes more complex and the number of people and relationships involved grows.

Ideally, in the stabilization phase, there is now the energy and attention available to deal with the ordinary development tasks of the family life cycle. This phase is often a time of quiet and calm, and it is here that the solutions to the various problems of the entire transition are tried and lived with. There is an acceptance of the new worked out. Children have a sense of freedom to move back and forth between two households, and into the outside world. Ex-spouses feel relatively comfortable in dealing with one another and in having other relationships. Often at least one of the parents ultimately does remarry (more often the father), thereby creating additional tasks around the issues of stepparents and siblings. Naturally the remarriage of one or both parents requires a major adjustment for all those affected. However, with the completion of the divorce process, there is every reason to expect that the family will be able to integrate these changes, as well as to accomplish the normative tasks of the family life cycle stages that lie ahead.

Interventions

Since by this time most of the tasks of becoming a single-parent family have been accomplished, families do not often present for treatment during this phase. However, some mothers will seek therapy as they begin to be more active socially and sexually. In addition, as the family reaches new stages of the life cycle, such as the launching phase, the family may come in for problems revolving around a spousal or parental child leaving the home.

At this time interventions center on solidifying the extrafamilial activities of each family member, and dealing more specifically with the triangle that keeps the child at home (Haley, 1980). For instance:

Marianne, 18 years old, called for an appointment because she felt extremely anxious abut her college plans, and felt unable to send her deposit money to the

college of her choice. When she arrived with her mother and younger sisters, it became clear that she felt very responsible for the family's welfare. In the session she frequently told her sisters, 12 and 14 years of age, what to do or not to do. Mother would permit this, remarking on how good Marianne was with the children. When questioned about the effects of Marianne's going to college on the household functioning, Mrs. L. stated that she thought things would be "very different." She said that the girls would have much less supervision; she also mentioned that money would be much tighter, since she not only would have some college-related expenses, but would also lose support payments for Marianne.

It was clear from this initial contact with Marianne and her family that her failure to pay her college deposit was related to her real fears about what mother and "the girls" would do without her and her support money. Typical of most parental children, Marianne took more responsibility for the problem than was appropriate for her age and family status. Also typical of the single-parent household is the inclusion of children in discussions that used to be parental,—i.e., money, educational expenses, etc. In the second session with this family three weeks later, several other issues, that were affecting Marianne's leave-taking emerged.

Mrs. L. and her three daughters came for the second session having followed the therapeutic suggestion that Marianne delay her sending of the deposit money until her mother had convinced her that she could handle things without her. Mrs. L. reported that because she wanted her daughter to have the opportunity for college, she had tried very hard and thought she "had handled mostly everthing" herself. Twice she had to keep her daughter from helping her with the kids. Mrs. L. went on to explain that she had a lot of opportunities to think since the last session. She felt that Marianne's leaving for school meant for the first time that she had to come to grips with her own single state. She would no longer have a companion. She also thought that Marianne's leaving home was like experiencing the divorce again. Both of the younger sisters expressed their anger that Marianne could leave and their worry that they wouldn't see her again. Mrs. L. was asked to reassure the younger ones on that point.

In contrast to families with two parents who may fear a divorce after the child leaves home, single-parent mothers may feel afraid that the child's departure will recreate the sadness of the original loss (the divorce itself) and necessitate yet another rebalancing of the system, with its associated stress. If a clinician is not sensitive to this matter, the family will remain impassive to any interventions he/she may use. For the L. family, further sessions are continuing to free Marianne up to go to college. After the fifth session, Marianne announced, laughingly, that she had paid her deposit money with a late fee. She also laughed at the prospect of finally being able to take a paying job while going to school. In subsequent sessions, Mrs. L. continued to work on how she herself could get unstuck and move her life past a divorce that had occurred four years before.

THE NONCUSTODIAL SINGLE PARENT

As the single-parent mother goes through the various transitions necessary to establish her competence and authority as both an individual and a custodial parent, her ex-husband goes through a different, though reciprocal, process. Most men tend to experience a loss of structure with the demise of their marriage, and with it the loss of a sense of home and family.

Traditionally marriage for men means economic responsibility in exchange for the companionship and emotional support of their wives, as well as built-in caretakers for their homes and children (Bernard, 1972). While men sterotypically complain about their wives nagging them to do household chores and their persistent requests for more "communication," men actually thrive better in marriage than their female or single-male counterparts (Bernard, 1971, 1972). Perhaps stemming in part from more personal and career freedom and lesser expectations regarding intimacy, married men experience lower rates of emotional and physical illness and report higher rates of personal happiness (Bernard, 1972).

In fact, as cited in many of the foregoing case examples, the noncustodial father often remains an active auxilliary member of the single-parent family. Moreover, at least legally, he carries some long-term financial responsibility toward his children, if not his ex-wife. It is worthwhile to consider his ongoing problems regarding money, parenting, and social relationships in the context of this discussion.

Money

The financial settlement and the need to support two households substantially reduces the economic base of the departing father. Although no one would argue that men are generally in a better position to rebuild after such a financial setback, there may be an initial sense of loss surrounding this issue. The more heavily invested the man has been defining his success on the basis of his net worth (or the more marginal his own financial security), the more threatened he is likely to be by the prospect of facing many years of child support and/or alimony payments. The fact that he must continue to support a household in which he no longer lives, and from which he no longer receives any personal benefit, may also contribute to make this economc issue an emotional one as well.

When a man has not initiated the separation, there may be an even greater resistance to paying support. Class issues often come into play here. The courts may require upper-middle-class fathers to pay higher portions of their earnings than their working-class counterparts. With rising real estate prices, fathers may be unable to purchase a second home, and be forced to live in an

apartment and/or to take in roommates. In effect, they may end up living like bachelors or students again.

> John had been separated for 18 months when he came for treatment. He had just been warned by his boss that his job was on the line because of his lateness and generaly poor work performance. When asked how he explained the job problem, John offered that he had been living with three single male friends in an apartment since his separation; he was unable to afford a house or apartment for himself, and seemed gloomy. Thus he and three "old buddies" had moved in together, having frequent parties and drinking nightly. He felt unable to have his children overnight since there wasn't enough room and he spent only one night a week and one day with them. He didn't know what to do. Because of expenses he had to continue living there but he couldn't do so and not party.

Self-employed men, in particular, may worry a great deal about economic issues, since divorce threatens the stability of their businesses (*Inc*. Magazine, 1986). The threat may come in two forms. Either a man may rightfully fear that his ex-wife will attack the resources of the business in the process of the legal settlement; and/or he may realize that the divorce will leave him too emotionally drained to handle the many critical functions an owner/entrepreneur must manage to keep a small business viable. (*Inc*. Magazine, 1986).

Thus a variety of financial concerns contribute to the current national problem in getting fathers to pay legally awarded sums When they do pay, they are often irregular in doing so (Bouton, 1984; Weitzman, 1985; Wright & Price, 1986). The larger judicial system has attempted to rectify this situation by garnishing the income tax returns and/or salaries of delinquent fathers. Although such procedures are time consuming and difficult to enforce, particularly across state lines, there has been some success reported using this procedure. (Wright, 1986). In most cases a father pays what he chooses to pay and can make collection procedures nearly impossible if he so desires.

Indeed, for men, money becomes the major source of power in the divorce process. Since men are in control of the money, both in the form of regular support payments and in decisions as to whether or not to grant requests for additional expenses, it is important that they consider the ways in which their use of money affects their relationships with their children and their ex-wives.

Parenting

Without the structure of the marriage and the efforts of their wives to define their parental relationships, fathers frequently become distant from their children because they lack the skills to conduct these relationships on their own. Generally those fathers who do pay support regularly also visit with their offspring more, and many see this money as insurance that their ex-wives will not "turn the children against them." Still the ex-spouse often finds it painful to enter the old home territory for visitation, as it reminds him of the old days. For similar reasons a man may experience a second loss when his ex-wife sells the marital home, which signals the true end of "the home" as he

once knew it. In the following case, the single mother had sold the house, and the client felt like an intruder in her new home.

> After Gene and his wife separated, he became very depressed. He frequently thought about "the fun they must all be having over there." He felt "left out" of the family, and responded by becoming more distant. He would not go to the house on visitation days, but would wait outside in the car, preferring to beep the horn for the children to come out.

Although one might not envy the noncustodial father's emotional distance from his children, it is worth noting that men still act as if they have an *option* regarding their participation in parenting. Women rarely consider parenting as a choice, and those who do must risk the negative consequences of society's view of them. As the role of fathers changes in society, there has been a slight increase in those who seek custody, as well as a rise in fathers engaged in joint-custody arrangements ("Changing USA Families," 1984; Rothberg, 1983). For this small minority, parenting issues parallel more closely those of the single-parent mother.

For example, a custodial father may also use his parents to an inappropriate degree to fill in the missing spouse in child care. However, men tend to view their mothers or girlfriends as convenient substitutes for their ex-wives, rather than as competitor. Due to their focus on work, men seem to experience less conflict over their roles as parents and are unlikely to seek treatment.

Possibly because they have not been socialized to nurture children directly, many fathers do not establish a viable "second home" for their children. The terms "circus daddy" and "zoo daddy" refer to the fact that most contact that fathers have with their children tends to be social or "play" time, with little discipline occurring in the limited time spent together. As in the case of the custodial father, the noncustodial father usually increases his involvement with his parents from the time of separation, as his parental home provides a convenient place for visits with the children and a break from dealing with them alone (Bloom, 1985; Nehls & Murgenhessty, 1980).

Although many fathers fail to establish a home like atmosphere of their own, many willingly continue to be the primary disciplinarians of their children for their ex-wives. As long as a man remains unattached, this may feel comfortable for both parties, but is likely to cause trouble when either of them remarry.

> Steve was still actively involved in the personal problems of his ex-wife, Judy. She frequently sought his help in "emergencies" ranging from "I need to talk to somebody" to solving fights between the couple's two children. His second marriage weas now on the verge of divorce because Linda, his new wife, resented Judy's many intrusions.

As time moves on, a father having difficulty maintaining contact with his children may drop out of their lives altogether. He may do this indirectly by taking a job in another state, or directly by simply failing to keep appointments for visitations. This tends to happen most often in families where the marital

conflicts are still quite alive, even if not discussed, and the father feels incapable of dealing with his ex-wife. Similarly, the ex-wife may also opt to remove the children from the direct influence of their father. She may do so either to pursue her own goals and/or follow a new spouse to a new state, or to eliminate the need for contact because the couple has not resolved the emotional divorce. When this happens the father may feel an overwhelming loss that leaves him powerless to seek other opportunities, such as school vacations, for visitations.

Social Relationships

While women become single parents after divorce, men become *single*. Since they do not have the responsibility for full-time parenting, men have more free time postdivorce. Despite the loss of family structure and its attendant convience, divorced men have an easier time socially than their female counterparts. Although they may lack the social supports of intimate friendships, they frequently have an already established social network at work.

In terms of social relationships with women, a divorced man is often viewed as a "catch." Men may at first feel inept at dating, but they frequently retain the benefit of being the initiators and can therefore "choose" whether or not to date, rather than wait to be asked. In addition they suffer no shortage of potential companions, since men traditionally have a broader range from which to select their dating partners. Lonely for emotional comfort, men often seek women for friends as well. Following divorce men marry sooner, and more often, than women, frequently to partners a decade or two younger than themselves (Glick, 1980).

Although most divorced men do not experience difficulty in finding new partners, they may enter a new commitment prematurely as a response to the loss of the "family." When they do so without resolving the issues surrounding the end of their first marriages, this move often exacerbates their problems. On the other hand, some men avoid intimacy altogether, focusing on sexual gratification in new relationships. As the involvement in one relationship grows, these men typically move into another new relationship. Often these are the men at the single-parent mother encounters when she begins dating. The following example illustrates problems associated with the first type of situation, "rapid remarriage."

Ralph came for treatment after the breakup of his second marriage of eight months. This marriage to Rita had occurred two days after his divorce from his first wife, Jane, became final. Ralph was extremely depressed—claiming he was a two-time failure and citing every misdemeanor he had committed. He had not wanted the second marriage to break up but felt that Rita's decision to leave was certainly understandable. He said Rita, 30 years old, had been complaining that since their marriage he had given her the responsibility for his three teen and preteen children. The children treated her poorly and he was too busy earning a living to intervene.

Ralph presents a fairly typical pattern when men try to recreate a family before they have become comfortable as parents alone, or have coped with the loss of their first marriage. The pressure to remarry, to provide a haven for themselves and a caretaker for their children, often creates immense pressure on the system, and especially on the new wife.

Interventions

It has been a fairly recent phenomenon for noncustodial fathers to enter treatment. Men generally do not seek assistance for problems related to finances. What ones does to solve money problems is to work harder, which is in itself a frequent "male solution" to any disruption in life. Men also tend not to seek help for relationship issues until they are married. At that point problems arise from the man's expectations of the new spouse with regard to his children and his ex-spouse. Or the new spouse's expectations about his relationships to her children may be the focus. These then become remarried family issues.

What does bring a noncustodial father to treatment with increasing frequency are issues regarding his parenting of his children. This is a fairly recent phenomenon and seems to be related to the more active role men are taking, in general, in parenting.

At times their distance from the children creates such anxiety in them that they need to be restrained from moving too fast without the necessary preparation regarding the system's reaction to a change. At other times they experience themselves as so far out that they feel powerless to change things and fear that they have permanently lost their children. Once assured that children almost never give up on their parents, they are ready to learn how to win them back. Often men are quite eager to learn, and a divorce may present the first opportunity to learn how to keep relationships alive and well.

GENERAL GUIDELINES FOR TREATMENT

Becoming a one-parent household is a process that spans three to five years. There is no method by which a family (or a therapist) can alter the amount of time it takes to stabilize after divorce. There appears to be something organic to the process, which is defined by a variety of physical, emotional, and legal markers. On the other hand, how the family negotiates the tasks required for reorganization is alterable. It appears that for both the family and the clinician, the primary issue that emerges early on is the idea that the father's absence has created an unfilled position in the family. With this operating viewpoint, the mother sees herself as needing to recruit others to fill

in the empty space. This definition of "something lacking" in the family structure perpetuates the attitude that this is merely a temporary situation that will ultimately be rectified by the appearance of a new "knight in shining armor." As with any family in crisis, the system is likely to close down and search among its members for recruits for the available position.

For the family the central issue is always how to manage all the instrumental and emotional roles for a two-parent family with only one adult in residence. The fact is, that it is not possible for the single-parent household to function as before. Attempting to do so leads inevitably to a continued sense of failure, and an ongoing effort to recruit available candidates (e.g., a child, a parent, the ex-spouse, the therapist) to fill in for the "missing" spouse.

What is necessary is that the single-parent mother develop a new vision of her family form, one that eliminates the perception of a "missing person" in the system and that allows her to see herself as the sole administration. Indeed one might compare the shift to a changing form of family government.

The central dilemma for the mother is how to enlist the help of others without allowing them to take over for her. As we have seen throughout the chapter, the long-term consequence of letting another "take over" is the decreased functioning of the parent. Quite understandably she might like nothing better and may require special encouragement to redefine her situation.

A therapist would be wise not to fall into the same trap in trying to help. Most mental health professionals are female and so most of these families will be seen by female therapists. For a like-aged female, the tendency may be to become a friend, a paid friend, who commiserates with the single parent and gives advice but does not do therapy. It is also possible for the older therapist to act like an overinvolved grandmother, thus decreasing the mother's functioning.

A family that ends up in a mental health agency, may be referred to a young female therapist who may tend to act like the parental child, attempting to help mother with the children, and often directing the children's activity in the therapy room. If the family is assigned to a male therapist, the dilemma for him is how not to fall into being the "man of the family," giving husbandly advice and support. Therapists of both genders need to remember that one's job is to increase the functioning of the client. Thus one might examine whether therapy is actually enabling dysfunctional behavior. While it is helpful to mother to have the children increase their instrumental functioning after divorce, it must be under her tutelage, at her request, and under her conditions. A parental child is one who no longer functions at the mother's request or under her supervision and derives his/her position vis-à-vis mother as a peer.

One simple practice offers tremendous reinforcement for the mother's developing vision of herself as the single head of the household: the family therapist must first examine the system as is—with a single parent—and view its functioning with only the custodial parent present. Often therapists assume that they must early on include fathers to understand how the system func-

tions. It is true that information about him is important to obtain a total picture of the system, as a father may be involved in symptom formation and more than a few triangles. However, it is helpful for a therapist to work first on other triangles within the household; e.g., a parental child, or interfering grandmother or grandfather. After the mother experiences herself as more sucessful in her own household, the father can and should be asked to attend a session with (or without) his children. This guideline does not apply to situations in which the relationship between parents is so conflictual and enmeshed as to impede any other family focus.

As we have seen, it appears that there is a strong positive relationship between the functioning of a single-parent household and the openness of relationships in the family and its social networks. Thus it is important for a clinician to help families develop open relationships within the nuclear and extended-family systems. It is also useful in this regard to work with various subsystems in treatment; for instance, doing a sibling session to work on strengthening the sibling relationships, or working with mother and her mother, or father and the children. By using an understanding of systems' potential triangles and themes in these families, it is possible for a therapist to coach a single parent on family-of-origin issues without the latter's presence. This process involves identifying one's part in the repetitive pattern and working on changing it, with the therapist acting as both a teacher and a systems analyst. The use of psychoeducational approaches and/or multifamily groups increases the family's social resources, and thus a sense of competence of the family, while affording the therapist additional treatment options.

CONCLUSIONS

It is the author's experience that these general guidelines, combined with the phase-specific interventions previously elaborated, will provide a framework for helping families negotiate the process of family reorganization postdivorce.

The family therapist also needs to address some of the broad issues that evolve from clinical work with single-parent households. One set of broader issues relates to the development of family policy and programs nationally that provide financial and occupational training opportunities for the mother and day care and other resources for the children. Since family therapists are most familiar with the problems of these households, it is important that they utilize their knowledge to address some of the social and economic conditions that perpetuate those problems.

Clinical work with these families forces us to rethink our models of family and family therapy. The notion that a family hierarchy must include two parents acting as a unit is clearly open to revision. The notion that a family can

and should perform all instrumental and emotional functions is also an open question, as are all the notions we have regarding clear boundaries.

Certainly, in terms of therapy models, our work with single-parent households suggests that we at least revise the typical family therapy interventions that call for backing off "overinvolved" mothers and involving distant fathers without regard for the metamessage thus delivered. In the broader sense, the work suggests that different family forms and structures may indeed generate not only some new family therapy techniques, but family theory development and research as well.

REFERENCES

Ahrons, C. R. (1980). Divorce: A crisis of family transition and change. *Family Relations* 29: 533–540.

Ahrons, C. R. (1980b). Redefining the divorced family. A conceptual framework for postdivorce family systems reorganization. *Social Work* 25: 437–44.

Ahrons, C. R. (1980) Joint custody arrangments in the post divorce family. *Journal of Divorce* 3 (Spring): 189–205.

Ahrons, C. R. (1981) The continuing co-parental relations between divorced spouses. *American Journal of Orthopsychiatry.* 51: 315–328.

Bernard, J. No news but new ideas. In P. Bohamman (Ed.), *Divorce and after.* New York: Anchor (1971).

Bernard, J. (1972) *The future of marriage.* New York: Bantam.

Biller, H. B. (1970) Father absence and the personality development of the male child. *Developmental Psychology* 2: 181–201.

Biller, H. B. (1974). *Paternal deprivation: Family school, sexuality and society.* Lexington, Mass.: Heath.

Biller, H. B. (1976). The father and personality development: Paternal deprivation and sex-role development. In M. E. Lamb (Ed.), *The role of the father in child development.* New York: Wiley.

Bloom, B. (1985). A prevention program for newly separated: Final evaluation. *American Journal of Orthopsychiatry.* 55 (1).

Bouton, K. (1984) Women and divorce. *New York Magazine* Oct. 8 p. 34.

Brandwein, R. A., Brown, C. A., & Fox, F. M. (1974). Women and children last: The social situation of divorced mothers and their families. *Journal of Marriage and the Family* 36: 498–514.

Cashion, B. G. (1982). Female headed families: Effects on children and clinical implications. *JMFT* 8 (2): 77–86.

Changing USA families (1984). *Family Therapy News,* 15(2): 16.

Chester, R. (1971). Health and marriage breakdown: Experience of a sample of divorced women. *British Journal of Preventive and Social Medicine,* 25: 231–235.

Chiriboga, D. A., Coho, A., Stein, J. A., & Roberts,J. Divorce, stress, and social supports: A study in helpseeking behavior. *Journal of Divorce* (1979). 3: 121–136.

Glick, P. C. (1979). The future of the family in current population reports. *Special Studies Series,* P-23, No. 78. Washington, D.C.: U.S. Government Printing Office.

Glick, P. C. (1980). Remarriage: Some recent changes and variations. *Journal of Family Issues* 1: 455–478.

Glick, P. C., & Sung-Ling, L. (1986). Recent changes in divorce and remarriage. *Journal of Marriage and the Family.* 48, 737–749.

Goldberg, M. L., & Dukes, J. L. (1985). Social support in black low-income, single parent families: Normative and dysfunctional patterns, *American Journal of Orthopsychiatry.* 55 (1).

Goldsmith, J. (1982) The postdivorce family system. In F. Walsh (Ed.), *Normal family process.* New York: Guilford Press.

Haley, J. (1980). *Leaving home.* New York: McGraw-Hill.

Herman, S. J. (1977). Women, divorce, and suicide. *Journal of Divorce* 1: 107–117.

Hetherington, E. M., Cox, M., & Cox, R. (1976). Divorced fathers. *The Family Coordinator* 25: 417–428.

Hetherington, E. M., Cox, M., & Cox, R. (1977). The aftermath of divorce. In J. H. Stevens, Jr., & M. Mathews (Eds.), *Mother–child, father–child relations.* Washington, D.C.: National Association for the Education of Young Children.

Hetherington, E. M., Cos, M., & Cox, R. (1979). Family interaction and the social, emotional, and cognitive development of children following divorce. In V. C. Vaughn III & Brazelton (Eds.), *The family: Setting priorities.* New York: Science & Medicine Publishers.

Kelly, J. B., & Wallerstein, J. S. (1976). The effects of parental divorce: Experiences of the child in early latency. *American Journal of Orthopsychiatry,* 46: 20–32.

Kressel, K., & Deutsch, M. (1977). Divorce therapy: An in-depth survey of therapists' views. *Family Process* 16: 413–443.

Kressel, K., Haffe, N., Tuchman, B., Watson, D., Deutsch, M. (1980). A typology of divorcing couples: Implications for mediation and the divorce process. *Family Process* 19: 101–116.

Lupnitz, D. (1982). *Child custody: A study of families after divorce.* Lexington, Mass.: Books.

Maxwell, J. W., & Andress, E. L. (1982). Marriage role expectations of divorced men and women. *Journal of Divorce,* 5: 55–66.

Mchanahan, S., Wedemeyer, N., & Adelberg., T. (1981) Network Structure, Social Support & Psychological Wellberg in the single parent family. *Journal of Marriage and Family* 43: 601–612.

National Center for Health Statistics (1984). *Monthly vital statistics report,* Vol. 32, No. 2, March 25, 1984. Washington, D.C.: U.S. Government Printing Office.

Nehls, N., & Morgenbesster, M. (1980). Joint custody: An exploration of the issues. *Family Process* 19: 2.

Norton, A. J., & Glick, P. C. (1976). Marital instability: Past, present and future. *Journal of Social Issues* 32: 5–20.

Norton, A. J. (1983). Family life cycle: 1980. *JMF* 45 (2) 267.

Rice, J. K., & Rice, D. G. (1986). *Living through divorce.* New York: Guilford Press.

Rothberg, B. (1981). Joint custody: Parental problems and satisfaction. *Family Process* 22 (1): 43–52.

Spanier, G. S. B., & Glick, P. C. Marital instability in the United States: Some correlates and recent changes. *Family Relations* 20: 329–338.

U.S. Bureau of the Census. (1977). *Current population reports,* Series P-60: 106. Characteristics of the population below the poverty level: 1975. Washington, D.C.: U.S. Government Printing Office.

Wallerstein, J. S., & Kelly, J. B. (1975). The effects of parental divorce: Experience of the preschool child. *Journal of the American Academy of Child Psychiatry* 14: 600–616.

Wallerstein, J. S., & Kelly, J. B. (1976). The effects of parental divorce: Experience of the child in later latency. *American Journal of Orthopsychiatry* 46: 256–269.

Wallerstein, J. S., & Kelly, J. B. (1977). Divorce counselling: A community service for families in the midst of divorce. *American Journal of Orthopsychiatry* 47: 4–22.

Wallerstein, J. S., & Kelly, J. B. (1980). *Surviving the break-up: How children and parents cope with divorce.* New York: Basic Books.

Weitzman, L. J. (1981). The economics of divorce: Social and economic consequences of property, alimony and child support awards. *UCLA Law Review* 28: 1181–1268.

Weitzman, L. J. (1985). *The divorce revolution*. New York: Free Press, 1985.

Wright, D. W., & Price, S. J. (1986). Court ordered child support payment: The effect of the former spouse relationship on compliance. *Journal of Marriage and the Family,* 48: 89–874.

Wojahn, Ellen (1986). *Divorce Inc.,* pp. 55–68.

conjunction with his or her ex-spouse, takes primary responsibility for raising or disciplining his or her own biological children. The relationship of the children and stepparent then remains to be defined and worked out in the light of such factors as the children's ages and primary residence, the circumstances of the divorce, and the desires of all concerned. Stepparents and stepchildren may then work out a relationship that resembles parent (or godparent) and child, aunt or uncle, friends, or whatever model of friendly relationship appeals to them.

This is a far cry from the assumptions of most people, both women and men, that the stepmother, because she is a woman, will be in charge of the home, the children, and the emotional relationships throughout the system. How she is to take charge of the children without getting into a hassle with their mother is not considered until it happens, and it is then labeled either her fault or the fault of the children's mother. Clashes between stepmothers and stepdaughters are common, as daughters feel a responsibility to protect their natural mother and get caught in the conflict over roles. Stepmother unhappiness with her new spouse and ambivalence about her parenting role is particularly acute when the stepchildren are young and remain in the custody of her husband's ex-wife. In this common situation, the stepmother feels less emotionally attached to the children; she feels disrupted and exploited during their visits and has to deal with the fact that her husband's coparenting partnership is conducted more with his ex-spouse than with her (Ambert, 1986). All of the facts of this situation are at variance with her assumptions about marriage and family and her role in the system. Neither her own family upbringing nor societal norms have prepared her to accept or to participate in family relationships that do not necessarily include primary emotional bonding. She does not feel empowered in the role, nor can she comfortably ignore the relationship issues that arise.

Of course, this new model of family rests on the assumption that ex-spouses are responsible adults who can learn to cooperate with each other for the sake of their relationships with their children. This is not always the case, and Elkin (1987) lists several contraindications to postdivorce arrangements of joint or shared custody. Among them are:

1. Mental illness or addiction in one or both parents.
2. A history of family violence and/or child abuse and neglect
3. Irreconcilable disagreement about child rearing.

This chapter will present an outline of the process of remarriage, discuss the implications of its occurrence at different stages of the family life cycle, and suggest clinical interventions for families who become stuck in this process. It is our experience that this is one of the most difficult developmental transitions for families to negotiate. This is so because of the wish for premature closure to end the ambiguity and pain, and because of the likelihood that the previous stage (mourning a death or working out the emotional

complexities of a divorce) has been inadequately dealt with, and will, in any case, be emotionally reactivated. Much therapeutic effort must be directed toward educating families about the built-in complexities of the process, so that they can work toward establishing a viable, open system that will permit restoration of the developmental process for future life cycle phases.

It is easy to understand the wish for clear and quick resolution when one has been through the pain of a first family ending. Unfortunately, however, the "instant intimacy" that remarried families expect of themselves is impossible to achieve and the new relationships are all the harder to negotiate because they do not develop slowly, as intact families do, but must begin midstream, after another family's life cycle has been dislocated. Naturally second families carry the scars of first families. Neither parents, nor children, nor grand-parents can forget the relationships that went before. Children never give up their attachment to their first parent, no matter how negative the relationship with that parent was or is. Having the patience to tolerate the ambiguity of the situation and allowing each other the space and time for feelings about past relationships is crucial to the process of forming a remarried family. However, the "battle fatigue" of family members quite naturally leads to a tendency to seek comfort, often resulting in the characteristic pseudomutuality (Goldstein, 1974) that denies difficulties and thus prevents their resolution.

STUDIES OF REMARRIAGE: CLINICALLY USEFUL FINDINGS

There follows a brief summary of some clinically useful findings from research done on remarried families over the past decade. For more thorough coverage, the reader is referred to the excellent books of Visher and Visher (1979, 1982 and especially 1987), Ahrons and Rodgers (1987), and Sager et al. (1983), and the *Stepfamily Bulletin,* published quarterly by the Stepfamily Association of America in Baltimore, Md.

We know that men remarry sooner and more often, and that whereas their first wives are on the average three years younger, their second wives are on the average six years younger than they are. The more income and education a woman has, the less likely she is to remarry. The reverse is true for men: the more income and education they have, the more likely they are to remarry, and to do it quickly. In general those with "incomplete" educations (e.g., some college but no degree) appear more likely to divorce, but those with more education seem less likely to redivorce. About half the remarrying couples have children, and the statistical average is for couples who divorce and remarry to do so within ten years of their first marriage.

In one of the few studies of nonclinical remarried families, Dahl and colleagues (1987) interviewed 30 remarried families in Connecticut. They were

Frank Furstenberg and co-workers (1983) found that remarriage of either spouse had a negative effect on the frequency of contact between fathers and their biological children. They found the level of contact between a divorced father and his children to be twice as high if he did not remarry, and even greater if the mother did not remarry. If both parents remarried, only 11% of the children had weekly contact with their fathers, compared with 49% of the children when neither parent had remarried.

Anderson and White (1986) studied 63 families, half of them remarried. They found in their stepfamilies that 69% of the children had contact with their fathers less than five times a year. They studied functional and dysfunctional first families and stepfamilies and found that:

1. Functional stepfamilies had less intense stepfather-child relationships than did fathers and children in intact first families.
2. Functional stepfamilies less often wanted to exclude a member.
3. There were fewer parent–child coalitions in functional stepfamilies.

E. Mavis Hetherington and colleagues (1977), in studying intact and divorce couples, found the following:

1. In 70% of divorcing-couples studies, one of the spouses was involved in an affair, but only 15% of them later married the person with whom they were having affair.
2. Remarriage of a former spouse was accompanied by a reactivation of feelings of depression, helplessness, anger, and anxiety, particularly for women. Men, possibly for financial reasons, and because they are usually less central to the emotional system, tended to be less upset by the remarriage of an ex-wife.
3. Remarriage often led to a renewal of financial and/or custody difficulties. Conflicting role expectations set mothers and stepmothers into competitive struggles over child-rearing practices.

Another study, by Stern (1978), of discipline and stepfather integration in 30 stepfather families found that it took stepfathers almost two years to become comanagers of their stepchildren with their wives. They had first to become friends of the children, and only gradually could they move into the role of active parenting.

In yet another study, by Estelle Duberman (1975), 88 remarried couples were interviewed to determine their level of "family integration." Duberman found that:

1. Family integration was better if the previous spouse had died rather than divorced.
2. Family integration was better if the new spouse had divorced rather than been a bachelor.

predominantly white, Protestant or Catholic, middle-class, two-income families. The researchers found that:

1. The "sense of belonging" in a remarried family took three to five years for most of its members, and longer if there were adolescents.
2. The families usually moved or did extensive redecorating in the first year or so to avoid the feeling of "living in someone else's house."
3. Both spouses preferred distant but cordial or courteous relationships with the ex-spouse and the ex-spouse's new marital partner.
4. Serious discipline issues with children and visitation arrangements for young children were handled by the biological parent. Men were actively involved in parenting and stepparenting.
5. Childhood experiences in a large family may be helpful in dealing with the complexities of a remarried family.
6. Marital satisfaction correlated with the stepparent's connection to stepchildren.

Asked what advice they would give to other stepfamilies, the families said:

1. Go slow. Take time. Settle your old marriage (divorce) before you start a new one. Accept the need for continual involvement of parts of the old family with the new. Help children maintain relationships with their biological parents.
2. Stepparents should try for mutual courtesy, but not expect a stepchild's love. They should respect the special bond between the biological parent and child.
3. Communicate, negotiate, compromise, and accept what cannot be changed.

White and Booth (1985) studied the role of stepchildren in remarriage. They found that remarried couples with stepchildren were more than twice as likely to redivorce. They found that the marriages themselves might be quite congenial, but the presence of stepchildren often meant that the couple had child-related problems that led them to separate. They found that stepchildren were much more likely to change residence or leave home early than children who lived with both biological parents.

Clingempeel (1981) and Clingempeel and colleagues (1984a, 1984b) also found that families in which stepfathers had left children behind in a previous marriage had difficulties in their step-relationships related to the lack of social role prescriptions to guide them. However, this did not necessarily make them less able than stepfathers with no previous parenting experience to developing relationships with their stepchildren. Stepdaughters appeared to have more difficulties than stepsons in dealing with their stepfathers, perhaps, again, because females are not socialized to maintain uninvolved family relationships.

3. The longer the new family had been together as a unit, the higher was the level of family integration.

4. Parent–child relationships were better when the remarried couple had children of their own.

5. Parent–child relationships were better when the wife's children from her first marriage were with her.

6. Men who had left children behind with an ex-wife did not relate to their stepchildren as well as bachelors did.

7. Stepmothers related better to young children than to teenagers.

8. Widows related to their stepchildren better than did divorcees.

9. The stepmother–stepdaughter relationship was the most problematic of all stepfamily relationships.

10. Remarried relationships were best when extended-family members approved or accepted the marriage, second best when they disapproved or were negative, and worst when they were cut off or indifferent.

Probably reflecting the fact that daughters feel more responsible for emotional relationships in a family, and thus get caught between loyalty and protection for their biological mothers and conflicts with their stepmothers, a recent study by Bray (1986) revealed that girls in stepfamilies reported more negative stress than boys in stepfamilies or girls in nuclear families.

Of special relevance to our view is the finding of Nolan (1977) and Ahrons (1980), substantiated by Isaacs and co-workers (1986), that children function best after divorce if they are able to maintain satisfactory contact with both parents.

PREDICTABLE EMOTIONAL ISSUES IN REMARRIAGE

The basic premise of family systems theory is that we all carry into our new relationships the emotional baggage of unresolved issues from important past relationships. This baggage makes us emotionally sensitive in the new relationships, and we tend to react in one of two ways: we become self-protective, closed off, and afraid to make ourselves vulnerable to further hurt (i.e., we put up barriers to intimacy) or we become intensely expectant and demanding that the new relationships make up for or erase past hurts.

Either of these stances complicates the new relationships. In first marriages the baggage we bring is from our families of origin: our unresolved feelings about parents and siblings. In remarriage there are at least three sets of emotional baggage:

1. From the family of origin.
2. From the first marriage.

3. From the process of separation, divorce, and the period between marriages.

To the extent that either or both remarried partners expect the other to relieve them of this baggage, the new relationship will become problematic. On the other hand, to the extent that each spouse can work to resolve his or her own emotional issues with significant people from the past, the new relationship can proceed on its own merits.

There are a number of major predictable emotional issues in remarriage that will be briefly summarized here. They have been dealt with in greater depth elsewhere (Visher & Visher, 1977; Schulman, 1972; Goldstein, 1974; Whiteside, 1982; Wald, 1981; Sager et al., 1983).

Complex, Conflicting, and Ambiguous New Roles and Relationships.

Instead of step-by-step progression from courtship to marriage to parenthood, remarried families must plunge into instant multiple roles, as a single young adult becomes a wife and stepmother of four. In such situations the parent–child relationship predates the couple relationship, with the obvious complications this entails.

The complexity of remarried families would probably not present quite so many problems for its members if our society provided guidelines for the roles and relationships, but we do not even have language or kinship labels to help orient the members of remarried families positively toward their newly acquired kin. These problems are by no means trivial, and they immediately invade every aspect of family life and contact with outsiders. How do children explain that their brother has a different last name and their mother yet another? How do they address their new stepgrandparents? And how do they learn to be middle children, when they have for years been the oldest?

Our cultural forms, rituals, and assumptions still relate chiefly to the intact first-marriage family, and the most ordinary event, such as filling out a form or celebrating a holiday, can become a source of acute embarrassment or pain for members of remarried families.

Complex and Ambiguous Boundaries of the System

Boundary difficulties include issues of:

1. Membership (Who are the "real" members of the family?)
2. Space (What space is mine? Where do I really belong?)

3. Authority (Who is really in charge? Of discipline? Of money? Of decisions? etc.)

4. Time (Who gets how much of my time and how much do I get of theirs?)

This cluster of issues is central and must be negotiated by remarried families, since one simple boundary cannot be drawn around the members of the household as in most first families. Great flexibility is called for to enable the new family constantly to expand and contract its boundaries, to include visiting children and then let them go, while also establishing its own stable life-style. An additional boundary problem arises when "instant incest taboos" are called for, as when several previously unrelated teenagers are suddenly supposed to view each other as siblings, or a new stepfather is not supposed to have sexual feelings toward his attractive stepdaughter.

Affective Problems:
Wishing for the Resolution of Ambiguity

Intense conflictual feelings, or their denial, are predictable problems in remarried families.

Guilt is an especially difficult issue. For example, if a father has left the children of his first marriage with his ex-wife, he may be moved by guilt to be a "better" father in the new family, bringing a special intensity to his relationships with his stepchildren. Or a wife may not really like her husband's children, may find them ill-mannered or intrusive, but at the same time may feel they are "part of the bargain," that they need her because of their previous losses, or that her husband is relying on her to do a good job with them. One of the injunctions most harmful to remarried families is that a person must love another's children as much as his or her own. "Overtrying" by the new parent is a major problem in such families, often related to guilt about unresolved or unresolvable aspects of the system. This is more often a problem for stepmothers because of our culture's special demands on women to take responsibility for the emotional relationships in a family.

Another major source of difficulty is loyalty conflicts. Children will always feel loyalty to their natural parents. One of the greatest strains on parents is to let their children have and express the full range of negative and positive feelings toward their parents and stepparents. A parent may prohibit a child from expressing negative feelings about a dead parent, or positive feelings about a parent who has divorced and left them. Often parents want the child's whole allegiance, and most children fear that if they love one parent, they will somehow hurt the other. If they don't love a new stepparent, they fear they will hurt and anger one parent; if they do love the stepparent, they fear disloyalty to the other.

The Tendency Toward Pseudomutuality or Fusion

Remarried families are formed against a background of hurt and failure. The sense of vulnerability, fear, and mistrust is very difficult to deal with. As a result families often cover over conflicts, fearing that their expression will lead to more hurt and separation. There is often a sense of, "Let's not rock the boat this time."

THE PROCESS OF REMARRIAGE

The process of remarriage must be viewed as part of an emotional process going back at least to the disintegration of the first marriage. The intensity of emotion unleashed by the life cycle disruption of divorce must be dealt with over and over again before the dislocated systems are restabilized. The emotions connected with the breakup of the first marriage can be visualized as a "roller-coaster" graph with peaks of intensity at the point of:

1. Decision to separate.
2. Actual separation.
3. Legal divorce.
4. Remarriage of either spouse.
5. Shift in custody of any of the children.
6. Moves of either spouse.
7. Illness or death of either ex-spouse.
8. Life cycle transitions of the children (graduations, marriage, illness, etc.).

Seen in this way, it should be clear that no amount of "dealing with" the emotional difficulties of divorce will finish off the process once and for all before remarriage, although it appears clinically that the more emotional work done at each step, the less intense and disruptive the subsequent reactivations will be. Failure to deal sufficiently with the process at each peak may jam it enough to prevent remarried family stabilization from ever occurring.

Chapter 1 describes the developmental steps required for a remarried family formation, and is similar in many respects to that described by Ransom and co-workers (1979). Their outline is particularly fortuitous in addressing the need to conceptualize the plan for the new marriage. Although it is certainly true that more advanced planning would also be helpful in first marriages, it is an essential ingredient for successful remarriage, because of the different conceptual model required, and because of the number of family relationships that must be renegotiated at the same time as the new marriage. We have

expanded Ransom and colleagues' outline to include conceptualizing and planning for the new family as well as for the marriage. This was done because, as they themselves have observed, "The presence of children at the earliest stages prevents the establishment of an exclusive spouse-to-spouse relationship which predates the undertaking of parenthood" (p. 37). We have also added to the framework extended-family relationships, which we consider vital to stabilization of the system.

It is our opinion that the emotional tasks listed in column 2 of our table are key attitudes in the transitions that permit the family to work on the tasks of column 3. If, as clinicians, we find ourselves struggling with the family over developmental issues (column 3) before the prerequisite attitudes (column 2) have been adopted, we are probably wasting our efforts. In addition to the emotional work, time is an essential ingredient in this process. Hetherington et al. (1977) found that an average of two years was required for restabilization of the family after divorce. Other studies have suggested (Stern, 1978), and we have observed clinically, that it takes at least two years for stabilization to occur in remarried families. This time for minimal stabilization is considerably shorter than the three to five years reported in the Dahl study for family members to develop a "sense of belonging."

From our clinical experience, we have outlined a number of predictors of difficulty in making the transition to remarriage:

1. A wide discrepancy between the family life cycles of the families.
2. Denial of prior loss and/or a short interval between marriages.
3. Failure to resolve the intense relationship issues of the first family—for example, if family members still feel intense anger or bitterness about the divorce or if there are still legal actions pending.
4. Lack of awareness of the emotional difficulties of remarriage for children.
5. The inability to give up the ideal of the intact first family and move to a new conceptual model of family.
6. Efforts to draw firm boundaries around the new household membership and push for primary loyalty and cohesiveness in the new family (thus excluding all other members of the family).
7. Exclusion of natural parents or grandparents or combatting their influence.
8. Denial of differences and difficulties and acting "as if" this is just an ordinary household.
9. Shift in custody of children near the time of remarriage.

THE IMPACT OF REMARRIAGE AT VARIOUS PHASES OF THE FAMILY LIFE CYCLE

Spouses at Different Life Cycle Phases

To be useful to clinicians, a family life cycle view of human development must provide for the variations in structure of remarried families. The same complexity that does not always provide a simple answer to questions such as "Who are your parents?" or "Where do you live?" applies equally to the clinician's attempt to locate the remarried family at a particular phase of the family life cycle. In fact the two subsystems now joined in remarriage may come from quite different phases, and this difference in experience and approach to current responsibilities may cause considerable difficulty if not explicitly addressed by the new spouses.

In general the wider the discrepancy in family life cycle experience between the new spouses, the greater the difficulty of transition will be and the longer it will take to integrate a workable new family. A father of late adolescent and/or young adult children with a new, young wife never previously married should expect a rather strenuous and lengthy period of adjustment during which he will have to juggle his emotional and financial responsibilities toward the new marriage and toward his (probably upset) children. His wife, looking forward to the romantic aspects of a first marriage, will meanwhile encounter instead the many stresses of dealing with adolescents who probably do not take kindly to her which is so whether the children live with the couple or not. If either spouse tries to pull the other exclusively into a life-style or attitude that denies or restricts the other spouse's family life cycle tasks, difficulties will expand into serious problems. Thus, if the husband expects his new wife to undertake immediately a major successful role in his children's lives, or to be the one who always backs down gracefully when her interests and preferences clash with those of the children, there will be serious trouble in the new marriage, as the formation of the new couple bond is continuously given second priority. On the other hand, if the new wife tries, overtly or covertly, to cut off or drastically loosen the tie between father and children, or if she insists that her claims always have his prior attention, thus forcing her husband to choose between them, there will also be serious trouble. Variations in which the new wife claims to support her husband but embarks on a battle with his ex-wife as the source of the difficulties are equally dysfunctional.

Since it is not possible emotionally either to erase or to acquire experience over night, it is useful to conceptualize the joining of partners at two discrepant life cycle phases as a process in which both spouses have to learn to function in several different life cycle phases simultaneously and out of their usual sequence. The new wife will have to struggle with the role of stepmother to teenagers before becoming an experienced wife or mother herself. The husband will have to retraverse with her several phases that he has passed through before: the honeymoon,—the new marriage with its emphasis on

romance and social activities, and the birth and rearing of any new children of their own. Both need to be aware that a second passage through these phases automatically reactivates some of the intensity over issues that were problematic the first time around. Attempts to "make up for" past mistakes or grievances may overload the new relationship. The focus needs to be on having the experiences again, not on undoing, redoing, or denying the past. With open discussion, mutual support, understanding, and a lot of thoughtful planning, this straddling of several phases simultaneously can provide rejuvenation for the older and experience for the younger spouse that can enrich their lives. If the difficulties are not understood and dealt with, they will surface as conflict or emotional distance at each life cycle transition in any subsystem of the remarried family.

Spouses at Same Life Cycle Phase

When the remarried spouses come together at the same phase of the family life cycle, they tend to have the advantage of bringing the same life cycle tasks and the same general previous experience to the new family. Their greatest difficulties will tend to be related to whether they are at a childbearing phase. Obviously spouses with no children from previous marriages bring the least complexity to the new situation. Families with grown children and grandchildren on both sides are complex systems with long histories and will require some careful thought to negotiate successfully. Neither of these circumstances, however, is likely to provide anything like the degree of strain involved at phases including either young or adolescent children, where the roles of active parenting and stepparenting must be included in the new family. Unfortunately the advantage of having similar tasks, responsibilities, and experiences is frequently swamped in a competitive struggle that stems from the overload of these tasks and concern (six children are not as easy to raise or support as three); the intense emotional investment in good parenting ("My methods are better than your methods"); and the need to include both ex-spouses in the many arrangements regarding the children ("Why do you let him or her dictate our lives?").

Reactions of Children to Remarriage

The most complex remarried families, and they are in the majority, are those in which one or both spouses have children under 18. In evaluating probable issues involved in remarried families with children, it is necessary to consider several important factors: the degree of recognition of previous profound loss (whether by death or divorce); the length of time that was available between marriages for dealing with the previous loss; the extent to which previous family loss and/or conflict has actually been resolved; and

recognition and acceptance of the emotional issues important to children at the time of remarriage, and their age-related methods of handling these issues.

Clinically we find that denial of the importance of prior loss, little time between marriages, failure to resolve intense relationship issues in the first family (including extended family), and expectations that the remarriage will be quickly or easily accepted by the children are all associated with poor adjustment of children in the stepfamily.

Visher and Visher (1979) have devoted several chapters of their book to the crucial issues for children of various ages. Their summary is based on their clinical work with this problem over many years and the small but important body of research on the subject, notably the work of Wallerstein and Kelly (1980). The Vishers identify the major issues concerning children at the time of remarriage as follows:

1. Dealing with loss.
2. Divided loyalties.
3. Where do I belong? (Shift in sibling position, role in family structure, family traditions.)
4. Membership in two households.
5. Unreasonable expectations.
6. Fantasies of the natural parents' reuniting.
7. Guilt over causing the divorce.
8. For adolescents, additional problems with identity and sexuality.

Children's struggles with these issues surface as school and/or behavior problems, withdrawal from family and peers, or "acting-out" behavior, any of which complicates or may completely obstruct, the process of stepfamily reorganization. There are indications that preschool children, if given some time and help in mourning their previous loss, adjust most easily to a new stepfamily, and that the adjustment is most difficult for stepfamilies with teenagers (Visher & Visher, 1979). Children of latency age seem to have the most difficulty resolving their feelings of divided loyalty (Wallerstein & Kelly, 1976), and benefit from careful attention to their need for contact with both parents. Clearly, children of all ages suffer when there is intense conflict between their natural parents and benefit when their parents maintain civil, cooperative, coparental relationships (Ahrons & Rogers, 1987; Ahrons & Wallisch, 1986); Ahrons' research (1981) indicates that if parents cannot be cooperative, structuring the relationships is the next best alternative.

Stepfamilies with Adolescents

Since the difficulties of most American families with adolescents are legendary, it is not surprising that the additional complications of this phase in stepfamilies can push the stress level beyond manageable bonds. We have found the following common issues in stepfamilies at this phase.

1. Conflict between the need for the remarried family to coalesce and the normal concentration of adolescents on separation. Adolescents often resent the major shifts in their customary family patterns and resist learning new roles for the new family constellation at this point, when they are concerned with growing away from the family.

2. Particular difficulty for a stepparent in attempting to discipline an adolescent.

3. Adolescents try to resolve their divided loyalties by taking sides (Wallerstein & Kelly, 1974) or actively playing one side against the other.

4. Sexual attraction between stepsiblings or stepparent and stepchild may be a problem, along with the adolescent's difficulty accepting the biological parent's sexuality.

The Impact of Remarriage in Later Life Cycle Phases

Although there is not the daily strain of living with stepchildren and stepparents, remarriage at a post-child-rearing phase of the life cycle requires significant readjustment of relationships throughout both family systems, which may now include in-laws and grandchildren. It is probable that grown children and grandchildren will accept a remarriage after a death of a parent more easily than after a late divorce. There will often be great relief throughout the family if a widowed older parent finds a new partner and a new lease on life, whereas a later-life divorce usually arouses concern and dismay throughout the family. One grown man spoke of feeling that all of his childhood memories had been challenged and required rearranging when his parents divorced in their 60s. He said he felt angry at both of them when they remarried for requiring him to try to figure out two new "foreign" relationships, and for depriving his children of "normal" grandparents. A grown daughter complained of the stress of sorting out the guest list for birthdays, graduations, and holidays, and was particularly upset when her father and his new wife remained in her childhood home, "changing and redecorating my past." A frequent problem for older remarried couples is negotiating with each other how their wills should be made and how much financial assistance should be given to which adult children. This is often more of a problem where the financial resources are large.

Clinically we find that the major factor in three-generational adjustment to remarriage in late middle or older age is the amount of acrimony or cooperation between the ex-spouses. Where the relationship is cooperative enough to permit joint attendance at important family functions of children and grandchildren, and where holiday arrangements can be jointly agreed upon, family acceptance of a new marriage tends to follow.

FAMILY THERAPY WITH REMARRIED FAMILIES: CLINICAL PROCEDURES AND ILLUSTRATIONS

A number of years ago, finding ourselves faced with increasing numbers of remarried families in our own clinical work and in the case loads of our trainees, we embarked on an informal project, discussing cases and developing clinical procedures for working with these families. The following is a summary of our work.

As indicated in column 2 of our developmental outline (Table 1-1), there are at least three key emotional attitudes that permit transition through the developmental steps involved in the formation and stabilization process for remarried families: resolution of the emotional attachment to the ex-spouse(s); giving up attachment to the ideal of first-family structure and accepting a different conceptual model of family; and accepting the time and space involved and the ambivalence and difficulty of all family members in moving toward stepfamily organization. Failure to achieve sufficient emotional grasp of these "enabling attitudes" will seriously hamper, delay, or prevent the reorganization and future development of the family.

Family therapists typically look back one or two generations to understand the presenting family problem. Thus difficulty with a child will involve an evaluation of the parental marriage and of the parents' relationships with the grandparent generation. Whatever the presenting problem in a remarried family, it is essential to look laterally as well as back and to evaluate the current and past relationships with previous spouses to determine the degree to which the family needs help to work out the patterns required by the new structure. Generally we take the position that the more open the lines are to all family members, and the clearer the roles, the more functional will be the new structure. Ongoing conflict or cutoffs with ex-spouses, natural parents, and grandparents will tend to overload the relationships in the remarried family and make them problematic.

In first-marriage families, the major problematic triangles involve the parents with any or all of the children and each parent with his or her own parents. In the more complex structures of remarried families, we have identified six of the most common triangles and interlocking triangles. For the purposes of this chapter, we have limited our clinical illustrations to those commonly presenting in the households and nuclear subsystems of remarried families. In no way do we mean to suggest by this focus that the triangles with the extended family and grandparental generation are unimportant to the understanding and the therapy of remarried families. However, this process has been fully explicated elsewhere (Bowen, 1978). In fact we consider genograms, as a basic tool for exploring structure and tracking process in all families, to be particularly essential in work with remarried families, because of the structural complexity that so influences the predictable triangles that exist in these situations.

(McGoldrick & Gerson, 1985). For a more extensive exploration of the use of genograms with remarried families, see Visher and Visher (1987). In our clinical work with remarried families, coaching of the adults on further differentiation in relation to their families of origin proceeds in tandem with work on current family problems. The extended-family aspect of the family therapy has been mostly deleted from the examples because of the focus of this chapter.

One final caveat: The brief case stories are meant to illustrate possible clinical moves. What they fail to convey is the enormous intensity aroused by attempts to shift these relationships, the extreme anger and fear that block change, the many, many slips back, and the recycling of old conflicts that accompany each move forward. Our experience indicates that families willing to work on relationships with their families of origin do better than those that do not.

Key Presenting Triangles in Remarried Families

1. *The husband, the second wife, and the ex-wife. Or: the wife, the second husband, and the ex-husband.*

Clinically the variations of this triangle will usually be presented directly as the main problem only when the remarried couple acknowledges its own marital difficulties and comes to therapy for that reason. (Actually, either or both variations of this triangle are usually present, though perhaps not acknowledged, in problems with children and stepchildren.) When this triangle is presented as the main difficulty, usually around financial issues or sexual jealousy, it is likely that an emotional divorce has not been accomplished by the ex-spouses. There may be conflict among all three in the triangle, or a spouse may defend or excuse an ex-spouse's intrusions, while claiming to have no emotional attachment to the ex-spouse. In either case therapy would need to focus on the completion of the emotional divorce between the ex-spouses. The first step in this most tricky clinical work is for the therapist to establish a working alliance with the new spouse, who will otherwise sabotage efforts to focus on the first marriage. Efforts to work on the resolution of the divorce by having either the ex-spouses alone or all three in sessions together will probably create more anxiety than the system can handle, and we have found that such work goes most smoothly when a spouse is coached in the presence of the new spouse to undertake steps outside of the therapy sessions that will change the relationship he or she currently maintains with the ex-spouse. This may require a lessening of contact, if the divorced spouses are still emotionally dependent on each other, or it may require becoming civil and friendly, if they have maintained their emotional attachment through intense conflict. Along the way the new spouse will have to learn to acknowledge the past importance of that bond to his or her spouse and to accept the fact that some degree of

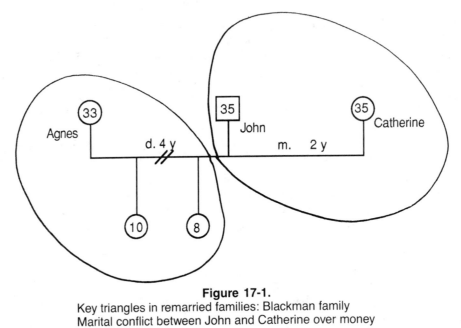

Figure 17-1.
Key triangles in remarried families: Blackman family
Marital conflict between John and Catherine over money
Triangle of husband–second wife–ex-wife

caring will probably always remain in the relationship, depending on the length of time the first marriage lasted and whether there were children.

Case Example: The Blackman Family.

Catherine and John Blackman, both in their mid-30s, came for marital therapy after two years of marriage. He had been married before; she had not. John's first marriage had ended in divorce two years prior to their marriage, and his two daughters, ages eight and ten, lived with their mother, Agnes. Catherine and John described their problem as "endless conflict over money," which was caused, Catherine said, because John put the needs of his ex-wife over hers and gave in to her every demand for extra money. John defended his ex-wife's need for money and her refusal to work on the grounds that the children needed her. He said he felt guilty for leaving his first marriage, even though it had been unhappy, and that Catherine refused to understand his financial obligations to his previous family. Agnes had been drinking since their divorce, found the care of the children a burden, had no social life, and he could not kick her while she was down. John said that Catherine's claims that he cared more about Agnes than about her were untrue, as he barely responded to his first wife's frequent phone calls and never saw her alone.

After several sessions Catherine agreed that John could not be free to plan a life with her until he had resolved the guilty attachment to his first wife, and that this would not be resolved, but exacerbated, by urging him to fight her or cut off all contact with her. Thereafter, with Catherine's somewhat ambivalent support, John arranged several meetings with Agnes during which he explained the limitation of his future financial support of her and offered to keep the children temporarily while she reorganized her life.

Since Agnes' angry accusations about the divorce had been predicted in a therapy session, John was able to hear them out fairly well without counterattacking. In joint sessions with Catherine alternating with outside meetings with Agnes and his children, John slowly rode out her angry tirades about the past, responded

to the children's questions about the divorce, took responsibility for his part in their marital problems and his decision to divorce, and became firmer in his insistence that Agnes work out a plan with him for the financial and emotional care of the children. Eventually, when her attacks on him provoked neither counterattacks nor guilty withdrawal, Agnes accepted the reality of the divorce and turned her attention to improving her life and the children's. With continued effort on John's part, their contact became both more friendly and less frequent. By the time they left therapy, Agnes phoned John only when necessary and had ceased criticizing Catherine to the children, who were now less hostile to her. During their joint sessions and in sessions with John's children, Catherine had heard John express his sorrow at the failure of his first marriage and had learned to accept that part of his past without reacting personally. She moved very cautiously with the children, leaving all disciplinary decisions to John and Agnes. Most difficult of all, Catherine gave up the expectation that John would support her financially, and they worked out a plan based on joint income and allocation of expenses.

2. *The "pseudomutual" remarried couple, an ex-spouse, and a child or children.*

In this triangle the presenting problem is usually acting out or school problems with one or more children, or perhaps a child's request to have custody shifted from one parent to another. The remarried couple presents itself as having no disagreements whatsoever, and blames either the child or the ex-spouse (or both) for the trouble. Although the request in therapy will be for help for the child, or for managing the child's behavior, the background story will usually show intense conflict between the ex-spouses, with the new spouse totally supportive of his or her spouse in conflicts with the stepchild. The first move in sorting out this triangle is to put the management of the child's behavior temporarily in the hands of the biological parent and get the new spouse to take a neutral position, rather than siding against the child. This move will probably calm things down, but they will usually not stay calm unless the pseudomutuality of the remarried couple is worked on, permitting differences and disagreements to be aired and resolved, and permitting the child to have a relationship with his or her biological parent that does not automatically include the new spouse every step of the way. Finally, work will need to be done to end the battle with the ex-spouse and complete the emotional divorce, the lack of which is perpetuated by the intense conflict over the child or children.

Case Example: The Bergman Family.

Bob and Nora Bergman came to therapy for help in dealing with Bob's son, Larry, age 14. They had been married for one year, during which Larry lived with his mother and visited on weekends. Nora Bergman's daughter from her first marriage, Louise, age nine, lived with the couple. Nora's first husband had died of cancer when Louise was five. The Bergmans reported that their marriage was extremely harmonious and that Louise was bright, cheerful, and pleasant, and had an excellent relationship with both her mother and her stepfather. They were worried that Larry was becoming "seriously disturbed" in that his school grades had suddenly dropped dramatically and he was becoming increasingly truculent

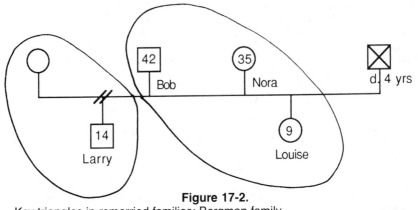

Figure 17-2.
Key triangles in remarried families: Bergman family
Remarried couple feared Larry was becoming mentally ill like his mother
Triangle of pseudo mutual couple–ex-spouse–child(ren)

and withdrawn during weekend visits, provoking endless fights with Louise and refusing simple requests from Nora to pick up his belongings. Since Larry's mother was "an unbalanced person" who used every opportunity to "harrass" them, the Bergmans wondered if Larry were "also becoming mentally ill."

Bob Bergman worked long hours and left the management of the household and children to his wife, who, he reported, dealt plesantly and "impartially" with both children. Nora agreed, saying that she loved Larry "as if he were my own son," and devoted herself entirely to the welfare of her "new family of four." She tried her best to be polite to the ex-Mrs. Bergman, but found her rude and almost impossible to deal with. She also felt the ex-Mrs. Bergman was a "harmful influence" on Larry, treating him inconsistently and occasionally leaving him alone when she went on dates. Larry reported that both of the Bergmans "hated" his mother, and he could not stand to hear them talk about her. He said his mother only phoned to check on his welfare because she knew that his father "left everything to that woman."

Therapy proceeded as outlined above. Bob Bergman agreed to be the liaison to his son's school and was put in total charge of his behavior during visits to the remarried household. He was also encouraged to take Larry on occasional trips alone. He admitted, after a lot of encouragement, that he and his new wife had some different ideas on raising boys, but that he had not wanted to argue with her, since she was doing such a great job generally. Nora, when given permission to do so, finally admitted that it was difficult to be a part-time mother to a stranger, and was encouraged to rethink her role, since Larry already had a mother. When Larry's behavior improved, the couple agreed to work on their relations with Larry's mother, although warning the therapist that she was "quite crazy." As the Bergmans stopped their end of the battle, the "crazy" behavior of Larry's mother diminished, although Bob was not willing to go very far toward resolving the old issues between himself and his ex-wife. The new Mrs. Bergman, however, did considerable work on resolving the mourning for her first husband, which had been incomplete, and was able for the first time to start telling her daughter about him and to share old picture albums with her. This work, she said, made it easier for her to enjoy her second family and not to try so hard to make everyone happy.

3. *The remarried couple in conflict over the child or children of one of them*

A. *The husband, the second wife, and the husband's children.*

This triangle, although not the most common household composition, is the most problematic, because of the central role the stepmother is expected to

play in the lives of live-in stepchildren. If the stepmother has never been married before, and if the children's mother is alive and has a less than ideal relationship with her ex-husband, it may be an almost impossible situation. Even the procedure of giving temporary complete management of the child or children to the natural parent is quite difficult if the father works long hours and the stepmother is the one who is at home. Nevertheless, some version of this is recommended, with the stepmother pulling back long enough to re-negotiate with both her husband and the children as to what her role realistically should be. She is in the very difficult position of being expected to be the primary caretaker although she cannot replace the children's mother. No woman can successfully function in this situation while being overtly or covertly criticized by the children's father. Rather than leave the stepmother and children to fight it out, the father will have to participate actively in making and enforcing such rules as are agreed upon. When their immediate household is in order, the husband will have to work on establishing a cooperative coparental relationship with his ex-wife, or the conflict with her will set the children off again and inevitably reinvolve his new wife.

If the husband's first wife is dead, he may need to complete his mourning for her and help his children to do so, in order to let the past go and not see his second wife as a poor replacement of his first.

Case Example: The Burns Family.

Sandy and Jim Burns came for marital therapy on the verge of divorce. Jim's first wife, Susie, had died of cancer when Jim's daughters were ages three and four. He had married Sandy a year later, and she had moved into their house, which Susie had decorated with exquisite taste. Although uncomfortable to be so thoroughly surrounded by signs of Susie, Sandy rationalized that it would be "wasteful" to redecorate the house and settled into it. She listened carefully while Jim explained the girls' routines and likes and dislikes, and tried to keep their lives exactly as they had been. As the years went by, with Jim criticizing every departure from "the way Susie did it," Sandy's nerves began to fray and she became, in her own words, "a wicked stepmother." She screamed at the girls and at Jim and they exchanged glances and whispered about her. Once she threatened to redecorate the house, but backed down under Jim's anger. Now, with both girls teenagers and increasingly rude to her, and Jim withdrawn and sullen much of the time, she thought perhaps she should admit to failure and leave the marriage.

The first turning point in therapy came when Jim realized that in his grief for his first wife and his concern for his children's welfare, he had never really "made a place" for Sandy in the tightly knit bereaved system of himself and his daughters. He had never supported her authority with them and had continued to join them in their rebellion against her. He then willingly took charge of the girls' behavior and started supporting Sandy against them. When Jim and Sandy's relationship was in better shape and the girls' behavior had improved, the therapy focused on the incomplete grief work of Jim and the girls, who visited Susie's grave several times together. On their third visit, Jim invited Sandy to join them. After that, Sandy redecorated the house and hung a picture of Susie with their other family pictures. Throughout this period Sandy worked on relationships in her family of origin, particularly with her mother, who had spent most of her life resisting Sandy's father's attempts to "tell her what to do."

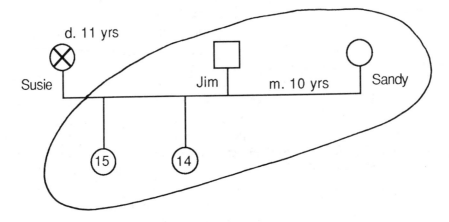

Figure 17-3.
Key triangles in remarried families: Burns family
Marital conflict over children
Triangle of remarried couple in conflict over child(ren)
Husband–second wife–husband's children

B. The wife, the second husband, and the wife's children

Numerically this is the most common triangle in remarried households. As in the above example, the new spouse is seen as both rescuer and intruder. He is supposed to help his wife with the burden of raising her children, but may be given no point of entry into their system, which has had a long history before his time, perhaps drawing closer in the interval between the mother's marriages.

Case Example: The Cooper Family.

Harold and Nancy Cooper sought treatment for Nancy's 17-year-old daughter, Susan, who had been arrested for shoplifting. Harold and Nancy had been married for three years, a second marriage for both. Harold's two daughters had remained in their mother's custody out of state, and Harold saw them infrequently. Not wanting to "fail at fatherhood twice," he had invested himself in making a good home for Nancy and her two children, Susan, 14 at the time of the remarriage, and Kevin, 12. Nancy's first marriage had ended in a bitter divorce and custody fight when the children were nine and seven, and they had spent the five years between the marriages as a tightly knit, beleaguered household of three, isolated from Nancy's parents, who did approve of divorce, and wracked by continuing legal battles between Nancy and her ex-husband. Harold complained that they have been in a state of turmoil since their marriage, in spite of great efforts to "become a 'real' family."

Harold blamed Nancy's "unruly" children, who did not know how to appreciate a good father, and Nancy alternately blamed Harold's "inconsistent handling" of her children and her ex-husband's harrassment of them. She was desperately afraid that the trouble with the police would enable her ex-husband to succeed in his periodic attempts to gain custody of the children.

In an attempt to calm down the household before going into the triangles involving both ex-spouses, the therapist used the usual crisis technique of putting the natural parent completely in charge of the symptomatic child or children. However, because of Nancy's feelings of helplessness with her children, and

because of Harold's overinvestment in being a father to them, this "simple" shift was not accomplished for a very long time. Nancy and Harold agreed to try it, but Nancy consistently complained about Susan to Harold, who then intervened, sometimes criticizing Nancy, sometimes lecturing Susan, and was then strongly criticized by Nancy for his "poor handling" of the situation. The therapist, in a separate session, coached Harold to stay out of the conflicts between Nancy and Susan. For months and months, Harold tried to hold this position, sometimes succeeding—sometimes failing.

While the attempt to shift the presenting triangle went on in the background, the therapist addressed the interlocking triangles with both ex-spouses. When Nancy admitted that she invested more emotional energy in fighting her ex-spouse than she did in getting along with her present spouse, the therapist wondered aloud if Nancy had dedicated her life to vengeance against her ex-husband. Several weeks later Nancy announced in therapy that she would stop battling him. Throughout these events the therapist discussed with Harold the history of his relationship with his natural children, bringing to the surface his agony after leaving and his attempt to replace them with Nancy's children. With the therapist's encouragement, and over frantic objection from Nancy, who felt threatened by his reconnection to his past, Harold began to write, phone, and visit his own children. At this point he was finally able to detach from the conflict between Nancy and Susan, and that conflict subsided. Finally, Nancy was helped to recognize her own competence with her children and she stopped calling on Harold for help in conflicts she had with them. Instead, in many concrete ways, Nancy "moved over" and invited Harold into the system in positive ways. Harold, having reinstated himself as father to his own natural children, now ceased demanding an overly intense relationship with Nancy's children and worked on defining for himself and with the children what a "stepfather" is. Nancy then worked out ways to "bury the hatchet" with her ex-husband and develop a cooperative relationship with him.

4. *The "pseudomutual" remarried couple, his children, and her children*

This triangle presents as a happily remarried couple with "no difficulties except that their two sets of children fight constantly with each other." The children are usually fighting out the conflicts denied by the remarried couple

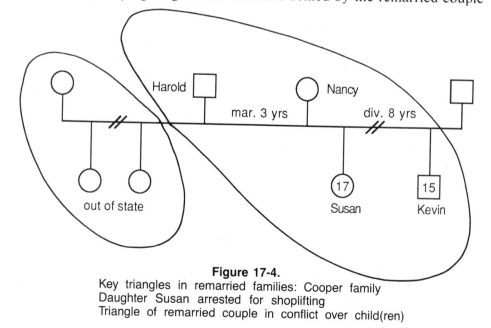

Figure 17-4.
Key triangles in remarried families: Cooper family
Daughter Susan arrested for shoplifting
Triangle of remarried couple in conflict over child(ren)

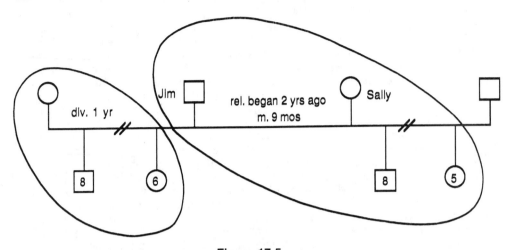

Figure 17-5.
Key triangles in remarried families: Brown family
Conflict between his and her children
Triangle of pseudomutual couple

either in the marriage or in the relationship with either or both ex-spouses. Since direct confrontation of the pseudomutuality stiffens resistance, and since the presenting request is made for the children, it is wise to begin with an exploration of the triangles involving the children and ex-spouses, focusing on the welfare of the children.

Case Example: The Brown Family.

Jim and Sally Brown requested family therapy because of the endless fighting between their children whenever Jim's children visited. Jim and Sally were in their 30s and had been married for less than a year. Their relationship had begun as an affair while Jim was still married, a fact that they believed was not known by Jim's ex-wife, or children—ages eight and six. Sally had been divorced two years prior to the affair with Jim and had custody of her two children, a boy of eight and a girl of five. The couple reported that they supported each other on all issues related to their ex-spouses; in fact Jim frequently arranged the visits for Sally's children to their natural father, since it "upset Sally to argue with him." Jim's wife was a "disturbed person," whom he could hardly deal with, but, again, they worked together not to let her cause trouble for them. Sally had assured Jim that if his ex-wife's "irrationality" became too disturbing for his children, she would support him in attempts to gain their custody and raise them with her own children.

Since none of this struck Jim or Sally as having anything to do with their children's battles with each other, the therapist spent several sessions educating them on children's loyalty conflicts and reactions to divorce and remarriage; their need, particularly at their ages, for support in the maintenance of relationships with both natural parents; and the time required for them to accept stepparenting. When this registered on Jim and he considered steps to improve his relationship with his ex-wife, their pseudomutual cover was blown as Sally collapsed in tears, threatening separation, termination of therapy, or whatever else she thought would deter Jim. In subsequent sessions, she confessed strong feelings of guilt and insecurity because of the affair, fearing that she had "taken him away from his wife, who would therefore be justified in trying to take him back." Very much later in treatment, Sally also recognized that the hidden agenda in her offer to raise Jim's children was the wish they both had to eliminate contact with Jim's ex-wife.

With the issues now out on the table where they could be dealt with, Jim and Sally were responsive to the therapist's suggestions that each take on, without the "help" of the other, the jobs of dealing with their respective ex-spouses, and managing their own children. When they both did this, the conflict between the two sets of children abated. The work of each of them in relationship to their ex-spouses was long and intense and they threatened to give it up, or divorce each other, many times during the process. The lack of time between Jim's marriages made his struggles with his guilty attachment to his ex-wife particularly intense, which then ticked off Sally's guilt and insecurity. Only after some period of work in their families of origin were they able to understand and take responsibility for their own contribution to the failure of their first marriages. Feeling less like "victims," they were able to reduce their tendency to huddle together helplessly against the "outside."

5. *A parent, the natural children, and the stepchildren.*

As in the above case, this triangle may present as "simple" household conflict with the parent caught in the middle between his or her natural children and stepchildren. It is, in fact, quite complex, always interlocking with the triangle involving the remarried couple (who may have either a pseudomutual or a conflictual relationship) and the triangles with both ex-spouses.

Case Example: The Green Family.

Florence Green sought a consultation to help her resolve a battle she was involved in with her 18-year-old-son, Donald, who was threatening not to go to college at all if he couldn't go to the expensive school of his choice rather than the moderately priced college Florence preferred for him. Florence said she wanted to clarify her own position on this issue, which, she said, kept shifting. When she argued with Donald, she pointed out the sensible choices and good work habits of her stepson, Jimmy, also 18; yet, in the frequent and bitter battles with her husband, she accused him of always favoring "his" son over "hers." Florence reported that in their 15 years of marriage they had not yet become a family. The main reason she stayed in the marriage, she implied, was that she and her second husband had a mutual son who was only 13.

The Green family is an example of a remarried family that has not achieved integation and restabilization even after the passage of many years. They had married within a year of the termination in divorce of their first marriages. Florence had cut off her ex-husband, who, she said, only disappointed and neglected their son, Donald. James Green, a wealthy physician, had engaged in a series of bitter custody battles with his ex-wife, which continued to the present day. A history of the attempts to integrate as a remarried family revealed that Florence, heavily invested in obtaining a "good father" for Donald, both pushed her husband toward her son and criticized his handling of the boy. In an attempt to make things work out, she made extra efforts to get along with her husband's son, Jimmy, which then aroused Donald's resentment. On his side, her husband's emotional energies went into the custody battles with his ex-wife and his professional practice, which was extremely demanding. He could not understand his wife's failure to appreciate the financial security he gave her and her son and became increasingly resentful of Donald's antagonism toward him and Jimmy. The family alliances were perfectly reflected in James Green's recently drawn will, which left the major share of his estate to his son, Jimmy; a secondary legacy to the couple's mutual son, Alex; a smaller amount to Florence; and nothing to

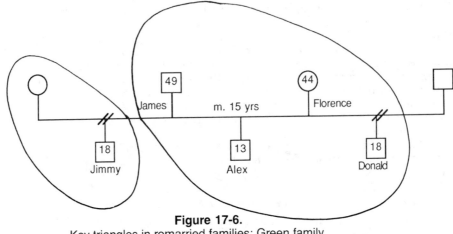

Figure 17-6.
Key triangles in remarried families: Green family
Mother–son conflict: comparison with stepson
Triangle of parent–natural children–stepchildren

Donald. Florence worried that the uneven inheritance would continue the family feud in subsequent generations, pitting her own two natural sons, Donald and Alex, against each other, as well as destroying any relationship between Donald and Jimmy.

Family therapy in this complex situation required motivation on Florence's part to go back to the unresolved tasks of 15 years ago and pull herself out of the triangles involving her husband and Donald, on the one hand, and Donald and Jimmy, on the other. Better progress would have been made initially if her husband could have been involved in the treatment and been persuaded to give up the battles with his ex-wife. Eventually Donald requested help in extricating himself from the scapegoat position and reconnecting with his natural father. Since the marital bond was in question, Florence had to find the motivation to initiate these changes for the sake of herself and her children. Only after she had confronted her husband on the negative effects his will would have and had convinced him that both their family relationships and the terms of his will must change did she decide that it was worth working toward stabilizing her second marriage.

6. *The remarried spouses and the parents of either*

This triangle features the in-laws as part of the presenting problem, but it should be remembered that relationships with the grandparental generation are as crucial in remarried families as they are in all other families, and their exploration should be a part of a routine evaluation. The presentation of the older generation as part of the current problem is most likely to occur if they have disapproved of the divorce and remarriage, and/or have been actively involved in caring for their grandchildren before or during the remarriage.

Case Example: The Hendrix Family.

Mr. and Mrs. Hendrix had been married for two years when they appeared for marital therapy. John was a businessman in his middle 40s and had been previously married. His ex-wife had custody of his three sons, the oldest of whom now lived with John's parents "because of the excellent high school in their town." Joan Hendrix was 15 years younger than her husband and had not been married before. John said that their major problem was that Joan constantly fought with his mother and put him "in the middle." Joan stated that John's mother had never

accepted John's divorce or their marriage, and that she talked and acted as if John were still married to his ex-wife, Ethel, with whom the older Mrs. Hendrix retained a very close relationship. Further, Joan complained, she had not yet had a honeymoon and every weekend was devoted to "entertaining" John's children in either their small New York apartment, or, worse, at John's parents' home in the suburbs. On the latter occasions, Joan said, her mother-in-law was cold and hostile toward her, interfered with every move she made toward John's children, and spoke constantly of Ethel's loneliness and financial difficulties. When they stayed overnight, John's mother insisted that the younger children share a room with them rather than "mess up" the living room. John never called his mother to task for any of this, but expected Joan to "understand that she meant well."

Since both John and Joan wanted their marriage to work, they negotiated a deal whereby John would clarify the boundary of his new marriage with his parents, his children, and his ex-wife, and Joan would stop criticizing and arguing with her mother-in-law. For openers John and Joan took a belated honeymoon trip over the objection of his mother that he should not leave his children for so long a period. Thereafter, however, John's part of the bargain was easier said than done. During the extended period that John spent renegotiating his visitation arrangements, resolving his guilty attachment to his first wife, and reworking his relationships with his parents, there were many eruptions throughout the system. One of his children started failing in school, the older boy returned to live with his ex-wife, his father had a heart attack, and his ex-wife was hospitalized briefly for depression. With each upsurge of tension, Joan was pulled back into conflicts with her mother-in-law. These occasions lessened considerably when she started serious work in her own family of origin, from whom she had been estranged since her marriage. Although very pleased with the outcome after several years of intensive work, Joan said that she had "aged ten years trying to work out a marriage to a whole family instead of just to a person."

During the course of treatment, the therapist involved all of the family sub-systems in sessions: the remarried couple alone, with John's children, and with John's parents: Joan and her parents; Ethel and the children; Ethel alone, Ethel and her parents; and once, Ethel, John, Joan, John's mother, and the oldest son.

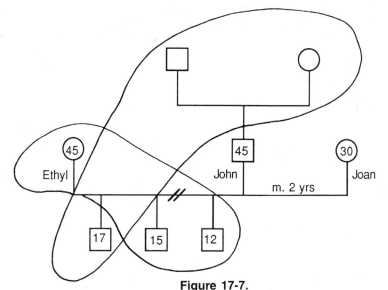

Figure 17-7.
Key triangles in remarried families: Hendrix family
Marital conflict over husband's mother
Triangle of remarried spouses and the parents of either

A few comments are in order here about our practice of involving ex-spouses in remarried family therapy. We include ex-spouses in joint sessions only when we have to deal with specific relatively serious child-focused agendas. Even in such situations, the level of tension and the lack of personal bonding between the first and second spouse often creates a climate of high anxiety and offers the therapist precious little leverage in his or her search for constructive resolution of family difficulties. Such a meeting may have primarily diagnostic value or be useful to underscore the seriousness of the child's situation. For some families only passage of time helps them accept the inevitability of having to deal with each other.

However, we routinely contact an ex-spouse and invite him or her to meet alone or with the children to hear a report on our opinion concerning the children's problems that have been brought to our attention by the remarried family. When we inform the family of our intention to do this, we are frequently warned that the ex-spouse in question does not care, won't respond, or is "crazy." Nevertheless such a phone call frequently locates a concerned parent who is perfectly willing to come in (although warning us that our client is "crazy"). These ex-spouses can frequently be engaged in subsequent sessions alone or with the children.

CONCLUSIONS

With the repeated warning that no list of do's and don't's can take the place of a clear theoretical framework and experienced clinical judgment, we would like to conclude with an outline of some attitudes and procedures that have helped us get a handle on the complexity of remarried families.

Our general goals involve establishing an open system with workable boundaries. This includes the following:

1. A working, open coparental relationship is developed between former spouses.

2. The emotional divorce between former spouses should be worked out. We assume this has not been resolved if they are not speaking or if they have continuous conflicts. Anger is, of course, a very strong bond. As Truman Capote put it: "You can lose a lot of good friends, but it is hard to lose a good enemy."

3. Children should never have the power to decide on remarriage, custody, and visitation. The parental boundaries and responsibilities need to be clear, although children's input into decisions obviously increases with age.

4. Parents need to help children have the full range of feelings for all parents—accepting the divided loyalties.

As more specific rules of thumb, we have outlined the following:

1. Get a three-generational genogram and an outline of the previous marriages before plunging into the current household problems.

2. Keep in mind particular difficulties related to (a) families being at different life cycle stages; (b) the emotionally central role of women in families and the special difficulties for them in moving into a new system; and (c) trying to maintain the myth of the perfect family.

3. Beware of families struggling with developmental tasks before they have adopted the prerequisite attitudes for remarriage (for example, parent pushing child and stepparent to be close without accepting that their relationship will take time to develop).

4. (Related to item 3) Help the family gain the patience to tolerate the ambiguity and not "overtry" to make thing work out. This includes accepting that family ties do not develop overnight. Encourage stepparents to understand that a child's negative reactions are not to be taken personally, and help them to tolerate guilt, conflicted feelings, ambivalent, divided loyalties, and the like.

5. Include the new spouse in sessions in which you coach a spouse to resolve his or her relationship with an ex-spouse, at least in the beginning.

6. Take the frequent characterization of an ex-spouse as "crazy" with a grain of salt. The list of the ex-spouse's outrageous behavior may reflect the client's provocations and/or retaliations.

7. Where the remarriage ends a close single-parent/child relationship, the feelings of loss, especially for the child, have to be dealt with and the shift to a new system will take time.

8. If the child is presented as the problem, try to involve all parents and stepparents as early as possible in therapy. If joint sessions are held, the discussion should be directed toward cooperative work to resolve the child's difficulties (we do not permit discussion of marital issues at these meetings).

9. In problems involving child-focused uproar, put the natural parent in charge of the child temporarily. When the uproar subsides, coach the natural parent on ways to "move over" and include his or her spouse in the system— first, as spouse only. Warn the family that the shift to active stepparenting may take several years and will require the active support of the natural parent. In the case of older adolescents, it may not be appropriate to expect the shift to occur to any great degree at all.

10. Look at the "hidden agenda" in sudden proposals to rearrange custody, visitation, or financial arrangements.

11. Include work on the spouse's families of origin as early in treatment as possible.

REFERENCES

Ahrons, C.H. (1980). Redefining the divorced family: A Conceptual framework for postdivorce family systems reorganization. *Social Work* 25: 437–441.

Ahrons, C. (1981). The continuing coparental relationship between divorced spouses. *American Journal of Orthopsychiatry,* 51: 315–328.

Ahrons, C. R., & Rodgers, R. H. (1987). *Divorced families.* New York: Norton.

Ahrons, C., & Wallisch, L. (1986). The relationship between former spouses. In S. Duck & D. Perlman (eds.), *Close relationships: Development, dynamics and deterioration* (pp. 269–296) Beverly Hills, Calif.: Sage.

Ambert. A. M. (1986). Being a stepparent: Live-in and visiting stepchildren. *Journal of Marriage and the Family* 48/4: 795–804.

Anderson, J. Z., & White, G. D. (1986). Dysfunctional intact families and stepchildren. *Family Process* 25/3: 407–423.

Bray, J. (1986). Reported in *Marriage and Divorce Today.* 12/9.

Bumpass, L. (1984). Some characteristics of children's second families. *American Journal of Sociology* 90: 608–623.

Cherlin, A. J. (1981). *Marriage, divorce, remarriage.* Cambridge, Mass.: Harvard University Press.

Clingempeel, W. G. (1981). Quasi-kin relationships and marital quality in stepfather families. *Journal of Personality and Social Psychology* 41: 890–901.

Clingempeel, W. G., Brand, E., & levoli, E. (1984a). Stepparent–stepchild relationships in stepmother and stepfather families: A multimethod study. *Family Relations* 33: 456–473.

Clingempeel, W., Glen, R., levoli, R., & Brand, E. (1984b). Structural complexity and the quality of stepfather–stepchild relationships. *Family Process* 23: 547–60.

Dahl, A. S., Cowgill, K. M., & Asmundsson, R. (1987). Life in remarriage families. *Social Work* 32/1: 40–44.

Duberman, L. (1975). *The reconstituted family: A study of remarried couples and their children.* Chicago: Nelson-Hall.

Elkin, M. (1987). Joint custody: Affirming that parents and families are forever. *Social Work* 32/1.

Furstenberg, F., Nord, C. W., Peterson, J. L., & Zill, N. (1983). The life course of children of divorce: Marital disruptions and parental contact. *American Sociological Review* 48: 656–668.

Furstenberg, F., & Spanier, G. (1984). *Recycling the family.* Beverly Hills, Calif.: Sage Publications.

Glick, P. C. (1980). Remarriage: Some recent changes and variations. *Journal of Family Issues* 1 455–478.

Glick, P. C. (1984). Marriage, divorce, and living arrangements: Prospective changes. *Journal of Family Issues* 46: 563–576.

Glick, P. C., & Lin, S. L. (1986). Recent changes in divorce and remarriage. *Journal of Marriage and the Family* 48/4: 737–747.

Goldstein, H. S. (1974). Reconstituted families: The second marriage and its children. *Psychiatric Quarterly* 48/3: 433–441.

Hetherington, E. M., Cox, M., & Cox, R. (1977). The aftermath of divorce. In Steven & Matthews (Eds.) *Mother-child relations.* Washington, D.C.: NAEYC.

Isaacs, M. B., Montalvo, B., & Abelsohn, D. (1986). *The difficult divorce: Therapy for children and families.* New York: Basic Books.

Kitson, G. C., & Lopata, H. A. (1980). Divorcees and widows: Similarities and differences. *American Journal of Orthopsychiatry* 50: 291–301.

McGoldrick, M., & Gerson, R. (1985). *Genograms in family assessment.* New York: Norton.

Messinger, L., & Walker, K. N. (1981). From marriage breakdown to remarriage: Parental tasks and therapeutic guidelines. *American Journal of Orthopsychiatry* 51:429–438.

Nolan, J. F. (1977). The impact of divorce on children. *Conciliatior. Courts Review* 15/2: 25–29.

Norton, A. J., & Moorman, J. E. (1987). Current trends in marriage and divorce among American women. *Journal of Marriage and the Family* 49/1: 3–14.

Ransom, J. W., Schlesinger, S., & Derdeyn, A. (1979). A stepfamily in formation. *American Journal of Orthopsychiatry* 49/1.

Sager, C. J., Brown, H. S., Crohn, H., Engel, T., Rodstein, E., & Walker, L. (1983). *Treating the remarried family*. New York: Brunner/Mazel.

Schulman, G. (1972). Myths that intrude on the adaptation of the step family. *Social Casework* March.

Stern, P. N. (1978). Stepfather families: Integration around child discipline. *Issues in Mental Health Nursing*.

Visher, E. B., & Visher, J. (1979). *Stepfamilies: A guide to working with stepparents and stepchildren* New York: Brunner/Mazel.

Visher, E. B., & Visher, J. (1982). *How to win in a stepfamily*. New York: Dembner.

Visher, E., & Visher, J. (1987). *Old loyalties, new ties: Therapeutic strategies with step families*. New York: Brunner/Mazel.

Wald, E. (1981). *The remarried family: Challenge and promise*. New York: Family Service Association of America.

Wallerstein, J., & Kelly, J. (1980). *Surviving the breakup*. New York: Basic Books.

White, L., & Booth, A. (1985). The quality and stability of remarriages: The role of stepchildren. *American Sociological Review*.

Whiteside, M. (1982). Remarriage: A family developmental process. *Journal of Marital and Family Therapy* 8: 59–68.

*Variables That Further Change
the Family Life Cycle*

CHAPTER 18

Chronic Illness and the Family Life Cycle

John S. Rolland M.D.

In the arena of physical illness, particularly chronic disease, the focus of concern is the system created by the interaction of a disease with an individual, family, or other biopsychosocial system (Engel, 1977, 1980). From the family point of view, family systems theory must include the illness system. Further, to place the unfolding of chronic disease into a developmental context, it is crucial to understand the intertwining of three evolutionary threads; the illness and individual and family life cycles.

To think in an interactive or systemic manner about the interface of these three developmental lines, one first needs a common language and set of concepts that can be applied to each and permits a trialogue. This chapter describes a conceptual framework that addresses this need. Two necessary preliminary steps are needed to lay the foundation for such a model. First one needs a language that permits diseases to be characterized in psychosocial and longitudinal terms—each illness having a particular "personality" and expected developmental life course. This is analogous to descriptive languages that portray individual and family personality types and development. Second, individual and family life cycle theoretical models need to be linked by culling from each its key overarching concepts. At present the developmental relationship between these different system levels remains mostly unexplored.

A schema to conceptualize chronic diseases is required that remains relevant to the interactions of the psychosocial and biological worlds and provides a common metalanguage that transforms or reclassifies the usual biological language. Two critical stumbling blocks to advancement in this area have been overlooked. First, insufficient attention has been given to the areas of diversity and commonality inherent in different chronic illnesses. Second, there has been a glossing over of the qualitative and quantitative differences in how various diseases manifest themselves over the time course of the illness. Chronic illnesses need to be conceptualized in a manner that organizes these similarities and differences over the disease course so that the type and degree

of demands relevant to psychosocial research and clinical practice are highlighted in a more useful way.

The first section of this chapter reviews a psychosocial typology of chronic or life-threatening illness (Rolland, 1984, 1987). The problems of illness variability and time phases are addressed on two separate dimensions. First, chronic illnesses are grouped according to key biological similarities and differences that dictate significantly distinct psychosocial demands for the ill individual and his or her family. Second, the prime developmental time phases in the natural evolution of chronic disease are identified. In the second section of the chapter, once one is equipped with a psychosocial language to describe chronic diseases, transgenerational aspects of illness, loss, and crisis will be considered. In the last section, which integrates key concepts from family and individual developmental theory, the interface of disease with the individual and family life cycles will be described.

PSYCHOSOCIAL TYPOLOGY OF ILLNESS

A disease classification that is based on purely biological criteria clusters illnesses in ways to meet the needs of medicine. This nosology fits the world of anatomy, physiology, biochemistry, microbiology, physical diagnosis, pharmacology, surgery, and so on. From a traditional medical point of view, the diagnosis of a specific illness is of primary concern because it dictates subsequent treatment planning. However a different classification schema may provide a better link between the biological and psychosocial worlds, and thereby clarify the relationship between chronic illness and the family life cycle.

Understanding the evolution of chronic diseases is hindered because clinicians often become involved in the care of an individual or family coping with chronic illness at different points in the "illness life cycle." Clinicians rarely follow the interaction of a family-illness process through the complete life history of a disease.

Any typology of illness is by nature arbitrary. The goal of this typology is to facilitate the creation of categories for a wide array of chronic illnesses. This typology is designed not for traditional medical treatment or prognostic purposes but rather, to examine the relationship between family or individual dynamics and chronic disease.

This typology conceptualizes broad distinctions of (1) onset, (2) course, (3) outcome, and (4) degree of incapacitation of the illness. These categories are hypothesized to be the most significant at the interface of the illness and the individual or family for a broad range of diseases. Whereas each variable is in actuality a continuum, each will be described in a categorical manner by the selection of key anchor points along the continuum.

Onset

Illnesses can be divided into those that have an acute onset and those with a gradual onset. Strokes and myocardial infarction are examples of illnesses with sudden clinical presentation. Examples of gradual-onset illnesses include arthritis, emphysema, and Parkinson's disease.

Diseases with a gradual onset present a different form of stressor to an individual or family than does a sudden crisis. Although the total amount of readjustment of family structure, roles, problem solving and affective coping might be the same for both types of illness, for acute-onset illnesses such as stroke, these affective and instrumental changes are compressed into a short time. This will require of the family more rapid mobilization of crisis-management skills. Some families are better equipped to cope with rapid change. Families that are able to tolerate highly charged affective states, exchange clearly defined roles flexibly, solve problems efficiently, and use outside resources will have an advantage in managing acute-onset illnesses.

The rate of family change required to cope with gradual-onset diseases, such as rheumatoid arthritis or Parkinson's disease, allows for a more protracted period of adjustment. For acute-onset diseases, there is relatively greater strain as the family divides its energy between protecting against further disintegration, damage, or loss through death, and progressive efforts that maximize mastery through restructuring or novel problem solving (Adams & Lindemann, 1974).

Course

The course of chronic diseases can take essentially three general forms: progressive, constant, or relapsing/episodic. A *progressive* disease (e.g., cancers, Alzheimer's disease, juvenile-onset diabetes, rheumatoid arthritis, emphysema) by this definition is one that is continually or generally symptomatic and progresses in severity. The individual and family are faced with the effects of a perpetually symptomatic family member, whose disability increases in a stepwise or progressive fashion. Periods of relief from the demands of the illness tend to be minimal. Continual adaptation and role change are implicit. Increasing strain on family caretakers is caused by both the risks of exhaustion and the continual addition of new caretaking tasks over time. Family flexibility in terms both of internal role reorganization and the willingness to use outside resources is at a premium.

A *constant-course* illness is one in which, typically, an initial event occurs, after which the biological course stabilizes. Examples include stroke, single-episode myocardial infarction, trauma with resulting amputation, and spinal cord injury with paralysis. Typically, after an initial period of recovery, the chronic phase is characterized by some clear-cut deficit, or residual, functional limitation. Recurrences may be seen, but the individual or family is faced with

a semipermanent change that is stable and predictable over a considerable time span. The potential for family exhaustion exists without the strain of new role demands over time.

The third kind of course is characterized as *relapsing or episodic*. Illnesses such as ulcerative colitis, asthma, peptic ulcer, migraine headaches, early stages of multiple sclerosis, and cancer in remission are typical. The distinguishing feature of this disease course is the alternation of stable periods of varying length, characterized by a low level or absence of symptoms, and with periods of flare-up or exacerbation. Often the family can carry on a "normal" routine. However, the specter of a recurrence hangs over their heads.

Relapsing illnesses demand a somewhat different sort of family adaptability. Relative to progressive or constant-course illnesses, they may require the least ongoing caretaking or role reallocation. But the episodic nature of an illness may require a flexibility that permits movement back and forth between two forms of family organization. In a sense the family is on call to enact a crisis structure to handle exacerbations of the illness. Strain on the family system is caused by both the frequency of transitions between crisis and noncrisis and the ongoing uncertainty of *when* a crisis will next occur. Also, the wide psychological discrepancy between periods of normality versus illness is a particularly taxing feature unique to relapsing chronic diseases.

Outcome

The extent to which a chronic illness will be a likely cause of death and the degree to which it can shorten one's life span are critical distinguishing features with profound psychosocial impact. The most crucial factor is the initial expectation of whether a disease will be a likely cause of death. On one end of the continuum are illnesses that do not typically affect the life span, such as lumbosacral disk disease, blindness, arthritis, spinal cord injury, and seizure disorders. At the other extreme are illnesses that are clearly progressive and usually fatal, such as metastatic cancer, AIDS, and Huntington's chorea. There is also an intermediate, more unpredictable category. This includes both illnesses that shorten the life span, such as cystic fibrosis, juvenile-onset diabetes, and cardiovascular disease, and those with the possibility of sudden death, such as hemophilia or recurrences of myocardial infarction or stroke. For life-threatening illnesses, the ill member fears life ending before living out his/her "life plan" and of being alone in death. Family members fear becoming survivors alone in the future. For both there exists an undercurrent of anticipatory grief and separation that permeates all phases of adaptation. Families are often caught between a desire for intimacy and a pull to let go, emotionally, of the ill member. The future expectation of loss can make it extremely difficult for a family to maintain a balanced perspective. A literal torrent of affect could potentially distract a family from the myriad of practical tasks and problem solving that maintain family integrity (Weiss,

1983). Also, the tendency to see the ill family member as practically "in the coffin" can set in motion maladaptive responses that divest the ill member of important responsibilities. The end result can be the structural and emotional isolation of the ill person from family life. This kind of psychological alienation has been associated with poor medical outcome in life-threatening illness (Davies et al, 1973; Derogatis et al., 1979; Schmale & Iker, 1971; Simonton et al., 1980).

For illnesses that may shorten life or cause sudden death, loss is a less imminent or certain an outcome than for clearly fatal and nonfatal illnesses. Because of this, issues of mortality predominate less in day-to-day life. It is for this reason that this type of illness provides such a fertile ground for idiosyncratic family interpretations. The "it could happen" nature of these illnesses creates a nidus for both overprotection by the family and powerful secondary gains for the ill member. This is particularly relevant to childhood illnessses, such as hemophilia, juvenile-onset diabetes, and asthma (Baker et al., 1975; Hamburg et al., 1980; Minuchin et al., 1975, 1978).

Incapacitation

Incapacitation can result from impairment of cognition (e.g., Alzheimer's disease), sensation (e.g., blindness), movement (e.g., stroke with paralysis, multiple sclerosis), energy production, and disfigurement or other medical causes of social stigma. Illnesses such as cardiovascular and pulmonary diseases impair the body's ability to produce raw energy. This can lower peak performance or the ability to sustain motor, sensory, or cognitive efforts. Illnesses such as leprosy, neurofibromatosis, or severe burns are cosmetically disabling to the extent that sufficient social stigma impairs one's ability for normal social interaction. AIDS is socially disabling because of the combined effects of its perceived high risk of contagion, long asymptomatic incubation/ carrier period, current status as incurable, and link with highly stigmatized groups in our society—homosexuals and intravenous drug abusers.

The different kinds of incapacitation imply sharp differences in the specific adjustments required of a family. For instance, the combined cognitive and motor deficits of a person with a stroke necessitate greater family role reallocation than a spinal-cord-injured person who retains his/her cognitive faculties. Some chronic diseases—such as hypertension, peptic ulcer, many endocrine disorders, or migraine headache—cause no, mild, or only intermittent incapacitation. This is a highly significant factor moderating the degree of stress facing a family. For some illnesses such as stroke or spinal cord injury, incapacitation is often worst at the time of onset and would exert its greatest influence at that time. Incapacitation at the beginning of an illness magnifies family coping issues related to onset, expected course, and outcome. For progressive diseases, such as multiple sclerosis, rheumatoid arthritis, or dementia, disability looms as an increasing problem in later phases of the illness.

This allows a family more time to prepare for anticipated changes. In particular it provides an opportunity for the ill member to participate in disease-related family planning.

In sum, the net effect of incapacitation on a particular individual or family depends on the interaction of the type of incapacitation with the preillness role demands of the ill member and the family's structure, flexibility, and resources. However, it may be the presence or absence of *any* significant incapacitation that constitutes the principal dividing line relevant to a first attempt to construct a psychosocial typology of illness (Viney & Westbrook, 1981).

By combining the kinds of onset (acute versus gradual), course (progressive versus constant versus relapsing/episodic), outcome (fatal versus shortened life span versus nonfatal), and incapacitation (present versus absent) into a grid format, we generate a typology with 32 potential psychosocial types of illness (see Rolland, 1984).

The extent to which illnesses are predictable has not been formulated as a separate category in the typology. Rather, predictability should be seen as a kind of metacharacteristic that overlays and colors the other attributes: onset, course, outcome, and incapacitation. In this regard there are two distinct facets in the predictability of a chronic illness. Diseases can be more or less uncertain as to the actual *nature* of the onset, course, outcome, or presence of incapacitation. And, they can vary as to the *rate* at which changes will occur.

Several other important attributes that differentiate illnesses were excluded from this typology because they seemed of lesser importance or were relevant only to a subgroup of disorders. When appropriate they should be considered in a thorough, systemically oriented evaluation. The complexity, frequency, and efficacy of a treatment regimen; the amount of home- versus hospital-based care required by the disease; and the frequency and intensity of symptoms vary widely across illnesses and have important implications for individual and family adaptation.

TIME PHASES OF ILLNESS

To create a psychosocial schema of chronic diseases, the developmental time phases of an illness need to be considered as a second dimension. Often one hears about "coping with cancer," "managing disability," or "dealing with life-threatening illness." These cliches can create a kind of tunnel vision that prevents sufficient attention to the phases of an illness. Each phase has its own psychosocial developmental tasks that require significantly different strengths, attitudes, or changes from a family. To capture the core psychosocial themes in the natural history of chronic disease, three major phases can be described: (1) crisis, (2) chronic, and (3) terminal.

The *crisis* phase includes any symptomatic period before actual diagnosis, when the individual or family has a sense that something is wrong, but the exact nature and scope of the problem are not clear. It includes the initial period of readjustment and coping after the problem has been clarified through a diagnosis and initial treatment plan.

During this period there are a number of key tasks for the ill member and his or her family. Moos (1984) describes certain universal practical illness-related tasks. These include (1) learning to deal with pain, incapacitation, or other illness-related symptoms; (2) learning to deal with the hospital environment and any disease-related treatment procedures and; (3) establishing and maintaining workable relationships with the health-care team. In addition there are critical tasks of a more general, sometimes existential, nature. The family needs to (1) create a meaning for the illness event that maximizes a preservation of a sense of mastery and competency; (2) grieve for the loss of the preillness family identity; (3) move toward a position of acceptance of permanent change while maintaining a sense of continuity between its past and future; (4) pull together to undergo short-term crisis reorganization; and (5) in the face of uncertainty, develop a system flexibility toward future goals.

The *chronic* phase can be long or short, but essentially it is the time span between the initial diagnosis and readjustment period and the third phase, when issues of death and terminal illness predominate. It is an era that can be marked by constancy, progression, or episodic change. In this sense its meaningfulness cannot be grasped by simply knowing the biological behavior of an illness. Rather, it is more a psychosocial construct, which has been referred to as "the long haul," or a phase of "day-to-day living with chronic illness." Often the patient and family have come to grips psychologically and/or organizationally with the permanent changes presented by a chronic illness and have devised an ongoing modus operandi. At one extreme the chronic phase can last for decades as a stable, nonfatal chronic illness. On the other hand, the chronic phase may be nonexistent in an acute-onset, rapidly progressive fatal disorder where the crisis and terminal phases are contiguous. The ability of the family to maintain the semblance of a normal life under the "abnormal" presence of a chronic illness and heightened uncertainty is a key task of this period. If the illness is fatal, this is a time of "living in limbo." For certain highly debilitating but not clearly fatal illnesses, such as a massive stroke or dementia, the family can become saddled with an exhausting problem "without end." Paradoxically some families' hope to resume a "normal" life cycle might be realized only after the death of their ill member. This highlights another crucial task of this phase: the maintenance of maximal autonomy for *all* family members in the face of a pull toward mutual dependency and caretaking.

The last phase is the *terminal* period. It includes the preterminal stage of an illness in which the inevitability of death becomes apparent and dominates family life. It encompasses the periods of mourning and of resolution of loss. It

is the predominance of issues surrounding separation, death, grief, resolution of mourning, and resumption of "normal" family life beyond the loss that distinguishes this phase.

Beyond their own significance, the three phases illuminate critical transition points linking each period. Apt descriptions in the adult-development and family life cycle literature by Levinson (1978, 1986) and Carter and McGoldrick (1980) have clarified the importance of transition periods. It is the same for the transitions between developmental phases in the course of disease. This is a time of reevaluation of the appropriateness of the previous family life structure in the face of new illness-related developmental demands. Unfinished business from the previous phase can complicate or block movement through the transitions. As Penn (1983) has pointed out, families or individuals can become permanently frozen in an adaptive structure that has outlived its utility. For example, the usefulness of pulling together in the crisis period can become a maladaptive and stifling prison for all family members in the chronic phase. Enmeshed families, because of their rigid and fused nature, would have difficulty negotiating this delicate transition. A family that is adept at handling the day-to-day practicalities of a long-term stable illness but is limited in its skills in affective coping may encounter difficulty if the family member's disease becomes terminal. The relatively greater demand for affective coping skills in the terminal versus the chronic phase of an illness may create a crisis for a family navigating this transition.

The interaction of the time phases and typology of illness provides a framework for a chronic-disease, psychosocial-developmental model. The time phases (crisis, chronic, and terminal) can be considered broad developmental periods in the natural history of chronic disease. Each period has certain basic tasks independent of the type of illness. In addition to the phase-specific developmental tasks common to all psychosocial types of disease, each "type" of illness has specific supplementary tasks. This is analogous to the relationship between a particular individual's development and certain universal life tasks. The basic tasks of the three illness time phases and transitions recapitulate in many respects the unfolding of human development. For example, the crisis phase is similar in certain fundamental ways to the era of childhood and adolescence. Piaget's (1952) research demonstrated that child development involves a prolonged period of learning to assimilate from and accommodate to the fundamentals of life. Parents often temper other developmental plans (e.g., career) in order to accommodate raising children. In an analogous way, the crisis phase is a period of socialization to the basics of living with chronic disease. During this phase other life plans are frequently put on hold by the family in order to accommodate its socialization-to-illness. Themes of separation and individuation are central in the transition from adolescence to adulthood. Erikson (1950) pointed out that adolescents are granted a moratorium or postponement period during which the identity of childhood gradually merges into that of adulthood. Eventually the adolescent must relinquish this moratorium and assume adult responsibilities. Similar to

life itself, the transition to the chronic phase of illness emphasizes autonomy and the creation of a viable, ongoing life structure adapted to the realities of the illness. In the transition to the chronic phase, a "hold" or moratorium on other developmental tasks that served to protect the initial period of socialization/adaptation to a life with chronic disease is reevaluated. The separate developmental tasks of "living with chronic illness" and "living out the other parts of one's life" must be brought together and forged into one coherent life structure. We will return to this concept of illness development later.

At this point we can combine the typology and phases of illness to construct a two-dimensional matrix (Rolland 1984).

By the addition of a family-systems model we can create a three-dimensional representation of the broader illness/family system. Psychosocial illness types, time phases of illness, and components of family functioning constitute the three dimensions. This model offers a vehicle for flexible dialogue between the illness aspect and family aspect of the illness/family system. In essence this model allows speculation about the importance of strengths and weaknesses in various components of family functioning in relation to different types of disease at different phases over the illness life course. As one specific application of this model, this discussion will look at stages of family development in relation to the type and time phases of illness.

At their core the components of the typology provide a means to grasp the character of a chronic illness in psychosocial terms. They provide a meaningful bridge for the clinician between the biological and psychosocial worlds. Perhaps the major contribution is the provision of a framework for assessment and clinical intervention with a family facing a chronic or life-threatening illness. Attention to features of onset, course, outcome, and incapacitation provides markers that facilitate integration of an assessment. The concept of time phases provides a way for the clinician to think longitudinally, and to reach a fuller understanding of chronic illness as an ongoing process with landmarks, transition points, and changing demands. An illness time line delineates psychosocial developmental stages of an illness, each phase with its one unique developmental tasks. Kaplan (1968) has emphasized the importance of solving phase-related tasks within the time limits set by the duration of each successive developmental phase of an illness. He suggests that the failure to resolve issues in this sequential manner can jeopardize the total coping process of the family. Therefore, attention to time allows the clinician to assess a family's strengths and vulnerabilities in relation to the present and future phases of the illness.

Taken together the typology and time phases provide a context in which to integrate other aspects of a comprehensive assessment. This would involve evaluation of a range of universal and illness-specific family dynamics in relation to the psychosocial type and time phases of illness. This discussion will focus on the interface of the illness with individual and family development; and the family's transgenerational history of coping with illness, crisis, and loss. Other important components of an illness-oriented family assessment

that will not be addressed in this chapter include the family's illness belief system (Rolland, 1987), the meaning of the illness to the family, the family's medical crisis planning, the family's capacity to perform home-based medical care, and the family's illness-oriented communication, problem solving, role reallocation, affective involvement, social support, and use and availability of community resources.

Equipped with this typological and developmental model of illness, we can return to our original task—to describe the interface of illness, individual, and family development.

TRANSGENERATIONAL HISTORY OF ILLNESS, LOSS, AND CRISIS

Systems-oriented theoreticians have emphasized that a family's present behavior cannot be adequately comprehended apart from its history (Boszormenyi-Nagy & Sparks, 1973; Bowen, 1978; Carter & McGoldrick, 1980; Framo, 1976; McGoldrick & Walsh, 1983; Paul & Grosser, 1965). They see historical questioning as a way to track key events and transitions in order to gain an undersanding of a family's organizational shifts and coping strategies *as a system* in response to past stressors. This is not a cause-and-effect model, but reflects a belief that such a historical search may help explain the family's current style of coping and adaptation. A historical, systemic perspective involves more than simply deciphering how a family organized itself around past stressors; it also means tracking the evolution of family adaptation over time. In this respect, patterns of adaptation, replications, discontinuities, shifts in relationships (i.e., alliances, triangles, cutoffs), and sense of competence are important considerations. McGoldrick and Walsh (1983) describe how these patterns are transmitted across generations as family myths, taboos, catastrophic expectations, and belief systems. By gathering this information, a clinician creates a basic family genogram (McGoldrick & Gerson, 1985).

A genogram oriented to chronic-illness involves the same basic tracking process, but focuses on how a family organized itself as an evolving system specifically around previous illnesses and unexpected crises in the current and previous generations. A central goal is to bring to light the adults' "learned differences around illness" (Penn, 1983).

The typology of illness and time phases are useful concepts in this part of the family evaluation. Although a family may have certain standard ways of coping with any illness, there may be critical differences in their style and success in adaptation to different "types" of diseases. A family may disregard the differences in demands related to different kinds of illnesses and thus may show a disparity in the level of coping with one disease versus another. If the

clinician inquires separately about the same or similar types of illnesses versus different types (e.g., relapsing versus progressive, life-threatening versus non-life-threatening), he or she will make better use of historical data. For instance, a family may have consistently organized itself successfully around nonlife-threatening illnesses but reeled under the impact of the paternal grandmother's metastatic cancer. This family may be particularly vulnerable if another life-threatening illness were to occur. A different family may have had experience only with nonlife-threatening illnesses and be ignorant of how to cope with the uncertainties particular to life-threatening diseases. Cognizance of these facts will draw attention to areas of strength and vulnerability for a family coping with cancer. A recent family consultation highlights the importance of tracking prior family illnesses.

Joe, his wife Ann, and their three teenage children presented for a family evaluation ten months after Joe's diagnosis with moderate–severe asthma. Joe, age 44, had been successfully employed for many years as a spray painter. Apparently exposure to a new chemical in the paint triggered the onset of asthmatic attacks that necessitated hospitalization and disability in terms of his profession. Although somewhat improved, he continued to have persistent and moderate respiratory symptoms. Initially his physicians had said that there would be some improvement, but remained noncommittal as to the level of chronicity. His continued breathing difficulties contributed to increased symptoms of depression, uncharacteristic temperamental outbursts, alcohol abuse, and family discord.

As part of the initial assessment, I inquired as to any prior experience in coping with chronic disease. This was the nuclear family's first encounter with chronic illness. In terms of their families of origin, they had limited experience. Ann's father had died seven years earlier of a sudden and unexpected heart attack. Joe's brother had died in a verified accidental drowning. Neither had had experience with disease as an ongoing process. Joe had assumed that improvement meant "cure." Illness for both had meant either death or recovery. The physician and family system were not attuned to the hidden risks for this family that was going through the transition from the crisis to chronic phase of his asthma—the juncture where the permanency of the disease needed to be addressed.

Tracking a family's coping capabilities in the crisis, chronic, and terminal phases of previous chronic illnesses will highlight complications in adaptation related to different points in the "illness life cycle." A family may have adapted well in the crisis phase of living with the paternal grandfather's spinal cord injury, but failed to navigate the transition to a family organization consistent with long-haul adaptation. An enmeshed family, with its tendency toward rigid overcloseness, may have become frozen in a crisis structure and been unable to deal appropriately with issues of maximizing individual and collective autonomy in the chronic phase. Another family with a member with chronic kidney failure may have functioned well in handling the practicalities of home dialysis. However, in the terminal phase, their limitations around affective expression may have left a legacy of unresolved grief. A history of time-phase-specific difficulties can alert a clinician to potential vulnerable periods for a family over the course of the current chronic illness. The following example of

a family coping with a current illness illustrates the interplay of problems that are fueled by unresolved issues related to disease experiences in one's family of origin.

> Mary, her husband Bill, and their son, Jim, presented for treatment four months after Mary had been involved in a life-threatening, head-on auto collision. The driver of the other vehicle was at fault. Mary had sustained a serious concussion. Also, for several months, there was some concern by the medical team that she might have suffered a cerebral hemorrhage. Ultimately it was clarified that this had not occurred. Over this time Mary became increasingly depressed and, despite strong reassurance, continued to believe she had a life-threatening condition and would die from a brain hemorrhage.
>
> During the initial evaluation, she revealed that she was experiencing vivid dreams of meeting her deceased father. Apparently her father, to whom she had been extremely close, had died from a cerebral hemorrhage after a four-year history of a progressive, debilitating brain tumor. His illness had been marked by progressive and uncontrolled epileptic seizures. Mary was 14 at the time and was the "baby" in the family; her two siblings being more than ten years her senior. The family had shielded her from his illness. This culminated in her mother deciding not to have her attend either the wake or the funeral of her father. This event galvanized her position as the "child in need of protection"—a dynamic that carried over into her marriage. Despite her hurt, anger, and lack of acceptance of his death, she had avoided discussing her feelings with her mother for over 20 years. Other family history revealed that her mother's brother had died from a sudden stroke and a cousin had died after being struck on the head by a streetlamp.
>
> Her own life-threatening head injury had triggered a catastrophic reaction and dramatic resurfacing of previous unresolved losses involving similar types of illness and injury. Therapy focused on a series of tasks and rituals that involved her initiating conversations with her mother and visiting her father's gravesite.

The family's history of coping with crises in general, especially unanticipated ones, should be explored. Illnesses with acute onset (i.e., heart attack), moderate–severe sudden incapacitation (i.e., stroke), or rapid relapse (i.e., ulcerative colitis, diabetic insulin reaction, disk disease) demand various rapid crisis-mobilization skills. In these situations, the family needs to reorganize quickly and efficiently, shifting from its usual organization to a crisis structure. Other illnesses can create a crisis because of the continual demand for family stamina (i.e., spinal cord injury, rheumatoid arthritis, emphysema). The family history of coping with moderate–severe, ongoing stressors is a good predictor of adjustment to these types of illness.

For any significant chronic illness in either adult's family of origin, a clinician should try to get a picture of how those families organized themselves to handle the range of disease-related affective and practical tasks. Also, it is important for a clinician to find out what role each played in handling these emotional or practical tasks. Whether the parents (as children) were given too much responsibility (parentified) or shielded from involvement is of particular importance. What did they learn from those experiences that influences how they think about the current illness? Whether they emerge with a strong sense of competence or failure is essential information. In one particular case,

involving a family with three generations of hemophilia transmitted through the mother's side, the father had been shielded from the knowledge that his older brother, who had died in adolescence, had had a terminal form of kidney disease. Also, this man had not been allowed to attend his brother's funeral. From that trauma he made a strong commitment to openness about disease-related issues with his two sons with hemophilia and his daughters, who were genetic carriers.

By collecting this information about each adult's family of origin, one can anticipate areas of conflict and consensus. Penn (1983) and Walker (1983) have described the frequency that unresolved issues related to illness and loss can remain dormant in a marriage and suddenly reemerge when triggered by a chronic illness in the current nuclear family. Penn (1983) describes the following vignette as a prototypical example of how particular coalitions that emerge in the context of a chronic illness are isomorphs of those that existed in each adult's family of origin.

> If a mother has been the long-time rescuer of her mother from a tyrannical husband, and then in her own family bears a son with hemophilia, she will become his rescuer, often against his father. In this manner she continues to rescue her mother but, oddly enough, now from her husband rather than from her own father. . . . In this family with a hemophiliac son, the father's father had been ill for a long period and had received all the mother's attention. In his present family, this father, though outwardly objecting to the coalition between his wife and son, honored that relationship, as if he hoped it would make up for the one he had once forfeited with his own mother. The coalition in the nuclear family looks open and adaptational (mother and son), but is fueled by coalitions in the past (mother with her mother, and father with his mother).

The reenactment of previous system configurations around illness can occur largely as an unconscious, automatic process. Further, the dysfunctional complementarity one sees in these families can emerge *de novo* specifically within the context of a chronic disease. On detailed inquiry couples will frequently reveal that a tacit, unspoken understanding existed that if an illness occurred, they would reorganize to reenact "unfinished business" from their families' of origin. Typically the role chosen represents a repetition of or an opposite of a role played by themselves or the same-sex parent in their family of origin. This process resembles the unfolding of a genetic template that gets switched on only under particular biological conditions. It highlights the need for a clinician to maintain some distinction between functional family process with and without chronic disease. For families that present in this manner, placing a primary therapeutic emphasis upon the resolution of family-of-origin issues may be the best approach to prevent or rectify an unhealthy triangle.

Families, like those just described, with encapsulated illness "time bombs" need to be distinguished from families that show more pervasive and long-standing dysfunctional patterns. For the latter, illnesses will tend to become embedded within a web of existing fused family transactions. Just as parents can enact a detouring triangle through an ill child in order to avert unresolved

marital conflict (Minuchin et al., 1975, 1978), so too the therapist can collude with a family's resistance by overfocusing on the disease itself. In this situation distinctions between the family's illness versus nonillness systems are, to a large degree, semantic. The illness serves to rigidify preexisting family dysfunction. In the traditional sense of "psychosomatic," this kind of family displays a greater level of baseline reactivity such that when an illness enters the system, this reactivity gets expressed somatically through a poor medical course and/or treatment noncompliance. These families lack the foundation of a functional nonillness system that can serve as the metaphorical equivalent of "healthy ego" in tackling family-of-origin patterns around disease. The initial focus on therapeutic intervention may need to be targeted more on the horizontal axis (nuclear family) than the vertical intergenerational axis. The prognosis for this kind of family is more guarded.

A third kind of symptomatic family facing chronic disease are those without significant intra- or intergenerational family dysfunctional patterns. Any family may falter in the face of multiple, superimposed disease and nondisease stressors that impact in a relatively short time. Progressive, incapacitating diseases or the illnesses occurring in several family members are typical scenarios. A pragmatic approach that focuses on expanded or creative use of supports and resources outside the family is most productive.

Interface of the Illness and Individual and Family Life Cycles

To place the unfolding of chronic disease into a developmental context, it is crucial to understand the intertwining of three evolutionary threads; the illness, the individual, and the family life cycles. This is a highly complex process that remains largely unexplored.

Because an illness is part of an individual, it is essential to think simultaneously about the interaction of individual and family development. To create a context for dialogue, a language is needed that bridges these developmental threads. A central concept for each is that of a life cycle. The notion of cycle suggests an underlying order of the life course whereby individual, family, or illness uniqueness occurs within a context of a basic sequence or unfolding. A second key concept is that of the human life structure. Although Levinson's (1978) original description of the life structure was within the context of his study of individual male adult development, the generic notion of life structure can also be applied to the family as a unit. By life structure, he means the underlying pattern or design of a person's/family's life at any given point in the life cycle. Its primary components are a person's/family's reciprocal relationships with various "others" in the broader ecosystem (e.g., person, group, institution, culture, object, or place). The life structure forms a boundary between the individual/family and the environment. It both governs and mediates the transactions between them.

Illness, individual, and family development have in common the notion of eras marked by the alternation of life-structure-building/maintaining and life-structure-changing (transitional) periods linking developmental eras. The primary goal of a structure-building/maintaining period is to form a life structure and enrich life within it based on the key choices an individual/family made during the preceding transition period. The delineation of separate eras derives from a set of developmental tasks that are associated with each period. As mentioned earlier, transition periods are potentially the most vulnerable because previous individual, family, and illness life structures are reappraised in the face of new developmental tasks that may require discontinuous change rather than minor alterations. Levinson (1978, 1986) has provided a pioneering effort in describing four major eras in individual life-structure development: childhood and adolescence, and early, middle, and late adulthood. Duvall (1977) and Carter and McGoldrick (1980) have divided the family life cycle into eight and six stages respectively. A primary distinction between Levinson's and the family life cycle models needs to be mentioned. In family life cycle models, marker events (e.g., marriage, birth of first child, last child leaving home) herald the transition from one stage to the next. Levinson's research elucidated a sequence of age-specific periods, five to seven years in length, during which certain developmental tasks for adult males are addressed independently of marker events. In this model marker events will both color the character of a developmental period and, in turn, be colored by their timing in the individual life cycle.

The concepts of centripetal versus ceutrifugal family styles and phases in the family life cycle are particularly useful to the task of integrating family, individual, and illness development (Beavers, 1982; Beavers & Voeller, 1983). Recent work of Combrinck-Graham (1985) elaborates the application of centripetal/centrifugal phases to the family life cycle. She describes a family life life-spiral model, in which she envisions the entire three-generational family system oscillating through time between periods of family closeness (centripetal) and periods of family disengagement (centrifugal). These periods coincide with oscillations between family developmental tasks that require intense bonding or high levels of family cohesion, like early child rearing, and tasks that emphasize personal identity and autonomy, like adolescence. Typically an individual will experience three oscillations in a lifetime: one's own childhood and adolescence, the birth and adolescence of one's children, and the birth and development of one's grandchildren. In a literal sense, centripetal and centrifugal describe a tendency to move respectively toward and away from a center. In life cycle terms, they connote a fit between developmental tasks and the relative need for internally directed, personal and family-group cohesive energy to accomplish those tasks. During a centripetal period, both the individual member's and the family unit's life structure emphasize internal family life. External boundaries around the family are tightened while personal boundaries between members are somewhat diffused to enhance family teamwork. In the transition to a centrifugal period, the family life structure shifts to

accommodate goals that emphasize the individual family members' exchange with the extrafamilial environment. The external family boundary is loosened while nonpathological distance between some family members increases.

From this brief overview of life cycle models, we can cull out several key concepts that provide a foundation for discussion of chronic disease. We can consider the life cycle to contain alternating transition and life-structure-building or maintaining periods. Further, particular transition or life-structure building/maintaining periods can be characterized as either centripetal or centrifugal in nature. The following discussion will use these overarching concepts rather than particular age- or event-specific periods as its central reference point.

The notion of centripetal and centrifugal modes is useful in linking the illness life cycle to the individual and family life cycles. One can think about this interface from the vantage point of chronic illnesses in general, or from the more finely tuned perspective of specific illness types or phases in the unfolding of chronic disease.

In general chronic disease exerts a centripetal pull on the family system. In family developmental models, centripetal periods begin with the addition of a new family member (infant), which propels the family into a prolonged period of socialization of and to children. In an analogous way, the occurrence of chronic illness in a family resembles the addition of a new member, which sets in motion for the family a centripetal process of socialization to illness. Symptoms, loss of function, the demands of shifting or new illness-related, practical and affective roles, and the fear of loss through death all serve to refocus on a family inwardly.

If the onset of an illness coincides with a centrifugal period for the family, it can derail the family from its natural momentum. If a young adult becomes ill, he or she may need to return to his or her family of origin for disease-related caretaking. Each family member's outside-the-family autonomy and individuation are at risk. The young adult's initial life structure away from home is threatened either temporarily or permanently. Both parents may have to relinquish budding interests outside the family. Family dynamics, as well as disease severity, will influence whether the family's reversion to a centripetal life structure is a temporary detour within their general outward movement or a permanent, involutional shift. A moderately fused or enmeshed family frequently faces the transition to a more autonomous period with trepidation. A chronic illness provides a sanctioned reason to return to the "safety" of the prior centripetal period. For some family members, the giving up of the building of a new life structure that is already in progress can be more devastating than when the family is still in a more centripetal period in which future plans may be at a more preliminary stage, less formulated, or less clearly decided upon. An analogy would be the difference between a couple discovering that they do not have enough money to build a house versus being forced to abandon their building project with the foundation already completed.

Disease onset that coincides with a centripetal period in the family life cycle (e.g., early child rearing) can have several important consequences. At the minimum it can foster a prolongation of this period. At worst it causes a permanent stuckness at this phase of development. In this instance, the inward pull of the illness and the phase of the life cycle coincide. The risk here is their tendency to amplify one another. For families that functioned in a marginal way before an illness begins, this kind of mutual reinforcement can trigger a runaway process leading to overt family dysfunction. Minuchin and colleagues' (1975, 1978) research of "psychosomatic" families has documented this process in several common childhood illnesses.

When a parent develops a chronic disease during this centripetal childrearing phase of development, a family's ability to stay on course is severely taxed. In essence the illness is added as a new infant member. This new member is like a child with "special needs" competing with the real children for potentially scarce family resources. For psychosocially milder diseases, efficient role reallocation may suffice. A recent case illustrates this point.

> Tom and his wife, Sally, presented for treatment six months after Tom had sustained a severe burn injury to both hands that required skin grafting. A year of recuperation was necessary before Tom would be able to return to his job, which required physical labor and full use of his hands. Prior to this injury, his wife had been at home full-time raising their two children, ages three and five. In this case, although Tom was temporarily handicapped in terms of his career, he was physically fit to assume the role of house-husband. Initially both Tom and Sally remained at home, using his disability income to "get by." When Sally expressed an interest in finding a job to lessen financial pressures, Tom resisted, and manageable marital strain caused by his injury flared into dysfunctional conflict.
>
> Sufficient resources were available in the system to accommodate the illness and ongoing child-rearing tasks. Their definition of marriage lacked the necessary role flexibility to master the problem. Treatment focused on rethinking his masculine and monolithic, definition of "family provider," a definition that had, in fact, emerged in full force during this centripetal phase of the family life cycle.

If the disease affecting a parent is more debilitating (e.g., traumatic brain injury, cervical spinal cord injury), its impact on the child-rearing family is twofold. The ill parent becomes for the family like another child with "special needs" competing with the real children for potentially scarce family resources. Second, a parent is "lost" and the semblence of a single-parent family is created. For acute-onset illnesses, both events can occur simultaneously. In this circumstance family resources may be inadequate to meet the combined child-rearing and caretaking demands. This situation is ripe for the emergence of a parentified child or the reenlistment into active parenting of a grandparent.

If we look at chronic diseases in a more refined way through the lens of the typology and time phases of illness, it is readily apparent that the degree of centripetal/centrifugal pull varies enormously. This variability has important effects on the family life cycle independent of family dynamics. The tendency for a disease to interact centripetally with a family grows as the level of incapacitation or risk of death due to the illness increases. Progressive dis-

eases over time are inherently more centripetal in terms of their effect on families than are constant-course illnesses. The ongoing addition of new demands as an illness progresses keeps a family's energy focused inwardly. After a modus operandi has been forged, a constant-course disease (excluding those with severe incapacitation) permits a family to enter or resume a more centrifugal phase of the life cycle. The added centripetal pull exerted by a progressive disease increases the risk of reversing normal family disengagement or freezing a family into a permanent state of fusion.

> Mr. L., age 54, had become increasingly depressed as a result of severe and progressive complications of his adult-onset diabetes that had emerged over the past five years. These complications included a leg amputation and renal failure that recently required the instituting of home dialysis four times a day. For 20 years Mr. L. had had an uncomplicated constant course, allowing him to lead a full active life. He was an excellent athlete and engaged in a number of recreational group sports. Short and long-term family planning had never focused around his illness. This optimistic attitude was reinforced by the fact that two people in Mrs. L.'s family of origin had had diabetes without complications. Their only child, a son age 26, had uneventfully left home after high school. He had recently married. Mr. and Mrs. L. had a stable marriage, in which both maintained many outside independent interests. In short, the family had moved smoothly through the transition to a more centrifugal phase of the family's life cycle.
>
> His disease's transformation to a progressive course, coupled with the incapacitating and life-shortening nature of his complications, had reversed the normal process of family disengagement. His wife took a second job that necessitated her quitting her hobbies and civic involvements. Their son moved back home to help his mother take care of his father and the house. Mr. L., disabled for work and his athletic social network, felt himself to be a burden to everyone and blocked in his own midlife development.
>
> The essential goal of family treatment in developmental terms centered on reversing some of the systems centripetal overreaction back to a more realistic balance. For Mr. L. this meant a reworking of his life structure to accommodate his real limitations while maximizing a return to his basically independent style. For Mrs. L. and her son, this meant developing realistic expectations for Mr. L. and reestablishing key aspects of their autonomy within an illness/family system.

Relapsing illnesses alternate between periods of drawing a family inwardly and periods of release from the immediate demands of disease. However, the on-call state of preparedness dictated by many such illnesses keeps some part of the family in a centripetal mode despite medically asymptomatic periods. Again, this may hinder the natural flow between phases of the family life cycle.

One way to think about the time phases of illness is that they represent to the family a progression from a centripetal crisis phase to a more centrifugal chronic phase. The terminal phase, if it occurs, forces most families back into a more centripetal mode. In other words, the so-called "illness life structure," developed by a family to accommodate each phase in the illness life cycle, is colored by each time phase's inherent centripetal/centrifugal nature. For example, in a family in which the onset of the illness has coincided with a centrifugal phase of development, the transition to the chronic phase permits a family to resume more of its original inertia.

One cannot overemphasize the need for clinicians to be mindful of the timing of the onset of a chronic illness with individual/family transition and life-structure building/maintaining periods of development.

All *transitions* inherently involve the basic processes of termination and initiation. Arrivals, departures, and losses are common life events, during which there is an undercurrent of preoccupation with death and finiteness (Levinson, 1978). Chronic and life-threatening illness precipitates the loss of the preillness identity of the family. It forces the family into a transition in which one of the family's main tasks is to accommodate the anticipation of further loss, and possibly untimely death. When the onset of a chronic illness coincides with a transition in the individual or family life cycle, one might expect that issues related to previous, current, and anticipated loss will be magnified. Because transition periods are often characterized by upheaval, rethinking, change, and increased family system entropy, there exists at those times a greater risk for the illness to become unnecessarily embedded in, or inappropriately ignored, when planning for the next developmental period. This can be a major precursor of family dysfunction in the context of chronic disease. If a clinician adopts a longitudinal developmental perspective, he or she will stay attuned to future transitions and their overlap with each other.

An example can highlight the importance of the illness in relation to future developmental transitions. Imagine a family in which the father, a carpenter and primary financial provider, develops multiple sclerosis. At first his level of impairment is mild and stabilized. This allows him to continue part-time work. Because their children are all teenagers, his wife is able to undertake part-time work to help maintain financial stability. The oldest son, age 15, seems relatively unaffected. Two years later father experiences a rapid progression of his illness, leaving him totally disabled. His son, now 17, has dreams of going away to college to prepare for a career in science. The specter of financial hardship and the perceived need for a "man in the family" create a serious dilemma of choice for the son and the family. In this case, there is a fundamental clash between developmental issues of separation/individuation and the ongoing demands of progressive, chronic disability upon the family. This vignette demonstrates the potential clash between simultaneous transition periods: the illness transition to a more incapacitating and progressive course, the adolescent son's transition to early adulthood, and the family's transition from the stage of "living with teenagers" to "launching young adults." Also, this example illustrates the significance of the type of illness. An illness that was less incapacitating or relapsing (as opposed to a progressive or constant-course disease) may interfere less with this young man's separation from his family of origin. If his father had an intermittently incapacitating illness, such as disk disease, the son might have moved out but tailored his choices to remain nearby and available during acute flare-ups.

The onset of a chronic illness may cause a different kind of disruption if it coincides with a *life-structure-building/maintaining period* in individual or family development. These periods are characterized by the living out of a

certain life structure that represents the outgrowth of the rethinking, formulation, and change of the preceding transition period. The cohesive bonds of the individual/family are oriented toward protecting the current life structure. Diseases with only a mild level of psychosocial severity (e.g. nonfatal, no or mild incapacitation, nonprogressive) may require of the individual/family some revision of the life structure, but not a radical restructuring that would necessitate a more basic return to a transitional phase of development. A chronic illness with a critical threshold of psychosocial severity will demand the reestablishment of a transitional form of life at a time when individual/family inertia tends to preserve the momentum of a stable period. This transition will be highly centripetal in nature because the illness will, like the addition of a newborn, require a period of socialization. An individual's or family's level of adaptability is a prime factor in the successful navigation of this kind of crisis. In this context the concept of family adaptability is referred to in its broadest sense—the ability of a family to transform its entire life structure to a prolonged transitional state.

For instance, in our prervious example, the father's multiple sclerosis rapidly progressed while the oldest son was in a transition period in his own development. The nature of the strain in developmental terms would be quite different if his father's disease progression had occurred when this young man was 26, had already left home, had finished college, secured a first job, had married, and had fathered his first child. In the latter scenario, the oldest son's life structure is in a centripetal, structure-maintaining period within his newly formed nuclear family. To fully accommodate the needs of his family of origin could require a monumental shift of his developmental priorities. When this illness crisis coincided with a developmental transition period (age 17), although a dilemma of choice existed, the son was available and less fettered by commitments in progress. Later, at age 26, he has made developmental choices and is in the process of living them out. Not only has he made commitments, but they are centripetal in nature—focused on his newly formed family. To serve the demands of an illness transition, the son might need to shift his previously stable life structure back to a transitional state; and the shift would happen "out of phase" with the flow of his individual and nuclear family's development. One precarious way to resolve this dilemma of divided loyalties may be the merging of the two households, thereby creating a single, super-large centripetal family system.

This discussion raises several key clinical points. From a systems viewpoint, at the time of a chronic illness diagnosis it is important to know the phase of the family life cycle and the stage of individual development of all family members, not just that of the ill member. This is important information for several reasons. First, chronic disease in one family member can profoundly affect developmental goals of another member. For instance, a disabled infant can be a serious roadblock to a mother's mastery of child rearing, or a life-threatening illness in a young adult can interfere with the spouse's task

of beginning the phase of parenthood. Second, family members frequently do not adapt uniformly to chronic illness. Each family member's ability to adapt and the rate at which he or she does so is directly related to each individual's own developmental stage and his or her role in the family (Ireys & Burr, 1984). The oldest son in the previous example illustrates this point.

Clinicians and researchers generally agree that there exists a normative and nonnormative timing of chronic illness in the life cycle. Coping with chronic illness and death are considered normally anticipated tasks in late adulthood. On the other hand, illnesses and losses that occur earlier are "out of phase" and tend to be developmentally more disruptive (Herz, 1980; Neugarten, 1976). As untimely events, chronic diseases can severely disrupt the usual sense of continuity and rhythm of the life cycle. Levinson's (1978) research showed that the timing in the life cycle of an unexpected event, like a chronic illness, will shape the form of adaptation and the event's influence on subsequent development.

This discussion suggests that the notion of out-of-phase illnesses can be conceptualized in a more refined way. First, as described earlier, diseases have a centripetal influence on most families. In this sense they are naturally "out of phase" with families in, or in transition toward, a more centrifugal period. From this vantage point, illnesses can be more disruptive to families in a centrifugal phase of their development. Second, the onset of chronic disease tends to create a period of transition, the length or intensity of which depends upon the psychosocial type and phase of the illness. This forced transition is particularly "out of phase" if it coincides with a life-structure-building/maintaining period in the individual's or family's life cycle. Third, if the particular illness is progressive, relapsing, increasingly incapacitating, and/or life threatening, then the phases in the unfolding of the disease will be punctuated by numerous transitions. In these conditions families will need more frequently to alter their illness life structure to accommodate the shifting, and often increasing, demands of the disease. This level of demand and uncertainty keeps the illness in the forefront of a family's consciousness, constantly impinging upon their attempts to get back "in phase" developmentally. Finally, the transition from the crisis to the chronic phase of the illness life cycle is often the key juncture at which the intensity of the family's socialization to living with chronic disease can be relaxed. In this sense it offers a "window of opportunity" for the family to correct its developmental course.

Some investigators believe that chronic diseases that occur in the childrearing period can be most devastating because of their potential impact on family financial and childrearing responsibilities (Herz, 1980). Again, the actual impact will depend on the "type" of illness and the preillness roles of each family member.

In the face of chronic disease, an overarching goal is for a family to deal with the developmental demands presented by the illness without the need for family members to sacrifice their own or the family's development as a system.

Therefore, it is vital to ask what life plans the family or individual members had to cancel, postpone, or alter as a result of the diagnosis. It is useful to know whose plans are most and least affected. By asking a family when and under what conditions they will resume plans put on hold or address future developmental tasks, a clinician can anticipate developmental crises related to "independence from" versus "subjugation to" the chronic illness.

CONCLUSIONS

This chapter has attempted to provide a conceptual base for thinking about the system created at the interface of chronic illness with the family and individual life cycles. The description of a psychosocial typology and time phases of illness is a necessary, preliminary step to the creation of a common language to bridge the worlds of illness, individual, and family development. This developmental landscape is marked by periods of transition, periods of living out decisions and commitments, periods of family centeredness, and periods less dictated by family group tasks. What emerges is the notion of three intertwined lines of development, during which there is a continual interplay of life structures needed to carry out individual, family, and illness phase-specific, developmental tasks. Families' intergenerational paradigms related to chronic disease, crisis, and loss play upon these three interwoven developmental threads and add their own texture and pattern.

REFERENCES

Adams, J.E., & Lindemann, E. (1974). Coping with long-term disability. In G.V. Coelho, D.A. Hamburg, J.E. Adams (Eds.), *Coping and adaptation*. New York: Basic Books.

Baker, L., Minuchin, S., Milman, L., et al. (1975). Psychosomatic aspects of juvenile diabetes mellitus: A progress report. *In Modern problems in pediatrics, 12*, White Plains, N.Y.: S. Karger.

Beavers, W.R. (1982). Healthy, Midrange, and Severely dysfunctional families. In F. Walsh (Ed.), *Normal family processes*. New York: Guilford Press.

Beavers, W.R. & Voeller, M.M. (1983). Family models: Comparing and contrasting the Olson circumplex model with the Beavers systems model. *Family Process* 22:85–98.

Boszormenyi-Nagy, I., & Spark, G. (1973). *Invisible loyalties*. New York: Harper & Row.

Bowen, M. (1978). Theory in the practice of psychotherapy. In *Family therapy in clinical practice*. New York: Jason Aronson.

Carter, E.A., & McGoldrick, M. (Eds.), (1980). *The family life cycle: A framework for family therapy*. New York: Gardner Press.

Combrinck-Graham, L. (1985). A developmental model for family systems. *Family Process* 24:139–150.

Davies, R.K., Quinlan, D.M., McKegney, P., & Kimball, C.P. (1973). Organic factors and psychological adjustment in advanced cancer patients. *Psychosomatic Medicine* 35:464–471.

Deogatis, L. R., Abeloff, M.D., & Melisartos, N. (1979). Psychological coping mechanisms and survival time in metastatic breast cancer. *Journal of the American Medical Association* 242:1504–1508.

Duvall, E. (1977). *Marriage and family development* (5th ed.). Philadelphia: Lippincott.

Engel, G. H. (1977). The need for a new medical model: A challenge for biomedicine. *Science* 196:129–136.

Engel, G.H. (1980). The clinical application of the biopsychosocial model. *American Journal of Psychiatry* 137:535–544.

Erikson, E.H. (1950). *Childhood and society.* New York: Norton.

Framo, J. (1976). Family of origin as therapeutic resource for adults in marital and family therapy. *Family Process* 15:193–210.

Hamburg, B.A., Lipsett, L.F., Inoff, G.E., & Drash, A.L. (Eds.) (1980). *Behavioral and psychological issues in diabetes.* U.S. Government Printing Office, NIH Publication no. 80-1993.

Herz, F. (1980). The impact of death and serious illness on the family life cycle. In E.A. Carter & M. McGoldrick (Eds.), *The family life cycle: A framework for family therapy.* New York: Gardner Press.

Ireys, H.T., & Burr, C.K. (1984). Apart and a part: Family issues for young adults with chronic illness and disability. In M.G. Eisenberg, L.C. Sutkin, & M.A. Jansen (Eds.). *Chronic illness and disability through the life span: Effects on self and family.* New York: Springer.

Kaplan, D.M. (1968). Observations on crisis theory and practice. *Social Casework* 49:151–155.

Levinson, D.J. (1978). *The seasons of a man's life.* New York: Knopf.

Levinson, D.J. (1986). A conception of adult development. *American Psychologist* 41:3–13.

McGoldrick, M., & Gerson, R. (1985). *Genograms in family assessment.* New York: Norton.

McGoldrick, M., & Walsh, F. (1983). A systemic view of family history and loss. In M. Aronson & L. Wolberg, (Eds.), *Group and family therapy 1983.* New York: Bruner/Mazel.

Minuchin, S., Rosman, B.L., & Baker, L. (1978). *Psychosomatic families.* Cambridge, Mass: Harvard University Press.

Minuchin, S., Baker, L., Rosman, B., Liebman, R., Milman, L., & Todd, T. (1975). A conceptual model of psychosomatic illness in children: Family organization and family therapy. *Archives of General Psychiatry* 32:1031–1038.

Moos, R.H. (Ed.) (1984). *Coping with physical illness, 2: New perspectives.* New York: Plenum.

Neugarten, B. (1976). Adaptation and the life cycle. *The Counselling Psychologist* 6:16–20.

Paul, N., & Grosser, G. (1965). Operational mourning and its role in conjoint family therapy. *Community Mental Health Journal* 1:339–345.

Penn, P. (1983). Coalitions and binding interactions in families with chronic illness, *Family Systems Medicine* 1:16–25.

Piaget, J. (1952). *The origins of intelligence in children.* New York: International Press.

Rolland, J.S. (1984). Toward a psychosocial typology of chronic and life-threatening illness. *Family Systems Medicine* 2:245–263.

Rolland, J.S. (1987). Family systems and chronic illness: A typological model, *Journal of Psychotherapy and the Family* (in press).

Rolland, J.S. (1987). Family illness paradigms: Evolution and significance. *Family Systems Medicine* 5:467–486.

Schmale, A.H., & Iker, H. (1971). Hopelessness as a predictor of cervical cancer. *Social Science Medicine* 5:95–100.

Simonton, C.O., Mathews-Simonton, S., & Sparks, T.F. (1980). Psychological intervention in the treatment of cancer. *Psychosomatics* 21:226–233.

Viney, L.L., & Westbrook, M.T. (1981). Psychosocial reactions to chronic illness related disability as a function of its severity and type. *Journal of Psychosomatic Research* 25:513–523.

Walker, G. (1983). The pact: The caretaker-parent/ill-child coalition in families with chronic illness. *Family Systems Medicine* 1:6–30.

Weiss, H.M. (1983). Personal communication.

The Impact of Death and Serious Illness on the Family Life Cycle

Fredda Herz Brown, R.N., Ph.D.

One thing we are certain of in our lifetime is that we will die. In fact it can be said that from the moment we are born we are dying. In view of the profound connections in history between members of a family system it is not surprising that adjusting to death seems to be more difficult than the adjustment to other life transition (Holmes & Rahe 1967). The majority of clinical research studies have focused attention on the dyadic relationship between an individual symptom bearer and the person who has died. However, there is much clinical evidence from family therapy that death is a systematic process in which all members participate in mutually reinforcing ways, with the symptom bearer being just one of those directly and indirectly affected by the loss of a family member.

Not only is the impact of death intense and often prolonged, but its affects are often not recognized by the family as related to the loss (Paul & Paul, 1982; McGoldrick & Walsh, 1983) Although death denial operates to keep us unaware of its eventuality and its effects, in fact, serve a positive function with families of the terminally ill to keep them going, to promote their continued hope of life.

There has been some recent societal moves to focus on the effects of positive thinking, imagery, and denial in the treatment of the seriously and terminally ill and to move the process of caring for dying individuals back to the family. However, there still remains a societal denial of death that affects not only treatment but the impact of dying on the family. Our society has created a variety of "death specialists" for dealing with all aspects of dying—hospitals to house the critically ill, morticians to handle the preparation of the body for burial, and funeral directors to deal with the details for burial. With all these individuals handling death, the family still tends to be distant from the dying person.

Since families generally operate to keep emotional tension down and an equilibrium stabilized, it is not unusual for family members to react automatically in a way that they view as least disruptive and least upsetting to

themselves and to each other. Thus it is often a typical reaction for families to want to distance from the reality of death and to permit the waiting death specialists to take over. At a time when open relationships can be most beneficial to the resolution of a life crisis and to the ongoing emotional functioning of the family, the effects of the joint societal, familial, and individual processes tend to render the family less capable of dealing with the stress and disruption of death.

The focus of the current chapter is threefold: (1) to elaborate on the factors affecting the impact of death on the family system; (2) to define some functional and dysfunctional family reactions and their consequences; and (3) to develop some clinical interventions for dealing with actual, anticipated, and unresolved mourning.

FACTORS AFFECTING THE IMPACT OF DEATH AND SERIOUS ILLNESS ON THE FAMILY SYSTEM

The death and serious illness of any family member lead to disruption in the family equilibrium. The degree of disruption to the family system is affected by a number of factors, the most significant of which are (1) the social and ethnic context of death; (2) the history of previous losses (3) the timing of the death in the life cycle; (4) the nature of the death or serious illness; (5) the position and function of the person in the family system; and (6) the openness of the family system.

SOCIAL AND ETHNIC CONTEXT OF DEATH

Since Kubler-Ross (1969) first wrote her book *On Death and Dying*, there have been many societal changes that have influenced families' reaction to death and the therapeutic treatment of it. Some of these are the changing role of women and the changing health-care methods for dealing with death. For generations women have been the caretakers of the ill and dying members of their families and of society; in fact the word family often meant women. As women had fewer children and their life became more mobile, they were no longer tied to the caretaking of the new and previous generation. With an increase in available time and a shift in the social and political context of Western society, such as the rise of feminism and the rising cost of living, women began to enter the workforce in greater numbers. The change of their family role has tended to create a vacuum in family functioning. "Who will care

for the ill and dying?"—just as "Who will care for the children?—becomes a question because of the centrality of women to family life. Women often feel guilty and upset because of the lack of desire or willingness to carry on such a role singly, and often without emotional reward.

In keeping with this view of women, it has been found that families tend to use hospice and home-care programs only if they are unable to have a principal care person (PCP) at home to care for them (Mor & Hiris, 1983; McCusker, 1983) and 70% of the PCPs were females. Families with higher incomes and individuals who were married were also more likely to die at home (Mor & Hiris, 1983; McCusker, 1983). It is the author's experience that while women will care for others or feel guilty about not doing so, they frequently do not expect their family to feel comfortable caring for them.

While women are leaving home to work, they are also changing their life expectancy and long-term low death rates (U.S. Vital Statistics, 1982). But although women still have lower death rates than men in most areas (Waldron, 1983), as they enter the workforce, they show an increase in morbidity and mortality rates in such areas as pulmonary dysfunction and breast and lung cancer. However, since men are exposed to more hazardous occupational conditions, they have higher accident rates than women. The greater exposure over time to industrial carcinogens contributes to the higher rates of some cancers in men (Waldron, 1983).

Women have higher rates of symptoms, and however, and therefore higher rates of physician visits than men (Waldron, 1983). If severity of illness is controlled, then men make as frequent visits to the health-care facility as women. Since women have frequently been at home and men at work, it is not unusual that men only seek treatment for illnesses that interfere with normal activities—that is, work—whereas women tend to seek preventative care. The long-term effect of the changing role of women (and men) on the type of health-care problems and utilization will probably not be totally clear for two decades when the women who have started to work start to match their male cohorts in number of years on the job.

The Changing Health-Care Methods for Dealing with Death

Over the past decade, there has been a beginning shift in the health-care philosophy and service available to the seriously and terminally ill. There has been a shift from a pathological view, which places care in the hospital and with the expert, the physician, to a more normative and acute view, which places responsibility for care and illness decisions on the individual and the family. In keeping with shift in responsibility there is some shift in focus to the techniques that give the individual more of a sense of control, such as positive thinking, imagery, and laughing (Cousins, 1979; Simonton, 1978.)

The development of the hospice and/or home-care movement has also

evolved from a shift in responsibility and has resulted in care being placed in the hands of the primary caretaking unit, the family. Some of the original fears regarding this movement were that families would be devastated by seeing a loved one die; that they would be unable to care for them adequately; and that the stress level would be extremely high. However, the opposite has been shown to be the case: families that decide to care for their seriously or terminally ill family member always do better on all the standard emotional measures than their hospital-based counterparts (Mulhern et al., 1983; Mor & Hiris, 1983; McCusker, 1983).

Families not only experience fewer psychological and psychosomatic symptoms but also view their time together as a time of growth (Lauer & Carnmitta, 1980; Lauer et al., 1983; Mulhern, et al, 1983). The selection of a hospice or home-care program depends in part on the availability of a primary caretaker, financial resources, and marital status. Although one might expect that the poor would choose this less expensive form of health care, they are frequently the families that choose hospital care. If offered enough supports and resources and increased availability of hospital services as needed, they might also utilize home care. Although it may be more work, it appears to be of less overall emotional consequence to the family over time.

THE ETHNIC INFLUENCE

Our ethnicity not only influences the way we view health and illness (McGoldrick, 1982; Schwartzman, 1982) but also, by extension, the way we view life and death. Some ethnic groups seem to be better prepared than others to deal with death, dying, and serious illness. Anyone who has seen "Ordinary People" cannot help but remember the scene in which the mother, played by Mary Tyler Moore, in a silent and very constrained manor, holds back her sobs as she packs to leave her home. With no rituals for dealing with death, a strong sense of autonomy, and a lack of verbal expressiveness, the white Anglo-Saxon Protestant ethnic group does not prepare families for dealing with life's tragedies. Often these families need a great deal of assistance in accepting and dealing with their feelings. Helping them to construct rituals that mark the event and ease the family way for the family to deal with the loss are important in preventing a rapid coverup and the resulting explosion or shock waves of divorce, suicide, or serious illness.

On the other end of the continuum are the Jews, who are well prepared to deal with life's tragedies and life's suffering. They have a strong concern with the ebb and flow of life, as demonstrated by their focus on life cycle ritual. They are also a very expressive ethnic group with a tradition of shared suffering; that is, expressing and sharing life's suffering with one another promotes the sense of a "people." These values and characteristics assist the Jews in dealing with death openly and directly. If they need assistance in this

regard, it is to get in touch with the personal aspects of the death ritual and to make it as meaningful as possible for all involved.

The History of Previous Losses

When considered at its moment of occurrence, that is, as an event, death appears to terminate an individual's life and imply that time moves in only one direction—from past through present to its end. It is only when time is viewed as evolutionary and circular in nature, that death can be viewed as part of an ebb and flow, of beginnings and ends, and not as an absolute final end. That all of life can be viewed as a motion from or toward death is the same as that all death can be viewed as a motion from or toward life. Past deaths and the family's relationship to them are always relevant to the current and future motion of a system, and as such form a temporal web or context for understanding the impact of current deaths.

The movement of at least three to four generations occurs along a transgenerational and developmental axis (Carter, 1978). The developmental movement in a system includes both the normative or predictable crises and the situational or unpredictable events that may disrupt the family life cycle process. Transgenerational movement consists of patterns of relating and functioning based on the family's past experiences that are trasmitted down through the generations. These include family attitudes, myths, themes, taboos, catastrophic expectations, and toxic issues. When developmental and transgenerational stresses intersect, the family experiences extreme stress, which dramatically increases the likelihood of dysfunction in the system. When a current situational stress intersects with one of life's normative transition, such as the death of a young adult, the ability of a family to maintain the current challenge is impaired. If these developmental and situational crises are further complicated by memories of past traumatic losses, the family's ability to handle the situation is impeded even further.

Past losses, and the family's ability to master them, have the potential of intersecting with a current life cycle loss and creating a life cycle impasse—an impasse in time, with the family being unable to move forward or backward toward a resolution. An overload of past losses and a history of difficulty in dealing with such losses seems to impede a family's ability to handle a current loss. By inhibiting their use of the past in the present, the family is prevented from learning from experience from understanding the similarities and differences between various losses.

The inability to make positive use of past losses in the present is often manifested in two ways: (1) the lack of knowledge regarding the concurrence of death with other life cycle events and (2) the lack of or differences in memory regarding particular losses in the family. McGoldrick and Walsh (1983) hypothesize that those previous losses concerning which family members show the most discrepancy of memory are often the most problematic and are likely to have rigidified family-response patterns. It is infrequent for families to volun-

teer information regarding past deaths since they frequently do not view them as significant to the problems at hand.

> Geri and Jim, a young couple, came to family therapy that had begun because of marital difficulties one and a half years previously and had culminated in Geri's discovering Jim's long-term affair. In conducting the evaluation session, it was learned that this couple had had an eight-month-old baby girl who died of a rare degenerative muscle disease two years before. Within two months of the baby's death, they adopted another child, now two years of age. Jim's complaint was that he felt somewhat numb toward Geri and their adopted child. Geri explained that she had felt unloved and unloving for several years. It was not until several sessions later that either was able to realize the impact of the loss of their baby or their experience of relationship "numbing."

When requested to elaborate on past deaths, families frequently not only do not remember the details of the event(s), but demonstrate an emotional overreaction to the memory. That is, they either are extremely emotional, sobbing while describing what they remember or remain placid and/or stoic while describing what seems a particularly traumatic event.

At times it is impossible for these families to move on, to deal with the impending or actual death of a loved one, without dealing with the past losses. (See interventions for unresolved mourning for strategies for dealing with this type of situation.) At other times the past losses can be dealt with indirectly in the context of the current loss by constructing interventions that link the past loss to the current situation. The situation with Geri and Jim was of this type.

> The impact of the death of their infant was made more intense for Geri and Jim because of the death of her mother during her pregnancy with the baby. Jim's mother had died many years before in suspicious circumstances and he refused to discuss the event or his reaction to it. He had become very close to Geri's mother, and not only missed her when she died, but agreed that he was reminded of his own mother's death. Geri longed for a mother throughout the pregnancy and infancy of her child and still thought of her frequently, crying as she did. Her family never discussed the mother's death (from cancer) and Dad has remarried. The dead infant was named for both mothers.
>
> Geri was interested in resolving the death of her child but did not see how the death of her mother further highlighted that death for her. Before making a visit to the grave of her daughter, she was asked to write a letter to her mother describing her experience as a mother losing a daughter and as a daughter losing a mother. She was asked to examine the similarities and differences in these experiences. This put her in touch with the impact of her mother's loss and her experience of her daughter's death. She chose to read this letter to her mother at the gravesight before visiting her daughter's grave.

TIMING OF DEATH IN THE LIFE CYCLE

Americans live longer than they did several decades ago; in fact most people live until their seventh or eighth decade of life (U.S. Vital Statistics,

1980–82). Generally the farther along in the life cycle, the less is the degree of family stress associated with death and serious illness. Death at an older age is viewed as a natural process. In fact coming to grips with one's mortality is a developmental task for the aged (Walsh, 1980). It is when a grandparent or great-grandparent dies that most people first become personally aware of death. Although most of us would rather death come in old age and prefer that it be sudden, nonviolent, quiet, and dignified, that is often not the case. Unfortunately statistics (U.S. Vital Statistics, 1982) indicate that the longer we live, the more likely we are to die to a debilitating and chronic illness—the most common of which are cardiovascular disease and cancer—and certainly not a sudden, quiet, or dignified death.

Although death of the elderly is viewed as an integral part of family life cycle, it is not without its stresses. Part of the stress evolves from the changes in the life-style needed to deal with the effects of the debilitating illness itself. For instance, what happens when the elderly, because of failing health, are unable to care for themselves? The answer to this question often creates a crisis for the succeeding generations, and frequently rests on the women's shoulder (Kramer & Kramer, 1976; Tobin & Leiberman, 1976). With the changing role of women in our country, women may not be available to perform the caretaking for the dying elderly family members. Their lack of availability has created a vacuum in this area of family functioning, engendered much guilt for women, and fostered the increased use of hospitals and old-age and nursing homes for our elderly.

> Mrs. James, a mother of five adult children, was an only child whose father had died five years to our meeting. Mrs. James was a professional woman with a very responsible job, which she found very fulfilling. After her father's death, she had moved her mother into the suburbs close to her home because she was afraid the area in which her mother lived was becoming increasingly unsafe. Her mother, 85 years old, had initially prospered, but that was short-lived as she became depressed without her friends. She complained continuously to her daughter, who felt guilty and finally suggested that her mother move back to the original home. Mother said no, she couldn't move again because, "it would kill me." From that point on, Mrs. James became a prisoner of her own guilt and her mother's resentment. She spent every spare minute taking care of her never-satisfied mother, who continued to complain that she was miserable. Mrs. James felt totally oppressed by the situation; her husband complained that they were unable to spend time together. Mrs. James said that she just couldn't continue like this anymore. "I'm exhausted and resentful, but if I don't do it, I feel guilty and miserable."

If the adult daughter decides to take the responsibility for caretaking, not only must she cope with the stresses of an additional household member, but also of continuous care. The expense of outside care is often great, and since the elderly are often also poor, the family must deal with the financial burden of their decision. However, a major portion of the family stress arises because the death of an elderly generation brings each successive generation closer to its own death. Often this occurs at a time when succeeding generations are

dealing with issues of movement toward life, that is, commitment, autonomy, and work.

Jeanine was a 25-year-old who sought treatment because she was very depressed and increasingly suicidal over the last week. When she was seen, she reported frequent thoughts of jumping out of her tenth-floor office window. She was unable to determine the reason for the intensity of her feelings; things had been going very well for her recently. She had an excellent job and was living away from home without any financial assistance from her mother. She had been dating and had a large network of friends. The only thing that seemed to be a problem was that her mother, a very isolated and angry woman since her own divorce 15 years before, had recently been diagnosed as terminally ill with cancer. While Jeanine felt that her mother could and wanted to care for herself, she also felt caught between her desire to maintain her newly found gains and her desire to help her mother. She found no solution to this and felt somewhat orphaned with the impending death of her mother, eight years after her dad's death. Sessions with her mother and sister helped to clarify the mother's needs and the daughter's ability and willingness to help. Both sisters alternated staying with mother during her last months and sessions were held at the home.

Whereas an eldery family member is viewed as having completed his/her life and has few remaining tasks and responsibilities, serious illness or death at another life cycle phase is considered to end an incomplete life; it does not follow the normative course of life. The timing is off; it is out of sync. In the author's experience, those deaths or serious illnesses whose victims are in the prime of life are the most disruptive to the family. This can be partly understood by the fact that it is at this phase of the life cycle that the individual has the greatest responsibilities. The death in serious or terminal illness of an individual at this point in the life cycle leaves the family with a gap in function that is difficult, if not impossible, to fill, and may therefore prevent the family from completing its life cycle tasks. In both earlier and later phases of the life cycle, the individual has fewer essential family responsibilities. So there appears to be a critical period of approximately 20 years in which, all things being equal, death and serious illness seem to have the greatest impact. Let us consider the family stresses engendered first by the death or serious illness of an adult family member, and then by the death and serious illness of a child or adolescent.

Recently a couple with an adult son and daughter sought treatment. The wife was dying a slow, painful death from cancer of the bone that had metastasized from a breast cancer six years before. The woman had become bedridden, and the husband continued therapy. He had expressed some concern about his 28-year-old son's reaction to the mother's death. When the father and son met jointly, the son attempted to explain to his father the concerns he had about his mom's death. First, the son said, "I think it is harder for you to lose your wife than for me to lose my mother. I know that since I've been married the relationship with a wife is different! Also, Dad, you and Mom have been looking forward to this time when you could be alone again—have time again for each other with no children around—just the two of you. I'll miss Mom; I think that she will not ever get to see her grandchildren. I also worry about what will happen to you."

The son expressed succinctly the issues and unfinished tasks for the family with young adult children in which a spouse/mother dies. Death ends a time in their lives when most couples are beginning to experience fewer family responsibilities and are looking forward to some time alone together to enjoy themselves and their children. When a marriage lasts until this time, death's greatest impact is on the spouse, who must consider spending the latter years of his/her life alone or beginning again with someone else. It has been shown in this regard that for the first year after the death of a spouse, the remaining spouse is vulnerable to suicide (Osterweiss et al, 1984) and serious illness. Men, partly because they do not utilize social-support systems and are used to being cared for, have a tendency to fare more poorly than women, with a significant increase in death from accident, heart disease, and some infectious illnesses and a greater likelihood of suicide in the first year (Osterweiss, et al, 1984).

This family's experience would be very different if the son were an adolescent, or even a young adult, still in the parental home at the time of his/her mother's illness and death. Serious illness and death of a parent with children still at home may result in the family's not resolving the tasks of these stages of the life cycle. In the family with adolescents or dependent young adults, the major life cycle task is the mutual weaning of parents and children. The serious illness or death of a parent may impede the completion of this process. The following is an example.

> The family of a 16-year-old girl sought treatment when the young woman's grades in school dropped from "A" or "B" work to "barely passing." In doing an overview of recent stresses on the family, the author was told by the mother that she had multiple sclerosis and had been hospitalized several times during the past two years (just when the girl's school work had gone down). The mother continued by saying, "I don't know what to do, I want my daughter to be able to be with her friends and do things like other kids her age do, but I also need her to help me with things around the house, I just can't do many things anymore. I tire easily; she needs to make dinner, put the kids (three other children) to bed very often. Maybe she's just too tired to do any school work." The daughter was quick to add, "But I don't mind."

Not only does the serious illness of a parent at this life cycle phase interfere with the adolescent's achieving independence through the usual rebellion and focus outside of the family, but it may set the adolescent up as a parental surrogate with siblings and thus hold him or her tightly within the family.

For the other spouse, the financial, domestic, and emotional responsibilities are more than double, as he/she not only must care for the spouse, but also do the spouse's share. Death after a prolonged illness may be a relief from caring for and trying to fill in for the mother or father, and "acting as if" one does not mind, or maybe even like doing so.

A couple I recently saw depicts the issues for a family with young children coping with the dying of an adult mother/father. The husband, 28 years old, was dying of leukemia. His two children were seven and five years of age. He often stated early in the course of treatment: "Day and and day out I am

confronted with the reality of never seeing my kids grow up. It's even hard to look at them, much less plan for their future." At a time when life should be in its prime, in terms of plans and dreams, it was coming to an end for him. The death of a mother or a father in a family at this life cycle phase leaves many child-rearing tasks and family responsibilities for the remaining parent. If the father is the main source of financial support, his death often leaves his spouse with the additional difficulty of establishing a new economic source of support. Since women have traditionally been responsible for the emotional and communication aspects of the family, it is not surprising that the death of a mother often leaves the father with a task for which he feels ill prepared and one that has great importance to the family's postdeath adjustment. In families where the father is unable to adapt to his new role as the center of communication and emotional responsibility, the family's adjustment is impaired (Cohen et al., 1977).

The reactions of a child to a parental death are varied, and appear to be influenced mainly by the child's age, level of emotional and cognitive development, and emotional closeness to the dead/dying parent and to the surviving parent (Bowen, 1976; Schiff, 1977; Kubler-Ross, 1976). A recent study (Elizur & Kaffman, 1983) suggests that initially it is the surviving parent's withholding of emotional expression, overrestraint, and an inability to share the child's grief that has the greatest impact on the child's adjustment. Later in the mourning process, it is the parent's proplexity, anxiety, and inconsistency—that is, the inability to move past his or her own initial grief into structuring the child's world—that seems to have the most effect on the child's adjustment. In the author's experience, both the initial and later parental reactions are manifestations of the parent's own grief and mourning, with the later reactions growing out of an inability to move on in the grief work. Thus it is not so much the parent's grief reaction, but the inability to express it in the system and thus letting it come between the child and the parent, that is problematic in the adjustment of both.

The death of a child is certainly viewed by most people as life's greatest tragedy. This view derives from the fact that a child's death appears so out of place in the life cycle. In terms of instrumental functioning of the family system, the young child is a family member with few responsibilities and emotional factors, and so such a serious illness or death does not leave an unfillable gap in the overall responsibilities of the family.

How then does one account for the drastic and lasting impact of a child's death or serious illness? The author believes a major portion of the emotional intensity can be accounted for in the family projection process through which children become the important emotional focus of the family. Since most parents view children as extensions of their hopes and dreams in life, the loss of the child is an existential wound of the worst kind. How does one get over watching the child one created and raised die? There is probably nothing as painful for parents. These families not only deal with the chronic sorrow and permanent uncertainty of outcome, but must also be the active caretakers of

the child. This very often means that at least one parent must remain at home full time (or have a flexible job that will permit the parent to deal with exacerbations of the illness) and perform painful caretaking responsibilities. The family is not only hit with the loss of one parent's salary but also with prohibitive medical costs. And the time and energy necessary to deal with the distress of the child's illness and/or death certainly have an impact on the relationships among the family members.

The effects of a child's death on the spouses' relationship is often profound, with separation or divorce resulting in an estimated 70% to 90% of all hospitalized cases (Kaplan et al., 1976; Payne et al., 1980; Schiff, 1977; Teitz et al., 1977). In recent home-care or hospice studies (Mulhern et al., 1983; Lauer & Camitta, 1980; Lauer et al., 1983) of the impact of a child's death, parents report a rapid reattainment of social functioning, fewer marital and personal problems, and less intense guilt, anxiety, or depression. They also did not appear to be socially withdrawn or dissatisfied with their decisions (Mulhern et al., 1983). Mulhern and co-writers (1983) attribute the positive effects of home care to the greater sense of power and control and decreased sense of helplessness that parents have over their child's terminal stage of illness.

It is the author's experience that often the impact of a child's death is even greater for parents whose attachment to that child has been dysfunctional. That is, the more significant the child is to the parents own sense of well-being or sense of self (Bowen, 1976), the greater is the degree of family disruption after the death of that child. Since the child's importance in dysfunctional relationship to the parent often involved a distant and/or conflictual relationship between the parents, it is not unlikely that the child's death represents a loss of self, a friend, and a buffer between the spouses. Since the intensity of this loss far outweighs that of the child himself or herself, it is not unusual for the loss to have a powerful impact on the family relationships.

Mr. and Mrs. Cunningham came to therapy because they were fighting violently since the death of their only son, Paul, in a car accident. Paul had been the "apple" of his mother's eye, her namesake, and the child who was bright enough to accomplish all those things Mrs. Cunningham felt she and her husband could not. Mr. Cunningham presented a totally different picture of Paul. He believed Paul's death resulted from his typically irresponsible behavior encouraged by Mrs. Cunningham. He related numerous instances in which Mrs. Cunningham had gone against their agreements regarding Paul and let him get away with an irresponsible act. His final irresponsibility was driving after drinking, going too fast, and going off the road down an embankment. The husband and wife fought continuously about who was responsible and who could have done something different, and the rest of their personal connections to children and other family were not acknowledged. At the time of the first session, they were about to divorce.

Siblings of a seriously ill or dying child may often experience a range of symptoms, from behavioral or school difficulties to somatic illnesses, depression, and even suicide (Kaplan et al., 1976; Payne et al., 1980) especially for a child next in line (Schiff, 1977; Teitz et al., 1977; Hare-Mustin, 1979; Bank & Kahn, 1982). Siblings are often affected in three major ways: (1) being haunted

by the dead sibling, (2) being fearful or counterphobic, and/or (3) resurrecting the dead sibling by leading two lives (Bank & Kahn, 1982). Conrad Jarret in the movie "Ordinary People" (1976) manifests each of these reactions and interactions with his parents vis-à-vis the accidental death of his older brother, the parents' more cherished child's siblings' reactions are not only affected by the parental response, but also by the circumstances surrounding the death—the degree of horror associated with the death; the length of time from diagnosis of the event to the death of the sibling; the degree to which the death could have been prevented; and the age of the surviving child/children (Bank & Kahn, 1982). Recent research (Mulhern et al., 1983; Lauer & Camitta, 1980) on the impact of a sibling death on the surviving children when a home-care or hospice program is involved suggests that the ability to interact and feel less isolated decreases the sibling's fears, anxiety, and depression. In some families a child is conceived to take the place of the dead child or the dead child's place is held open by the family, creating further complication for the surviving sibling(s) (Teitz et al., 1977).

For most families adolescence is a time of great turmoil. In fact, there are probably few other times in the family life cycle in which such turmoil is viewed as normative. Most of the upheaval of this stage centers on the difficulties of accomplishing the life cycle task of the mutual weaning of parents and children. These difficulties arise because, although the adolescents are entering into adulthood, they still must live in a family in which they experience themselves as being alternately treated as adults (when there is a job to be done) and as children (when they want to do something else). Thus the particular dilemma of family life at this time is one in which the family cast does not change but a reshuffling of the hierarchy begins. The serious illness of death of an adolescent can be viewed as the addition of a great deal more stress/upheaval to an already stressful life phase. The fact that most adolescents who die do so suddenly as the result of an accident or by suicide (*Monthly Vital Statistics Report,* 1981) further compounds the degree of family disruption. The symptoms of this family disruption are often enduring, and range from the dissolution of a family through separation/divorce to emotional symptomology, such as depression or physical illness, often in another adolescent child.

Several years ago a young woman came to me for help in dealing with the consequences of her younger brother's suicide two years before. She said that she and her family had not told anyone about the suicide nor did they discuss it frequently among themselves. She thought that, in addition to feeling ashamed because of what her brother had done, she also felt that she and her other siblings were guilty and/or responsible for it. She felt that she should have been able to help him, but yet she felt his behavior was irresponsible and an affront to her own values. Her mother and father had divorced; her mother and one sister suffered from depressions. All she wanted to do was to get it over with. "I don't want to continue suffering. I keep wondering what he would have been like now, and what was terrible enough anyway to lead to him killing himself."

For this family and others like it, the weaning process is paradoxically abruptly and never terminated. That is, they are often left in a state of suspended animation, never truly able to complete their life cycle task, but yet having the task and process cut short. In addition, these families, as in the example above, usually experience tremendous guilt and anger about the suicide, trying at once to understand it, explain it to others, and accept their own and the adolescent's responsibility.

In contrast to this type of suspended animation of the family life cycle are those instances in which the adolescent is chronically or seriously ill. In such instances the adolescent and the family are engaged in a prolonged weaning process. The family, fearful and concerned about the child's health, often acts to protect the adolescent by keeping him/her within the family fold. The parent's need to keep the adolescent within the family confine is extreme when the extrafamilial contacts or activities may pose a real or imagined threat to the adolescent's health. Furthermore, there are some types of chronic or serious illnesses that will impede the adolescent's leaving the family, such as arthritis, mental retardation, or cancer. The seriously ill adolescent may rebel against the curtailments of the disease and/or the family by doing such things as refusing to take medication and eating prohibited foods, or may accept the curtailment and become the family patient. The family, especially the parents, may alternate between overt power struggles, anger, and helpless confusion. Siblings are often resentful of the attention shown the ill child, and feel guilty that they do. The manifestations of this prolonged weaning process can be varied, but the process in the family remains essentially the same.

This had been by necessity a brief overview regarding the timing of death in family life cycle. However, it should be clear that understanding the life cycle tasks and issues for the family at each stage are crucial to understanding the effects of death and serious illness on a family.

THE NATURE OF DEATH

Death can be expected or unexpected, and may or may not involve periods of caretaking. Death can even take place before birth, as in the case with stillbirths, miscarriages, and abortions. Each type of death has implications for the family's reaction and adjustment. Sudden deaths give the individual and/or family little warning. The family reacts with shock. There is no time for farewells or the resolution of relationship issues. There is no anticipatory mourning. In cases such as homicide (1.2% of the total deaths) and accidental deaths (5.1% of the total deaths), (*Monthly Vital Statistics*, 1981), the intensity of the initial grief reaction has been found to be more intense than for more prolonged and natural deaths, and to be displayed more by those people less than 60 years of age (Prouty, 1982).

In addition to the lack of psychological preparation for the death, there may also be a lack of preparation for the realities of death, such as the will, insurance, or other financial arrangements. After the initial intense reaction to these deaths, the loss is often covered over and tends to become a "taboo" subject, as described by Solomon and Hersch (1979). These families tend to begin a long course of family difficulties usually viewed as unrelated to the death. Although the person most directly affected by the death may develop symptoms, it is not uncommon for another member who is sensitive to the family's anxiety to develop symptoms also. The following is an example.

> The client, a 36-year-old divorced mother of three children, began treatment for depression that she related to a marital separation of three years. In the course of obtaining a family history and genogram, it was noted that the client's father had died suddenly of a heart attack four years before. The woman described her relationship to her father as intense and close. "In fact, this may sound dumb, I am really embarrassed, but I keep a box of candy he gave me before he died. I know it's silly, but I can't seem to throw it away." This woman then described similar difficulties in her third and favorite child, her only son. A major part of the treatment was focused on the resolution of her father's death. After a year, the client reported in a somewhat embarrassed way, that she was finally able to throw away the box of candy.

While sudden deaths form only a small proportion of the total among 15 leading causes of death, and have as a major disadvantage the difficulty of resolving the loss, an advantage of this type of death is that it is not preceded by long periods of stress. This period of long-term stress is the major difficulty associated with expected deaths resulting from debilitating illnesses (Cohen et al., 1977). Families in which a member has a long illness (nine of the 15 leading causes of death) such as cancer suffer from the stresses of permanent uncertainly. They are never sure of the course of the illness. Every remission brings the hope of life, and every exacerbation the fear of death. This constant uncertainty can wear the family out emotionally. Watching a family member dying in pain is very draining for everyone. Being helpless to do anything about the comfort of the family member, as when the person is hospitalized, only increases the emotional stress on the family. And the emotional drain is intensified by the financial drain of a long-term illness. Toward the end of such a long process, it is not unusual for the dying individual and the family to wish for death (Shanfield et al., 1984). The intensity of long-term illness is hard for any family to deal with on a continuing basis because of the difficulty in maintaining a balance between living and dying. Often the family and the dying individual, acting to protect each other from anxiety, stop communicating. The resulting inability to deal with the tension creates distance and further tension manifested in a variety of symptoms. However, if the family members are willing to work at it, the terminal illness of another family member (unlike sudden death) does allow the family, if the system remains open, to resolve relationship and reality issues, and to say a final goodbye before death. The following is a special example of a family in which these goals were not achieved.

A father in his late 30s was dying of leukemia. Numerous times throughout the course of the man's illness, he had attempted to talk with his wife about his feelings and his plans. When she distanced because of her own anxiety, he gave up. A fixed distance developed between them. The wife became involved in an affair. Their six-year-old son began experiencing difficulties in school, and their nine-year-old daughter began thinking and speaking about dying.

A special category of family reactions to the nature of death belongs to those deaths that occur around the time of birth. Although the rate of such deaths has consistently decreased since 1930 (U.S. Vital Statistics, 1930–1982), their significance are different enough from other types of death to warrant a separate consideration.

Stillbirths, abortions, and miscarriages all occur before a mutual relationship system is established between the family. However, this very fact is what makes them different. In contrast to other expected or unexpected deaths in which the dying or dead individual has formed a relationship with the family, the family has formed an emotional connection to (and has feelings about) the unborn child. The following example illustrates the issues for a family suffering this type of death.

A midwife asked for consultation regarding a family—mother, 32, father, 34, and two children—that had just experienced a stillbirth. The five therapy sessions took place three months after the experience. The midwife was concerned about the mother's depression and inability to relate to her children, who were anxiously asking about their baby sister. During the second session with the husband and wife, the wife described her repetitive dreams of losing the baby and her other children. A great deal of her thinking was devoted to wondering what the child looked like, why it had died, and what she had done to "make" it die. Although she wanted to see the baby after birth, the hospital staff and physician had said it was better that she did not. Their refusal only solidified her belief that the child was defective and that she was too weak (or inadequate) to handle the situation. When she told her husband of her request, he could not understand her request to see the child. She went on to describe her ambivalence about the conception of the child and her pregnancy. When she attempted to discuss these feelings with her husband, he would say it was no use in discussing it. A fixed distance developed in which the wife became increasingly involved in her thoughts about the child and less involved with the family.

All family members develop certain expectations, wishes, fantasies, and so on, during the course of a pregnancy. The possibility of a relationship is abruptly terminated with the death of a child at or before birth. Furthermore, the expectations and fantasies tend to continue after the death, unless the process is terminated in some way, such as by seeing the baby and doing some grief work. In this respect the reactions to stillbirth are often similar to the reactions in those instances in which the family elects not to have the child (abortion) or in which the mother is unable to carry through to term (miscarriage). In general, the differences in reaction are often those of intensity. The more the mother wants the child (for whatever reasons), or the greater the ambivalence in either parent, or disagreement between the parents regarding the pregnancy or birth and the longer the duration of the pregnancy, the more severe will be the family stress and disruption.

Births that result in infants who have anomolies, or chronic or serious illnesses have also decreased for the past five decades (U.S. Vital Statistics, 1982). Whether or not an infant dies immediately from the effects of these disorders, the knowledge of the "imperfections" often represents a loss of dreams, expectations, and hopes for the child who was to be. Parents often go through a period of mourning following such births; this period is complicated by the fact that they are often also required to make decisions regarding the child's care, and are actively relating to the child, which make it difficult to mourn. Furthermore, such a birth often begins a long period of permanent uncertainty and tremendous financial and emotional responsibilities. The concordance of the normative life cycle event of the birth (and its stresses) and the situational stress of an infant's disability and potential death often create an intense period of stress for the new parents and the extended families.

THE OPENNESS OF THE FAMILY SYSTEM

Many family emotional reactions and long-term adjustment difficulties arising from death originate in the lack of openness in the system. By openness the author means the ability of each family member to stay nonreactive to the emotional intensity in the system and to communicate his or her feelings to the others without expecting the others to act on them. According to Bowen's theory (1976a), two interrelated continua determine the degree to which a family system is open. The first continuum defines a family system according to the level of differentiation (roughly equivalent to the level of emotional maturity). Differentiation defines people according to the degree of distinction between emotional and intellectual functioning. Briefly, this concept suggests that those individuals whose lives are more or less dominated by emotional reactions are those in which the emotional and intellectual functions are fused. The actions of these individuals are based on what "feels" right or comfortable, and/or upon the reactions of others. A more differentiated individual can remain nonreactive to the emotionality of others. This person is able to define his/her position on the basis of thought or principle and can hear the others' thoughts without overreacting. The individual's level of differentiation is determined by the degree to which he or she is caught in the emotional process in the family of origin. The lower the level of differentiation of the spouses, the less able they are to express directly to each other divergent or anxiety-provoking thoughts and feelings without either becoming angry or upset. The more undifferentiated they are, the more likely it is that when stress is high, marital conflict, fusion, and dysfunction in a spouse or child will develop.

The level of family stress, the second continuum, is the crucial element in the evolution of family symptomatology. A family can be relatively undifferentiated, have little stress, and be free of symptoms. On the other hand, a well-

differentiated family can develop symptoms when stress is high. In several studies of the effects of family stress on the development of illness, Holmes and Masuda (1973) found that the death of a spouse is the life event associated with the greatest degree of stress. Furthermore, they found a high degree of association between reported health changes and family life cycle events, one of which is death of a spouse.

In families dealing with death or terminal illness, the author has found that there is a greater likelihood of emotional and/or physical symptom development when family members are unable to deal openly with one another about the death. However, no matter how well differentiated the family, the ability to remain open to express one's thoughts and feelings, and to remain nonreactive to the other's anxiety, is related to the intensity and the duration of stress. The longer and more intense the family stress is, the more difficult it is for the family relationships to remain open and the more likely it is that dysfunction will develop. In addition, the very nature of death and terminal illness often isolates the family from external support networks such as friends and work. This isolation further closes the system. Families that are able to communicate with one another, share information and options, and utilize outside sources of support for these functions seem to restabilize better after death (Cohen et al., 1977; Mulhern et al., 1983; Shanfield et al., 1984). The author is becoming more firmly convinced that anything the therapist can do that helps family members stay connected to each other and to extended families and extrafamilial resources will have a profound impact on the long-term postdeath adjustment of the family. The author's experience suggests that exacerbation of symptoms in the terminally ill often relates to the degree of openness or connectedness between family members at the time. For example:

> A couple came to a cancer group because the wife was finding it difficult to cope with the impending loss of her husband, who at 50 was dying of pancreatic cancer. Her life had been spent in total devotion (fusion) to her husband. As his death began to appear imminent, she became increasingly anxious about living without him. As she became more anxious and more verbose, her husband began to distance from her. His distance further increased her anxiety and the process continued to escalate. Their two sons, 16 and 20, also did not communicate their thoughts and feelings directly to their father, but rather to their mother. The end result was a system in which each member was isolated from the other and in which anxiety continued to escalate. Physical symptoms began to develop in each of the family members, leading to frequent hospitalizations of various members.

THE FAMILY POSITION OF THE DYING OR DEAD FAMILY MEMBER

Not all deaths have equal importance to the family system. In general the more emotionally significant the dying or dead family member is to the family, the more likely it is that his or her death will be followed by a ripple effect up

and down the generations. The reason for this effect is twofold: the disruption in the family equilibrium and the family tendency to deny emotional dependence when that dependence is great.

An individual significance to the family can be understood in terms of the functional role in the family and the degree of emotional dependence of the family on the individual. For instance, the loss of either parent when the children are young removes the functional and emotional positions of breadwinner and/or parent when the family is most dependent upon these functions. The death of a grandparent who functions as the head of the clan is another example of a serious functional loss in the family. In general the more central the dying or dead individual's position, the greater will be the family's emotional reaction.

It can also be observed that the more the family depends emotionally on the dying or dead family member (McGoldrick & Walsh, 1983; Mueller and McGoldrick-Orfanidis, 1976), the greater will be the reaction. For instance, in couples with extreme marital fusion or dependence, the loss of the spouse usually represents the emotional loss of self to the other spouse. The same is true of families in which there is emotional dependence on a child. Any family member who functions in an emotionally overresponsible position is likely to have others in the family who are emotionally dependent on him or her, and who will thus react strongly to the death.

The impact of a functional and/or emotional loss is expressed in the phenomenon of an emotional shock wave, first described in the literature by Bowen (1976). This can be a series of underground aftershocks to the emotional/functional system. They are most likely to occur in families in which emotional dependence is denied and therefore not dealt with directly. The symptoms in a shockwave can be any problem (emotional, social, or physical) in multiple family members. The family often views these events as unrelated and denies the significance and impact of the death that preceded them.

FAMILY TREATMENT INTERVENTION

Of the six factors affecting family reaction and adjustment to death and serious illness, the only one the family or the family therapist has the ability to shift is the openness of the system. There is no way for the family (or the therapist) to change the timing or the nature of the death, or the position of the dead or dying family member. Therefore, most family interventions before, at the time of, or after the death are directed toward opening up family emotional systems.

Interventions Before or at the Time of Death

The major purpose of family interventions in these situations is the prevention of family symptomatology and dysfunction during the illness and after death. There are seven interventions that are often helpful in dealing with the stress and disruption of serious illness and death: (1) viewing the family in context; (2) using open and factual information and terminology; (3) establishing at least one open relationship in the family (4) respecting the hope of life and living; (5) remaining human yet nonreactive to the family pain; (6) dealing with symptoms and stress; and (7) acknowledging and helping the family to use rituals, customs, and styles to deal with death.

Viewing the Family in Context

Not all families enter treatment because they are aware of the impact or potential impact of the death of a family member. In fact some families enter treatment for symptoms they view as totally unrelated to the serious illness or impending death. As in all such situations, a careful and thorough three-generational assessment not only will elaborate the current life stressors, but will also place these in the context of the family's history. Furthermore, this type of assessment, which places the symptoms in a nuclear and three-generational context, helps the family and the therapist to define a familial network and sources of ongoing support. Other sources of support can be defined and elaborated when the therapist explores the family's relationships with other systems such as school, job(s), friends, and church.

Without conducting a complete assessment, the therapist will not develop a sense of a family's "fabric," its texture, and its style, and the ability to understand the impact of the serious illness and death will be decreased, as will the ability to develop relevant hypothesis and interventions.

Using Open and Factual Terminology and Information

It is important that the family therapist avoid using terms or expressions that are indirect, such as "decreased," "passes away," or "passes on." These terms imply that the therapist is unable to speak directly about death and so the family should not either. Using direct words such as death and dying suggests to the family that the therapist is able to be open and relatively comfortable with such a discussion. The same principle is true of the presentation of information. Families with a seriously ill individual are often confronted with health professionals who control the relevant information about the illness. The health professionals—doctors or nurses—decide what and how much to tell the patient. Furthermore, families often themselves decide to withold information from the patient. It is important for the therapist to be a model by presenting information in a factual way to the family, including the patient, and letting them make decisions regarding the use of information. In

this way the therapist encourages the family, including the dying person, to take maximum responsibility for life decisions.

Establishing at Least One Open Relationship in the Family System

One of the major contributions of Kubler-Ross's (1969) work was not only to define stages of dying, but also to make death "a subject" that it was okay to talk about. The reader will notice that the focus of the author's interventions is on a relationship *within* the family system. An open discussion of death between the therapist and any one family member in isolation from the others is not opening up family relationships. It may lower anxiety enough to prevent the family members from dealing with each other. In fact it often invites dysfunction because the therapist becomes involved in a triangle with the family. For individuals to gain from an open discussion of death, it must occur in the context of the intimate family relationships. Since one of the major difficulties all families have is being able to communicate directly about a toxic or taboo issue, it is not surprising that the discussion of death provokes much tension in the family members. It is not uncommon that as the tension increases between any two of the family members around the death issue, the most uncomfortable individual will draw in a third to relieve his/her tension. Another variant of the same process is that the twosome will collude in avoiding a discussion of the impending death.

The family therapist is often confronted with either one of these variations of a triangle (a dysfunctional relationship in which the relationship of any two depends on the relationship with a third). The task is to help each person to talk directly to the other. One can accomplish this task in several ways. One way is to work with the most uncomfortable person, who may be the most motivated to change his or her role in the process. By coaching this person to control his or her emotions and to plan a method to broach the death issue, the family therapist is often successful in opening up the system to deal with the death. At other times the utilization of displacement material may open up the death issue. For instance, the author has played Bowen's taped lecture on death (Georgetown University Medical Center Videotape) for families as a way of helping them start to talk about the death issue. The author has also found that giving the family reading material can be helpful. Families respond positively to material such as the work of Anderson (1974) and Schiff (1977), and popular films such as, "I Never Sang For My Father," (Columbia Pictures) and the TV movie "Death Be Not Proud." The use of multiple family and self-help group settings has also been helpful in the process. It is always amazing how much these groups normalize the family's experience of death and dying.

Respecting the Hope for Life and Living

Very frequently the author is confronted by the following statement by a family therapy trainee: "But that parent only has three months to live and the

family is still discussing the son." No one knows exactly when someone will die, except perhaps the dying person, who often senses the time of death. Often patients outlast the predicted survival time; often they live a shorter length of time. Since families are constantly living on an emotional seesaw of uncertainty, it is very difficult for them to deal continuously with death. I have found that clients will not deal with some death-related issues during a remission, but will discuss the same issues during exacerbations. Each family develops a timing and style of accomplishing their work, much like the timing Kubler-Ross (1969) defines for the individual's work. Although the mental health professionals may want the family to deal with the death issues at all times, they need to develop a respect for the family's timing and the need for hope and the fact that the family moves back and forth in stages.

> One client, a widowed mother of four children, began treatment four years after her lung cancer was diagnosed. This woman would attend sessions irregularly— only when she had some difficulty with the children. I kept asking about her plans for the children and herself. Each time she would say that there were too many other problems to deal with and that she would deal with her death when that was imminent. After a two-year course of irregular sessions, this woman announced that she would die shortly and that she had a number of issues to deal with for herself and her kids. She died six months later when her plans for the children were complete. The children, three years later, are doing very well emotionally.

This example illustrates the necessity to balance issues relating to dying with those related to living, and to understand that tasks have their sequence in the life cycle. Although we are all eager and impatient to assist families with dying, we must respect their hopes to continue living and to deal with their life issues.

Remaining Human Yet Nonreactive to the Family Pain

To be of assistance to families dealing with death and dying, the therapist must be able to remain calm and to think clearly. Families dealing with anticipated or actual death are not only coping with the normal life cycle stresses, but also have the additional stresses of living with dying. Families often seek treatment when the stress is high and they are unable to decrease it. A family therapist who is unable to remain calm increases the family stress even further. The author does not mean that the therapist cannot experience emotions, but only that his or her actions should not be guided by emotions.

If death is a toxic issue for the therapist, then he or she will often tend to be reactive and to cut off discussion, and collude with the family in not discussing the issues or, conversely, insist that the family deal with the death. The therapist who begins behaving in one of these ways must examine his or her own feelings about and experiences with death. At the same time, a therapist who remains impassive and devoid of any emotion, "professional" as families call it, is also not helpful to families dealing with death and serious illness. Family members will no longer discuss their pain with someone whom they

think is unable or unwilling to feel it. They can teach one about death, and will grow from such an experience, if the therapist can stay connected to them and his/her own feelings, while assisting them to remain open and to deal with each other.

Dealing with the Symptoms of Stress

With the stress level so high in these families, it is not unusual for the therapist to be presented with numerous "sideshows." Sideshows are what the author calls symptoms developing is some part of the system because tension is not being dealt with in another area. For instance, a young wife whose husband has terminal cancer begins to have an affair, or a child begins to develop symptoms. The sideshows are not to be ignored; they are an indication of stress. However, the family therapist should be aware of getting sidetracked into spending too much time on the symptom. It is important to check on the family's progress in dealing with major stress in the relationships.

One family that the author was seeing over a three-year period would present a new "symptom" every month or two. Each time the author would spend a brief amount of time in questions about the new symptom and any plans for dealing with it. Then the author would check on how the family was doing in dealing with a previous issue. After a short period of time, the family began making the connection and used the symptom or dysfunction as a signal of some stress to be dealt with more directly.

Acknowledging and Encouraging Families to Use Their Own Style, Customs, and Rituals to Deal with Death

All families have personal and/or religious rituals or customs for dealing with death. In obtaining a family genogram, it is always useful to ask families about the ways in which deaths have been handled in the extended families. Not only does one obtain a picture of the rituals, but one also gains information regarding the way families deal emotionally with death, whether it be angry fights over money, cutoffs, or depression. Another area that should always be discussed with families is the client's plan for his or her death, funeral, and burial. That is, where does the client want to die, who does he or she want present, where will he or she be buried, and what will the funeral be like? The author is always interested in having these plans discussed in the family. In this discussion process, the therapist is able to observe the family's reactiveness to the plans and begin coaching them. Therapists should never take a position on the "right" way or the "best" way since what is right or best is what the family wants and agrees to. There are some general guidelines for coaching the family on the funeral ritual (Bowen, 1976b; Friedman, 1980).

First, rituals are important because they mark an event. Second, the rituals should be in keeping with the religious and philosophical beliefs of the family. Third, they should be as personalized as possible. Fourth, family members

should see the individual after death in order to make death more real. Fifth, children need to be told of the death and given the opportunity to attend the funeral, see the dead family member, and say goodbye. (Most children want to go when given the choice.) Last, the family should talk frequently of the dead individual. When given the options, most families can carry these guidelines through to completion.

Intervention in Unresolved Mourning

Families do not generally seek treatment for issues relating to a recent or past death. Treatment is often sought for a problem or dysfunction in a family member or relationship. Although the symptoms are part of the emotional shockwave following death, the family does not view the death as the important issue in the current problem and so will not mention it. Unless the therapist routinely does a genogram and a chronology of important life events, he or she may not suspect that a death has occurred in the family. If the therapist mentions the relationship between the symptom development and the death, the family will deny it or say it is coincidence. Pushing the issues will only bring more denial, and possibly withdrawel from treatment. The family therapist must remain relevant to the problem presented by the family, coaching the family in that area and beginning to ask questions about the dead family member's relationships. Frequently, after the initial problem has been relieved to some extent, the focus of the sessions begins to shift. The goal of treatment becomes a resolution of the past relationship. In this regard several common factors about these situations are important.

First, the dead family member tends to be either idealized or bastardized, but is not seen as a person with both strengths or weaknesses. Second, there are some issues that were not resolved in the relationship with the dead family member, and this lack of resolution interferes with other relationships. Third, the facts surrounding the death are often confused, uncertain, or unreal. Fourth, the client either never speaks of the dead family member or over-focuses on the person, often as though he or she were still alive. The following example illustrates how the knowledge of these factors can be used in treatment.

A 42-year-old mother of two children, 13 and 16 years of age, began treatment for a depression she viewed as related to her husband's sudden death three years previously. After much effort this woman was able to reestablish contact with her dead husband's family and friends, to view him as a human being, not as an idol, and to visit his grave to say good-bye. She refused to bring the children in for a session throughout this time, and discontinued treatment after a year. One year later she became seriously interested in a man and they began to plan their marriage. At this point her daughter, then almost 18 years of age, began to be argumentative with her mother and refused to leave her alone with her fiance. The mother and daughter sought treatment. During the first session, the daughter began to cry. She expressed her wish that her father was still alive, and described how she would fantasize him holding her when things got bad in school or with the

mother's boyfriend. She said that as far as she was concerned, her father would always be there when she needed him. The author suggested that unless she put her father in his grave, she would not be able to get on with her life.

We outlined a plan that necessitated contact with her father's old friends, business associates, and family; a visit to the grave with and without her mother; and a discussion with her mother of the events on the night of her father's death. We also decided that she seek out occasions to mention her father several times a day. She came back for two more sessions, two weeks apart, to report on her progress in following through with the plan. She was not only pleased with herself, but was pleased with her new relationship with both mother and soon-to-be stepfather. She began the last session by saying, "I put my father to rest—I don't need him to be here to rescue me anymore."

This example illustrates several interventions that are useful in helping family members deal with unresolved mourning. The first is to help the family members obtain a clear view of the details around the death, and a balanced view of the person who died. Often accomplishing these goals means that the therapist must coach the individual to make the "dead person" and the death real; visits to the grave site (Friedman, 1980; Williamson, 1978; Carter, 1978), and to relatives and friends of the deceased are often helpful in this endeaver. It is also extremely important for the family therapist to take time to deal with the intensity of the feelings that these tasks engender in the individual and to respect the pacing and timing necessary to accomplish these goals. The benefits of giving a piece of history its appropriate and relevant place in one's life are important to the ability to move on with life.

REFERENCES

Anderson, R. (1974). Notes of a survivor. In S. Troop & C. Green, (Eds.), *The patient, death and the family.* New York: Scribner's.

Anonymous (1973). A family therapist's own family. *The Family* 1:26–32.

Anonymous (1977). Taking a giant step: First moves back into my family. In J. E. Loria & L. McClenathan (Eds.), *Georgetown symposia: Collected papers.* Vol. II. Washington, D.C.: Family Center, 1977.

Anonymous (1982). Annual summary of births, deaths, marriages and divorces: U.S. 1982. *Monthly Vital Statistics Report.* vol. 31, no. 13. Center for Health Statistics.

Bank, S. P., & Kahn, M. D. (1982). *The sibling bond.* New York: Basic Books.

Bowen, M. (1976a) Theory in the practice of psychotherapy. In P. Guerin (Ed.), *Family therapy: Theory and practice.* New York: Gardner Press.

Bowen, M. (1976b). Family reaction to death. In P. Gueren (Ed.), *Family therapy: Theory and practice.* New York: Gardner Press.

Bowling, A. (1983). The hospitalization of death: Should more people die at home? *Journal of Medical Ethics* 9:158–161.

Carter, E. A. (1978). Trangenerational scripts and nuclear family stress. In R. R. Sager (Ed.), *Georgetown family symposia.* Vol. 3, 1975–76. Washington, D.C.: Georgetown University Press.

Cohen, P., Dizenhuz, I. M., & Winget, C. (1977). Family adaptation to terminal illness and death of a parent. *Social Casework* 58:223–228.

20

Alcohol Problems and the Family Life Cycle

Jo-Ann Krestan, M.A., C.A.C., and Claudia Bepko, M.S.W.

Alcoholism is a problem of epidemic proportions and one that no family therapist can avoid treating. Conservative figures estimate that 4% of the total population or 8.8 million Americans are alcoholic (Royce, 1981). Within specific segments of the population this estimate may climb to 8% or 10%. Every alcoholic directly affects the lives of at least four to five other people. Problem drinkers are included in 42% of all automobile fatalities and abuse of alcohol is implicated in 67% of child-abuse cases, 40% of rape cases, 51% of felonies, and 38% of suicides (Royce 1981). Given the sobering realities of this widespread tendency to abuse alcohol in our culture, a clinician is well-advised to assume the existence of an alcohol problem somewhere in a family until thorough assessment proves otherwise.

Alcoholism typically represents a progressive sequence of events that may continue through several successive life cycle phases. If drinking begins in an early developmental phase, dysfunction may be obvious, or it may remain more insidious, and consequently go unidentified. Nonproblematic drinking may arise early in the life cycle and become dysfunctional in later phases and tend to resolve itself in later ones (Vaillant, 1983). Dysfunction for the individual and the family occurs *over time* and its pace is different for different individuals and families. Frequently the pacing and intensity of dysfunction are related to life cycle stresses occurring at the onset of problematic drinking.

For instance, drinking frequently becomes problematic for women at such developmental points as menopause or at life cycle stages such as early marriage or early parenthood that stress role concept and adjustment. Or parental drinking may increase significantly in response to stresses imposed by a child's reaching or moving out of adolescence.

Assessment of the impact of an alcohol problem must take developmental issues into account. The life cycle model is clinically relevant to an understanding of alcohol problems because the family's developmental stage and the individual's developmental stage intersect to become a context in which an alcohol problem may become both a cause and effect of dysfunction. Drinking

Coleman, S. B., & Stanton, M. D. (1978). The role of death in the addict family. *Journal of Marriage and Family Counseling* 4:79–91.

Cousins, N. (1979). *Anatomy of an illness.* New York: Norton.

Elizur, E. & Kaffman, M. (1983). Factors influencing the severity of childhood bereavement reactionsm. *American Journal of Orthopsychology* V. 53: 668–676.

Evans, N. S. (1976). Mourning as a family secret. *Journal of American Academy of Child Psychiatry* V. 15: 502–509.

Friedman, E. H. (1980). Systems and ceremonies. In E. A. Carter & M. McGoldnick (Eds.), *The family life cycle a framework for family therapy.* Gardner Press.

Hare-Mustin, R. T. (1979). Family therapy following the death of a child. *Journal of Marital and Family Therapy* 5: 5.

Herz, F., & Rosen, E. (1982). Jewish-American families. In M. McGoldrick, J. Pierce, and J. Giordano, (Eds.), *Ethnicity and Family Therapy.* New York: Guilford Press.

Holmes T., & Rahe, R. H. (1967). The social adjustment rating scale., *Journal of Psychosomatic Research* 11: 17–21.

Holmes, T., & Masuda, M. (1973). Life change and illness susceptability., In *Separation and depression: Clinical and research aspects.* Washington D.C.: American Association for the Advancement of Science,.

Juncker, A. G., & McCusker, J. (1983) Where do elderly patients prefer to die? *Journal of American Gerontological Society* 31: 457–461.

Kaplan, D. M., Grobskin, R., & Smith, A. (1976). Predicting the impact of severe illness in families. *Health Social Work* 1:71.

Kowalski, K. & Bowes, N. (1976). Parents' response to a stillborn baby. *Contemporary Obstetrics and Gynecology* 8:53–57.

Kramer, C., & Kramer, J. (1976). *Basic principles of long term patient care.* Springfield, Ill.: Charles C. Thomas.

Kubler-Ross, E. (1969). *On death and dying.* New York: Macmillan.

Kubler-Ross, E. (1976) *Death and dying.* Interview on Public Broadcasting System.

Kuhn, J. (1981). Realignment of emotional forces following loss. *The Family* 5:19–24.

Lauer, M. E., & Camitta, B. M. (1980). Homecare for dying children: A nursing model. *Journal of Pediatrics* 47: 1032.

Lauer, M. E., Mulhern, R. K., Wallaskog, J. M., et al. (1983). A comparison study of parental adaptation following a child's death at home or in the hospital. *Pediatrics* 71:107.

Lester, D. & Blustein, J. (1980). Attitudes toward funerals: A variable independent of attitudes towards death. *Psychological Reports* 46(3).

Lieberman, M. D. (1973). New Insights into the crisis of aging, *University of Chicago Magazine* 66:11–14.

Melgis, F. T., & DeMaso, D. R. Grief resolution therapy: Reliving revising, revisiting. *American Journal of Psychotherapy* 34:51–61.

McCusker, J. (1983). Where cancer patients die: An epidemiologic study. *Public Health Reports*, 98(2):170–176.

McGoldrick, M. (1982). Normal families: An ethnic perspective. In F. Walsh (Ed.), *Normal family process.* New York: Guilford Press.

McGoldrick, M., & Walsh, F. (1983). A systemic view of family history and loss. In L. R. Wohlberg & M. L. Aronson (Eds.), *Group and family therapy.* New York: Brunner/ Mazel.

Monthly vital statistics report (1984). Advance Report of Final Mortality Statistics, 1981, PHS. National Center for Health Statistics, Vol. 33, No. 3, Supplement, June 22.

Mueller, P., & McGoldrick-Orfanidis, M. (1976). A method of co-therapy for schizophrenic families. *Family Process* 15:179–192.

Mor, V., & Hiris, J. (1983). Determinants of site of death among hospice cancer patients. *Journal of Health and Social Behavior* 24: 375–385.

Mulhern, R. K., Lauer, M. E., & Hoffman, R. G. (1983). Death of a child at home or the hospital: Subsequent psychological adjustment of the family. *Pediatrics* 71:743–747.

Osterweiss, M., Solomon, F., & Green, M. (Eds.) (1984). *Bereavement reactions, con-sequences and care*. Washington, D.C.: National Academy Press.

Payne, J. S., Goff, J. R., & Paulson, M. A. (1980). Psychological adjustment of families following the death of a child. In J. Schulman & M. Kupst (Eds.), *The child with cancer*. Springfield, Ill.: Charles C. Thomas.

Paul, N., & Paul, B. B. (1982). Death and changes in sexual behavior. In Walsh, F. (Ed.) *Normal family process*. New York: Guilford Press.

Prouty, E. N. (1983). The impact of race, age and other factors in experience of bereavement *Dissertation Abstracts International* Vol. 44, No. 5, Sect. b, 1605.

Rosen, H., & Cohen, H. L. (1981). Children's reactions to sibling loss. *Clinical Social Wor Journal* 9: 211–219.

Schiff, H. W. (1977). *The bereaved parent*. New York: Crown.

Schneidman, E. S. (1971). You and death. *Psychology Today* 5:44.

Schwartzman, J. (1982). Normality from a cross-cultural position. In P. Walsh (Ed.), *Norm Family Process*. New York: Guilford Press.

Shanfield, S. B., Benjamin, A., & Swain, B. (1984). Parent reactions to the death of an ad child from cancer. *American Journal of Psychiatry*. 141:1092–1094.

Shanfield, S. B., & Swain, B. (1984). Death of adult children in traffic accidents. *Journal Nervous and Mental Diseases* 172:533–538.

Simonton, C., & Simonton-Matthews, S. (1978). *Getting well again*. Los Angeles: Tarcl

Solomon, M., & Hersch, L. B. (1979). Death in the family: Implications for family devel ment. *Journal of Marital and Family Therapy* 5:43.

Teitz, W., McSherry, L., & Bratt, B. (1977). Family sequelae after a child's death du cancer, *American Journal of Psychotherapy* 31:417–425.

Tobin, S. S., & Lieberman, M. A. (1976). *Last home for the aged: Critical implication institutionalization*. San Francisco: Jossey-Bass.

U.S. vital statistics. (1980–1982). U.S. Department of Health, Education, and Welfare.

Vargas, L. A. (1983). Early bereavement in the four modes of death in whites, blacks, Hispanics, *Dissertation Abstracts International* Vol. 43, No. 11, Sec. B. 3746.

Waldron, I. Sex differences in human mortality: The role of genetic factors. *Social Sci and Medicine* 17(6).

Walsh, F. (1978). Concurrent grandparent death and birth of schizophrenic offspring intriging finding. *Family Process* 17:457–463.

Walsh, F. (1980). In E. Carter & M. McGoldrick (Eds.), *The family life cycle: A frame for family therapy*. New York: Gardner Press.

Williamson, D. S. (1976). New life at the graveyard: A method of therapy for individu from a dead former parent. *Journal of Marriage and Family Counseling* 4: 93–

both disrupts accomplishment of developmental tasks and may be a response to stresses imposed by specific developmental phases.

ALCOHOLISM AND THE LIFE CYCLE: GENERAL TREATMENT ISSUES

The lack of a universally agreed-on definition of alcoholism presents a stumbling block in assessment to most clinicians and frequently results in the misdiagnosis of or the failure to identify a drinking problem in families. One major recent text on alcoholism (Pattison & Kaufman, 1982) devotes six chapters to the issues of definition and diagnosis. Rather than belabor the point here, for the purpose of this chapter we will adopt the National Council on Alcoholism's definition: "The person with alcoholism cannot consistently predict on any drinking occasion the duration of the episode or the quantity that will be consumed" (National Council on Alcoholism, 1976). Along with this inability consistently to predict drinking behavior on the part of the drinker, the clinician will note various somatic, psychological, and interpersonal symptoms in the family that may range from disturbances in job functioning, marital conflict, and infidelity, to problems in children's school functioning, and may also include depression, social isolation, abuse of prescription or other drugs to combat anxiety, or a host of physical disorders in all family members. Presenting problems are rarely seen as related to drinking behavior by the family. Whenever incest or physical abuse is present in a family, alcoholism should be a suspected diagnosis.

Considerable controversy exists regarding the classification of alcoholism as a disease. Our operating premise is that alcoholism is a systemic process that affects and is affected by interaction that occurs between the drinker and the alcohol, the drinker and himself or herself, and the drinker and others. The effects of drinking result in adaptive changes at all systemic levels, and because it is ultimately highly destructive at all these levels, as well as potentially life threatening, alcoholism is most efficiently referred to as a disease.

As Valiant (1983) comments, "The point of using the term *disease* is simply to underscore that once an individual has lost the capacity consistently to control how much and how often he drinks, then continued use of alcohol can be both a necessary and a sufficient cause of the syndrome that we label alcoholism" (p. 17). This view suggests that the activity of ingesting alcohol acquires a self sustaining, self-reflexive, and destructive impetus that requires outside treatment or intervention for its interruption.

Other important assumptions are that, as a psychoactive drug, alcohol consumption produces highly predictable effects in the drinker (allowing for cultural and ethnic differences), and that over time it distorts patterns of

interpersonal feedback within the family system. Treatment of other family problems may stop or alleviate the drinking behavior in some families (Bowen, 1978). In these cases it is usually true that drinking behavior is more situational and not addictive, and would not generally be classified as alcoholic drinking by any standard diagnostic indicators of alcoholism. In other families, however, drinking behavior will have become addictive and will have assumed such central importance that it becomes the fulcrum of interactional sequences. This type of family may be referred to as an "alcoholic system" or one that is "organized around" alcoholism (Steinglass, 1979). In this type of family, abstinence from drinking is an necessary but insufficient goal. Abstinence must be maintained if the distorted and dysfunctional interaction in the family is to be treated, but dysfunctional interaction must also be treated if abstinence is to be maintained and other symptomatology prevented (Meeks & Kelly, 1970).

Assessing behaviors that maintain drinking is always more important than hypothesizing about causes of drinking behavior. It is important to understand the oscillating quality of alcoholic interaction from drunk to sober states (Berenson, 1976) and to view treatment as a process of rebalancing these behavioral extremes.

It is not sufficient to generalize family systems treatment principles to alcoholic families. A specific understanding of the dynamics particular to alcohol addiction is imperative and treatment should be undertaken with consultation or training by professionals knowledgable about alcoholism. Treatment in conjunction with referral to the programs of Alcoholics Anonymous (AA) is optimal since family therapy alone is not sufficient to address the complex issues represented by alcohol addiction. In the sense that addiction represents a process that occurs on an interactional level that includes a level of feedback generated between the drinker and the alcohol, treatment is best accomplished within a context that includes acknowledgment of this aspect of the problem. Thus AA currently provides the most effective context available for addressing the compulsive, self-correcting nature of drinking behavior. With its focus on peer support, mutuality, "correct" thinking, behavioral change, and spiritual surrender, AA fosters change in the drinker's experience of himself or herself that cannot typically be achieved within the context of therapy.

In terms of the effects of drinking on developmental phases, it is important to distinguish between early-onset (drinking that begins early in the life cycle) and late-onset (drinking that begins in later life cycle stages) drinking in terms of the disruption imposed on family developmental tasks. Late-onset drinking may have caused only minor disruption in the developmental progression of family life whereas a long-term (early-onset) drinking problem will usually have severely impaired the family's capacity to accomplish transitions from one stage to another.

The time lapse between the onset of drinking and the point at which the family seeks treatment is also significant. Once several years of chronic alcoholic drinking have elapsed, dysfunction is usually quite severe, while early

intervention and treatment suggest both a less intense degree of impairment as well as a better prognosis for the family's future adjustment.

Alcoholism differs from other problems or illnesses that may affect family life in that the family, as well as the drinker, develops a rigid system of denial in an attempt to avoid acknowledgment of the problem. The effects of alcoholic drinking are insidious, and both distort and erode self-confidence and self-esteem in the family. Denial becomes a defense against acknowledging the increasing loss of control that typically occurs on both emotional and functional levels. Denial may be considered one of the major symptoms of the alcoholism itself and may extend to denial of both the problematic drinking and the impact of that drinking on other family members (Vaillant, 1983).

Finally, it is important to conceptualize alcoholism as a disorder that has an intergenerational impact. The occurrence of an alcohol problem at any point within at least a three-generational time frame of the immediate nuclear family presenting for treatment significantly affects behavioral and emotional patterns evolving within that family. It is important for the clinician to assess the effect alcoholism may have had on earlier generations in the family and to recognize its relevance to the family or individual's current issues of differentiation. One cannot work with a young adult presenting typical problems of separation/differentiation, for instance, without understanding the particular influence an alcoholic grandparent may have had on current interactional patterns in the family. Whether or not the family defines alcoholism in the past generations as a problem, it must be assessed as influencng the current functioning of the family.

Wolin and colleagues (1980) recently conducted research that assesses the impact of the disruption of family rituals on the intergenerational transmission of alcoholism. They hypothesize that families that protect their rituals from the disruptive influence of the drinking parent are less likely to transmit alcoholism to the next generation. In other research now in progress, they are examining the significance of birth order and other factors as these relate to intergenerational transmission.

STAGING

Staging, the process of assessing and defining phase-related aspects of dysfunction and their treatment, is crucial in the treatment of any problem and the process of staging in the evaluation and treatment of an alcoholic system (any family in which problematic drinking has occurred or is occurring within three generations) is particularly complex. This complexity relates to the fact that two interacting sequences of events are taking place—the progression of the alcoholism within the individual as it is influenced by and influences the developmental progression of the family itself. Various authors have attempted

to describe the developmental history of the family influenced by alcohol (Steinglass, 1979), the physiological and psychological progression of the alcoholism within the individual (Jellinek, 1960), and the adjustment process of the family to alcoholism (Jackson, 1954).

Appropriate assessment of alcoholism and staging of treatment should include a clear understanding of the following points:

1. In what life cycle stage is the individual who is drinking? An adolescent drinker represents different family dynamics and requires different treatment approaches than an elderly drinker, for instance.

2. In which generation of the family is the individual who drinks (grandparent, parent, child) *and* in what stage of the life cycle is the family this drinker is affecting?

3. What is the time lapse between the onset of the early warning signals of alcoholism and the presentation of the family for treatment? How many life cycle phases have occurred since drinking began and how have they been or not been resolved?

4. In what stage of alcoholism is the individual drinker? Jellinek (1960) identifies three phases of progression of alcoholism: the prodromal, middle, and chronic phases. Briefly, the prodomal phase is characterized by increased tolerance for alcohol, preoccupation with drinking, using alcohol for effect, and personality changes after a few drinks. The middle stage is characterized by blackouts, inability consistently to predict drinking behavior, drinking alone, more marked personality changes, increased physical and psychological dependence including early symptoms of withdrawal, and increased rationalization or denial about drinking. Finally, the late stage is characterized by job loss, social isolation, medical problems, moral and ethical deterioration, irrational thinking, extreme mood swings, vague fear, anxiety, paranoia, decreased tolerance for alcohol, and frequent or constant inebriation. Are there physical symptoms present and will medical treatment be required to deal with potential complications of withdrawal? Is the alcoholic sober or still actively drinking? (A system in which there is a sober alcoholic is still an alcoholic system.)

5. In what phase of adjustment or adaptive response to drinking is the family? Joan Jackson (1954) suggests some of the following sequence of reactions to a drinking problem on the family's part. While her model is based on a family in which the husband is the drinker, the adaptive responses outlined can be somewhat generalized to a family in which any member drinks.

a. Strained marital interaction in response to drinking—tendency to minimize or avoid problems not related to drinking.

b. Increasing social isolation of family—family interaction becomes more reactive, interaction becomes "organized" around drinking behavior. Marital adjustment deteriorates. As self-esteem is eroded, attempts to control drinker or to "keep the family going" intensify. Children adopt dysfunctional roles.

c. Family behavior swings to an opposite extreme as attempts to control

the drinker are abandoned and responses become geared toward relief of tension. Children may exhibit acting-out or disturbed behavior while the spouse becomes highly anxious about his or her own ability to function adequately. He or she feels "to blame" for the drinking.

d. Spouse becomes responsible for all functional and parental tasks and the drinker is no longer viewed as a responsible adult member of the family. The family now tends to protect and "feel sorry for" the drinker. The spouse becomes more confident in his or her ability to manage the family and a new family organization evolves that is geared toward minimizing the disruptive influence of the drinker. The drinker and spouse may or may not separate. Whether or not they do, when and if the alcoholic becomes sober and attempts to reestablish his or her role in the family, the family experiences difficulty in reorganizing and accepting the new roles required by sobriety.

These questions provide the clinician with a means of assessing the ways in which the family and the individual have adapted and changed in response to drinking and the ways in which the drinking is influenced by stresses related to normal developmental change in the family. They define the specific stage of the drinking behavior within the context of family development.

Treatment based on an understanding of these factors may occur in one of three phases which we define as follows:

• Presobriety: the drinker is still actively drinking and the family functions in a state of sustained crisis that intensifies as the drinking progresses. Interactional patterns in the family usually become more rigid and extreme. Family members assume roles that are reactive and survival oriented. Social isolation intensifies and increasing inability to negotiate and resolve developmental transitions occurs. The predominant characteristic of the family in this phase is a dysfunctional complementarity of role behavior in which one or more family members overfunction or are overresponsible while the drinker becomes increasingly underresponsible. Treatment goals in this phase include reducing the isolation and rigidifying of family boundaries through referral to AA programs and other community resources, addressing the rigid complementarity of role behavior by reducing the overresponsibility in key family members, and motivating the drinker to achieve abstinence preferably in an alcoholism rehabilitation program or in AA. Other family problems become secondary in this treatment phase and cannot be effectively addressed while drinking continues. Little effective work on family problems can take place while interaction continues to be distorted by the presence of alcohol in the system, in much the same way that marital problems are unlikely to be resolved while the continued presence of an extramarital affair is permitted.

• Adjustment to sobriety: Once the alcoholic has achieved sobriety, the family and the drinker face the "crisis" of sobriety. This phase may continue for six months to two years after sobriety is achieved. General treatment goals involve helping the family to stabilize itself in response to the radical unbalancing represented by sobriety. It is important to keep reactivity within the

family to a minimum. Primary issues to be addressed involve encouraging differentiation and self-focus for the spouses rather than focus on marital interaction, and helping to restructure previously dysfunctional roles assumed in terms of parenting. Intensified resentment on the part of spouse and children, and potential depression, acting out, or shift of symptomatic behavior to another family member should be predicted and explained. The family should be helped to understand the changes and dynamics that are normal consequences of the shift to sobriety.

• Maintenance of sobriety: This phase occurs after about two years of maintained sobriety. The family is typically now stabilized enough to encourage a rebalancing of the interactional extremes that occurred before sobriety. The ultimate goal is to shift family dynamics in a way that will prevent a relapse to drinking or symptoms in other family members. The family must be helped to understand how drinking functioned to help avoid or distort interactional conflicts and issues of power, dependency, and sex-role conflict in the family.

CHARACTERISTIC ISSUES AT SPECIFIC LIFE CYCLE STAGES

Although a general understanding of staging and treatment phases provides an overall context for approaching the alcoholic family, alcoholics and related family members present particular issues at various life cycle points that are useful to bear in mind. Our discussion of these categories is based on the concept of life cycle stages already outlined in previous chapters and our intention is to highlight specific developmental tasks and treatment goals as they relate to specific life cycle stages.

THE UNATTACHED YOUNG ADULT

The major task at this life cycle phase is that of the differentiation of self from one's family of origin. The degree to which this task is completed will profoundly influence subsequent life choices.

The presence of alcoholism in a family—in whatever generation—complicates the task of differentiation for all family members. Family boundaries are often either too rigid or too diffuse, roles are frequently reversed or otherwise inappropriate, and dysfunctional triangles are activated and shifted depending on whether the system is in a dry phase or a wet phase (Berenson, 1976). If the alcoholism is advanced and the family is in an advanced stage of reorganization around the alcohol, cutoff and isolation from both extended family and the

community are prevalent. The alcoholism is frequently a secret, as are violence, incest, and other potential complications of the alcoholism.

It is in this dysfunctional family environment that the young adult has spent some of his or her formative years and it is from this dysfunctional family system that he or she must differentiate. The problem is that, at best, he or she may have developed the skills to survive within the family system without having developed the skills to separate from it.

Where alcoholism is found in the young adult's family of origin, one of three potential solutions to the problems of differentiation tends to predominate. The individual may become alcoholic or otherwise addicted himself or herself, assuming a pseudodifferentiated stance; he or she may perpetuate a family role of overresponsible functioning and marry an alcoholic; or he or she may simply become cut off from the family emotionally.

The effects of growing up in an alcoholic system influence the young adult's adaptations and coping skills throughout the life cycle and are obviously not confined to the early adult years. Treatment during this particular life stage, however, may help significantly to restore the individual's capacity to negotiate adequately the developmental stages that follow.

When the young adult in treatment is abusing alcohol or drugs, it is important to suggest a period of abstinence even if it is not clear that the drinking or drug problem has progressed to actual addiction.

Since alcoholism distorts both thinking and affect, and alcoholic drinking frequently supports a pseudoindependent stance or image of self, drinking cannot help but complicate the process of differentiation. The achievement of the tasks of this age—occupational choice, choice of future partner, and solidification of a sense of identity—requires skills that alcohol abuse renders unusable or unobtainable.

Once abstinence from alcohol is achieved, work on differentiation issues may proceed as it would in other clinical situations with family-of-origin coaching (Carter & Orfanidis, 1976) being a primary focus of treatment. Various writers (Woititz, 1983; Black, 1982) have commented on the characteristic "loss of childhood" that dominates the personality development of the child who grows up in an alcoholic system. As an adult such an individual may experience emotional isolation, a fear of intimacy, and a tendency to react passively rather than act in his or her own self-interest.

Consequently both the alcohol-abusing young adult and his or her nondrinking counterpart frequently have either over- or underfunctioned in their family of origin, and unless disrupted, these patterns of over- and underresponsibility may perpetuate themselves into his or her new family and set the stage for alcoholism in future generations. This role reciprocity of over- and underresponsibility is a key dynamic in alcoholic systems, and part of treatment for the young adult in either category is to restore more self-focused, self-responsible behavior.

It is important to be aware that adults who have grown up in an alcoholic family become alcoholic, marry alcoholics, and produce alcoholics at an

alarming rate, and that they have frequently been the victims of incest or physical abuse (Black, 1982; Herman, 1981; Kempe & Helfer, 1972). In our clinical experience, they are more likely than other groups to develop eating disorders, phobias, depressive problems, and addictions to other drugs.

Having experienced intense dysfunction in their families and a distorted sense of self as a result, most adult children of alcoholics are tenaciously unaware that alcoholism had a significant influence in their lives. Denial and an intense pride or defensiveness tend to block an acknowledgment of the influence of parental drinking. The very defenses that enabled the adult child to survive eventually block the accomplishment of adult relational tasks.

One 26-year-old phobic woman in treatment described the profound distortion of roles and reality characteristic of most alcoholic homes. When she was ten, her mother lined her and her siblings against a wall to question them about the breaking of a vase. As each child responded in turn, the intoxicated mother slapped the child in the face. Later that afternoon all the children played in the backyard as if nothing had happened. No one talked about the incident.

In the present an alcoholic brother fell and injured himself seriously. The parents stood by helplessly while the client took her brother to the hospital. The next day the parents ignored the doctor's diagnosis that their son had an alcohol problem and sat down to their before-dinner cocktails as usual. Part of the issue in treatment for the client herself, apart from dealing with the problems of the overresponsible, parental role she has assumed in the family, is her inability to accept that her parents are alcoholic. To the degree that she cannot, she will continue to have a distorted, dysfunctional view of herself and her own role and responses within the family.

The daughter's genogram illustrates some of the potential intergenerational patterns that may occur in alcoholic systems.

Both the father's parents were nondrinking whereas both the father and sibling became alcoholic. The mother's father was alcoholic. In the father's family, overfunctioning and rigidity on the parental level resulted in underfunctioning of both males. In the mother's family, one daughter became an overfunctioner and her two siblings became alcoholic. For the daughter herself and her siblings, there tended to be an alternating sequence to the occurrence of over- and underresponsible roles.

In general, in families where one or both parents are alcoholic, it is typical for oldest children, especially oldest female children, to assume the overfunctioning role. In the father's family in this case, the complementarity of overfunctioning by parents versus underfunctioning in children was extreme— neither child assumed an overresponsible role. In the mother's family, however, note that the oldest male became alcoholic and the oldest daughter became the overfunctioner. Her sister, the patient's mother, responded by underfunctioning, and became alcoholic as well. In the third generation, the oldest son (patient's oldest brother) has assumed an overresponsible role, and as the oldest daughter, the patient stepped into this role as her older brother became less involved with the family. In general gender and birth order affect patterns

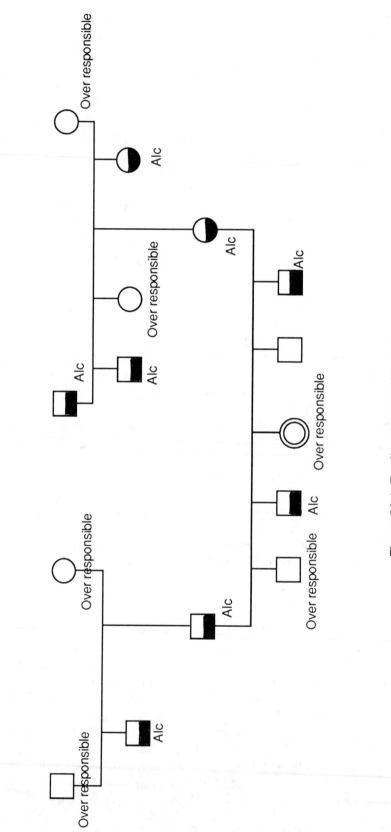

Figure 20-1. Family patterns with alcohol abuse.

of over- and underresponsibility—females primarily become the overresponsible emotional caretakers in families, unless the male is a first-born or the timing of the alcoholism and the triangulation surrounding it has its primary impact developmentally on a male child born at a later point in the family's history. Both males and females may respond to the pressures of the overresponsibility. One could make the generalization that the person in the predominately underresponsible role probably begins drinking in early life cycle phases such as adolescence whereas the person in the overresponsible role typically starts drinking later in life as a response to responsibilities and pressures imposed by the added demands of developmental stresses in his or her own adult life.

The treatment of young adults in alcoholic family systems can be conceptualized as assuming two phases. In the first it is crucial to encourage what may be viewed as a linear nonsystemic process in which the client is helped to experience and express the profound anger and despair that are an inevitable part of growing up in an alcoholic home. Affective experience must be dealt with in treatment because a purely cognitive approach perpetuates the process of having feelings deadened or ignored that is characteristic of the alcoholic system itself. The adult child must move emotionally through a grieving process to an acceptance of the particular degree of parental limitation imposed by alcoholic drinking.

Second, a focus on responsibility for self must be encouraged through a more systemic approach, including coaching of new role behaviors and the encouragement of a more cognitive understanding of family roles and dynamics. The young adult needs to learn new skills for achieving intimacy, to develop a more realistic appraisal of personality strengths and limitations, and to achieve a more functional balance with regard to the tendency to be either over- or underresponsible.

THE NEW COUPLE

As McGoldrick suggests in Chapter 5 of the first edition, the major pitfalls for couples at this phase of the life cycle are an expectation of Utopia, boundary problems with extended family, and a tendency to "triangle" to stabilize the marital relationship by an overfocus on a third person or issue, including alcohol.

Alcohol use is a frequent regulator of such issues as closeness and distance in the couple. Alcoholism interferes with the formation of appropriate boundaries both between the partners and between the couple and other parts of the system. Alcoholism also distorts the formation of appropriate roles and rules within the marriage. Therefore, alcohol abuse powerfully interferes with tasks at this phase of the life cycle and the interactional sequences that form around

the alcohol use set the stage for the inability to resolve later issues of difference, power, and intimacy.

When couples seek marital counseling during the first few years of their marriage, drinking is frequently mentioned as a problem, and as the cause of conflict, but alcoholism and the implications of a diagnosis of alcoholism are often rigidly denied. If alcoholism is overtly and quickly accepted as a significant factor in marital dysfunction, the prognosis for resolution either through achievement of sobriety or divorce is good. However, it is much more typical that intense denial continues to block therapeutic progress. Marital relationships affected by alcoholism may be characterized by intense symmetrical conflict, competitiveness, a high degree of overt or covert dependency on the part of both spouses, and extreme imbalances of role complementarity such that one partner overfunctions for the other partner, who underfunctions. A typical presenting problem when the couple seeks treatment is marital infidelity. Even if problem drinking is identified as a source of concern, it is typical that an affair is perceived as more problematic and upsetting. It is important to note that in marriages where either one or both partners are children of an alcoholic parent, similar dynamics may occur in the marriage even if there is no alcoholic drinking present.

Alcohol frequently functions in a marriage to regulate or suppress conflict regarding sex-role behavior. Expectations of self and partner regarding appropriate expressions of "maleness" and "femaleness" are heightened by the necessity to evolve rules regarding role functioning early in a marriage.

Although there appears to be a trend in today's society toward the acceptance of more androgynous, nontraditional sex-role behavior, with men assuming caretaking functions for children and more women entering the work force (Romer, 1981, Travis, 1977), the more traditional views of sex-role functioning continue to be strongly reinforced by many families. Couples who appear to have adopted more nontraditional expectations of sex-role functioning often revert to more stereotyped male and female role definitions after the birth of a first child (Romer, 1981).

The relevance of an individual's notions of appropriate sex-role behavior to a discussion of alcoholism and the family life cycle is that alcohol use can function to allow the individual to suppress or express impulses that contradict a prevalent notion of what constitutes acceptable male or female behavior. For instance, if a woman has learned that the expression of anger or direct attempts to assert power are unfeminine, alcohol may function to allow these impulses in a face-saving way. For a male, drinking may permit dependency or emotionality that would be unacceptable in terms of stereotyped notions of masculine behavior if acted out in a sober state.

In this sense alcohol abuse represents a commentary on constrictions that are imposed by the larger social context, and it also seriously distorts the process of differentiation in terms of the individual's ability to evolve a clear sense of his or her own behavioral preferences and sex-role identity. Neither partner operating under these assumptions of traditional sex-role constraints

is free to express more "masculine" or more "feminine" aspects of his or her personality. A marriage in which this type of confusion is operating is predictably conflicted and it is common that the couple fails to evolve a functional structure for dealing with the demands and constraints of family life because clear communication or awareness of actual needs and feelings is distorted.

Treatment of the couple with an alcohol problem is complex and is influenced significantly by the nondrinking spouse's denial and evolving sense of inadequacy. Primary steps in treatment involve the drinker's achieving abstinence from drinking, helping the spouse to "hit bottom" (that is, to experience his or her despair at being powerless to affect or change the drinker's behavior despite extreme overfunctioning), coaching the spouse to give up overfunctioning for the drinker, and eventually, once stable sobriety has been achieved, helping the couple to acquire new skills that will permit intimacy, clear role definitions, and enhanced capacity for conflict resolution.

THE FAMILY WITH YOUNG CHILDREN

Problem drinking does exist in young children although, there is inattention to this age group in the literature. One study found 3% of second-grade children and 8% of third-grade children had been drunk at least once and some had experienced hangovers (Rice, 1982).

When the family with young children presents itself for treatment, however, it is more typical that the presenting problem reflects parental alcoholism. It is estimated that 15 million school-age children (Booz-Allen & Hamilton, 1974) are affected by parental alcoholism and a high percentage of school-related problems may have alcoholism implicated as a determining factor. The role of maternal alcoholism in the etiology of intellectual, physical, and academic disabilities in children has become prominent as a research issue, the Seattle Research of 1969–1972. The components of fetal alcohol syndrome include mental deficiency, growth deficiency, and altered morphogenesis. The syndrome is easily recognized at birth (Streissguth, 1976). Alcoholic families with young children are often referred by other agencies for school problems, learning disability, delinquency, neglect, or abuse, or they are self-referred with a focus on either marital dysfunction or difficulties related to the child's behavior. In either case the presence of parental alcoholism should always be assessed.

One of the most tragic effects of parental alcoholism on young children is that it robs them of childhood (Black, 1982). One of the functions of family life is to guarantee the child emotional and physical safety and an environment within which normal developmental tasks can be completed. Alcoholism, whether in a sibling or a parent, distorts normal family processes, skews family roles (Wegscheider, 1981; Black, 1982), often parentifying the children,

and creates a climate in which fear, anger, mistrust, guilt, and sadness prevail. Wegscheider (1981) identifies four roles that children assume—hero, scapegoat, lost child, or mascot. Black (1982) breaks down children's roles to include the "responsible one," the "adjustor," and the "placator." Each role generally identifies either an over or underresponsible pattern of behavior that represents the child's attempt to address the disorganization and emotional inconsistency of the family environment. Normal dependency needs of children go unmet, and the child may experience a sense of chronic grief and loss that manifests itself in depression and a sense of being "different" or isolated from others.

Sexual abuse and both battering and neglect may be the common experiences of the child in the alcoholic home. Black (1982) asserts that over 50% of known incest victims lived in alcoholic homes, and in various studies (Korcok, 1979; Behling, 1979; *New York Times*, 1974) 69% of reported cases of battering and neglect were related to alcohol abuse. The alcoholic family tends to be alcohol focused rather than child focused. While children in such families may respond with acting-out or delinquent behavior, it is more often the case that they become highly compliant, quiet, and withdrawn, and thus tend to go unrecognized by school authorities or other professionals.

While it is typically perceived that the damage to young children is more intense if the drinker is the mother, this perception often reflects social bias regarding drinking as being more deviant for women than for men. The effects of drinking and the adaptive behaviors evolved by the spouse in response to drinking tend to create damaging interactional patterns that may be equally intense whether the drinker is the mother or the father. Current studies fail to differentiate adequately between the effects of maternal and paternal drinking (Williams & Klerman, 1984) and one study (McLachlan et al., 1973) indicated that children were more negatively affected by the presence of an actively drinking father than by either a recovered or unrecovered mother.

The birth of a first child is commonly a stressful life cycle event that may set the stage for alcoholic drinking. Parents frequently feel trapped by and ill equipped to deal with the responsibilities of child rearing. As noted previously, the birth of a child may arouse sex-role conflict that was more easily resolved when caretaking functions were not a part of the marriage. Distance tends to increase between partners when a child demands attention and drinking often represents either spouse's attempt to cope with increased feelings of isolation or decreased feelings of adequacy related to parenting.

When treating the family in which young children are affected by alcoholism, primary goals should include the following:

Before Sobriety

1. Validate the child's feelings of anger, fear, and loss—address the child's fear that he or she is responsible for the problem—educate the child about alcoholism.

2. Encourage the drinking parent to assume more of the parenting responsibility but track behavior carefully to ensure that the child is not being treated punitively or abusively. In some cases, depending on the severity of the drinking, the parent may resume or assume some effective role with the child. If he or she fails, the therapist can use this fact for leverage to point out that drinking is affecting his or her ability to parent adequately and can make a strong case for the need for abstinence.

After Sobriety

1. Teach parenting skills and help the parents to repair the damage done by the absence of nurturing of the children that occurred before sobriety.

2. Help the family as a whole to adjust to the role losses and gains that are seen with sobriety. For instance, if a child has been functioning as a surrogate spouse and parent, the parent's resumption of his or her appropriate role will displace the child. The child in this instance loses both the special emotional relationship with the nondrinking parent and the adult status he or she enjoyed. Depression or acting-out behavior may be a result.

3. Continue to validate the children's anger and hurt even if denied. Help the family to achieve the ability to be more responsive emotionally without the need for dysfunctional and rigid rules dictated by perceived needs for power and control.

THE FAMILY WITH ADOLESCENTS

It is common that an inherent dysfunction in family structure fails to emerge until children reach adolescence. Often inappropriate rules, boundary violations, triangling, and conflicts between spouses can be sustained and the family can operate with a certain tenuous equilibrium until adolescent problems and challenges to the hierarchical rules of the family emerge.

In this phase alcoholism or alcohol abuse may present as a problem either in the adolescent or in the parental generation. Often the two are correlated. A study by Jessor and Jessor (1975) found that alcohol use by parents increases the chances of alcohol use by both sons and daughters and that parents have a greater influence on the drinking habits of girls than of boys. Some clinical evidence suggests that an adolescent daughter's drinking, related as it may be to sexual promiscuity and unplanned pregnancy, often has more disruptive effects on the family than a son's drinking behavior and is a more frequent precipitant for a family's decision to seek therapy (Williams & Kleman, 1984). Sex of the drinking parent in the study cited earlier (McLachlan, et al., 1973) appears to have more effect on the quality of the parent–child relationship specifically than on the general personality characteristics or drinking

behavior of the adolescent male or female. In general, in this study, adolescents were less affected by maternal drinking than by a drinking father. Miller and Lang (1977) found, however, that as adults, sons were heavier drinkers than daughters despite the sex of the parental drinker, but that daughters tended to drink more heavily if the mother had been alcoholic.

The intensely demanding nature of adolescent behavior and the emergence of separateness and difference in the family all serve to seriously threaten a parent's sense of adequacy, and may rekindle identity conflicts unresolved in his or her own adolescence. Certainly issues concerned with response to authority, autonomy, and sexuality begin to dominate family life during this phase. This period, with its attendant anticipation of separation and change in the family, is, clinically, the most frequently identified phase during which parental drinking is reported to have become problematic (Rouse, 1981). Adolescent drinking during this period often represents the child's intense conflict about separation, sexuality, and sex-role adequacy (Wilsnack, 1977)

Young people are drinking at ever-increasing rates (Blane and Hewitt, 1977). Some studies indicate per capita consumption rates to be increasing even faster than rates of use are increasing in adults (U.S. Dept. Health, Education & Welfare, 1974). Parental influences on adolescent drinking are complex and multilevel (Zucker, 1976). The sociocultural environment has consistently been found to be highly significant as a determinant of adolescent alcohol abuse (O'Leary et al., 1976; Kamback et al., 1977; Schuster, 1976).

Adolescent alcohol abuse is also more highly correlated with other drug abuse (Royce, 1981) and is less likely to represent physiological addiction. This latter observation raises questions about whether abstinence is a necessary treatment goal for all adolescent abusers (Coyle & Fisher, 1977). In view of the prevalence of heavy drinking behavior in adolescence, differential diagnosis is much more difficult than it is for other age groups.

If the adolescent alcohol abuser presents as a problem and alcohol abuse is ruled out in the parents, it is highly likely that there was alcoholism in either of the parents' families of origin. Frequently, however, the parents are active or recovering alcoholics themselves.

The major choice that needs to be made regarding treatment direction for the adolescent abuser is that between coaching the parents to totally back off and leave the full responsibility for consequences of the chemical abuse, once the youngster is educated, on the adolescent, versus coaching the parents to take full responsibility for the adolescent's abuse (Haley, 1980: Stanton et al., 1982), including forcing him or her into treatment involuntarily.

For instance, in one case, Mary, a single parent, had four adolescent children, all of whom were involved with alcohol and drugs. The daughter in question, Joan, had been admitted to a number of treatment programs unsuccessfully and had been hospitalized a number of times for detoxification and drug overdose. Mary's response in each case was to become highly anxious, overinvolved, and, consequently, to prevent the daughter from ever experiencing the consequences of her drinking. She continually bailed the daughter out

by giving her money, taking her back, and in general, accepting responsibility for all the daughter's irresponsible behavior. Mary was coached slowly and consistently to back off to the point where eventually she was not even involved in arranging Joan's last admission to a treatment program.

Joan managed to stay sober for six months, but during a slip one day, vomited, aspirated and died. Although the outcome of this particular case was ultimately negative, the six-month period of sobriety was the most prolonged that Joan had experienced since the onset of drinking. It appeared evident that, in this situation, Mary's disengagement from her overresponsible position represented a shift that established the optimum likelihood of change in the system given the history of failure related to her previous overfunctioning. Joan's age (19), Mary's status as a single parent with no involvement with the child's biological father or supportive parent surrogate and the history of repeated hospitalization, were all factors that indicated a backing-off approach.

In another case the parents of Susan, a 15-year-old adolescent, were coached to arrange admission to a treatment program after a session in which both parents jointly agreed that Susan must have inpatient alcoholism treatment and that they, and not she, would control where she would be admitted. Susan's bags were packed and she was taken to the program directly from the therapy session. She continues to be sober two years later.

There is no hard and fast rule other than clinical judgment that determines which course to follow. Age of the adolescent and history of prior attempts at treatment are important factors. In some less extreme cases where alcohol or drug abuse is in its early stages, it is effective to coach parents to be firmer in their parenting and limit setting based on age-appropriate expectations for the adolescent, while backing off in terms of their overfocus and overresponsibility for decisions that are appropriately left to the adolescent. One mother, for instance, had set exceedingly rigid limits for her adolescent son, and at age 17 he was not allowed to make judgments about what curfew would be appropriate and she kept his savings in her account to help him control how he spent his money. She was coached to help him to be more responsible for himself by making his decisions about curfews, savings, and school performance, while she made very clear what consequences would be imposed for evidence of his further abuse of drugs or alcohol. Eventually, as their communication and his sense of independence improved, the substance abuse receded.

As a general operating principle, it is important to remember that extreme overresponsibility in the parent will typically result in extreme underresponsibility, including abuse of alcohol or drugs, in the adolescent. The fine line between appropriate responsibility for the feelings and behavior of the child is often difficult to pinpoint. It is crucial that the therapist be comfortable with, clear about, and consistent in whichever approach he or she takes, as well as willing to weather the crises that will inevitably arise in the course of treatment.

One of the major determinants of this choice, finally, is whether or not

parental alcoholism does exist or has existed. If the parent is actively drinking, the parental alcoholism must be addressed, along with the adolescent alcoholism. If the parent is either a recovering alcoholic (sober) or an active one, it is likely that any limit setting done with the adolescent will be ineffective without the reparative nurturing mentioned earlier, and without permitting the adolescent verbally to express his or her anger at the parents for the parental alcoholism.

Many problems of adolescence, including anorexia, bulimia, school-related disorders, and unplanned pregnancies, mask parental alcoholism. Although the presenting problem must be treated, and can sometimes be treated without treating the alcoholic parent, the adolescent problem should not be treated without acknowledging the alcoholism of the system. This means that even if the alcoholic does not acknowledge a problem or achieve sobriety, dealing with the alcoholism with the spouse and significant others, and acknowledging the pain the parental alcholism causes the adolescent, should always be part of the treatment plan. It is important to confront the spouse with his or her role in maintaining the other parent's alcoholism. The role shift that is required of family members after the alcoholic achieves sobriety can be particularly problematic for the adolescent.

Debbie, an attractive 17-year-old and middle child who achieved average grades in school and was popular with her peers, came into therapy because of a highly conflicted relationship with her mother, Roberta, who had entered AA and achieved sobriety when Debbie was 12. Before that Debbie had developed good autonomy skills, and never required much attention from Roberta or Roberta's second husband, Hank, also an alcoholic. The home was characterized by an absence of parenting rather than actual neglect or abuse. When Roberta and Hank became sober, they were exceedingly concerned to be good parents. Roberta inconsistently tried to set very firm limits with Debbie. The setting of limits, however, coincided with Debbie's entry into adolescence, a time when she should have had increased autonomy, not less. Since she had had more than usual autonomy prior to Roberta's sobriety, and since she had not had appropriate nurturing and still longed for it from her mother, the adolescent dilemma of wanting to be a baby and an adult at the same time was highly exacerbated by the shift in the family rules subsequent to sobriety.

LAUNCHING CHILDREN AND MOVING ON

This phase typically takes place when parents are in their mid-40s to mid-60s and is commonly referred to as the "empty nest" phase. It is a stage that begins with the departure of the children from the home and ends with the couple living alone in preretirement. Vast changes are seen in the family during this time, with some members leaving (marriage, college, death) and new members entering (in-laws, children).

The impact of alcoholism is significant in this period because, in re-establishing themselves as a marital dyad, a couple is forced to face issues that may not have been resolved earlier in the marriage. Alcoholic drinking may represent an attempt to avoid these issues, it may replace children as a triangle in the marriage, or it may be the case that having been tolerated earlier, drinking now becomes a focus of concern to the nondrinking spouse. Changes in the expectations of or needs to avoid intimacy often occur at this stage and, in general, the equilibrium formerly evolved in the relationship changes radically. While a high degree of fusion (Bowen, 1978) may be tolerable in a relationship when children are present, it tends to become more intense and, consequently, less tolerable with the children gone. Midlife also forces most couples to cope with the death of parents and loss of extended family supports.

A 56-year-old man, a prominent architect, was court ordered to seek therapy with his 50-year-old wife due to his physical abuse of her. It was clear from the outset that he had been drinking alcoholically for 15–20 years. They had four children, the youngest of whom was 17.

The onset of the abuse seemed related to the wife's attempt to change the marital power balance. John, who was very angry about the court-ordered therapy, was clear with the therapist about his expectations. "In any situation there has to be a leader. Yes, ma'am, and I am the leader and I always will be."

John's wife, however, had begun to assert herself and to challenge John's alcoholism. When the therapist asked her about the precipitant of her desire to change the rules, she said, "It is more apparent to me because the kids are grown up and gone."

While the onset of problematic drinking may have been much earlier, midlife is the stage at which both men and women are most likely to seek help for alcohol-abuse problems (Collier, 1982). Differences between male and female drinkers have been ill defined and not thoroughly researched, but again, sex-role-related conflicts and differences tend to be important determinants of drinking behavior.

Estimates of the prevalence of women alcoholics as compared with men range from one in five to one in one (Schuckit, 1976; Homiller, 1977; Sandmaier, 1977). Most studies indicate that women's alcohol abuse has increased over the past ten years (McCrady, 1982) and that women tend to relate the onset of their drinking to specific life stresses more than men do (Curlee, 1969). There has also been a tendency to connect alcoholism in women with physiological changes such as those associated with gynecological problems and menopause (Wilsnack, 1973; Beckman, 1977). These changes also include children leaving home, death of a parent, and marital problems, all typical issues of midlife.

Other common findings that are clinically significant include the fact that depression is more commonly associated with alcoholism in women, as is concomitant use of other drugs, and that men leave alcoholic women more than women leave alcoholic men (Fraser, 1973). From clinical observation it appears to be the case that husbands of alcoholics rarely seek help for the wife's drinking and that this tendency to deny the problem or to act protec-

tively toward the wife is more typical of husbands than of wives of alcoholic husbands. Fox (1956) finds that husbands of female alcoholics tend to be less patient and accepting of the wife's problem than is true of a wife of a male alcoholic. These differences reflect social biases and constraints (depression is a "woman's" disease, women are more frequently tranquilized by doctors than men are, and men are more economically capable of leaving a marriage).

In any case it appears that economic and physiological factors affect patterns of drinking between women and men, and that as social constraints have changed, different patterns of drinking may emerge. Women are more on the edge of social change and, consequently, may experience more changes in terms of the function of alcohol in their lives. As one writer (Ellis, 1984) describes the problem, "The nurturing instinct dies hard. We are conditioned entirely by our own 1950's view of how things must be done. We are trying to develop our new lives within the framework of [providing] continuing support systems for husband, homes, far flung children and aging parents. In many cases, husbands are talking retirement as we edge toward the starting gate . . ." It is at midlife that differences in expectations regarding role functioning and in personal needs may become most apparent in a marriage. The couple needs to be helped to adapt to change without the need for alcohol. In many instances couples need help to acknowledge irreconcilable differences as well as the possibility that the marriage is unworkable.

ALCOHOLISM AND DIVORCE

Divorce is a frequent result of alcoholism and, particularly for women, may be an antecedent of alcoholism as well. Clinically it appears that divorce occurs most often not while drinking is active, but in the early stages of sobriety when the reaction to the removal of alcohol as a stabilizer in the marriage is most intense. Available studies report a higher rate of divorce and separation among female alcoholics. Divorced women, as well as men, experience increased risk of developing alcohol problems. From clinical impression it appears that the life cycle phase in which divorce is most likely to occur is that in which the family is coping with the adolescent children. It may be the case that the acute stress on the family of this life cycle phase, as well as the tendency for alcoholism, particularly in men, peaks at midlife.

THE FAMILY IN LATER LIFE

Although alcoholism in any generation affects all generations, this discussion is confined primarily to the impact of alcoholism on the elderly person and the problems it may pose for younger relatives.

The 65-and-over age group is the fastest growing in American life as longevity increases and the effects of postwar increases in birth rates become more apparant. In this life phase, both the older adult and other family members must adapt to the shifting of power from older to younger family members. Loss is a concurrent and equally important theme. The middle generation faces the loss of parents through death or impaired functioning. The older generation faces multiple changes that may involve loss of role status, of physical and mental capacity, of work identity in retirement, of power and, most affect-laden, of spouse or partner.

In general a growing isolation from family and peer supports tends to characterize the elderly and this isolation could be defined as the major problem affecting the older person's adjustment to this life phase. These problems tend to be compounded by social patterns in which the difficulties of the aged are often ignored. Alcoholism in the elderly appears to be a growing problem and a frequent response to it on the part of the medical and mental-health professions and family members reflects a pessimism that suggests that the best solution is to ignore it.

Esther, an 80-year-old widow, living in a retirement village for "seniors," started keeping company with Pete, three years her senior, after her husband's death. Lunch on Sundays progressed to a situation in which Pete effectively moved in with Esther. One day she called her neighbor, distraught. Pete was on the floor, apparently in convulsions. The neighbor called an ambulance and Pete was taken to the nearest emergency room. The hospital released Pete with a diagnosis of alcoholism, but failed to make any attempt to arrange treatment. Esther went to the manager of the retirement village to ask whether he could help her find a nursing home or other help for Pete. He not only was unwilling to help, but informed Esther that she was violating the rules of the retirement village by having an unmarried man living with her, and would be evicted if the situation continued.

Estimates of prevalence of alcoholism in the elderly are especially confusing. On the one hand, the two age peaks that some studies report in alcohol abuse are the 45–54 age group, with a rate of 23 per 1000 (Bozzetti & MacMurray, 1977; Pascarelli, 1974; Mishara & Kastenbaum, 1980) whereas Vaillant and others indicate a number of studies reporting a return to asymptomatic drinking or spontaneous abstinence in later life (Vaillant, 1983; Maletta, 1982). The confusion of alcoholism with the physical deterioration of the aging process, the underreporting of alcoholism in the elderly, (Royce, 1981; Maletta, 1982), the issue of polydrug abuse (Royce, 1981), and the fact of mortality (i.e., some alcholics do not live long enough to be counted in the statistics) all make prevalence estimates highly questionable.

Drinking may first become problematic for the elderly person in retirement, it may become exacerbated during this phase, or it may recede as a problem. As noted previously, alcohol may function to suppress conflicts related to changing role expectations in the marriage during this time, or it may function to help the older person cope with increasing feelings of isolation and the sense of inadequacy associated with a loss of role. Even if extended-family

members live nearby, less frequent contact with them, or an experience of having no meaningful part in their lives, may heighten the tendency to drink. Retirement or increasing physical incapacity may bring with it the expectation of a role reversal in which children are expected to become overresponsible for the parent. The middle-aged child may react to this expectation by distancing or cutting off, while the disappointment of this expectation may prompt further, underresponsible drinking behavior in the parent. Drinking tends to heighten the isolation that may have set it in motion. Family members tend to distance further from a drinking relative and the effects of the alcohol render the older person more and more physically incapable of functioning in social situations. While most family members would seek help for an acknowledged drinking problem in a younger member of the family, it is often the case that drinking in an older relative is tolerated because it is viewed as a hopeless situation.

It is useful to classify alcoholism of the elderly into two subgroups: (Maletta, 1982; Zimberg, 1978); early-onset alcoholism, defined as that beginning prior to age 65 and as having progressed since, and late-onset alcoholism, which began after age 65. The most distinctive feature of the early-onset drinker is the almost total social isolation that has occurred by age 65. Often the person in this category makes sudden unpredictable attempts to repair cutoffs.

Joan's father, who had deserted the family when she was 15 and who had been alcoholic as long as she could remember, made perhaps five or six phone calls to the family between 1960 and 1979. At Christmas 1979, he called her and asked for $25 toward his rent. In the fall of 1983, Joan sought therapy. Her father was placed in a Salvation Army flophouse after being taken off skid row with an ulcerated leg. He had contacted Joan and her mother and asked her mother, who had never divorced him, if he could live with her again. Her mother was considering taking him back despite the almost total lack of contact for 24 years.

This early-onset drinker was almost totally socially isolated, although, in his mind a tie remained with his family. Joan evaluated her relationship with her father and decided to have limited contact with him, but his wife did not take him back and he remained the community's responsibility. The isolation so many elderly people experience had been made almost total by his alcoholism.

The late-onset group is thought to be larger (Maletta, 1982) and is viewed as having a better prognosis. Drinking in this group is considered (Rosin & Glatt, 1971) to be related more specifically to the stresses of aging and is seen as more responsive to therapeutic attempts to relieve those stresses.

It is important for the clinician working with alcoholism to make a differential diagnosis between alcoholism accompanied by organic mental disorder and either organic mental disorder or alcoholism as an isolated condition (Maletta, 1982). Many of the effects of chronic alcohol abuse on intellectual functioning may be mistakenly attributed to organic brain disorder (Maletta,

1982). Use of alcohol also intensifies already existing somatic complaints and problems and consultation on these issues is advised.

There is also reason to believe that a considerable amount of alcoholism in the aged is iatrogenic (Blume, 1973); that is, alcoholism set in motion by a well-meaning physician who recommends alcohol as a tranquilizer.

Finally, abuse of the elderly has become a cause for concern in recent years. Abuse may involve outright physical violence, verbal assault, neglect, self-neglect, and financial exploitation. Some estimates indicate (Parness, 1984) that between 50% and 70% of reported cases of abuse involve alcoholism either in the older person or in the middle family generation having the greatest direct contact with the victim. While society may wish to ignore the issue of alcoholism and the elderly, alcohol use significantly affects the quality of life experienced by the elderly person. Even if the older person is not the drinker, alcohol may seriously disrupt the relationships between that person and other family members.

The approach to the elderly person who has an alcohol problem is to attempt to decrease isolation by helping the family to evolve solutions for providing the person with contact and support. The issue of who is responsible for what or whom must be dealt with, as should the emotional factors in the family related to loss, grief, and unresolved anger. Both the family and the older person need to make productive use of community supports, and it should never be assumed that referral to AA or Al-Anon is an unproductive suggestion because of the person's age. Some individuals may require detox-ification and medical treatment for the physiological consequences of abusive drinking. Many studies (Zimberg, 1978) suggest that group therapy is one effective modality for addressing the isolation of the older person, but cer-tainly family therapy has much to offer as a resource to families who experi-ence difficulty adjusting to this life phase.

GENERAL GUIDELINES FOR TREATMENT

(For a full description of the course of treatment, see Bepko with Krestan, 1985.)

1. Make a careful assessment of the degree to which drinking is a current problem or has affected the family in the two prior generations. For instance, in a young married couple, assess whether drinking has become problematic as a current issue in the marriage or whether the marital relationship is being influenced by the effects of parental alcoholism of one or both spouses.

2. If alcoholic drinking is a current problem in the family and is the primary focus of interaction, abstinence is crucial to the success of treatment.

The therapist must be attentive to the family's need, as well as the drinker's, to deny the seriousness of the problem. Therapist gullibility in terms of believing the family's reports about the extent of drinking and drinking-related dysfunction can be the greatest block to effective treatment. Abstinence is best achieved in AA with the family attending related family Al-Anon or Al-Ateen groups.

3. Four general concepts are important to effective treatment.

a. Educate the family about alcoholism—the family needs information to correct its misperceptions and to break through its denial. Refer to or consult with a trained alcoholism counselor if necessary.

b. Open the system up as much as possible by charting the degree to which drinking is a secret from other family members and by encouraging open discussion of the problem with other family members. Encourage participation in all outside resources available in the community for alcohol-involved families.

c. Assess and help the family to understand the ways in which alcoholism may have been a response to specific life cycle transitions or stresses within the family and/or the individual. A three-generational genogram and mapping of significant developmental blocks, prior coping patterns, and triangular interaction within the family are crucial. Assessment of the developmental phase at which drinking became problematic in a family can alert the therapist to family dynamics that need to be addressed *after sobriety is achieved*. For instance, it is often the case that sons of alcoholic males become alcoholic themselves. While inconclusive evidence points to a genetic basis for this phenomenon, it may also be true, for instance, that drinking in the son's parental system became problematic when the father was newly married and starting a family, indicating a difficulty adjusting to the role changes required by the developmental tasks of this life cycle phase. It is typical that, since the son of the alcoholic had no role model for developing his own idea of himself as a husband and father, abuse of alcohol becomes a likely solution for his own difficulty with this transition. If this developmental breakdown can be pinpointed generationally within the family, it gives direction to the therapist's work as he or she evaluates how the inability to resolve this life cycle phase for the drinker affects or intersects with the spouse's family patterns to create dysfunction that sustains a drinking problem. Clearly, work on sex-role behavior and an appropriate sense of responsibility are at issue in this type of family and a general focus postsobriety will involve the issues of this particular developmental phase.

d. Finally, the therapist must be alert to the medical needs of the alcoholic—late-middle- or end-stage drinking frequently requires medical detoxification and referral to an alcoholism treatment program is generally indicated.

4. The process of therapy involves, as outlined earlier under staging, three distinct phases. General guidelines for each phase include the following:

Presobriety

1. Deal with denial.
2. Help the drinker to achieve abstinence, optimally in AA.
3. Reverse patterns of over and under responsibility.

In this phase it is primarily important to have the major overfunctioner in the family "back off" or give up the overresponsible role in both the functional and emotional dimensions. Coach the spouse very specifically to accomplish this and track behavior carefully. A knowledge of triangles in the family is important since an overfunctioning spouse may give up his or her role only to have a second, typically an oldest child, step in. Anticipate resistance to the process of reversing overresponsibility but convince the family of its importance. All family members should be asked to make a commitment to attend at least six meetings of AA or Al-Anon. If the drinker does not achieve abstinence and leaves treatment, continue to work with other family members on issues of over- and underresponsibility.

Adjustment to Sobriety

The clinician's task in this phase is to stabilize the family around sobriety. The prior organization and role behaviors that the family assumed are no longer workable. Since sobriety is tenuous at this point, it is important to step down conflict and to encourage self-focus for each family member. Family members should be coached to operate in ways that address basic tasks of family functioning. Some work on parenting issues is important at this phase but marital issues generally should be avoided. It is important to help the family to anticipate resentment, disappointed expectations of sobriety, and loss of role that early sobriety may represent. Frequency of therapy may be lessened during this phase, particularly if a strong involvement with AA and Al-Anon is operative. Conditions under which more intensive therapy is indicated include (1) drug or alcohol involvement of a child, (2) severe depression of any family member, (3) physical abuse, (4) incest, or (5) insistence of either spouse on dealing with marital issues. In any of these cases, the therapist should predict for the family that relapse is likely to occur.

Maintenance of Sobriety

Once the family has made a stable adjustment to sobriety, preferably with AA and Al-Anon, the therapeutic task is to rebalance the system in ways that promote greater flexibility of role functioning and that allow family members to express feelings or behavior that were previously expressible only through

drinking. Additionally the therapist can work on helping the family to resolve developmental blocks that have arisen as a result of drinking or those that have created stresses for which drinking became a solution. Important issues in this phase include (1) sex-role concepts and behavior; (2) sexuality; (3) emotional intimacy; (4) issues of power, dependency, and control; (5) pride and perfectionism; (6) handling anger, accepting limitation; (7) achieving a "correct" interactional balance in which dependency is acknowledged and marital "bargains" in terms of complementarity in the relationship are overt and agreed to by both spouses.

Important Points to Keep in Mind

• Alcoholism has an intergenerational effect—do not assume that because drinking is not current in the system, the family is not affected by it.
• A drinker may not be currently drinking, but if drinking has been untreated (AA, a rehab or treatment program), presobriety or adjustment issues may need to be addressed and the family organization may be more characteristic of those early stages even if drinking has been stopped for a number of years. This often occurs in families where the drinker attended AA briefly and then stopped.
• Children who grow up in alcoholic homes have special needs, even as adults. Life cycle issues are crucial to assess and it is important to pinpoint the specific developmental stages at which drinking occurred in the parental system when working with children of alcoholics.
• Alcoholic families benefit most from treatment that is directive and provides information about the nature of alcoholism, its effects on the family, and concrete steps that can be taken by each family member to address it.

REFERENCES

Beckman, L. J. (1975). Women alcoholics: A review of social and psychological studies. *Journal of Studies on Alcohol*, 36:797–824.

Beckman, L. J. (1976), Alcoholism problems and women: An overview. In M. Greenblatt & M. A. Schuckit (Eds.), *Alcoholism problems in women and children*. New York: Grune & Stratton.

Behling (1979). Alcohol abuse as encountered in 51 instances of reported child abuse. *Clinical Pediatrics*, 18.

Bepko, C. with Krestan, J. A. (1985). *The responsibility trap: A blueprint for treating the alcoholic family*. New York: Free Press.

Berenson, D. (1976). Alcohol and the family system. In P. Guerin (Ed.), *Family therapy: Theory and practice*. New York: Gardner Press.

Black, C. (1982). *It will never happen to me*. Colorado: MAC.

Blane, H. T., Hewitt, L. E. (1977). Alcohol and youth: An analysis of the literature, 1960–

1975. NIAAA, Rockville, Md. (U.S. Dept of Commerce, National Technical Information Service, PB-268, 698).

Blume, S. B. (1973). Iatrongenic alcoholism. *Quarterly Journal of Studies on Alcoholism,* 34:1348–1352.

Booz-Allen & Hamilton, Inc. (1974). An assessment of the needs of and resources for children of alcoholic parents. NIAAA, Rockville, Md. (pp. 14c, 15).

Bozzetti, L. D., & MacMurray, J. P. (1977). Drug misuse among the elderly: A hidden menace. *Psychiatric Annals* 7:95–107.

Bowen, M. (1978). *Family therapy in clinical practice.* New York: Jason Aronson.

Carter, E., & Orfanidis, M. (1976). Family therapy with one person and the family therapist's own family. In P. Guerin (Ed.), *Family therapy: Theory and practice,* New York: Gardner Press.

Cahalan, D., Cisin, I. H., & Crossley, H. M. (1969). *American drinking practices: A national study of drinking behavior and attitudes.* New Brunswick, N.J.: Rutgers Center for Alcoholic Studies.

Collier, H. V. (1982). *Counseling women.* New York: Free Press.

Corrigan, E. M. (1980). *Alcoholic women in treatment.* New York: Oxford University Press.

Coyle, B., & Fischer, J. (1977). A young problem drinker's program as a means of establishing and maintaining treatment contact. In J. H. Madden, R. Walker, & W. H. Kenyon (Eds.), *Alcoholism and drug dependence—a multi disciplinary approach.* New York: Plenum, pp. 227–238.

Curlee, J. (1969). Alcoholism and the "empty nest." *Bulletin of Menninger Clinic,* 33:165–171.

Curlee, J. (1970. A comparison of male and female patients at an alcoholism treatment center. *Journal of Psychology,* 74: 239–247.

Deutsch, C. (1982). *Broken bottles, broken dreams.* New York: Teachers College Press, Columbia University.

Ellis, J. (1951). From work in progress based on lives of women at Vassar.

Fallup, C. (1974). The rising number of drinkers. *Washington Post* B2, June 10.

Fifeld, L., Latham, J. D., & Phillips, C. (1978). Alcoholism in the gay community: The price of alienation, isolation, and oppression. Sacramento, Calif. Division of Substance Abuse.

Fox, R. (1956). The alcoholic spouse. In V. W. Eisensteid (Ed.), *Neurotic interaction in marriage.* New York: Basic Books.

Fraser, J. (1973). The female alcoholic. *Addictions,* 20:64–80.

Greenblatt, M., & Schuckit, M. A. (Eds.) (1976). *Alcoholism problems in women and children.* New York: Grune & Stratton.

Haley, J. (1980). Drinking attitudes and behaviors among college students. *Journal of Alcoholic Drug Education,* 19:6–14.

Hawley, Richard A. (1983). *The purposes of pleasure.* Wellesley Hills, Mass.: The Independent School Press.

Herman, J. L., with Hirschman, L. (1981). *Father–daughter incest.* Cambridge, Mass.: Harvard University Press.

Homiller, J. D. (1977). *Women and alcohol: A guide for state and local decisionmakers.* Washington, D.C.: Alcohol and Drug Problems Association of North America.

Jackson, J. (1954). The adjustment of the family to the crisis of alcoholism. *Quarterly Journal of Studies on Alcohol,* 15 (4:562–586.

James, I. P. (1966). Blood alcohol levels following successful suicide. *Quarterly Journal of Studies on Alcohol* 2:23–29.

Jellinek, E. M. (1960). *The disease concept of alcoholism.* New Haven, Conn.: College and University Press.

Jessor, R., & Jessor, S. L. (1975). Adolescent development and the onset of drinking: A longitudinal study. *Journal of Studies on Alcohol* 36 (1):27–51.

Kamback, M. C., Bosma, W. G., & D'Lugoff, B. C. (1977). Family surrogates. The drug culture or the methadone maintenance program. *British Journal of Addiction,* 72:171–176.

Kempe, H., & Helfer, R. E. (1972). *Helping the battered child and his family*. New York: Lippincott.

Korcok, M. A. 81979). Alcoholism is a family affair. *Focus on alcohol and drug issues* 2:4.

Lawson, G., Peterson, J. S., & Lawson, A. (1983). *Alcoholism and the family*. Rockville, Md.: Aspen Systems Corporation.

Lisansky, E. S. (1957). "Alcoholism in women: Social and psychological concomitants: Social history data. *Quarterly Journal of Studies on Alcohol*, 18:588–623.

Lohrenz, L. J., Connelly, J. C., Coyne, L., & Spare, K. E. (1978). Alcohol abuse in several midwestern gay communities. Unpublished paper.

Maletta, G. (1982). Alcoholism and the aged. In E. Pattison & E. Kaufman (Eds.), *Encyclopedic handbook of alcoholism*. New York: Gardner Press.

McGoldrick, M., & Carter, E. (1982). The family life cycle. In F. Walsh (Ed.), *Normal family processes*. New York: Guilford Press.

McCrady, B. S. (1982). Women and alcohol abuse. In M. R. Notman & C. C. Nadelson (Eds.), *Aggression, adaptations, and psychotherapy*. Vol. 3 of *The woman patient*. New York, Plenum, pp. 217–244.

McLachlan, J. F. C., Walderman, R. L., & Thomas, S. (1973). A study of teenagers with alcoholic parents (Research monograph No. 3). Toronto: Donwood Institute.

Meeks, D., & Kelly, C. (1970). Family therapy with the families of recovering alcoholics. *Quarterly Journal of Studies on Alcoholism*, 31:399–413.

Miller, D., & Lang, M. (1977). Children of alcoholics. A 20 year longitudinal study. *Social Work Research and Abstracts*, 13(4):23–29.

Mishara, B., & Kastenbaum, R. (1980). Treatment of problem drinking among the elderly. In B. Mishara & R. Kastenbaum (Eds.), *Alcohol and old age*. New York: Grune & Stratton.

National Council on Alcoholism (1976). Definition of alcoholism. *Annals of Internal Medicine* 85:764.

New York Times (Feb. 1974) 17.

O'Leary, D. E., O'Leary, M. R., & Donavan, D. M. (1976). Social skill acquisition and psychosocial development of alcoholics: A review. *Addictive Behavior*, 1:111–120.

Parness, J. (1984). Protective Services for the Elderly, F&CS, Long Branch, N.J. Personal communication.

Pascarelle, E. F. (1974). Drug dependence: An age-old problem compounded by old age. *Geriatrics*, 29:109–114.

Pattison, E, Mansell & E. Kaufman (Eds.) (1982). *Encyclopedic handbook of alcoholism*. New York: Gardner Press.

Rada, R. R. (1975). Alcoholism and forcible rape. *American Journal of Psychiatry*, 132:444–446.

Rice, M. M. (1982). Alcohol use and abuse in children. In E. Pattison & E. Kaufman (Eds.), *Encyclopedic handbook of alcoholism*. New York: Garder Press.

Romer, N. (1981). *The sex-role cycle*. Old Westbury, N.Y.: Feminist Press.

Rosin, A., & Glatt, M. (1971). Alcohol excess in the elderly. *Quarterly Journal of Studies on Alcoholism*, 32:53–59.

Rouse, B. A. (1981, April), Stressful stages in the family life cycle and ethanol intake of husbands and wives. Paper presented at the National Alcholism Forum of the National Council on Alcoholism. New Orleans, La.

Royce, J. E. (1981). *Alcohol problems and alcoholism*. New York: Free Press.

Saghir, M. T., et al. (1970). Homosexuality IV: Psychiatric disorder and disability in the female homosexual. *American Journal of Psychiatry*. 127: 147–154.

Sandmaier, M. (1980). *The invisible alcoholics, women and alcohol abuse in America*. New York: McGraw-Hill.

Schuster, R. (1976). Trust: Its implication in the etiology and treatment of psychopathic youths. *International Journal of Offender Therapy*, 3:128–133.

Smart, R. G., & Finley, J. (1975). Increases in youthful admissions to alcoholism treatment in Ontario. *Drug and Alcohol*, 1:83–87.

Stanton, D. et al. (1982). *The family therapy of drug and alcohol abuse.* New York: Guilford Press.

Steinglass, P. (1979). Family therapy with alcoholics: A review. In E. Kaufman & P. N. Kaufman, (Eds.), *Family therapy of drug and alcohol abuse.* New York: Gardner Press, pp. 147–186.

Streissguth, A. P. (1976). Maternal alcoholism and the outcome of pregnancy: A review of the fetal alcohol syndrome. In M. Greenblatt & M. A. Schuckit (Eds.), *Alcoholism problems in women and children.* New York: Grune & Stratton.

Travis, C. (1977). Men and women report their views on masculinity. *Psychology Today,* 10:34–42.

U.S. Department of Health, Education and Welfare: Second special report to the U.S. Congress of Alcohol and Health. New knowledge. Washington, D.C.: DHEW.

Vaillant, G., E. (1983). *The natural history of alcoholism.* Cambridge, Mass.: Harvard University Press.

Wegscheider, S. (1981). *Another chance: Hope and health for the alcoholic family.* Palo Alto, Calif.: Science and Behavior Books, Inc.

Williams, C., & Kleman, L. (1984). Female alcohol abuse, its effects on the family. In S. Wilsnack & L. Beckman, (Eds.), *Alcohol problems in women.* New York: Guilford Press.

Wilsnack, S. (1973). Sex-role identity in female alcoholism. *Journal of Abnormal Psychology,* 82: 253–261.

Wilsnack, S. C. (1977). Women are different: Overlooked differences among women drinkers. Keynote address, Symposium on Alcoholism and Women. Institute of the Study of Women in Transition, Portland, Maine.

Wilsnack, S., & Beckman. L. (1984). *Alcohol problems in women.* New York: Guilford Press.

Wolin, S., Bennett, L., Noonan, D., & Teitelbaum, M. P.H. (1980). Disrupted family rituals. A factor in the intergenerational transmission of alcoholism. *Journal of Studies on Alcohol* 41 (3): 199–214.

Zimberg, S. (1978). Psychosocial treatment of elderly alcoholics. In S. Zimberg, J. Wallace, & S. Blume (Eds.), *Practical approaches to alcoholism psychotherapy.* New York: Plenum Press.

Zimberg, S., Wallace, J., & Blume, S., (Eds.) (1978). *Practical approaches to alcoholism psychotherapy.* New York: Plenum Press.

Zucker, R. A. (1976). Parental influences on the drinking patterns of their children. In Greenblatt, M. & M. A. Shuckit (Eds.), *Alcoholism problems in women and children.* New York: Grune & Stratton.

CHAPTER 21

The Family Life Cycle of Poor Black Families

Paulette Moore Hines, Ph.D.

Undoubtedly, poor families are among the most needy and difficult populations to work with. Unfortunately, they have not attracted the attention of many theorists or clinicians in the family therapy field. At first thought, this is somewhat suprising, given the relatively greater proportion of poor families who seek or are referred for clinical services compared to other populations (e.g. anorexica) and that the poor are growing at a faster rate than the middle class (Norton, 1985). The ranks of the poor are increasing not only because of a growing number of single parent households but also due to an increasing proportion of elderly, middle-aged women with responsibility for a growing number of children and non-working young adults.

In this chapter we have limited our focus to multiproblem, generally non-working, poor families of African-American heritage. More than all other ethnic/racial groups in America, Blacks have struggled for basic freedoms and opportunities and have been thwarted continually by the institutions created to assist them. The once legal physical and psychological enslavement of Blacks has resulted in their being overrepresented among the poor more than 100 years after the "Great Emancipation." Black families still average 58% of the income of White families (Noble, 1984) and one out of every two black children grows up in poverty.

Poor Black families can expect nothing but sporadic, menial work. The life cycle of these families is blighted by unemployment, malnutrition, premarital births, family instability and violence, mental disorder, delinquency, substance abuse, a high rate of infant mortality, physical disability, untimely death, and the ongoing stresses of inadequate housing and constant indebtedness. There is always too little money to meet basic needs and too few recreational outlets.

In contrast to middle-class families, whose concerns with government structures relate to taxes, federally assisted housing, college loans, the military

The author gratefully acknowledges the contribution of Fernando Colon whose chapter in the first edition of this book served as the basic framework for this paper.

draft, and life-threatening environmental issues such as toxic waste, poor Black families interface with the government to ensure their basic subsistence. Various agencies participate in, and intrude upon, their daily lives, affecting their basic survival, world view, and decision making. They depend upon governmental agencies for rental assistance, family planning, basic income, food supplements, energy assistance, transportation, medical benefits, education, and job training. Their life cycle constitutes a virtually endless series of crises and their adaptive capacities are often pushed beyond human limits. Thus emotional impoverishment becomes a part of their profile as well. Although they share similar problems with the growing numbers of poor families of all races, discriminatory attitudes in the prevailing power system set them apart in some ways from the non-Black poor.

While various authors have considered the cultural issues in doing family therapy with Black families (e.g., Hines and Boyd-Franklin, 1982; Pinderhughes, 1982), relatively little attention has been paid in the family therapy field to multiproblem poor Black families and their adaptive responses to their harsh environment since the work of Minuchin and colleagues (1967) and Aponte (1974, 1976). These families are not merely families in one or another kind of trouble. They face complex, often extreme and unrelenting conditions related to race and poverty, that go far beyond the experience of most helping professionals. It is easy to resist working with this population, or to become overwhelmed by their multiple problems, since our traditional treatment methods often fail miserably with them.

Those embedded in a context of chronic unemployment and discrimination seem to be most limited in their abilities to function in ways that allow family members to thrive. When they are referred for mental-health services, they present multiple problems and ambivalence about the value of therapy. They may repeatedly fail to show up or terminate prematurely. The complexity of the issues that surround poverty seems to promote helping agents' assumption that family therapy is of little value in helping poor families to effect change in their lives. However, members of multiproblem Black families are interdependent financially as well as emotionally. Survival as well as success for one person depends on others. Stress is persistently high and families are consistently experiencing demands for change and flexibility. When the impact of these external stressors is heightened by normal developmental stressors and the vertical stressors of unresolved family issues, the odds are great that developmental movement forward will be thwarted for both individual family members and the family unit as a whole. Any demand for adaptation or change will be most stressful when families move from one stage to another, and will be successful only if previous developmental needs have been adequately met. Certainly, family therapists cannot operate as though we and the families that we treat exist in a vacuum. Family therapy is no panacea but it can help families achieve a healthier level of functioning within the limits of their context. In particular, the family life cycle framework is a valuable tool in assessment and intervention with this group.

The observations set forth are intended to provoke thought rather than to be conclusive. On one hand, the author is concerned that the reader recognize the individuality of every individual and family. Far too often, distorted views of African-American families have been perpetuated by a literature written with insufficient attention to social, political, and economic contexts and heterogeneity within the group. Yet, there is a need to acknowledge that dysfunctional poor families do exist; they are alike *and* different from working and middle class families.

This chapter describes the cycle of poverty and the family life cycle of multiproblem poor Black families, offers recommendations for assessment and treatment, and discusses therapist "burnout" in work with these families. Case examples are provided to illuminate the life cycle issue. Although focused on those most severely oppressed by virtue of poverty and racism, the discussion has relevance to family therapy with other multiproblem poor families, particularly for those who have lived with poverty for more than one generation.

THE CYCLE OF POVERTY

The relationship between socioeconomic status and level of family functioning is not linear. To be poor does not automatically mean that one's family is dysfunctional. Some of the features of poverty in urban, poor Black populations are shared by the poor in vastly different cultural contexts: In all of these settings, there are poor families that struggle to make ends meet with inadequate resources but who manage to fulfill the basic developmental needs of their members. Yet I want to emphasize the importance of poverty as a factor that can force the healthiest family to buckle under, especially when there are societal features that serve to maintain them in the position of poverty and powerlessness.

I believe that the cycle of poverty is multiply determined and that it is *circular* rather than *linear*. The structure of society renders certain groups subject to a situation of chronic poverty. Black Americans in particular have secured equal choice but not equal opportunity. They learn a variety of responses to cope with a persistently impoverished and hostile environment. Many of these adoptive responses are a reflection of great creativity and strength. However, some responses are maladaptive and tend to perpetuate their condition. While these behaviors can become ingrained, they are learned responses and family members can modify them.

A clear example of how poverty is perpetuated in a circular fashion is evident in how self-esteem is assaulted by the pervasive absence of adequate jobs. Life has become more complex in the past two decades and there are fewer unskilled jobs available. While higher education and technical skills have

become critical, this group often lacks the opportunity to acquire them. They are the last hired and first fired.

For these reasons members of multiproblem poor Black families may develop a pervasive sense of impotence, rage, and despair. Their world view is shaped by their overexposure to tragedy and suffering (Lefever, 1977). Their rage may be directed at society, at members of their own families, or at themselves (Coles, 1970, 1978). Pinderhughes (1982) suggested that those who are most severely victimized adapt to their powerlessness by adopting behaviors that include: preference for immediate emotional expression, manipulation in relationships, withdrawal or passive aggression, oppositional or rebellious behavior, and identification with the aggressor. In this regard Minuchin and Montalvo (1967) state: "Families that experience chronic frustration and impotence and fail to see how they can affect their own environment either remain immobile in situations in which directed differentiated movement is indicated or else respond by fast, random activity that serves only as a crude way of alleviating stress" (p. 885).

CHARACTERISTICS OF THE FAMILY LIFE CYCLE

There are a wide variety of family structures among the poor. In this regard they are not different from their middle-class and upper-class counterparts. Gans (1968), in a dated but still relevant article, observed that there is as much variety among the poor as there is among the affluent.

> Some have been poor for generations, others are poor periodically. Some are downwardly mobile, others are upwardly mobile. Many share middle-class values, others embrace working-class values. Some, because of chronic deprivation, have difficulty in adapting to new opportunities, and some are subject to physical and emotional illness which makes them unable to adapt to nonpathological situations. The research has not been done to tell us what percent of poor people fit into each of these categories (Gans, 1968, pp. 205–6).

Multiproblem poor Black families also vary enormously in whether their ongoing familial interconnectedness is active, infrequent, or nonexistent.

The blueprint for work with poor families has been strongly influenced by the work of Minuchin and colleagues (1967), who attempted to observe, assess, intervene, and document both their sucesses and their failures in working with poor ghetto families. They described the families that they studied as disorganized and lacking in clear generational boundaries and differentiated communication patterns. They delineated the organization of two kinds of families: the "disengaged" and the "enmeshed."

Aponte (1974, 1976b), who spent many years working with such families,

has noted that while they have often been referred to as "disorganized," he prefers to use the term "underorganized" to suggest not so much an improper kind of organization as a deficiency in the degrees of constancy, differentiation, and flexibility of the structural organization of the family system. He has distinguished three structural underpinnings of operational patterns in social systems: alignment, force, and boundary. Alignment refers to the joining or opposition of one member of a system to another in carrying out an operation. Force defines the relative influence of each member on the outcome of an activity. Boundary tells who is included and excluded from the activity. Aponte describes underorganized families as lacking in the development and elaboration of these organizational underpinnings.

Lewis and Looney (1983) conducted a study of 18 inner-city, Black, working-class, two-parent families in an effort to explore the usefulness of Beaver's (1976) concept of a continuum of family competence. Competence was defined in terms of two tasks: stabilizing parental personalities and developing autonomous children. The families spanned the full range of family functioning. In spite of their low income and continuous external stresses, there were optimal functioning families. The families who fell the farthest below the poverty line were rated as least competent; however, the data did not suggest a simple linear relationship between income and family functioning.

We observe four distinguishing characteristics in the life cycles of poor Black families: (1) Their life cycle seems more truncated than that of middle-class families, and transitions are not clearly delineated. (2) Households are frequently female headed and of the extended-family type. (3) Their life cycle is puncutated by numerous unpredicatable life events and the associated stresses they engender. (4) They have few resources available to assist them in coping with these stressors and must rely extensively on governmental institutions to meet even basic needs.

Truncated Life Cycle

There is generally less calendar time in poor Black families for the unfolding of various developmental stages and they face numerous unpredictable life crises at each stage. Family members leave home, mate, have children, and become grandparents at far earlier ages than their middle-class counterparts. A shortened life cycle means that there is inadequate time to resolve the developmental tasks of each stage, and individuals are often required to assume new roles and responsibilities before they are developmentally capable of doing so. Shifts from child and adolescent roles to marital, parental, and grandparental roles may be blurred and without clear transitional demarcation or rites of passage. Subsequent stages become increasingly difficult to traverse because the solid underpinnings of previously resolved tasks are not there, resulting in a family system that may be inadequately organized to cope with its needs.

Female-Headed Households

Frequently, if there is a mate/father present, his participation and length of stay in the family are tenuous. Single-parent households among the Black population had increased to 47% by 1980 from 21% in 1960 and 8% in 1950 (Noble, 1984). Often a mother, her children, and her daughter's children live together, or within a short distance of each other, without clear delineation of their respective roles. This adaptation to circumstances can create additional problems, including an incredible economic and emotional burden on the mother-grandmother, and difficulty for younger mothers in assuming parental responsibility. Indeed the overrepresentation of females as heads of poor households has resulted in the terms "the feminization of poverty." Certainly not all poor Black families headed by woman are dysfunctional. Those that are functional tend to have maintained access to contextual resources and retain rich, viable ties with their extended families and communities (Hill, 1977; Klausner, 1978; Goldberg & Duke, 1985).

Unpredictable Stress

Multiproblem families are subject to abrupt loss of membership through family disruption, death, imprisonment, and alcohol and drug addiction. Along with the basic fact of poverty, these create additional barriers to normal development. The potential for emotional conflict is greatly increased by the concrete realities of poverty, such as overcrowding. Informal resources are continually taxed by crises, making it that much more difficult for the family to respond to everyday demands.

Reliance on Institutional Supports

Poor Black families are often forced to seek public assistance to meet their basic needs, which ultimately contributes to further deterioration of an already stressed emotional system. The most salient example is the father, with too little or no money, who knows that leaving his family will actually improve their situation since they may then become eligible for medical benefits or governmental support. These institutionalized solutions supplement, but cannot replace, the social and emotional support available in even the most limited family structure (Colon, 1973; 1978). As Lefever (1977) suggests, primary relationships are of even greater importance for low-income people because the family unit may be their only source of favorable evaluation.

STAGES OF THE FAMILY LIFE CYCLE

The shortened life cycle described can be loosely divided into three stages: adolescence/unattached adulthood, the family with young children, and the family in later life. By attempting to compare normative tasks in these stages with the reality of multiproblem families, one can gain some insight into the difficulties these families experience in going through this life cycle. While the stages are described largely in terms of the experience of the family members for whom the stage is named, the case studies that follow provide a three- or four-generational perspective on the multiple problems of the representative families in each stage.

Stage 1—Adolescence/Unattached Young Adulthood

Family theory posits that the young person's ability to negotiate the tasks of this stage is influenced by his or her observation of adult family members; but since boundaries between adolescence and young adulthood are typically blurred, the normal middle-class goals of this stage may seem impossible goals from many adolescents' observations of the world around them. Often there is an "all-or-nothing," "do-or-die," "make-it-or-break-it" quality to the poor adolescent Black experience, as all too quickly they find themselves with adult responsibilities. Moreover it would seem that poor Blacks are confronted with this stark reality at increasingly young ages, as what used to occur at 16 or 17 years of age is now taking place at 10 or 11.

Although they are based on the normative psychological development of middle-class families and may not correspond to the reality of ghetto living, for the sake of discussion we will define the tasks of this stage as: (1) differentiation of self (2) establishment of self in work, and (3) development of intimate peer relationships.

Differentiation of Self

Adolescents from multiproblem poor Black families are often either pushed out of the home to fend for themselves, or clung to desperately as a source of concrete assistance. Still others continue to live at home with a definitive need to hold onto the support and affirmation that the family provides. Yet inevitably most find the pressures of home unbearable and seek distance from the burden of the family. The pull of their peers is powerful and they may precipitously attempt to make their own way, or remain at home but refuse to contribute in any way to the family situation. This sense of burden does not allow them to grow away from their families but tears them away, leaving them ill equipped to do well in later stages.

Establishment of Self in Work

It is extremely difficult for poor young Blacks to develop a sense of commitment to the world of work. They may have high aspirations (Hines, 1978), but a poor Black youth's expectations for achievement may be limited by observations of the ever-present reality of failure. Poor Blacks are over-represented among high-school dropouts, and in 1985, unemployment statistics for Black youth were as high as 39%—two and one-half times the rate for White youth (Norton, 1985). Those who find menial work are fortunate, and what is most available to them is illegal activity. The underground economy promises to put a quick end to poverty, and its appeal is powerful.

Some, but far too few, are lucky. They happen to meet the right people at the right time, and are able to get a glimpse of their talents and a sense of possibility. With the support of concerned people, they manage to avoid the minefields that are all around them and to raise themselves into the middle class. Yet even these precious few may have to cope with deep feelings of guilt and confusion related to leaving their families and peers behind.

Development of Intimate Peer Relationships

Young Blacks from multiproblem families have little time to develop the skills essential to negotiating intimate relationships successfully, as the previously cited emotional concomittants of poverty fail to support relationships. In addition adolescent sexual experimentation is likely to be quickly replaced by parental responsibility.

Although adolescent Black females are less discriminated against in some ways than their male counterparts, they often see their only chance for positive identity as becoming mothers. As Gibbs (1984) writes, "These are children having children with profound physical and psychsocial consequences for the girls themselves, as well as for . . . their babies and their families" (p. 10).

The adolescent male, because of limited job options and dismal odds for being able to fulfill the functions of adult males in this society, often becomes a transient figure in his heterosexual relationships. In fact he may have seen few adult men function in a marital/parental capacity with a stable job. Consequently he asserts his masculinity by serving a procreative function but frequently cannot go beyond this point.

Case Example: The Gary Family

The child protection agency referred 13-year-old Natalie, a fifth grader, because of her refusal to attend school, her poor achievement and peer relationships, and family conflicts. Five years previously she had been referred for school problems. The year before she had been hospitalized for a suicide attempt, in which she took six types of medication, and several months earlier she had spent two weeks in an adolescent treatment center after stabbing her sister. She was also a juvenile

arthritic. Her brother Ronnie also had a history of psychiatric hospitalizations and was sporadically attending follow-up sessions. Her sister Jill, an unmarried mother, was pregnant with her second child and had recently been abandoned by the father of both children. Depressed and withdrawn, Jill had frequent suicidal thoughts, and the children's mother, Mrs. Gary, now took her along whenever she left the house. Mrs. Gary also cared for Jill's child (while the teenager attended school), in addition to two younger children of her own and two children of an "irresponsible" mother in the neighborhood. Mary had reportedly moved as a result of an argument with her mother, involving the identified patient, Natalie. The oldest daughter, Hazel, also lived outside the home.

These data were gathered at a home visit, which followed Mrs. Gary's last-minute call canceling her appointment at the agency due to a leg injury. Several observations were made during the course of a rather haphazard two-hour interview, conducted admid the normal routines of the Gary household. Natalie was unfriendly and uncooperative with the interviewers. She assumed a parental role in relation to her siblings, who seemed relatively happy and well cared for. Mrs. Gary suggested that she had no right to complain as her problems did not measure up to those her mother had faced with 11 children. Mrs. Gary said she had always been in the caretaker role, and while she reported much depression about her own life, including the breakup of a relationship the previous year, she did not have time to "worry about it." Her biggest concern at present was Jill's state of mind and the younger children, whom she insisted on caring for at home despite the availability of day care. She informed us that she would also take Jill's second child rather than see the child put up for adoption, and we learned that she received no financial assistance for the visiting children. Jill expressed some interest in treatment, and Ronnie said he had found his own therapy of some value.

Strongly invested in her parenting role, Mrs. Gary presented an ambivalent message regarding Jill's choice about teenage motherhood. We also hypothesized that the children in this family could only leave their mother through anger and cutoffs. The usual transitional struggle between parent and adolescents seemed intensified by the simultaneous but conflicting tasks Ms. Gary faced. She had the task of letting go and fostering the independence of her older children while reinforcing her position as parent with the younger children. The difficulty of pulling off these two tasks at once may contribute to what we frequently observe—parents giving up on their parental responsibility for their adolescents.

The therapy team accepted Mrs. Gary's definition of the problem, and at the conclusion of the session, she agreed to send Jill to a second session, and to attend herself when appropriate. As expected there was no follow-through. The intense, easily overwhelming nature of the Garys' daily lives, the limited outlets for channeling or even being alone to examine their frustrations, along with the legacy of "family strength" transmitted by Mrs. Gary, contributed to the family's propensity to deny or diminish the varying developmental needs of its members. (Adolescents and young adults suffer most in such an instance, given the fact that it is in this stage that their need to separate from the family emotionally and physically is greatest.) As the Gary youth approached young adulthood, the ambiguous and ambivalent messages regarding their privileges and responsibilities served to intensify the normal adolescent struggles and they became even more vulnerable to acting out their conflicts and to negative peer influence. Given the multiple demands on Ms. Gary, they were most successful in gaining attention and new options for separation from their overwhelming situation when they became sick or bad. The Garys were contacted by letter and did not respond. In the Garys' case, the crises had clearly passed and the agencies involved with the family were in greater distress about the circumstances than were the family members. Less than a year later, the family resurfaced. Mrs. Gary had remarried, and Natalie had run away and had been rehospitalized.

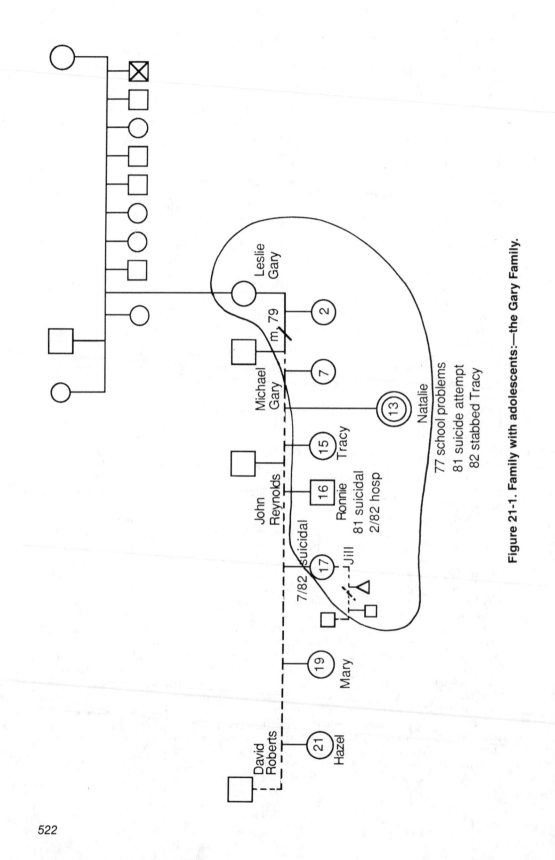

Figure 21-1. Family with adolescents:—the Gary Family.

Stage 2—The Family with Children

Significantly, for two-thirds of Black women this phase begins without benefit of marriage (Cherlin, 1981). While this statistic includes mature working- and middle-class Black mothers who opt to have children out of wedlock, many of these mothers are still in their teens and unmarried. In 1981 83% of babies born to Black teenage mothers were born out of wedlock. Fursenberg (1986) conducted a study of 300 Black, adolescent mothers and found that even in high-risk families teenage childbearers could escape poverty if they limited the number of subsequent births and became involved in educational programs involving counseling, child-care education, health, and family planning. The majority of those who were doing well were married or living with a male who provided extra income. Nonetheless those who do marry are likely to divorce or separate. For example, Teachman (1983) found that Black women who marry before age 16 face a 57% increase in the likelihood of marital dissolution. He also found that premarital births decrease the chances of successful marriage by 33%, even compared with postmarital births occurring within seven months after marriage. The subsequent search for a mate for the unmarried mother is difficult, as she is limited by her responsibilities. If she does marry a man older than the child's father there is also greater potential for marital friction over roles, which contributes further to the rate of marital breakup.

The implication for a poor Black woman is that her role may become constricted at an early age to that of caretaker. She is likely to interrupt her education, and to become dependent on Aid for Dependent Children (AFDC) for support and medical benefits. If and when she does enter the job market, child care and transportation costs may be prohibitive, and she faces few options as she presents no previous work history and few, if any, salable skills.

In terms of normal development, the tasks of this phase combine the major tasks of both "the newly married couple" and "the family with young children." These are (1) forming a marital system, (2) taking on parental roles, and (3) realignment of relationships with family. The related tasks of adjustment that include the older generation take on a different meaning as the grandmother becomes a primary source of assistance, if not the actual head of the family.

Forming a Marital System

In 1982 the divorce ratio for Blacks was 220 per 1000 married persons—double the rate for Whites (Cherlin, 1981). While it is unclear how many poor people are represented in this statistic, male–female relationships among poor Blacks (married or unmarried) are inherently unstable. It is extremely difficult to sustain a relationship in the context of chronic stress. The pressures of daily life prompt husband/wife transactions that are typically unfinished, vague, and unresolved. Conflictual issues that involve use of time and money are so fluid

that couples find it difficult to explore, negotiate, and modify these areas of their lives.

Conflict between spouses seems to arise from a host of unfinished role definitions, as neither has had the opportunity to complete the tasks of child-hood and adolescence. There may be gaps, inconsistencies, confusion, and uncertainty as to how adult roles are carried out. This is often a function of their parents' impoverished interpersonal, social, and emotional histories. Although some may have stable models for marital roles in the extended family, for many the only model is television families, whose resources are so much more abundant than their own. The pull of the old, more exciting single life is powerful when compared with the drudgery of a future filled with the overwhelming needs of young children and menial work.

Another significant factor that greatly influences male/female relationships is that of the male/female ratio. Black females between the ages of 20 and 40 outnumber Black men in that group by almost 700,000. These are differences significant enough to affect the potential for marriage when considered to-gether with the ways that Black males are otherwise unavailable. Staples (1981) writes: "Many a black male's shortcomings must be tolerated for the sake of affection and companionship. In a sense, many black women have to take love on male terms" (p. 32). When tensions and conflicts do surface, as they inevitably do, they may be related to this imbalance. In any case there are fewer options for resolution.

Taking on Parental Roles

While procreation is about the only source of continuity for poor Black couples, the arrival of children when parents do not have jobs spells trouble for the new family. Still primarily identified with their adolescent peer groups, they tend to avoid adult parenting roles; the functions of adult mutuality and shared responsibility for children may be slow to develop. Generally the mother is forced to obtain AFDC, and the father becomes the peripheral male. In some cases both the parents remain juvenile and the children are left to fend for themselves (Minuchin et al., 1967).

As this system evolves, the female, who has the greater economic opportu-nity, becomes the central, organizing force within the family. Marital disrup-tion and long separations are common. However, Cherlin (1981) notes that this does not mean a total absence of contact between the partners or between the father and the children, a fact often overlooked in therapy. With her inter-nalized belief that males cannot be trusted or depended upon, the female may actually contribute to her mate's peripheral status. Thus she may maintain distance as a mate and restrict his involvement with the children (some of whom may not be his biological offspring) in order to protect them from hurt if he should depart. If the husband/father does stay in the picture, the spouse subsystem may be vaguely delineated or undefined (Minuchin et al., 1967)

because, in a context of scarcity, the male's role as breadwinner supersedes any other role he might have.

In time the children may come to view the father/mate as a useless member of the family. Male children, in particular, are handicapped by this derogated concept of maleness and the inability to visualize a role for them in the family. The numbers man and the drug pusher may become the persons with whom they identify and further confuse male children by equating irresponsibility and violence with masculinity. However, without a consistent male adult figure, children of both sexes lose a rich source of identification with the marital subsystem and the father role.

The mother left with sole care of young children is soon overburdened, and eventually a "parental child" may emerge who attempts to assist her. Such children are in a difficult position, and with inadequate skills or power can easily become the object of the siblings' rage. They may be jealous of the parental child's special favor with the mother or enraged at the mother for failing to be an adequate parent (Minuchin et al., 1967). Just as important, the needs of the family conflict with the youth's own developmental needs, setting the child up to repeat the family pattern.

In general school-age children of multiproblem families face a grim life and are high risk for maladjustment. The mother, chronically overburdened and depressed, may be unable to respond to any of her children on an individual basis. Expectations may shift abruptly without any change in a child's readiness to respond. Without adequate attention such children often fail to develop vital cognitive, affective, and communication skills. Given this reality, they easily fulfill the negative expectations of teachers in a middle-class-oriented school system.

Discipline tends to be authoritarian in an effort to toughen children's survival skills. Physical punishment is the major mode of limit setting. Embedded in a harsh environment, parents demand quick responses and may be impatient with a failure to obey. Many find it even more difficult to shift to another mode of discipline as children reach adolescence, and thus may feel more out of control than they might otherwise when the family reaches this stage.

Realignment of Relationships

The integration of mates and/or children into the family is not necessarily experienced as a major stress given the extended-family context of Black families. Boundaries are easily relaxed to accept newcomers; emotional and functional inclusion in a system of mutual exchange may begin even during courtship. The arrival of children prior to or early in a couple's relationship hastens the acceptance of a family member's mate into the extended-family network. New couples often live in the household of a parent or family member, or they establish residence nearby and interact almost daily. The

extended-family network provides a necessary cushion, particularly for the family with children. However, the level of interconnectedness leaves room for some predictable problems. The usual negotiations of everyday decisions are complicated by the need to factor in the impact on the larger extended-family network. Family members must struggle with issues of loyalty between the newly created family and one or both extended-family systems. Marriage and/ or children may result in shifts in roles and relationships but the generational hierarchy is maintained. Young adults who have not taken sufficient time to establish their separate identities are predisposed to continue functioning without full regard for the role demands that marriage or parenthood dictate. This may further tax an already burdened family system.

Case Example: The James Family

Ms. James, a 22-year-old single mother of two boys on welfare, contacted the clinic because of her concern about seven-year-old Marshall. The family also included Anthony, five, from another relationship of Ms. James. After repeated questioning about his tardy arrival home from school by Ms. James' live-in boyfriend, Mr. Newton, Marshall reported that he was being sexually abused by several older youths in his school.

The perpetrators included a cousin who had moved to the South several years earlier. Accordingly Ms. James estimated that the abuse had begun at least prior to this point in time. More recently Marshall also reported that he had been victimized by two young men who had transported him and his brother to a church program. Marshall indicated he had been afraid of being beaten by the boys in his school and he was concerned that they would stop being his friends. He also admitted that he derived some enjoyment from the sexual contacts, and that he feared punishment by his mother. Ms. James was fearful that Marshall would continue to be victimized because of his fear of rejection by other children and his reluctance to turn to her for help with problems. The abuse was denied by all accused. School authorities agreed to transfer Marshall from the school where the incidents took place since they had allowed a dectective to escort Marshall from class to class to identify the accused boys.

Overwhelmed, Ms. James responded by spanking Marshall until he was bruised for previously withholding the truth, and was reported to the child protection agency. Intimidated by the school, the police, and the agency, she became depressed about her family's lack of support and guilty about her own inadequacy. She also reported problems with Mr. Newton, who did not have a positive relationship with either child. A harsh disciplinarian, he was an occasional drug user and did not contribute financially to the home.

Ms. James had moved north, after quitting high school, when Marshall was a year old. Prior to that time, her mother had cared for the child. Ms. James felt much guilt about "taking Marshall" from her mother. When Ms. James was 14, her mother had left her own husband and children. Their relationship had been strained ever since. The grandmother was now openly critical of Ms. James' relationship with Mr. Newton and undermined his discipline efforts with the children. Although she worked as a volunteer at school, Ms. James did not have a social network and said that because of her lack of transportation and money she could not pursue any interests. In addition, she felt that her sisters made constant demands for assistance that detracted from her energy and concrete resources.

Considering the family life cycle paradigm, the therapist hypothesized that Ms. James' ability to nurture, reassure, and protect her sons against the realities of

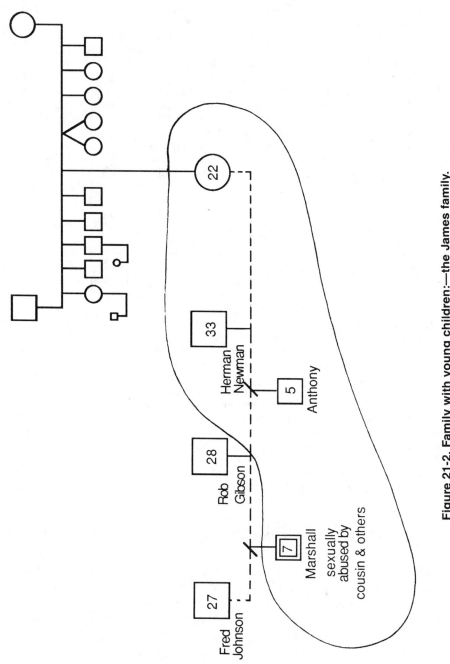

Figure 21-2. Family with young children:—the James family.

their environment was hampered by her sense of guilt, depression, and powerlessness. Common to most women who become mothers during their teen years, she had long felt inadequate about her ability as a parent. Her connectedness with her mother had been abruptly disrupted during her teen years. Marshall and his brother had filled an emotional vacuum for both women, who had never been able to resolve their conflicts with one another. Aware of the triangle and invested in proving herself competent as a mother, Ms. James had never developed the usual peer relationships as a teen or young adult. These factors, along with the desire to protect her children from the evils of their urban environment, contributed to harsh disciplining that rendered her unapproachable by her children, and finally subject to supervision by the child protection agency; inevitably this heightened her sense of inadequacy and powerlessness. The issue for the therapist was clearly one of understanding the adaptiveness of the mother's and son's behaviors in relation to their needs, interrupting the problem–response– problem spiral, and strengthening Ms. James' ability to help her son prevent further abuse. The therapist was clear that the locus of the problem went beyond the family to the refusal of the larger system to intervene with the alleged abusers to ensure that other children would not also be abused. The therapist successfully empowered Ms. James to assert her rights to the school and police authorities by highlighting her strengths and educating her about options for action. She was also encouraged to pay more attention to her own needs, and seemed relieved by the therapist's confirmation of the multiple stresses in her life. Suggestions for alternative methods of disciplining her sons were offered, and it was suggested that she enroll her boys in an after-school recreation program. Marshall entered individual therapy and a social skills training group. He benefited from the opportunity to improve his social skills and develop positive peer connections. His complaints about peer acceptance decreased accordingly.

Ms. James made a great deal of progress in therapy, but continued to have difficulty with Mr. Newton, who would not attend sessions. During the course of treatment, she received her general equivalency diploma, enrolled in a nursing program, and secured a part-time job. Her handling of her sons improved. The couple's conflicts escalated after Ms. James' mother died and her sister moved into the apartment for several months. At one point she obtained a court order to have Mr. Newton removed, although she subsequently reunited with him. She was afraid of being alone, and of exposing her sons to a series of relationships that she feared would be no more satisfactory. At last contact she reported that Mr. Newton's relationship with the boys had improved significantly, though the couple's interactions were still unsatisfactory.

Stage 3—The Family in Later Life

In contrast to middle-class families, this stage for multiproblem, poor Black families does not signify a lessening of daily responsibilities and a shift into the issues surrounding retirement for the older generation. Elderly family members are great sources of human wisdom and strength by virtue of their survival. However, males in particular often die before or soon after retirement. Many elderly persons continue working to make ends meet in spite of poor health. There is not likely to be an "empty nest"; in fact, because of the level of interconnectedness between family members, the elderly are likely to be active members of expanding households and family systems. The task of shifting generational roles often has arisen before midlife when the female parental child described in stage 2 may attempt to escape her family by

becoming a mother herself. However, once the baby is born, she may be unable to shift from being a "parental" daughter to being a mother. Her own mother may also be unable to allow this shift to occur, or to make the shift into the role of grandmother. The baby may experience his or her mother as an "older sister" while the new mother remains primarily a daughter.

At this point what often evolves is a three- or four-generational family system that is headed by a grandmother who is responsible for caring for both her younger children, some of her grandchildren, and possibly her great-grandchildren as well. Given the debilitating effects of poverty over a lifetime, in many cases she reaches later life with severe medical problems that influence her ability to manage this overwhelming task successfully. For the larger family system, the issues remain similar to earlier stages, as there are usually adolescent and young adult members in the household, as well as young children to be cared for. Additional adult growth for the grandmother is blocked by these continuing responsibilities and the forward thrust of the family life cycle for all family members may become stalled.

The role of the nonevolved grandmother in such an environment requires her to be an exceptional human being. Although roles are typically blurred in these families, the nonevolved grandmother's status is often the most well defined. However, her capacity to perform her role is taxed by the persistence of economic crises, and poor Black families can become totally fragmented, or forced to live together in crowded, inadequate dwellings. Indeed recent statistics indicate that poor Black women in this stage are likely to be in poor health and have an income below $3500 per year. Daily life is further complicated by conflicts surrounding the unresolved issues between the various family members in the extended family system.

Case Example: The Arnold Family

Following a stroke, Mrs. Arnold, 79, a once-divorced and twice-widowed great-grandmother, was referred to the family service agency by her public-health nurse. Confined to a wheelchair, she lived with Margaret, 30, her grandaughter, and her great-grandaughters, Ann, 11, and Lisa, nine, whom she cared for while Margaret worked. Margaret's mother, Flo, 61, was Mrs. Arnold's only daughter. Mrs. Arnold and Flo had a highly conflictual relationship marked by several periods of lapsed contact. Margaret and Flo also had a poor relationship, and so the younger woman turned to her grandmother rather than her own mother for assistance with her children. Mrs. Arnold owned her one-bedroom home and marginally supported herself on Social Security and disability payments. Margaret, who worked full-time for minimum wages, was supposed to contribute financially but did not. Instead, she spent most of her time drinking at the local bar with her friends. At this point Mrs. Arnold, who had recently stopped drinking herself, was threatening to stop caring for Ann and Lisa.

It became apparent that Mrs. Arnold's problems with Flo stemmed from the older woman's marital history. Mrs. Arnold had married Flo's father at 17, and Flo was the couple's only child. After four years they divorced because of his "immaturity," and the following year she married her second husband. Flo was raised for some time with two younger stepbrothers. A relatively stable figure at home, the second husband died after nine years. When Flo was 17, her mother married again.

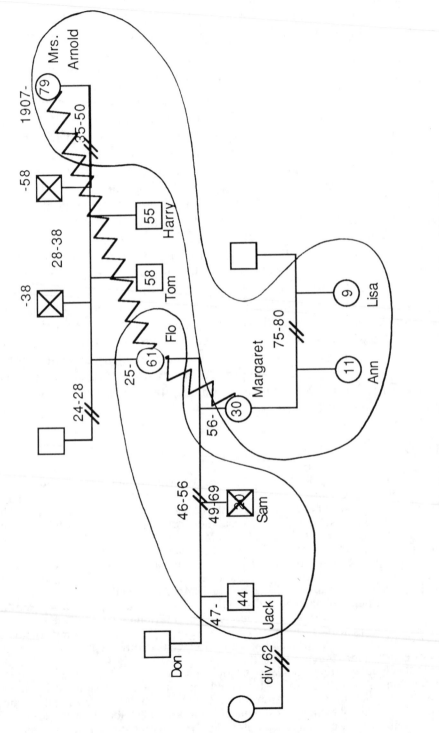

Figure 21-3. The family in later life—the Arnold family.

The third husband died 15 years later. Flo was intermittently close to Mrs. Arnold when her mother was divorced or widowed. However, each time she remarried, Mrs. Arnold tended to exclude Flo from the relationship.

Flo married Don, Margaret's father, one year after her mother's third marriage. The couple had two other children, Sam and Jack. Sam died at 20 of heart failure, and Jack now lived with Flo, following his divorce. Margaret felt that Flo favored Jack, which, given Flo's intense attachment to her son, was not an unreasonable assessment. Again the pattern of poor mother–daughter relationships was repeated. Margaret married at 19, had Ann and Lisa, and divorced after six years. She initially moved in with Mrs. Arnold and received AFDC, saying she was unable to manage the children and job. When she took employment, the children were temporarily placed in foster homes, but were subsequently placed with Mrs. Arnold with whom they had lived for four and a half years.

The therapist first assisted Mrs. Arnold with a practical problem in daily living by arranging for a ramp to be built onto her house for her wheelchair. Therapy then focused on facilitating mother–daughter relationships across the four generations. With some difficulty Flo was engaged in the therapeutic process, and she and her mother spent some time reviewing their experiences surrounding the three husbands/fathers in their shared history. After seeing movement in her relationship with her own mother, Flo was able to take steps toward her daughter Margaret. This, too, was a long-term project, as Margaret was at first suspicious and unresponsive to her mother's efforts.

The last step involved bringing all three women together to further differentiate their respective roles, as well as to solidify and integrate the gains they had made. As Flo and Margaret worked out their issues with their mothers, they became more effective mothers to their own daughters. When this happened, Mrs. Arnold was able to let go of some of her responsibility for Ann and Lisa, and Flo, who was also not working, picked up more of the grandparenting tasks. Meanwhile Margaret began to take a more active interest in her children and the momentum of the cross-generational process was reactivated as parenting roles were once again handed from one generation to another.

This case illustrates how the transitional tasks of later life for the older generation in poor, multiproblem Black families are often colored by the interdependence that poverty and cultural values impose. The active, daily involvement of multigenerational households magnifies the interplay of their own life-phase tasks. Family members can span three to four generations; thus intergenerational conflicts have a high probability of arising. Reality demands that the aged assume meaningful roles; the therapeutic task is to help them to be useful without overfunctioning. Family therapy facilitated a shift toward new options that freed the multigenerational family system to proceed with their intertwined lives without repetition of patterns that had led to triangling of younger family members.

ASSESSMENT AND INTERVENTION

Adequate assessment of multiproblem poor families, as of all families, requires gathering of information for a genogram (Bowen, 1978; McGoldrick & Gerson, 1985). This demographic information and accompanying details regarding life events and systems involved with a family assist the therapist in deciding who should attend the family sessions. The data also offer insight into the family's strengths and connections to its ecosystem. Unfortunately the

issue is not only whether or not such a family can viably connect with the sources of support and continuity that lie outside itself but whether such external supports exist.

A family may be referred because of one member's presenting problems, but share numerous other concerns regarding others in the family. Often families appear reluctantly, contending that they have no problems, and expressing little or no understanding about why they were referred. Therapists can assume generally that these families have little or distorted information about what to expect, how the process can be helpful, and the nature of the therapist's relationship with other agencies involved in their lives. History and their contemporary experience dictate distrust, and, at best, a posture of ambivalence about seeking help (Hines & Boyd-Franklin, 1982).

A therapist enters the room with the task of engaging the family, narrowing the field of inquiry so as not to become overwhelmed, understanding the presenting problem(s) within the context of the family life cycle and its larger ecology, and intervening in such a way that the family is mobilized to think differently about the identified person, the problem, and the worthwhileness of returning where appropriate. Relevant questions include the following:

1. What is the family's definition of the problem that brought them to therapy?

2. Where is the problem occurring and what systems are involved?

3. At what point in the life of the problem and in the life cycle of the family is the family seeking help?

4. How does the identified problem relate to the current life cycle phase or transition as well as to unresolved issues in the family life cycle of the multigenerational system?

5. Who has the power to influence the outcome with regard to the problem?

6. What is the family's relationship with the referring agent and how consistent are the family members' perceptions of the problem?

7. What experiences and attitudes do the family members have about helping agents in general and about therapy in particular?

8. Based on the data available, what is a plausible hypothesis about what is maintaining the problem?

9. How can the presenting problem be redefined in a way that shifts the family's perception of the identified client and the "problem"?

10. What will be the consequence of all members of the family if the problem is resolved?

11. What are the individual and family strengths as well as community resources that can be mobilized?

Inquiry in these areas should assist the therapist in pinpointing the family's strengths as well as the information, attitudes, emotional shifts, behavioral skills, and extrafamilial resources that the family needs to exercise alternative

ways of addressing the problem. The distinction between assessment and intervention can become artificial in that both need to take place during the first session to maximize therapeutic impact. Clinical interventions may be grouped into four general categories; (1) structural, (2) larger systems, (3) educational and rehabilitative, and (4) extended-time models.

With concrete and other social services as backup, the practitioners of the structural method move in rapidly to shore up the family's sagging hierarchy (usually reliant on mother and grandmother) and to define generational boundaries (Minuchin et al., 1967, 1976; Haley, 1976).

There are also approaches that emphasize larger systems that have clear applications for work with poor families. Aponte (1974, 1976) expanded the structural model to include the interrelatedness between the family and larger systems. The "ecostructural" approach acknowledges that the locus of a family's problems may lie outside of the family system. Thus the therapist may invite relevant people from outside the family system to participate in family sessions in order to facilitate assessment and intervention and/or conduct therapy sessions outside of the clinic (e.g. in the schools).

Palazzoli and co-workers (1980) describe effective uses of systemic interventions with the attendance of the referring person in the session or with interventions that take the relationship with the referring agent into account. Coppersmith described a model where a consultant is invited in, usually by the family therapist, to conduct a series of interviews with the family, the family therapist and larger systems representatives in the presence of each other (Coppersmith, 1983b, p. 40). This model offers numerous advantages when treating multiproblem families. Families are less likely to be triangled into conflicts of opinion and advice by their numerous "helpers." Second, all of the family's helpers are spared the anger, frustration, and burnout that accompanies working toward conflicting goals and duplication of effort.

Anderson et al.'s (1986) psychoeducational approach, though developed for the chronically disabled and their families, may have some utility for work with low income, multiproblem families. The psychoeducational approach involves assembling multiple family units and intervening through a structured, educational process about medication management and relational processes. The process allows for an exchange between the professional(s) and family members that facilitates informational, attitudinal, and behavioral shifts within the family. Families are able to extend help to one another in solving relational and concrete problems. They develop the skills and confidence to be advocates on their own behalf for services.

Multiple-Impact Family Therapy

In the author's experience, many multiproblem poor families, Black and others, have been lost referrals as a result of our adherence to the traditional, one-session-per-week therapy model that ignores so many realities in the lives of the poor. The aforementioned approaches served as a cornerstone for the development of the Multiple-Impact Family-Therapy (MIFT) model, an alternative approach for multiproblem families who have no interest in ongoing, weekly therapy (Richman, et al., 1984). Our formulation of this model also draws on the work of MacGregor and colleagues (1964), Alexander, et al. (1981, 1982), and the Milan schools. Essentially the model combines (1) immediate response to a request for service; (2) a brief, problem-oriented treatment approach; (3) use of a team of therapists who work directly with the family; (4) the involvement of agency representatives connected with the family; and (5) an extended session format.

Within a week of a call for services, a family is seen by a team of three therapists for a daylong session, which is divided into four phases—presession strategizing, assessment, treatment planning, and intervention. A six-week follow-up visit is scheduled, with interim and subsequent assistance (e.g., systems advocacy) provided by one of the therapists as needed.

Before the family's arrival, the team meets to formulate hypotheses on the basis of intake data. The family life cycle framework allows the team to zero in on what is maintaining the family's problems. This hypothesis allows the team to narrow the field of inquiry and to deal with what can otherwise become an overwhelming amount of information from the family and other agencies. It reduces the chance of getting sidetracked by the family's multiple problems and multiple storytellers.

During the assessment phase, the team meets with the family as a group and subsequently in individual and/or subsystem groupings to gather additional information and to test their hypotheses, expanding upon the field of inquiry as needed. The subgroup meetings are an important component of the model's application to multiproblem, poor Black families since they permit clarification of the blocks to meeting individual life cycle needs within the multigenerational system. When needed, and with the family's permission, representatives from agencies involved with the family are included in the family group interview.

After the morning session, caseworkers from external agencies leave and the family takes a lunch break. The team meets to share information gathered during the subsystem interviews. It refines or reformulates the working hypothesis and develops a plan of action for assisting the family with major problem(s) and mobilizing system changes to enhance the family's ongoing functioning. The lunch break also affords the family a time to discuss the morning session and to do further relational work and problem solving on their own.

The team draws upon a variety of family therapy approaches during the

intervention phase. However, the team consistently offers families a straight-forward, consumer-oriented reframing of the problem(s) presented. Empowerment and opening up communication have been cornerstones upon which all strategies are built for these families, who are suffering from systems overload and a sense of hopelessness. The family life cycle framework provides a useful way of presenting issues that are within the family's ability to affect regardless of their impoverished context and forces that are beyond their control. Whether or not family life cycle issues are the primary problem, by using this paradigm therapists can quickly focus on central emotional issues that are crucial to the family's ability to proceed developmentally.

Six weeks following the all-day session, a two-hour interview is scheduled with the family and any additional persons or agency representatives judged appropriate. The status of the problems that were targeted for intervention is reviewed. If the family has achieved or moved towards resolution of the identified problems, the family is advised that its case will remain active for a three-month period should any problems or questions arise. They are, of course, free to contact the center beyond this period if necessary. If there has been little or no change with the identified problems, further interventions are made and, if appropriate, a date and time for follow-up later is established. Ironically, families requiring additional intervention beyond the six-week, follow-up have frequently become quite engaged and proved willing to meet on a more frequent basis if recommended.

The uniqueness of the MIFT model resides not in any one of its parts but in its whole. Because "three heads are better than one," the team is able to assess and intervene more efficiently than a single therapist. Moreover the varying personalities, life cycle phases, and skills of the team members increase the chances that the family will be engaged. The potential for burnout and loss of therapist objectivity and focus is also reduced. The daylong meeting facilitates the joining process and permits greater impact than is afforded by weekly therapy sessions of one hour with numerous missed sessions. It also increases the potential for all relevant family members to be present at the time when the family system is most open to change by virtue of the crisis that precipitated the referral.

Case Example: The Goodwin Family

Ms. Goodwin, a 34-year-old single mother, called the clinic for help with her seven children. Her physical condition had been gradually deteriorating over two years as a result of multiple sclerosis, and she indicated that, "My children give me a hard time and show me no respect." She was particularly concerned because Cindy, 17, was refusing to assist with the care of the younger children. Also, her ten-year-old son, Charles, had started staying out until 3:00 o'clock in the morning and her two-year-old, Laurel, had been suspended from nursery school because of her behavior.

The family failed to keep two appointments. The therapist learned from the public-assistance and child-protection caseworkers that Ms. Goodwin and the

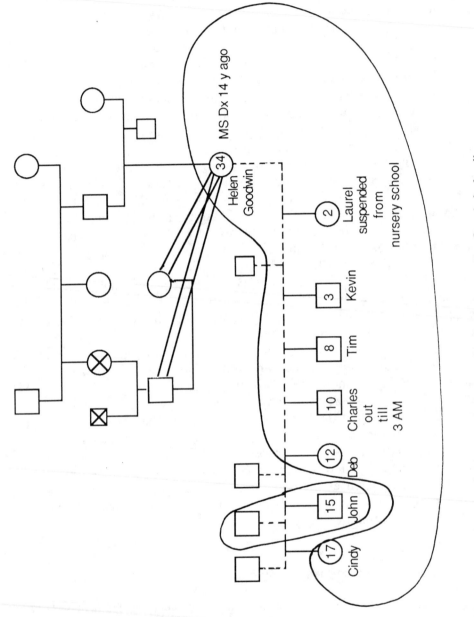

Figure 21.4. Multiple-impact family therapy—the Goodwin family.

children frequently missed appointments because she needed assistance in dressing and getting down the three flights of steps from her apartment.

Concluding that the family would be unlikely to follow through with traditional therapy, arrangements were made for the case to be seen by a team of therapists using the multiple-impact family-therapy model previously described.

The team of three therapists met prior to the family's arrival to review information and formulate a working hypothesis. From the family life cycle framework, the family's life cycle course had been seriously disrupted by unexpected, serious, and irreversible illness. Ms. Goodwin's ability to carry out her parental functions had been greatly diminished, resulting in an emotional and functional loss for the family. Exhausted and frustrated by their failure to fill the power vacuum and restore order from chaos, the older children had retreated, but in a manner that allowed them neither to proceed with their lives in a healthy fashion nor to give the family the support they could otherwise provide.

The assessment consisted of a family interview and separate but simultaneous interviews with Ms. Goodwin and the children. We learned that Ms. Goodwin's condition had been diagnosed 14 years earlier but had worsened during her pregnancy with three-year-old Kevin. Her condition had rapidly deteriorated, and her children seemed neither to understand nor to accept her condition. Unhappy with her present medical care, she often ignored medical advice. John (15) had moved out three months earlier to live with his father, complaining about the overwhelming responsibilities. Since that time Cindy, described by her siblings as "beat woman" because she constantly threatened to smack them for their misbehavior, was refusing to help her mother with the most minor tasks. Cindy had missed many days from school in order to escort her siblings to clinic appointments for medical care.

Debby (12) was not doing as well as she could at school; otherwise no concerns were voiced concerning her, Tim (8), or Kevin, except for their tendency to be unresponsive to the disciplining efforts of Cindy and Ms. Goodwin's relatives.

Charles, called the "street runner," was described as the most problematic. Failing in school, he had become totally noncompliant at home as well. He would frequently bang his head without apparent provocation. Ms. Goodwin had threatened to have him placed in a foster home because she feared he would be killed if he continued to roam around the neighborhood at night.

During both the sibling and family interviews, the children tended to deny the seriousness of their mother's illness. Cindy attributed it to her mother's failure to exercise; she had also blamed her two youngest siblings since she had read that multiple sclerosis could be aggravated by pregnancy. Charles felt that his mother could not walk because she had stopped going to church and drank too much. All of the children seemed angry at John: "He thinks he's bad because he lives in a mansion—all them fancy clothes—and a big bed like a king."

There were frequent references to promises made by their own various fathers. Cindy clearly expressed her upset about the frequent criticism she received from her siblings and mother and how this led to her current refusal to help. Cindy wanted her mother to get help so that she (Cindy) could go on with her life, saying, "These kids are too far gone and it's not my responsibility."

In the individual interview with Ms. Goodwin, we learned that she also had many fears and misconceptions about her disease. She was still sexually active and had refused contraception and a tubal ligation. Reluctant to place any of her children in foster homes, with great ambivalence she had recently permitted her relatives to care for the younger children during the day. According to the caseworkers, there was much conflict between her and her sister and brother-in-law. She often sabotaged their efforts to discipline the children even when she asked for their help. She confirmed that she was both angry and anxious about the extent to which her life and the lives of her children were increasingly beyond her control.

During the daylong meeting, the family was provided lunch while the therapists

met to share data and impressions. The data were supportive of the initial hypothesis, that the family's ability to function adequately had been diminished by the activation of Ms. Goodwin's illness. Besieged by anger, depression, and a growing sense of powerlessness, Ms. Goodwin fluctuated between totally relinquishing her parental responsibilities and resisting the assistance that her older children and relatives attempted to give. She feared losing her children physically and emotionally, and they feared that she would die from her disease. The adolescents in the family experienced much ambivalence about pulling away to pursue their own interests and needs; yet they were unsuccessful in taking on the parental role for the younger children, who needed new resources to be integrated into the family system. Ms. Goodwin, Cindy, John, and Tim demonstrated different coping responses but essentially each was attempting to retreat from an overwhelming situation that none could escape but John.

From the family life cycle perspective, the family could not restabilize and proceed until all had accepted the implications of Ms. Goodwin's illness. Their hesitancy to avail themselves of the concrete and emotional support that their extended-family and church network could provide further restricted their abilities to make the necessary transition. The children were assuming a level of responsibility and independence for which they were not developmentally prepared. Additionally, the various agencies involved with the family were adding to the chaos and lack of structure rather than remedying it. A lack of coordination resulted in a failure to secure many available resources. The team assumed that further "helping" would be useless unless Ms. Goodwin could feel competent and in charge, even if only from the director's chair.

The team established the following priorities: (1) clarify the family's misconceptions regarding Ms. Goodwin's illness; (2) encourage the family to reconnect with its natural support system; (3) assist Ms. Goodwin in securing additional resources; (4) create a forum to coordinate services; and (5) support Ms. Goodwin in her right and ability to provide support and direction for her children.

The team met with the Goodwin family and shared its observations and recommendations. The therapists emphasized that they were highly impressed by the level of caring that seemed evident in the face of a situation that would be stressful and frustrating for anyone. They suggested that the various behavioral and relationship problems seemed to be misguided ways in which the family members tried to protect themselves from further stress and that the attempted solutions had complicated the more concrete problem of being without adequate resources. They impressed upon Ms. Goodwin that her children lacked her maturity and experience and that the response of each was partially related to his or her own developmental issues.

The nurse on the team was particularly helpful in educating the family about the realities of multiple sclerosis. As the discussion evolved, there was a noticeable decline in name calling, interruptions, threats, and incomplete communications. Ms. Goodwin asked, without prompting, for assistance in finding a support group for people with multiple sclerosis and in securing transportation. The team commended Cindy on her academic and sports achievements and her realization that talking would not be enough to resolve the home situation. They also reinforced Ms. Goodwin's position as the executive decision maker.

The team took a break while Ms. Goodwin directed a family discussion. A short while later, team members met with her alone to discuss what, if any, assistance she would like beyond connecting with a multiple sclerosis support group. She had been impressed by the children's interest in reconnecting with their former church and volunteered that perhaps this would help her to feel less depressed and to stop drinking.

The team facilitated a meeting several weeks later between Ms. Goodwin and the family's various helpers. A sense of frustration, but also increased empathy with the family's dilemma, was experienced by the team as the group wrestled with

numerous logistical problems. For example, Ms. Goodwin was eligible for visiting nurse and homemaker services but the social service agency worker anticipated that it would be difficult to find such personnel who would be willing to work during early evening hours because the family lived in a high-crime area. The absence of a telephone and the housing authority's refusal to repair the elevator limited Ms. Goodwin's ability to arrange transportation services when needed. Nonetheless, at the completion of the session, the role of each agency had been clarified in terms of funding, coordination, and provision of physical therapy, day care, disability, supplemental nursing, homemaker services, transportation, and the temporary care of the children should Ms. Goodwin require hospitalization.

At the six-week follow-up session, Ms. Goodwin reported that John was still living with his father but had reconnected with the family. She and the children had resumed church attendance and she had reduced her drinking. The church members had provided much needed kitchen appliances. Ms. Goodwin was being more cooperative with her sister, who continued to keep the younger children during the day. However, a new conflict had arisen between these relatives and the child protection agency, which was refusing to pay them for child care. Cindy shared her excitement about a potential college basketball scholarship. Her level of cooperation had improved but she restated clearly that she could not play parent. The team reinforced Ms. Goodwin's ability to parent, though differently from physically mobile parents. It also predicted, in Cindy's presence, that in spite of her surface anger and frustration, Cindy's ambivalence about leaving the family might lead her to find ways to sabotage her college scholarship. It was suggested that only Ms. Goodwin could help Cindy with this struggle.

One of the therapists assumed responsibility for further follow-up, which evolved in the form of periodic home visits and continued advocacy on the family's behalf.

This case example is typical of the kinds of dilemmas faced by multiproblem poor Black families and their therapists. Often there are no simple solutions. In the Goodwins' case, there was task overload prior to Ms. Goodwin's illness. Previously existing problems were intensified since the family members had not begun to deal openly and realistically with the realities of the illness. The concrete needs of the family demanded an immediate response that could not be adequately met by the traditional helping system. Enlarging the system to include the informal network of the family was a crucial part of the multilevel intervention required in this case.

GENERAL GUIDELINES

In summary, we have presented a number of assessment and therapeutic guidelines for therapists:

1. Provide an orientation for families so they understand what kind of help is available and what your relationship is to others in the human services network.

2. Examine the problem within the context of the multiple systems in which the family is embedded. Involve the essential persons and systems in your thinking, if not in the actual therapy sessions.

3. Develop focused treatment goals that are significant to the family.

    4. Offer hope—think, say, and do something positive (Ford et al., 1986).

    5. Help family members to reclaim repressed feelings through subgroup meetings and shifting attention to feelings below the surface (Minuchin & Montalvo, 1967).

    6. Empower them in whatever ways possible to deal with their circumstances. Pinderhughes (1983) states the issue eloquently: "Using empowerment strategies with our clients would emphasize teaching them about power dynamics and the systems in which they live. They can come to understand the way in which the social system supports or undermines their functions as individuals and as a family. They can learn to sort out the factors in their predicament that belong to external systems and those that belong to them. In doing so, they will not assume blame for systemic influences but will take responsibility for ways in which they collude in reinforcing their own powerlessness" (p. 335).

    7. Work to strengthen families. Ramirez (1978), in a review of the factors that affect the utilization of mental health services, notes: "There is the probability that our present strategies of professionalizing and institutionalizing every problem may cause damage to those natural systems and in the long run exacerbate rather than better our situation. The professionalization of problems which remove people from the natural setting may provide temporary relief, but it also depletes a community of experience and resources for dealing with this and similar problems in the future. My argument is that in bypassing existing helping structures (or failing to create them with the people) we may systematically lower the adaptive capacity of many human populations and weaken those indigenous resources which in times of crisis may be the only ones available and cooperative" (pp. 58–59).

    8. Think politically. Kantor (1984) offers excellent advice in this regard: Avoid one-way give-and-take situations as they reinforce powerlessness and do nothing to alter the family processes. Always be concerned about the adaptive aspects of behaviors, as the individual family may need to retain the behavior as part of its repetoire but exercise more selective use or modify its form.

    9. Avoid trying to solve every family crisis that arises. Crises are an ongoing part of a poor family's existence. Focus rather on those processes and patterns that are maintaining the problems and symptoms that require treatment.
ment.

    10. Accept that families may drop out and return at a later point. The revolving door is not necessarily a negative indicator if a family exhibits evidence of gains.

    11. Use time flexibly.

    12. Do not assume that families can change based on their feeling or thinking differently, as they may require skills training.

    13. Protect yourself from burnout. Connecting with other therapists to work with families and to provide consultation and support is crucial.

    14. Advocate for systems changes that reduce the stress on families seek-

ing services and on those family therapists who accept the challenge of trying to help.

AVOIDING THERAPIST BURNOUT

There are many understandable reasons for therapist "burnout" or emotional exhaustion and diminished job satisfaction in working with multiproblem families. Those doing this kind of work need greater flexibility and administrative support in order to function effectively. The cost of service delivery is always an important consideration. However, it is not necessarily more expensive to utilize a treatment or consulting team rather than a single therapist—considering the cost of therapist burnout, which leads to frequent staff turnover, decreased proficiency, and, in turn, increased client dropouts.

Administrative support can be extended by caseload assignment policies and performance evaluations that do not put undue emphasis on the number of cases that have to be seen. A single multiproblem family case may consume numerous unplanned hours as a therapist follows up with school and other agency contacts and responds to calls for assistance, because of unanticipated events in the lives of these families. Home visits may also be required, necessitating more time than usual. In addition, families may adopt the therapist into their network and request assistance with issues that may not formally relate to the presenting problem or "planned" session goals. For example, a recent visit to the home of an incorrigible 14-year-old girl led the therapist to become involved in the red tape surrounding the grandmother's claim for veteran's benefits from her deceased husband; in a letter regarding housing code violations that threatened the family's sense of security, in the failure of the Social Security Administration to follow up on the disability claim of the identified client's psychiatrically disabled 19-year-old son; and in the failure of school staff to follow up on securing a special placement for the client's younger brother.

Family therapists are constantly challenged to define our role and boundaries, and clearly our best efforts are not always enough. It is undoubtedly a rare therapist who has not faced moments of doubt about such work. Even when families are successfully engaged, they may leave treatment without termination interviews, only to reemerge on the agency's rolls after another crisis. Therapists can be assisted by supervision to see this revolving-door phenomenon as an opportunity to help families to reach higher levels of functioning at various stages rather than as treatment failure.

At times therapists may experience stagnation because they cannot justify their own affluence in the face of a client's poverty. Poorly paid community workers may overidentify with poor clients, thereby rendering themselves equally ineffective. Attempts to operate on the basis of guilt or a "bleeding

heart" will inevitably fail. A useful goal is to stay personally connected with the poor, but also to stay connected with one's own viable contextual base. This means staying in regular, active contact with one's own extended family, which provides a continuing base for the therapist's own hope and vitality.

Administrators and therapists would also benefit by heeding Beels (1976) advice to those working with families of schizophrenics:

> One must be able to retreat sometimes. No one can do this work all week long or every year of his life. The working life of the staff must include times of retreat and reflection. Otherwise they get burned out—permanently turned off from too much coping. (p. 281)

Most therapists who work with multiproblem families have a genuine commitment to assisting the population and the need to retreat even in the form of lunch away from the office often is ignored. Agency mandates in this regard may be insufficient as it becomes incumbent on the therapist to recognize the need to refuel his or her own tank, as they so often caution families to do who succumb to too much coping.

CONCLUSIONS

In this chapter we have reviewed aspects of the family life cycle for poor, multiproblem Black families. Along with ethnic traditions, the triple jeopardy of being economically poor, politically bankrupt, and discriminated against because of race is a significant factor in the way that these families organize themselves and function. The need to be flexible and to adapt to ongoing stresses have resulted in great heterogeneity among families even in the same setting. Research is sorely needed to tease out those factors that allow some individuals and families to cope with, and even mobilize themselves to overcome, the harsh conditions that poverty and racism impose.

A family life cycle perspective provides a useful framework for assessment and intervention since it does not dismiss or focus solely on the impact of context and external stressors. It permits an understanding of how these exacerbate the stress of normal developmental needs and unresolved family issues and, most important, provides direction for intervention.

Multiproblem, poor Black families face and present many challenges. Success in meeting these depends in part upon their ability to maintain hope. The author's belief is that those who lose the ability to hope lose the ability to perceive and act on the choices and resources available to them, however limited. Therapists' success in having and conveying hope depends on their ability to bridge differences in experience connected with social class, race, ethnicity, gender, and so on. Thus the question "How do you know where I'm going if you don't know where I'm coming from?" is deserving of attention.

The average family therapist may not be able to connect with poor Black families on the basis of race or shared oppression. However, his or her own family life cycle has at some time been punctuated by experiences of powerlessness in one form or another (Pinderhughes, 1984). Through whatever means, therapists must find ways to deal with their own complex and delicate feelings of anger, guilt, confusion, and a desire to turn away from the pain of the poor's intimate lives and the nonesthetic trappings of their surrounding external world. In doing so therapists become freer to communicate genuine respect and compassion, and ultimately to empower.

REFERENCES

Aging America (19?). U.S. Senate Special Committee on Aging in Cooperation with the American Association of Retired Persons.

Alexander, J. F., & Parsons, B. V. (1982). *Functional family* therapy, Monterey, Calif.: Brooks/Cole.

Anderson, C. Reiss, D., Hogarty, G. (1986) *Schizophrenia and the family.* New York: Guilford Press.

Aponte, H. (1974) Psychotherapy for the poor: An eco-structural approach to treatment. *Delaware Medical Journal,* 46:432–448.

Aponte, H. (1976a). The family school interview, an eco-structural approach. *Family Process* 15/3:303–312.

Aponte, H. (1976b). Underorganization in the poor family. In P. J. Guerin, Jr. (Ed.), *Family therapy: Theory and practice.* New York: Gardner Press, pp. 249–283.

Beels, C. (1976). Family and social management of schizophrenia. In P. Guerin (Ed.), *Family therapy: Theory and Practice.* New York: Gardner Press, pp. 249–283.

Bowen, M. (1976), *Family therapy in clinical practice* New York: Jason Aronson.

Cherlin, A. J. (1981). *Marriage, divorce, remarriage.* Cambridge, Mass.: Harvard University Press, pp. 93–112.

Coles, R. (1970). *Uprooted children.* Pittsburgh: University of Pittsburgh Press.

Coles, R., & Coles, J. (1978). *Women of crisis.* New York: Delacorte.

Colon, F. (1973). In search of one's past: an identity trip. *Family Process* 12(4): 429–438.

Colon, F. (1978). Family ties and child placement. *Family Process* 17(3); 289–312.

Ford, R., Gregory, H., Merriweather, J., Brown, G., & Norman, R. (1985), Expanding perspectives on the black family. Eighth Annual Family Network Symposium, Arlington, Va.

Furstenberg, F. (1986). Teen mothers 17 years later—They've recovered but their children are maladjusted. *Professional Newsletter for Family Therapy Practicioners.* 11(46).

Gans, H. J. (1968). Culture and class in the study of poverty: An approach to anti-poverty research. In D. P. Moynihan (Ed.), *On understanding poverty,* New York: Basic Books, pp. 205–206, 216, 219.

Gibbs, J. (1984). Black adolescents and youth: An endangered species. *American Journal of Orthopsychiatry,* 54(1): 6–21.

Haley, J. (1976). *Problem solving therapy.* San Francisco: Jossey-Bass.

Hill, R. (1977). *Informal adoption among black families.* Washington, D.C.: National Urban League.

Hines, P., & Boyd-Franklin, N. (1982). Black families. In McGoldrick, M., Pearce, J., & Giordano, N. (Eds.), *Ethnicity and family therapy.* New York: Guilford Press, pp. 84–107.

Imber-Coopersmith, E. (1983). The family and public service systems: An assessment method. In J. Hansen & B. Keeney (Eds.), *Diagnosis and assessment in family therapy.* Aspens Systems Corp., pp. 84–99.

Imber-Coopersmith, E. (1983b). The family and public sector systems: Interviewing and interventions. *Journal of Strategic and System Therapies.* 2:38–47.

Kantor, D., Peretz, A., & Zander, R. (1984). The cycle of poverty—Where to begin? *Family Therapy Collections,* 9:59–73.

Klausner, S. (1978). *Six Years in the lives of the impoverished: An examination of the win thesis.* Philadelphia: Center for Research on the Acts of Man.

Lefever, H. (1977). The religion of the poor: Escape or creative force? *Journal of the Scientific Study of Religion* 16 (3):225–236.

Lewis, J., & Looney, J. (1983). *The long struggle: Well functioning working class black families.* New York: Brunner/Mazel.

Lindblad-Goldberg, M., & Dukes, J. (1984). Social support in black, low-income single-parent families: Normative and dysfunctional patterns. *American Journal of Orthopsychiatry* 55 (1): 42–58.

MacGregor, R., Ritchie, A., Serrano, A., & Schuster, F. (1964), *Multiple impact therapy with families.* New York: McGraw-Hill.

McGoldrick, M. & Gerson, R. (1985), *Genograms in family assessment.* New York: W. W. Norton.

Minuchin, S., & Montalvo, B. (1967). Techniques for working with disorganized low socioeconomic families. *American Journal of Orthopsychiatry* 37/5, Oct: 880–887.

Minuchin, S., Montalvo, B., Rosman, B. L., & Schumer, R. (1967). *Families of the slums.* New York: Basic Books, p. 368.

Noble, K. (1984). Plight of black family is studied anew. *New York Times,* Jan. 29.

Norton, E. (1985). Restoring the traditional black family. *The New York Times Magazine.* June 2: 43–93.

Palazzoli, M., Boscolo, L., Cecchin, G., & Prata, G. (1980). The problem of the referring person. *Journal of Marital and Family Therapy,* Jan.: 3–9.

Parsons, T., & Bales, R. (1955). *Family, socialization and interaction process.* Glencoe, Ill: Free Press.

Pinderhughes, E. (1982). Afro-American families and the victim system. In McGoldrick, M., Pierce, J., & Giordano, J. (Eds.), *Ethnicity and family therapy.* New York: Guilford Press, pp. 108–122.

Pinderhughes, E. (1983). Empowerment for our clients and for ourselves. *Social Casework,* 64(6):331–338.

Pinderhughes, E. (1984). Teaching empathy. Ethnicity, race and power at the cross-cultural treatment interface. *American Journal of Social Psychiatry,* 4(1).

Ramirez, O. (1978). Chicano mental health status and implications for services. Preliminary examination paper. Ann Arbor, Mich: Department of Psychology, University of Michigan, pp. 58–59.

Richman, D., Hays, N., Hines, P., & Maxim, K. (1984). Beyond outreach—Engaging the multi-problem family. Presented at the Family Networker Conference, Washington, D.C.

Staples, R. (1981a). The myth of the black matriarchy. *The Black Scholar,* Nov./Dec.: 26–34.

Staples, R. (1981b), Black manhood in the 1970s. A critical look back. *The Black Scholar.* May/June: 2–9.

Teachman, J. (1982). Early marriage, premarital fertility and marital dissolution. *Journal of Family Issues* (4(1):105–126.

22

Lower-Income and Professional Families: A Comparison of Structure and Life Cycle Process

Richard H. Fulmer, Ph.D.

This chapter deals with a segment of the family life cycle—the years when the family's children are between the ages of 12 and 35—as it is passed by two different types of families in our society: two-career professional families and lower-income families that receive public assistance.

The author made the clinical observations that formed the basis for this chapter in three different work settings. He worked with future professionals in the psychological counseling service of an ivy league college from 1979 to 1981. He has also seen older professionals in his private practice on the upper west side of Manhattan in New York City from 1976 to the present. These groups are overwhelmingly white, have middle or upper middle levels of income, and plan to (or have already taken) at least one higher degree. His contact with lower-income families has occurred as he has conducted live supervision of families at a community mental health center in the south Bronx, New York City, from 1980 to the present. The group served there is 55% Hispanic (mostly Puerto Rican), 30% Black, and 15% White. Eighty-five percent of these families receive public assistance.

SOURCES OF DATA

A discussion of family structure and social class ideally requires the citation of marriage and birth data in relation to level of income. Unfortunately many relevant national level statistics are not gathered or reported in relation to level of family income (Children's Defense Fund, 1985, p. 6). Marriage and birth data are reported in relation to race, although often only for Blacks and

Whites. Because poverty is disproportionately concentrated among racial minorities in the United States, studies of family structure and social class can adopt the admittedly imperfect strategy of considering the Black statistical subgroup to represent the lower-income group and the White statistical subgroup to represent the middle-income group. This method, of course, confounds the effects of race and class, a serious but currently unavoidable shortcoming to which all such analyses are subject.

Further complicating this analysis is the fact that the Hispanic people in the author's clinical population have become a sizable minority relatively recently. Many statistics still reflect only Black and White races and only now are being gathered on Hispanics as a separate group. Whether "Hispanics" in the United States (including Mexicans, Cubans, Puerto Ricans, and people from Central and South America) are sufficiently uniform in culture and social class to be considered a "group" is a matter of some scholarly debate. At any rate, although the author's observations of lower-income families were made of mixed racial group, not enough statistics are available to distinguish between the different cultures represented.

An additional difficulty is that American sociological scholarship on minorities has studied Black families much more extensively than Hispanic families. Although the lower-income members of these two minorities now share many of the same residential areas and environmental conditions in urban areas, they differ in their history in the United States and in the history of their family structure. Therefore, to cite sociology of the Black family to make a point about the predominantly Hispanic families in the author's clinical population may be questioned. The author has observed, however, some similarities between Hispanic and Black families in the function of the extended family. For instance, in both Black (Stack, 1974) and Puerto Rican (Garcia-Preto, 1982) families, children are seen as the responsibility of the whole kinship network, not just the biological mother. Fosterage and informal adoption of kin are common. In addition, Rogler and co-workers (1983) write that Puerto Rican families in Puerto Rico "enmesh their members in a system of help-giving exchanges" (p. 22). This is very similar to the sociological and anthropological descriptions of lower-income Black families that will be cited below. It thus appears that enough similarities exist between Black and Puerto Rican lower-income families to permit *some* generalization, but the clinician should proceed cautiously in applying the general conclusions of this chapter to any specific family.

BIRTH AND MARRIAGE PATTERNS

A central difference between the two groups being compared in this chapter (other than socioeconomic) is the age at which females characteristically become mothers. In the professional class, women born in the 1950s are

delaying this transition substantially in relation to women born 20 years earlier. In a recent report on the relationship between delayed childbearing and employment, David Bloom (1986) uses U.S. Bureau of the Census statistics from 1985 to show that for women now aged 30–39, "Professional working women are most likely to have delayed childbearing until after their 27th birthday, whereas women managers and executives are most likely to [still] be childless." He goes on to say that 52% of women who are still childless at age 30 are projected to have children. Between 1970 and 1983, the first-birth rate for women aged 30–34 increased 120%. The rate for women 35–39 increased 105%.

Bloom also asserts that:

> The phenomenon of delayed childbearing is almost exclusively associated with the fertility behavior of white women. The mean age at first birth has been remarkably steady across cohorts of black women born from 1935–1960.

Educational attainment, not race, seems to be a major factor in the delay of childbearing, however. Bloom notes that up to half of the difference in age at first-birth is eliminated when Black and White women with the same level of education are compared. Staples (1985) contends that college-educated (and so, presumably, middle-income) black women "have their children later and in smaller numbers than any other socioeconomic or racial group in the United States" (p. 1011).

In the lower-income group, average age at first birth tends to be much lower and out-of-wedlock births much more common. The average age at first birth for Black women is about 21. Staples (1985) uses 1984 U.S. Census figures to report that among women who had turned 20 between 1975 and 1980, 41% of Blacks and 19% of Whites had already given birth. Staples goes on to say:

> Within that same group of young black women, about 75% of all births were out-of-wedlock, compared with only 25% of births to white women. (p. 1006)

Although the absolute proportion of out-of-wedlock and adolescent births is still much higher for Blacks than Whites, Whites are closing the gap. The Children's Defense Fund (1985) cites the fact that between 1970 and 1981, birth rates to unmarried White women rose by one-third and White adolescent birth rates rose by 57%. For unmarried Black teenagers, the rate dropped 10%. Thus race is not the sole determinant of teenage pregnancy or out-of-wedlock birth. In a later publication, the same source (Children's Defense Fund, 1986) contends that the out-of-wedlock birth pattern is a function of social class.

> Disadvantaged young women, whether black, white or Hispanic, are three to four times more likely to become unwed parents than non-poor teens. Single parenthood among teens is much more strongly linked to poverty than to race or other indicators. (p. 6)

These two groups thus pass the life cycle milestones at ages that are widely different from each other. They also differ structurally in that when a child is born out-of-wedlock, a family is formed of mother and child that later adds a

husband/stepfather. In contrast, the professional family begins with the couple and adds children only after substantial delay. The normative model for family life cycle development may thus be relevant to the largest single group of families in America today, but it must be revised to create norms for these two minorities. The therapist must work with different expectations for what is "normal" and "healthy" for the developmental pace and structure for these two groups. This implies different techniques of assessment, intervention, and expectation about outcome. The same theories of pathology apply: families with problems are not performing a certain developmental task; family members are either too close or too distant from each other, and most problems can be seen as a function of a disordered hierarchy. Two important differences are:

1. Pathological patterns will be enacted by different players and at different times for these two minority groups.

2. Lower-income families suffer much more severe environmental pressures than do professional families. Any theory of lower-class family dysfunction must consider the harsh environment of poverty as a cause of family disorder or developmental disturbance.

ADDITIONS TO A THEORY OF THE FAMILY LIFE CYCLE

These two variations on the life cycle—the extreme elongation of the process of forming the family in the professional class and the extreme acceleration of the lower class—suggest an addition to life cycle theory: the time it takes a family to pass a certain stage affects the structure of the family. In the lower-income family, the acceleration of pregnancy makes it impossible to go through the stages of "launching pad," "single adult," and "couple formation" without children involved. Thus "launching pad" must often be achieved while the young girl stays in her mother's home. "Single adult" is certainly a misnomer for an adolescent mother with children. And since the husband/wife bond does not precede child rearing, it is not likely to be emphasized as the central relationship around which the family is built. With this acceleration the central relationship will probably be mother/daughter, in both the generation of grandmother/mother and of mother/daughter. The family will also be larger, not only because each woman will have several children, but because she will have them when she is young, so that several generations will be alive at the same time.

On the other hand, the elongated professional model creates a very different structure. The extreme delay of pregnancy and emphasis on higher education creates a very clear break during the "launching pad" phase, after which children have virtually no family responsibilities. If they travel away from home to college, they have very little actual family contact. The stage of

"single adult" may stretch on for many years. During these years the profession, not family relationships, is still the primary focus. Because "couple formation" always precedes child rearing, a great deal of attention can be given to that stage. Both partners are often quite selective, trying out a number of serious but childless relationships before marrying. Once married the primacy of the couple is asserted over relationships to parents. Children are not yet a focus. When children do arrive, two-career parents may assign a substantial portion of their care to hired professionals, with grandparents as visitors. Rarely does another relative raise the children or does a mother take in children other than hers for long periods. Because childbearing begins so late, few couples have more than two children and at such a late age that no more than three generations are alive at once. The extended family thus is smaller and, relative to the children, much more aged. Divorce and remarriage occur quite often, but usually when parents are in their late 20s and 30s. When divorced, parents still usually live independently of grandparents. The number of family members is fewer and everyone is further apart, both in space and time.

A second possible addition to life cycle theory suggested by this comparison concerns the theory of symptom formation. Terkelsen (1980) posits that symptoms occur when family structure lags behind the developmental needs of its members (p. 46). Evidence of this pathological process is commonly exemplified by overattentive parents who are moving too slowly through the life cycle and do not accommodate their child's developing need for independence and autonomy. The child responds with immature behavior, confirming the parents' idea that more supervision is necessary and a pathological loop ensues. It is possible that this slowness of structural change is a class-related characteristic. It may be more common in the elongated, professional-class life-cycle model. The highly compressed, lower-class model might illustrate another process by which symptoms are formed.

Lower-class families are subject to sudden structural changes due to environmental pressures. Mother loses a job, father leaves, an apartment is burned out, or a sister becomes pregnant. All these require a sudden change in the membership and caretaking structure of the family. In a situation so subject to emergencies, changes in structure may precede rather than lag behind the developmental needs of children and other family members. The children may be expected to grow up too fast, rather than too slowly. For instance, young children may be expected to supervise themselves at home because some survival need draws the mother away. Such premature self-reliance might lead to the children defensively detaching themselves from caregivers, making it difficult for parents to influence them when they are adolescent.

This structural acceleration can occur in professional families as well if parents are too preoccupied with their own careers to spend time caring for their children. The author has also certainly seen structural lag in lower-income families in which mothers, afraid to be left alone, act as though their children are not growing up. But it may be that each culture is especially

vulnerable to a different source of symptom formation because of the unique pace with which it passes through the family life cycle.

LIFE CYCLE STAGES FOR "PROFESSIONAL" FAMILIES

This is a group that not only graduates from high school and college, but takes at least one higher degree as well. It is distinguished by a fairly continuous and lengthy school attendance and a delay of pregnancy. Such a pattern holds for this group regardless of race.

"Professional" Identity

An original meaning of the verb "to profess" was "to confess or own a religious belief" (*Shorter Oxford*, 1959). It is in this way that a profession is distinguished from a job. Not only is it a way to support oneself, but it also constitutes a set of beliefs, a mission, a way to practice meaning in life. The specific professional activity and the product of that activity become centrally important to the happiness and self-esteem of the practitioner.

The second, more popular meaning of "professional" is to distinguish it from "amateur." That is, professionals are paid for practicing their skill. Everyone needs these two elements in life—a way to practice meaning and a way to support oneself. Professionals are fortunate to be able to combine both activities in their daily work.

Junior and Senior High: Ages 12–17

The preparation for a profession requires lengthy concentration on non-wage-earning tasks. Middle-class income makes this possible for children in these families. The central focus is on school achievement. This means that school attendance and daily homework are expected by the parents for both sexes. Both of these are monitored, and unexplained school absences of a day or two are cause for a family crisis.

Grades are also monitored and "underachievement" (that is, grades that may be passing but are lower than expected) often results in parents conferring earnestly with their children, their children's teachers, school officials, private tutors, and, finally, mental health professionals. It is assumed that both sexes will receive a high school diploma on time and that both sexes will make multiple college applications. During this period (and even before) parents (and grandparents) save money to help finance at least four years of college.

Comparison of Family Life Cycle Stages

Age	Professional Families	Low-Income Families
12–17	a. Prevent pregnancy b. Graduate from high school c. Parents continue support while permitting child to achieve greater independence	a. First pregnancy b. Attempt to graduate from high school c. Parent attempts strict control before pregnancy. After pregnancy, relaxation of controls and continued support of new mother and infant
18–21	a. Prevent pregnancy b. Leave parental household for college c. Adapt to parent–child separation	a. Second pregnancy b. No further education c. Young mother acquires adult status in parental household
22–25	a. Prevent pregnancy b. Develop professional identity in graduate school c. Maintain separation from parental household. Begin living in serious relationship	a. Third pregnancy b. Marriage—leave parental household to establish stepfamily c. Maintain connection with kinship network
26–30	a. Prevent pregnancy b. Marriage—develop nuclear couple as separate from parents c. Intense work involvement as career begins	a. Separate from husband b. Mother becomes head of own household within kinship network
31–35	a. First pregnancy b. Renew contact with parents as grandparents c. Differentiate career and child-rearing roles between husband and wife	a. First grandchild b. Mother becomes grandmother and cares for daughter and infant

Pregnancy is incompatible with the expectation of good school achievement and a college career, so it is prevented. This is accomplished partly by parental supervision of both sexes. Eventually it is done by the adolescents themselves, who either practice sex play without intercourse or practice intercourse with some form of birth control. Pregnancies that do occur are usually terminated by abortion (Zelnick et al., 1981). This control of pregnancy is motivated not so much by morality about sexual activity as by utility. Professional preparation requires childlessness, so that is what prevails.

Characteristic Issues

Most common presenting problems for this group are underachievement in school, disobedience at school and home, drug and alcohol abuse, and anorexia/bulimia.

Possible Interventions

Most theories of family therapy will view these problems as functions of parental disharmony that has disturbed the hierarchy of parents over children. Therapists will try to heal the parental division and restore appropriate limit setting. Parental impotence, anxiety, hypervigilance, neglect, or perfectionism will be seen as functions of insufficient cooperation between the two halves of the parental dyad. Problems are not seen as resulting from an absence of parental resources but from conflict between the parents in using those resources.

College: Ages 18–21

In the majority of cases, both sexes will leave home to go to college, becoming single adults. Developmental tasks for these young adults are to become independent from their parents in life-management functions, decision making and social choices. They are not expected to be independent financially.

College students may work to supplement their parents' support, but they are not usually beginning their "careers" with the jobs they take. They may be expected to "live poor" with the understanding that this is a temporary arrangement. Their primary work is schoolwork. An important developmental task is to learn to work very hard without parental supervision.

They are also expected to develop a personal identity, experiment intellectually, and develop a vocational direction. They are expected to be sexually active. Parents who worried when they *were* active during ages 12–18, will now worry if they are not. Intercourse is more common, but pregnancy is still avoided, now by active, medically sanctioned birth control methods (usually) initiated by the woman. Serious liaisons are developed and couples sometimes live together, but few marry.

Parents must adjust to their child being permanently out of the house. This requires them to invest in their marital relationship, their younger children, or their work (Fulmer, et al., 1982). During this period they do not have grandchildren in whom to invest, a situation they tolerate willingly.

Characteristic Issues

Many college students present with work-related problems: poor concentration, lack of motivation, inability to study, writer's block, or sleeping through classes. They may also present with social difficulties—shyness or loneliness—or with drug or alcohol abuse. Characteristic problematic family processes are the tension between the parents' necessary loss of authority and their continued financial responsibility, readjustment of the sibling subsystem remaining at home, intensification of marital dysfunction as parental roles

become less demanding, and the young adult's conflicts over asserting a differentiated position while maintaining continuity with family ideals.

Possible Interventions

The family therapist must understand these issues as functions of the task of older adolescents separating from their families. Therapy is then focused around the whole family's resistance to that task (Fulmer & Medalie, 1987). Students are often geographically separated from their families, and so current family influence is less obvious. Therapy with the whole family present is not always easy to arrange.

Because of college students' youth and financial dependence on the parents, it is too early to expect them to become fully individuated. Sessions alone with students can help, however, to begin to resolve identity conflicts and challenge the degree to which their behavior is provocative to or unnecessarily dependent on their parents. Sessions alone with their parents (if possible) can focus on their changing roles as parents and normalize some of the ambiguities of their still being financially responsible for but having little control over their child.

In certain very difficult circumstances, therapists may consider convening the whole family, no matter how geographically dispersed (Whiting, 1981). Sessions with students, parents, and siblings all together can deal with new patterns of functioning in the changing family structure. These sessions should focus more on communication and understanding than on limit setting. In general the parents should be less protective than in the past and limits should come from the general community or school. Limit setting is an appropriate focus, however, if the student is abusing drugs or is schizophrenic and intends to live at home.

Graduate School: Ages 22–25

The professional class by definition goes on to graduate school, sometimes for two years (social work, law, business) and sometimes for four to eight years (psychology, medicine). At the end of college, students move out of the dormitories or university apartments and move in with a roommate or two, but leave the adolescent "gang." They tend to become more financially independent, working to support themselves, taking out student loans, and receiving stipends. Often parents decrease their financial contributions after college, so the student's separation from the family is more complete.

Couples begin to "live together" quite seriously, but many still delay marriage. For "living together" couples, pregnancy and childbearing are rigorously avoided. Women living alone also are sexually active but avoid pregnancy, and elect abortion if they do get pregnant. Very few women choose single parenthood at this time. The focus of the relationship is the satisfaction

of each member of the couple with each other—the further development of each individual within an intimate, day-to-day relationship with a member of the opposite sex. These relationships are not casual, but are more easily begun and dissolved than marriages. They are conducted at a greater remove from parental comment or involvement than earlier dating or subsequent marriages. If they dissolve, there is no social censure for either participant.

The academic focus shifts from intellectual searching to practical preparation for a specific profession. Students do not "experiment" with courses outside their major field. They are taking a relatively unvarying program designed to teach them a "trade" at which they will earn a living.

Characteristic Issues

This is a period when the environment provides the least structure for these adult children. They are relatively distant from their families of origin and have not yet formed families of their own. They are no longer part of the more intensely structured rhythms of undergraduate life (dorms, spectator and participant athletics, regular parties). They are not yet in jobs that require full-time, regular attendance. Some time is spent in attending classes, but even more on solitary study and writing. A major task for individuals is to learn to structure their own time, become self-reliant, and learn to work independently. Their intrinsic interest in their field is expected to be their primary motivation, not the authority of parents, teachers, or bosses.

If graduate students have conflicts within themselves or with their parents about this task, they can lose traction in their development, neither advancing to their degree nor accepting a regular nonprofessional job. They may become stalled for awhile in a provisional state, never quite reaching the "starting line" (a higher degree and licensure) of adult life.

Sometimes the student's parents received bachelors' degrees themselves, but did not take higher degrees. Conflicts about achievement that had not emerged before may emerge now. This is especially true for women in that it is especially unlikely that their mothers received higher degress or prepared for a life with professional activity at its center. Professional women of this generation, therefore, often lack family role models. Gender expectations that may not have been so apparent in college may now begin to become quite apparent when the purpose of education is to develop a central identity as someone who works outside the home. For women especially, success may mean difficulty in finding or holding a mate, since women with advanced degrees are among the last to marry and the first to divorce (Norton & Moorman, 1987).

For parents this may be a poignantly frustrating era because their children are delaying a developmental stage in a way that is unfamiliar to them. It also greatly prolongs the period of being "unsettled," a condition that is hard for parents to bear. Children no longer have their protection, but do not yet have the protection of marriage and regular income. Parents are also now more

urgently waiting for grandchildren, but don't even see the preconditions for grandchildren developing.

Possible Interventions

Therapy at this stage will probably not focus so much on the concrete issues of leaving home as on the conflicts of the children over living out the life scripts they feel their parents want for them. Unless the separation problems are literal and severe, family therapy with one person (Carter & Orfanidis, 1976) is indicated, with focus on themes of how the family views "success," separation, and attitudes toward sex roles. The adult children may now be old enough and sufficiently independent financially to expect them to work toward individuation. Because such a process is neither more nor less than the appropriate developmental task for the era, the work will probably proceed slowly. Progress will be incremental and could be lengthy. If problems are more severe, it may be useful to convene the family to focus on the parents feeling they still must take care of their child and children feeling they must take care of their parents.

After Graduate School: Ages 26–30

After completing graduate school, professionals enter a period of intense work involvement as they begin their careers. They also begin to shift their social arrangements from "living together" to marriage. For the first time, they may begin to show anxiety or depression if they are *not* married. They are likely to marry other professionals, however, so that even when married they may each practice their profession and still prevent pregnancy for some years. In their book on different patterns of the timing of parenthood, Daniels and Weingarten (1982) refer to this "late timing" process as "programmatic postponement."

Characteristic Issues

The problems of this stage involve finding a balance between self-assertion and accommodation in intimate relationships. This process is common for all new couples, but is complicated by the symmetrical nature of the husband's and wife's roles. Both expect to pursue their professions as the central source of life meaning. Neither expects to focus on home or marriage as central. In two-career marriages, our society as yet has no model for how to distribute money-making and relationship-maintenance functions. Men may expect to work outside the home and be taken care of by their wives as their fathers were. Women may find themselves doing as much caretaking as their mothers did, but without allowing for the fact that they have neither the time nor the

energy to do so. Power struggles over who does caretaking and whose career is more important may result. The woman's career is often seen as less important because she may be paid less money than the man and because both have the unspoken anticipation that when they *do* have children, she will take care of them and more financial responsibility will fall on the man. Thus even in early-stage two-career families, there is a pressure for this type of sex-role differentiation and the power inequities that result from it.

Possible Interventions

Couples often have implicit and unconscious assumptions about marriage that they did not have about their relationship when they were cohabiting. These assumptions are a product of social belief and two main family influences: an imitation of or reaction against their parents' marriages, and the spouses' respective sibling positions. Careful inquiry into these areas will often reveal such expectations. Each spouse will consider some of them to be ego-syntonic, nonnegotiable aspects of reality. The other spouse may regard the same ideas as self-indulgent, arbitrary whims. For professional couples, blending these different assumptions may raise special difficulties. Their sense of almost religious commitment to their professions permits them to justify many desires not as their own idiosyncratic wishes but as requirements of their work. The way leisure time is used, who does household chores, and how much time is spent together are all righteously defended as necessities dictated by the demands of professions. This seems to be especially true of those in the "helping" professions. The professionals feel themselves to be sacrificing so much already to their professions that they are entitled to their spouses' accommodation.

To reframe their righteous demands as ordinary personal desires (expressed in statements such as "I want . . ." or "I feel . . .") is a very difficult but necessary therapeutic maneuver (Lerner, 1985). It is sometimes nearly impossible, however, because the practice of the profession is so much a part of the professional's identity. To accept the idea that one's own desires are just like everyone else's and deserve neither more nor less than equal consideration can be a serious blow to one's self esteem. It seems to question the sense of a unique mission that sometimes underlies the idea of profession.

Birth of a First Child: Ages 31–35

Here is where sex roles really diverge. Families that attempt to divide money-making and child-rearing tasks symmetrically between the spouses have a hard struggle to maintain their balance, beginning with the facts that only the woman carries and bears the child and the man is usually paid at a higher rate. Even after birth primary child-care responsibilities (even if this

means arranging for baby-sitters) is still usually given to the mother (O'Don-nell, 1984) and primary breadwinning to the father, at least for some years.

Characteristic Issues

The tasks of making money and finding meaning in a profession continue, but now the couple also faces the task of providing consistent parenting. How this new task is distributed is sometimes the source of power struggles in which both parties feel exploited and that choices are being denied them. For individuals whose lives have been based on the experience of choice (choosing a college, a major field of study, a profession, an apartment, a mate, a job, timing of pregnancy), this feeling of being "forced" by the powerful "obliga-tions" of parenthood may be especially poignant. Mothers may feel they are not getting enough support as mothers from their husbands, while fathers may feel they are not getting enough emotional appreciation for being breadwin-ners. Women may be reluctant to interrupt the careers in which they have invested so much and may look to their husbands to make it up to them. Sometimes neither parent really accepts the parenting responsibility, which has serious consequences for the child. Because this professional household is affluent enough to be independent of (and often geographically distant from) the parents' families of origin, and because birth has been delayed so long, the now relatively elderly grandmothers cannot be expected to provide daily child care, nor are they likely to be free or willing to do so.

Possible Interventions

Because it is a relatively recent phenomenon for two-profession couples to be so numerous, virtually all such couples come from families that did not provide a model for a two-profession family. Each brings complementary models to an allegedly symmetrical relationship. Getting them to recognize the difference between the explicit values they profess and the implicit assump-tions on which they actually behave is a major task. Once this is done, couples may be freer to decide deliberately how they want to apportion tasks. The family therapist is most helpful in clarifying how they decide what they decide, and in validating the difficulty of creating a new model of family.

LIFE CYCLE STAGES FOR LOWER-INCOME FAMILIES

Lower-income parents are often unemployed outside the home. They work hard, but usually at raising their families. When they do have outside, paying

jobs, these are not "professions," or even "careers." That is, the jobs rarely express a belief the parents have about themselves that gives special meaning to their daily activity. They may work for a paycheck, or for the social contacts at work, or because they like to be purposefully active, or because they gain self-esteem by being self-supporting, but they usually do not see the specific activity of the job as a source of personal meaning in their lives. One job might do as well as another if they are equal in difficulty, social stimulation, status, and pay.

Because the work available to the lower-income group is sometimes difficult to invest with meaning, preparing for it by going to school may not be seen as especially meaningful either. That is, knowledge is not acquired to enhance the practice of meaning, but rather to ensure better job opportunities. When few jobs are visibly available, even for high-school graduates, school seems even less meaningful. When work (in the form of job or profession) is not available as a source of meaning or financial support, other sources of meaning must be sought. One of the richest sources of meaning available to lower-income families is the activity of the family itself, specifically the raising of children.

In lower-income families, the structure of the family going through the life-cycle stages is different than that of the professional classes. It often appears to be a "single-parent" family. In fact the basic family unit is more usually an extended three- or four-generational network of kin. If the only model for "family" that we are expecting to observe is the "nuclear" one based on the marital couple, such families seem deficient and "disorganized" in that the fathers are absent (Frazier, 1948, Moynihan, 1965, 1986). Recent sociological scholarship contends that these families are not necessarily disorganized if the unit observed is the extended family (Gutman, 1976; Martin & Martin, 1978; Stack, 1974).

These writers describe low-income black families as large networks of kin who exchange a great deal of material and service resources through "swapping" of goods and "child keeping" (Stack, 1974). The activities of these kinship organizations are seen as adaptive strategies to the conditions of poverty. It might be more accurate to call these "multiple-parent" families. Far from being underorganized or chaotic, they are seen as predictable groups bound by loyalty and reciprocal obligations in which (when they are functioning well) meager resources are shared as efficiently as possible.

Application of Theory to an Extended-Family Model

If the family unit is not "nuclear" but "extended," ideas about hierarchy, generational boundaries, and separation that apply to a middle-class family model must be revised. We must also modify our theory of symptom forma-

tion. Several theories of symptom formation for lower-income families have been advanced by different workers.

Environmental Pressure

In investigating a large sample of White English women, Brown and Harris (1978) found that those from the working class became depressed four times more often than middle-class women. Belle and colleagues (1979) report a similar finding with a sample from the United States. They attribute this difference to the greater number of negative life events among the lower-income women. The accumulated impact of these events produces a chronic hopelessness, rendering them more vulnerable to depression when further losses occur. Mother's depression may also have serious psychic effects on other members of the family, especially children. Thus the environmental effect of poverty itself is seen as an important source of symptomatic behavior in lower-income families.

Isolation from Kin Support

While it may be normative for middle income nuclear families to be relatively separate from their extended kin in terms of exchange of goods and services, such a separation may be disastrous for lower income families. Morawetz and Walker (1984) theorize that symptomatic "single-parent" families are those cut off from their kinship networks by migration and urbanization (p. 322).

Nonreciprocity of Relationships

Lindblad-Goldberg and Dukes (1985), however, compared the kinship networks of Black single mothers who had symptomatic children with those whose children were nonsymptomatic. They found that there were no differences in the size or the network of the amount of contact with networks. They did discover that mothers with symptomatic children reported less reciprocity from their kinship networks. That is, those mothers felt they gave but did not receive in equal amount. These findings suggest that it is not the number of people with whom the mother is involved but the quality of these relationships that is associated with whether her children will be symptomatic. Brown and Harris (1978) found that working-class women who lacked (as one of several factors) "a confiding relationship with a husband or boyfriend" were more likely to become depressed. Again, the finding is that symptoms were not associated with whether the woman *had* a husband or boyfriend, but the quality of her relationship with him.

Underorganization

Aponte (1986) proposes a fourth theory of the source of symptoms in poor families: an "underorganization" of the family in terms of "number, . . . complexity, . . . coherence, . . . continuity, . . . and flexibility" (p. 547). He explicitly differentiates this phenomenon from "family conflict, the dynamic that is more commonly discussed in family therapy literature" (p. 547).

Conflict Between Mother and Nonparental Executives

This is a variant of the structural model (Minuchin, 1967, 1974) of parental discord coupled with inappropriate cross-generational alliances. Instead of discord between mother and father, however, the break is between mother and grandmother or mother and aunt, depending on who in the network's executive system has disciplinary rights over a given child.

It is likely that individuals in lower-income families become symptomatic because of some combination of these influences, from the larger society to the family itself. The therapist must assess the family for the following possibilities:

1. The mother is so overwhelmed by environmental pressures—an eviction, a robbery, a dangerous school, unemployment or illness of a family member—that she cannot give full attention to child care. This is primarily a problem between environment and family, not between mother and children. The therapist should concentrate on helping the family to utilize concrete services until the crisis is past.

2. The mother does not have a kinship network on which to rely because of being cut off from it by migration or because the network has disintegrated as a result of the pressures of urban life. This is again a problem "outside" the subsystem of mother and children. Here the therapist can help the family recreate a social network of peers for itself to replace the missing support.

3. The mother has an intact kinship network but is not receiving support because of a nonreciprocal relationship with it. This is a problem between the extended family and the mother. It may be a product of conflict between adult peers or an issue of unresolved loss. Here the therapist must discover the reason for the breakdown of mutual aid. Rather than helping the mother construct a new network, the task will be to resolve the cut-off between her and her existing network.

4. The family itself is underorganized, thereby putting too much responsibility on one person. This may be a problem within the household of mother and children. No two family members are in a conflict for power, but the family is governed by the activity and presence of a single overburdened executive rather than by rules and shared expectations. Too little responsibility is systematically delegated. Here the therapist can lend support to the family's

executive while working to clarify and differentiate roles for others in the family.

5. The mother is in conflict with someone else within the kinship network's executive subsystem over how the symptomatic child should be raised. Single mothers often present for treatment as depressed, isolated, and overwhelmed with child-care responsibilities. The majority of symptomatic lower-income families have difficulties at the environmental level that require good casework before any family dynamics can be approached. On closer inquiry (including the gathering of a genogram), it often becomes clear that the child in question is also receiving different disciplinary messages from different executives or that the mother's child-rearing practices are being sharply criticized by her own mother. It emerges that executive conflict has led to apparently chaotic organization and has undermined the mother's morale. In such cases the therapist must address the conflict.

Assessing a kinship network requires some special technical procedures. One of them is discovering the actual (which may differ from the nominal) executive subsystem for each child. The child who grows up in a family of the same mother, father, and siblings living alone together for 18 consecutive years is the exception in this group, not the rule. Any of the relatives who have cared for a child may feel they have disciplinary rights over that child. Even if they do not supply direct discipline, they may be implicitly authorized to comment on the mother's attempts at discipline. Each child, therefore, may be responding to a different set of executives. For instance, a mother of an ex-husband may have rights to discipline the children her son fathered, but not their stepsiblings.

An executive subsystem in a kinship network is, of course, vulnerable to the same pressures (power struggles, different philosophies of child rearing, cross-generational alliances, etc.) as any two-parent nuclear family. Once the subsystem is located, the next assessment task is to search for such dysfunction.

History of Separations

Another special issue for kinship systems is assessing the effect of the history of each child's movement within the system. Not all children are raised exclusively by their parents; some are raised by whoever in the kinship network is best able to take care of them at the moment. As some executive acquires extra burdens or develops more resources, children might move from one caretaker to another. At its best such movement can give the child a feeling that multiple resources are available for support. But abrupt changes of residence or caretakers do have some psychic impact, even if the child's most important physical needs are thereby satisfied. Separations made necessary

by environmental conditions may lead to fears of abandonment, defensive detachment, or premature self-reliance. The caretaking adults who have struggled to make sure the children are taken care of may not be especially tolerant of such feelings. They may understandably feel that they have saved the child from becoming a ward of the state and that the child should be satisfied with that.

Informal adoption and child-taking in these extended networks may also change the sibling arrangements for children in such families very abruptly. Siblings may be separated. Cousins may suddenly become stepsiblings, requiring a rearrangement of "pecking order" or displacing a child from a familiar and privileged position as eldest or youngest. Such changes often affect sleeping arrangements also. No child has his or her own room. Few have their own beds. The author supervised a family in which the identified patient, an eight-year-old boy, no longer wanted to sleep with his 92-year-old aunt when she became enuretic. He began sleeping with his mother, intensifying their already enmeshed relationship. His sisters began to call him "faggot" and his obstreperous behavior in school increased. After some family therapy, he began sleeping on a couch in the living room. When his eldest sister (who had been living on her own) suddenly returned to the house, she reclaimed the couch (it had been her old bed) and he went back to sleep with his mother.

The fact that poor families are familiar with such events does not mean that they are insignificant in their emotional impact. They would be considered to have much explanatory value if discovered in the history of a middle-class patient. Because they are so necessary, in a concrete, physical sense, parents may not be motivated to think about their psychological effects. They thus may not think to mention them to the interviewer.

Junior and Senior High: Ages 12–18

In this life cycle stage, an important transition may be taking place in the executive subsystem of the family. If mother had her first children when she was a teenager, she may have received considerable help from her own mother in raising them. The executive subsystem in such youthful single-parent families is not mother/father but grandmother/mother, with grandmother naturally having more authority than her teenage daughter. As the mother matures, however, she takes on more authority. As her children reach their teenage years, grandmother becomes less involved in direct care and full responsibility is coming to bear on mother, who is now in her early 30s.

As children become more independent as adolescents, two-parent families have the developmental task of reviving the marital relationship that may have been less central when the children demanded most attention. In the single-parent family, however, there is no marital bond in which to reinvest. The grandmother/mother subsystem, while it is a very useful *parental* unit, cannot satisfy the same needs as a *marital* unit.

Thus as children become more independent, mother and grandmother must both find peers (or a job, or the church) to fill the gap. Nothing is easy about such a task. While the life cycle task requires increasing peer involvement for both mother and children, this may not occur if the mother has no one else with whom to bond. Supervision that was once experienced as nurturant is now experienced by teenagers as interference. Boys and girls may respond to this unwelcome attention in characteristically different ways, which will be considered below.

Another transitional task is to transfer authority from grandmother to mother at a time when the adolescent's challenge to authority is most intense and consequential. Children, particularly the oldest ones, may have difficulty accepting mother as a full authority when they may have seen her in earlier years more as an older sister. They may even have been placed in an institution or raised for a time in another household when mother was young and are now returning and really getting acquainted with her for the first time. Problems may arise if the mother does not fully grasp the thankless job of disciplining adolescents and if the grandmother remains involved as the mother's critic.

Attitudes Toward School

Schools for lower-income children are notoriously poor, disorganized, and physically dangerous for students. Opportunities beyond school are limited, particularly for boys. Staples (1985) reports that even college-educated Black males earn less income than White male high-school dropouts. Mothers themselves were often school dropouts. It is hard to imagine how, under such conditions, school could become the central focus for children of such families. Yet it is a highly invested activity, taken very seriously by mothers. School is mainly viewed, however, as an opportunity to get a high-school diploma and thereby enhance employability. For this purpose little more than regular attendance is necessary. Learning something interesting or useful or working for high grades for college entrance (as in the professional class) is rare.

Gender expectations in relation to school differ widely and earlier for the lower-income groups—girls are more likely to graduate from high school while boys are not necessarily expected to. Neither sex, however, applies to college in large numbers. Parents have no money to save to support them. Because not all finish high school on schedule (and many not at all), the end of high school does not serve as the clear marker of the "launching pad" stage that it does in the professional class.

Issues for Adolescent Daughters: School or Pregnancy?

One major determinant of whether a girl will stay in school is whether she becomes pregnant. Because schooling understandably does not command

much respect from adolescents in the lower-income community, it does not constitute a very attractive alternative to having a baby.

Mothers are often explicitly against early pregnancy before it happens—not so much on moral grounds as on the grounds of utility. Mothers appreciate how difficult it is to complete high school with young children, and often strongly warn their daughters against it. Their attempts to supervise their daughters to prevent it are a main reason for conflict that leads families to the clinic.

But while they are explicitly against it, they unfortunately must hold themselves up as an example of what *not* to do, not the strongest position for an authority. And the children they are advising owe their very lives to their mother's early pregnancy. Notman and Zilbach (1975) recount that in some families there is relatively unambivalent pressure on the adolescent daughter to have a baby. They see one reason for this arising from the mother's need to replace the dependency relationship that she is losing with her daughter.

Before their daughter's first pregnancy, mothers often do not acknowledge their daughter's sexual activity. Virtually the only method of birth control they encourage is abstinence. They will not even discuss other methods, fearing that to do so will provide an implicit approval of sexual activity. If they do take their daughters for the gynecological examination necessary for the prescription of a diaphragm or pills, the daughters sometimes refuse it out of embarrassment.

Boys and Sexual Activity

Mothers do not expect to deter their sons from sexual activity at all, except by warning them that they will not care for any babies the sons may father. Stack (1974) writes, however, that mothers in the Black kinship network she studied did not even issue such warnings. They "encourage(d) sons to have babies," (p. 121), hoping it would "make them more responsible." They took great pride in being paternal grandmothers and tried to care for the children when they could. At any rate, boys are not usually expected to be abstinent or to use condoms when they are sexually active.

Issues for Adolescent Sons: School or Delinquency?

Because unmarried teenage fathers are usually not involved with child care and cannot get jobs to contribute to child support, their becoming fathers is not what deters them from finishing school. Yet they do drop out earlier and in higher numbers than girls.

Lower-income mothers nurture and supervise their preadolescent sons just as they do their daughters. But when they become adolescents, they often consider them lost to the world of unreliable, uncontrollable adult men. They cease to expect them to be responsible and make few attempts to influence them. They thus lose intimate contact with them as well.

A son's developmental task is different from that of his sisters. He must become more separate from his mother in order to identify himself as a man and may find that dropping out of school is a convenient way to defy his mother's stated wishes. Attending school may be seen as unmanly compliance. Adolescent boys of any social class often identify with "outlaws" in order to feel free of their parents' rulings. In the lower-income group, the tendency is increased because *real* outlaws may be the only visibly successful males in the neighborhood. Acting tough so as not to be thought a "mama's boy" will draw any adolescent male to the streets. But the streets of an impoverished neighborhood are dangerous. Normal adolescent rebellion may lead boys into serious delinquency with adult-level consequences.

Dornbusch and colleagues (1985) studied the effect of different family structures on the control of adolescents. After controlling for the effects of poverty, they found that in households where the mother was the only executive, boys began to make decisions without any parental input as early as age 13. Girls, however, continued to accept their mothers' decisions or participate in joint ones until age 16 or 17, at which time they began to show more autonomy. In single-parent households in which an extended-family member was present, however, the mother had greater influence over children of both sexes, establishing "a level of parental control that is closer to the control of adolescents found in two-parent households" (p. 336).

These findings confirm the author's clinical impression that single mothers may lose confidence in their ability to influence their sons as the sons reach adolescence. But they also make the point that the influence can be retained with the support of the extended family. It should be noted that the findings of Dornbusch and co-workers do not apply to stepfathers, however, whose presence actually *increased* adolescent boys' rebelliousness (p. 333). Thus if lower-income single mothers feel they cannot control their adolescent boys, it may be because their relationship with their kinship network is disturbed, by either being cut off or in conflict.

Possible Interventions

1. Focus family therapy on the difficulties in the task of passing authority from the grandmother to the mother. It may be necessary to recruit the grandmother to come to sessions. Boundary issues between the generations will have to do with who is in charge of the children.

2. Try to get the executive subsystem to continue to provide nurturance and supervision for children (monitor school attendance, homework) rather than prematurely drafting them into parental roles in relation to the younger children. If the mother is to continue to nurture her adolescents, she will need support for herself as well. This may require recruiting sisters, aunts, or her own mother to reassure her, to advise her, or to present a unified policy toward rebellious adolescents. If the family is too distant geographically, she can be

connected to mothers' groups, PTA, or church groups (Douglas & Jason, 1986; Parker, Piotrkowski, & Peay, 1987).

3. Try to clarify ambiguous communications about sexual activity. Get mothers to accept it as a reality and to support adolescents in an effective plan to prevent pregnancy. This must include visits to the gynecologist, filling of prescriptions, and use of methods prescribed, not just dramatic exhortations. This may require convincing mothers that giving advice about birth control does not necessarily increase sexual activity.

In a review of literature on the family's role in pregnancy prevention, Fox (1981) found that parental communication about contraception, "however minimal or inaccurate," tended to delay or forestall a daughter's sexual activity. Among those daughters already active, it was related to more effective contraception. Furstenberg (1981) also found that "the likelihood of an adolescent's using contraception was strongly related to the degree to which her sexual activity was openly acknowledged and accepted by her parents" (p. 143).

Unfortunately early pregnancy is no longer the only "danger" for sexually active men and women. The acquired immune deficiency syndrome (AIDS) threatens people of all social classes. It is especially prevalent, however, in neighborhoods with a high frequency of intravenous drug use. Until late 1984 the majority of people with AIDS in New York City were gay white males. Since then the frequency of the illness has declined in that group but has accelerated among intravenous drug users. Citywide since early 1985 the majority of AIDS sufferers have been heterosexual and nonwhite—that is, either black (31%) or Hispanic (23%). Of all the boroughs, the Bronx has the largest proportion of women with AIDS in relation to men (1:4) and the largest number of children with AIDS (New York City Department of Health, 1987). To protect themselves and their children from this catastrophic illness, parents and adolescents should be instructed in how AIDS is passed on and in the practice of safer sex, particularly the use of condoms.

4. Mothers will discuss contraception more willingly with daughters, of course, but it is worth the effort to attend to the mother–son relationship as well. The extended family may be enlisted to support the mother in this unfamiliar and anxiety-provoking task. Firm and nonjudgmental encouragement of their sons' contraceptive and health-care responsibilities by instructing them to use condoms is a way for mothers to communicate their continuing respect for their sons.

5. Make a special effort to support mothers in continuing to guide their adolescent sons. Very often mothers have the idea that because they are women they simply cannot raise boys, and that boys need a "strong male hand." This idea is often supported by popular belief. Such women in desperation sometimes enlist grown sons, boyfriends, or stepfathers to administer physical discipline to their young adolescent sons. This usually has disastrous and explosive consequences. Physical discipline is not appropriate for adolescents, and discipline of any sort can be effectively applied only by an ex-

ecutive the son accepts. A mother must therefore use her relationship and powers of persuasion to influence her son.

Encourage the mother to turn to her extended family for moral support and advice for herself. She may be able to enlist more distant but respected family members (male or female) to serve as advisors or mentors to the boy. She can use the social pressure of the kinship network by asking other family members to encourage the boy to comply with her. She can also plug leaks in the network by getting other family members to refuse favors to the boy until he complies. Coordinated, persistent application of nonindulgent concern by the mother and the boy's relatives may keep the boy connected to and influenced by the family.

If the daughter becomes pregnant:

1. Although this is difficult, it is worth encouraging continued schooling.

2. If the family shows an interest in abortion or formal adoption, the therapist can help them consider it. These options are rarely exercised, however, because the values of lower-income families reject them and because the baby will serve an important function in the family.

3. If the baby is retained, school attendance can be supported by efforts to secure reliable child care, either within the kinship network or in day care or with a homemaker. Many schools and agencies now have special programs for young parents (Forbush, 1981).

4. After birth, help clarify who is in charge of childcare. For a 15-year-old mother, *her* mother will still direct the family.

5. Focus on grandmothers' training their childbearing daughters in appropriate expectations for infants and toddlers. The pattern to avoid is their being harshly critical of their daughters and simply taking over the entire mothering function. Often this was done to them by their mothers, so an inquiry into their families of origin may be useful.

6. Establishment of a functioning young couple is rare, but explore the possibility of enlisting paternal responsibility. This might be done by the couple living together with one of the families. If such an arrangement is impossible, the father might continue to live with his network, but be expected to make contributions of money and time to the support of his child. This again is a long shot, but the possibility should be at least considered, if only as a way to demonstrate respect for the idea that fathers have a role in family life. Ooms (1981) suggests that these young men may be more involved in the adolescent mother's life than was once thought and that any family assessment should include the current relationship, and attempt to discover his needs as well. Furstenberg (1981) found that a primary factor in the young father's involvement with his child was the mother's parents' willingness to include him.

Young Adulthood: Ages 18–21

For lower-income families, this period is not the moratorium that it is for college students in the professional class. It is "experimental" in that young adults must attempt things they have not attempted before, but the consequences of each "experiment" are felt with full force. College students may try a course or a part-time job or an affair and drop it if they do not like it. Lower-income mothers, however, are playing for keeps. A lost job may mean a missed meal or rent payment and a precipitous relocation. A romance gone sour may mean being left alone to support another child. Finding out that one is not yet ready to care for preschoolers all day has lifelong consequences for both mother and child.

Tasks for Women

This is the period when young mothers should be expected to gain more authority in relation to their own mothers, becoming heads of their own families. It is unrealistic to expect a poor single mother with young children to find her own apartment (or college dormitory) and leave home, so the question for this phase is: "How do adult children gain adult status while still living in their mother's home?" Mothers can either accept more child-care responsibilities or, if the grandmother agrees to continue to do childcare, get a job and contribute to home expenses. Either way, grandmother and mother should move toward something like equality in the household, with equal influence and responsibility for the two tasks of money making and child rearing.

Possible Interventions

The homemaking "couple" that must be preserved here is not husband/wife, but grandmother/mother. Thus the boundary to be monitored is not so much the one dividing the generations (as it would be in the professional class) but the one dividing those who make the home from those who do not. It is, of course, appropriate for both the mother and grandmother to have contact with men who are peers, but the access of these men to the home should be orderly. Children will find it difficult to distinguish between temporary boyfriends and stepfathers. Indeed mothers cannot be expected to know if a casual romance will become a serious relationship or not. But an important task of this era is for mothers to maintain a reasonably predictable household for their children by sensibly regulating who sleeps at home, not giving a boyfriend babysitting responsibility, and maintaining as good a relationship as possible with the fathers of her children.

This is the developmental stage when women may try to leave their mother's home and set up a nuclear family in a separate household with a man. Stack (1974) and Kenkel (1981) write that the kinship network often views marriage as dangerous to both the wife and the stability of the network itself,

and so may resist it. Because the mother so often has children already, this marriage will create a stepfamily, even if it is the first marriage for both partners. The partners often expect it to function like a first marriage and are disappointed when the relationships between children and parents prove unexpectedly problematic. The relationship with in-laws is always an issue in middle-class marriage, of course. It can however, be even more crucial in the lower-income groups, because the kinship network is so much stronger and so necessary for survival. Few marriages will survive long without its blessing. If the therapist has a chance to treat a lower-income couple, very careful attention must be given to the acceptance of the husband (and his network) by the mother's kin, and vice versa.

Tasks for Men

This is the age when lower-income men are expected to enter the workforce full-time. This is a notoriously difficult task, given the high probability of inadequate academic preparation and the low number of unskilled jobs available. They are more likely to leave home than women, but rarely establish their own households. They circulate among members of the extended family, living where they can. The extended family can be very useful in this phase by supplying support for the anxiety-arousing, discouraging, lengthy task of finding a stable job. Not finding a job is a dangerous situation. Boys must have some way to demonstrate that they are men. If they cannot do so by finding a job and earning a living, they are left with two other methods: demonstrating sexual potency and having daring adventures. The former is best accomplished by actually fathering children and the latter by using drugs and committing crimes—activities that expose them to serious danger. In the several life cycle periods between ages 15 and 35, Black men are ten times more likely to be murdered than White men (*Health Hazard Appraisal,* 1972).

Possible Interventions

Men in this era rarely present for treatment. The most common family members to present are young mothers who have some problem with their children. The therapist often must recruit the grandmother into treatment. An inquiry at that time into the whereabouts of all members of the family will at least identify the men.

The biggest family danger for men in this life cycle stage is that the kinship system will allow them to underfunction and overindulge them until they are angrily ejected into the street, only to be allowed to return some months later in a deteriorated condition. They should be asessed with special attention to possible depression. Organizing the family to support these men (provide shelter and respect), *and* to require adult behavior of them (early rising, no drug use in the home, persistent job search), is a difficult but worthwhile job. It is especially worthwhile in relation to the larger social system, because these

young men are the fathers of the children of the single young mothers who make up the rest of the therapist's caseload.

Ages 22–30

While this era begins in the professional class with graduation from college and ends with the completion of a graduate program, it is not as clearly delineated for the lower-income group. There are some similarities, however, in that it is in this era that men and women have the best chance to form stable couples, regardless of income level. Maturation may make the participants less needful of self-assertion and more capable of accommodation. Frequency of pregnancy may decrease as families get larger and mothers (and grand-mothers) acquire the knowledge and maturity to prevent it. The existing children are getting older, attending school, and needing less care. Men have had more time to find a job, and may even have had a chance to establish some seniority. Stack (1974) reports that some young couples do not even plan to live together until their *second* child is born but that they do do so then.

During this developmental era, fathers can sometimes contribute more to their stepfamilies than to their original ones. An unemployed father may be humiliated by his inability to meet society's expectation that he support his children. He may reduce this humiliation by simply abandoning that family. But as a stepfather, he owes nothing to his stepchildren. In that context even a small contribution appears generous, is appreciated, and enhances his status in the community.

Possible Interventions

The difference between lower-income and professional class in this era is that the couple in the lower-income group is almost always a stepcouple. Often mother's children have two or three different natural fathers. The family must thus face the special issues of stepfamily formation. These are detailed in McGoldrick and Carter (1980), and include the resolution of previous marriages, the blending of different sibling subsystems, competition between husband and children for the wife's attention, and the slow development of relationships between the stepparent and stepchildren. An additional issue for the lower-income group is that "previous marriage" may include the grand-mother/mother dyad that raised the children when they were young. A step-father entering a grandmother/mother executive system may have special difficulty becoming enfranchised as a father because a grandmother/mother partnership will certainly not dissolve as fully as an ex-husband/ex-wife team can. It is often better to develop his role as husband and not to expect him to exercise fathering responsibility, except for his own children.

Ages 31–35

During this era the mother's oldest children are reaching adolescence and the cycle already described under "Junior High and Senior High: Ages 12–18" begins to repeat itself. Hill (1986) sees this as one of two eras (the other being when the children are of preschool age) when "single-parent families find themselves most vulnerable to critical role transitions" (p. 28).

If the mother has recently married or begun living with a man, adjustments to stepchildhood and stepparenthood (already difficult) are aggravated by children becoming adolescent and searching for their own identity. This is especially true for adolescent males. Their increased rebelliousness should be an expected consequence of forming a stepfamily. The mother should not expect the stepfather to do any limit setting with her older children especially, but should indicate that she expects them to be polite to her husband. Under these conditions positive step-relationships at least have a chance of developing.

If the mother is not with a man and is living with the grandmother, she has no marital dyad in which to become reinvolved as her children begin to become more independent. Both grandmother and mother must find some way to compensate for their role loss as mothers. At a time when the mother and grandmother may be reluctant to let them go, the children must begin to function more independently. To identify themselves as separate from their families, middle-class adolescents can become involved in school activities or organized athletic teams. Such outlets are often unavailable to lower-income adolescents. Boys, seeking to disidentify with their mothers, are likely to go to the street and join an informal group of adolescent peers who gain status by committing petty crime.

A quite different pattern is possible in this transition if the mother attempts to compensate for impending loneliness (and the adolescent's characteristic lack of gratitude) by becoming preoccupied with the problems of her younger children, thereby virtually abandoning the older ones. In this case the neglected adolescent may feel deprived and show some immature behavior in an unacknowledged effort to elicit guidance and reenter the family while still striving for the privileges of age.

The Function of Early Pregnancy for the Extended-Family System

A solution for many of the family tensions of this life cycle era is for the young daughter to become pregnant. Some attempts to explain causes for early pregnancy have focused on the girl's inner motivations (Schaeffer & Pine, 1972). These authors saw the girls as struggling both with wishes to be mothered and wishes to mother. Fisher and Scharf (1980) contended that some girls had experienced early deficits in nurturing and became pregnant to compensate for feelings of emptiness or to make an attempt at mastery. Such hypotheses can be very useful to the clinician in making an empathic connec-

tion to such a girl. Systemic thinking, however, requires us to consider how an early pregnancy might also be a function of forces in the whole kinship network and the socioeconomic context in which it is embedded.

The pregnancy does meet several of the girl's needs. It meets her need for sexual activity, for adult status, and to have a baby. It provides a meaningful purpose to her life (Buchholz & Gol, 1986). But it also has important effects on the other generations in the family as well. It may gratify the girl's mother in several ways. By giving her a baby to care for and increasing her daughter's dependency on her, it relieves her of the loneliness she might face if her children were to leave and live independently. Once her daughter is pregnant, battles over makeup, hair style, curfew, and homework become irrelevant, to the relief of both mother and daughter. Because she was too young when she had *her* first children, the mother may not have raised them herself. She may thus welcome the opportunity to nurture her daughter's children. She now has a chance to "do it right" (Rodman Hill, 1977). The mother also attains the moral superiority of being a grandmother. Now that the child is not her own, she receives no condemnation for bearing it and receives extra gratitude and approval from the community by caring for it.

Great-grandmother may also be gratified by an early pregnancy in that she can begin to function as a "true" grandmother, spoiling her great-grandchildren without primary responsibility for their care. Thus the several tensions—personal and intergenerational—that are aroused when the youngest generation reaches adolescence are resolved by the teenage girl becoming pregnant.

Clinical Implications

Loss of Traction

If there are two parents in the family, an early pregnancy can occasion severe conflict. The father may accuse his daughter of being morally lax and the mother of having been insufficiently strict in her supervision. The mother may join in condemnation of the daughter, and may also accuse the father of having been too distant. The daughter may be urged to have an abortion.

In a single-parent family, there may also be an initial storm of protest, but eventually the prospect of a new infant is so gratifying that families often lose interest in their symptoms. Issues of disordered hierarchy seem to become trivial as the adolescent daughter is suddenly promoted to womanhood. Behaviors that once seemed too "grown up" (staying out late, having sex, refusing school) do not disappear, but are suddenly redefined as "womanly" and are no longer an occasion for family conflict. Pregnancy now absorbs the interest of the family and it is often difficult to keep them in treatment.

Sibling Imitation and Competition

As younger siblings achieve adolescence, they are tempted to repeat the successful childbearing strategy of their older siblings. Sometimes older sib-

lings who have avoided pregnancy but who have not been particularly successful otherwise will be provoked by a younger sibling becoming pregnant. The older sister may now be stimulated into getting pregnant in the hope of regaining attention and status she has lost. Preoccupied by the first pregnancy, the mother may not think of this possibility for her other daughters.

STRENGTHS AND VULNERABILITIES

The author has tried to describe these two family types naturalistically, working from clinical experience. But in fact they represent family types already identified in the sociological literature. Skolnick and Skolnick (1971) make it clear that the nuclear family and the life cycle model built around it is not a universal family grouping. They cite Aries (1962), who contends that "adolescence" has not been a fixed concept throughout history but rather is a recently invented construct that has developed with the rise of mass public education and the decline of apprenticeship. Just as the family life cycle is not an unchanging given, the family structure itself varies with circumstances. Goode (1963) sees family structure as changing during the past century from the "kinship group" to the "conjugal" (or nuclear) model as industrialization spreads. Winch and Blumberg (1971) contend that the "kinship group" model is especially typical of agrarian societies in which the family is settled on a plot of land that remains family property through the generations. The conjugal or "nuclear" family, however, has a "peculiar fit" with industrialized society. Couples are separate from the family unit and can move where jobs are available. Jobs are (or at least can be) awarded on merit rather than family ties (Skolnick & Skolnick, 1971). Thus the nuclear family is not seen by these authors as an ideal, primary, traditional, basic form. It is simply a form that has evolved to accommodate the requirements of industrialization.

Demos (1986), however, opposes the "myth" that the "extended-family" *household* was the norm in premodern times. He cites the fact that "mean household size" has been no more than five or six persons for centuries (declining very slowly after industrialization) in Western countries. He does grant that premodern communities—villages or neighborhoods—"supported a density of kin-contacts unknown in our day" (p. 5).

Gutman (1976) carefully analyzed plantation records and census data over the period 1750–1925 to study changes in the size and shape of the American Black family from the time of slavery until after the great migration of Black people from southern farms to northern cities. Unlike scholars who have seen slavery as having a disorganizing effect on the Black family that has kept it disorganized into modern times (Frazier, 1948; Moynihan, 1965, 1986), Gutman focused on the slaves' response to slaveholders' practices. He agrees with

an abolitionist who wrote of some Sea Island Blacks in 1862 that "we abolitionists had underrated the suffering produced by slavery among the negroes, but had overrated the demoralization" (p. 474). Gutman contends that slave families were not disorganized by slavery but developed marital, childbearing and extended-kin customs of their own that created as stable and predictable an environment as possible under the circumstances. He would agree with Demos that the rural, premodern family was nuclear in shape (p. 443) and supported by a dense kinship network. When he traces the movement of Blacks to the cities, however, he sees a shift. By 1925 in New York City only two in five Black households were nuclear in composition, and extended families living in the same household had increased in importance (p. 454). He adds, however, that this change was "not accompanied by any increase in the male-absent household" (p. 454). He sees these extended households as organized, predictable units that were a necessary adaptation to the massive unemployment that confronted Blacks moving to urban areas. He attributes the more recent loss of male presence in urban poor families between 1950 and 1970 to the cumulative effects of 35 more years of continued unemployment, not to structural distortions in the Black American family that began during slavery.

It thus seems clear that when urban families of any race find employment and are financially successful, they tend toward a nuclear model. When they are unemployed and oppressed by poverty, Black and Hispanic families attempt to draw on their kinship network model to share meager resources and provide for their children. The latter model is an organized and predictable adaptation, not a broken, disorganized version of a nuclear family.

By using Skolnick and Skolnick's view of family form in relation to its surrounding socioeconomic structure, it is possible to calculate the costs and benefits of the different family models. The extended-family form provides a large number of caretakers for the children. Individuals in need can find support from the network rather than the state. Few resources (goods or labor) are wasted, because someone can always be found who can use them. If one person is lost or disabled, another has been "trained" and is drawn by ties of mutual obligation to take his or her place.

But such a model does not encourage the extreme individuation expected of job holders in an industrialized society. In the preindustrial agricultural model, children are trained by other family members to do farm and child-raising chores. As they grow they are expected to support others as they have been supported. In the city, however, they are trained by outsiders (teachers) to take jobs that have nothing to do with the family. They must be mobile enough to even move away from the family to find such jobs. This is the dilemma of the lower-income group. The ties of mutual obligation that permit them to survive pull against the very differentiation required to prepare for jobs that would permit exit from poverty.

The professional class, by contrast, has the capital to render family obliga-

tion less important and so can become highly differentiated. It is almost as though the goal of the professional family (with its emphasis on delay of pregnancy, extended adolescence, etc.) is to maximize discontinuity between parents and children. And indeed, such generational discontinuity does serve the formation of the couple.

While the isolated couple creates a highly mobile support unit for husband and wife that is ideal for meeting the demands of professional employment, its costs become more apparent when the couple has children. An extremely heavy child-care burden falls on the mother. She may have to give up or sharply curtail the career she has worked so hard for. If she has no help, she must bear the unremitting burden of child care alone, without the relief and support that a kinship family can offer every day. The children must also bear the burden of being raised by an inexperienced, isolated, overworked mother. In a study comparing child rearing in several different cultures (including an American suburb and some agrarian societies), Minturn and Lambert (1964) found that the suburban mothers whose affluence permitted them to be most isolated tended to be less patient with children than in cultures where other women were present. To solve this problem, the nuclear family tries to change itself to resemble the kinship model, both by reestablishing actual kinship ties (grandparents are recruited as babysitters) and (to a much greater degree) by hiring "kin" in the form of professional domestics. Again, these families' financial success permits them to work, raise children, and still keep relatives at a distance.

All professional couples with children struggle with the following calculus in their attempts to revise the nuclear model to accommodate children: Is it better for parents to raise their own children? Is it worth giving up a profession to do so? Or is it better to retain the profession as an essential satisfaction to sustain the parents' morale and hire a stranger to care for one's children? How much should grandparents (whom parents have striven to separate from) be reinvolved to help with child care (assuming they are willing)?

In addition to the relative scarcity of resources for child care in the professional family, another cost of that family model stems from the fact that there are so few participants. The loss of any family member is felt very acutely because there are few kin and few kinship ties to replace whatever role that person performed in the family group. If a husband/father is lost in a divorce, for instance, a professional mother cannot expect (and may not want) her mother or sister to take care of her children while she works. The lost role must be made up by hiring a helper rather than by another family member. Thus this family form requires affluence to counteract its vulnerability.

The strengths of these family forms are their weaknesses as well. The interdependence of lower-class families that enables them to survive in deprived circumstances makes it hard for them to develop a nuclear model that maximizes employability. The highly individuated professional families are well designed to permit the long preparation necessary for high-paying jobs,

but really have no one to do child care. Their lack of kinship ties requires them either to decrease their professional activity or to hire outsiders to augment their child-care capabilities.

REFERENCES

Aponte, H. (1986). If I don't get simple, I cry. *Family Processes* 25:4, 531–548.

Aries, P. (1962). *Centuries of childhood: A social history of family life.* New York: Vintage.

Belle, D., et al. (1979). Depression and low-income female-headed families. In E. Corfman (Ed.), *Families today: A research sampler on families and children,* Vol. 1. Washington, D.C.: NIMH Science Monographs 1. DHEW Pub. No. (ADM) 79-815.

Bloom, D. (1986). The labor market consequences of delayed childbearing. Paper presented at the annual meeting of the American Statistical Association, Chicago.

Brown, G., & Harris, T. (1978). *Social origins of depression: A study of psychiatric disorder in women.* New York: Free Press.

Buchholz, E., & Gol, B. (1986). More than playing house: A developmental perspective on the strengths in teenage motherhood. *American Journal of Orthopsychiatry* 56:3, 347–359.

Carter, E., & Orfanidis, M. (1976). Family therapy with one person and the family therapist's own family. In P. Guerin (Ed.), *Family therapy: Theory and practice.* New York: Gardner Press.

Children's Defense Fund (1985). *Preventing children having children.* Clearinghouse paper number one, Washington, D.C.

Children's Defense Fund. (1986). *Adolescent pregnancy: Whose problem is it?* Adolescent Pregnancy Prevention Clearinghouse, Washington, D.C. (January).

Daniels, P., & Weingarten, K. (1982). *Sooner or later: The timing of parenthood in adult lives.* New York: Norton.

Demos, J. (1986). *Past, present, and personal: The family and the life course in American history.* New York: Oxford University Press.

Dornbusch, S., Carlsmith, J. M., Bushwall, S., Ritter, P., Leiderman, H., Hastorf, A., & Gross, R. (1985). Single parents, extended households, and the control of adolescents. *Child Development,* 56: 326–341.

Douglas, J., & Jason, L. (1986). Building social support systems through a babysitting exchange program. *American Journal of Orthopsychiatry* 56:1, 103–108.

Fisher, S., & Scharf, K. R. (1980). Teenage pregnancy: An anthropological sociological and psychological overview. *Adolescent Psychiatry* 8: 393–403.

Forbush, J. (1981). Adolescent parent programs and family involvement. In T. Ooms (Ed.). *Teenage pregnancy in a family context: Implications for policy.* Philadelphia: Temple University Press.

Fox, G. (1981). The family's role in adolescent sexual behavior. In T. Ooms (Ed.), *Teenage pregnancy in a family context: Implications for policy.* Philadelphia: Temple University Press.

Frazier, E. F. (1948). *The negro family in the United States.* Chicago: University of Chicago Press.

Fulmer, R. & Medalie, J. (1987). Treating the male college student from a family systems perspective. In J. Coleman (Ed.), *Working with troubled adolescents: A handbook.* London: Academic Press.

Fulmer, R., Medalie, J., & Lord, D. (1982). Life cycles in transition: A family systems perspective on counselling the college student. *Journal of Adolescence* 5: 195–217.

Furstenberg, F. (1981). Implicating the family: Teenage parenthood and kinship involve-

ment. In T. Ooms (Ed.), *Teenage pregnancy in a family context: Implications for policy*. Philadelphia: Temple University Press.

Garcia-Pretro, N. (1982) Puerto Rican families. In McGoldrick, M., Pearce, J., & Giordano, J. (Eds.), *Ethnicity and family therapy*. New York: Guilford Press.

Goode, W. (1963). *World revolution and family patterns*. New York: Free Press of Glencoe.

Gutman, H. (1976). *The black family in slavery and freedom: 1750–1925*. New York: Vintage.

Health hazard appraisal (1972). Probability tables of deaths in the next ten years from specific causes. Methodist Hospital of Indiana, Indianapolis.

Hill, Reuben. (1986). Life cycle stages for types of single-parent families: Of family development theory. *Family Relations* 35: 19–29.

Hill, Rodman. (1977). Personal communication.

Kenkel, W. (1981). Black-white differences in age at marriage: Expectations of low-income high school girls. *Journal of Negro Education* 50:425–438.

Lerner, H. (1985). *The dance of anger*. New York: Harper.

Lindblad-Goldberg, M., & Dukes, J. (1985). Social support in black, low-income, single-parent families: Normative and dysfunctional patterns. *American Journal of Orthopsychiatry* 55:1, 42–58.

McGoldrick, M., & Carter, E. (1980). Forming a remarried family. In E. Carter & M. McGoldrick (Eds.), *The family life cycle: A framework for family therapy*. New York: Gardner Press.

Martin, E., & Martin, J. M. (1978). *The black extended family*. Chicago: University of Chicago Press.

Minturn, L., & Lambert, W., et al. (1964). *Mothers of six cultures*. New York: Wiley, pp. 291–292.

Minuchin, S. (1974). *Families and family therapy*. Cambridge, Mass.: Harvard University Press.

Minuchin, S., Montalvo, B., Guerney, B., Rosman, B., & Schumer, F. (1967). *Families of the slums: An exploration of their structure and treatment*. New York: Basic Books.

Morawetz, A., & Walker, G. (1984). *Brief therapy with single-parent families*. New York: Brunner/Mazel.

Moynihan, D. (1965). *The negro family in America: The case for national action*. Washington, D.C.: U.S. Government Printing Office.

Moynihan, D. (1986). *Family and nation*. New York: Harcourt, Brace, Jovanovich.

New York City Department of Health (1987). AIDS surveillance update (2/25/87).

Norton, A., & Moorman, J. (1987). Marriage and divorce patterns of U.S. women. *Journal of Marriage and the Family* 49:1.

Notman, M. T., & Zilbach, J. J. (1975). Family aspects of nonuse of contraceptives in adolescence. In H. Hirsch (Ed.), *The family. 4th International Congress of Psychosomatic Obstetrics and Gynecology*. Basel: Karger, pp. 213–217.

O'Donnell, L. (1984). *The unheralded majority: Contemporary women as mothers*. Lexington, Mass.: Lexington Books.

Ooms, T. (1981). Family involvement, notification, and responsibility: A personal essay. In T. Ooms (Ed.), *Teenage Pregnancy in a family context: Implications for policy*. Philadelphia: Temple University Press.

Parker, F.; Piotrkowski, C.; Peay, L. (1987) Head Start as a social support for mothers: the psychological benefits of involvement. *American Journal of Orthopsychiatry,* 57:2, 220–233.

Rogler, L., Cooney, R., Costantino, G., Earley, B., Grossman, B., Gurak, D., Malady, R., & Rodriguez, O. (1983). *A conceptual framework for mental health research on Hispanic populations*. Monograph No. 10, Hispanic Research Center, Fordham University, New York.

Schaffer, C., & Pine, F. (1972). Pregnancy, abortion and the developmental tasks of adolescence. *Journal of American Academy of Child Psychiatry* (3):11, 511–536.

Shorter Oxford English Dictionary (3rd ed.) (1959). London: Oxford.

Skolnick, A., & Skolnick, J. (1971). Rethinking the family. In A. Skolnick & J. Skolnick (Eds.), *Family in transition*. New York: Little, Brown.

Stack, C. B. (1974). *All our kin: Strategies for survival in a black community*. New York: Harper.

Staples, R. (1985). Changes in black family structure: The conflict between family ideology and structural conditions. *Journal of Marriage and the Family* (Nov.), 1005–1013.

Terkelsen, K. (1980). Toward a theory of the family life cycle. In E. Carter & M. McGoldrick (Eds.), *The family life cycle: A framework for family therapy*. New York: Guilford Press.

Winch, R. F., & Blumberg, R. L. (1971). Societal complexity and familial organization. In A. Skolnick & J. Skolnick (Eds.), *Family in transition*. Boston: Little, Brown.

Whiting, R. (1981) The practice of family therapy at a college counseling center. *Journal of College Student Personnel, 22*, 558–559.

Zelnick, M., Kantner, J., & Ford, K. (1981). *Sex and pregnancy in adolescence*. Beverly Hills, Calif.: Sage.

Author Index

Abarbanel, A., 345
Abeloff, M.D., 437
Abelsohn, D., 405
Adams, J.E., 435
Adelberg, T., 373, 381
Adelson, J., 263
Aguirre, B.E., 35, 36
Ahrons, C., 21, 22, 337, 338, 339, 342, 343, 344, 345, 350, 351, 358, 359, 362, 381, 402, 405, 412
Alexander, J., 49, 534
Altman, I., 290
Anderson, C., 294, 319, 533
Anderson, J.Z., 404
Anderson, R., 476
Anzieu, D., 166, 179
Aponte, H., 24, 514, 516, 533, 560
Apter, T., 34, 211
Aries, P., 10, 573
Ashby, W.R., 93, 96, 97
Asher, S.J., 337
Asmundsson, R., 399, 402
Avis, J., 30, 43
Aylmer, R.C., 199, 200, 201, 212

Bach-Peterson, J., 319
Bacon, L., 231
Baker, L., 437, 446, 449
Baldwin, C., 36
Bank, S.P., 467, 468
Barbour, L.S., 36
Barker, D.L., 222
Barko, N., 239
Barnett, R., 30, 31, 35
Baruch, G., 30, 31, 35
Bateson, G., 91, 100
Beavers, W.R., 447
Beck, R., 312, 317
Becker, G., 231
Beckman, L.J., 501
Beels, C., 542
Belenky, M.F., 32, 64
Belle, D., 30
Belsky, J., 243
Bengston, V.L., 297
Benjamin, A., 470, 473
Bennett, L., 486
Bennett, S.A., 149
Bepko, C., 60, 61, 218, 505
Berenson, D., 485, 489
Berheide, C.W., 36
Berman, W.H., 340

Bernard, J., 11, 30, 32, 34, 41, 60, 192, 210-211, 374, 389
Bianchi, S.M., 12, 29, 31, 36, 37
Biener, L., 35
Black, C., 490, 491, 495, 496
Blane, H.T., 498
Blau, T., 297
Blenkner, M., 312, 320
Bloom, B., 337, 391
Bloom, D., 547
Blos, P., 259, 260
Blumberg, R.L., 573
Blume, S.B., 505
Blumstein, P., 35, 36, 61, 218
Bodstein, E., 265
Bohrstedt, G.W., 260
Booth, A., 231, 403
Borgatta, E.F., 260
Boscolo, L., 153, 157, 296, 533
Bosma, W.G., 498
Boss, P., 62
Boszormenyi-Nagy, I., 199, 247, 442
Bouton, K., 372, 373, 375, 390
Bowen, M., 8, 14, 72, 116, 199, 203, 213, 216, 242, 290, 291, 295, 299, 306, 366, 414, 442, 466, 467, 472, 474, 478, 485, 501, 531
Boyd-Franklin, N., 71, 514, 532
Bozzetti, L.D., 503
Bradt, J., 241, 248, 290
Brand, E., 403
Bratt, B., 467, 468
Bray, J., 405
Briscoe, C.W., 337
Brodsky, A.M., 30
Brody, E., 31, 312, 319, 320
Bronfenbrenner, U., 240
Broverman, D.M., 32, 260
Broverman, J.K., 32, 260
Brown, G., 540, 559
Brown, H.S., 265, 402, 406
Browne, A., 76
Buchholz, E., 572
Bumpass, L., 231, 336
Burchinal, L.G., 231
Burke, R.J., 232
Bushwall, S., 565
Butler, R., 312, 316, 321, 322, 329

Camara, K., 344
Camitta, B.M., 467, 468, 481

Campbell, A., 5
Cantor, M., 319
Caplan, J., 8
Carlsmith, J.M., 565
Carper, M., 319
Carter, E.A., 8, 151, 199, 203, 261-262, 300, 440, 442, 447, 461, 480, 490, 555, 570
Cashion, B.G., 373
Caspi, A., 326
Casto, R.F., 338, 339, 342
Cecchin, G., 153, 157, 296, 533
Cherlin, A.J., 523, 524
Chester, P., 345
Chiriboga, D.A., 314, 340, 376
Chodorow, N., 44, 260
Christensen, H.T., 231
Cicirelli, V.G., 5
Clark, R.W., 166
Clarkson, F.E., 32, 260
Clinchy, B.M., 32, 64
Clingempeel, W.G., 403
Cohen, M., 323
Cohen, P., 466, 470, 473
Cohler, B., 30
Coho, A., 376
Coles, R., 516
Collier, H.V., 501
Colon, F., 518
Combrinck-Graham, L., 5, 447
Contratto, S., 44
Cooney, T., 344, 358
Cousins, N., 459
Cowen, C.P., 44
Cowgill, K.M., 399, 402
Cox, M., 22, 345, 349, 373, 376, 378, 379, 383, 404, 409
Cox, R., 22, 345, 373, 376, 378, 379, 383, 404, 409
Coyle, B., 498
Crohn, H., 265, 402, 406
Crouter, A., 243
Curlee, J., 501

Dahl, A.S., 399, 402
Daniels, P., 32, 43, 44, 555
Davies, R.K., 437
Dell, P., 91, 92
Demos, J., 573, 574
Derdeyn, A., 408, 409
Derogatis, L.R., 437
Deutscher, I., 312
Dickman, J.R., 258

Dinnerstein, D., 32, 44
Dizenhuz, I.M., 466, 470, 473
D'Lugoff, B.C., 498
Doherty, W.J., 36
Dohrenwend, B.S., 30
Donavan, D.M., 498
Dornbusch, S., 565
Douglas, J., 566
Douvan, E., 263
Drash, A.L., 437
Duberman, L., 404
Dukes, J.L., 373, 518, 559
Duszynski, D.R., 8
Duvall, E., 5, 288, 447

Edwards, J.N., 231
Eissler, K.R., 181
Elder, G., 326
Elizur, E., 466
Elkin, M., 401
Ellis, J., 502
Ellman, B., 63
Emery, R., 344
Engel, G.H., 433
Engel, T., 265, 402, 406
Epstein, N.B., 64
Erikson, E., 5, 32, 49, 94, 192,
    260, 312, 326, 440
Eskew, R.W., 290
Evans, R.R., 260

Feikema, R.J., 297
Feiring, C., 44
Feld, S., 211
Ferree, M.M., 36
Fischer, J., 498
Fisher, S., 571
Fogarty, T., 212-213
Forbush, J., 567
Ford, R., 540
Forrest, V., 71
Fox, G., 566
Fox, M.F., 34, 36
Fox, R., 502
Framo, J., 305, 442
Fraser, J., 501
Frazier, E.F., 558, 573
Freeman, L., 181
Freud, E., 179
Freud, S., 259
Freud Lowenstein, S., 181
Friedan, B., 35, 37, 64
Friedman, E., 74, 83, 119, 128,
    212, 216, 222, 478, 480
Fulmer, R., 552, 553
Furstenberg, F., 336, 345, 350,
    404, 523, 566, 567

Gans, H.J., 516
Garcia Preto, N., 80, 271, 272, 546
Gaskin, F., 337
Gelfand, D.E., 10, 84, 85, 326
Gelfand, E.G., 79
Gerson, R., 165, 186, 415, 442,
    531
Gibbs, J., 520

Gibson, R., 79, 326
Gigy, L., 340, 341, 346
Gilligan, C., 3, 5, 32, 33, 34, 49,
    64, 192, 198, 199, 237, 238,
    260, 263, 291, 292
Giordano, J., 335
Glatt, M., 504
Glen, R., 403
Glenn, N., 292
Glick, P.C., 21, 211, 232, 288, 336,
    337, 359, 371, 392, 399
Glicklhorn, R., 166
Goff, J.R., 467
Gol, B., 572
Goldberg, M.L., 373, 518
Goldberger, N.R., 32, 64
Goldfarb, A., 320
Goldner, V., 3, 29-30, 35-36
Goldsmith, J., 341, 342, 376
Goldstein, H.S., 402, 406
Goode, W., 6, 573
Goodman, J.T., 64
Goodrich, T.G., 63
Goodrich, W., 231
Goolishian, H., 91, 92
Gorney, R., 240
Gould, R., 5
Gove, W.R., 30
Grainger, R., 153
Gramsci, A., 98
Greeley, A.M., 79
Green, M., 81, 465
Gregory, H., 540
Greif, J.B., 345
Grobskin, R., 467
Gross, R., 565
Grosser, G., 8, 442
Groves, L., 313
Grunes, J., 313
Guerin, P., 303
Guerney, B., 24
Gurin, G., 211
Gutman, H., 558, 573, 574
Gutmann, D., 313n, 326
Gutmann, J., 313n

Hadley, T., 8
Hagestad, G., 288, 344, 358
Haley, J., 95, 151, 295, 296, 387,
    498, 533
Hall, J.S., 296
Halsted, C., 63
Hamburg, B.A., 437
Handelsman, M.M., 76
Hansen, D.A., 95
Hare-Mustin, R.T., 3, 29, 30, 50,
    64, 113, 467
Harkins, E., 292
Harris, T., 559
Harry, J., 5
Hartman, A., 46
Hastorf, A., 565
Hausman, S., 340, 341, 346
Hays, N., 534
Helfer, R.E., 491

Heller, S., 256
Hendrix, L., 232
Herman, J.L., 491
Hersch, L.B., 470
Herz, F., 81, 453
Herzog, E., 81, 343
Hess, B.B., 6, 31, 35, 36, 56
Hess, R., 344
Hesse-Biber, S., 20, 34, 36, 53,
    113
Hetherington, E.M., 22, 335, 338,
    339, 341, 342, 344, 345, 349,
    356, 373, 376, 378, 379, 383,
    404, 409
Hewitt, L.E., 498
Hewlett, S.A., 37
Heyman, D., 314
Hill, R., 5, 95, 518, 571, 572
Hines, P., 71, 80, 514, 520, 532,
    534
Hiris, J., 459, 481
Hirschman, L., 491
Hoffman, L.W., 35, 46
Hoffman, R.G., 467, 468, 473, 481
Hogarty, G., 533
Holmes, R., 473
Holmes, T., 95, 338, 457
Homiller, J.D., 501
Hoorwitz, A.N., 153
Hopkins, J.R., 258, 259
Horner, M.S., 38
Howard, K.I., 261
Huston, T., 41

Ievoli, E., 403
Iker, H., 437
Imber-Black, E., 153
Imber Coppersmith, E., 153, 157,
    159
Inhelder, B., 261
Inoff, G.E., 437
Isaacs, M., 350, 405

Jacklin, C., 45, 237
Jackson, J., 487
Jacob, T., 8
Jacobs, J., 345
James, K., 34
Jason, L., 566
Jellinek, E.M., 487
Jessor, R., 260, 497
Jessor, S., 260, 497
Johnson, V.E., 314
Jones, E., 172, 181, 185
Jordon, B., 74

Kaffman, M., 466
Kafka, J.S., 212, 228, 231
Kagan, J., 44, 46
Kahana, R., 320
Kahn, M.D., 467, 468
Kamback, M.C., 498
Kantor, D., 540
Kaplan, D.M., 441, 467
Kastenbaum, R., 503
Kaufman, E., 484

Kegan, R., 194, 198, 199
Kelly, C., 485
Kelly, J., 339, 340, 341, 343, 344, 345, 346, 349, 351, 353, 378, 383, 412, 413
Kempe, H., 491
Kenkel, W., 568
Kessler, R.C., 30, 34
Kim, B-L., 71
Kimball, C.P., 437
Kivnick, H.Q., 338
Klausner, S., 518
Klerman, L., 496, 497
Klock, R., 344, 358
Kohlepp, K.A., 290
Korcok, M.A., 496
Kotsonis, M., 44
Kramer, C., 322, 463
Kramer, J., 322, 463
Krestan, J., 60, 61, 218, 505
Krull, M., 172, 173, 181
Kubler-Ross, E., 458, 466, 476, 477
Kuhn, M., 327
Kulys, R., 322
Kutzik, A.J., 10, 84, 85
Kuypers, J., 326

Lambert, W., 575
Lang, A.M., 31
Lang, M., 498
Lappin, J., 84
Lauer, M.E., 467, 468, 473, 481
Lee, E., 80
Lefever, H., 516, 518
Leiblum, S.R., 218
Leiderman, H., 565
Lerner, H., 38, 302, 556
Lever, J., 45
Levin, S., 64, 320
Levinger, A., 337
Levinson, D.J., 5, 33, 60, 192, 193, 198, 291, 292, 293, 326, 440, 446, 447, 451, 453
Lewin, T., 239
Lewis, J., 517
Lewis, M., 44, 45, 312, 316, 321, 322
Libow, J.A., 3
Lieberman, M., 10, 30, 313n, 463
Liebman, R., 437, 446, 449
Lin, S.L., 399
Lindblad-Goldberg, M., 559
Lindemann, E., 94, 435
Linsk, N., 319
Lipsett, L.F., 437
Looney, J., 517
Lopata, H., 316
Lord, D., 552
Lowenthal, M., 314
Lowery, C., 344
Luepnitz, D., 344, 346
Lynch, J.J., 290

Maas, H., 326

Maccoby, E.E., 45, 237
MacGregor, R., 534
MacMurray, J.P., 503
Maletta, G., 503, 504
Marten, S., 337
Martin, E., 558
Martin, J.M., 558
Martin, M., 257
Mas, C.H., 49
Masson, J., 181
Masters, W.H., 314
Masuda, M., 473
Mathews-Simonton, S., 437
Matthews, S., 317
Maxim, K., 534
McCrady, B.S., 501
McCullough, P., 302, 306
McCusker, J., 459, 481
McGill, D., 70, 82, 85, 267
McGoldrick, M., 3, 12, 34, 70, 71, 73, 74, 80, 87, 108, 151, 165, 185, 186, 212, 230, 271, 272, 281, 299, 316, 323, 326, 335, 415, 440, 442, 447, 457, 461, 474, 481, 531, 570
570
McKegney, P., 437
McLachlan, J.F.C., 496, 497
McLanahan, S., 373, 381
McLeod, J.D., 30
McRae, J.A., 34
McSherry, L., 467, 468
Mead, M., 317, 318
Medalie, J., 552, 553
Medley, M., 314
Meeks, D., 485
Melisartos, N., 437
Merriweather, J., 540
Messinger, L., 351
Miller, D., 498
Miller, J.B., 3, 5, 32, 34, 64, 192
Milliones, J., 8
Milman, L., 437, 446, 449
Minturn, L., 575
Minuchin, S., 24, 107, 273, 373, 376, 437, 446, 449, 514, 516, 524, 525, 533, 540, 560
Mishara, B., 503
Moitoza, E., 267
Montalvo, B., 24, 405, 514, 516, 524, 525, 533, 540
Moore, S.F., 231
Moorman, J., 399, 554
Moos, R.H., 439
Mor, V., 459, 481
Morawetz, A., 559
Morgenbesster, M., 383, 391
Morsbach, H., 73
Moss, H.A., 46
Mott, F.J., 231
Moynihan, C., 241, 248, 290
Moynihan, D., 558, 573
Mueller, C.W., 337
Mueller, P., 474
Mulhern, R.K., 467, 468, 473, 481
Murphy, R., 296

Nadelson, C., 5
Nehls, N., 383, 391
Neugarten, B., 292, 297, 298, 299, 313, 315, 317, 325, 327, 453
Newfield, N.A., 18, 279
Newman, B.M., 263
Newman, P.R., 263
Nichols, M., 218
Nicholson, S., 273
Noble, K., 513, 518
Nolan, J.F., 405
Noonan, D., 486
Nord, C., 345, 350, 404
Norman, R., 540
Norton, A., 373, 399, 554
Norton, E., 513, 520
Norton, S.J., 336, 337
Notman, M.T., 564
Nowakowski, L., 329

O'Connor, J., 153
O'Connor, M., 296
O'Donnell, L,, 557
Offer, D., 261
Olcamura, A.I., 71
O'Leary, D.E., 498
O'Leary, M.R., 498
Olson, D.H., 212, 228, 231
Ooms, T., 567
Orfanidis, M., 199, 203, 266, 299, 490, 555
Osterweis, M., 81, 465
Ostrov, E., 261
Ozawa, N., 71

Padan, D., 35
Palazzoli, M., 153, 157, 296, 533
Papp, P., 153
Parker, F., 566
Parker, R.D., 349
Parsons, B.V., 534
Pascarelli, E.F., 503
Pattison, E., 484
Paul, B.B., 299, 457
Paul, N., 8, 299, 442, 457
Paulson, M.A., 467
Payne, J.S., 467
Pearce, J.K., 70, 82, 85, 267, 335
Pearson, W., 232
Peay, L., 566
Penn, P., 440, 442, 445
Peplau, L.A., 260
Peretz, A., 540
Perry, R., 296
Perry-Jenkins, M., 243
Peterson, J.L., 345, 350, 404
Piaget, J., 261, 440
Pinderhughes, E., 514, 516, 540, 543
Pine, F., 571
Pinkston, E., 319
Piotrkowski, C., 35, 566
Platt, J., 92-93
Pogrebin, L.C., 60
Pope, H., 337

Prata, G., 153, 157, 296, 533
Prause, G., 173
Preto, N.G., 70, 73, 74, 87, 230
Price, S.J., 390
Prosen, H., 257
Protinsky, H.O., 18, 279
Prouty, E.N., 469

Quinlan, D.M., 437
Quinn, W.H., 18, 279

Rabkin, R., 99
Radetsky, D.S., 76
Rahe, R.H., 95, 338, 457
Rainwater, L., 241
Ramirez, O., 540
Rampage, C., 63
Ransom, J.W., 408, 409
Raschke, H., 344
Raschke, V., 344
Rausch, H.L., 231
Reever, K.E., 319
Reiss, D., 533
Repetti, R.L., 35
Rice, D.G., 378, 383
Rice, J.K., 378, 383
Rice, M.M., 495
Richardson, L., 41
Richman, D., 534
Rilke, R.M., 213
Rindfuss, R., 336
Ritchie, A., 534
Ritter, P., 565
Rivers, C., 30
Roberts, J., 340, 376
Robins, E., 337
Rodgers, R., 5, 21, 402, 412
Rodstein, E., 402, 406
Rolland, J.S., 434, 438, 441, 442
Romer, N., 33, 45, 46, 494
Rosen, E.M., 81
Rosenkrantz, P.S., 32
Rosin, A., 504
Rosman, B.L., 24, 437, 446, 449,
    514, 516, 524, 525, 533
Ross, H.L., 337
Roth, S., 61, 218
Rothberg, B., 391
Rotunno, M., 71
Rouse, B.A., 498
Royce, J.E., 483, 498, 503
Rubin, L., 60
Rutter, M., 344
Ryder, R.G., 212, 228, 231

Sager, C.J., 265, 402, 406
Saltz, R., 317
Saluter, A.F., 41
Sandmaier, M., 501
Santa-Barbara, J., 64
Santrock, J., 346
Sassen, G., 38
Satir, V., 213
Sawhill, I.V., 337
Schaeffer, C., 571
Scharf, K.R., 571

Schiff, H.W., 466, 467, 476
Schlesinger, S., 408, 409
Schmale, A.H., 437
Schram, R., 5, 286, 290
Schulman, G., 406
Schulz, B., 260
Schumer, R., 24, 514, 516, 524,
    525, 533
Schuster, F., 534
Schuster, R., 498
Schwartz, P., 35, 36, 61, 218
Schwartzman, J., 149, 481
Schydlowsky, B.M., 60
Scott, S., 84
Seiden, A., 237
Seltzer, M., 153
Seltzer, W., 153
Serrano, A., 534
Settle, S., 344
Shanfield, S.B., 470, 473
Sheehy, G., 198
Simonton, C., 459
Simonton-Matthews, S., 459
Simon, R., 112
Simonton, C.O., 437
Simos, B.G., 298
Sinott, J.D., 326
Skolnick, A., 573, 574
Skolnick, J., 573, 574
Sluzki, C., 12, 85
Smith, A., 467
Smith, J.B., 337
Smyer, M., 288, 344, 358
Soldo, B.J., 36, 56
Solomon, F., 81, 465
Solomon, M., 5, 19, 294, 470
Spain, D., 12, 29, 31, 36, 37
Spanier, G.B., 338, 339, 342
Spark, G., 247, 312, 320, 442
Sparks, T.F., 437
Spitz, D., 8
Sprey, J., 317
Stack, C.B., 71, 546, 558, 564,
    568, 570
Stanton, D., 498
Staples, R., 524, 547, 563
Stein, J.A., 340, 376
Steinglass, P., 485
Steinman, S., 346
Stern, P.N., 404
Sternberg, R., 41
Stierlin, H., 265
Strean, H.S., 181
Streib, G., 312, 317
Streiner, D.L., 64
Streissguth, A.P., 495
Strube, M.J., 36
Sudia, C., 343
Swain, B., 470, 473
Swales, P., 168, 173, 175, 181
Sweet, J., 231
Swensen, C.H., 290

Taeuber, M., 312, 327
Taggert, M., 3, 29
Tarule, J.M., 32, 64

Taylor, D., 290
Teachman, J., 523
Teitelbaum, M.P.H., 486
Teitz, W., 467, 468
Terkelson, K.G., 151, 549
Thomas, C.G., 8
Thomas, S., 496, 497
Thurner, M., 314
Thurow, L., 9, 10, 37
Tobin, S., 322, 463
Todd, T., 437, 446, 449
Toews, J., 257
Toman, W., 116, 198, 229, 247
Travis, C., 494
Treas, J., 312
Troll, L., 312, 326
Turk, D.C., 340

Vaillant, G.E., 33, 60, 192, 291,
    292, 293, 483, 484, 486,
    503
Van der Hart, O., 153, 154
Van Gennep, A., 150
Veroff, J., 211
Viney, L.L., 438
Visher, E.B., 402, 406, 412, 415
Visher, J., 402, 406, 412, 415
Voeller, M.M., 447
Vogel, S.R., 32

Wald, E., 406
Walderman, R.L., 496, 497
Waldron, H., 49
Waldron, I., 459
Walker, G., 445, 559
Walker, K., 351
Walker, L., 265, 402, 406
Wallaskog, J.M., 467, 481
Wallerstein, J., 339, 340, 343,
    344, 345, 349, 351, 353, 359,
    378, 383, 412, 413
Wallisch, L., 412
Walsh, F., 8, 185, 212, 266, 299,
    316, 319, 323, 324, 326, 442,
    457, 461, 463, 474
Warburton, J., 49, 64
Ware, L., 319
Waring, J.M., 6
Warshak, R., 346
Watzlawick, P., 161, 279
Wedemeyer, N., 373, 381
Wegscheider, S., 495, 496
Weiner, J.P., 62
Weingarten, K., 32, 43, 44, 555
Weinstein, K., 317
Weintraub, M., 45
Weir, T., 232
Weiss, H.M., 436
Weiss, R.S., 34, 60, 339, 340
Weitzman, L.J., 35, 342, 371, 372,
    375, 390
Welts, E.P., 86
Westbrook, M.T., 438
White, G.D., 404
White, K., 37, 41
White, L., 403

White, S.W., 337
Whiteside, M., 406
Whiting, R., 553
Williams, C., 496, 497
Williamson, D., 305, 480
Williamson, J., 20, 53, 113
Wilsnack, S., 498, 501
Winch, R.F., 573

Winget, C., 466, 470, 473
Woehrer, C.E., 10, 78, 79, 80, 319, 326
Wolin, S., 149, 486
Woodward, C.A., 64
Wright, D.W., 390
Wright, L.M., 296
Wynne, L., 101

Zander, R., 540
Zarit, J., 319
Zarit, S., 319
Zborowski, M., 81
Zilbach, J.J., 564
Zill, N., 345, 350, 404
Zimberg, S., 504, 505
Zucker, R.A., 498

Subject Index

Abortion, 471
Abuse
    alcoholism and, 496
    of elderly, 505
Accession, crisis of, 95
Achievement, professional families and, 550, *see also*
    Professional families
Acquired immune deficiency syndrome, *see* AIDS
Adaptability, women and, 33
Adolescence, family system in, 17-18, 255-282, *see
    also* Pubescence
    alcohol problems and, 497-500
    attachment and, 264
    autonomy and, 262-264
    clinical intervention with, 270-281
    conceptions of time in, 271-273
    death of adolescent and, 468-469
    divorce and, 355-358
    ethnicity and, 76, 267-270, 278-280
    genograms and, 173-174
    identity and, 260-262
    loss and, 265-267
    lower-income families and, 562-568
    meeting with adolescents in, 276
    meeting with other relatives of, 278-279
    meeting with parents in, 273-276
    meeting with siblings in, 277-278
    parental illness and, 465
    poor Black families and, 519-522
    professional families and, 550-552
    remarriage and, 412-413
    separation and, 264-265
    sexuality and, 258-260
    sociocultural factors and, 267-270
    subsystems in, 273
    tasks of adolescent and, 257-270
    therapeutic rituals for, 279-280
    three-generational view of transformation and,
        256-257
    uses of self and, 280-281
    women in, 49-52
Adult development, life cycle theory and, 191-193
Adulthood, young, 13-14, *see also* Launching phase;
    Young adulthood
Affective problems, remarriage and, 407
Ageism, 329
Aging, *see* Later life
AIDS
    homosexual couples and, 218
    lower-income adolescents and, 566
Alcohol problems, 483-508
    adaptive responses to, 487-488
    Alcoholics Anonymous and, 485

denial of, 486
divorce and, 502
family in later life and, 502-505
family with adolescents and, 497-500
family with unattached young adult and, 489-493
family with young children and, 496-497
general treatment issues with, 484-486
intergenerational impact of, 486
launching phase and, 500-502
new couple with, 493-495
progression of, 487
staging of, 486-489
statistics on, 483
treatment guidelines for, 505-508
Alzheimer's disease, 319
Ambiguity, remarriage and, 406, 407
Anxiety, *see also* Stress
    career development and, 197
    family stresses and, 8-9
    rites of passage and, 141, *see also* Rites of pas-
        sage
Attachment
    adolescence and, 264
    autonomy and, 199
    female development and, 34
Autonomy, *see also* Launching phase
    adolescents and, 262-264
    attachment and, 199
    illness and, 448

Babies, death of, 471
Bar mitzva, 140-142
Battering, alcoholism and, 496
Birth defects, 472
Birth order
    marital stability and, 229
    therapist and, 116
Birth practices, ethnicity and, 74-75
Black families, *see* Ethnicity; Poor Black families
Blended families, *see* Remarriage; Stepfamilies
Bowen coaching, 72, 203-207
Bowen systems theory, fusion in, 213
Boys, *see* Gender
Brothers, *see* Siblings
Burnout, therapist, avoidance of, 541-542

Career development, *see also* Work
    parental reactions to, 194
    in young adulthood, 197-198
Caretaking, women and, 31
Centripetal phase, centrifugal phase versus, 447-450
Ceremonies, *see also* Rites of passage
    ethnic, 83

myth about, 124-128
Change, discontinuous, 91-104, *see also* Discontinuous change
Child(ren), *see also* Infants; Parent *entries*
  adolescent, 17-18, *see also* Adolescence, family system in
  adult, 194-197, *see also* Launching phase
  alcoholic parents and, 496-497
  custody of, 58-59, 345-346, 351-353
  death of, 466-469
  divorce and, 343-346, 349-355, 366, 384, *see also* Divorce; Postdivorce *entries*
  filial role of, 320
  grown, 293-296
  launching of, 18-19, *see also* Launching phase
  migration and, 84
  remarriage and, 411-412, *see also* Remarriage
  socioeconomic status and, 546-548
  space for, 240-242
  of working mothers, 35
  young, 16-17, *see also* Parenthood
Child abuse, alcoholism and, 496
Child care, conflicts about, 17, 246
Child-focused family, 248
Childless couples, divorce of, 347-348
Childlessness
  decision for, 241
  old age and, 327
Child rearing, *see also* Parenthood
  ethnicity and, 75-76
  gender and, 44-45, 237-239
  illness during period of, 449
  remarriage and, 400-401
Child support, postdivorce, 342-343, 389-390
Christmas, anxiety surrounding, 141
Chronic illness, 433-454, *see also* Illness
Chronologies, *see also* Genograms
  Freud family, 187-188
Clinical intervention, *see* Family therapy
Coaching, 72, 203-207
Cohabitation, 211
  marriage after, 217-218
College students, 552-553
Communication
  lack of, in marriage, 217
  paradoxical injunction in, 98-104
Community, adolescents and, 267-268
Conflict, *see also* Triangles
  adolescents and, 256
  grandparenthood and, 318
  lower-income families and, 560-561
  loyalty, 407
  marital, 291
  parental, children's adjustment to divorce and, 344
  poor Black couples and, 523-524
  women and work and, 17, 34-36
Contraception, lower-income families and, 566
Control, adolescence and, 265
Counseling, *see* Family therapy
Couples, 14-16, *see also* Marriage
  ethnicity and, 72-73
  homosexual, 61, 218-221
  remarried, *see* Remarriage
  unmarried, 211
Crises, *see also* Nodal events; Transition points; *specific crisis, e.g.,* Divorce

dual, 380
  expectable, 94-96
Culture, *see also* Ethnicity; Rites of passage
  adolescence and, 267-270
  divorce and, 335-336
  family life cycle and, 10
  family process and, 122-124
  marriage and, 230
Custody issues, 58-59, 345-346, 351-353
  noncustodial parent, 389-393
Cutoff, 203-204
  launching phase and, 295

Death, 457-480, *see also* Illness; Widowhood
  of adolescent, 468-469
  of adult family member, 464-466
  changing health-care methods and, 459-460
  of children, 466-469
  establishment of open relationship and, 476
  ethnicity and, 80-82, 460-461
  family context and, 475
  family position and, 473-474
  family treatment intervention and, 474-480
  funerals and, 128-134
  hope and, 476-477
  information about, 475-476
  nature of, 469-472
  openness of family system and, 472-473
  perinatal, 471
  previous losses and, 461-462
  rituals and, 478-479
  sequential order of, 185
  social context of, 458-460
  stress and, 478
  sudden, 469-470
  therapist's reaction to, 477-478
  timing of, in life cycle, 462-469
  unresolved issues and, 299
  unresolved mourning and, 479-480
Delinquency, 564-565
Dementia, senile, 319
Demographics
  divorce and, 336-337
  midlife phase and, 287-289
Dependency, old age and, 318-323
Design for a Brain, 96
Detriangling, 204
Developmental stress, 9
  death and, 461
Differentiation, family system, 472
Discontinuous change, 91-104
  evolutionary feedback and, 91-92
  expectable life-stage crises and, 94-96
  hierarchical growth and, 92-94
  paradoxical injunctions and, 98-104
  step mechanisms and, 96-98
Disease, *see* Illness
Dismemberment, crisis of, 95
Distance-sensitive triangle, 200, 201
Divorce, 12, 20-23, 143-144, 335-367, *see also* Postdivorce *entries*
  adjustment process in, 338-340
  adolescent children and, 268-270
  aftermath of, 374-381
  alcoholism and, 502
  children and, 343-346, 349-355, 366

clinical implications of, 364-367
coparental relationship and, 341-342
as crisis of transition, 337-338
demographics of, 336-337
economic consequences of, 342-343
emotional, 366, 374
families with adolescents and, 355-358
families with young children and, 349-355
family metacognition phase in, 339
gender and effects of, 31, 58-59, 340
impact on family of, 338-343
individual cognition phase in, 339
later life and, 361-364
launching phase and, 358-361
legal aspects of, 366-367
life-cycle stage and, 346-364
mediation of, 365
middle age and, 288
newly married childless couple and, 347-348
parenting arrangements after, 345-346
poor Black families and, 523-524
predecision phase of, 339, 364-365
rate of, 336
realignment after, 381-386
redefinition phase of, 343
reorganization phase of, 341
separation phase of, 339, 365-367
social network and, 340-341
stabilization after, 386-388
trial separation before, 365
Domestic sphere, see Home
Double bind, 98-104
Dual-career families, see also Professional families;
   Work
   with young children, 17, 245-246
Dual crises, 380
Dying, see Death; Terminal illness

Eastern cultures, Western cultures versus, 69
Economic context, 9, see also Poverty; Socioeco-
      nomic status
   adolescents and, 267
   divorce and, 342-343, 356, see also Postdivorce
      entries
   middle age and, 288-289
Economic independence, women and, 35-36
Education, childbearing and, 547
Egalitarianism
   parenthood and, 237-239
   sibling rivalry and, 247
Elderly, see Later life
Elementary-school-age children, divorce and, 353-355
Emotional baggage, remarriage and, 405-408
Emotional divorce, 366, 374
Emotional issues, men and, 52
Emotional pressure, see also Stress
   divorce and, 21-23, 339-340
Emotional shock wave, 474
Employment, see Career development; Work
Empowerment strategies, 540
"Empty nest" phase, 53, see also Midlife phase
Enmeshment, 203
   illness and, 443
Enmeshment-sensitive triangle, 200
Environment, see also Socioeconomic status
   children and, 240-242

Erikson's theory of human development, gender and,
      32-33
Ethnicity, 69-89, see also Poor Black families
   adolescence and, 267-270, 278-280
   ceremonies related to, 83, see also Rites of pas-
      sage
   death and, 80-82, 460-461
   families of adolescents and, 76
   family concept and, 70-71
   immigration and, 83-86
   intermarriage and, 73-74
   launching of children and, 77-78
   life cycle stages and, 70-71
   old age and, 78-80
   parenthood and, 74-76
   problems related to, 82
   rituals and, 83, see also Rituals
   therapy and, 86-89
   unattached young adult and, 71-72
   young couple and, 72-73
Evolutionary feedback, 91-92
Ex-spouse, see also Postdivorce entries
   family therapy including, 426
   remarried couple and, 415-417
Extended family
   early pregnancy and, 571-572
   intimacy issues and, 199-201
   lower-income model of, 558-562
   marriage patterns and, 224-228
   parenthood and, 243-245

Family
   child-focused, 248
   ethnic concepts of, 70-71
   myth of breakdown of, 121-122
   of therapist, 116-117
Family chronologies, see Genograms
Family home, postdivorce sale of, 382
Family identity, illness and, 451
Family life cycle
   changes in, 10-13
   dislocations of, 22
   illness and, 446-454
   major variations in, 20-25
   perspective of, 3-4
   "pressure cooker" phase of, 12
   socioeconomic status and, 548-550
   stages of, 5, 13-20, see also Life cycle stages;
      specific stage, e.g., Launching phase
Family life-spiral model, 447
Family Policy Panel, 253
Family process
   culture and, 122-124
   rites of passage and, 119-147, see also Rites of
      passage
Family projection process, 199
Family size, reduction of, 287-288
Family structures, current, 13
Family system
   alcoholism and, 485, see also Alcohol problems
   death and, 472-473
   illness and, 441, see also Illness
   launching phase and, 194-197
   moving through time, 4-10
   remarriage and, 400, see also Remarriage
   three-generational, 6-7, 256-257

transformation in adolescence, 17-18, 255-282, *see also* Adolescence, family system in
Family therapy, 107-117, *see also* Therapeutic rituals; Therapist
  adolescents and, 270-281, 276
  alcohol problems and, 505-508
  coaching in, 203-207
  death and, 474-480
  divorce and, 364-367
  elderly and, 327-329
  ethnicity and, 86-89
  ex-spouses in, 426
  fit between therapist and family in, 107-112, 114-115
  framework for, 3-25
  lower-income families and, 565-570
  midlife phase and, 299-306
  multiple-impact, 534-539
  noncustodial parent and, 393
  parents of adolescents and, 273-276
  parents with young children and, 249-253
  poor Black families and, 533-541
  postdivorce, 378-381, 385-386, 387-388, 393-395
  reframing family's conception of time in, 271-273
  relatives of family in adolescence and, 278-279
  remarried families and, 414-426
  siblings of adolescents and, 277-278
  with therapist and family in same life cycle stage, 109- 110
  with therapist not yet at family's life cycle stage, 108- 109
  with therapist past family's life cycle stage, 110-112
  uses of self in, 280-281
  women and, 62-64
Fatal illness, *see* Terminal illness
Father(s), *see also* Parent *entries*
  postdivorce parenting and, 345-346, 350-351, 389-393
  with young children, 44-45
Father-daughter relationship, adolescence and, 50
Feedback, evolutionary, 91-92
Female development, male development versus, 31-34
Feminism, *see* Women
Filial role, 320
Financial context, *see* Economic context; Socioeconomic status
Flexibility, successful aging and, 326-327
Freud family, chronology for, 187-188, *see also* Genograms
Friendships, *see also* Social network
  marriage and, 224
  women and, 60
Funerals, 128-134, *see also* Death
  opportunities related to, 129
Fusion
  intimacy and, 212-218
  remarriage and, 408

Gay couples, *see* Homosexuality
Gender, *see also* Women
  adjustment to divorce and, 340
  adolescence and, 49-52
  adolescent autonomy and, 263
  adolescent sexuality and, 259-260
  adult development and, 192

alcohol problems and, 497-498, 501-502, *see also* Alcohol problems
  Black ratio of, 524
  career issues and, 198
  child rearing and, 44-45
  of children, divorce and, 344
  earnings and, 9-10
  economic context of divorce and, 342-343, 356
  established differences between, 237
  ethnicity and, 72-73, 78
  friendships and, 60
  health-care behavior and, 61-62
  human development and, 31-34
  identity structure and, 260, 261-262
  later-life divorce and, 362
  lower-income adolescents and, 563-565
  male-female relationships, 112-114
  marriage and, 30, 41-43, 211
  midlife divorce and, 359
  midlife maturity and, 292
  old age and, 326
  parenthood and, 237-239
  professional families and, 556-557
  views toward marriage and, 16
Generations
  death and, 463-464
  in family system, 5-6
Generation to Generation, 128
Genograms, 165-188
  families with adolescents in, 173-174
  later life in, 182-185
  marriage in, 165-168, 177-179
  midlife phase in, 175-177
  parenthood in, 168-172, 179-182
  predictable triangles and, 168
  second generation in, 177-182
Geographical uprooting, 145-146, *see also* Migration
Girls, *see* Gender
Government assistance, poor Black families and, 514, 518
Graduate school students, 553-555
Grandchildren, 296-297
Grandparents, 17, 244, 297, 317-318
Grief, 94, 129, *see also* Death; Loss
  divorce and, 366
Grown children, adult relationships with, 293-296
Growth, hierarchical, 92-94
Guilt, remarriage and, 407

Healing rituals, 157-159
Health, *see also* Illness
  midlife marital status and, 290-291
  old age and, 318-323
Health-care behavior, of women, 61-62, 459
Health-care methods, serious illness and, 459-460
Hierarchical growth, 92-94
Hispanics, *see* Ethnicity
Home
  sale of, after divorce, 382
  work balance with, 236, 245-246, *see also* Parenthood
Homeostasis, 91, *see also* Discontinuous change
Homosexuality, 218-221, *see also* Idiosyncratic transitions
  female, 60-61
Households, 36-37

dual-career, *see* Dual-career families
postdivorce, *see* Postdivorce families
Housework, 37
Human development, *see also* Adult development
gender and, 31-34

Identity, *see also* Self
adolescent, 260-262
ethnicity and, 70, 83
family, illness and, 451
gender and, 32-33, *see also* Gender
"professional," 550
vocational, 197-198
Identity-redefinition rituals, 159-161
Idiosyncratic transitions, 150-153
rituals and, 153-162, *see also* Rituals
symptom emergence and, 151-153
Illness, 433-454, *see also* Death
of adolescent, 469
alcoholism as, 484
centripetal versus centrifugal family style and,
447-450
chronic phase of, 439
constant-course, 435-436, 449-450
course of, 435-436
crisis phase of, 439
episodic, 436, 450
family identity and, 451
family life cycle and, 446-454
human life structure and, 446
incapacitation and, 437-438
infants and, 472
life-structure building/maintaining periods and, 448,
451- 452
old age and, 318-323
onset of, 435
outcome of, 436-437
out-of-phase, 453
progressive, 435
psychosocial typology of, 434-438
relapsing, 436, 450
stress due to, 470-471
terminal phase of, 439-440
three-dimensional matrix with, 441
time phases of, 438-442
women and, 61-62
Illness life cycle, 443-444
Immigration, 83-86
In a Different Voice, 192
Incapacitation, illness and, 437-438
Infants, death of, 471
Injunctions, paradoxical, 98-104
In-laws, 228, 296-297
Institutionalization, elderly and, 322-323
Income, *see* Economic context; Socioeconomic status
Independence, *see also* Launching phase
adolescents and, 262-264, *see also* Adolescence,
family system in
economic, 35-36
Intermarriage, ethnic groups and, 73-74
Intervention, *see* Family therapy
Intimacy
definition of, 237
fusion and, 212-218
parenthood and, 243
single young adults and, 198-203

Jewish rites of passage, *see also* Ethnicity; Rites of
passage
bar mitzvah, 140-142
Joint custody, 58-59, 345-346

Kinship network, *see* Extended family

Labor force, *see* Work
Language, sexist bias in, 33
Later life, 19-20, 311-329
abuse in, 505
alcohol problems and, 502-505
childlessness and, 327
crossgenerational interplay of life cycle issues
and, 324-326
death in, 463-464
dependency in, 318-323
difficulties in, 19-20
divorce in, 361-364
ethnicity and, 78-80
genograms and, 182-185
grandparenthood and, 317-318, *see also* Grandchildren; Grandparents
illness in, 318-323, 463-464
invisibility and, 328-329
life-review therapy and, 321
middle-aged children of parents in, 297-299,
303-306
migration in, 85
myths about, 19
poor Black families in 528-531
remarriage in, 413
retirement and, 144-145, 314-315
role flexibility and, 326-327
setting the stage for, 312-313
stereotyping and, 329
treatment issues in, 327-329
widowhood and, 315-316
women in, 55-58
Launching phase, 18-19, 191-207, 285-307, *see also*
Midlife phase
adult development and, 191-193
alcohol problems and, 500-502
career issues in, 197-198
coaching in, 203-207
divorce in, 358-361
ethnicity and, 77-78
family system factors in, 194-197
in genograms, 175-177
individual factors in, 193-194
intimacy issues in, 198-203
migration in, 85
transition to later-life phase and, 312-313
trouble with, 295-296
women in, 52-55
Leap theory, 99
Legal proceedings, divorce and, 366-367
Lesbians, 60-61, 219-221
Life cycle
alcoholism and, 484-486
life-structure building/maintaining periods in, 448,
451- 452
timing of death in, 462-469
Life cycle events, family stress and, 8
Life-cycle issues, cross-generational interplay of,
324-326

Life cycle perspective, *see also* Family life cycle
  adult development and, 191-193
  cautions about, 3-4
Life cycle stages, *see also* Family life cycle, stages of;
    specific stage, e.g., Midlife phase
  ethnicity and, 71
  remarriage and, 410-413
  therapist's versus family's, 107-112, 114-115
Life cycle transitions, idiosyncratic, 150-153
Life expectancy, increase in, 12, 287
Life-review therapy, 321
Life-stage crises, expectable, 94-96
Life-threatening illness, *see* Terminal illness
Living together, *see* Cohabitation
Loss, *see also* Death; Grief; Illness
  adolescence and, 265-267
  divorce and, 366
  healing rituals and, 157-159
  terminal illness and, 323
Lower-income families, 557-573, *see also* Poor Black
    families; Poverty; Socioeconomic status
  ages 22-30 in, 570
  ages 31-35 in, 571-573
  conflict between mother and nonparental
    executives in, 560-561
  environmental pressure and, 559
  extended-family model and, 558-561
  history of separations in, 561-562
  isolation of, 559
  junior and senior high school age and, 562-568
  nonreciprocity of relationships in, 559
  professional families versus, 551
  sibling arrangements in, 562
  underorganization of, 560
  young adulthood in, 568-570
Loyalty conflicts, remarriage and, 407

Male development, female development versus, 31-34
Marriage, 14-16, 209-232, *see also* Divorce; Intimacy;
    Remarriage
  adjustment issues in, 231-232
  age at, 211-212
  alcohol problems in, 493-495, 501-502
  career versus, 37-38
  cultural differences and, 230
  death of child and, 467
  decisions involved in, 209-210
  ethnicity and, 72-74
  evasiveness in, 217
  extended family patterns and, 224-228
  friendships after, 224
  fusion and intimacy in, 212-218
  gender and satisfaction in, 30, 41-43, 211
  in genograms, 165-168, 177-179
  in-laws and, 228
  later life and, 314-315
  living together before, 211, 217-218
  midlife and, 18, 289-291, 303
  parental reactions against, 135-138
  parenthood effects on, 243, 246
  poor Blacks and, 523-524
  professionals and, 555-556
  rates of, 12, 211
  as response to family process, 134
  sibling issues and, 228-230
  socioeconomic status and, 546-548
  weddings and, 134-139, 221-224

  women and, 41-43, 232
Maternity leave, 239
Maturation
  adolescent, 140-142, 258-260
  midlife, 291-293
Men, *see also* Gender
  emotional issues and, 52
  friendships and, 60
  lower-income, 569-570
  with young children, 44-45
Menarche, 258
Menopause, 53
Middle-class family, *see also* Socioeconomic status
  life cycle stages of, 13-20
"Midlife crisis," 18
Midlife phase, 18-19, 285-307, *see also* Launching
    phase
  adolescents and, 257
  alcohol problems in, 500-502
  clinical considerations for, 299-306
  demographic changes in, 287-289
  divorce and, 288
  duration of, 286, 288
  economic status in, 288-289
  genograms and, 175-177
  marriage and, 289-291
  maturity in, 291-293
  new relationships in, 296-297
  older generation and, 297-299
  relationships with grown children in, 293-296
  responsibility for other generations in, 303-306
  two-part process in, 288
  unresolved issues in, 299, 300-303
  working women and, 289
MIFT (multiple-impact family therapy), 534-539
Migration, 12, 83-86, 145-146
Mind and Nature, 91
Miscarriage, 471
Money, *see* Economic context; Socioeconomic status
Moral development, female, 34
Morphostasis, morphogenesis vs., 99
Mother(s), *see also* Parent *entries*; Women
  low-income, conflict between other family members
    and, 560-561
  working, 35, 239
Mother-in-law, 228
Mourning, *see also* Grief
  unresolved, 479-480
Multiple-impact family therapy, 534-539

National Council on Alcoholism, 484
National origin, *see* Ethnicity
Neglect, alcoholism and, 496
Networking, 115
Network stresses, women and, 30
Nodal events, 143
  individual development and, 200-201
Noncustodial parent, 389-393
  interventions for, 393
  money and, 389-390
  relationships between children and, 390-392
  social relationships of, 392-393
Nuclear family, size reduction of, 287-288
Nuclear-family triangle, 242
  distance-sensitive, 200, 201
  enmeshment-sensitive, 200
Nursing homes, elderly and, 322-323

Old age, *see* Later life

Paradigms, collison of, 237-240
Paradoxical injunctions, "sweat box" and, 98-104
Paranormative transitions, 150-153
Parent(s), *see also* Father(s); Mother(s)
  aging, 320, *see also* Later life
  chronic illness of, 449, *see also* Illness
  death of, 464-466, *see also* Death
  noncustodial, 389-393, *see also* Noncustodial parent
  postdivorce relationship of, 341-342
  postmarriage relationships with, 224-228
  reactions to marriage of children, 135-138, 223
  of remarried spouses, 424-425
  response to adolescents of, 256, *see also* Adolescence, family system in
  young adults' relationships with, 194-197
Parent-child relationships, overcloseness in, 240-241
Parent and Disability Leave Act, 253
Parental conflict, children's adjustment to divorce and, 344
Parenthood, 16-17, 235-254, *see also* child(ren)
  alcoholism and, 496-497
  child-focused family and, 248
  collision of paradigms and, 237-240
  decisions for or against, 241
  ethnicity and, 74-76
  extended family and, 243-245
  in genograms, 168-172, 179-182
  home/work balance and, 236, 245-246
  intervention guidelines for, 249-253
  intimacy and, 243
  lower-income families and, 560-561
  poor Black families and, 523-528
  postdivorce aftermath and, 376-377
  postdivorce realignment and, 383
  professional families and, 556-557
  sexual equality and, 237-239
  sexuality and, 242
  sibling rivalry and, 246-248
  single, *see* Single parenthood
  space for children and, 240-242
  women and, 43-48
Parenting arrangements, postdivorce, 345-346, 350-351, *see also* Custody issues; Divorce
Peer relationships, *see* Friendships; Social network
Personal power, gender and, 114
Person-to-person contact, 204
Physical illness, *see* Illness
Political context, 9
  poor families and, 23-25
Poor Black families, 513-543, *see also* Poverty; Socioeconomic status
  adolescence/unattached young adulthood stage in, 519-522
  assessment of, 531-533, 534
  characteristics of, 516-518
  children and, 523-528
  cycle of poverty and, 515-516
  empowerment strategies for, 540
  female-headed households in, 518
  general guidelines for, 539-541
  institutional supports of, 518
  intervention in, 533-541
  later life and, 528-531
  multiple-impact therapy for, 534-539

  truncated life cycle of, 517
  unpredictable stress in, 518
  world view of, 516
Postdivorce aftermath, 374-381
  interventions in, 378-381
  money in, 375-376
  parenting in, 376-377
  social relationships in, 377-378
Postdivorce families, 371-396, *see also* Divorce; Remarriage; Single parenthood
  aftermath phase of, 374-381
  noncustodial parent of, 389-393
  process of becoming, 372-373
  realignment phase of, 381-386
  stabilization phase of, 386-388
Postdivorce realignment, 381-386
  intervention in, 385-386
  money in, 381-383
  parenting in, 383
  social relationships in, 384-385
Postdivorce stabilization, 386-388
  intervention during, 387-388
Poverty, *see also* Poor Black families; Socioeconomic status
  adolescents and, 267
  cycle of, 515-516
  feminization of, 343
  life cycle of families in, 23-25
  single parenthood and, 372
Power, gender and, 114
Pregnancy, *see also* Parent *entries*
  adolescent, 563-564, 567, 571-573
  early, extended-family system and, 571-572
  loss of, 471
Pre-school-age children, divorce and, 349-353
"Pressure cooker" phase, 12
Prison Notebooks, 98
Professional families, 550-557, *see also* Socioeconomic status
  college and, 552-553
  graduate school and, 553-555
  identity of, 550
  junior and senior high school and, 550-552
  low-income families versus, 551
  parenthood in, 556-557
  postgraduate school stage in, 555-556
Pseudolaunching, 295
Pseudomutuality, remarriage and, 408, 417-418, 421-423
Pseudo-self, 199
Psychopathology, divorce and, 337
Psychosocial development, illness and, 440-441
Pubescence, 140-142, 258-260, *see also* Adolescence, family system in
Public assistance, poor Black families and, 514, 518

Race, *see* Ethnicity; Poor Black families
Reconnecting, 204-205
Relationships, *see also* Friendships; Social network
  with grown children, 293-296
  intimate, 198-207, *see also* Marriage
  new, in middle age, 296-297
  nonreciprocity of, in lower-income families, 559
  with young children, 240-241, *see also* Parenthood
Relatives, *see also* Extended family; *specific relationship*
  of family in adolescence, 278-279

Religion, *see* Ethnicity
Remarriage, 20-23, 24, 399-427
    affective problems and, 407
    boundary difficulties in, 406-407
    child rearing responsibilities in, 400-401
    children's reactions to, 411-412
    clinically useful findings on, 402-405
    emotional issues in, 405-408
    family integration in, 404-405
    family makeup in, 402
    family therapy and, 414-426
    fusion tendency in, 408
    in genograms, 165-168
    goals in, 426-427
    in later life, 413
    model of family in, 400
    predictors of difficulty in, 409
    premature, 392-393
    process of, 408-409
    pseudomutuality tendency in, 408
    rates of, 399
    role of children in, 403
    roles and relationships in, 406
    with spouses at different life cycle phases, 410-411
    with spouses at same life cycle phases, 411
    triangles in, 415-426, *see also* Triangles
    after widowhood, 316
    women and, 58-60
Reminiscence, 321
Retirement, 144-145, 314-315
    alcohol problems and, 503-504
    dysfunctional adaptation to, 315
Reversals, 204
Rites of passage, 119-147, *see also* Rituals
    ceremonies versus, 124-128
    continua of time periods around, 126-127
    divorce, 143-144, *see also* Divorce
    funerals, 128-134, *see also* Death
    geographical uprooting, 145-146
    myths inhibiting family process view of, 121-128
    natural versus nodal, 143
    pubescence, 140-142
    retirement, 144-145
    weddings, 134-139, 221-224, *see also* Marriage
Rituals, 149-150, *see also* Rites of passage
    death and, 478-479
    ethnicity and, 83
    healing, 157-159
    identity-redefinition, 159-161
    therapeutic, 153, 161-162, 279-280
    transition, 154-157
Role flexibility, successful aging and, 326-327
Role reversals, 204
Rural community, adolescents and, 268

Saltology, 99
School achievement, professional families and, 550,
        see also Professional families
School, attitudes toward, lower-income families and,
        563-564
Self, *see also* Identity
    children versus, 241
    differentiation of, poor Black adolescents and, 519
    individual versus interdependent orientation of, 199
    uses of, 280-281
Senile dementias, 319
Separation, *see also* Divorce; Launching phase

adolescence and, 264-265
    history of, lower-income families and, 561-562
    trial, 365
Sex, *see* Gender; Women
Sexism, *see also* Women
    language and, 33
Sexual abuse, alcoholism and, 496
Sexuality
    adolescents and, 258-260
    lower-income adolescents and, 564, 566
    parenthood and, 242
    professional-family adolescents and, 551
Shock, emotional, 474
Siblings, *see also* Sisters
    adolescent pregnancy and, 572-573
    of adolescents, 277-278
    death of, 467-468
    lower-income, 562
    marriage and, 228-230
    position of, *see* Birth order
    rivalry between, 172, 246-248
Single parenthood, *see also* Divorce; Postdivorce *entries*
    adolescent children and, 268-270
    increase in, 371
    noncustodial, 389-393
    poor Black families and, 518, *see also* Poor Black
        families
    process of becoming a one-parent family, 372-373
    stress of, 349-350
Single young adult, 13-14
    alcoholic family system and, 489-493
    ethnicity and, 71-72
    female, 37-40
    launching of, 191-207, *see also* Launching phase
Sisters, relationships of, 55
Social context, 9
    of death, 458-460
    poor families and, 23-25
Social network, *see also* Friendships
    of noncustodial parent, 392-393
    poor young Blacks and, 520
    postdivorce aftermath and, 377-378
    postdivorce family and, 373
    postdivorce realignment and, 384-385
Sociocultural factors, *see also* Culture; Ethnicity
    adolescence and, 267-270
    divorce and, 335-336
Socioeconomic status, 545-576, *see also* Economic
        context
    and additions to family life cycle theory, 548-550
    birth patterns and, 546-548
    data sources on, 545-546
    lower-income, 557-573, *see also* Lower-income
        families; Poor Black families; Poverty
    marriage patterns and, 546-548
    professional, 550-557, *see also* Professional families
    strengths and vulnerabilities and, 573-576
    symptom formation and, 549-550
Stepfamilies, 23, 24, 59-60, *see also* Remarriage
    with adolescents, 412-413
    advice for, 403
Stepfamily Bulletin, 402
Stepfathers, 404
Step mechanisms, 96-98
Stepmothers, 59-60

expectations of, 401
Stigma
  identity-redefinition rituals and, 159-161
  single mothers and, 384
Stillbirth, 471
Stress, *see also* Emotional pressure
  career development and, 197
  cultural differences and, 230
  death and, 472-473, 478
  expectable crises and, 94-96
  illness causing, 470-471
  intimacy issues and, 201
  launching of children and, 53
  poor Black families and, 518
  transition points and, 4-5, 8-10, *see also* Rites of
    passage
  women's susceptibility to, 30
Students, *see also* Children
  college, 552-553
  graduate school, 553-555
Suburban community, adolescents and, 268
Suicide, adolescent, 468-469
Supervision, 115
"Sweat box," 98-104
Symptom emergence
  idiosyncratic transitions and, 151-153
  socioeconomic status and, 549-550

Teenagers, *see* Adolescence, family system in
Terminal illness, 323, 436-437, *see also* Death; Illness
Therapeutic rituals, 153
  design of, 161-162
  family system in adolescence and, 279-280
Therapist, *see also* Family therapy
  burnout of, avoidance of, 541-542
  choice of model by, 115
  family of origin of, 116-117
  family system in adolescence and, 280-281
  networking and, 115
  not yet at family's life cycle stage, 108-109
  past family's life cycle stage, 110-112
  at same life cycle stage as family, 109-110
  stance of, 115
  supervision and, 115
Three-generational family system, 6-7, 256-257
Transgenerational stress, 9
  death and, 461
Transition points, 149-150, *see also* Rites of passage;
    specific transitions, e.g., Divorce
  family stress and, 4-5, 8-10, *see also* Stress
  idiosyncratic, 150-153
  illness and, 440
Transition rituals, 154-156, *see also* Rites of passage;
    Rituals
  discussion of, 156-157
Treatment, *see* Family therapy
Trial separation, 365
Triangles, 204
  adolescents and, 256, 264
  couple-sibling, 228-230
  death and, 476
  distance-sensitive, 200, 201
  enmeshment-sensitive, 200, 201
  husband–second wife–husband's children, 418-419
  in-laws and, 228
  nuclear-family, 242
  parent–children–stepchildren, 423-424

postdivorce aftermath and, 376-377, 379, 380
postdivorce realignment and, 385-386
predictable, 168
pseudomutual remarried couple and, 417-418,
    421-423
remarried spouses and parents of either, 424-425
spouse–second spouse–ex-spouse, 415-417
wife–second husband–wife's children, 420-421
"Trigger family," 108
Twins, 246-247
Two-income families, *see* Dual-career families; Profes-
    sional families

Urban community, adolescents and, 268

Vocational identity, 197-198, *see also* Work

Weddings, 134-139, 221-224, *see also* Marriage
Western cultures, Eastern cultures versus, 69
Widowhood, 56, 315-316
Women, 29-64
  caretaking and, 31
  changing role of, 11
  divorce and, 58-59, *see also* Divorce; Postdivorce
    entries
  earnings of, 9-10
  ethnicity and, 78
  in families with adolescents, 49-52
  family therapy and, 62-64
  friendship networks of, 60
  health care and, 61-62, 459
  households and, 36-37
  human development and, 31-34
  launching children and, 52-55
  lesbian, 60-61, 219-221
  lower-income, 568-569
  marriage and, 30-31, 41-43, 211-212, 232
  old age and, 55-58
  remarriage and, 58-60
  single parenthood and, 349-350, *see also* Single
    parenthood
  stresses and, 30
  work and, 9-10, 34-36, 239, 289, 382-383
  young adulthood of, 37-40
  with young children, 43-48
Work, *see also* Career development
  lower-income men and, 569
  parenthood and, 236, 245-246, *see also* Parent-
    hood
  poor young Blacks and, 520
  professional, *see* Professional families
  women and, 9-10, 34-36, 239, 289, 382-383
Workplace, adaptations necessary in, 253

Young adulthood, 13-14, *see also* Launching phase
  alcoholic family system and, 489-493
  career development in, 197-198
  ethnicity and, 71-72
  lower-income families and, 519-522, 568-570
  parental death and, 464-465
  parental relationships in, 194-197
  poor Black families and, 519-522
  women in, 37-40
Young children, 16-17, *see also* Parent *entries*
  alcoholic parents and, 496-497
  divorce and, 349-355

ABOUT THE EDITORS

Betty Carter, M.S.W., is the first woman in the field to direct a major training institute, The Family Institute of Westchester, founded in 1977.

She is the Codirector of the Women's Project in Family Therapy with Peggy Papp, Olga Silverstein, and Marianne Walters. Since 1979, this group has given workshops throughout the United States and in Europe on the dilemmas of women in families and methods of dealing with these dilemmas in treatment. Their book on feminist issues will be published next year.

In addition to training and supervision, Mrs. Carter sees 15 to 20 couples and families per week, specializing particularly in marital therapy and therapy of remarried families.

She regularly lectures, appears on panels, and gives workshops on family therapy topics throughout the United States and in Europe, and has published numerous articles and book chapters on theoretical and clinical subjects.

Mrs. Carter is married to a musician, Sam Carter, who recently retired from record producing at CBS Masterworks. They have two young adult sons.

Monica McGoldrick, M.S.W., is an Associate Professor and Director of Family Training for the Department of Psychiatry, UMDNJ-Robert Wood Johnson Medical School, and the Community Mental Health Center at Piscataway. She is cofounder of the Family Institute of Westchester. Her books *Ethnicity and Family Therapy* and *Genograms in Family Assessment* are best sellers. In addition to the new edition of *The Changing Family Life Cycle,* she is currently working on two other books, *Women in Families; A Framework for Therapy* and *You Can Go Home Again,* a popular book on family systems. Other areas of her work include family therapy with one person, remarried families, and dual career families. She is Vice President of the American Family Therapy Association, former secretary of the American Orthopsychiatric Association, and a fellow of AAMFT. She is on the Editorial Boards of *Family Process, The Journal of Marital and Family Therapy, The Family Networker, Family Systems Medicine, The Journal of Family Psychology,* and *The Journal of Divorce.*

Ms. McGoldrick is married to Sophocles Orfanidis, a professor of electrical engineering at Rutgers University, and she is the mother of a three-year-old, John Daniel.